W9-CDH-905

MANAGING: A Contemporary Introduction

second edition

man

PRENTICE-HALL, INC., ENGLEWOOD CLIFFS, NEW JERSEY 07632

aging

a contemporary introduction

JOSEPH L. MASSIE
Professor of Business Administration
University of Kentucky

JOHN DOUGLAS
Raymond E. Glos Professor of Business
Miami University, Oxford, Ohio

Library of Congress Cataloging in Publication Data

Massie, Joseph L.
Managing: a contemporary introduction.

Includes bibliographical references and index.
1. Industrial management. I. Douglas, John, (date) joint author. II. Title.
HD31.M337 1977 658.4 76-22521
ISBN 0-13-548545-2

MANAGING: A Contemporary Introduction

second edition

Joseph L. Massie and John Douglas

Printed in the United States of America

10 9 8 7 6 5 4 3 2 1

Prentice-Hall International, Inc., *London*
Prentice-Hall of Australia Pty. Limited, *Sydney*
Prentice-Hall of Canada, Ltd., *Toronto*
Prentice-Hall of India Private Limited, *New Delhi*
Prentice-Hall of Japan, Inc., *Tokyo*
Prentice-Hall of Southeast Asia Pte. Ltd., *Singapore*
Whitehall Books Limited, *Wellington, New Zealand*

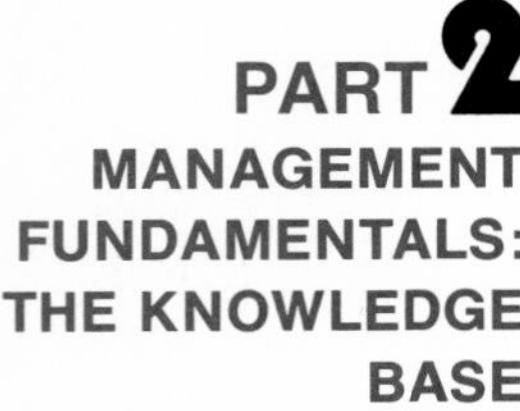
PART 2
MANAGEMENT FUNDAMENTALS: THE KNOWLEDGE BASE

preface to the second edition

The style, organization, and special features of the first edition were favorably received by the many users; therefore, this revision retains the same general format. Nevertheless, the second edition revises the content in a majority of chapters, further develops some of the features of the first edition, and supplements the approach with added features.

Three chapters have been completely rewritten—Chapter 6 on the Design of the Organization Structure, Chapter 7 on Management Systems, and Chapter 14 on Interpersonal and Organizational Communications. One chapter has been dropped reducing the total chapters to twenty one; yet the overall length of the book has been increased slightly. New topics appear in the areas of motivation, techniques for adjustment to pressures in organizations, and international management.

The number of vignettes at the beginning of chapters has been increased so that in this edition there is a vignette for each chapter. Users of the first edition indicate that these vignettes helped the students understand managerial problems before they study the alternative answers; thus, the vignettes help to show the student the relevance of the academic content.

New features increase the focus on the practice of management and offer additional help to the student in his study of the subject. The

Situational Episodes at the end of each chapter include realistic incidents, practical problems, and business situations in which the topics of each chapter can be applied. These episodes are relatively short and to the point, and they provide the foundation for lively class discussion.

The new Student Resource Manual prepared to accompany the text is not only a study guide but it contains summary information to help the student relate an academic education to the world of work. Part I of the Student Resource Manual offers concise statements of key ideas, summary of terms defined in the text, and extensive reinforcement opportunities including not only study questions but also detailed answers to the questions that guide the student by means of author feedback. Finally, several short cases are provided for each chapter that offer opportunities for applying ideas developed in the text. Part II of the Student Resource Manual helps the student both in studying for classes and for beginning his career in management. Study aids include hints on taking notes, guides for reading, help in preparing for exams, and means of locating additional information. Preparation for a career includes information on the labor market, how a new applicant can fit in to his job, how to make a career choice, how to prepare for job search, and how to evaluate job offers.

acknowledgments

The purpose of this book is to present a meaningful experience of a complex and dynamic activity, to show the contemporary nature of the subject, and to develop a classroom situation that allows student participation. The first edition was the result of the joint efforts, over a period of three years, of a number of people in Prentice-Hall and many instructors in both two year and four year colleges. The preparation of the second edition started immediately after the publication of the first edition with the help of feedback from users of the text in diverse institutions.

This edition is thus the product of contributions from many people —reviewers, former users, practicing managers, academic colleagues, students and editors. The authors wish to thank the many people who have made these contributions.

Key personnel in Prentice-Hall deserve special mention. The original idea of the book came from Chester C. Lucido, a former editor of Prentice-Hall; Frederick K. Easter assisted in planning and implementing the production of the first edition; Earl Kivett, Editor, Management; Ann Marie McCarthy, College Book Editorial-Production Department; and Lee Cohen, designer, were most valuable in the development of the revised edition.

Several colleagues contributed significantly to the revised edition: William C. Pavord, Indiana University East, helped with both chapter revisions and the teachers' manual; Victor F. Phillips, Jr., Charles E. Watson, and John D. McNeill, Miami University, offered suggestions for improvements.

The authors have received continued help from a number of colleagues through their suggestions and contributions to individual chapters. Dr. Elias Awad, Ball State University, provided creative help particularly on the subject of data processing and systems. Colonel Dewey Johnson, USAF Systems Development Agency, Department of the Army, Monterey, Calif., provided innovative ideas on educational techniques in management. Dr. John Lloyd, Monroe Community College, Rochester, N.Y., was helpful in the development of plans for the Student Resource Manual. Professor Robert Miller, Hillsborough Community College, Tampa, Fla., provided enthusiastic support for the first edition and for its effective use in the classroom.

We gratefully acknowledge those who have critically reviewed the manuscript: Dr. James Gatza, Director of Management Education, American Institute for Property and Liability Underwriters; Prof. Robert G. Murdick, Department of Management, Florida Atlantic University; Prof. Jamieson H. B. Newell, Chairman, Department of Management, San Antonio College.

Our thanks also go to those who assisted in the typing of the manuscript: Phyllis J. Bryant, Gail Phelps, Sara Lee Douglas, and Rachael Massie.

To our wives we owe more than words. Chris and Marilyn made critical inputs and provided insights. Perhaps their most important contributions were in keeping the work in proper perspective, and helping us to maintain our sanity through the years of endeavor.

Introduction for the Student

This book has been written specifically for you. Your instructor can help you understand the ideas developed in the text, but—in the last analysis—it is up to *you* to learn. Nobody can teach you if you don't want to learn.

We have concentrated on a style and format that should help you to learn when you study the chapters. In class, you can reinforce this learning and see what others have to say or what questions they raise. Your instructor can supplement this process through the assignments, lectures, and testing. We hope that the experience will be satisfying for you.

How can the authors help you? Let's summarize some specific aids in this book:

1. The objectives stated at the beginning of each chapter establish specifically what you are to learn. Use these to check whether you have studied well.

2. We haven't introduced language just to impress you with the academic acceptability of the subject; in fact, we have avoided unnecessary academic jargon. However, when you learn a new language, a new athletic game, or any other subject, you always find some special words that you must understand. In management there are key words that have a common meaning among managers. These words have been placed in the margin and printed in color. Whenever you see one of these words you will find that its meaning is contained nearby. After you learn this meaning, you won't have

to bluff anyone—yourself, the teacher, a fellow student, or a prospective employer—you will know what is being said when the term comes up.

3. The marginal questions indicate the relevance of the adjacent text discussion. We don't want to give you a lot of answers in the text and then have you wondering what questions we meant them to answer. In some cases, the marginal question will be a very important and significant question that no one has the answer to. Yet just asking the question can be very helpful to you in developing your understanding of the relationship of management to other things that you feel are important.

4. The montages preceding each of the five parts have been carefully selected to stimulate thought and generate reactions. You should spend some time with these montages and take note of the specific ideas that they bring to mind. In class these ideas can be used as the basis for a wide-ranging introductory discussion for each part.

5. The charts, tables, and other illustrations are included to help you quickly understand a particular subject. If your tendency is to skip over such additions in a textbook, don't! In fact, if your time for study is short, concentrating on the illustrations can give you more help per minute than reading the text.

6. The summary and propositions (the section at the end of each chapter) include a set of management propositions that are generalizations related to the chapter just read. These will help you review the subject and give you concise statements of the basic ideas that you should master.

7. The study assignments for each chapter will help you to state key ideas in your own words and to make practical applications of your knowledge. Careful attention to these assignments will help you succeed both in the classroom and in later life.

8. We have provided real life situations for three stages of your study. First, you will find short vignettes preceding each chapter. The purpose of these vignettes is to orient you to the types of situations a manager faces so that you can appreciate the relevance of the text material. Second, at the end of each chapter you will find Situational Episodes that offer you incidents in which you can practice applying the ideas in the chapters. Third, in the Student Resource Manual accompanying the text, you are provided longer business cases in which you can develop in more depth your managing skills.

You now have some of the "secrets" on how to do well in the course. Moreover, you are ready to learn some things that can help you in everyday experiences during your entire career. When you know a subject, you can really enjoy doing things that make use of it. The structure of this book will help you develop such a knowledge. Each of its parts has a definite purpose, as follows.

Part 1 is, of course, introductory. Its two chapters describe the role and functions of a manager and also the social and physical setting in which the manager operates. When you have finished Part 1, don't go ahead into Part 2 unless you feel that you have met the objectives stated at the beginning of each of these first two chapters.

Part 2 summarizes the knowledge that is fundamental to managers. The subject of management is built on a wide variety of knowledge obtained over the years, often under different headings such as psychology, economics, organization, and computer sciences. Knowledge of the basic ideas drawn from this vast and interesting reservoir serves as a foundation for managing.

Part 3 discusses the processes performed by a manager. If you are to be a manager, you should get a clear idea of what you will do. Our analysis of management processes or functions gives you a pattern for the activities of any manager; it also includes aids to performing these activities. Together the chapters in this part will give you an overview of the details of what managers *should do.*

Part 4 focuses on management in action. In Part 3, we supply the prescription at the drugstore; you can't get any benefit from it, however, unless you take the medicine. In management, all of the research and theory can do little good unless you, as a prospective manager, understand how this prescription relates to actual practice. Part 4 introduces you to the real world of practicing managers. After you take a managerial position, you will continue to expand on the knowledge you've gained from this part by learning from your own experiences.

Part 5 prepares you for adjusting to a rapidly changing world. It focuses on the broader aspects of management, on personal and social values and the place that management takes in molding a better world. Change is an important subject throughout the book but is a special theme in this part. A manager can have any number of ideas lying around in his mind but to be effective he must assemble them into a meaningful framework. Thus integration and innovation are among our concluding subjects. It is this ultimate problem of putting knowledge, functions, and practice together that will require continual study and work throughout your life. The final chapter then is the connecting link between your formal education in this course and your practical education after you successfully complete this book. Are you ready to start? Then Chapter 1 it is!

MANAGING: A Contemporary Introduction

the manager in the modern world

I

Part 1 invites you to enter the world of the manager. It is an attractive world for those of you who like to be a part of a group that gets things done, and the opportunity to enter it is wide open. It is not restricted to the rich, or to persons of any special race, creed, or sex. The keys to entry are a well-balanced education and a burning desire to get where the action is. We provide a general admission ticket with education—you must have the desire.

The professional manager is a dynamic force in today's society, through his expert participation in a wide variety of organizations ranging all the way from business firms, to nonprofit community-oriented associations, to athletic groups. To give you the feel of the atmosphere you will enjoy when you become a manager, and to help you to understand just what you are getting into, we begin in Chapter 1 with a description of the many forces that shape and define a manager's job.

To complete your introduction to this exciting world of management, Chapter 2 presents an overview of what a manager does. You already have some samples of a manager's duties; for example, you may have seen the manager of your favorite baseball team walking slowly to the mound when his pitcher is in trouble. Such glimpses of managers in action may have given you some idea of what a manager does. In Chapter 2 we show you other functions that you would not normally be aware of.

Forces shaping the manager's job

ONE

OBJECTIVES YOU SHOULD MEET

Give *a general definition of management.*

Name *at least three forces that shape a manager's job.*

State *an example, from your personal experience, of the value of knowing an organization's tradition.*

Support, *with illustrations, an argument against a simple definition of management.*

List *three limitations and constraints of management jobs you know.*

THE FIRST CLASS IN MANAGEMENT

It had been a big day for Gale. She was new on the campus, having transferred from the Bloomfeld Secretarial School to one of the many state universities. Gale had done well in her secretarial classes, and a number of her instructors had suggested she transfer to the four-year school. After many phone calls, letters, and personal visits with the registrar, she was ready to start her course work, although she had to admit to herself she was apprehensive about the whole experience.

Accounting courses had always come easily for her, even in high school, so she listed herself as an accounting major in the College of Administration, Business, and Economics. The requirements were clear for her program and, on the recommendation of her advisor, she had enrolled in the business core course, Management 100.

Although the class listing had read 6:30, Gale arrived at 6:20 in the auditorium. It was a large room, and she looked for a seat in the middle—not in the back where it might be hard to hear, and not in the front where it's too easy to be seen. She recognized two fellow students who had stood in lines with her and sat next to them.

"Hiya," said the guy with the Budweiser Beer T-shirt. "You in this course?"

"Yes," Gale answered. "It's a requirement for me, and I thought I'd get through it as fast as I could."

"I'm a psy major," said the girl with "Mr. Bud." "I needed an easy elective—so I came over to ABE."

"What is ABE?" asked Gale.

"Administration, Business, and Economics," both replied. "You must be new here."

Meanwhile, the hall was filling up rapidly. By 6:30, the room was about full. As Gale turned back to the front, she saw a man—apparently the professor—stand up and tap the mike.

"Testing. One, two, three, four. . . . Good evening, students of Management 100. I'm Professor George Banner of the department; I function as the coordinator of this course—a course with an enrollment of 410, plus or minus the floaters."

The students laughed at this comment—more as a release of tension, Gale thought, than out of amusement.

"Tonight," the professor went on, "we want to introduce you to the topic of management, and our approach is to look at this field through the eyes of three different people—all managers in organizations. First we'll hear from the vice-president of the university, who will describe for us a day in his life as a manager of many diverse units in an organization. Second, we'll hear from one of his subordinates' subordinates—the head football coach. . . . Did you notice the reaction of the vice-president and the coach when I used the term 'subordinate'? There are many people in universities who believe that the vice-presidents are the subordinates of the football coach, and that everyone works for the alumni!"

Again the audience responded with laughter—this time, with more genuine enjoyment.

"The coach will speak to us about 'Managing to the nth *degree.' In other words, how he manages the day-to-day activities to get the team ready for Saturday's game."*

Gale could sense the audience responding to the prospect of hearing from the coach. Even she had heard of the university's football reputation, and even though her mother had discouraged her from watching football games, Gale felt she could easily become a fan at this school.

"Our last speaker is a woman executive, from one of the largest companies in this part of the state and one of the top ten in its industry. She'll speak to us on the topic, 'A female executive in a male-intensive industry.' "

Gale's interest was really high now. She was especially interested in hearing from a woman executive—she had never seen or heard one speak before.

Each speaker was very well organized and clear. Gale heard each one identify the forces in his or her environment that had great influence on how they managed. The vice-president spoke of the many populations he served or came in contact with: students, parents, employers, taxpayers, faculty, other professional administrators, all kinds of pressure groups, student and local press, alumni, and the state and federal government people who were responsible for education, employment of personnel, and the allocation of funds and grants. He mentioned a few of the new laws affecting education and how he had to manage within ever-changing constraints.

Gale admitted to herself that she had never realized how complex the job was and how much change there was in his world.

The managerial life of the football coach seemed similar to the vice-president's, but the coach had less time to decide on many issues. He illustrated this point by explaining the factors behind what the fans think is a simple problem: After a touchdown, does your team try to score two points, or kick for one point, when the score is 14–12 in favor of the opponent? The coach explained that he must relate to his other coaches, the players, the student body, the faculty, the alumni, the press, pro scouts—and even federal and state police officials, if gangsters pressure the players to shave points during a game.

The woman executive said two things that stood out in Gale's mind: that successful executives, male or female, work very long hours; and that the Affirmative Action Program of the federal government is opening up more and more opportunities for women.

Gale's attention was redirected to the professor now. "You have heard a brief description of the forces that shape a manager's job. Even though the jobs of our three guests differ, there were important similarities in terms of managing in each case. Our objective tonight was to whet your appetite for the subject and to form the background for the first chapter, "Forces Shaping the Manager's Job." You'll find this chapter touches in a different way many of the points mentioned tonight. You're now on your way to understanding the field of management. We'll see you next week."

As Gale got up to leave, she reflected on the evening and found it hard to understand why, when she was so excited about this course, her fellow student, "Mr. Budweiser T-Shirt," had slept through most of the class.

This book is a contemporary introduction to the fundamentals of managing. You may feel as Gale did, wondering, How can there be fundamentals in a field that comprises as diverse organizations as a university, a football team, and a major industrial firm? How can all the differences be lumped under the term *management?* Are women really becoming managers? How do you manage an organization when all its parts seem to have different participants and separate objectives?

We intend to answer many of the questions you have about managing. For example, we'll offer you the opportunity to learn some of the language of management—a language that will enable you to converse with practicing managers of organizations. You'll also have the opportunity to add to what you already know about managers. You may know something about managers of manufacturing plants but not managers of service institutions. You may have knowledge of management in small firms but not large firms; in profit-making organizations but not nonprofit organizations. By depicting management in a very broad context, we intend the coverage to be as complete and real as possible.

Before getting into the topic of management fundamentals, we feel that an overview of the manager's world is needed. Since each of you comes to this text with different experiences, expectations, and attitudes, the first two chapters will give you all a similar orientation to the manager's world and what he does. We try to create this shared experience base in Chapter 1 by looking first at who the managers are, then at the factors that shape the manager's activities in organizations, and finally at the role the organization plays in defining the manager's job.

MANAGERS AS A CLASSIFICATION

Managers

Managers are people who are primarily responsible for seeing to it that work gets done in an organization. This very simple and broad statement includes all kinds of managers—the president of a large steel corporation, a day-care-center director, or an administrator of an educational institution. In most instances, the work of managers differs markedly from the work of nonmanagers.

The president of the steel firm does managerial work; he does not operate a machine. A football coach manages his staff and players; he does not play the game himself. A day-care-center director sees that revenues equal or exceed costs, that health-care standards are maintained, that parents are satisfied with the care, and that a qualified staff follows a planned program; she does not necessarily deal directly with the children. An academic administrator anticipates the student enrollments for the next few years, develops committee assignments for the faculty, represents the higher administration to the faculty and the faculty to the higher administration, prepares budgets and reports, and manages one or more secretaries and perhaps student help; she may or may not teach in the classroom. There is a distinctive set of activities performed by managers and administrators. In Chapters 2–21 we set forth what managers do, what knowledge they use, and the context and problems they face.

subordinates

Nearly all managers of organizations have one common denominator—*subordinates,* those people who work under them. In most cases, nonmanagers of organizations also have some common denominators—they usually have no subordinates but rather work with tools or equipment. Thus, the presence or absence of subordinates may be a useful factor in helping us define who the managers are. The relationship between managers and others in the organization can be seen in the very simple diagram of Figure 1.1.

The managers of an organization, as a group separate from nonmanagers, can be broken down further. Organizations differ in the language they use to define, describe, and classify that group of people who perform the management activity of the firm. Figure 1.2 shows three different sets of terms used to identify the management work force. Each set is interchangeable with the others;

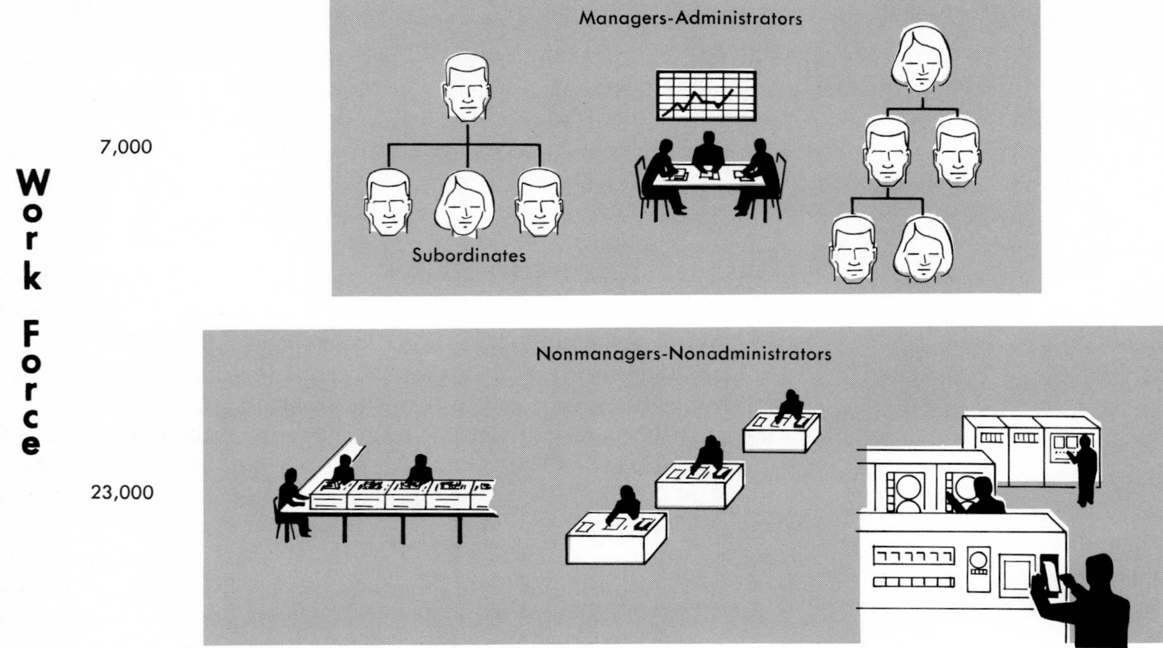

FIGURE 1.1 Organizational classification of work force (numbers represent a Midwest utility)

Are supervisors managers?

that is, the executive group in a firm may also be called the top managers, or the fourth level of management (if the fourth is the highest level). Exact definitions for these classes, however, are still difficult and vary in different organizations. For example, where does the middle-management level begin and end? Are all top managers included when the president of the firm calls for a meeting of his executives? Even with these difficulties and differences, it is possible to group managers using the ideas of classification and subordinates.

Generally speaking, supervisors, first-level personnel, and the

FIGURE 1.2 Three sets of terms used to classify managers

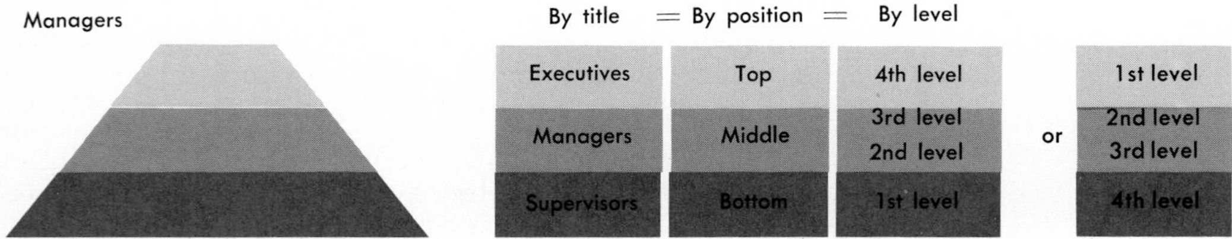

bottom segment of management are all part of the same class—a group that usually has subordinates in the hourly work force. And middle management, managers, and second- and third-level personnel are frequently the bosses of other managers. Thus, having subordinates tells us you are a manager, and the kind of subordinates tells us what level of manager you are.

It is important to realize the flexibility in using the term *manager*. Although you would be more specific if you called the president of General Motors an executive or a member of top management, you would also be right if you called him a manager. For the present, we shall refer to the entire class—from top to bottom—as managers.[1]

You can see, then, that the term *manager* subsumes a varied and diversified population. Indeed, it is often impossible to specify and describe a manager's role completely. One reason for this impossibility is the difference in the specifics of the manager's work world. Managers operate with different personal work worlds, with different internal work environments, and with different external work environments. A brief description of the work world will highlight these differences and reveal forces that shape the manager's job.

THE MANAGER'S WORK WORLD

Figure 1.3 shows the three different dimensions of a manager's work world. Every manager relates or responds to his job and to others in a very *personal, unique* way. At every moment in time, dealing with every situation and problem, he does so in the context of his own person. Who he believes he is, whom he wants to become, what forces exist in his home life—all these forces impinge on him. (This topic is developed more fully in Chapters 3, 4, 15, and 20.) Since no two managers share identical backgrounds and personality, no two managerial jobs can be performed in the same way.

The second dimension of the work world also contains ele-

[1] Our emphasis in this book is on the first, second, and third level of management, the supervisors and middle managers of organizations. Many of the "management fundamentals" are applicable to the higher levels of management, but there are some activities of top management that are beyond the scope of this book: dealing with the international dimensions of their organization, long-range planning, the lobbying functions in politics, union management strategy, money markets, legal relationships, boards of directors, etc.

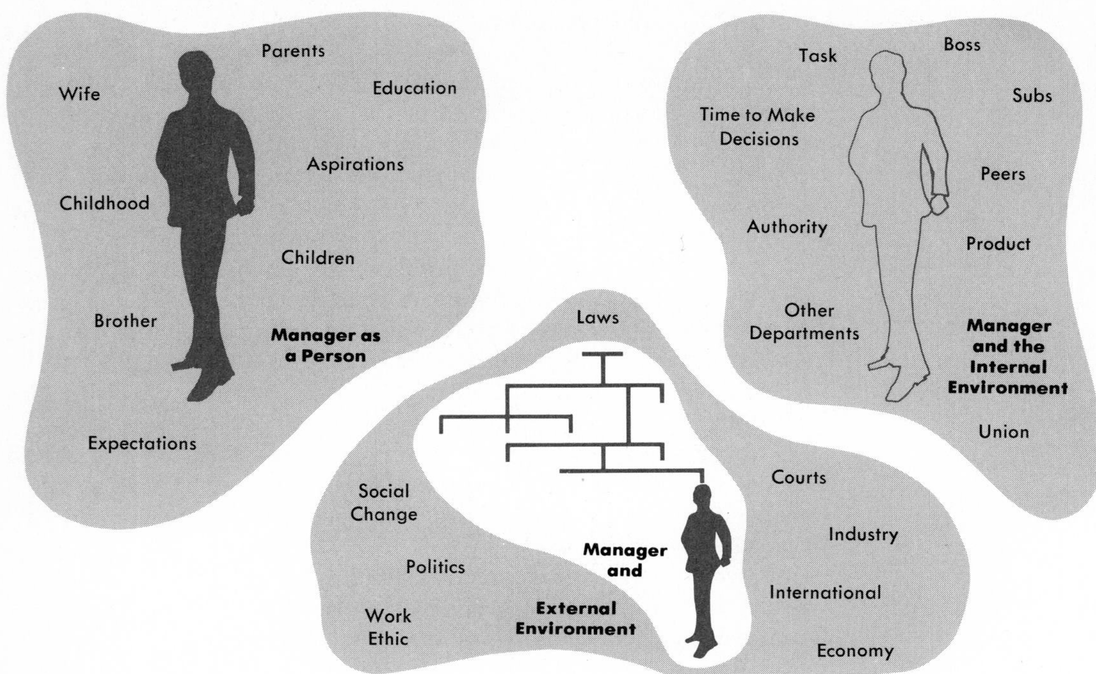

FIGURE 1.3 Three dimensions of a manager's work world

ments that demand we approach the study of management with respect for differences. The manager, personal and unique, finds his job influenced by other forces than himself. In the immediate, *internal environment* of his work world, he finds important items: the type of work required of his subordinates, the nature and number of subordinates, the interrelationships between his department or work unit and others, the amount of authority he has in his position, the methods used to determine acceptable or unacceptable performance, his relationships with other managers at his own level, and so on. These forces and many others work toward defining what managers can and cannot do. You can see that the internal work environment, although different for each job, has more similarity among managers than the personal dimension has.

internal environment

external environment

The *external environment* describes the last of the dimensions. This environment contains all those forces, factors, and information in the world that interact with the manager's organization. The nature and number of competitors, customers, or markets would be included in the external environment. The nature of the economy or society, the legal requirements affecting the industry, the degree of its technological development, and the ideological factors of the work population in general have an impact upon what the manager should do in his job to be effective. Obviously, a manager ignorant of recent labor legislation may perform illegal acts and quickly become an ineffective manager.

The manager's work world, therefore, becomes a most significant force shaping his job. Even though we will become more detailed in other sections of this chapter and throughout the book, you can see already one condition a manager must live with. The work world is dynamic and changing.

FACTORS THAT SHAPE THE MANAGER'S WORK

First we want to focus on those topics that are closer to the day-to-day operations of a manager. In most instances, we discuss items that the manager has very little direct control over, although these items do have an impact upon what he does or how he responds or how successful he will be. The recognition of these characteristics is a first step in understanding the manager's world, as well as what a manager does.

Change and Resistance to Change

Is there much change in the manager's world?

The manager's world is changing and yet is resistant to change. No two days are the same to a manager of any organization, whether he manages the staff of a YMCA in a downtown area or a group of lumbermen in the Pacific Northwest. There are so many variables impinging upon the manager's day—he cannot know what phone call will come in the next minute, what machine will break down, what customer will register a complaint, what boss will give a commendation, or what plan will fail.

The manager will find that there are many surrounding him who want change. He will not fully know why they want it; he will only sense a desire for change. Some want change to improve the present situation, yet the manager will find some resisting such change. For example, organizations are encouraged to hire women managers; at the same time, there is some resistance to accepting them. Change can be very costly. The expense sheet of a manager can run out of control if change runs wild. Change brings on the unknown and people sometimes fear the unknown. And so one of the first factors that shape the manager's world is that he simultaneously faces conditions for change and conditions resisting change.

Knowns and Unknowns

Can a manager expect to know what's going on?

The manager's world is made up of unknowns and knowns. Since he must anticipate the future, it is almost certain that a great deal of what he has to do focuses on dealing with the unknown, the future, which no person can predict. For example, the recent oil crisis was largely unpredicted. The manager may not always know himself; his motives, his career plans, the outcome of a particular decision—all may be unknown to him. He does not know that one decision is better than another. Neither does he know all he needs to know about the people around him. People send guarded communication signals to him, and thus he is always less than fully informed.

What does a manager know?

And yet there is much about the job that is known. The manager knows what authority he has, or what authority his people will allow him to have. He knows what may be expected of him by his office. He can see the income and expense of his operation. He is made aware through feedback from other sources of whether his decisions were successful or unsuccessful. He is a thinking animal and is able to take many of the knowns and do something with them.

Controllables and Uncontrollables

The manager's world consists of controllable and uncontrollable elements. A manager may be able to influence a particular subordinate but have very little influence over a group of them when a union issue is involved. A manager may be able to influence his boss in a decision-making problem but have little influence in affecting the decisions of his peers. A manager may be trapped—he may have not enough authority and too much responsibility—if materials that he must process in his department are not under his control and yet higher management holds him responsible for the work and the productivity of these materials. The manager may be able to control the pay rate and scale of the people who work for him, yet he cannot control the aspirations that his people have for work or promotion in the company. A manager may have control over the work methods of people but little control over the effort that people put into these work methods.

A manager does not always know what constitutes successful performance for promotion. "Being in the right spot at the right time" may well be beyond his control, and yet this condition leads to promotion for many managers in organizations today. A manager may be able to control the conditions under which employees work but be unable to control the face-to-face contact that his people may have. There is a realm of elements, some uncontrollable and some controllable, both constantly changing. Thus, a person who believes that a manager has great control is in for surprise, disappointment, and a frustrating managerial life.

Limits and Freedom

What kinds of limits does a manager face?

Although the manager's world is full of constraints, the opportunity for individual freedom does exist. In all organizations, managers assume the responsibility for productivity—some kind of output. The economic concept of profit has one meaning to all managers, even those in nonprofit organizations: In order for an organization to survive, the amount of output must be greater than the amount of input. In profit-oriented organizations, managers are held responsible for running profitable units—the revenues produced by their unit must be in excess of the expenses. There are some variations of this, of course, but basically, no organization can survive over time if the energy to sustain its operations is greater than the return that it receives.

Within this profit limitation, most managers of organizations have found a great deal of freedom to manage as they best see fit. Except when the work of employees and managers is constantly controlled by machinery, managers are generally free to create the plans and methods and to direct and supervise operations in a way that will be beneficial to the organization.

Behavioral Insight and Performance Competence

Must a manager be a political animal?

Besides the specific job performance required from the manager, his world includes relationships requiring behavioral sensitivity and organizational reality. The manager's world in organizations involves give-and-take behavior. The saying, "I will do this for you if you do this for me," applies very well to organizations. There are managers who have tremendous drives for power and use the organization and its people as stepping-stones to the power thrones. There are managers, either competent or incompetent, who recognize the importance of the politics within organizations; "getting on the right side of the boss" is part of the real world of managers.

Does performance pay off?

As stated earlier, an organization that does not show results will soon die or cease to exist in its present form. The corporate officials of most organizations have been so conditioned that, in the last analysis, performance is usually valued more than political awareness. We do not want to depict the world as "either—or"; rather, we want to indicate that in the manager's world there is a realm of political maneuvering as well as objective evaluation.

Opportunities and Risks

The manager's world is filled with both opportunities and risks. Most managers are not members of any union. They do not bargain collectively for wages, nor are they guaranteed any rights through the power group of large numbers of organized workers. It is uncommon for managers to have legally binding contracts. This means that a manager may be released on a Friday and find he is unemployed and looking for a job on the weekend. Individual-to-organization relationships in the managerial world are very, very different from those in the work world of the organized employee.

Managers who at an early stage showed much promise, career growth, and mobility may find themselves classified as nonpromotable for any of a dozen reasons—when they have a bad performance year, or when their boss suddenly changes jobs. Once labeled nonpromotable, a person is frequently put on a shelf and only tolerated within an organization. Thus, there is great potential for the development of insecurity and fear in a manager in an organization, since he has few legal rights for his protection and must develop himself so that the organization continually views him as a valuable asset.

To develop and become an asset is not easy, for as our manager grows and matures, he may well decline in many of the attributes that made him attractive to an organization. He may not have the same energy. He may not show the same freedom to criticize. He may not be as willing to pick up and move to new locations, because his wife or children do not want to make the move. For whatever reason, the assets of a manager vary throughout his career because he changes, as does the organization. But the picture is not all pessimistic.

Is management all dark and gloomy?

There is a short supply of capable managers in organizations, so that a manager who finds himself cut off in one organization has the freedom and mobility to affiliate with another firm. A manager is usually broadly trained, and thus the skills developed in one organization are frequently transferable to another. If a manager has the ablilty to perform and manage his unit, it is possible that he will advance, develop, and find a satisfying sense of accomplishment and achievement.

In the preceding paragraphs and pages we have discussed some factors important to the manager's work. We have intentionally steered clear of many management "sayings," for we feel that what is important to the practicing or potential manager is a grasp of the reality of his world rather than a series of truisms that dissolve when put to the test. We believe the world of the manager is an exciting one. We contend that the demands placed upon the managers in organizations are legitimate demands; that the problems the manager faces are amenable to solutions. We admit that there are many unknowns concerning the management of organizations. This is an important limitation that a manager must always carry with him. We also submit, however, that much is known and that a manager has a responsibility to make himself aware of this information.

All the factors just discussed are present in varying degrees in all managerial jobs and are common to much work, managerial or otherwise. There is another important factor that we shall treat separately, which is not as nebulous as the others. The manager will gain much by spending considerable time thinking about those characteristics of the specific organization for which he works that relate to his job.

THE ROLE OF THE ORGANIZATION IN DEFINING THE MANAGER'S FUNCTIONS

Many characteristics of an organization are beyond the influence and control of a manager, yet are critical to the life he must live in the organization. One characteristic is the idea of the life cycle of organizations.

The Life Cycle of Organizations

life cycle

In a very simple way you might say that organizations have three major stages in their *life cycle*—a start-up stage, a keep-going stage, and a slow-down or start-again stage. Organizations obviously *get started.* Once created, they tend to expand and get larger. The second stage in the evolution, then, is the period that could be labeled the *stabilizing stage,* when an organization, finding itself in the industry or economy, is making adjustments to changes and is attempting to survive in perhaps a very competitive situation. The third stage of organization has two possibilities. An organization that has been unable to adjust will move to a *slow death* or bankruptcy stage and terminate its existence. Or it may *innovate* with new ideas and new approaches to its problems, or merge with other firms to start another growth cycle in its history. Organizations, therefore, have a *starting point,* a *stabilizing point,* and a kind of *termination–start-again point.*

Books about the history of business management are filled with case histories of defunct companies. Although small businesses are most susceptible to failure, giant firms are not immune. W.T. Grant, a firm in the retail merchandising industry, closed its doors in the mid 1970's and the Penn Central Railroad struggles for survival in the transportation industry. No industry is protected against "organizational cancer," for there are failures in the aircraft, automobile, fast-foods, utility, and banking industries, and even in the educational industry.

A knowledge of the life-cycle position of a company may help a manager with a number of career-cycle decisions. Only three examples of such decisions will be offered here; they are related to the idealized life cycle of an organization in Figure 1.4.

Do you know what your assets are?

THE VALUE OF KNOWING ABOUT LIFE CYCLE Knowing the life-cycle position of a company may help a manager *match his own needs* with those of the company. For example, if a manager's primary assets are innovating, contributing new ideas, and accepting change, a company in the early stages of growth would value that manager. A company that has stabilized its growth (and is thus in its second stage) would find such managerial characteristics disruptive. On the other hand, a manager who does not particularly like constant change might enjoy working with an organization that is in the stabilizing stage; in such a stage, his particular assets would match those of the company. At any point of a growth cycle, the manager would do well to make an assessment of his own abilities and characteristics to see if they match those demanded by the situation.

The knowledge of a company's life cycle can help a manager *direct his own efforts.* A manager should reassess what he has been

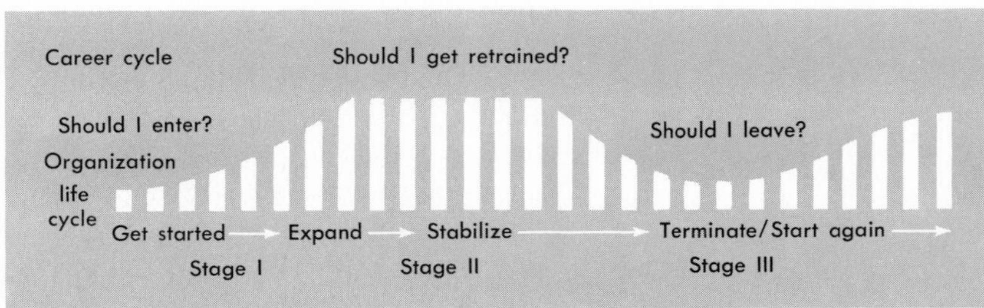

FIGURE 1.4 Relationship of career cycle to an organization's life cycle

doing in terms of the company's stage of growth, and ask whether what he has been doing relates to what the company seems to need at that point in its life cycle. If there is no match from the re-assessment, the manager may be able to train or develop himself more in line with the company's stage of growth.

The knowledge of the life-cycle position of a company can be very helpful to a manager in knowing *when to make a change* in jobs. The worst time for a manager to go into the job market searching for other managerial opportunities is when he has been released from a company in its last stage. The best time to move is when he is still mobile and the organization is still respected as a source of employment. It is possible for a manager to sense the characteristics of "organizational cancer" and to make plans for moving to other organizations before the final stage is reached.

The life-cycle concept is not restricted to industries or corporations. The idea has meaning in terms of departments or functions. For example, during a time of high employment, the personnel manager is very important because he has to search for capable managerial talent. Similarly, when an organization is in the early stages of growth with a new union, a great deal of uncertainty exists and the personnel function is again vital. At a later stage in the growth of the company and the union, the personnel function may not be as critical. The knowledge of life cycle as an organizational characteristic is important in terms of both matching a manager to the organization and directing his efforts.

The Environment of an Organization

Are all organizations the same?

What is it that a manager of a tax firm and a manager of a mortuary have in common? Regardless of the economic conditions of the country, most people have to pay taxes, and all eventually die; so both these managers face a dependable group of customers with considerable certainty.

As mentioned earlier, organizations exist in a particular setting or *environment*. One way that organizations differ is in customers. The customers for durable goods are very different from the customers for nondurable goods. Moreover, even within an industry, each organization exists in a particular environment. For example, the customers in the automobile industry differ; thus, each company attempts to establish brand loyalty, so that a Ford customer remains a Ford customer over the years. Attempts are made to capture the customers of other products; for instance, the American automobile industry attempts to capture the American consumer of foreign imported cars. A decision by a foreign manufacturer to invest, produce, and distribute goods in the United States might well affect one American firm in the industry and yet leave another untouched.

The illustration about death and taxes highlights the insensitivity of both these occupations to the economy. But an organization that deals with luxury or specialty items might well be affected by a recession or depression, whereas a firm dealing with staple goods would not be affected as much. Perhaps the best example of the action-reaction picture that we are describing is the clothing industry, where the particular demands of social groups drastically affect the marketability of a product. Other factors that give rise to a particular environment include legal statutes, differences between states and their interpretations and enforcement of laws (especially dealing with the questions of pollution control), and the intensity of competition. Thus we see that one characteristic of an organization is that it does not exist in a vacuum. In addition to an organization's having a life cycle, it also has an environment that conditions, constrains, and tempers a great deal of its action. No organization is totally independent of the economy, the society, the legal environment, its customers, and its competition.

THE VALUE OF ENVIRONMENT INSIGHT TO A MANAGER The relevance of this knowledge to the manager is probably very clear. A manager of a corporation who believes he can operate independently of his competition may have successive unprofitable years, for he is waging an upstream, uphill fight. A manager who does not recognize the nature of his customers—their idiosyncracies, desires, moods, and so on—will soon find himself in that final, dark stage of the life cycle. As mentioned earlier, the manager can match his particular assets with the organizational environment. If he is highly trained in a legal area, then he would be underutilizing his talents if he affiliated with a firm that had little responsiveness to the legal changes in the industry. A manager who knows the dependence his firm has on the economy will attempt to anticipate changes in the economy and make appropriate plans.

The Tradition, Life-style, and Image of Organizations

Every person is unique. Each one has a personality and behavior that belong to that individual. So, too, with organizations.

tradition

The U.S. Marine Corps, for example, has developed a *tradition* from the experiences and behavior of its men throughout the years. The psychological expectation that others have of marines gives it its tradition and *life-style*. The same process applies to other organizations.

Many corporations attempt to develop a life-style among their managers by insisting that they wear similar types of clothing on the job, that they drive similar automobiles, and even that they reside in certain areas within a city. Perhaps an example will highlight what we mean by this tradition or life-style.

Do clothes make the banker?

Many people consider banking a rather conservative industry. That is, you do not expect to walk into a bank and find the employees wearing loud, wild, or bizarre clothing. Their managers usually greet you in business suits. There are some banks that even insist upon white shirts as part of the uniform that generates a particular *image*. What they are trying to convey to the customer is the idea and feeling of stability, credibility, and security. These managers feel that casual clothes and eccentric behavior suggest flightiness, uncertainty, and rapid change—features that might be perceived negatively by potential customers. Thus, the tradition and life-style are perpetuated through the behavior, practices, policies, and procedures of management.

image

In every industry, then, you find a different but definite tradition. There are some industries that tend to lead in terms of innovation and risk taking. Some companies within an industry lead in establishing prices, in introducing new products, and in moving against the trend. In many such industries, there are also followers—those firms that have decided that the leadership costs are too high and whose heritage dictates to them a follower role. This is not to say that only in the leader role can an organization be profitable. What we are saying here is that there is a niche or place that an organization fits best into, and it is an intelligent organization that is able to identify the features that give it its definite tradition and life-style.

THE VALUE OF TRADITION INSIGHTS TO A MANAGER The awareness of life-style and tradition is valuable to managers who are in the position of developing objectives and establishing the long-range plans of organizations. The manager who does not know of his company's tradition or life-style may be making decisions that are counter to the productivity of the company; for, as mentioned earlier, industries, companies, departments, and functions all have an interdependence. A follower of the sports world is aware of what we mean by tradition and life-style, for certain teams are primarily known as offensive teams in football, or run-and-shoot teams in basketball, or pitching teams and low-hit teams in baseball. What holds true in the world of athletics also exists in the organization world.

The life-style of an organization can be changed. A basketball manager who has had to play defensive basketball because of the inability of higher management to recruit tall basketball players may change his life-style with some successful recruits—a number of seven-footers. *Fortune, Business Week,* and *The Wall Street Journal* are filled with stories of organizations that have changed trends inherent in the tradition and life-style with managerial innovations.

We have just looked at three characteristics of the organization that have rather fixed effects upon the particular managerial job. Knowledge of the organization's life cycle, its particular environment, and its tradition are valuable to a manager who wants to take advantage of such information.

SUMMARY AND PROPOSITIONS

In this chapter we introduced you to the manager. Our description has been broad and varied so that you will expect to encounter no stereotypes. This open-ended definition was necessary in view of the many factors that shape the manager's work. Some of these factors were discussed in the second part of the chapter. Then, in contrast to these nonspecific factors, the third part of the chapter included three important aspects of a very definite influence on a manager—the specific organization for which he works. Thus, having met the manager at the start, you went on to focus attention on forces shaping the manager's functions. You are now ready for a closer look at the manager's job in the next chapter.

As we complete each chapter in this book, we shall propose some useful generalizations to help in the management of an organization. These statements or propositions are composed of summary ideas from the chapter, and provocative ideas that have not yet been completely tested but that offer explicit guides for your own reflection and some clues as to "how to do it." You can use these propositions in your personal study and in class discussions as (1) a summary for review, (2) tentative statements upon which further thought and discussion can evolve, and (3) checklists for your own practice of management. In Chapter 1, we offer the following propositions:

1. The idea of managers as a class is useful to understanding the manager's job.
   a. Middle managers in all organizations tend to perform similar management functions.
   b. Managing nonmanagerial subordinates is easier than managing managerial subordinates.
2. Certain managers "fit better" with certain types of organizations.

   a. Innovative managers thrive in rapidly changing organizations.
   b. Aggressive managers create friction in stabilized organizations.
3. Change is the most common factor in all management positions.
   a. Organizations must change or they die.
   b. People frequently resist change.
   c. Managers deal with both organizations and people.
4. One of the most important jobs for a manager is identifying his own and his company's niche or place in this world.
   a. Companies in the wrong niche underachieve.
   b. Managers in the wrong niche become nonpromotable.
5. The better manager is aware of the forces that shape his job.
   a. The better manager accepts many forces as the givens of a situation and responds accordingly.
   b. The better manager responds to the forces by trying to influence the force or the impact of the force on the situation.
6. Every organization has an image or tradition.
   a. The real test of an organization's image is what others believe it to be.
   b. What you believe an organization's image is affects how you behave in that organization.

STUDY ASSIGNMENTS

1. *What are our objectives in writing this book?*
2. *Do you think our plan (see the Table of Contents) will enable you to meet the objectives? Explain your answer.*
3. *Notice the contents of Part 4, "The Reality of Managing," and then answer these questions:*
   a. *In what ways is Part 4 different from the other parts?*
   b. *What is Part 4's role in the overall objectives of the book? Explain.*
   c. *Why do you think the other parts differ from Part 4? Why isn't the whole book a focus on the "reality of managing?"*
4. *Why does "having subordinates" help in defining managers?*
5. *What are some differences among different levels or classes of management?*

6. *Why is it important for you to know some of the forces that shape a manager's job? What is the value of this information to you?*

7. *Give examples of companies or organizations from your own community that may fit into the stages of the life cycle shown in Figure 1.4.*

8. *Think of three organizations that have an image, tradition and life-style.*
   a. *What is the image of each?*
   b. *How does this image get expressed through specific behavior or organizational policies or procedures?*
   c. *In what ways would an organization's image be important to you if you were thinking of joining it?*

9. *Do you accept Proposition 1(*b*) as true? Explain your answer.*

10. *Explain why Propositions 2(*a*) and 2(*b*) may be true. Use examples of innovative or aggressive managers to prove these propositions, or use some form of logical argument.*

11. *What do you think is the image of your educational institution from the viewpoint of the following?*
    a. *The faculty*
    b. *Yourself*
    c. *Other students*
    d. *The administrators*

12. *Are any of the viewpoints in question 11 similar? Discuss why, or why not.*

situational episodes

1. Joe had been first in his family to attend college and now held a managerial position. His older brother had stayed in the army and his father had been a union member for thirty years. Both had very definite ideas about who managers are and what they do. If you were Joe, how would you answer two questions from your father and brother:

   a. Who are the managers in an organization?

   b. What do managers do?

2. Charlie was home on vacation, and Uncle Harry stopped in to visit. Uncle Harry owned a small company in Rochester, New York. "Charlie," said Harry, "one of the things that helped me get where I am was a suggestion from a friend of mine to identify personal goals and objectives early in life. What are your goals or objectives? What do you expect to receive from a career in management?" Write up a statement of *your* answers to Uncle Harry's two questions.

Defining the manager's job

TWO

OBJECTIVES YOU SHOULD MEET

List *some of the elements of the management concept emphasized by leading management writers.*

State *the basic functions performed by a manager.*

Identify *the chief problems faced by managers.*

Summarize *the most important types of knowledge needed by managers.*

Restate *in your own words some useful generalizations about management development.*

WHAT IS MANAGEMENT?

"There's nothing like a late breakfast, is there, honey?" Bob Allison says to his wife, Carol. "In a way, I'm glad my day off is Wednesday, when the kids are in school. I can sleep late and we can have our coffee together."

"I know what you mean," Carol replies. "The last few months have almost been too much for me. You've been working such long hours, we hardly see each other. Yesterday I saw your mother in town and she said you're looking so much older than 31. Gosh, we all do. . . . Are things any better at the office? What about that trip you took to Detroit? . . . Did you talk to the professors?"

"Yeah, and did they shake me up!"

"Gee, the profs I had at the community college were nice. How did these upset you?"

"Well, you know, the company is sending all of us to the university for three weeks of training—and me with only a high school education. For some reason, these profs wanted to talk with us district directors from the Midwest—Sandy from St. Louis; Harry from Chicago; Red from Detroit. Things went fine at first. There were three profs: Sam Timer, Peter Smith, and a guy, Andy, with a funny last name. I was surprised how young they were and how easygoing they seemed—really put us at ease.

"At first, each of us told something about our background. I told them how after high school we got married and I went to electronics school in the navy . . . how after the navy I worked as an electronics technician at two different companies, getting laid off each time because of defense-contract cancellations. Boy, were they surprised to hear how I got started with Ole Harpey's Hams—yeah, I told them how I was working as a bartender and got interviewed on the job. The profs

thought I was putting them on, but the other guys had had similar experiences. Remember, I told you how Red got interviewed while he was driving a cab in Chicago.

"It was when the profs started asking us questions about our jobs that we all got shaky. Each guy had had a kinda similar experience . . . bounced around from one job to another until we joined Harpey's. Of course, I started with the franchise instead of company-owned stores. But even with Mr. Thomas's franchise, our training was the same. Remember how I started as a management trainee and worked over the stoves for four weeks, learning how to cook the hams and fries? Then I became an assistant store manager, cooking and selling to customers and occasionally opening the store at 11 A.M. or closing at 11 P.M. And it wasn't until I became a store manager six months later that I figured out why my manager never let me check the tapes on the cash register—he was keeping some of the money for himself. I told the profs how I heard him tell someone that if I knew all the secrets of the business—the special recipes and ways of cooking the hams—I'd be able to replace him. His training approach was to keep everybody below him in the dark and complain to his boss how dumb we were.

"I went on to explain that once E.J. Thomas realized I wouldn't cheat him, I got promoted to assistant and then supervisor. I had five stores under me. Remember how I had to spend all those hours visiting the stores, checking on the managers to see that everything was OK?

"It was at this point that I explained how Ole Harpey's Hams started to buy back the franchise owners . . . how Mr. Thomas became a vice-president and I became a district director, all these promotions through the levels of management in just six years."

"But, Bob, why did you say that the questions from the professors shook you up? So far, everything you've said seems innocent enough."

"Well, they asked us questions about our future in the company. Where did we think we were going? Did we have people trained to take our places? What did we think was different between managers and nonmanagers? What kind of planning did we do? Had we any thoughts of innovation to improve our sales picture? Why did we spend so much of our time driving around town visiting the stores and the people?

"Carol, all of a sudden it seemed to dawn on all of us there that in spite of our time and experience with the company, in spite of our good salaries (I'll bet the range of the district directors was from $28,000 to $42,000), in spite of our loyalty and desire, we don't know what the hell we're doing. And now, because of the tightness of the economy and increased competition, there's a profit squeeze and we don't know what to do but to tell our people to try harder."

"Maybe you'll learn what management is during the three weeks of training at the university course."

"I don't know. Maybe the profs will try to snow us with big words and diagrams."

"If you don't understand something, you should ask questions."

"And show how dumb I am. Listen, the company doesn't fool me.

They'll have some spies in the group who'll report back to top management on all of us. I'm not going to play into their hands."

"Maybe you should think about looking for another job, in a different kind of work."

"What can an ex-bartender and nonmanager do for a living?"

Many of us are like Bob Allison and find that we have opportunities to be a manager even though we might not know just what the position really is. We may be flattered by the offer of a manager's position because we know that the pay opportunities are very attractive and the title sounds good when we tell our friends about our work. Even if we have been in a managerial position for some time, as Bob has, we may not have realized that the qualifications for a position of manager are different from those for engineers, technicians, scientists, doctors, lawyers, or craftsmen.

Do you really want to be a manager?

If a person likes to do things himself, without worrying about directing the activities of others, he might find that accepting a manager's position does not fit his basic interests. Yet the obvious advantages of being a manager often cause a person to accept the position in spite of a feeling of insecurity due to lack of knowledge about management and its processes. The objective of this chapter is to make available more knowledge about what a manager does, for those who aspire for managers' positions and for those who, like Bob Allison, find themselves in positions with the "bear by the tail."

A manager normally has greater freedom and authority than a nonmanager to get things done. He may be in a better position to know what is going on and to feel a real satisfaction in being where the action is. He can have an assistant, come and go as he pleases (when he feels that he has others working as they are expected to), and have many fringe benefits that go with the manager classification. He is looked up to (and criticized) by his subordinates. He is considered part of the "establishment" and thus develops inner conflicts when he must carry out certain duties for the good of the organization that may adversely affect friends to whom he feels obligations. He may not do physical labor (and may thus become flabby and overweight), but he may become tired mentally (and need a psychiatrist). In short, there are good and bad characteristics in the manager's position. Whether a person wants to be a manager or not depends upon how he views the opportunities and costs in the light of his own interests and abilities.

In this chapter, we supply information about the position of a manager so that you will have a better idea of what a manager does. First, we summarize how others have viewed the field of management; second, we outline the processes of management; third, we look at some problems managers face; fourth, we identify the knowledge that managers need; and finally, we present our approach in this book for developing management fundamentals for a changing world.

CONCEPTS OF MANAGEMENT AS VIEWED BY OTHER WRITERS

Writers on management have developed various focuses on the problems, knowledge, and functions of managers. In their integration, they tend to distill their ideas into their own key focus. It will be useful for you, even at this early stage, to try to restate your present understanding of the concepts of management in a short statement that has meaning to you. To help you with this practice of your conceptual ability, we shall paraphrase some of the key ideas of a number of well-known leaders in the development of management thought and shall ask you to place each of these viewpoints into one or more of the seven processes to be discussed in the next section. Our advice is not only to borrow some of these ideas from us and from the leader discussed but also to steal these ideas and make them your own. (This is one time that taking something from someone else is ethically and educationally sound.)

management

First, we define *management* as the process by which a cooperative group directs actions of others toward common goals. This process is handled by a distinguishable group (managers) that coordinates activities of others. Managers seldom actually perform the activities themselves. Recently, the management concept has been broadened to include the process of setting the common goals (objectives) and relating them to the goals of society.

Now let us look at what some outstanding writers have identified as the central focus of their view of management.

Concepts of Early Thinkers on Management

What did the pioneers of management say about management?

1. Mary Parker Follett: The essence of management is *coordination.* Follett was a well-known lecturer on management in England and the United States in the 1920s and 1930s. She has recently been "rediscovered" by modern writers, and modern thinking increasingly relates to her emphasis on coordination.

2. Frank Gilbreth: There is a *"one best way"* of performing any activity. Gilbreth is known as the father of motion study and methods analysis. His intense efforts toward improving efficiency have been described by two of his twelve children in a humorous book that was made into a successful motion picture, *Cheaper by the Dozen.* Many of the current improved methods used in industry come from Gilbreth's work on searching for the best way.

3. Oliver Sheldon: A manager must determine the *proper balance* between things of production and the humanity of production. Sheldon was one of the group of classical management writers in the early decades of the twentieth century. His attention to proper balance makes us feel that this concept is from a person writing in the last decade about protecting the environment while increasing oil and coal production.

4. Ralph C. Davis: The primary objective of any corporation is *service;* if service is given, profits will follow. Davis, as a management teacher at a well-known graduate school in the 1930s and 1940s, was the chief mentor of many now teaching in business schools. He predated such well-known activists as Ralph Nader in pressing corporations to focus on service.

5. Frederick W. Taylor: The *scientific method* can be applied to work problems. Taylor is often called the father of scientific management. He was both a practicing manager and writer-researcher; thus he is always listed as one of the "big names" in management.

6. Henri Fayol: Management is a process of *functions,* with planning being the most important. Fayol, a French management pioneer, improved administrative processes in France in the first two decades of the twentieth century, but his book was first translated into English in 1949. Fayol is often credited with the first focus on processes of management.

Concepts of Modern Scholarly Writers on Management

Have modern writers added to a better understanding of management?

1. Douglas McGregor: The way a person manages others depends on his assumptions about the *basic nature of man.* McGregor was one of those who emphasized the human side of management in the 1950s and 1960s.

2. Leonard Sayles: Much in a manager's world is beyond his control and planning; the manager must learn to make marginal decisions and accept *uncertainty* as part of the job. Sayles is a current provocative and stimulating writer of scholarly books.

3. Chester I. Barnard: The executive is the critical person to establish a climate where *cooperation* can exist among subordinates and work groups. Barnard was probably the most influential practicing executive and scholarly writer in laying the foundation for the change in approach from the early to the modern writers.

4. Rensis Likert: High-producing managers are viewed by their subordinates as being *supportive* in their supervisory relationships. Likert is a modern management thinker who bases his comments on extensive research.

Concepts of Modern Popular Writers on Management

Do popular writers have something to add to our understanding?

1. Peter Drucker: Managers should see to it that *objectives* get set in those areas that affect the survival and prosperity of the organization and in *measuring* results. Drucker is probably the writer most widely read by modern business executives. His books tend to interpret philosophical issues to practicing executives.

2. William H. Whyte, Jr.: The *organization man* must fight the organization; he must not surrender his individuality. Whyte has for a number of years written in popular business journals, and he received unusual attention in the early 1960s for his writing on the subject of the "organization man."

3. C. Northcote Parkinson: An official wants to *multiply subordinates,* not rivals; officials make work for each other. Parkinson originated the popular approach of humorous and hard-hitting observations about administration in practice with a number of so-called Parkinson's laws.

4. Robert Townsend: Since most people are mediocre, the true *leader* can be recognized because, somehow or other, his people consistently turn in *superior performances.* A successful business executive, he wrote a best selling book, *Up the Organiza-*

tion, which appealed to the general public and emphasized certain simple truths about management.

5. Lawrence J. Peter and Raymond Hull: In a hierarchy, every employee tends to rise to his level of *incompetence.* The "Peter Principle" was developed by a sociologist and appealed to practicing managers because of its concentration on the realities of modern organizations.

Each of these statements concentrates on an important aspect of the management concept. They show that different management experts view the important components of management with different degrees of emphasis; yet they do not conflict. You will find most of these concepts of management elaborated upon later in this chapter. As we develop the discussion, you may find that checking back on these concepts will help you form your own balanced concept of management.

THINGS MANAGERS DO

How does a manager use his knowledge to solve his problems?

Managers tend to be problem-oriented. Managers need a great deal of knowledge. Yet managers are really people of action. They don't just talk about doing things, they get them done.

processes of managing

Management books usually concentrate on management functions and processes. In fact, the subject on management is frequently defined in terms of the types of things managers do. Part 3 of this book is devoted to a description in some detail of not only what a manager does but how he does it. To keep our attention on all functions as a group, let us summarize here the *processes of managing* that are later discussed in more detail (Figure 2.1):

1. Managers *make decisions;* that is, they develop a process by which a course of action is consciously chosen from available alternatives for the purpose of achieving a desired result. Chapter 9 outlines the decision process. Chapter 10 summarizes some of the tools, techniques, and aids that can be used in this process.
2. Managers *focus on objectives.* Chapter 11 discusses how to set definite goals and objectives.
3. Managers *plan and set policies;* that is, they anticipate the future and discover alternative courses of action; then they set guidelines for future decisions. Chapter 12 elaborates on these functions.

4. Managers *organize and staff* the positions; that is, they use a process by which the structure and allocation of jobs is determined and then place people in these jobs. Chapter 6 discusses the design of organization structure, and Chapter 13 focuses on staffing the positions called for in the structure.
5. Managers *communicate* with subordinates, colleagues, and superiors; in other words, managers transmit ideas to others for the purpose of effecting a desired result. Chapter 14 covers this linking function.
6. Managers *direct and supervise;* that is, they secure actual performance from subordinates toward common goals and objectives. Chapter 15 talks about this action phase and the qualities of leadership.
7. Managers *control activities;* that is, they utilize processes that measure actual performance and guide it toward some predetermined goal. Chapter 16 explains the essentials of all control systems and outlines the specific characteristics of particular types of control systems.

These seven processes are closely interrelated and often occur in different sequences or simultaneously. The list will help you analyze mentally the different parts of a manager's job, and to identify just what management is and what managers do. The list can be expanded or contracted; some writers include coordinating,

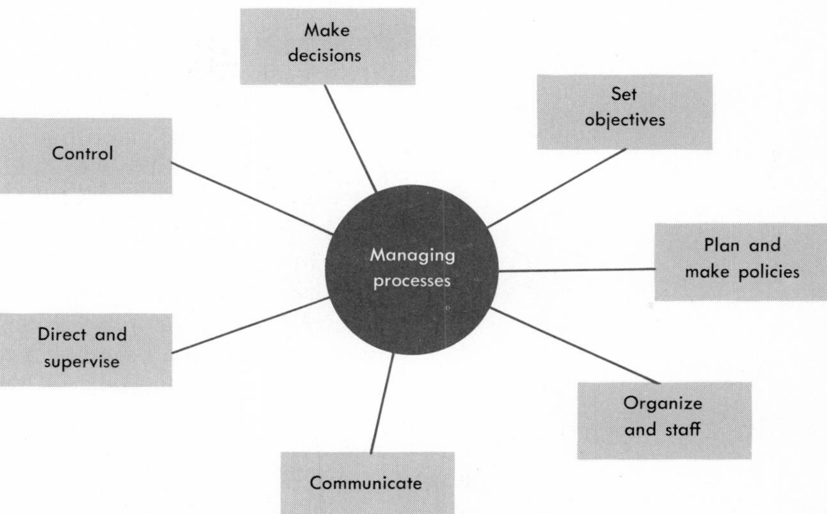

FIGURE 2.1 Processes of managing

leading, motivating, and so on. The preceding list, however, is complete, as you will find when you read the individual chapters. The important thing at this stage is that you get an idea of just what the subject is about.

PROBLEMS MANAGERS FACE

Managers are specialists in solving problems for the organization. We emphasize in later chapters that the ability to recognize potential problems soon enough, the ability to face up to the problems as they appear, and the ability to shift attention quickly from one problem to another are all critical to successful management. Initially, therefore, the potential manager needs to recognize the value of developing these abilities; our first step, then, is to identify the nature of the problems managers face daily.

Human and Organizational Problems

Why should you worry about other people's problems?

A manager cannot avoid dealing daily with a variety of people, some acting rationally, some irrationally. Yet the first and foremost human problem for a manager is to recognize that he himself is a human being and that he must live with himself. He must seek to understand himself. At times, he might feel that the organization certainly would be easier to manage if he could eliminate human problems—yet to do this would eliminate himself!

A manager cannot avoid problems of "getting along with people" and telling others what to do. In short, a manager assumes the role of leadership. Although all leaders are not managers, and although managers perform other functions in addition to leading, the ability to meet human and organizational problems as a leader has received major attention in recent years. We shall discuss the knowledge necessary for handling human problems in the next three chapters and the subject of leadership in Chapter 15, but at the outset you should understand the relationship between human problems and other managerial activities. Figure 2.2 graphically shows how human and behavioral problems relate to managing. Later, we shall use this diagram to focus on the different components as we present them in greater detail.

When a person first becomes a manager, or when he is promoted to a different manager's position, the way others view him changes. He must act like a manager. Even a side remark may be interpreted by others differently from the way they would have interpreted it if he were not a manager. Within a ten-minute period, his role is interpreted (by telephone, personal contact, or written memos) differently by several types of human contact.

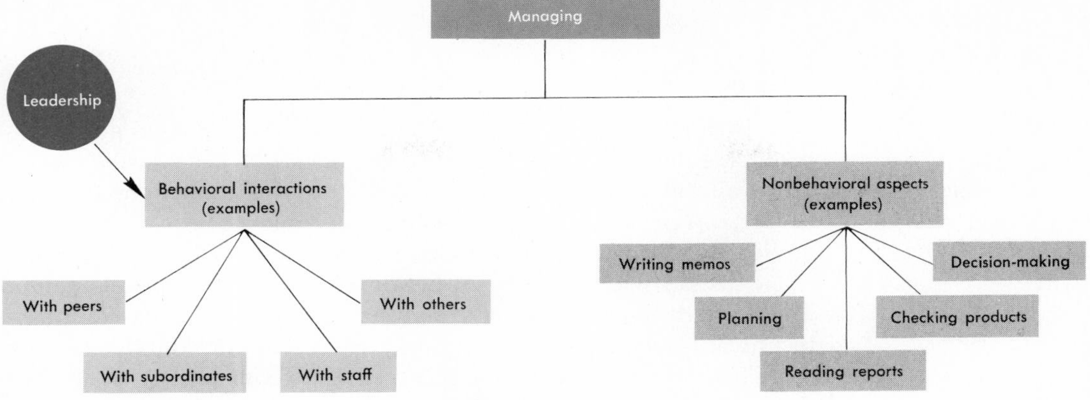

FIGURE 2.2 Relationship of leadership to managing

Does becoming a manager change your behavior with other people?

As a superior to his own work group, the manager is viewed as a "boss" who can reward or penalize subordinates. He is not just Bob Allison; he is Bob Allison, the one to whom his subordinates look for guidance, for an example of behavior, and for supportive help. He is not just "one of the boys." He may appear as a "regular guy," but he is the No. 1 regular guy. He must answer questions or find ways to obtain answers. He must listen and communicate with his subordinates. He may deliberate, but he must give the appearance of being decisive and a man of action. In short, human problems of subordinates need to be met whether they involve individual or group problems.

As a subordinate to his superior, the manager is viewed as an extension of upper management. He is expected to assume the responsibility for mistakes by any member of his work group. He is assumed to identify with the good of the organization and to have loyalty to his superior. He is expected to interpret directives from higher management from the viewpoint of the organization. Although he may have considerable discretion in these interpretations, he must fit in with upper management and its ideas while keeping it informed of what his work group thinks and does. In short, he is a representative of management to his work group; he is *a man in the middle* (Figure 2.3).

FIGURE 2.3 The manager as a man in the middle

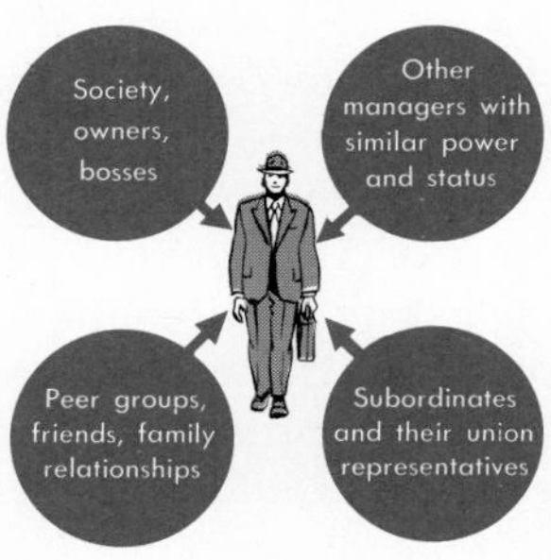

When he deals with people outside the organization, the manager is viewed as a representative of his organization. Often his action is the organization's action. He is a public relations representative of the organization (even though it may have a separate Public Relations Department). In short, human problems with people outside the firm involve the relationships of his own organization to the community and society in general.

Technical Problems

Do you really need to worry about "nut and bolts"?

Increasingly, the technical aspects of the manager's job pose problems he must face. The manager does not necessarily need to know all the technical answers, but he must know where to get the answers. When he meets a technical problem, he obtains expert advice from technical specialists, but the manager is the one who must decide which course of action to take on technical matters. The underlying problem for him is to know enough about the technical issues to be able to judge whose technical advice to take.

The technical problems of a manager cover such a wide scope that we can only outline the general classes of these problems:

1. Problems relating to the physical aspects of the workplace, such as building and equipment design, layout, working conditions, work flow, and handling of products
2. Product design and efficiency of the service rendered by the organization, such as the technical characteristics of the product or service, the reliability and serviceability of the output, the choice of materials and parts, the warranties and guarantees to the customer, the unintended social effects of pollution, risks to the safety of the user, and environmental effects
3. The choice of the technology to be used, including the type of machines, automatic controls, and transportation equipment
4. The rate of depreciation and obsolescence of the equipment and processes employed
5. The maintenance of the physical resources of the organization
6. The risks from natural forces, such as wind, fire, and floods
7. The legal problems imposed by government regulations pertaining to competition, labor relations, racial matters, and so on

Let us illustrate these classes of technical problems by assuming that you have recently been hired to be a service manager of a medium-sized garage and service station. Immediately, you want to improve the working conditions, the flow of cars into the workplace, the location of tools, and the means of making best use of your skilled mechanics. You will face problems of diagnosing auto mechanical problems, so you should obtain testing equipment to help your workers go directly to an auto's problem. In cases where you have a number of similar types of automotive problems, you may consider special automatic equipment that will help you become known as a specialist for a particular type of problem—for example, mufflers, transmissions, or wheel alignment. As you start to use more specialized types of capital equipment (such as auto lifts and car-washing equipment), you will face the questions of depreciation and obsolescence of the equipment and the problems of maintenance. Fire is one specific natural risk you face, so you will want to emphasize safety measures and insurance in the event that a disaster occurs. You will want to comply with regulations for minimum wages, length of workday, price collusion with other garages, equal-opportunity laws, health and safety regulations, and many other legal issues. Furthermore, if your garage can become known as one that stands by its repair responsibilities to the customer, you may be able not only to avoid the large amount of criticism heaped on your competitors, but also to use this image of honest workmanship to greatly increase your clientele.

Technical problems tend to require greater attention of managers at lower levels of the organization, whereas middle and top managers spend more of their time with other problems. At the early stages of the development of management, the scientific managers focused on technical problems. In recent years, these have received little or no attention in the management literature. Throughout your managerial career, you will continue to build on your technical knowledge base.

Budgetary and Financial Problems

How do you get funds to do what needs to be done?

A manager is usually responsible for securing and disbursing funds through his own efforts. He must be able to present his case to his superiors so that they will understand the financial needs of his work group. For example, he may need to seek a raise for a good subordinate. He needs to work within the budgetary allocations set by his superiors. If he overspends, he must explain the reasons for his actions; if he comes up with excess funds, he may lose them in the next allocation unless he shows that it was the result of his own skill and not because he had too much in the first place. Budgetary and financial problems have often been assumed to be assignments for top management; however, the recent trend is to spread budget problems to all managers, including first-line supervisors.

A manager need not be an accountant or an economist, but he needs to understand how his financial problems can be answered successfully. Maintaining accounting, production, and budgetary records is a part of his job. In short, the way he faces the problems of using scarce resources economically can have a great effect on his ability to handle human, organizational, and technical problems. Since all levels of managers need a basic understanding of financial problems, we elaborate in Chapters 10 and 12 on techniques to help meet these problems.

Integrating and Conceptual Problems

How can you put all the parts together?

As a manager moves up in his organization, he faces increasingly the conceptual problems of dealing with individual problems as part of a larger, broader, and more complex set of problems. Throughout this book, we analyze different aspects of management, but we continually look at the forest in addition to each tree. Therefore, we refer throughout to systems, relationships, interfaces, integrations, comprehensive understanding, coordination of parts, connective tissues, and so on. In short, management problems ultimately involve *conceptually integrating* specific and identifiable parts into a whole. Studying the vignettes and actual situations presented in this book will increase your awareness of this integrating problem.

Recently, the view of management as a system with interlocking components has improved the knowledge base for conceptually interrelating parts to the whole, and so we discuss this view early in Chapter 7. Our last chapter concentrates on helping meet conceptual issues, but meeting this type of problem requires continual practice. We thus mention it early in the book, refer to it constantly throughout, summarize it in Chapter 21, and suggest your continued attention to it throughout your practice of management.

KNOWLEDGE MANAGERS NEED

Does a manager need to know everything?

Our summary of the problems faced by a manager gives us a clue to the types of knowledge he needs. As a first approximation, we can see that the manager needs knowledge in many areas. These needs make it desirable that he have a well-balanced general understanding of many subject areas. If he has been a specialist in his past experience and education, he will probably need to broaden the scope of his knowledge. One fault often observed in a person in a new managerial position is his tendency to continue to give too much attention to doing the work himself in his own area of specialization, rather than leaving that to someone else (managers call this *delegating*) and developing skills in his nonspecialty.

According to Robert L. Katz, effective administration rests on *three basic developable skills,* which obviate the need for identifying specific traits and which may provide a useful way of looking at and understanding the administrative process. The three basics are technical skill, human skill, and conceptual skill.

Technical skill

Technical skill implies an understanding of, and proficiency in, a specific kind of activity, particularly one involving methods, processes, procedures, or techniques.

Human skill

Human skill is the executive's ability to work effectively as a group member and to build cooperative effort within the team he leads. As technical skill is primarily concerned with working with "things," so human skill is primarily concerned with working with people.

Conceptual skill

Conceptual skill involves the ability to see the enterprise as a whole: It includes recognizing how the various functions of the organization depend on one another, and how changes in any one part affect all the others.

Part 2 of this book develops in more detail the subjects about which a manager must have knowledge, but let us look at the broad scope of this knowledge as an introduction.

Psychology and Sociology

Can science and research supply useful ideas to a practicing manager?

To help answer problems of human relationships and group behavior, the manager needs to know as much as possible about human psychology and the social aspects of groups. He has learned from experience since his childhood about how people react to his behavior. He has picked up a number of platitudes, many of which have little factual basis. He has developed biases from his own social surroundings. With these bases of knowledge, he must develop a program of continuous learning. The increase in his knowledge can best be achieved through study of research findings of social scientists and through his own research and experimentation in his work relationships. Chapters 3 to 5 concentrate on the basic knowledge needed for handling the human aspects of the manager's job.

Organizational Structure

The subject of organization pervades all managerial activities. Many social organizations (clubs, gangs, teams) develop without special help. However, a manager has the power to organize special groups that will aid in his job. The knowledge of organizational design and structure is fundamental; the topic is studied in detail in Chapter 6. In addition, we can learn from management in practice, and Part 4 supplements this knowledge base.

Management Systems

A manager operates in an organization within an environment that is changing rapidly because of a number of technological breakthroughs. He does not have time to become a technical specialist himself, but he must become an expert in making use of technical knowledge of others. In Chapter 7 we shall see how the systems approach can help him tie together the operations of different technical groups through information systems built around computer technology. Using systems thinking, the manager can serve as a connecting link for technological change.

Environmental and Cultural Influences

Why should you worry about society?

The manager operates within an environment that has direct impact on his own activities. Knowledge about this environment and the society in which he operates has become much more important as population explodes, contacts with others become more frequent, and society becomes more complex. This knowledge is important regardless of whether the manager is self-centered and profit-minded or whether he is concerned with moral issues. The pioneer of a century ago had fewer pressures from society; the manager today finds that social unrest, social action, and social change directly affect his own job.

Federal laws constrain the manager's actions in even the smallest firm by requiring compliance with restrictions on employment practices (HEW), health and safety standards (OSHA), record keeping (IRS), environmental impact (EPA), competitive practices (FTC, Justice Dept.), conservation of energy, and other laws and executive orders that increase social control over managerial actions. Since these constraints are continually changing, the manager must keep up with the details through periodicals and government releases; however, in this book you will find the framework for handling this information and illustrations of specific requirements. Chapter 20 summarizes some of the knowledge about society and culture that has become necessary not only for each manager but for each citizen in his desire for his own survival or that of society as we now know it.

The Language of Management

Why is it important to know the meaning of the key words listed in the margin of this book?

The study of management provides one additional type of knowledge that becomes especially important as a manager talks with other managers and specialists—the knowledge of the jargon, terminology, and language used by his colleagues. We have made special efforts in this book to discuss ideas in clear, simple language; however, at the same time, we have introduced those generally used words, terms, and phrases typically used by other managers. Throughout the book, the reader will pick up additional knowledge about the jargon of managers, without which he might feel that others are "talking in tongues" or merely trying to show off in their use of big words. The questions in the margins, the propositions at the ends of chapters, and the marginal placement and color used to emphasize key words will all help the reader acquire the necessary language for management.

STUDY OF MANAGING IN THIS BOOK

With this introductory discussion of the world in which management functions and a knowledge of what managing is, we are ready to proceed in a logical manner to dig deeper into those topics that will enable you to develop as a manager. Figure 2.4 outlines your educational process as you proceed through this book.

In Part 2 we shall discuss in some detail the knowledge a manager must have. This knowledge base becomes the foundation

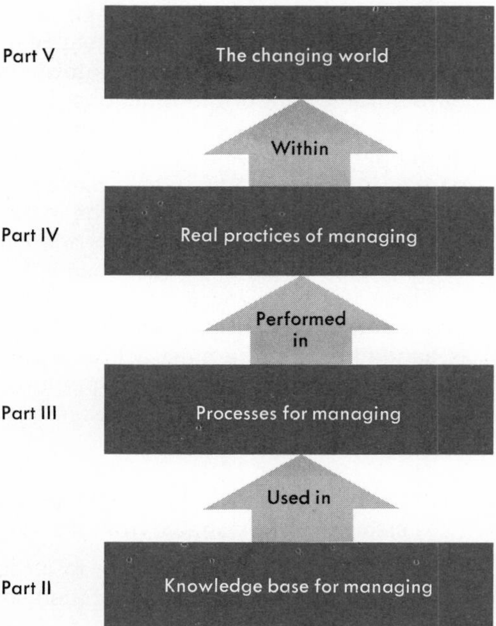

FIGURE 2.4 Process of development of the study of managing in this book

interdisciplinary

upon which we view the managerial process. The knowledge is *interdisciplinary*—that is, the facts and ideas available for improved management come from many fields of academic study. A manager, therefore, tends to need a broad and general base of knowledge.

In Part 3 we shall discuss the different functions or processes of management. This traditional approach in studying management is the theme around which the various topics relating to the processes of management are developed. In this part you will learn in some detail what managers *should* do. You will want to master the terminology of these functions so that you will be able to talk with other managers and to fit into the managerial team.

In Part 4 we put the discussion into real-life terms by showing how this knowledge and the managerial process are *implemented* by operating managers. The art of management can continually be improved in practice if you will take these groups of essentials into the managerial world and use them as a basis for building your knowledge from your own managerial experiences.

In Part 5 we shall conclude the study of the details of managerial actions by describing the broader issues faced by managers as they fit into society and its rapidly changing conditions. Since change can be expected to accelerate, you should view this part as a point of departure for further study of management.

SUMMARY AND PROPOSITIONS

We have seen in this chapter that managers are skilled in identifying problems that various types of knowledge help to solve. Also, you now have a framework of the functions performed by managers: making decisions, setting objectives, planning, organizing, staffing, communicating, directing, and controlling. With this outline, we are better prepared to understand what managers do and the concepts of management generally held by the leading writers.

Since managers are action-oriented, they need explicit guidelines to help them meet their responsibilities. Science has contributed few truths in this area and thus management remains, in large part, an art. The manager cannot just wait around until a set of laws and principles is handed to him; he must act. In order to meet his daily problems, he continually develops his own hypotheses and tentative conclusions. We shall do likewise—through propositions. In Chapter 2 we offer the following propositions:

1. The duties, activities, problems, and functions of a manager are clearly distinguishable from those of nonmanagers.
   - *a.* Managers are oriented to problem solving; they continually search for problems and then seek answers, often with the help of expert advisers.

b. Managers are continually alert to new opportunities and develop means by which they can exploit the best ones.

c. Managers delegate and thus "get things done through other people."

d. Managers' functions consist of decision making, setting objectives and policies, organizing, communicating, planning, controlling, staffing, and directing.

e. To some people, management represents a class with its own culture and behavioral characteristics.

2. The behavior of a manager can be taught and learned.

   a. "Learning by example" and more formal apprenticeship programs have been partly successful in the past, but these methods for developing managers do not supply the vast pool of managerial manpower that is needed.

   b. A body of information about the management process offers important help to those who want to be managers.

   c. Professional managers have developed in the last half century through formal study; these persons have become distinct from capital owners, entrepreneurs, and workers.

3. The need for managerial behavior exists at all levels of an organization.

4. Management behavior has basic similarities regardless of the type of organization in which it is found.

   a. Business management is one area to which much recent study has been directed.

   b. Public administration has a long history and is one important category of management behavior.

   c. Military management has long recognized some of the functions of managerial behavior.

   d. Educational administration has recently concentrated on managerial behavior; however, most practicing top educational executives come from many different backgrounds and professions and thus do not yet comprise a professional management group.

STUDY ASSIGNMENTS

1. Make a list of those "forces shaping the manager's job" (discussed in Chapter 1) that are illustrated in the vignette, "What is Management?"

2. How could Bob Allison have gotten significant help from reading Chapter 2?

3. *Explain how the concepts of early thinkers in management are still relevant to your learning about management today.*
4. *What aspects do contemporary writers tend to focus on? How do these writers add to the knowledge base built by the early writers?*
5. *Do the popular writers offer new viewpoints not covered by the early thinkers or contemporary scholars? Are some of their ideas inconsistent with one another, or do they further develop a common theme?*
6. *List our seven processes of managing.*
   a. *Which ones would you have identified before reading this chapter?*
   b. *Compare the seven processes of managing with your answers to Bob Allison's problem of defining what a manager does. What differences exist?*
   c. *Rank the seven from most important (1) to least important (7). Explain your reasons for the ranking.*
7. *What pressures and tensions result from the manager's being the "man in the middle?" See Figure 2.3.*
8. *Must a manager always face "being in the middle"? Explain your answer.*
9. *Of the problems a manager faces, which ones are easiest to train a manager to solve? Which do you think are the easiest to overcome?*
10. *The type of organization often affects the management processes involved with it. For example, show how the managing of a high school by a principal is* similar *and* dissimilar *to the managing of the following:*
    a. *Managing a government department (e.g., a local employment agency)*
    b. *Managing a book store*
    c. *Managing a gas station*
    d. *Managing a hospital*
11. *Set up the conditions that would make the following jobs (1) managerial; (2) nonmanagerial:*
    a. *A high school teacher*
    b. *A professional football coach*
    c. *An executive secretary of a large corporation*
    d. *A police guard at an elementary school*
    e. *An employee of a department store*
    f. *A newspaper carrier*

situational episodes

1. Your closest friend accepted a job, immediately after high school, with a local delivery firm as a truck driver. In six months he was brought into the office as a dispatcher, and after a year he was made the office supervisor over six office employees. He now feels that he has learned how to manage with only two years' experience. In talking with you, he raises the questions of why you have chosen to go to college during those two years, and why you feel that your college experience will give you advantages that he doesn't have. He comments, "I know that you have two years of course credits, but I have two years of experience. I am learning to manage by doing it. You are just reading books and talking about the subject. It will be interesting to see which of us is better off five years from now."

   a. What can experience teach him that you can't learn in a classroom?
   b. What can education do for you that you couldn't get from working in a job?
   c. Do you think that your friend can learn how to manage in two years without knowing just what managing involves?
   d. Assuming that you complete a management degree, what advantages do you feel you will have over your friend? Will he soon reach a stage from which his opportunities are more limited than yours?

2. John and his brother Frank have the opportunity of entering their father's successful building-supply firm. Their father assures them that in a few years he will want to retire from the business and he will leave them to manage it. When he retires, he will retain ownership of the business, but he will pay each of his sons a salary if each will assume managerial duties.

   a. What duties do you think the father has in mind?
   b. After the father retires, what would be the difference between the father's role and the role of his sons?
   c. What roles are available for one of the sons in the event that the other does not want to be a manager?

TECHNOLOGY
SMALL BUSINESS
MANAGED CHANGE
ORGANIZATION
COMPUTERS
CHANGE
SOCIOLOGY-GROUPS

2 management fundamentals: the knowledge base

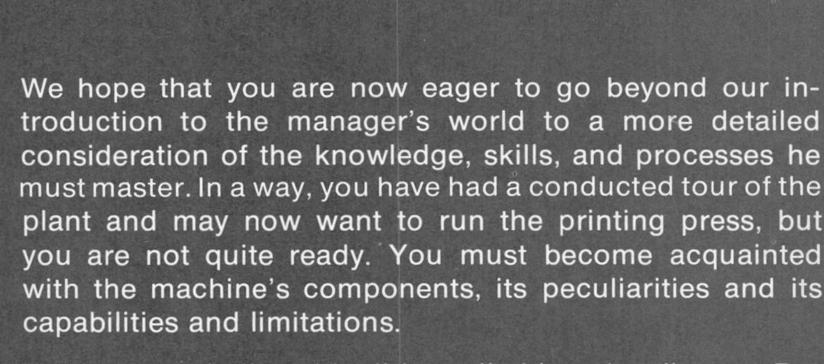

We hope that you are now eager to go beyond our introduction to the manager's world to a more detailed consideration of the knowledge, skills, and processes he must master. In a way, you have had a conducted tour of the plant and may now want to run the printing press, but you are not quite ready. You must become acquainted with the machine's components, its peculiarities and its capabilities and limitations.

The manager's "machine" is really his subordinates. Before he can effectively accomplish goals through the work of his subordinates, the manager must attempt to understand human behavior—given the limitations of our knowledge about it—in the same way that the printer must understand the press. The next chapters are therefore geared to making the behavior of people in the manager's world more intelligible to him and thus more amenable to his modifications.

Of course, the manager must consider more than the behavioral processes of his subordinates. After Chapters 3 to 5, the emphasis of Part 2 shifts from people to the organizational structure and its relationship to the manager (Chapter 6). Another important consideration receives attention in Chapter 7, when present-day technology and information systems are explored. Chapter 8 ends Part 2 with a view of all these elements of the manager's world within a changing context.

Human motivation

THREE

OBJECTIVES YOU SHOULD MEET

Diagram *the relationship between motivation and job performance.*

List *at least four of the basic generalizations on motivation.*

Summarize *the six motivation theories.*

Identify *the similarities and dissimilarities in the six theories.*

State *any two personal experiences illustrating the usefulness of any motivation theory.*

THE "WHY" OF BEHAVIOR

"Prof, you got a minute?"

I turned to the door and saw Sue, one of the stay-awake students of my org. behavior class. Sue was married to a graduate student and the mother of a small boy, and she always seemed prepared, rarely asked stupid questions, and stayed with you when you tried to develop a point. She had a good attention span and a good mind.

"Come on in and sit down, Sue," I said, moving the pile of unread Wall Street Journals *from the big chair to the floor. "What can I do for you?"*

"I'm sorry I missed class this morning. The flu bug hit our family last night, and I had to be sure my son would be all right before I came to school."

"Is he OK now?"

"Yes, it must have been the 24-hour variety. I tried to get notes from other students, but you know how some students keep notes. Fortunately, I've had some courses in psychology and sociology, and I'm familiar with Maslow's theory but not Herzberg's or Vroom's. Would you have time to give me the highlights or summary of your lecture on motivation? That way, I can take my own notes."

I had some time before Stu, my faculty colleague, and I were to go for coffee, and Sue was a good student.

"Well, let me run through the illustration I gave on car buying so that some characteristics of motivation might show up. You remember, I set up the example in the form of a student in a marketing-research class whose job it is to find out why people buy automobiles, a rather common purchase here in Detroit. When the student reported back to the class, he told them and the professor that he was confused. He had

gone back to his hometown after the class assignment, developed a good sample, and put together a good interview schedule. It was the answers to his questions that had confused him. He remembered that the marketing professor had told him to probe after a person gives his first answer; that frequently the first answer is not always the answer the respondent himself really believes but is more of a convenience answer, or an answer that is expected."

"I know what you mean," Sue said. "I know people who live at the housing complex who'll give any answer just to get rid of an interviewer."

"Exactly. Well, when the student probed, he found people giving some strange reasons for the purchase of their last car or an anticipated one. One manager of a paint company said that his type of car was part of the total management fringe package of the company. Since it was a supplier to GM, the different levels in the company received different types of cars. Some drove Pontiacs, some Olds or Buicks; he drove a Chevy and would continue to do so until he moved up in the company.

"Another respondent was concerned with the economy of the car. This person said he checked Consumer Reports *and other journals comparing cars and usually picked the car recommended by these groups."*

"Isn't that interesting?" commented Sue. "My husband Tom is just like that. He won't let me buy just any toothpaste; it has to be the one that's been rated best."

"Sue, I gave another example of a woman with three children, who said her family belonged to a very active church group, all in their thirties, and that they liked to camp in the Upper Peninsula, so they needed a wagon. Most of the other families drove Ford, Chevy, or Plymouth wagons. This young mother felt that the kind of car you drive or park in front of your house tells a lot about the people who live inside. If you drive an old, beat-up clunker, you're probably a kind of messy person who walks around in a fog. 'You definitely don't work for anyone connected with the automobile industry if you drive a piece of junk.'

"Another young man said that ever since he was a struggling kid in graduate school, he had promised himself that one of the first luxury purchases he'd make would be a sports car. If he's depressed, a spin lifts him.

"Now, Sue, why do you think I gave all those examples to my class? What do you think was my intention and my major point?"

"You asked me before I got a chance to ask you. I guess I really don't know what your point would have been. I know that if I had been in class, this is the place where I would raise my hand. . . . I thought the purpose of studying motivation was so that managers of organizations could know why people behave as they do. If the manager knows why the people around him do what they do, then he can predict their behavior. Managers are able to get away from the 'art' in management and become more 'scientific.' If every answer is different, how can you possibly predict responses?"

"I gave those examples to show that the specific reason or motive for purchase behavior is very difficult to isolate. Look at all the motives that seemed expressed through car purchases: to appear younger and attractive; to appear respectable; to gain acceptance from others; to maintain the acceptance already gained through similar income levels and church affiliation; to satisfy economic values; to reinforce company-created status differentials. Motives can't be accurately inferred from behavior, since the same behavior may be used to fulfill different individual motives. An understanding of the field of motivation may help us interpret behavior and give us possible insight into the reasons people do what they do. We are a long way from being able to predict scientifically why specific people will select specific bits of behavior."

study of motivation

Basic to any discussion of motivation is the assumption that most of our behavior occurs for some reason. Behavior is purposive. Larry shouts at Joe . . . Gail gets up from her desk and paces the floor . . . Vic steps between two of his subordinates to change the subject in a heated argument. In each instance, the person acts for some reason. A *study of motivation* is a study into the reasons for behavior.

The vignette, "The 'Why' of Behavior," illustrates a very basic characteristic of motivation. At first glance, the more you know, the more confused you become; the student who wanted to generalize on the motives for buying cars may have come back from his interviews more confused than before. But at second glance, we can see that our student learned two things: First, he learned that motives are widely varied, and second, he did learn about some specific motives that culminated in car purchases. Although our student could not report a neat, concise formula as the answer to his question, he knew more than he did before and would have a more valid basis for designing an advertising campaign.

We now go from the specific question of why people purchase cars to a much broader topic: Why do people behave as they do? The "why" of behavior is a very general concept of motivation. In this chapter, motivation is approached first by discussing the relation between performance and motivation. This puts motivation into a context relevant to managers. From that point, we shall try to establish the utility of continuing the discussion of motivation by considering the basic question of managing motivation.

The remainder of the chapter contains the content material that gives you information needed to deal with the subject. Generalizations commonly held as being true are followed by various theories concerning motivation. The limitations of these theories are mentioned before the chapter ends with the summary and propositions.

MANAGERS AND MOTIVATION

Why do we want to know about motivation?

Managers value performance—their own and that of others. Performance serves many functions. For example, performance is the most usual means for determining compensation. Performance is frequently an important factor in determining who gets promoted. Performance can give a person a feeling of pride and of higher status if others also value performance. In the preceding chapter, one main section was devoted to "Things Managers Do." These "things" all add up to performance. Sometimes performance, or output, translates into different, concrete items. In manufacturing firms, for example, output may be a product that is worked on by many people along an assembly line. In marketing, on the other hand, output may be the sale of a product or service to a customer.

Performance or output takes many shapes and can generate many different responses. The performance may be viewed as the best or the worst ever seen. Or the evaluation may place the output into the marginal-acceptance class. What usually follows the evaluation of performance is an explanation as to the cause or reason. "Shirley sure was turned on to perform as she did. . . . Bill just didn't seem to have it today. . . . Why can't we motivate others to be like Harold, he really puts out." In each of these statements, there is the assumption that the performance depended on the motivation of the person. Just what is the relationship between performance and motivation?

Relationship of Motivation to Performance

Managers must frequently answer these questions about two aspects of individual or group performance: If the performance is high, the question is, How do I keep it high? If the performance is marginal or low, the question is, What do I do to improve the performance, and why is it unacceptable?

With either question, the concern is the same—the knowledge of the factors contributing to performance and output. To a casual observer, the factors are usually seen clearly. "John is just not putting forth the effort. . . . Vicky is trying to impress people. . . . Fred's working hard for his promotion. . . . Lynda has two kids and needs the money." No one needs extensive training in the behavioral sciences or advanced degrees to realize the complexity of human beings and how incomplete simple answers are. In Figure 3.1, we diagram possible relationships between performance and motivation sources. This figure needs further elaboration if the topic of motivation is to be placed in a meaningful setting.

At this point in the discussion of the manager and motivation, we are primarily interested in the individual and group behavior that results in organizational performance, output. Obviously, not all behavior in an organization contributes directly to unit goals or objectives, but a discussion of noncontributory be-

FIGURE 3.1 Motivation–performance model

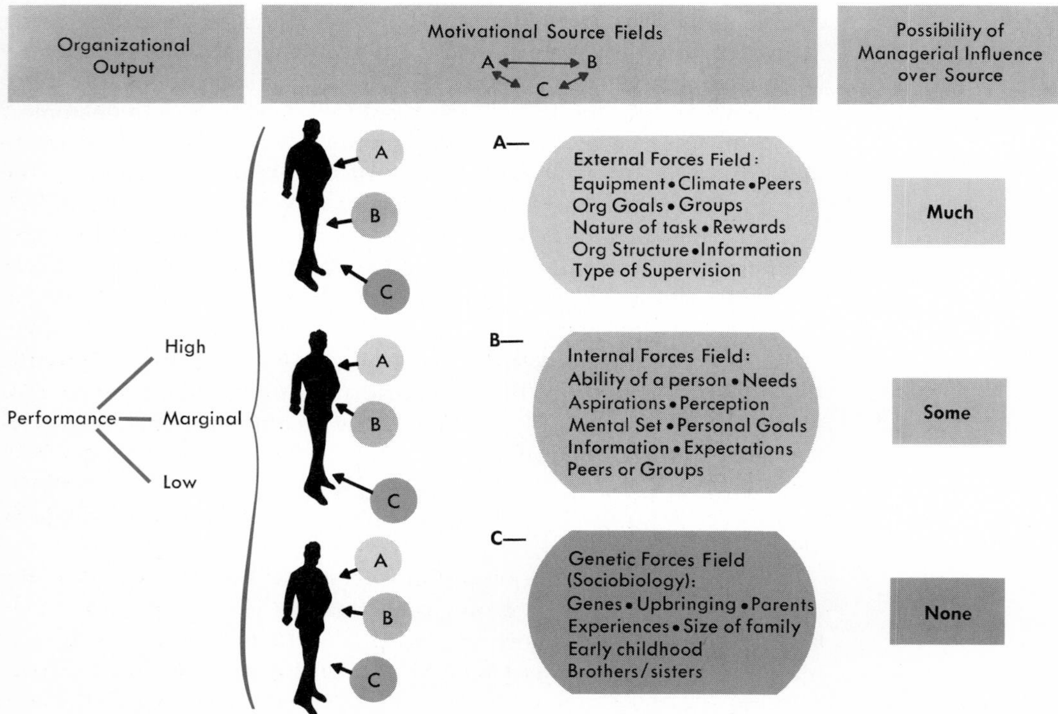

havior is delayed until later sections of the book. In the first column of Figure 3.1, therefore, the behavior we want is that leading to organizational outputs.

Motivation Source Fields

The section on *Motivation Source Fields* in Figure 3.1 contains three subdivisions. The first subdivision has examples of forces external to the individual but possibly contributory to the output. Assume that your secretary's performance is unsatisfactory. Managers using the motivation–performance model would see that one possible explanation for this performance might be her equipment—perhaps her typewriter is faulty, or her task calls for demanding attention and she is continually interrupted by phone messages. No matter how hard she tries, her performance will not reach the expected level. Or assume that a new staff manager shows remarkable performance during the first few months of employment. It is possible that he is in a job calling for only 60 percent of his potential ability. Or it's possible that other members of the work force have not been able to get to the new manager and explain the necessity for more controlled and lower output. Some of these explanations come from the second subdivision, where the examples are of internal forces. The third force, sociobiology, is important to understand, for some of our behavior is moderated by our genetic structure and elements given to us and is therefore difficult to change or control.

How much influence does a manager have over the motivational sources?

The last column is important to managers, for it shows both the limitations and the opportunities for managerial action. It is our belief that the manager has much control and influence over the external forces in the person's work world. The manager has much to say about the type of equipment, the nature of the task, the organizational structure, the amount and kind of information sent through regular channels, and the climate in which the subordinate works. The manager also has some influence over the person's internal forces, even though this area is highly dependent upon the person's way of interpreting the external forces of the work world.

These three forces work in combination with each other. Figure 3.2 depicts the interrelationship of the forces: Your sociobiological makeup determines much of the means you use to interpret the world, as well as your inner needs and aspirations. Your internal state shapes the way you react and respond to forces in the external environment. A piece of equipment will not have the same meaning or influence upon two people in the same work unit.

The motivation–performance model serves as a partial overview of the remaining sections of this book. A great deal of man-

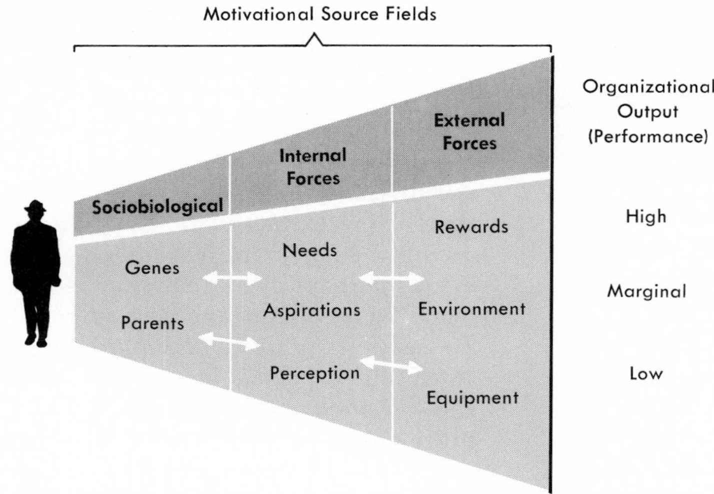

FIGURE 3.2 Interrelationship of motivational source fields

aging activity aims at influencing through external forces the internal forces of individuals. The remaining portions of this chapter focus on these motive forces. In Chapters 4–7, the topics highlighted are to be viewed as modifiers of behavior.

The Management of Motivation

The manager of an organization does not sit in an armchair and spend his time speculating about behavior. He does not have the time to deal with analysis that is not related to action. Thus, of primary importance to any manager is the operational character of motivation. If information from the behavioral sciences is limited to speculation and individual analysis, the manager may find the process interesting but not very useful. For this reason, let us consider the following question: Can the motivations of people be managed?

managed behavior

This question is basic, for it deals with the daily problems of motivation or behavior. Do not be misled when the term *managed behavior* is used. We are not suggesting an organization filled with puppets. To say that you are influenced by another is not to say that when that person pulls a string, you always respond in the same way. The manager's world, however, is one where predictability of behavior is valued, and although specific behavior may be very difficult to predict, the manager has a right to ask the behavioral scientists whether motivations can be managed; whether behavior can be influenced.

The term *managed behavior* should not be foreign to you. Reflecting upon your own experience for a moment should show that you frequently anticipate what other people want from you. If you take advantage of such behavioral information, you know what behavior pleases other people and thus you may behave in that manner. In a simple way, is this not managing behavior? You are managing the response of the other person (favorably) by behaving in a way you know he wants.

There are more obvious and direct methods in the management of behavior. The manager has both the control over the rewards (salary, promotion, recognition) in an organization and the ability to influence through specific day-to-day behavior with others. Some of the interpersonal techniques of influence are developed in this chapter and in Chapters 4, 8, 15, 18, and 19. Nonpersonal techniques are mentioned throughout the book in terms of objective setting, control, policies, and organizational structure.

Now that we see why the manager wants to study motivation, we next consider what it is. The generalizations below, most of which run throughout the theories that follow, may be described as accepted axioms regarding the concept of motivation. Another word for these generalizations might be *assumptions.* The assumptions appear to be true in the light of the present state of knowledge about man, but they are not all established as fact.

SOME USEFUL GENERALIZATIONS ABOUT HUMAN MOTIVATION

The reason these generalizations appear before the theories are discussed is that they help to define a concept that is difficult to specify. In the theoretical framework that comes after this section, we explain the world partly described and bounded by these generalizations.[1]

Motives

Motives Are the Energizing Forces within Us. These forces are invisible and impossible to measure. Because all of us are different, the motives energizing us at any moment differ. All

[1] The framework for this section is similar to that developed in John Douglas, George A. Field, and Lawrence X. Tarpey, *Human Behavior in Marketing* (Columbus, O.: Charles E. Merrill, 1967), pp. 55–58.

that is possible is to observe and measure the behavior we choose and, from this behavior, make a kind of *backward causation* statement to the possible motive. Observing someone's behavior may show that a certain need is present in this person, motivating him onward.

One Motive May Result in Many Different Behaviors. The desire for prestige may lead a person to run for political office, give money away, get additional educational training, steal, join groups, grow mustaches and sideburns, or shave off facial hair. A person wanting acceptance will behave differently in a car pool, an office secretarial pool, and a swimming pool.

The Same Behavior in Different People May Come from Many Different Motives. In the vignette, "The 'Why' of Behavior," the illustration about car buying supports this generalization. You may remember that the same behavior (purchasing a car) could be seen as coming from a number of different motives. Recall the motives that seemed expressed through car purchases: to appear younger and attractive; to appear respectable; to gain acceptance from others; to maintain the acceptance already gained through a similar income level and church affiliation; to satisfy economic values; and to reinforce company-created status differentials. Managers would commit a bad mistake if they tried to classify the same behavior in different people as coming from the same motive. People join unions, get married, attend class, and laugh at professors' jokes for many different reasons (motives). Thus, a motive cannot always be identified from the specific behavior.

What's the difference between estimating and predicting?

Behavior Can be Used as an Estimate of an Individual's Motive. This statement may seem to be in direct opposition to the preceding generalization, but there is an important difference. There we said that the same behavior does not always follow the same motive. Here we are saying that it is possible after repeated observations of one person's behavior to make an estimate of the cause of that behavior. For example, there is truth in the statement that some people always seem to feel insecure and thus behave continuously in a manner reflecting that insecure feeling. You know other people who behave in a way that radiates confidence. They are confident in many different social settings, so that what you see is a constant and repeated behavior, behavior from which people probably estimate the motive of the person. Obviously, if a person is at a state of near starvation, most of his behavior will be related to the need for food. Although it is dangerous to categorize people, it is also wrong to believe that individual behavior, when looked at in some time perspective, cannot be used as an estimate for motivation.

Motives May Operate in Harmony or in Conflict. Behavior is frequently the result of the interplay of several motives. These motives may push a person in one direction or in a number of directions. For example, a girl may want to get high grades in school while also wanting to appear "dumb" to her boyfriend. An athlete may desire an outstanding performance but may also be sensitive to being shunned by his fellow teammates if he performs too well and receives too much of the credit. Behavior, therefore, is the result of many forces differing in direction and intent.

Do your own motives ever vary?

Motives Come and Go. It is very rare that a motive has the same energy potential over a long period of time. The boy who buys a paper route in the spring so as to get money may sell the route during the football season because the monetary need takes second place to the need to play football. The girl who is extremely concerned about her hair and clothes during adolescence may turn her attention to other things once she grows up. Because human beings are constantly growing, the motive at one point in time will not be as intense as at another.

The Environment Influences Motives. The situation at a particular time may trigger or suppress the action of a motive. You have probably experienced situations where you did not realize the intensity of your hunger needs until your sense of smell picked up the odor of food cooking. Similarly, many of your sociological needs become stimulated when you are in a situation filled with the sociological factors. Thus, needs that may be latent can quickly be stimulated by the environmental situation.

We have now identified a number of generalizations that are useful in understanding the concept of motivation. Notice the similarity in the generalizations. Few of them are simple statements: "One motive may result in many behaviors. . . . Motives may operate in harmony or conflict. . . . Motives come and go." You may feel as confused as the marketing-research student in the vignette. Yet managers cannot escape a complex world.

How do you cope with the complexity of motivation?

One way to cope with the complexity of understanding orga-

model

nizational behavior is to study analytical models. Rarely is a *model* (a simpler-than-real-life representation) thought to be complete or totally accurate. It is a depiction that shows how someone *believes* a thing works. Although crude and rough, models form one starting point for managers to answer the "why" question of behavior—the behavior of others and of themselves.

MOTIVATIONAL MODELS FOR MANAGER UNDERSTANDING

What is a motivational model?

In one sense, *motivational models* are very common. Adam probably had some explanation for Eve's behavior in the Garden of Eden; Cain had some explanation for Abel's behavior; and so on through the ages. There are motivational models that find their foundations in religious thought or in the statements of philosophers. You probably have your own model that describes your basis for explaining the behavior of others.

There are several theories that have received a great deal of discussion in recent business literature, and it is to these theories that we now turn our attention. The theories selected for review can be classified as theories built upon assumptions of man's basic nature and similarities, theories ignoring inner man but focusing upon man's environment, and a theory containing parts of both. The first description, therefore, is of those theories whose authors suggest the universal application of their ideas, since they are developed from assumptions basic to all people.

Universal Theories

ABRAHAM H. MASLOW AND DOUGLAS MCGREGOR[2] In 1954, Maslow published a basic theoretical work built upon his interpretation of man's basic needs. These needs are in a specific order or hierarchy, so that one level of need satisfaction must be met be-

[2] Abraham H. Maslow, *Motivation and Personality* (New York: Harper & Row, 1954); Douglas McGregor, *The Human Side of Enterprise* (New York: McGraw-Hill, 1960). Douglas McGregor is best known for his ideas about the basic assumptions of man and the managerial implications of these assumptions. For example, if a manager assumes that his subordinates are lazy, uncreative, and motivated by money and fear (theory x), he will manage accordingly. But if a manager assumes that her subordinates want responsibility and involvement and are creative beings (theory y), she will manage in a different manner. McGregor's theory x and y are treated in greater detail in chapters 6 and 15.

fore a person progresses to the satisfaction of a different level of need.

This basic notion was adopted by McGregor, who related it to the practice of management. (See Figure 3.3.) The following nine points summarize the basic ideas of Maslow, together with some application to management practices that come from McGregor:

1. Man has as least five sets of basic *needs.*
   a. *Physiological*—hunger, thirst, sex, and so on
   b. *Safety*—protection against danger, threat, deprivation, and so on
   c. *Social*—belonging, association, acceptance by others, giving and receiving friendship and love
   d. *Ego*—self-esteem (self-confidence, independence, achievement, competence, knowledge) and personal reputation (status, recognition, appreciation, respect)
   e. *Self-fulfillment*—realizing one's own potential, continued self-development, creativity

hierarchy

2. These needs exist in an order, or *hierarchy,* with the physiological being the most basic.
3. The needs at any level emerge only when the more basic needs have been gratified.
4. One hundred percent satisfaction is not required for a need to no longer be dominant.
5. Most people in organizations are past the physiological-need level.

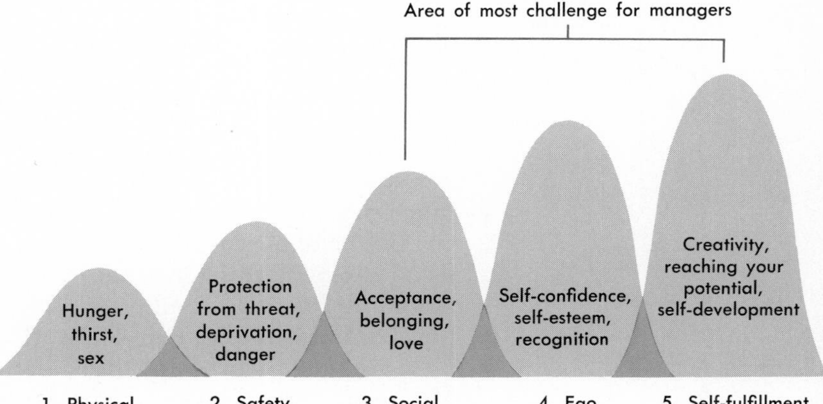

FIGURE 3.3 A general view of the Maslow-McGregor needs hierarchy

6. The challenge to managers is in dealing with the egoistic and self-fulfillment needs.
7. People operating at the higher need levels are healthier people.
8. The irresponsible behavior of some people in organizations is a symptom of illness—of deprivation of social and egoistic needs. The negative behavior observed is the *result* of poor management.
9. There are management techniques that result in the satisfaction of physiological and safety needs and many of the social needs. Managers in organizations can perform in a way that enables others to function in the higher and healthier areas of behavior.

How would you make use of these statements?

These statements by Maslow and McGregor are very positive. They envision a person who wants to be healthy, who wants to be responsible, who wants to make a contribution to others. Both Maslow and McGregor feel that a mismanaged organization causes sick and unhealthy behavior in its participants. The solution, discussed and developed primarily by McGregor, is for a new management approach that unleashes the human potentialities of organizations' participants. Many of McGregor's ideas are developed in a later chapter dealing with directing and leadership (Chapter 15).

The Maslow-McGregor model has found great favor and use among many practicing managers, although care must be taken not to overgeneralize from it. This model is elaborated on in Figures 3.3 to 3.5. Figure 3.3 diagrams a needs hierarchy and indicates the normal movement from the most basic (1, on the left) to the highest (5, on the right) needs. Note that there is overlap in each need area, for it would be far too simplistic to think that one area has abrupt starting and stopping points. Figure 3.4 compares the needs hierarchy of two different people (Howard and Vicky), who vary substantially in the amounts of need in different areas that each must satisfy before the complete set of needs can be brought into harmony. As Figure 3.4 emphasizes, Howard will have to expend much more energy and time than Vicky to have his dominant social or "belongingness" need (level 3) gratified before he can move on to satisfying higher needs. Vicky, in contrast, will probably be searching for opportunities to satisfy her ego or self-esteem need (level 5) much sooner than Howard will.

FIGURE 3.4 Real-world needs of Howard and Vicky. The curve heights represent the minimum amount of need in each area that must be gratified before the next area becomes dominant. The numbers correspond to the five basic needs of Figure 3.3.

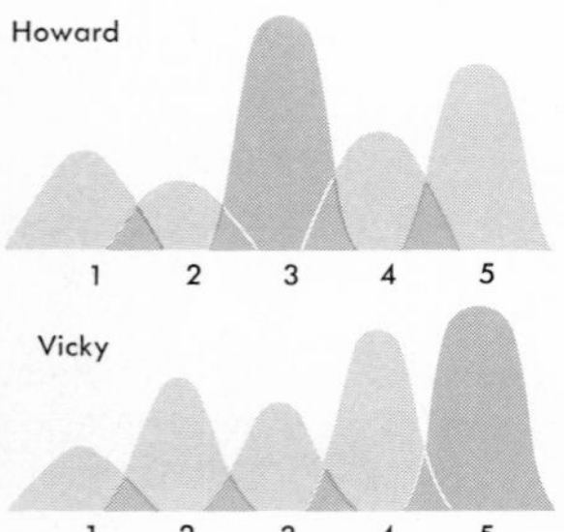

Figure 3.5 illustrates the situational character of the Maslow-McGregor model. A person may be fulfilling his ego needs (level 4)

TABLE 3.1 The Atkinson-McClelland Three Motive Table

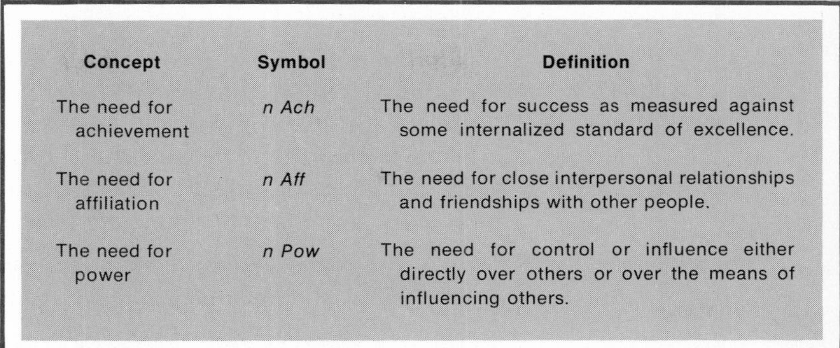

Concept	Symbol	Definition
The need for achievement	*n Ach*	The need for success as measured against some internalized standard of excellence.
The need for affiliation	*n Aff*	The need for close interpersonal relationships and friendships with other people.
The need for power	*n Pow*	The need for control or influence either directly over others or over the means of influencing others.

achievement

affiliation

power

when a fire suddenly breaks out in his department. The safety need (level 2) may then become dominant, and behavior will be directed toward that goal until the safety need is gratified.

J.W. ATKINSON AND DAVID C. MCCLELLAND[3] Several motives have been identified and studied by Atkinson and McClelland. Three have particular relevance to organizations. To these men, the individual personality is assumed to be composed of a network of three basic motives, as outlined in Table 3.1. Given that people have the need for *achievement*, the need for *affiliation*, and the need for *power*, it is possible to think of specific types of behavior that are likely to be associated with each kind of motive. McClelland found that people with a high need to achieve tend to (1) seek and assume high degrees of personal responsibility; (2) take calculated risks; (3) set challenging but realistic goals for themselves; (4) develop comprehensive plans to help them achieve their goals; (5) seek and use concrete measurable feedback of the results of their actions; and (6) seek out business opportunities where their desire to achieve will not be thwarted.[4]

People with affiliation needs, on the other hand, seek to find warm relationships and friendship. They are not as concerned as the higher achievers with getting ahead, but rather, they enjoy jobs that have many interactions with other people.

People who seek power also seek positions of power or influence. These are people who enjoy jobs where authority and power rest within the position they have.

FIGURE 3.5 The effect of situation on a person's needs hierarchy

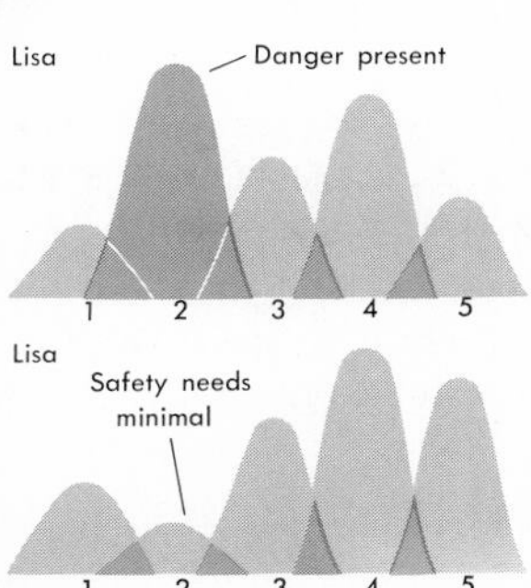

[3] See David C. McClelland, *The Achieving Society* (New York: Van Nostrand Reinhold, 1961); and J.W. Atkinson, *An Introduction to Motivation* (New York: Van Nostrand Reinhold, 1964).

[4] McClelland, *The Achieving Society.*

Can you influence these three needs?

Much in the same way that McGregor talked about establishing a management style that allows people to reach higher need levels, Atkinson and McClelland, and more recently Stringer,[5] talk about the creation of the right kind of climate that will have an impact upon the motives of other people. The specific techniques for creating this climate are considered in later chapters.[6] What is important here is that both these analytical models give the manager an insight into the kind of motives and needs that operate in both themselves and others.

VIKTOR E. FRANKL The first two analytical motivation models dealt with the idea of motives and the type of motivated behavior that a manager may apply to other people. Frankl, in his book, *Man's Search for Meaning,*[7] writes more directly to the individual person and his own motivation. Frankl believes, for example, that a great deal of man's basic frustration derives from his inability to find what Frankl calls the "will to meaning." He believes that people have a basic need to do meaningful things, and thus, when put into an environment that does not allow for meaning, people become frustrated and develop neurotic behavior. In this sense, Frankl is similar to Maslow, who feels that unsatisfied needs result in unhealthy behavior. Frankl urges his readers to search for the *why* of life, for if a person can find a why, he can bear with almost any type of situation he confronts. His theory of finding meaning rests on the values that pull man, rather than the needs and drives that push him.

Is "will to meaning" like Maslow's "self-fulfillment"?

Frankl speaks from a very difficult personal experience; he was imprisoned in a Nazi concentration camp and had to suffer the hardships of the inhumane treatment of Jews during the Second World War. His insights came from experiencing personal trauma and observing men, women, and children under conditions that tested the question, Why go on living, why survive? Yet Frankl believes that to most—not all—people, "the striving to find a meaning in one's life is the primary motivational force in man."[8]

[5] Robert A. Stringer, Jr., "Achievement Motivation and Management Control," in *Motivation and Control in Organizations,* eds. Gene W. Dalton and Paul R. Lawrence (Homewood, Ill,: Irwin-Dorsey, 1971), pp. 329–36.

[6] Notice the similarity between the description of the manager's job in Chapter 2 and items 3, 4, and 5 cited by McClelland. These items cover the same activities as planning, objective setting, and control, to be discussed in Part 3.

[7] New York: Washington Square Press, 1963.

[8] Frankl, *Man's Search for Meaning,* p. 154.

Most managers and organizational employees never face the intense hardships of concentration-camp life. Yet, since the work world makes up a large percentage of adult life, is it not appropriate for managers to apply the insights from Frankl's logotherapy (search for meaning) to their jobs and employment relationships? Many recent developments in job engineering (enlarging a job, enriching a job, redesigning a job to match personal qualities) aim to generate more *meaning* in the job. Even with these developments, Frankl's insights help, for he believes that you possess "the last of the human freedoms—the ability to choose one's attitude in a given set of circumstances."[9] *You ultimately determine the meaning of work.* Managers should not be amazed, therefore, when "meaningfully developed jobs" are not viewed as meaningful by all workers.

Managers today are not as familiar with Frankl's ideas as they are with Maslow-McGregor or Atkinson-McClelland. But Viktor Frankl's concept of ultimate choice, a search for meaning and values form much of the framework for the chapters in Part 5 dealing with personal conflicts within an organization.

Environmental Motivation Theories

In the universal theories that we have been discussing, the emphasis has been on man, particularly on the inner states of man. In the environmental motivation theories, there is a shift in emphasis: Factors or conditions in the environment are viewed as contributing to man's behavior, and the analysis, or diagnosis, thus moves away from individual needs. Two recent examples are the "two-factor" theory of Frederick Herzberg and the "conditioning and reinforcement" theory of B.F. Skinner.[10]

FREDERICK HERZBERG[11] Herzberg identifies two factors in his motivation theory. These factors are described as conditions on the job that relate to employee dissatisfaction and satisfaction.

maintenance or hygiene factors

The first set of job conditions is called *maintenance or hygiene factors.* Some examples of these factors are salary; working conditions; interpersonal relations with supervisors, peers, and subordi-

[9] *Ibid.,* p. xiii.

[10] The authors, not B.F. Skinner, classified his contributions as motivational.

[11] Frederick Herzberg, Bernard Mausner, and Barbara Bloch Snyderman, *The Motivation to Work* (New York: John Wiley, 1959).

nates; job security; and company policy. If present, *they will not lead to employee satisfaction; they will just prevent dissatisfaction.* If not present, their lack will lead to employee dissatisfaction. The maintenance-hygiene factors are thus not motivators.

motivational factors

The other set in the two-factor theory, the *motivational factors,* are those job conditions that, when present, lead to job satisfaction and high levels of motivation. The following are examples of these motivational factors: achievement, recognition, the possibility of growth, advancement, responsibility, and the work itself. If absent, however, *their lack will not lead to employee dissatisfaction.*

Have you ever felt the two-factor theory applying to your job?

One way to view the relationship between the two factors is pictured in Table 3.2. The dissatisfaction-satisfaction factors are seen as outputs of the environmental conditions of maintenance or motivational factors and not as two opposite points on a continuum, as is usually thought.

Like many of the other models, the Herzberg model has received its share of criticism, but it does bring our attention to the reservation that not all factors in the workplace have the same potential for positively motivated behavior. Herzberg presents us the generalization that gets immediate support from any who have ever worked: Any job, from the viewpoint of the employee, can be and usually is both satisfying and dissatisfying. There are conditions in the job that allow both states of motivation to exist. The factors leading to satisfaction on a job are different from the factors leading to dissatisfaction.

A word of caution is appropriately raised by Herzberg for the manager who assumes that by increasing salary or improving work conditions, for example, he is automatically developing motivated growth behavior. He may be in error. What such managerial action usually does is to remove possible sources of dissatisfaction for employees; the action does not create a state of employee satisfaction.

TABLE 3.2 Relationships in the Two-factor Theory

Factor	State		Motivational Force
Maintenance or hygiene	If present	→	0
	If absent	→	Dissatisfaction
Motivational	If present	→	Satisfaction
	If absent	→	0

Does it seem appropriate to you to use data from animal experimentation to generalize about man?

B.F. SKINNER[12] Skinner is best known as an animal psychologist whose interest is in the behavior of an organism in terms of its effect on the environment. Skinner's explanation of man's behavior differs from Maslow-McGregor-McClelland-Frankl. Absent from Skinner's approach are concepts such as needs, values, drives, power, achievement, or affiliation. Present are terms like *operant learning, stimulus, response,* and *reinforcement.* To understand the contribution of Skinner to the managerial knowledge base of motivation, we need to review briefly the history of behaviorism.

FIGURE 3.6 Classical conditioning (S-type)

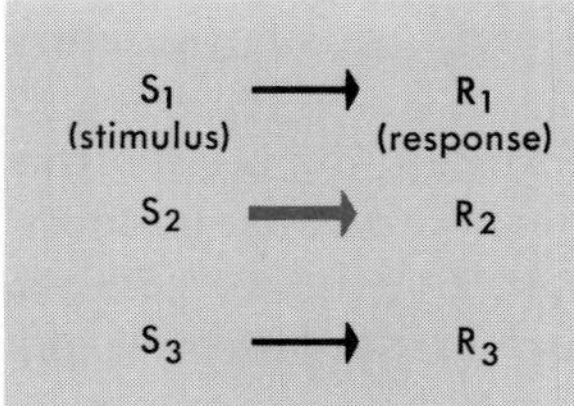

Behaviorists of the early 1900s were greatly influenced by the work of Pavlov.[13] Behavior, to the classical conditioning scientists, was a reflex to a previous stimulus. Thus, to get the desired response, attention was directed at generating the right stimulus. Notice the emphasis on the stimulus in Figures 3.6 and 3.7. They show not only the S-type classical reflex conditioning model, but also an example of applying the theory to an organization. It is easy to see how managers and supervisors would receive support from the scientific community when they assumed that money or some other stimulus brought about the desired performance (a re-

[12] These thoughts come from an article by Walter R. Nord, "Beyond the Teaching Machine: The Neglected Area of Operant Conditioning in the Theory and Practice of Management," reproduced in Dalton and Lawrence, *Motivation and Control,* pp. 352–77. For a more detailed recent statement of Skinner's thoughts, see B.F. Skinner, *Beyond Freedom and Dignity* (New York: Knopf, 1971).

[13] Glenn E. Snelbecker, *Learning Theory, Instruction Theory, and Psychoeducational Design* (New York: McGraw-Hill, 1974), pp. 286–317.

FIGURE 3.7 Example of S-type conditioning

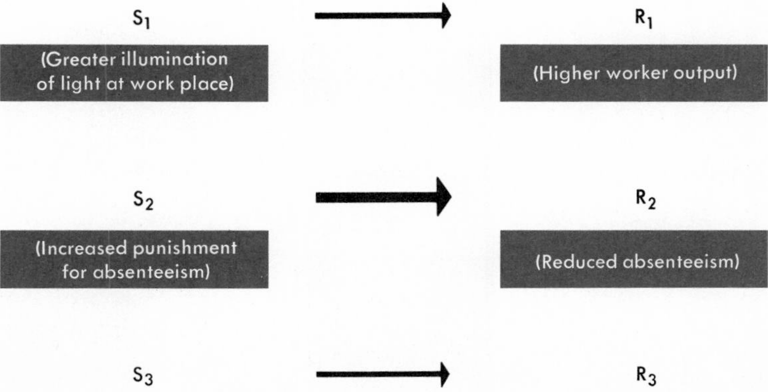

sponse). Philosophers had said that man was an economic animal, behaviorists supplied an S-R model with experimental findings, and organizational practitioners managed others under these assumptions.

operant behavior

Figures 3.8 and 3.9, on the other hand, show the Skinnerian basic model, as well as the application of the concepts to a management setting. Skinner is less concerned with the stimulus and possible internal states of man. He rejects the traditional S-R theory and places emphasis on *operant behavior*—that is, behavior that is voluntary, learned, and a *function of its consequences.* The behavioral focus is now the response and subsequent interaction with its environment. In the work world, managers have great influence over that environment.

reinforcement

Managers influence the environment through managing the reinforcement factors. By *reinforcement* we mean the consequences that follow a response. Managers may give positive reinforcement through reward sanctions (praise, money, more responsibility) and thus increase the probability that the behavior will be repeated. Or they may give negative reinforcement, an act that increases the probability of the desired behavior by presenting an unfavorable consequence. For example, an employee may change her behavior to keep her shouting boss quiet. Punishment, a third intervention

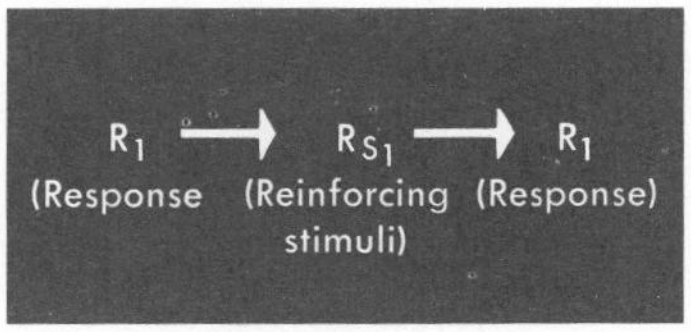

$R_1 \longrightarrow R_{S_1} \longrightarrow R_1$

(Response (Reinforcing stimuli) (Response)

FIGURE 3.8 Operant conditioning (R-type)

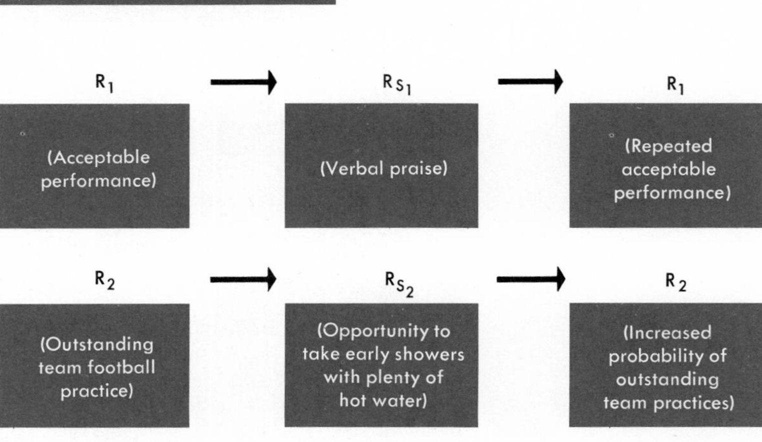

FIGURE 3.9 Example of R-type conditioning

strategy, decreases the probability of the behavior's recurring. Some managers favor a do-nothing approach, thinking that little harm will come to the situation. This approach, called extinction, does have an impact upon subsequent behavior. Responses not reinforced will eventually disappear.

Skinner believes positive reinforcement is the most effective long-run strategy, and we will explore this dimension of behavior for managers later, when discussing behavior modification in Chapters 8 ("Change") and 15 ("Leadership"). We have spent quite a bit of time and space in explaining Skinner's behaviorism because we feel the ideas have direct application to the managerial world. You also have experienced many events that you can recall now as illustrations of behaviorism: in the home with your parents, in the classroom with your teachers, on athletic fields with your coaches, or even in the work situation with your bosses.

A Composite Theory

Are the universal and environmental theories combined here?

VICTOR H. VROOM The Vroom model of motivation is the most recent of the models described. Victor Vroom developed his thoughts and published them in an important work in 1964.[14] To Vroom, motivation is a process governing choices. For example, a person may have a goal that he wants. In order to get to that goal, he must perform some behavior. According to Vroom, the person weighs the likelihood that the behavior or performance will enable him to reach his goal successfully. If he thinks or *expects* that a particular act will be successful, he is likely to select that type of behavior.[15] Thus, this theory of motivation has been labeled the *expectancy model.* (In Chapter 15, you'll see how the path-goal theory of leadership rests upon the Vroom expectancy model.)

expectancy model

An example of career selection may illustrate the thinking of Vroom. There are many reasons why you might select one career over another. One could be the fact that your father is a very successful businessman and steers you into his area, or even offers you employment in his company. (Of course, his occupation could also steer you away from the career—very few children whose fa-

[14] Victor H. Vroom, *Work and Motivation* (New York: John Wiley, 1964).

[15] The expectancy, effort-reward probability aspects of this model have received further attention and research work. See Lyman W. Porter and Edward E. Lawler III, *Managerial Attitudes and Performance* (Homewood, Ill.: Richard D. Irwin, 1968); and Richard M. Steers and Lyman W. Porter, *Motivation and Work Behavior* (New York: McGraw-Hill, 1975).

thers are members of the clergy select the clergy as their own career.) If your goal is to achieve success in business quickly, then the likelihood of your reaching that goal is much improved, as you might expect, if you work in your father's firm rather than elsewhere.

Do you see the importance of individual differences?

Another idea in this motivational model is that people differ in terms of seeing the desirability of certain organizational behavior. Not all workers in an organization place the same value on job security, or promotion, or high pay, or pleasant working conditions. Vroom believes that what is important is the perception and value that the individual places upon the organizational behavior. Suppose a person wants to be promoted from his present job and feels that high performance is the best way of reaching that goal. It follows that he will then perform in a superior way so as to get the promotion. But also assume that this worker knows of others who have performed in a superior way but have not received promotions. In fact, it appears to the worker that the political behavior of a man is more important than his performance. Obviously, if promotion is important to our man, superior performance will not necessarily be the avenue he selects to achieve the promotion. Thus, Vroom highlights the importance of individual perceptions and assessments of organizational behavior. *What the individual perceives* as the consequences of the behavior is far more critical than what the manager thinks he *should* perceive. Vroom's model explains how people's goals influence their effort, and that the behavior the individual selects depends upon his assessment of its probable success in leading to the goal.

Research and study continue in the area of the expectancy theory of motivation. As we approach the 1980s, social and behavioral scientists believe that performance is a function of three things: the *motivational levels* of people, their *abilities and traits,* and their *role perceptions.* From the material already presented about Vroom, we see that a person must want to perform—that is, must expect something worthwhile to come from performance. Vroom, Porter, and Lawler added that desire alone is not sufficient to explain performance; ability or capacity to perform must also be considered. In their 1968 book, Porter and Lawler expanded the theory to include *role perceptions,* a person's idea of what he is supposed to do on the job. Examples will summarize this theory. (See also Table 3.3.)

role perceptions

Charlie may have the motivation force (desire) to perform but not the ability, whereas Susan has the desire and ability but is confused about her role. Effective performance would seem to require the motivation, the ability and traits, and the clear understanding of the job demands. Proper organization, screening and

TABLE 3.3 Performance Factors—Expectancy Theory

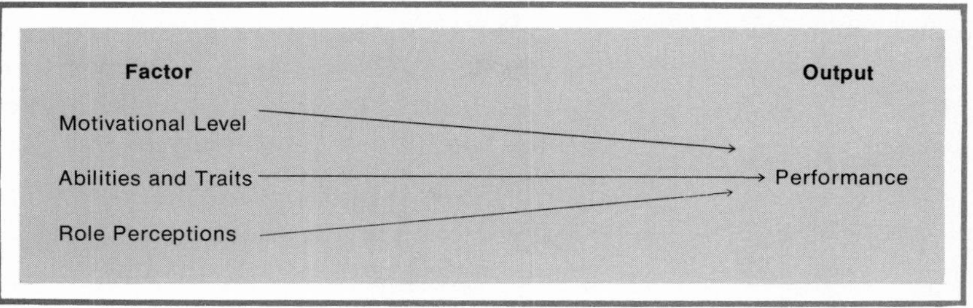

training of employees, and communication of work demands all fall under the responsibility of the manager.

SOME LIMITATIONS OF THE MOTIVATIONAL MODELS

THERE ARE FEW "LAWS OF MOTIVATION" Human subjects are difficult to research. Unlike animals, who are more amenable to experimentation and observation (because they have no choice), humans are themselves an obstacle to rigorous scientific investigation. What we call knowledge, then, consists of observations that have been found to be in agreement by a number of researchers and scientists.

Who has the edge on motivational truth?

ANSWERS TO QUESTIONS OF BEHAVIOR COME FROM MANY SOURCES The work of Maslow has not had a great deal of empirical support and is viewed by some as a philosophical statement. McGregor's contributions are similarly philosophical in nature. Frankl's work comes from his own introspection and experiences and may or may not be applicable to all people. Nevertheless, the explanations of motivation that these three men offer can have strong validity and practical usefulness as each of us attempts both to understand himself better and to practice explaining the behavior of others. The models described by Vroom and Skinner have had considerable research in support of the theory; Herzberg has performed a number of studies in support of his theory; and even though there is some question as to the applicability of the research to other populations, the contributions from all these sources add insight into this most complex and difficult topic.

Is there one motivation theory?

MANAGERS SHOULD NOT ASSUME THAT ALL THINGS MEAN THE SAME TO ALL PEOPLE The behavior a person selects is dependent upon the behavior that is available. Thus, the environment is a very critical factor in motivation. But the behavior that is available in the environment also depends upon the individual's perception of the value of that behavior, or the relationship that the behavior has to the goal that is to be achieved. The topic of motivation, therefore, is an interrelationship type of topic, in that the worker and the job are continually in interplay, one with the other.

NOT ALL PEOPLE CONSIDER WORK THEIR CENTRAL LIFE INTEREST There is a temptation, when talking about the management of motivated behavior, to assume that the work world is the dominant place for motivation. For a great many, their work is their life (some even have been called "workaholics"). For others, however, their sense of growth and satisfaction comes from associations and activities outside their workplace. If a majority of the rising generation of workers and managers should fall into this latter group, the notion of "motivation at work" will be difficult to translate into action.

SUMMARY AND PROPOSTIONS

We began this chapter by explaining why a manager in the course of his work must be concerned with the motivation of his subordinates: The manager must acquire the direct efforts of his workers to reach his own goals.

With this necessity in mind, we considered a basic question: Can the motivation of people be managed, and can a manager know and control himself sufficiently to get desired results from others? We hope this discussion stimulated you to find out something more about motivation, and that our seven generalizations about what is known or assumed in this area will be of value to you.

Following this section, we summarized six theoretical models and considered some of their limitations. The various approaches to the concept of motivation were included for two reasons. First, these theories illustrate that no one theory of motivation exists. While they all have merits and limitations, these theoretical models are current attempts to sort out and order the complex elements inherent in the concept of motivation. They illustrate the kinds of analyzing processes others have used in dealing with motivational problems.

Second, these models give the practicing manager a place to begin his own diagnosis of a particular problem. Since the manager deals in a changing environment, no one model could work even if it were completely true at the time of its creation. The manager must literally contrive his own models. The motivational material included in this chapter gives him a basis on which to begin.

In Chapter 3, we offer the following propositions:

1. There are several useful theories explaining the motivational side of a person's behavior.

a. General explanations have more utility than specific explanations.

b. No one theory is "truest" of them all.

2. Every person has a unique behavioral output even though processes may be similar.

   a. Managers will always have to do their own analysis and interpretation of specific motivational situations.

   b. Managers must learn to deal with the "most likely" approach to motivation and the understanding of behavior.

3. Many motivation theories may be helpful for self-analysis.

   a. Knowing your own motives will help you understand the possible motives of others.

   b. Knowing the processes of motivation when dealing with others may help you understand your own reaction to your bosses' management intervention.

   c. What you find to be true about yourself through introspection may not be true when applied to others.

4. The most productive area for motivational success is through nonpersonal techniques.

   a. System interventions attempting to motivate behavior usually cover many people; thus individual interpretation will have peer support.

   b. Individuals in groups respond better to motivation attempts.

5. The organizational climate is primarily under the control and influence of the manager.

STUDY ASSIGNMENTS

1. What is the relationship between motives, personal goals, jobs, and performance?

2. How does a manager manage motivations? Give examples from your personal experience in which you managed another person's behavior.

3. Select any four of the seven generalizations about human motivation. Give two examples, different from those in the text, of your four generalizations.

4. Briefly summarize the Maslow-McGregor theory. Does this theory explain any of your own behavior? Explain.

5. In what ways are the McClelland and Maslow theories similar? Dissimilar?

6. *Why do you think Frankl includes suffering as necessary for discovering meaning in life?*
7. *What is the significance of Herzberg's two-factor theory to managers?*
8. *Briefly explain the B.F. Skinner theory and its usefulness to managers.*
9. *Evaluate the Vroom model of motivation. Give examples of its value to you in understanding either your own behavior or the behavior of another.*
10. *Do you accept Proposition 3(a)? Why, or why not?*
11. *Why is Proposition 3(c) especially important to a manager?*
12. *How can you explain Proposition 4 in a chapter on human motivation?*
13. *What need does money satisfy?*

situational episodes

1. The performance of a secretarial typing pool is not meeting the expectations of the office manager, Mary Ann Bassier. She knows you are taking a course in management and asks you to help her understand the behavior of the typists. What *information* do you need from Mary Ann before you can help her?
2. A friend of yours works the night shift in a trucking firm. He was just promoted to assistant foreman and brings you a problem he faces. The men he manages are a mixed group: some old, some young. The older ones have been with the company quite a while. Many of the young ones are like he is—going to school in the daytime. His problem is this: How does he know what explanation of behavior to use when all his people are so different?

Individual Behavior Processes

FOUR

OBJECTIVES YOU SHOULD MEET

Define *perception, as used in this chapter.*

Diagram *the relationship of motivation–perception–behavior.*

Describe *the four components of the self-concept.*

Describe *four factors that affect an individual's perception process.*

Cite *three examples of predictable perception responses.*

Identify *three sources of attitudes and opinions.*

Define *and give an example of a defense mechanism.*

I'VE GOT HIS NUMBER

I knew it would happen. Sooner or later these profs were going to find out some stuff about us, and the info will probably get back to the new people. I wish I'd never come here. . . . I don't mind being with the guys—most of them, anyhow—but I don't like answering questions or even asking questions in front of the other people. These profs take everything too seriously . . . and with Arthur from headquarters sitting there, there's no telling what he's writing down to report back.

Now what are they talking about? . . . Geez, the last time the prof with the mustache tried to do some of that group dynamics stuff, we fixed his wagon. When he told us he had a degree in psychology, I glanced over to Dave, then Tom, then Marv—the oldtimers in the group—and you could see that we all silently agreed to teach this guy a lesson. We weren't going to let him practice his stuff on us. That was on Monday of this two-week training program, and the prof got so disgusted with us that he dropped his plans for group dynamics—we got him off our backs. Who did he think he was, trying to make asses out of us by asking those stupid questions. It was funny how the four of us were able to foul his whole plan up. What's really funny is that the prof will never be able to figure out why his little games fail, 'cause he can't find anything common about us. Marv played pro ball for a couple of years before a bad knee ended his athletic career; Tom is from Texas and has been in and out of more businesses than all of us put together; Dave is the only one who went to college, but he was a jock; and I'm the only "professional" of the group. When we were introducing ourselves during the first session, I told the profs that my previous experience was in the CPA field—and boy, the group broke up when I explained that I drove a truck for a Cleaning, Pressing, and Alterations outfit.

Now the professors are talking about the different leadership styles professors find so interesting—things like production-oriented, people-oriented, and theory X–theory Y. "It might be interesting and instructive if all you men take our little test. Then we can plot your scores and discuss the different meanings to the distribution."

Boy, does some of this stuff begin to ring bells! Our company is a young one in its industry, and we've been very successful because we have a bunch of guys who started with nothing and really had nothing to lose. Man, the crazy ideas we had and the silly things we did and got away with! Our competitors couldn't keep up with us because they could never figure us out—we were unpredictable. I guess it really was a miracle that a bunch of guys who knew nothing about business but a lot about long hours, hustling, and playing odds could have come out of those first years smelling like a rose. Since then we've become so large and successful that the top man, a guy who plays a mean poker game and drinks like the rest of us, decided to bring in a more "professional" group of managers. Hell, they're more like a professional group of gangbusters—they've got a bunch of us running scared. They all have college training and came into the company with fancy titles. They don't like our jokes, and they don't drink or play cards with us. Geez, they hardly ever even come out to the field to visit us—but boy, do they ever ask for reports! At first we were worried, until Johnnie in Dallas called us to say that the top boys weren't reading the reports. In one, where they asked us to spell out any special requests, Johnnie had written that he needed two Sherman tanks and seven go-go girls to help increase his sales. On every report he writes that stuff, and he's never gotten any flak from anyone. We all felt better after hearing that.

But then came this training thing. We got a memo saying we were being sent to this conference center for "management training." At first, I couldn't figure out why we were going. Was it because we were dumb and needed some help from the brains, or was it because they wanted to get us away from our jobs with the thought of firing us because our work could go on without us? When I called the other guys about this, they all thought it was the second reason, so we made sure the work couldn't be done without us. I wonder if the profs notice how often we have to go to the phone and make big decisions for our offices?

"What we'll do is ask you to fill out this Leadership Opinion Questionnaire as honestly as possible, and then we'll score the answers and have some discussion." That's the tall and slightly bald prof talking now, a good Joe though. Even though he doesn't play cards with us at night, he sure can consume the suds. He put away thirteen the other night!

I look around at the other guys to get some clue on how to outfox the psychology prof. Geez, they're all listening to the guy. What's the story? Sure, I know it's the last day of the first week, but I didn't think the guys would let these intellectuals con them. Well, here's my copy of the questionnaire. Let's see what I'm supposed to do.

Hey, how about that! This is the thing that guy was talking to me about at that cocktail party I went to in Houston. Yep, it's got those silly letters on the left side that we're supposed to circle—A for Always, F for Frequently, O for Occasionally, S for Seldom, and N for Never. Now if I can just remember how the guy said I was supposed to fill this thing out. . . . How can I figure out how to get a good score? I've got it! He said to fill it out as if I were one of my own subordinates in terms of the things my subordinates would like to see in me. Whoopee! I'll fix their goose! There. I'm all finished and now they can score the damn thing.

Geez, most of the guys are scoring in the lower left side of that thing on the board. Well, here goes—the prof is calling for my score. "On the Task score I had 16 and on the Person score I had 12." There, that'll show those dumb clucks.

"Very interesting," says the smart-aleck prof, "Yours is the only score that falls in the 9,9 category, a category depicting a manager with the unusual combination of the best features of both styles of leadership."

"You described me to a T, Doc . . . to a T."

In the vignette, "I've Got His Number," we have the three basic elements of this chapter. First, our trainee responded and reacted to the situation in a unique way. The way he "sees" the world is truly his own. Second, his feelings and attitudes toward himself, others, and the company contributed to the way he sees his world. Third, he behaved in a way to cope with his situation. His humor and his approach to taking the leadership test are his method of adjusting to his discomfort. You have witnessed specific behavior through this vignette and have seen some of its subtleties; we shall now explore individual behavior processes in a more formal manner.

The preceding chapter, on human motivation, might be called a first step toward understanding the why of behavior. In that chapter we said that people behave as they do for certain reasons, and that a manager of an organization becomes more effective if he is able to understand the factors determining the behavior of himself and others.

We may never really know the answers to behavior questions, for people are very complex, and studying them does not lend itself to traditional rigor and scientific investigation. We are able to develop *partial answers,* and thus the theories of motivation should be viewed as *partial explanations* of behavior.

What are some of the other factors, then, that we should examine to gain a better understanding of behavior? Of the many that we could list, we have chosen three to discuss at this point. They are mental states or processes that influence the selection of behavior. The three concepts we want to add to motivation are perception, attitudes, and defense mechanisms.

These three concepts are very personal and highly individualized. No two people perceive the world the same way; no two have identical attitudes or preferences about the objects of their work world; no two people react the same to the consequences of their behavior—each has individualistic defense mechanisms. Managers can play a large role in influencing all three.

This chapter's first main section deals with the basic mental process of perception. Next, we turn to attitudes, with the emphasis on the process of filtering experience through our predispositions or biases. The chapter ends with a section on the process used when a person has behaved a certain way and received a response or feedback about this behavior (defense mechanisms).

PERCEPTION: A CONCEPT FUNDAMENTAL TO BEHAVIOR ANALYSIS

The treatment of perception in this chapter is oriented to the manager's use of the concept. Frequently, psychology texts describe the perception processes in very sophisticated and scientific language. This is not our method. We offer instead a condensed and, we hope, useful presentation of the concept of perception.

Perception

Perception is the way a person experiences the universe, the process by which he interprets the experiences around him. All kinds of sensations and stimuli exist around us, but we take in or see only certain elements in every situation. Simple illustrations abound to highlight the commonsense understanding of perception.

> *Although two people may share the same event, each one's perception of the experience will be different.* You may have read two different newspaper accounts of one event and been amazed at how different they were. You may have told a joke to a group of people and found it hard to understand how some people fully understood the joke and others gave you a blank stare. You may even have become upset with fellow students when they did not take things as seriously as you do—for example, when cheating occurs in a classroom and they want to pass it off as the "guerrilla tactics" of a youthful, resentful generation. In many different ways, the truth about perception comes through. Individuals are just that—each

person experiences the world in a very personal and individualistic manner.

We experience the world subjectively; that is, we interpret it. There is a difference between what is sent out and what is received. Someone concerned with management and organizational behavior who feels that other people *should* understand what he says or what he writes is naive; he obviously doesn't understand the process of perception. *What is, is what people believe it to be.*

The "same" event is not "read" the same by two different people. Our manager in the vignette "read" behavior and events in the training session in a unique way. He was even surprised when others seemed to show behavior suggesting a different interpretation of the professor's techniques.

We might say that human behavior is actually responses to perceptions. After behaving, we respond or react to our "mental image" of that outside world at any given moment. Differential perception and patterns of reaction exist for complex reasons. After studying the complex perceptual picture, you may find a new understanding of yourself and others.

Factors Affecting the Perceptual Process

Factors influencing perception processes are innumerable—thus, innumerable books are written on this topic alone.[1] The factors shown in Figure 4.1 were chosen to give you a sample of some of the significant factors that affect the perception process. You may be able to add some of your own to this classification system, for all of us are constantly involved in the act of perception.

How do inner needs relate to perception?

INNER NEEDS What you see in the universe depends partly on your inner needs. When you are hungry, for example, you pick up the aroma of hamburger or bakery goods far more quickly than when you have just finished a pizza with pepperoni. Your basic needs affect the way you perceive objects as desirable or repugnant. Maslow's five basic needs, discussed in Chapter 3, serve as a good illustration of the relationship of motivation and perception. The same needs are basic to both concepts. People with different

[1] This section's organization comes from John Douglas, George A. Field, and Lawrence X. Tarpey, *Human Behavior in Marketing* (Columbus, O.: Charles E. Merrill, 1969), pp. 22–45.

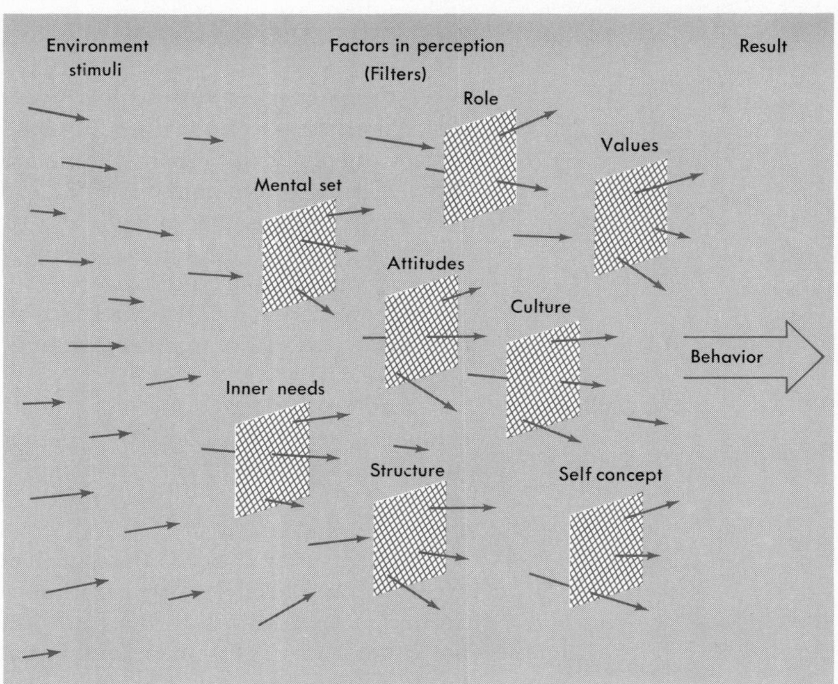

FIGURE 4.1 Some factors in perception.

needs usually experience different motivational stimulants. Similarly, people with different needs select different items to remember or respond to.

A manager must be aware, therefore, that the inner needs of a person have an impact upon what that person sees or takes away from any situation. Since all people have different needs and are at different need levels, all people by definition perceive similar situations differently. The task of understanding perception is not overwhelming; it will come more easily by using some of the insights developed in the earlier chapter on motivation.

Mental set

MENTAL SET *Mental set* means the tendency you have to act or react in a certain way to a given stimulus. For example, suppose you are a contestant in a track meet and are positioning yourself in your starting blocks as you hear the preparatory commands, "Get ready! Get set!" When you hear the command, "Go!" you take off at once, since you are already set and ready to react to this command. This is a very simple illustration of what is meant by mental set.

expectation

You have been aware of the mental-set feature of perception, although you may not have used this language. You may have talked in terms of expectation. When we use the term *expectation*, we mean that people tend to perceive what they expect. For example, your parents may expect you to be smarter when you return home for vacation after the first term. Production managers may erroneously anticipate that marketing managers know little about quantification and work only with ideas. There are those who expect professors to speak "intelligently," women "softly," and union officials "roughly." Many of these examples of mental set are changed soon after direct contact, and the perception process does not remain distorted. But a mental set about ideas, beliefs, and values filters perception and may be lasting and difficult to change.

stereotyping

Another aspect of the mental set is *stereotyping*, the tendency to have a mental set about a person's behavior based upon some previous classification of that person. There are many classic stereotypes: the redhead with a fiery temper, the jolly fat man, the absent-minded professor.

Stereotyping is a major source of distortion in perception. It is very pronounced in organizations with many different natural groupings. In addition to the traditional male–female stereotyping that occurs, managers in organizations are faced with the stereotypes of education, age, race, management level, membership affiliation (as with the union member), and function (such as production personnel, engineering, or marketing). To each of these classifications, people give their own perceptual interpretations and then tend to perceive what they expect to perceive.

halo effect

Is the halo effect a "good" effect?

Very closely related to the idea of stereotyping is the *halo effect*. In the halo effect, an individual believes that a person with one good or bad trait must have certain other good and bad traits. For instance, someone who speaks with rough tones will be perceived as cold, domineering, and bossy. One who is well liked may be judged to be more intelligent than another who is not liked.

In both stereotyping and halo effect, the perceiver makes a judgment, which then creates an expectation that helps filter the environment so that the perception agrees with the expectation or mental set. The mental-set factor is fundamental in perception and is obviously very important in the perceptual process.

Since the mental set or the expectation is developed primarily from past experiences, the manager of an organization does have the potential of influencing the experiences of others and thus influencing the mental set or expectation.

How do you use mental set?

You can influence the perception of a group, for example, by introducing a friend with very appropriate and descriptive titles. The commonsense language of this effort is called "impressing others," and what is obviously happening is the development of a mental set or expectation that may or may not prove true through later experience. Do not misinterpret our intention here. Our homey illustrations only point to the importance of mental set and expectation in the perception process, and also to the way in which the perception process can be influenced.

self-concept

SELF-CONCEPT The way a person views the world depends a great deal on the concept or image he has about himself. The filtering of the experiences around a person is done to meet the *self-concept,* the expectations that the person has of himself. The term or concept *self* has a number of components, depicted in Figure 4.2.[2]

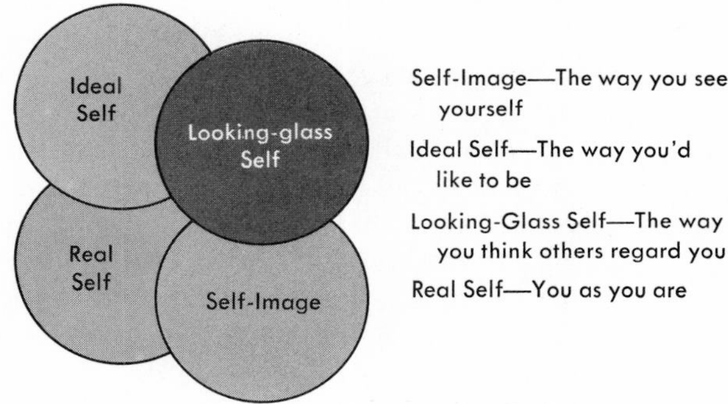

FIGURE 4.2 Components of self-concept

First there is the *self-image*—this is *the way you see yourself.* For example, you might consider yourself to be well liked by others, a forceful person, honest, sincere, and responsible. Second, there is the *ideal self*—this is *the way you'd like to be.* Perhaps you would like to be brave or tough or strong or looked up to. Third, there is *the way you think others see you*—this is the *looking-glass self.* The emphasis here is still on your perception of others' perceptions, for this is not the way people actually see you, but rather the way that you *think* they see you. These three components are all a function of individual perception, and they may be the same as, or different from, the last component, the *real self,* or *the way you really are.* Some observations about self-concept theory are needed.

[2] John Douglas, George A. Field, and Lawrence X. Tarpey, *Human Behavior in Marketing* (Columbus, O.: Charles E. Merrill, 1969), p. 65.

Why is self-concept important?

Perhaps the key to most of your behavior is your self-concept.[3] Establishing a mental picture of yourself—your pluses and minuses—is essential for mental health. This process continues as one changes and adjusts his concept throughout his life. The urge to preserve a relatively stable, somewhat flattering, and steadily more satisfying self-concept is the driving and organizing force behind a large portion of human activity. Each of these components is an important feature in the development of a healthy, mature individual. For example, you might be said to have some disorientation if your self-image, ideal self, and looking-glass self are the opposite of the real self. You may undergo a great deal of stress and frustration and may have to resort to a kind of personality fantasy in order to maintain the self-concept. There are people in mental hospitals who consider themselves to be famous personalities of past ages: a Napoleon, a George Washington, a Sitting Bull. In one way of thinking, these people are viewed as having personality disorders because of the difference between the components of the self-concept.

What is a good balance in self-concept?

The healthy, developing, maturing type of concept might be one where the similarity among all these components is great. This would mean that you have a pretty good picture of the real world and are not trying to escape from the reality of interpersonal feedback. If you feel an urge for power and some form of domination, and people see you behaving in that way, then there is a match between the two components and, most likely, adjustments and accommodations will not have to be made in perception or in behavior.

All of you have experienced the changes in your personal search for identity, for the self-concept you had as a child was probably revised throughout the stages of your growth. This concept is under constant rearrangement; we frequently express this in words by saying that a person "finds" himself or "really knows who he is." What is meant by this is a form of agreement in the components of self-concept.

What is important here is to realize that your self-concept in-

[3] Interest in the self-concept continues in both the popular and scientific communities. For example, Dr. Thomas A. Harris, author of the best selling book *I'm OK—You're OK* (New York: Avon Books, 1973), speaks of the remarkable change in a child at 10 months of age. The child experiences the power of locomotion and shows signs of personal awareness and original thought. Professor A.K. Korman, in works published in 1970 and 1971, proposed a theory of motivation based on one's attitudes about oneself (the self-image). See A.K. Korman, "Toward an Hypothesis of Work Behavior," *Journal of Applied Psychology*, 54 (1970), 31–41; and "Expectancies as Determinants of Performance," *Journal of Applied Psychology*, 55 (1971), 218–22.

fluences the perception process. You will tend to screen and filter the world around you so as to meet your personal goals of self-image and ideal self. You may even accuse others of prejudice and bigotry if the looking-glass self differs from the ideal and self-image. In short, the self-concept is a pivotal factor affecting the perception process.

What else affects perception?

Structural factors

STRUCTURAL FACTORS *Structural factors* relate to the objective world that exists in concrete form. For instance, if you are reading this chapter in a room, the objects in the room constitute structural factors in perception. There may be a radio, a number of chairs, a desk, several books, and perhaps some dirty clothes around the room. These are objective structural factors. When someone walks into the room and assigns meaning to these structural factors, then individual perception is occurring. If the dirty clothes, for example, are on the floor near a laundry basket, someone might perceive that structural factor to mean you were a bad thrower of dirty clothes and missed the mark. If the dirty clothes were all around the room, a different interpretation might be forthcoming.

Two illustrations in housing projects bring this point out. In one housing project, there were a number of bicycle racks that were not being used, and yet bicycles were being dropped all over the grounds. Letters to parents and threat of punishment did little to change the behavior of most of the children; the problem was solved only when the manager put the bicycle racks where most of the children were dropping their bicycles.

In another situation, the large dumpster trash cans were moved to a different location, and the tenants still behaved as if they were at the former location. Efforts had to be made to change the behavior and perception of the tenants in order to get their trash into the trash cans. Bicycle racks and dumpsters are the structural factors in these examples.

Although the structural factors may be easy to change, there is often a tendency to ignore them. The clue to problem behavior may reside in these factors.

role

ROLE DEMANDS The term *role* refers to the behavior associated with a particular position. All positions in organizations have a written or unwritten expectation of behavior. It helps, for example, if you know what are the "legitimate," accepted behavior possibilities of your boss, your peers, and yourself.

In addition to the formal demands of role behavior made by the organization, there are also informal role demands. There may be nothing in any formal policy statement about manager involvement in community affairs, but you may quickly learn that such involvement is expected of managers who want to move up in the organization.

role conflict

Role demands can create perception problems when there is *role conflict.* Conflict exists when the demands from two roles are incompatible within one situation. Suppose you were brought up in a steel town. Your father has worked for years as an hourly employee. You are hired into the company as a management trainee and soon become a foreman over hourly employees. It may be the company's expectation that foremen are to be "tough" with the hourly workers. You see much of their "playing-around" behavior as a natural release from the tensions and pressures of the job and believe it is all done in fun. Your management peers and boss perceive the same behavior as "goldbricking" or "slowdown tactics" and insist you tighten up your management methods. Thus, your role as manager conflicts with your role as son.

We need not expand the illustration for you to see the implications and perceptual complications arising from role conflict. It is obvious that an organization will try to minimize role-conflict situations in both the formal and informal settings.

Culture

CULTURE *Culture,* which is defined as everything that is learned and passed on from one generation to the next, obviously affects every aspect of the perception process. Culture includes such things as language, value system, religious beliefs, and other patterns of behavior. Societies have a culture, organizations have a culture, and groups have a culture. The individual, as a participant in all these areas, is thus a composite of many culture elements. If we look at particular cultures within organizations, groups, or societies, we are looking at what sociologists call the *ethos.* The ethos is the image, the character, or the personality of the unit. In what ways does the culture or ethos of a unit affect the perception processes?

ethos

What do we learn from our culture?

Think for a moment of the ethos you are familiar with. The United States of America has an ethos that may include such terms as strong, powerful, invincible, unselfish, protective. (The terms you use depend upon who you are—people of other nations might offer a different set of terms to describe our ethos.) If an American accepts these terms and the meanings behind them, you can understand how difficult it would be for him to interpret government action as weak, irresponsive, exploitive, and so on. There will be a tendency, therefore, for people to perceive events and defend actions in terms of their ethos positions. The same analysis holds for communist, nationalistic, commonwealth, common-market, and neutral, emerging countries.

The Marine Corps has a definite character and personality that shapes behavior. So too with corporations. General Motors has a different ethos from the Ford Motor Company, International Business Machines is different from American Airlines, and Harvard University is different from Heidelberg College.

What is true for corporations is true for smaller groups or classes. The ethos of the Production Department differs from that of the Personnel Department, which differs from that of the Marketing Department. The union membership differs from the management membership.

The ethos and culture of organizations are developed and maintained through the transmission of *language* and *values.* Each group or class has its own language and values. These get communicated and reinforced through rewards and punishment of the unit. What a company values, for example, is communicated to its managers through the qualities that are rewarded by salary increases or promotions. Deviants from the organizational ethos are either removed or not rewarded, thus reducing their effectiveness. Organizations, through language and value efforts, try to have the perceptions of all their members become similar.

Culture and ethos operate in another behavioral process when they become the standards or criteria for evaluating environment responses. Managers frequently "explain away" reactions to the environment (competitors, customers, or the government) in terms of the established ethos or culture of the organization. So in both the perceptions leading to behavior and the explanations for environment feedback, culture and ethos play an important part.

We have seen that many factors affect the perceptual process. As stated earlier, the factors explained in this chapter do not represent all possible factors affecting perception. Being selective, we have identified those most critical to organizations and those having the potential of being influenced by managers. Look back at Figure 4.1, keeping three considerations in mind: (1) We do not indicate which of the filters or factors comes first—this varies with every individual; (2) we do not diagram the interplay between the factors; and (3) the order and interplay of the factors vary a great deal, depending upon the situation.

Predicting Perceptual Responses

How do you predict behavior?

It is possible to predict perceptions of other people and then predict their behavior or responses to stimuli. This statement is not made to shake you up or to create some kind of expectation about mysterious wands, magic words, or fantasy sessions with the spirits of another world. It would not be difficult to predict, for instance, that the residents of Kentucky would respond with "University of Kentucky" to the stimulus initials UK, whereas residents of England would more readily respond with the words "United Kingdom." It similarly follows that the capital letters SEC would generate different responses in different parts of the world. To people on the East Coast, SEC might mean Securities and Exchange Commission. To the followers of athletic activities in the Midsouth, it stands for Southeastern Conference. And to Australians, it would mean State Electric Commission.

The two examples given to illustrate the connection between behavior and perception are oversimplified ones. The ease in predicting word associations in terms of stimulus–response does not mean that it is easy to predict an employee change in work procedure. That the problem is more difficult does not mean the attempt at prediction should be disregarded. Prediction of behavior from knowledge of others' perceptions is possible.

ATTITUDES

Attitudes, a subject that was mentioned in the earlier part of this chapter, also relate to perception. Attitudes may be seen as a moderating concept or variable. For instance, if you see two people arguing and you stand at a distance so you cannot hear what is said, your perception of that event will be affected by attitudes that you have if one of the people is of a different race from the other. If we tell you that one of them is from Italy and you have an attitude about Italians, your perception of the event will be moderated or affected by that attitude. Thus we turn to an important idea that deals with an individual behavior process, the concept of attitudes.

The many factors described in the perception process make each person unique in the way he relates to his world. The attitudes that people have also contribute to the uniqueness and the differences among people.

Clarification of Terms

Three terms usually cover this area of study: *opinions, attitudes,* and *values.* In each case, the term represents your preference, your position, your bias for or against something. A distinction is usually made between the first two terms and the last. Opinions and attitudes are similar in that they deal with the preferences you have about an object. *Opinions* on topics or subjects usually take some thought but are not necessarily long-lasting—they change rather frequently. *Attitudes* are also preferences, not necessarily for subjects but rather for objects; they are of longer duration and usually more resistant to change. *Values* deal with deeper, perhaps more philosophical subjects and are usually the most enduring of these three. (See Table 4.1.) We discuss values in Chapter 20; here, we discuss opinions and attitudes, two terms that we accept as being very similar.

Opinions

Attitudes

Values

Where does an attitude come from?

It is important to understand how opinions and attitudes are formed and what impact they have on perception and ultimately on behavior. At the present stage of understanding in this field, it is not possible to say that attitudes are necessarily the direct cause of behavior. In other words, knowing a person's attitude is no guarantee that his behavior can be predicted. At this time, we are not really interested in whether behavior affects attitude or attitude affects behavior; probably each has an impact on the other. We might start this discussion of opinions and attitudes by looking into some of the sources of attitudes.

Sources of Attitudes

How does the family create attitudes?

The *family* is probably the most common source of the development of opinions and attitudes. Your opinions and beliefs about the topics of religion, of fairness in play, of honesty and cheating are usually similar to those held by your parents. Similarly, people's voting patterns and career choices are very closely linked with those of their parents.

TABLE 4.1 Personal Preferences Classification

Term	Definition	Quality	Example
Opinion	Preference on a topic or subject	Short duration, changeable	U.S. involvement in foreign affairs
Attitude	Preference about an object	Mixed time duration, somewhat difficult to change	Conservative, protective; liberal
Value	Preference on belief	Long time duration, very resistant to change	Loyalty, honesty, responsibility

ethnic status

A second source of attitudes is the *ethnic status* of individuals. Catholics, Jews, and blacks have been known in times past to vote for the Democratic Party in much larger numbers, proportionally, than have white Protestants. Although this is an example of behavior and not attitude, the ethnic groups were probably identifying the Democratic Party as holding values, attitudes, or opinions on certain issues that were similar to their own.

class

A third important source is *class*. Each of you is a member of a class that has defined status. For example, you may be affiliated with the working class, or the middle-income class, or the upper class, or the educated class, or the young-generation class. Each class is measured by various criteria, including income, occupation, education, or some combination. People within classes tend to share similar attitudes, perceptions, and behaviors.

A person's geographic location can also be a subtle source of attitudes and opinions. For example, people from the same region tend to hold similar, although not necessarily identical, opinions. Residents of large cities tend to be more alike in their attitudes than people who come from either rural or suburban areas.

Most of the sources of attitudes mentioned are part of a person's given set of characteristics; you have little choice in being born into a family with an ethnic status, class, and geographic location. To look to others as a source of attitudes, opinions, and values is a natural individual behavior process as well as a bench mark for decision making. A good deal of behavior depends on identifying with others. When we analyze behavior in terms of the impact from others, we are using a theory or explanation called

reference theory

reference theory—whom it is you identify with or refer to when making behavioral decisions.

In some cases, the referent is a person you know and probably admire. Examples would include one or both of your parents, a successful aunt or uncle, an older brother or sister, a revered teacher or athletic coach, an older employee, a union official, your boss, a successful manager of a technical unit, and so on. You may seek out this person's advice or help when faced with problems, and your attitudes and opinions will most likely be shaped by those of this other person.

In other instances, you may never come in contact with the other person, or that person may not be living. Martin Luther King's life stands as a model for many, young and old; U.S. presidents serve as referents, as do professional athletes; the same is true for organizational officials. In all illustrations, you can see the value of knowing a person's referent—the values, attitudes, and

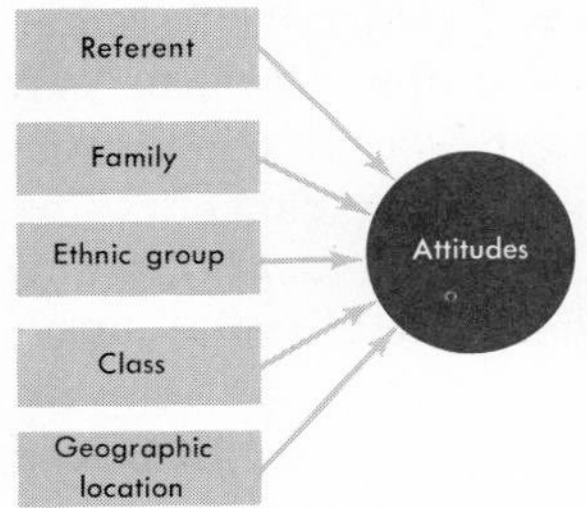

FIGURE 4.3 Summary of some attitude sources

opinions of one help you understand the values, attitudes, and opinions of the other.

The referent can easily be a group as well as a person, and the influence on behavior can be as important. The group reference is a topic more fully developed in Chapter 5, "Human Groups."

Attitudes play an important role in behavior. A manager is one step closer to effective managing if he has insight into sources of attitudes for himself and others. He is better able to anticipate the consequences of organizational action if he has some knowledge of the factors affecting behavior. He may even be able to change the referents people use and thus improve organizational performance so that rewards can go to both the individual and the unit. A manager in an organization can reduce possible friction in his interpersonal behavior if he has some knowledge of attitudes and opinions and their sources (Figure 4.3).

DEFENSE MECHANISMS

Defense mechanism

Once you have displayed behavior, there is likely to be some consequence. The consequence can be rewarding or punishing or confusing. Consequences of your initial behavior invariably lead to some further behavior. You can either accept the consequences for what they are or reject the consequences and go through a behavioral process to maintain a balance and constancy or congruity with your self-concept or organizational ethos. This behavioral response to a threat to self, when the feedback of your behavior does not match your expectations, is called a defense reaction. *Defense mechanisms* are the ways people defend themselves from threat.

How do you behave if you don't like the feedback?

Defense mechanisms are based on a very simple idea and basic assumption: when confronted with experiences of anxiety, conflict, frustration, or failure, you would rather be psychologically comfortable than psychologically uncomfortable. It is natural for you to dislike personal embarrassment, personal rejection, personal attack. The healthy person strives for a balance in his interpersonal life so that there is psychological comfort. When discomfort occurs, when stress and tension arise out of the conflict between what you want and what is happening, you may resort to a defense mechanism—a process that the organism uses to protect itself and maintain the balance (see Figure 4.4).

Suppose a young man believes he has the ability to be an

outstanding basketball player but fails to make the team. He is basically faced with two options with this information. First, he can accept the evaluation judgment of the basketball coach and perhaps decide that he will get enjoyment from playing basketball as a hobby even though he is not good enough for the school team. Or he may create a defense mechanism by deciding that the coach was prejudiced against him or that he was not given a fair chance to show his ability. If a person experiences a number of these tryouts followed by failures, he will probably stop trying out.

cognitive dissonance

A very useful way of thinking of these defense mechanisms is to use a theory of *cognitive dissonance*. Simply stated, this theory says that you will be motivated to match up two elements of knowledge if these two elements are "objectively" in disagreement with one another. For example, if you want to buy a small sports car yet are faced with the statistics of accidents of small cars and their tendency to turn over, you may add the conclusion that the small car gives you greater maneuverability and thus reduces the likelihood of an accident ever happening. Or if you enjoy smoking, you will do a kind of psychological manipulation with the facts and statistics showing the relationship between smoking and cancer. The theory is helpful in understanding behavior, for it assumes that humans cannot tolerate inconsistency and thus will use some defense mechanism to bring elements back into agreement.

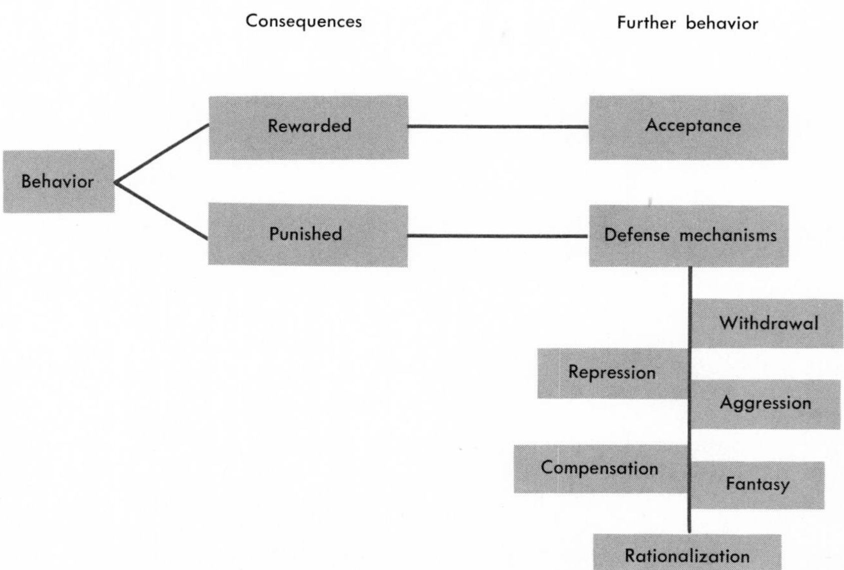

FIGURE 4.4 Defense mechanisms as behavior processes

How would you cope with unreasonable goals?

Frequently, such unproductive defenses are started by an organization. Organizations often impose *unreasonable goals* on their executives. It is probably assumed that the managers would have set lower, easier goals. Higher management thus goads its subordinates into giving better performance and then criticizes the failure. Managers respond by building slacks into their budgets, underestimating output and sales, and overestimating personnel needs and expenses. They arm themselves with all sorts of "objective data" to explain the failure to meet goals. Much of this defensive behavior is organizationally unproductive. Although defense mechanisms counter threats to the self-concept and are perhaps necessary for mental stability and balance, intentional creation of tension and failure situations may not result in productive adaptive behavior.

SUMMARY AND PROPOSITIONS

This chapter has discussed three concepts relating to the individual's process of selecting behavior. Perception, attitudes, and defense mechanisms are all basic to the "why" of behavior; they explain, in part, why the same set of circumstances can affect everyone differently. Every person differs; yet every person uses similar processes. The manager who wants to take advantage of this process information will be the one who does not jump to quick conclusions about the behavior of others. He will not attribute all kinds of bizarre motives to a piece of behavior that he has just observed; rather, he will attempt to analyze the context of attitudes and perceptions and see the cycle by which every individual processes behavioral decisions. He will recognize the variety of factors possibly affecting individuals' perceptions and will use his knowledge to guide and influence others' work behavior toward his own goals. You should now be ready to reflect on the following propositions.

1. Self-concept is the most valuable and meaningful factor in perception.
   a. In the final analysis, a person must "live with himself"—that is, ultimately answer to his self-concept.
   b. The self-concept of a person gives meaning and interpretation to the significance of the other perception factors.
2. It is possible to understand the perception process of others.
   a. Many of the simple factors have been tested in psychology laboratories and a body of accepted knowledge exists.
   b. Where motives and attitudes are important in perception, individual differences and complexity enter in.

3. Understanding of perception is not the same as controlling behavior.
   a. Understanding helps define the set of choices from which the behavior will come.
   b. "Predicting behavior" in organizations may have to be viewed as "influencing the set of choices." Specific behavior prediction is probably an impossibility for managers.

4. Managers control or influence the important environmental forces of perception.
   a. Managers decide what the structural and technological stimuli will be. Even though the individual filters the stimuli, the type of stimuli available to be filtered influences the resulting behavior.
   b. Managers, through the organization, define the ethos. Managers determine sanctions and thus establish the reward or punishment context of behavioral consequences.

5. Defense mechanisms should be expected by a manager.
   a. No organization is ever perfect, and employees must resort to defense mechanisms to cope with failure and frustration.
   b. A manager may have to create information so as to provide a subordinate with a way of saving face.
   c. Since not all defense mechanisms are organizationally healthy, the manager must be aware of the process and adjust to reduce their costs.

6. Attitudes are more difficult to change than behavior is.
   a. Behavior change without attitude change is compliance and thus has a short life.
   b. If you can get attitude change, then the behavior change will be longer-lasting.

STUDY ASSIGNMENTS

1. What individual behavior processes do you see operating in the vignette "I've Got His Number"?

2. Why is perception a concept fundamental to behavior analysis?

3. Write out a statement describing your own ideas of your self-image, ideal self, and looking-glass self.

4. Give four examples, from your personal experience, of structural factors affecting your perception.

5. Name three factors that contribute to mental set.

6. *Define the term* role. *Describe three different roles you must play. Define a role for a boss and one for a subordinate that will result in conflict; repeat for two managers on the same level but in different departments.*

7. *Describe the ethos of your educational institution.*

8. *Give one example of how you can predict a perceptual response and one example of predicting a behavioral response.*

9. *What is an attitude? Give two examples of your attitude about something.*

10. *Are defense mechanisms a necessary aspect of behavior? Explain.*

11. *Give two examples in which defense mechanisms are costly to an individual or organization and two examples in which they are good.*

12. *Explain Proposition 3*(b).

13. *Describe an instance where the manager's ability to determine sanctions influences perception.*

14. *What is meant by Proposition 5*(b)*?*

15. *Do you agree with Propositions 6, 6*(a), *and 6*(b)*? Explain.*

situational episodes

1. Your boss calls you into the office one day and gives you the following assignment: "I want you to change our orientation program for new employees. They join us expecting to be order takers in the fast-foods industry. We want them to be salesmen and women." What would be your program or plan for changing expectations?
2. You have a number of people working for you. They all work on individual projects but frequently get help from each other. They work in one large room. Sissy Marshall is an older woman who has returned to the work force since her children have left home. She seems very sensitive about her work and frequently questions her own ability. She works well and receives praise from you and the others in the office. Is there anything you can do to improve this situation?

Human Groups

FIVE

OBJECTIVES YOU SHOULD MEET

Describe *why groups form, and state three of their functions.*

Name *two types of groups, and give personal examples of each.*

Identify *six characteristics of all groups.*

Explain *how individual behavior can be changed in the context of a group.*

Describe *three schemes for analyzing groups.*

Give *three properties that an ideal, highly effective work group possesses.*

Give *three ways a manager uses the organization structure to influence group behavior.*

List *three gains and three losses related to the use of informal organizations.*

THE GAMES PEOPLE PLAY IN ORGANIZATIONS

"I wish you the best of luck in this job. It about got me down. Perhaps a younger man will have more patience, or whatever it takes." Tony Risso was headed back to Detroit, still in personnel work, but with a new company. The Adam-Carey Company had denied his request for transfer, so Tony had contacted some of his friends in Detroit to find a new job. Harv Bell was his replacement.

"I think my problems began even before we opened our plant here. The company spent a bundle planning the new plant and making this move—we wanted to find a locale free of the labor problems we were having in Warren, Michigan. We wanted a town where the tax base was suitable and rail transportation was good, and we wanted an inexpensive supply of untrained people. The Industrial Development people and Chamber of Commerce really put on a show. You'll soon realize that this section of Kentucky is a recreational area that is expected to grow. We became the major employer in the whole area, and with a brand new plant, you'd think we wouldn't have had the problems we had."

"Tony, why don't you spell out some of the problems you had and give me some idea of what I'm walking into."

"Well, the first problem was housing—they had some bad weather down here and it delayed construction on our houses. Most of us left our wives and families in Detroit and rented motel rooms. Then, when the weather got better, you'd expect the construction people to get busy, right? When the weather got better, the construction foreman had trouble getting workmen because the fish were biting! That should have been my first clue that the so-called available nonunion labor in the area might not be available on our terms.

"The next problem was the trouble with the wilderness weirdos—you know, the hairy ones who complained about our proposed source of water and the possible pollution to the water and their damn fish. Well, all that trouble with the scenic bunch cost us two and a half months in delay for getting the plant ready to go.

"So, we finally get open with a big parade, the kids from the consolidated school band, a talk by the mayor and the Industrial Development guy from the governor. We had an open house for everyone in the area, and I thought that things were looking up and that everything might work out, right? Harv, what happened to me shouldn't have happened to anyone! I mean I've been in the business a long time. I've attended courses at Wayne State in collective bargaining, labor relations, and all the rest. How come no one told me that the first big labor action I was going to get here was a wildcat strike? And this so-called nonunion, available, semiskilled work force not only didn't know what a wildcat strike was—they didn't even care! A small group of them got sore and before I could get to the problem, they walk off the job to go fishing or whatever they do around here when they walk off a job. To make a short story long, Harv, the labor situation is touch-and-go.

"Well, after we got the labor situation toned down, I conducted a survey among our 56 first- and second-level managers to see what kind of development they needed. Most of those men are from around this area: Southern Ohio, West Virginia, Tennessee, and, of course, Kentucky. There's a mixture of college and noncollege, and some of the younger men have these new two-year associate degrees from the community college. What the company needed, so these guys thought, was management training courses. I checked with Detroit and they said to go ahead and use local talent if I could find any. And I did find some capable guys at the state university in their business school. These profs came down and put on a two-day program for supervisors on both shifts for six weeks.

"I really enjoyed these guys. Yes sir, they did a hell of a good job. Even though only one of the profs was from Kentucky, our first- and second-level supervisors really got to know them, enjoyed meeting with them for two hours at a stretch, and even looked forward to their visits each week. When the training was over, I invited the profs to dinner and asked them to give me all the feedback they could.

"They said that the plant contained two different cultures: an industrial culture (primarily the men from Detroit) where the emphasis was on performance, efficiency, hard work, monetary rewards, status, position, argumentation, directness, openness, and playing all your cards from the chest. Most of the workers and many of the first- and second-line managers, on the other hand, were of a different culture—one where fishing, tobacco, and politics were more important than the Detroit Tigers; where a quieter style of life was honored; where Baptists and religious principles are a primary force in the development of attitudes and values; and where, on a bright, sunny, clear day in early spring, they will go fishing. These people don't like to be yelled at and they don't like the abrasive character of the Detroit managers. The profs

said we were going to continue to have trouble and resistance to our efforts at productivity because we were dealing with a nonindustrial culture.

"And for what it's worth, Harv, I pass on one bit of information that your friends in Cleveland won't believe. Bourbon County, Kentucky, is a dry county. No alcohol can be sold here. Harv, you have my blessings. I'll think of you when I'm in Detroit."

Tony Risso, personnel manager, wanted to be a good manager. He had probably been effective in Detroit, yet his experiences in Kentucky overwhelmed him, and resignation from the Adam-Carey Company seemed the only way to cope—a very expensive way, since personal contacts and power within the company would be of little value to him in a new job, and seniority, pension rights, and other fringe benefits had to be sacrificed to keep personal sanity, emotional stability, and self-respect. Could Tony have avoided such a problem?

The professors from the state university described an aspect of organizational life foreign to Tony. They talked to different cultures in the plant, cultures that might explain why the workers responded in unpredictable ways. Perhaps the workers' behavior seemed unpredictable only because of the management's erroneous concept of what people's behavior should be. If the plant management had a better understanding of how individual behavior is modified and influenced by groups, intergroup processes, and different cultures, many of the frustrations and conflicts might not have had the same intensity and impact.

In this chapter, the individual (manager or hourly worker, superior or subordinate) is put into the dynamic mix of the organization. This mix contains many kinds of groups, and these groups form the topic of this chapter. Managers need to know what groups exist, how groups influence their own behavior, and, if possible, how groups can be managed.

To begin our study, we look first at some groups and their functions. After the concept of "group" is established, we consider some schemes for the analysis of group behavior. Finally, we turn from the analysis of groups to the possibilities open to the manager for solving problems emerging from the groups within his organization.

A DESCRIPTION OF GROUPS

Like individuals, groups come in many sizes, shapes, and forms. A few examples will illustrate this point. These examples do not exhaust all the types that exist; they are given to represent types you can relate to.

Illustrations of Group Types

FORMAL WORK GROUP Assume that you are part of a formal work group of five members, all of whom are charged with the responsibility of developing a feasibility study for a housing development corporation in a rapidly growing metropolitan area. The group is formed in September and has a December 30 deadline.

In this work group are five different people: Tom is on loan from the city commissioner's office and has expertise with budgets. Bessie, a black woman who has just completed a two-month scholarship training program in Washington sponsored by HUD (Department of Housing and Urban Development), is an assistant director of a housing corporation in the city. Jerry is on loan from the county planning commissioner. Carol, a volunteer worker and housewife, has a great deal of knowledge and experience in developing feasibility studies for funding purposes. And Paul is a volunteer representative from the university, whose major interest is housing. Of the five, therefore, you have three paid workers and two volunteers on this temporary formal work group committee with the responsibility to produce the study report. The project group is to report to the director of the local OEO (Office of Economic Opportunity) unit, and the work group's first organizational meeting is supposed to develop its structure.

How would you organize this group?

One of the hired employees of the city is designated as chairman of the group and conducts its first meeting. (The agenda items he develops deal with the description of the task at hand, the assignment of specific duties, and the planning of work to meet the deadline.) When the group meets for the first time, the two women know each other from previous associations on other committees, as do the men from the planning commission and the budget section. Only the volunteer from the university is unknown to the other four. The agenda is discussed, the issues and missions of the committee are clarified, the resources necessary to get the job done are identified and committed, the work is allocated and responsibilities are assumed, and an overall plan is generated, with early checkpoint dates for feedback and correction if necessary. This sounds like a well-oiled and fundamentally effective work group. The people are committed; they sense the importance of the feasibility study for housing; there is a recognition of the need for a leader; the leader has been able to emphasize the importance of the mission; and on paper it appears that all will run smoothly. There is a *formal group*. It has structure, a mission authority from OEO, and organizational legitimacy.

formal group

INFORMAL WORK GROUP There are three teams of three men each working in the pasteurizing section of a large brewery. These three teams are organized on the basis of the technology of the company: The cans of beer come out of the pasteurizer, are inspected, go to one station for weighing, and go to another station for packing and shipping. Every thirty minutes, the men at each of these stations rotate, so that no particular group is overcome by the boredom and the routine of the operation. Charlie is a junior-college student who has come in for the summer months and apparently was very eager to find the job. He received instructions about work methods from the foreman who is responsible for the three stations on the pasteurizer and the other stations up and down the assembly line. So far, we have described a formal work group.

What is an informal group?

At first Charlie works very rapidly, perhaps trying to impress the foreman that he is worthy of the job. But Charlie's efforts prove somewhat embarrassing to the other men on the merry-go-round operation, for Charlie weighs cans far too fast and creates a backlog for Hal; then Charlie packs cans far too fast and creates a backlog for Sam, and so on. During the second break period, Tony, who has worked in the breweries for years and was once a union officer in the Teamsters, gets Charlie off to the side and gives him some of the "unofficial rules" of the work team. Tony explains to Charlie that the rest of the guys have to work there for months and years, whereas Charlie may only be working there for the summer. They do not want Charlie to work at his own rate. As Tony says to Charlie, "It's a good job and a good deal, and the union protects us and gives us this good deal. You owe it to us to do it our way." If Charlie agrees to go along with Tony's suggestions and gets accepted by the other members, he is thus a member of both the formal and the informal work group. This is an *informal group*. It has structure, a mission, no authority from the formal organization, and no legitimacy from management.

informal group

We could go on with many other illustrations of formal and informal groups—family, fraternity, Girl Scout troop, bridge club. Basic to all groups, however, you would find certain fundamental and similar processes. These are listed here for clarification:

All groups have leaders.

All groups have followers.

All groups seek to get some "work" done.

All groups have feelings and ideas about how work is to be done.

Most groups operate within the minimal performance requirements of the organization.

All groups exhibit behavior (i.e., emergent behavior) above and beyond the minimal behavior expected by the organization.

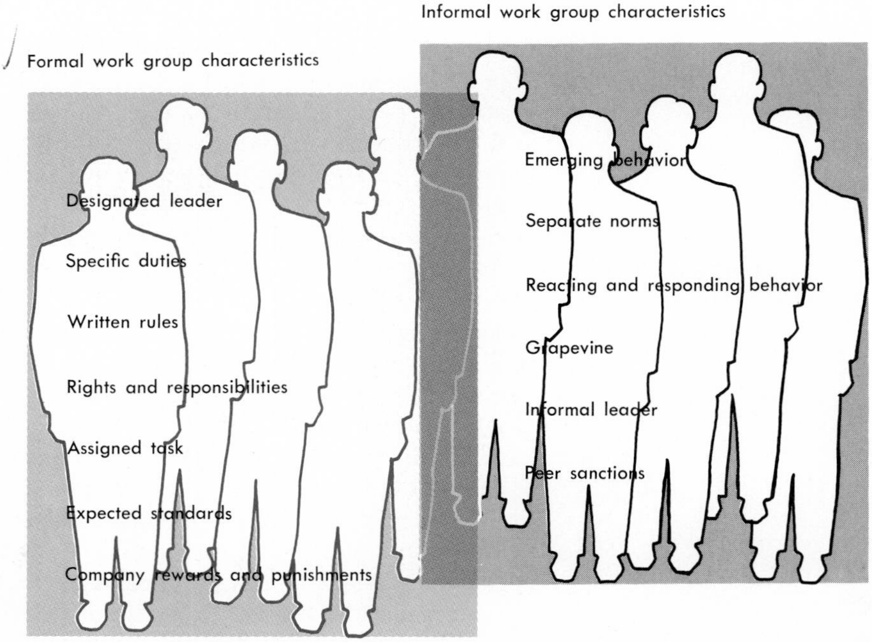

FIGURE 5.1 The dual character of work groups. A person who joins a *formal* work group with its prescribed characteristics may find his actual behavior modified by the same group's *informal* work-group characteristics.

These six conclusions about group behavior indicate the dual character of groups (see Figure 5.1). In formal groups, the structure is dictated from outside the group. Who is to be the boss and how many followers there are, what kind of work is to be done, how the work is to be done, what kinds of output can be expected and what kinds of rewards and punishments are to flow are all part of what can be classified as an *authority system*. The other side of the coin from the formal authority structure is the behavior that generates from an informal, unofficial type of organization. Even though the example about Charlie was identified as an informal work group, you could probably sense that in all groups there are both the formal and informal aspects; that is, there is a designated, recommended, and expected type of behavior coming from the authority source, and there is also the emerging, reacting, or responding behavior in the group that may or may not match the expected behavior. All groups have both these dimensions working within them, so that the behavior of an individual in a group is modified by the interaction of both these forces.

authority system

Functions of Groups

SATISFYING THE INDIVIDUAL'S EXPECTATIONS Groups can be said to perform two functions for individuals: a *production* function and a *social* function. Assume that a person voluntarily joins a group—he becomes a working member of the local police department, he becomes an assistant foreman in a lumberyard, she becomes an assistant department head for a small unit of the state's personnel department, she becomes a manager-in-training for a downtown department store. The individual voluntarily gives up many of his individual rights when he affiliates with an organization. He agrees to come in on time, to follow the rules and regulations of the organization, to work within the structure of the organization, and to conduct himself with some degree of responsibility and honesty. If he violates any of these rules and regulations, he is apt to find himself unemployed. When the individual joins an organization and begins a job, he has to integrate his work with the work of others. To the extent that all the people within a unit are working for some kind of a goal, a group exists. What our new person wants from the group is the following:

What rights do you give up?

What do you want from the group?

1. He wants the group to help him produce some kind of *measureable product*, since the organization will reward or punish him in terms of what he produces.

2. She wants the group to help her *achieve satisfaction* in what she does. She is a human being, and as such, has human emotions, with all the needs and motive drives described in Chapter 3.
3. He has a need to grow as an individual. He expects the group to give him that latitude to *grow and develop* as a human being and an individual.

What does the group want from you?

IMPOSING GROUP NORMS The relationship obviously works two ways, so that the group has certain expectations of the individual. Some of these expectations might be simply stated as follows:

norms

1. The group expects the individual to *obey the "house rules."* Each group has some idea of what should or should not be done by its members. It has an idea of the range of acceptable behavior *(norms)* for its members. The group has an expectation of the allowable behavior for a newcomer (this could be called the role behavior). A long-time member in a group is allowed to deviate from the group norms in his personal behavior, but if a newcomer tries the same deviation, the group will probably respond with negative sanctions—punishment. Every group has definite house rules or norms, and in order for it to maintain its character as a group, the behavior of its members must conform to certain expectations.

sanctions

2. The group expects the individuals to *support the sanctions* that get developed. There are various kinds of *sanctions* in a group, ranging from violent physical sanctions (e.g., punching) to subtle social sanctions (e.g., cooling out). Members must accept the value of even extreme sanctions, for they are expected to realize the importance sanctions play in maintaining the character of the group.

   If a group of secretaries, for example, is part of a work group and has established some informal and unofficial house rules, the secretaries might treat a "rate buster" as a social outcast; this outcast will be unable to find anyone to have conversation with at lunch. In many, many ways the group will accept and implement the sanctions that have been created so as to maintain the character and integrity of the group.

3. The group expects the individual to *give up some of his individual rights.* A group of five men playing basketball will become a team when each of them has accepted some of the group rules and regulations. For example, the notion of "passing to the open man" is a group expectation that the individual will knowingly give up the "glory of scoring" so that the team may eventually win the contest. A collection of individuals playing basketball will usually have a number of "hogs" or "gunners"—people who use the others for their own purposes and are not giving up some of their individual rights.

How do outside forces influence group behavior?

BEING A REFERENT We talked earlier about reference theory and reference groups. In all the illustrations given so far in this chapter, the individual is working within the group. Frequently, however, individuals look to others for assistance in decision making, and it is when the help of others is sought that the concept of reference develops. Man is a social animal and uses others to get bench marks for behavior. He learns what is right and what is wrong through experimentation of behavior and the ensuing feedback from its consequences. Nearly all of us at times use, in connection with our behavior, a bench mark or reference point outside the immediate work group.

Consider a person who is unable to find satisfaction (especially social or growth satisfaction) from his immediate group; he may then search for an identity with a group or a class of people outside his immediate work group. Assume that you are a salesman in a tire store. Every salesman in the store is paid according to his individual sales for the week. The salesmen realize that a customer will frequently come into the store and spend quite a bit of time with one salesman then perhaps realize he needs additional information about his tire size or the condition of his present tires, or even want to shop around for other prices. When that customer returns to the store, the very sticky problem of sales credit emerges. The usual practice is for the salesman to give the customer his card, so that if the customer returns, he can search him out. But if the salesman is busy or on his lunch hour, another salesman may wait upon that customer and close the sale in just a few minutes. Now, if you follow the group norms, you will give the credit for the sale to the first rather than the second salesman. However, there is no way that the store knows which customer is coming in for the first time and which one has already talked with

Have you ever sensed group norms?

a salesman—the effectiveness of this practice rests entirely with the social control of the group.

As the salesperson, you may not respond to the efforts of social control by the group. Perhaps you identify with a group of people with a higher social status. To maintain your desire to be part of that reference group, you might intentionally deviate from the social control so as to remain separate from the sales personnel.

You can see through this example that the individual may be a member of a work group in the formal and traditional sense and yet not abide by its house rules, its sanctions, its norms. Even though the behavior from the other members of the group will be nasty and abrasive, it is possible for people to resist such sanctions and operate as individuals apart from the group. To most people, however, the significance of anything they do in an organization is not just the behavior or act itself, but rather the *meaning* that the others give to it. Individuals are thus affected by groups in a number of ways and are almost always in constant relationship with them.

THE ANALYSIS OF EMERGENT GROUPS

In most of the illustrations given so far in this chapter, you have been asked to assume the role of an individual going into a group or as a member of the group. Suppose, however, you are a manager in an organization and are interested in analyzing or understanding the groups that report to you. What kinds of insights are available to help you understand what groups are, how they operate, and how they can be managed?

Can you analyze work group behavior?

We have already spoken of the two major inputs to the behavior of any work group. Repeated in simpler form, these are (1) the behavior that is *required* by the external forces in order to get the job done, and (2) the behavior that *emerges above and beyond* this required behavior. In the first case, required behavior is set by the organization and is usually known. It is the emergent behavior that is most puzzling to the manager. Here are some schemes for analysis that might help solve the puzzle.

A-I-S Method

Both George C. Homans and William F. Whyte have written extensively about the elements of group behavior, especially the element of emerging group behavior.[1] They have identified three basic ingredients for this emerging behavior: activities, interactions, and sentiments.

activity
interaction

An *activity* is just that—it is something that the group or individual does. An *interaction* is a communication between people. There are verbal and nonverbal communications and interactions. You have frequently had someone speak to you or tell you of an event, and, without your giving any verbal response, the other person is able to "read" your reaction. Your reaction might be in the form of a frown, a raised eyebrow, a snarl, a laugh, or a smile. What is important is that you are giving feedback to the other person and he is interpreting and reading this feedback. Thus, interactions are either verbal or nonverbal communications.

sentiment

The last element is the *sentiment;* this is an idea, a belief, or a feeling that you have about something. A synonym for sentiment might be attitude or opinion—it is a liking or a preference you have.

How do A-I-S act on each other?

In all groups, individuals perform activities, some required and some not required (emergent). Simultaneously they are communicating with each other (interactions) about their sentiments toward the activities. Homans and Whyte suggest that there is a mutual dependence among these three elements (Figure 5.2) and that it might work in the following way. Assume that the sentiments people have can be classified as either positive or negative. For example, one person might have a very positive attitude toward baseball, whereas another might have a very negative attitude toward baseball. (This illustration could also apply to attitudes toward communism, politics, religion, alcohol, smoking, or anything.) Now if these two people, one with a positive and one with a negative attitude, are put into a work situation where both are performing similar activities, you may find that the interactions they have are kept to a bare minimum because of the differences in their sentiments. If, on the other hand, you put two people together who start out with neutral sentiments, it follows that the association in similar activities will probably result in increased interactions, which then may develop into a positive sharing of sentiments. So it is a two-way street. The activities of two

FIGURE 5.2 The mutual dependence among activity, interaction, and sentiment.

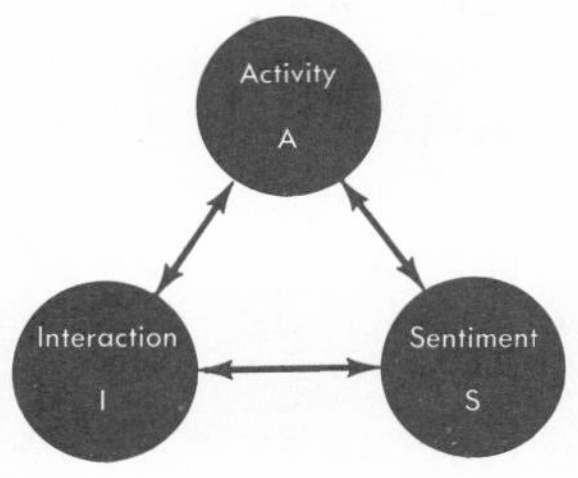

[1] These two men have especially enriched the literature with their writings. See George C. Homans, *The Human Group* (New York: Harcourt Brace Jovanovich, 1950); and William F. Whyte, *Men at Work* (Homewood, Ill.: Richard D. Irwin, 1961).

people affect the interactions, and the interactions are affected by the activities and the sentiments that each person holds.

Exchange Theory

Another scheme for analyzing groups is given by Homans;[2] it has been classified as a kind of exchange theory. Homans sees groups as always having a purpose; they exist to satisfy certain needs. He believes that it is possible to describe behavior in terms of economic concepts such as value, cost, profit, and marginal utility. To Homans, it is possible to think of behavior between two people as consisting of activities that are valued but are achieved at a cost. The surplus of reward over cost yields profit, but an insufficiency may produce a deficit.

How does exchange theory work?

For example, assume that we are thinking of two people in a workplace, Harry and Wanda. Assume further that Harry is the manager and boss of Wanda. Harry will reward Wanda for performing to the standards of the organization, but the reward obviously costs money. Wanda will reward Harry for the compensation by producing so many units per hour, or so many sales per day, or whatever the productive unit is. But as we mentioned earlier, there are many nonmonetary and social rewards such as acceptance, recognition, and pride. Harry can now reward Wanda by being more pleasant to her—in other words, by giving her a feeling of approval and acceptance. This effort costs Harry in time and thought, but Wanda may well respond and reward Harry for the effort by showing greater loyalty to the company, and greater cooperation and interest in what she is doing. Obviously, this costs Wanda effort. If the reward outweighs the efforts, each has a psychic profit. This same kind of scheme can be used in a non-boss–subordinate relationship; it can be used between individuals.

Although the example of exchange theory described two individuals (Harry and Wanda), the concept can be used to analyze behavior within a group. If your own work group is not performing as expected, you might look at the behavior of individual members in terms of what each values and what costs and profits each sees in the interpersonal relationships. A particular work group may not value certain organization goals and may thus view any extra effort on their part as too costly.

Thus, the activity–interaction–sentiment model plus the ex-

[2] George C. Homans, *Social Behavior: Its Elementary Forms* (New York: Harcourt Brace Jovanovich, 1961).

change theory gives the manager some insight into the way groups tend to behave.

Equity Theory

Closely related to the Homans exchange theory is the theory of equity. People frequently evaluate their possible behavior in terms of what it will cost or in terms of what they will gain. This cost or gain is perceived cost or gain, and the equity theorists believe the perception is moderated by comparison with other people.[3] For example, Merrill believed his announced salary increase (outcome) for the past year's performance (input) was satisfactory until he related it to Jo Ann's increase. Faced with this inequity between perceived inputs and outcomes, Merrill behaves in such a way as to create balance and restore equity. Figure 5.3 shows the states of the relationship. At first Merrill is pleased; then he is displeased. To get balance, he may reduce his inputs in relation to the outcomes (that is, work less for the same pay so that he feels he's earning more).

This theory is at an early stage of development and may have limited application toward explaining performance. But you can sense the application to understanding dissatisfaction and the use of defense mechanisms. The following illustration shows how the use of the equity explanation can prevent costly organizational error.

The manager in this instance was a chairman of an academic department in a university. He was surprised one morning when a delegation of three students handed him a petition signed by fifteen students complaining about the teaching of a faculty member who taught one of the sections of a basic required course. In the petition, the students used words like "unfair," "caustic," and "too demanding" to describe the teacher. The chairman accepted the petition and set up a meeting with the faculty member and the spokesperson of the students.

At the meeting, the chairman asked the faculty member to describe the course—the outline, the exams, and the standards for grading. The climate of the discussion was not hostile, and after more probing by the chairman, the student brought out the real is-

[3] Richard M. Steers and Lyman W. Porter, in *Motivation and Work Behavior* (New York: McGraw-Hill, 1975), pages 135–79, devote a full chapter to equity theory. J. Stacy Adams' article, "Inequity in Social Exchange," and the article, "An Examination of Adams' Theory of Inequity," by Paul S. Goodman and Abraham Friedman, make up Chapter 5.

FIGURE 5.3 Equity

sue. Fellow students in other sections did less reading and less exam preparation, yet they received higher grades. The issue was one of perceived inequity. One set of students had greater perceived inputs but received lower outcomes (grades) and thus did what they thought would bring back balance.

This illustration points to some important benefits to using theory (that is, possible explanations) before taking managerial action or jumping to false conclusions. If students (or managers, secretaries, machine operators, or whatever) perceive inequity in a situation, frustration is likely, and the subsequent reactions to frustration may cause additional organizational problems. Personal output may suffer; negative feelings may be generated—first toward the initiator (such as the faculty member), then toward the organization (the chairman, college, and university), and finally toward the other members of the society (fellow students). Inequity is almost inevitable because of the normal errors in any organization and the differing perceptions occurring daily. Managers can use the equity model to gain a better understanding of behavior by individuals within and between groups.

Formal and Informal Leader Relationship

Another scheme for analyzing groups is to identify the objectives or goals common to most groups. In one way or another, the individuals in groups want to perform some kind of task, want to have some kind of social satisfaction, and want to feel some sense of contribution and growth. This language may sound very familiar to you, since it sounds like the theories of motivation describing need for achievement, power, and affiliation. We also know that in most work groups, there is a *formally designated leader*, appointed by the organization. This leader has an option of focusing on one or more of the group objectives, for the manager also has personal and career objectives. He may attempt to be a task-oriented manager, placing most of his emphasis, behavior, and sanctions to meet the achievement need. If the group has the same kind of achievement need, he may find a perfect match in the productivity and effectiveness of the group; but in most instances, the needs of the formal leader are not perfectly matched with the needs of the group. What will probably happen is that the group will develop *emergent behavior* to compensate for the deviation. The group will even develop an emergent or *informal leader*. This leader will be someone in the group to give it direction, to identify the appropriate sanctions, or perhaps to help in the creation of the group norms.

What is an informal leader?

Harmony will probably result in a work group if the formal leader is emphasizing behavior for one basic need while the informal leader is stressing behavior for the other need. Confusion may exist if both leaders are vying for the same kind of objective. For example, if the formal leader is task-oriented and the informal leader is oriented toward the social needs of the group, a balance exists and harmony probably results. But if the formal leader is giving orders and directions for productivity and the informal leader is giving directions for productivity, the possibility of a conflict between the two leaders is very pronounced. Similarly, if both the formal and the informal leader are too concerned about the social needs of the group at the expense of getting the task done, no balance exists and dissatisfaction is likely to follow.

The preceding pages have pointed to a number of ways a manager can approach group behavior. A manager is a fool if he thinks that he can perfectly control and predict the informal and emerging behavior of a group, that groups should not be allowed to have an existence of their own, and that the word "unofficial" or "informal" is a dirty word, not to be allowed in his department. The informal, unofficial, emerging aspects of group behavior are very valuable and sound features of any work group.

After recognizing these groups and analyzing behavioral situations, the manager must turn his attention to using the tools available to him in order to solve his problems. What can he do to cope with situations that need changing?

THE MANAGEMENT OF GROUPS

Leadership Techniques

The first method we explore for changing group behavior is leadership technique. Although this subject receives detailed examination in Chapter 15, some leadership possibilities are given here.

TABLE 5.1 Comparison of the Gains and Losses of Informal Organization

Gains	Losses
Fills in gaps of the formal structure.	Is more difficult to predict and control compared to the formal structure.
Opens up new channels of communication.	Friendships developed are difficult to break, thus creating a form of rigidity.
Develops the social cement for members.	Can result in a loss of power and authority and thus respect, accountability, and responsibility in the work group.
Clarifies behavioral expectations.	Requires a very competent manager to handle and has much potential for flare-ups and disaster.

Note: The idea for this comparison comes from Edwin B. Flippo, *Management: A Behavioral Approach* (Boston: Allyn and Bacon, 1970), pp. 197–214.

Would you know how to manage groups?

The manager has the freedom to put certain people in various positions along a line of activities. He may even have insight into the sentiments that people bring with them to the workplace. If he wants to create conflict and disruption, he can probably do so by taking two people with extreme and incompatible attitudes on a topic and forcing them to work together. He may find greater success by matching sentiments of people and work assignments, or by staffing his unit with people whose sentiments are not as extreme. The field of the control of work groups is still in its infancy, and we do not want to suggest that it is simply a matter of putting round pegs in round holes. But the manager does make structure and staffing decisions, and the knowledge of the relationship between interactions, activities, and sentiments could work in his behalf.

Must you work with the informal group?

The manager may recognize the limitations upon himself and perhaps understand that as a formally designated manager he cannot satisfy all the needs of the work group. If he does, he might encourage the development of informal and emergent leadership, so that the balance exists between the formal and the informal leader. A summary of some of the advantages and disadvantages of the informal organization as previously discussed can be seen in Table 5.1.

Another leadership approach would be to use the criteria of effective work groups as the manager's leadership goal. A great deal of research has been done on the topic of work-group behavior and the methods to achieve the most effective work groups. Rensis Likert of the University of Michigan identifies the "nature" of highly effective groups.[4] He identifies at least 24 separate properties and performance characteristics of the ideal group. It is possible to summarize these properties through a few generalizations.

What are some generalizations about effective work groups?

The ideal highly effective work groups behave in such a way as to produce a *supportive* atmosphere and relationship. There is a great deal of *confidence and trust* between the formally designated leader and the members of the group; there is also confidence and trust among the members of the group, so that the concept of "our group" rather than that of "my group" predominates. *Fear and distrust are removed,* so that there is very *open and frank communication* by all members of the group. The values of each person, the values of the group, and the values of the leader are all moving toward a balance and agreement.

[4] Rensis Likert, *New Patterns of Management* (New York: McGraw-Hill, 1961), pp. 162–77.

This model by Likert is, of course, ideal, but it is the kind of model that a manager of an organization might want to move toward. It sounds like a very free and open and relaxed group but one that is fully aware of the reason for its existence and the expectations that are being held for it by the organization.

The description by Likert of the nature of highly effective groups sounds very natural. If individuals were to share common sentiments, values, and attitudes, then their communication processes would not be distorting data and their efforts would be moving toward the satisfaction of task, social, and growth needs. But we know this is not the way most work groups operate. We know that there are other forces and factors that create differences and perhaps barriers to such effective work groups. Fortunately, the manager has additional tools to use in coping with problem situations. A great deal can be accomplished through the use of organizational structure.

Why aren't all groups effective?

Techniques for Using Organizational Structure

How does the organization set norms?

All organizations make at least two decisions that in time affect the behavior of work groups. Someone in the organization decides on the *design of the work flow*—the technology of the organization. The second decision made in the organization is the one dealing with the *authority system*—who is to have the authority over whom, who is to do what, who is to receive what rewards and punishments, how these are to be administered, and what the house rules are for employees. The technology factors are important to the development of group and individual behavior, and reference to a research study will uncover this importance.

STRUCTURE AND TECHNOLOGY Leonard Sayles has made some important observations on certain group behavior based upon the technology of the organization.[5] Sayles looked at factories that frequently experienced strikes and work stoppages. He found that the troubles and problems seemed to come from the same departments, even though the personnel in both the leader and the follower roles changed. He concluded that there must be some other factor causing the similar and persistent type of behavior. This factor he found to be the *structure* or *technology* of the work flow.

The workers studied performed different tasks and thus were

[5] Leonard R. Sayles, *The Behavior of Industrial Work Groups* (New York: John Wiley, 1958).

members of different groups. Sayles found that the groups doing certain kinds of jobs tended to show very similar behavior, which Sayles was able to classify. He identified this behavior and talked about it in terms of the four different groups he found. He classified the workers into the four categories of apathetic, erratic, strategic, or conservative because of the behavior that emerged from the structural features of the technology.

This finding is significant to the study of work groups, because what Sayles suggests is that the behavior of a work group does not depend upon the leadership style or even the individual personalities of the workers—rather, the *type of job or technology of the workplace determines much of the behavior.* Thus, if you were a manager in one of these factories, your effectiveness as a leader would depend more on which of these four groups you were managing than on any particular style you used. The manager therefore must be aware that the technology and the flow of work has an impact upon the behavior of a group.

AUTHORITY SYSTEM The second big decision that managers make in an organization deals with the authority system—the roles that are to be designated throughout the organization. Whenever one group defines what it is that it expects from another person or

role

group in terms of behavior, we use the word *role.* Role is usually related to a specific position with job duties and functions to be performed. The organization also manages and influences the

status

status that a person receives from the role that he has. Status is a relative concept—it refers to the individual's position within a group, compared to those of his fellow employees.

The managers of organizations have the authority to design the role positions as well as give the rewards and punishments for certain kinds of attributes. One attribute that tends to give a person status, for example, is age. If a company does not want age to be given status, it will have promotion and reward policies that favor youth and work against age. Status and status symbols are important management factors of organizational life that affect the behavior of individuals and groups, and we should look at what status can and cannot do for an organization.

Can you manage status?

STATUS As mentioned earlier, you may receive status from one of two sources: from the organization or from others. For you to have status, others must value your attributes; these include education, age, sex, training, experience, and seniority. As a manager of an organization, you can definitely affect the status of a person in terms of the job that you give him, or, as we have said earlier, you can affect the perceptions that others have toward his personal attributes. The way in which you do both of these is through the use of status symbols. A *status symbol* is a *visible sign* of one's social position, and you can think of many kinds of status symbols. The military gives status symbols in terms of insignia, on the shoulder or sleeve. Other status symbols are the type of furniture in your office, the number of square feet in your reception room, whether you have a personal secretary, the type of car the company allows you to drive, the proximity of your office to the head man, your privacy, and even the location of your parking space. The use of status, the authority system structure, and technology are a few of the ways the manager can work through the organizational structure to achieve behavior change. This subject receives greater attention in Chapters 6 and 7.

status symbol

MANAGEMENT GROUPS

In the material described so far about human groups, you are placed in the role of manager. Information about formal and emergent groups helps make the management of groups easier; however, there are other instances where managers relate with groups in a totally different context. They relate without formal authority.

Managers, especially at the middle and higher levels of an organization, spend many hours and much effort as members of committees and project teams. There is not a great deal of empirical research on this topic—most of the insights on human groups come from research using hourly workers and operatives as the data base. Yet there are some observations common to most managerial groups that provide a better understanding of the world managers face.

Observations

Many groups are *temporary* in nature. Oriented to a specific task or project, these groups function until the task is completed, and then their life is terminated.

Peers, or people in horizontal relationships, are the participants in such groups.

The chairman or leader of the committee or project team is usually *appointed* by some higher management level.

There are *few written rules* for the behavior or roles of group members.

Much of the behavior is *political.* You must be aware that behavior in the temporary group frequently becomes the basis for out-of-group decisions and recommendations. Satisfactory committee behavior, for example, may result in involvement on other important organization projects and indicate that you are a member of the "management team."

More particulars on this aspect of groups will be presented in Chapters 14, 15, 18, and 19. At this point, it is enough to know the purposes of formal and informal groups and the relationship managers have with groups.

SUMMARY AND PROPOSITIONS

This chapter has been full of ideas about individual behavior in groups. We have seen how individuals make up groups and how groups relate to individuals. In the beginning of the chapter, the concept of the group was described through the use of examples and a discussion of group functions. Then, several ways of systematically examining emergent group behavior were explained. With this background in mind, you were asked to turn your attention to the practical alternatives for managerial action when relating to group behavioral problems. Leadership and the organizational structure were the source of the manager's plan of action. You are now ready to think about the propositions.

1. The lower and middle levels of management spend much of their time dealing with groups.
   - *a.* The higher the level, the fewer the subordinates, and thus the smaller the group.
   - *b.* The higher the level, the higher the compensation, authority, and responsibility, and thus less the need for control and supervision of subordinates in groups.
2. All organizations have informal work groups.
   - *a.* Managers in formal leadership positions cannot possibly satisfy all the needs of individuals; thus, informal groups emerge to meet these needs.
   - *b.* Managers are more effective if they maintain a certain "psychological distance" from their subordinates; thus, groups form to take up the slack in relationships.
3. An organization with strong informal groups will be more effective than an organization with weak informal groups.
   - *a.* Needs not met by formal and informal groups will create frustration and disrupt organizational objectives.
   - *b.* Strong informal groups frequently handle vital information faster than do the formal channels of communication.

4. Managers influence formal and informal groups.
   a. The manager usually staffs his department and thus has a voice in the kind of people who will make up both formal and informal groups.
   b The manager also has information about an individual's attitudes (sentiments), which can be used in the formation of groups.
   c. The manager controls formal rewards and punishments and can use these sanctions to influence formal and informal group behavior.

STUDY ASSIGNMENTS

1. *In what specific ways might the cultural factors in the vignette get expressed by the workers in the plant?*
2. *Do all formal groups have informal groups? Explain.*
3. *State your ideas of what informal, emerging behavior might develop from the illustration of the formal work group (the temporary committee on housing).*
4. *Think of your class as a group.*
   a. *What are some formal rules governing it regarding absences, homework, and taking tests?*
   b. *What are the informal norms regarding asking questions in class, "hogging" the classroom discussion, seating arrangement, length of written papers, cheating on tests?*
   c. *Are there subgroups in the class? If so, describe their composition and reasons for forming.*
5. *Discuss the following statement: "Since managers rarely belong to formal work groups, they rarely form informal work groups."*
6. *What are your definitions of activities, interactions, and sentiments?*
7. *What sentiments do you share with your friends or members of other groups? Do you have more interactions with people sharing your sentiments, and fewer interactions with those with dissimilar sentiments? Describe.*
8. *What is the relationship between the topics of groups and human motivation?*
9. *Can a group have an identity independent of the identities of its members? Explain your answer.*

10. *If you were a foreman, would you encourage the development of an informal group and informal leader? Explain.*

11. *Based on the comparison in Table 5.1, are you in favor of or opposed to informal organization? Explain.*

12. *What conditions do you feel must exist for groups to be highly effective? If you use the techniques suggested by Rensis Likert, will you have a highly effective work group?*

13. *In what ways can a manager attempt to change the status of another person?*

14. *Give your own explanation of propositions 2(b) and 3(b).*

situational episodes

1. You were surprised to read the memo. The vice-president has asked you to serve on the Community Health Project and you're concerned. You know the committee has 15 members and the chairman is someone who works under you in the department. What problems do you foresee? What should you do?
2. You find yourself in a bind. You have just been hired at the operative level in a plant. You have aspirations of going into management but felt that experience first, followed by schooling, would be better than schooling, then experience. The work group you're assigned to does not put out all the time. In fact, you know you could produce much more. You're worried at the reaction of your fellow workers. What should you do?

Design of organization structure

OBJECTIVES YOU SHOULD MEET

State *the reasons for the existence of formal organizations.*

Construct *an organization chart illustrating line, staff, and functional authority.*

State *six traditional principles of organization.*

Identify *the basic characteristics of Weber's bureaucratic model.*

Outline *the assumptions of classical organizational theory.*

Name *three determinants of organizational structure in current contingency models.*

Describe *three concepts fundamental to Likert's System Four theory of organization structure.*

WHO'S BOSS?

Now, in the fourth day of a management training conference, it was time to find out just what managers thought their jobs were. Larry, a doctoral student, was picking up a few summer dollars by working with us on this management training program. He and I divided the group of thirty managers into three groups and put them in three rooms. In one group we had all the managers who worked in staff jobs: personnel, marketing, international operations, warehousing, distribution, accounting and data processing, and finance. In a second group were top line executives, the executive staff at the very top of the company. Most of the staff and most of the line executives reported to them. We call them executive staff because they're not directly involved in the line operations or in the creation of advisory data and information. Their decisions have line authority behind them. The third group of managers, the executive vice-presidents, were the ones who held line responsibility and authority over different geographic but fundamentally similar territories and stores.

To each group we posed the same question: What are the major problems facing the company at this time? To each group we gave the same instructions: On the 6" by 4" cards in front of you, simply list all the problems. When you have completed your list, hand the cards in. Please put no names on the cards.

Each conference leader collected the cards and put the problems on the chalkboard. All managers gathered in a large room to review the problems of each group, and we saw that each of the groups tended to see problems from their own experience base. For example, the staff people saw that the company's major problems were those directly affecting the staff activity. Larry read some of the problems to the group:

"The General Office thinks they're the good guys and we're the bad guys"; "They [G. O.] visit us to tell us what to do—rarely do they listen to us"; "The line managers have a great deal of authority; their problem is that they lean on us too much."

After discussing the problems, we had the executive vice-president group of managers develop specific and real solutions and plans for solving one of the company's problems. While they were out of the room working on their solutions, I had asked the staff group to identify the resources they had that would enhance the success of any solution developed by the vice-presidents. I was pleased to see the staff personnel respond to such a request, and they came up with quite a list of the resources and talents that would be available.

We were all surprised and a bit embarrassed when the vice-presidents presented their solution and plan. They made no use of any staff assistance in either the development of their solution or in the implementation of their plan of action. Beyond that, they were taking an action that had tremendous impact on other segments of the company, and as far as we could see, there were no plans to inform the other divisions that would be affected. Many managers told us that although the vice-presidents had been the ones to show an absence of line–staff awareness, resources, and impact areas, the same lack of awareness was true of all groups—line or staff.

After the group left, Larry looked amazed. "You know, Prof, I'd never have believed what I just heard and saw. I've read about line and staff conflict and I've taught about it in basic management courses. But to hear and see the conflict come out so dramatically is something else. Some of those cards showed that managers were not even aware other departments existed!

"About the best one I found appeared on cards of managers in both staff and line positions: 'If they [whoever the other group was] had to work with the problems I have, they would understand better and not try to appear to lord it over us.' "

"Larry, this is just the attitude I see over and over at these conferences. Everybody's looking out for himself."

"Gee," said Larry, "in organizations, who's the boss—line or staff?"

In the last three chapters, we concentrated on the individual human being and his relationships in groups because people constitute the foundation of any organization. Groups evolve into informal organizations spontaneously, but a manager must be able to coordinate the group effort toward its objectives. To meet these objectives, individual tasks need to be identified, the tools and technology must be provided, and a predetermined structure of relationships should be designed. The manager has the important function of designing an organization structure that will best coordinate people in performing their tasks using appropriate technology so that organizational objectives are achieved. What knowledge is useful to aid the manager in this design? This chapter provides the guidelines for establishing these formal relationships.

Having read the preceding vignette, you may have wondered how the conflicts between line and staff people developed. Before you can attempt to seek an answer, you first need to understand certain concepts of organizational structure.

THE MEANING OF ORGANIZATION

The terms *organizing* and *organization* are widely used by everybody, but each use may represent a different meaning. In economics and political science, we find "organization" used in a broad (macro) sense relating to the interrelationships of consumers and producers and the establishment of some system of government to avoid a state of anarchy. In the physical and biological sciences, "organization" relates to the structure of the atom or the universe. The recent attention to ecology involves the idea of the wonderful balance in nature's organization and to the possible ultimate disaster that would result if man naively upset this balance.

Do we naturally tend to organize?

entropy

Problems of organization are thus inherent in all of nature. In fact, one fundamental physical law—the second law of thermodynamics—can be stated in simple terms as being the tendency in all of nature toward randomness or disorganization *(entropy).* A fundamental reason for human beings to organize is to oppose this natural tendency. A second reason is that man is a social animal: He is not a loner or hermit by nature; he tends to seek interaction with other human beings. Thus, the subject of organization is central to sociology, social psychology, and anthropology. In fact, man may learn something about his own tendency toward socialization and organization in a variety of biological sciences through the study of the habits of baboons, ant hills, and schools of fish.

Organizing

Informal organization

Formal organization

In this chapter we concentrate on a rigorous definition of organizing, informal organization, and formal organization. *Organizing* is defined here as a conscious process of management that focuses attention on the predetermined structure and process of allocating tasks to achieve common objectives. *Informal organization* is any human group interaction that occurs spontaneously and naturally without conscious design. (Much of the discussion of groups in the preceding chapter relates to informal organizations.) *Formal organization* refers to *planned* patterns of group cooperative relationships made to achieve a common purpose.

Managers perform the function of organizing whenever they consciously attempt to design, map out, or overtly predetermine human relationships. Managers must understand the informal organizations and adapt their formal structures to them. The staffing of the organization is discussed in Chapter 13; the knowledge necessary to develop the formal organization is the subject of this chapter.

Why do we have formal organization?

The reasons for formal organizations are:

1. To establish efficient and logical patterns of interrelationships among members of the group
2. To secure advantages of specialization or division of labor whereby the optimum utilization of talents can be realized
3. To coordinate activities of the component parts in order to facilitate the realization of the goals of the organization

Problems of formal organization become more difficult as the number of component parts increases, as technology changes, and as the organization takes advantage of specialization of talents. This is the reason that in a small business firm with one or two managers, the managers tend to give less attention to designing the organization than do the managers of large firms. Small firms tend to depend primarily on the already-existing informal organizations and on simple formal structures.

ORGANIZATION CHARTS

organization chart

Although it is possible for a manager to plan an organization structure without drawing an organization chart, generally the initial evidence of a planned structure is the existence of such a chart. The *organization chart* is nothing more than a map of positions in an organization and their authority relationships, indicated by boxes connected by straight lines.

How useful is an organization chart?

The existence of an organization chart does not indicate the existence of a good formal organization, just as a geographical map does not necessarily indicate good terrain. Furthermore, a chart may be poor, just as a map may be poor when it does not represent the actual situation. In fact, even when the organization chart is an accurate representation of formal relationships, it may have limited use or may indicate the wrong emphasis, since it merely identifies the planned organization and cannot show all organizational relationships. For the same reason, a small-scale map of a country gives no information concerning how one might proceed from one place to another within a city. Detailed charts or maps are required, depending upon the needs of the individual. A first-line supervisor may wish to construct his own organizational chart, showing each of his subordinates, in the same way that he might want to construct a large-scale map to show him how to travel to his friend's house for supper.

Figure 6.1 is a typical chart; it includes formal organizational positions (symbolized by boxes) and lines of authority (symbolized by straight, solid, connecting lines). Such a chart is useful in the following ways:

1. It identifies the existence of certain positions.
2. It is a useful charting tool in planning organization, since a number of types of organization structure can be simulated on paper, thus aiding the manager's mental processes.

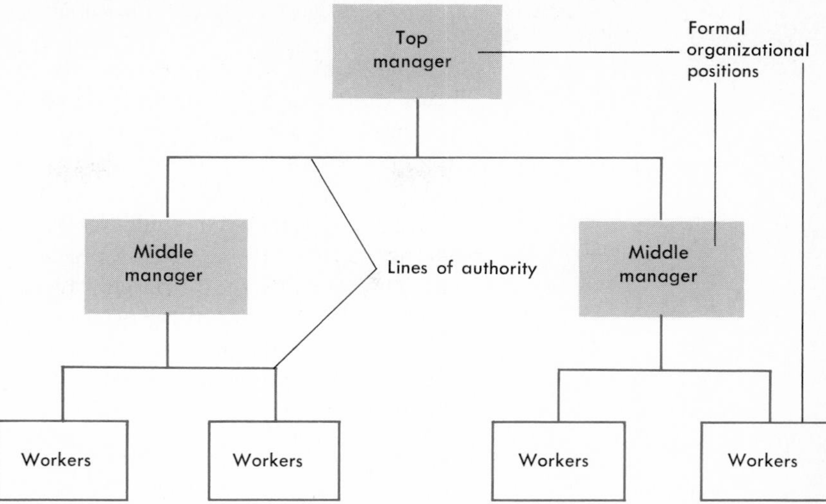

FIGURE 6.1 Prototype of an organization chart; only line authority is indicated.

3. It is very useful as a first approximation for orienting a new person in the organization or in explaining the formal organization to interested outsiders (e.g., customers, suppliers).
4. In cases of reorganization of formal authority, charts are shorthand methods for identifying the changes.

An organization chart can be abused if one attempts to use it for purposes for which it was not designed. It does *not* provide a pictorial diagram for showing the flow of formal communications in an organization. It does show the "chain of command," but it does *not* imply that this chain must be used for all communications. Furthermore, the vertical lines provide little insight into the degree of control over subordinates, decision making, and actions. In fact, the chief weakness of a good organizational chart showing formal authority relationships lies in some viewers' misinterpretation of the pictorial diagram caused by their psychological reactions to it.

Some organizational specialists have attempted to expand the concept of a simple organization chart through the development of elaborate organizational manuals and a collection of subcharts. These specialists concentrate on explicitly diagramming and elaborating through textual notes for the purpose of planning formal relationships in greater detail. The resulting elaborate manual can be very helpful when it is possible to plan the formal structure in great detail. The problem with such efforts is that human organizations tend to change rapidly in actual practice and to be affected by many human relationships discussed in the previous chapters.

The traditional theory of organization consists of observations about the design of a formal structure and the organizing process by which specialization can be applied. The basis for this approach is in the proposition that planning of positions and departments should precede consideration of the particular people who fill the positions. We shall see in Chapters 13 and 17 how the structure is staffed using this proposition.

The remainder of this chapter discusses the essentials for understanding the designing of a formal structure: (1) a clear definition of some types of formal organization; (2) traditional principles prescribing an organizational plan; and (3) some organizational models.

CONCEPTS OF FORMAL ORGANIZATION

Authority

Traditionally, organization has been analyzed as a structure of authority relationships. *Authority* is defined as the right to decide or to act. Authority is assumed to flow down from the top in an organization; yet the basic test for the existence of authority is whether one's colleagues will *accept* instructions from a person or position that assumes it. Thus, a superior delegates authority from the top to the bottom of an organization; the subordinates recognize this authority if they accept the instructions and responsibilities.

We shall see in Chapter 18 that authority is only one type of power, the legitimate power vested in a position. Early organizational theorists overemphasized the role of formal authority in their effort to develop rational organizational designs without recognizing the importance of behavioral characteristics of people in organizations. This emphasis on authority tended to result in mechanical and static propositions about organization structure that have been modified by modern behavioral studies. The manager, in designing an organization structure, attempts to influence the behavior of members of the organization to achieve coordination by establishing relatively fixed authority channels; however, he

influence

may find that other types of *influence* may reinforce his efforts. He can develop a structure to accommodate persuasion and suggestions from colleagues and thus to achieve cooperation from organization members in meeting their individual human needs. This view of organizational design retains the idea that authority relationships serve as the skeleton in the anatomy of the organization without neglecting the nerves and muscles of other behavioral interactions.

responsibility

Implied in the formal structure is the assumption that organization members will assume *responsibility* consistent with their authority. Classical theorists stated this assumption as an organization principle: Responsibility for the execution of work must be accompanied by the authority to get the job done. However, recent discussions on organization have neglected studies of this moral element. Chester I. Barnard, generally recognized as the pioneer in attacking classical principles, nevertheless emphasized the place of executive responsibility in management as the "quality which gives dependability and determination to human conduct."[1] Recent disclosures in both governmental and business organizations indicate that responsibility for actions by managers will receive renewed attention. Furthermore, the question of a manager's social responsibility is becoming a critical issue concerning the external pressures on any organization structure.

Once authority has been established and the responsibility of each organization member is accepted, the manager needs a system of accountability by which he can monitor actions of each member. *Accountability* involves the process by which a subordinate reports to a superior the use of resources for which he is responsible.

Accountability

In practice, an efficient formal organization is dependent upon the skill with which a manager *delegates* authority. A suitable structure provides the framework by which a superior can allocate duties to subordinates with sufficient authority to achieve the desired results. When managers find that they do not have time to perform their jobs effectively, it often means that they have failed to give sufficient attention to delegation. When subordinates become frustrated in their ability to meet their responsibilities, it may mean that they have not clarified with their superior exactly what authority has been delegated. Since the superior always retains the ultimate responsibility for the decisions and actions of subordinates, the superior may tend to hesitate in allowing subordinates sufficient authority to encourage initiative in qualified members of the organization.

delegation

Organizational structure establishes the pattern for delegation of authority. It provides the means by which the superior and subordinate achieve a common understanding of the degree and type of authority that is delegated. We saw in the vignette of the discussion between Larry and his professor that confusion may exist

[1] Chester I. Barnard, *The Functions of the Executive* (Cambridge, Mass. Harvard University Press, 1938), p. 260.

as to the nature of authority delegated. A superior has a number of alternatives for explicitly assigning duties: (1) He may ask the subordinate to find out the facts about a problem and seek available alternatives so that he can make the decision; (2) he may instruct the subordinate to take action but to inform him immediately of his action; (3) he may delegate authority to take action but require a report if action is unsuccessful; or (4) he may delegate complete authority for action, with no immediate report necessary.

To help clarify the exact type of authority held by each member of the organization, three classifications have been used in organization design:

Line authority

1. *Line authority* is the simplest, with each position having direct and general authority for taking actions and complete authority over lower positions in the hierarchy. A manager with line authority is the unquestioned superior for all activities of his subordinates. The flow of authority is simple, direct, and uncomplicated, so that conflicts of authority are reduced and quick action is possible.

Staff authority

2. *Staff authority* is purely advisory to the position of line authority. A person with staff authority studies a problem, seeks alternatives, and makes recommendations, but has no authority to put the recommendations into action. A position with staff authority may be generalist in nature (as an "assistant to") and may serve as an extension of the line position to relieve the line position of any details it has limited time to handle. Staff authority also provides specialists who have expert abilities for such functions as planning, fact finding, and analysis.

Functional authority

3. *Functional authority* focuses on achieving advantages of specialization and permits the specialist in a given set of activities (such as accounting, engineering, or law) to enforce his directives within a limited and clearly defined scope of authority. Staff becomes desirable when the line needs advisory help; however, the coordination of a staff complicates the problems of the superior. Functional organization is developed to reduce such problems by permitting orders to flow directly to lower levels without attention to routine technical problems by the line superior.

Figure 6.2 shows how all three types of authority can appear in an organization chart.

Line authority is the backbone of hierarchy; staff and functional authority merely supplement the line. In an actual organization, a single person might serve as line, staff, and functional at the same time but for different phases of the organization's activities. For example, the chief accountant in a business firm might give tax accounting advice (staff) to the chief line officer, supervise his own accounting department (line), and set specific accounting procedures for the factory manager with his own specialist authority (functional). (See Figure 6.3.) The practical value of the distinction among the three types of authority is in focusing attention on the different types of authority delegated to individual managers (see Table 6.1). Failure to perceive and appreciate the distinctions by members of each group often results in conflicts between line and staff, as we observed in the actual situation reported at the beginning of this chapter.

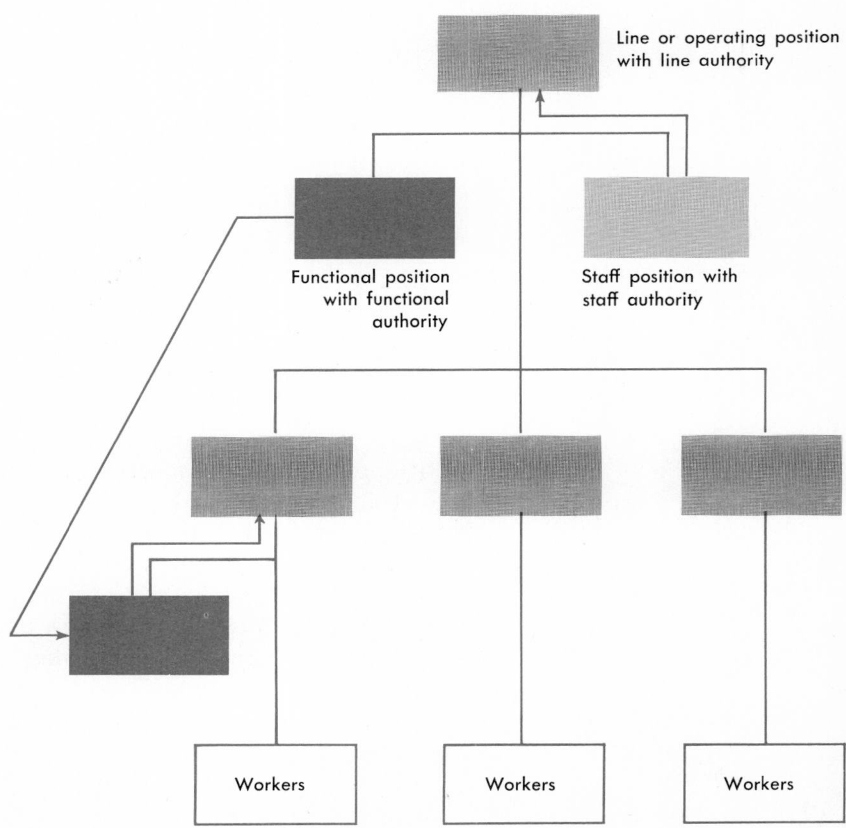

FIGURE 6.2 The three types of authority in organizations

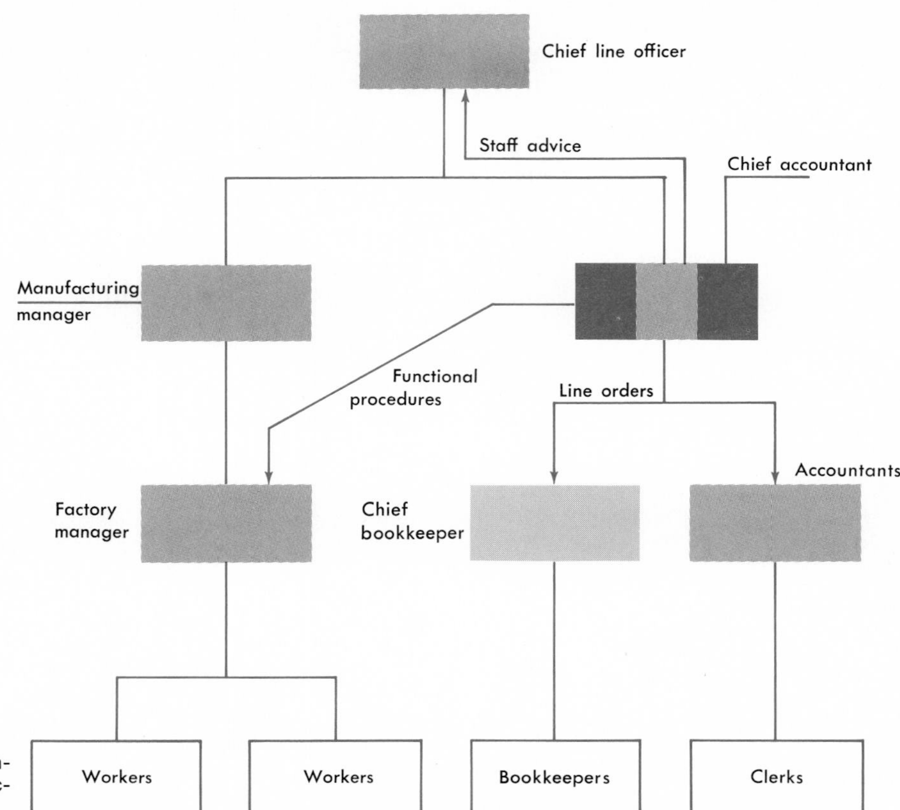

FIGURE 6.3 A position combining line, staff, and functional authority

PRINCIPLES OF ORGANIZATIONAL DESIGN

In the early development of management thought, writers and practitioners developed a set of organizational principles that they claimed to be universal prescriptions of how an organization should be designed. Although these prescriptions have been criticized because they were not based on empirical investigations and because their lack of necessary qualifications caused them to be contradictory at times, they remain useful first approximations as criteria for describing and diagnosing organizational design. Later, we shall indicate the qualifications needed if they are to serve in designing specific structures for different people, technologies, and environments.

The classical principles have been valuable because:

Why are classical principles useful?

1. They are inevitably the point of departure for newer ideas.

2. They provide the apprentice manager a group of first approximations from which he can proceed to develop organizational ability.

A good beginning for an apprentice manager is to understand exactly what some of these principles are as a first step toward evaluating their usefulness in his own situation. The most important of these principles are unity of command, the exception principle, span of control, the scalar principle, departmentation, and decentralization.

Underlying all these principles is the ageless idea of what Adam Smith referred to as division of labor and what F.W. Taylor called *specialization*. In designing an organizational structure, the manager must continually consider the balance between the benefits derived from specialization and its costs. One of the reasons that no universal structure has been found is that the optimum degree of specialization tends to differ for different people, technologies, and environments.

specialization

TABLE 6.1 Comparison of Line, Staff, and Functional Authority

Advantages	Disadvantages
Line Authority	
Maintains simplicity.	Neglects specialists in planning.
Makes clear division of authority.	Overworks key men.
Encourages speedy action.	Depends on retention of a few key men.
Staff Authority	
Enables specialists to give expert advice.	Confuses organization if functions are not clear.
Frees the line executive of detailed analysis.	Reduces power of experts to place recommendations into action.
Affords young specialists a means of training.	Tends toward centralization of organization.
Functional Authority	
Relieves line executives of routine specialized decisions.	Makes relationships more complex.
Provides framework for applying expert knowledge.	Makes limits of authority of each specialist a difficult coordination problem.
Relieves pressure of need for large numbers of well-rounded executives.	Tends toward centralization of organization.

Should a subordinate have more than one boss?

unity of command

Unity of Command

One of the traditional principles of organization, generally referred to as *unity of command,* states that no member of an organization should report to more than one superior on any single function. The application of this principle is easy in a pure line organization, in which each superior has general authority; however, it becomes a complex problem in actual cases in which some form of staff and/or functional organization is used. In practice, instructions may be received from several sources without loss of productivity. The central problem is to avoid conflict in orders from different people relating to the same subject. You should recognize immediately that the actions of a subordinate may be *influenced* by many people who are not recognized in the formal hierarchy of authority; for example, emergent groups (discussed in Chapter 5) have powerful influence. The principle of unity of command may be useful in the planning of an organization if it helps to keep relationships between superior and subordinate simple and direct; it is not realistic if it is interpreted as an immutable law that would eliminate useful relationships among a number of managers. It is sometimes argued that the modern family has developed serious problems because of the retreat of the father as the single manager of the household. When a father and a mother give conflicting orders to children, the children are understandably frustrated.

How can a manager get the important things done?

exception principle

Exception Principle

The *exception principle* states that recurring decisions should be handled in a routine manner by lower-level managers, whereas problems involving unusual matters should be referred to higher levels. This principle emphasizes that executives at the top levels of an organization have limited time and capacity and should refrain from becoming bogged down in routine details that can be handled as well by subordinates. Thus, it is an important concept concerning the *delegation* of authority in an organization.

The exception principle can be very useful to a manager by focusing his attention on those matters that should receive his attention first. It is applicable at all levels and, if kept in mind, can help the inexperienced manager compensate for a human tendency to concentrate on the immediate, concrete, and detailed problems at the expense of the more fundamental, difficult, and abstract issues.

The principle has remained important in modern applications because of the distinction it makes between programmed and nonprogrammed decisions. *Programmed decisions* are those that are repetitive and routine and can be handled by a definite procedure. *Nonprogrammed decisions* involve new, one-shot, and unstructured elements that require tailored handling by superiors. Programmed decisions may be easily delegated; nonprogrammed decisions often need the attention of the superior.

Programmed decisions

Nonprogrammed decisions

Is there a limit to the number of persons a manager can handle?

Span of Control

span of control

A third traditional principle involves the *span of control* of a manager: There is a limit to the number of subordinates that one superior should supervise. Often, this principle is stated in terms of the exact number of subordinates that should report to a superior and thus has become highly controversial. The determination of the optimum number depends on many factors in a given organization and should always be tied directly to the question of the number of levels in the hierarchy. If it appears that a small span of control for each manager is desirable, then the number of necessary levels will be larger than would be the case with a larger span of control. The organization with more levels is considered "tall," whereas the organization with a larger span of control is "flat." Figures 6.4 and 6.5 illustrate tall and flat organizations.

Span of control focuses attention on the basic fact that any

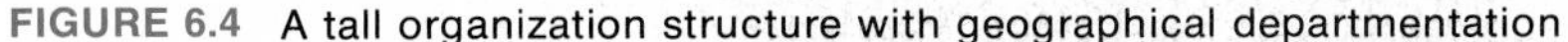

FIGURE 6.4 A tall organization structure with geographical departmentation

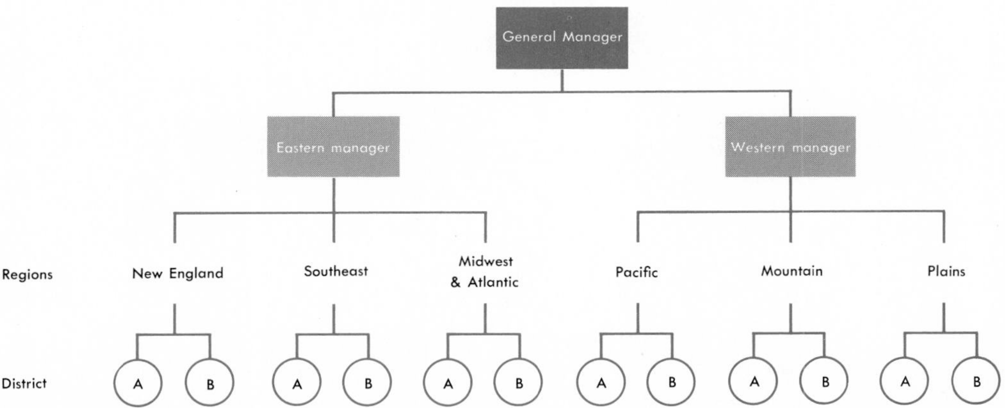

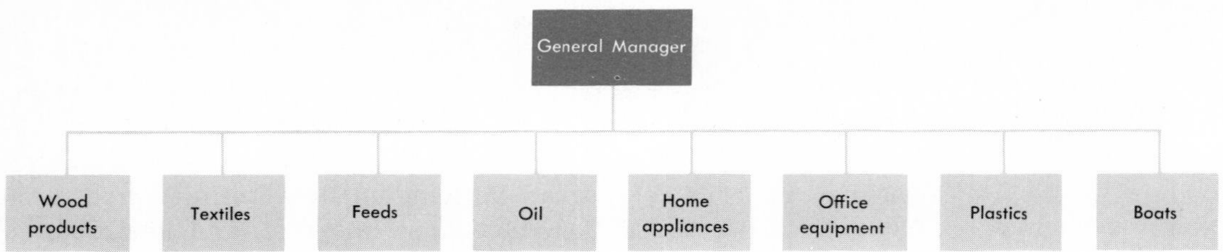

FIGURE 6.5 A flat organization structure with product departmentation

human being has limitations. First, he has limited *time available* for his activities. Second, he has limited *available energy* and must depend on others to supplement his energy. Third, the number of subjects to which a manager can give his *attention* is limited. These limitations not only support the concept of span of control but indicate that the optimum span of control varies among situations.

The appropriate span depends upon four major factors:

1. The *competence* of managers in delegating authority and responsibility varies, and thus the optimum span in an organizational structure depends on the qualifications of the managers. Span for those who delegate can be much larger than for those who do not delegate.
2. The level of *motivation* of subordinate personnel is both a determinant and a result of the span of control. Increased motivation permits larger span, but it has also been found that a larger span increases motivation.
3. The existence of a good *information* system and free communication flow provides the basis for increased span. If subordinates have access to necessary information, they can take action without close supervision from above.
4. The nature of the *job* affects span, since a routine, stable operation can be handled by subordinates without close supervision, whereas a diverse and changing job requires a smaller span of control.

One useful approach in applying these factors is to analyze the need of subordinates for services of their superior and the rate at which the superior can supply those services. The optimum span can be determined by balancing the cost of the subordinates' waiting time against the cost of the superior's time.

Span of control refers to the number of people that one person can supervise directly. A related and probably more useful idea is the *span of managerial responsibility*, which refers to the number of people whom one superior can assist, teach, and help reach their objectives—that is, the number who *have access to* the superior. The span of managerial responsibility can probably be larger than the span of control.

span of managerial responsibility

Scalar Principle

Is a chain of command necessary?

scalar principle

A fourth traditional principle, the *scalar principle*, states that authority and responsibility should flow in a clear, unbroken line, or chain of command, from the highest to the lowest manager. One writer describes this vertical relationship as a job-task pyramid. The principle simply states that an organization is a hierarchy. The importance and usefulness of the principle is evident whenever the line is severed. The splintering of one organization into two or more results from a permanent breach of this principle. Temporary breaches, however, are not uncommon, although they are frequently subtle and unrecognized. The tendency of an aggressive executive to fight the control of superiors can create a situation in which he attempts to form his own "empire" instead of remaining a part of the larger organization.

Departmentation

How can activities be grouped in an organization?

departmentation

The manner in which activities should be divided and formed into specialized groups is usually referred to as *departmentation*. The purpose of departmentation is to specialize activities, simplify the tasks of managers, and maintain control. Several types of departmentation are possible: geographical, by customer, by process or equipment, by product, or to take care of a large number of subordinates. Often, different types are used at different levels of the organization structure. For example, Figure 6.6 illustrates geographical departmentation at the top level, product at the second level, and process at the third.

No single formula for departmentation applies to all situations. The following criteria may help the organization planner:

1. Similar activities may be grouped together, based upon likeness of personal qualifications or common purpose—for example, medical and dental personnel.
2. An activity may be grouped with other activities with which it is used—for example, safety with production.

3. Functions may be assigned to that executive who is most interested in performing them well.
4. Activities may be grouped to encourage competition or to avoid friction among departments.
5. If it is difficult to make definite distinctions between two activities, they may be grouped together.
6. Certain functions that require close coordination would increase problems of higher-level managers if they were separated; such functions should be grouped together.

Decentralization

How can an organization plan make each person really important?

Since World War II, the concept of decentralization has been an important organizing principle, especially in large corporations. However, the concept has been confused by the use of the term to describe different ideas. It sometimes refers to operations at different geographical locations; in this sense, decentralization describes physical characteristics of a company but does not indicate the type of organization structure used.

Decentralization, as an organizational idea, refers to the pro-

FIGURE 6.6 An organization chart with different types of departmentation

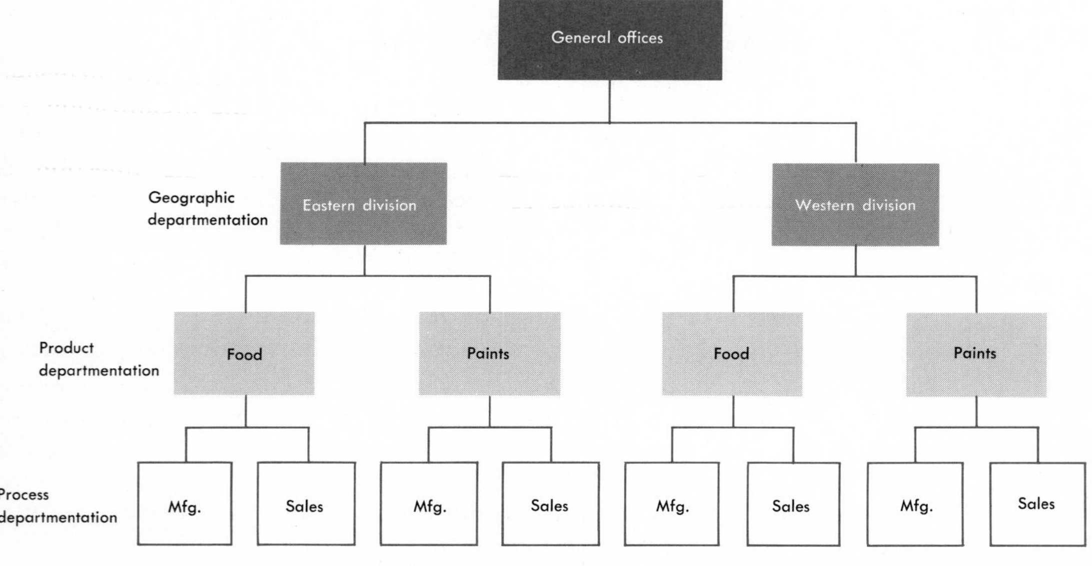

Decentralization

cess of pushing decision making to lower levels of the organization. It is closely related to the delegation of authority to the broader base of executives who are at the lower levels of the hierarchy. Decentralization is a matter of degree. Basic decisions and policies must receive attention at the top levels. Although delegation is generally recognized as an important art by most operating executives, in practice it involves significant cost and risks. Two important considerations determine the degree of decentralization desirable in a given situation. First, the amount of skills and competence possessed by subordinate managers influences the success of any program of decentralization; managers must be developed who can adequately handle the decisions delegated to them. Second, the distribution of the necessary information to points of decision is critical to any delegation process; unless an executive has sufficient information available for making a decision, he will have little chance to make a good one.

Decentralization has certain advantages: (1) Decision making can be spread and actions can be implemented quickly without awaiting approval from higher levels; (2) managers at the lower level have more flexibility to adjust to changing conditions; (3) managers tend to develop more quickly and initiative is encouraged by a more challenging situation.

On the other hand, the disadvantages are significant: (1) Control and coordination at the top level is more difficult, since the top manager may not be aware of critical problems as they emerge; (2) duplication of effort by the more autonomous divisions tends to reduce the advantage of specialization on certain activities provided by the organization as a whole, and operating managers may overlook the value of expertise within the organization but not within their individual divisions.

A practicing manager continually faces the question of whether to centralize or decentralize. Centralization is warranted when the decision *must* be made at a higher level, when status in dealing with outside people is important, when consistency of policies and procedures is of special importance, and in some cases of extreme emergency, such as fire or civil disturbance. The reason that the principle of decentralization has become increasingly important is that in modern society more people are becoming highly educated and thus more competent to make decisions, and these people continually press for greater "democratic" participation in organizations. In Chapter 17 we shall see how this organization principle has been particularly significant in such companies as General Motors and General Electric.

WEBER'S BUREAUCRATIC MODEL OF ORGANIZATIONAL STRUCTURE

The organizational model most consistent with the principles stated thus far was originally developed by Max Weber, a German social scientist and philosopher of the early twentieth century.[2] It was developed during a period in which organizations were increasing in size and in which there was a need for a rational and planned design. It has continued to influence design for large organizations under relatively stable conditions.

bureaucracy

Weber noted that three types of authority can be observed in society: (1) the authority vested in tradition or heritage; (2) the authority that flows from charisma or personal leadership qualities that cause certain people to attract a large number of followers; and (3) the concept of *bureaucracy*, which he defined as a set of offices invested with authority to perform specific functions. The first type evolves from tradition and is not subject to a manager's planning and design, and the second cannot be passed on independently of the life of the charismatic individual; so bureaucracy was viewed as the rational and efficient basis for managers to consciously design an organizational structure.

Weber's bureaucratic model has the advantage of having clear and explicit characteristics, which he viewed as universal guidelines for design:

1. There is an explicit structure that functions by clear and explicit *rules*.
2. Regular activities of an organization are distributed as fixed *official* duties.
3. The organization follows the principle of *hierarchy*, in which each lower office is under the supervision of a higher one.
4. The incumbent in an office is placed in the position on the basis of his *competence*, not on the basis of a natural right or ownership.
5. Employment is based on *technical* qualifications and not subject to arbitrary termination.
6. Administrative acts, decisions, and rules are recorded *in writing*.

[2] Max Weber, *The Theory of Social and Economic Organization* (New York: Oxford University, 1947).

These characteristics are consistent with the previously stated principles and have been described as a mechanistic approach to organizational design with little attention to the people in the organization. A critic, Douglas McGregor, identified the assumptions about human nature implicitly made for classical principles and Weber's bureaucracy, and referred to them as Theory X:[3]

Classical-theory assumptions

> Members of an organization are unable to work out relations among their positions without thorough guidance and planning.
>
> Some members are aggressive and will tresspass on the domain of others unless clear boundaries are drawn. This arouses hostility that may reduce the effectiveness of the undertaking.
>
> Some members are reluctant to assume responsibilities unless assigned a definite task.
>
> Members generally prefer the security of a definite task to the freedom of a vaguely defined one.
>
> Delineation of clear-cut responsibilities offers an incentive by providing a more exact basis for evaluation.
>
> It is possible to predict in advance the responsibilities that will be required in the future.
>
> Members are prone to conflict; and if this conflict is permitted to arise, it takes a toll in personal energy and productivity.
>
> Justice is more certain if the enterprise is organized on an objective, impersonal basis.

Although Weber failed to identify many of the factors discussed in Chapters 3 and 5, he provided the first consistent model for seeking efficiency and justice in an administrative structure. Weber argued that in a bureaucratic structure, each person would know exactly what was expected of him; each person could depend upon the power of impersonal rules and regulations rather than the whims of unpredictable human beings. The result would be precision, speed, reduction of friction, and the selection of the best qualified person for each position. Weber's model provides a clear and definite statement of assumptions and expected results.

[3] Douglas McGregor, *The Human Side of Enterprise* (New York: McGraw-Hill Book Co., 1960).

Weber's theory has been blamed for social dissatisfaction, in spite of its efficiency. Nevertheless, many present-day organizations design their structures employing elements of the classical and bureaucratic model. Several reasons may explain the persistence of classical theory. For years it was the only theory that was available, and practitioners were searching for guides for designing increasingly complex formal organizations. In addition, during a period of relative stability, with a minimum of rapid changes and a shortage of educated personnel, the theory provided a systematic, efficient guide for maintaining an orderly and unambiguous approach to collective efforts. It fitted a particular time and situation. Its chief enemy was change. Social, technological, and political change overtook it, and the pendulum swung to the other extreme of emphasis on human factors, which deemphasized hierarchy and structure.

HUMAN AND PARTICIPATIVE THEORY'S EFFECT ON ORGANIZATION DESIGN

Weber's model contributed objectivity and efficiency to design to replace the traditional idea, held for centuries, that organization evolved from an elite who found themselves at the top as a result of their birth into the "right" family or through the ownership of property. These past structures resulted in what Frederick Harbison classifies as dictatorial (authoritarian) or paternalistic philosophies. However, the bureaucratic model, with its emphasis on rules and nonpersonal offices, met increasing opposition by human-relations proponents and, later, behavioral scientists. Management was viewed by these revisionists as purely dealing with people, without focusing on structural design. Individual propositions that offered some elements for a revisionist theory were collected, but the empirical evidence often lacked cohesion; that is, the practitioner could understand the criticisms of classical organization design, but he had no design theory to replace it.

In the 1960s, Douglas McGregor and Rensis Likert contributed to a general theory that, they claimed, had universal applications.[4] This theory tends to be directly opposed to the classical theory; and since both claimed universality, the battle lines were drawn. The essential difference between the two extremes was that

[4] Rensis Likert, *New Patterns of Management* (New York: McGraw-Hill Book Co., 1961).

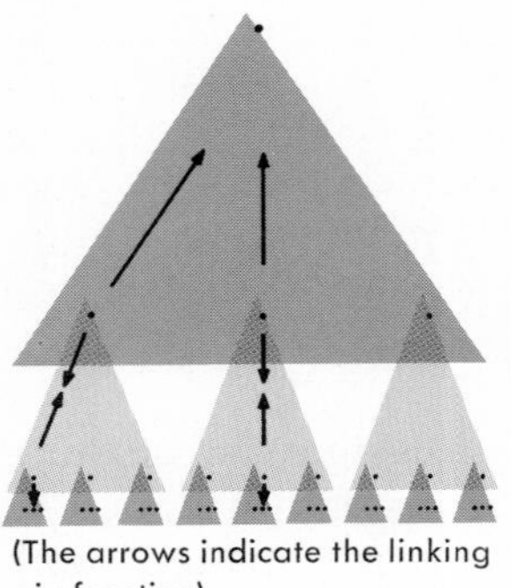

(The arrows indicate the linking pin function)

FIGURE 6.7 The linking pin

the classical school focused on work, efficiency, and order; the human participative theory focused on the human component, motivation, and satisfaction. As the behavioral theory attempted to shift from description to prescription, the proponents tended to overgeneralize and to leave their propositions open to the same criticisms that their proponents had directed at the classical propositions. The major difference was that these theories had been built on a sounder foundation of empirical evidence.

Behavioralists early tended to study and describe an organization's behavior without focusing on structure. The subject of design was a residual in their thinking, and since they opposed classical design, any conscious structural model is not essential. H.A. Simon developed his thinking around decision making, with a system of decision centers indicating structural aspects.[5] Silverman, a sociologist, concentrated on action centers, with structural implications evolving around the fact that when people get together to do something, structure tends to emerge.[6]

McGregor's *Theory Y,* discussed in Chapter 3, does not concentrate on design of formal structure as much as it argues for a general management thinking that would emphasize generalized, not specialized, jobs and departments. Span of control would be wide, not narrow, in order to grant independence to the human being. Emphasis on hierarchy would be replaced by emphasis on group participation, autonomy, self-direction, and decentralization of authority. Formal, official authority would give way to power and influence of the individual.

System Four

linking pins

The most explicit contribution to structural design using the assumptions of Theory Y has been made by Rensis Likert.[7] His *System Four* theory is based on the *principle of supportive relationships,* the idea that high performance goals are more important than job descriptions and formal authority in organizational relationships, and his concept of "linking pins" as an explicit structural concept. He believes that the charting of hierarchical relationships should provide *"linking pins"* among groups (not individuals), and that these relationships should be overlapping (not in a tight chain of command). As illustrated in Figure 6.7, he says that "management should deliberately endeavor to build ef-

[5] Herbert A. Simon, *Administrative Behavior* 3rd ed. (New York: Macmillan, 1976).

[6] David Silverman, *The Theory of Organizations* (New York: Basic Books, 1971).

[7] Rensis Likert, *The Human Organization* (New York: McGraw-Hill Book Co., 1967).

fective groups, linking them in an overall organization by means of people who hold overlapping group membership."[8] In this view, every manager finds himself in at least two groups, one in which he participates with his superiors and one in which he participates with his subordinates, thus serving as a linking pin between groups. The aim of the concept is to reduce the impersonality of hierarchical positions and to integrate the work of different levels through interlocking groups.

Behavioral contributions to organization design can be summed up as a focus on organization behavior instead of structure. The structural aspects emerge from increased participation, both informally and formally, in committees, conferences, and consultative schemes. In such a design, shared leadership is made possible by making no sharp distinction between the roles of superiors and subordinates. All participate in reaching goals through group action in which various roles may be assumed by different individuals in the organization.

Since there is disagreement between schools of management thought, then what type of structure is best? The answer is that it depends. First, it depends on the assumptions of human nature. Second, it depends on the preferences and educational background of the manager and members of the organization. Third, it depends upon the situation. Contemporary views of design can be summarized as recognizing the truth in both classical and participative theories and identifying the factors in the different situations that affect structure. These factors compose the current trend in developing contingency theories of design. Figure 6.8 summarizes the relationships among classical, human participative, and contingency theories of organization.[9]

CONTINGENCY THEORIES OF ORGANIZATION

Both in practice and in the results of empirical research, no single universal optimum structure can be distinguished; yet in our search for the best design for a specific organization, we do have additional guidelines for our choice. Our choice depends on four

[8] Rensis Likert, *New Patterns of Management* (New York: McGraw-Hill Book Co., 1961), p. 105.

[9] W. Warren Haynes, Joseph L. Massie, and Marc J. Wallace, Jr., *Management: Analysis, Concepts and Cases,* 3rd ed. (Englewood Cliffs, N.J.: Prentice-Hall, Inc., 1975), p. 75. Reprinted by permission of Prentice-Hall, Inc.

groups of factors: the nature of the people in the organization, the type of task and technology, the environment within which the organization operates, and the degree of change and uncertainty faced by the organization. Behavioral studies, as we have seen, offer insights into the nature of human beings, both individually and in groups. Contingency theories have generally focused in the last decade on the latter three factors.

Task and Technology Determinants of Structure

Rapid changes in technology have created conditions that have required numerous reorganizations in many large firms. The introduction of computer systems usually demands a restructuring of authority channels. Machine-paced production in place of worker-paced operations requires a new look at organization design. Increasing the ratio of indirect labor to direct labor changes the demands on organization structure. Continual changes in products to capture new markets create pressures for built-in flexibility in structure. Organization theory compatible with dynamic technology differs from the theory that may work satisfactorily in a stable situation.

Results of research by Joan Woodward and her associates in Great Britain offer more specific elements by which technology af-

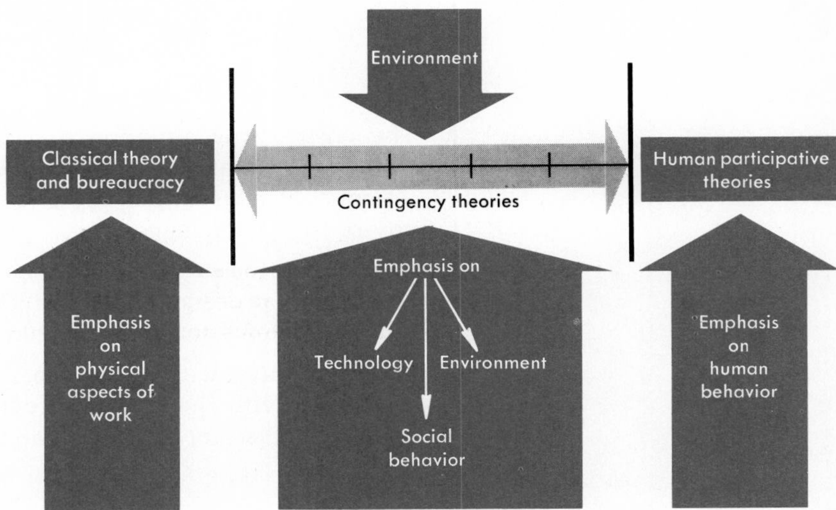

FIGURE 6.8 Theories for design of organization structure

fects organization structure.[10] Woodward classified production technology into three types: (1) small-batch production, (2) large-batch and mass production (assembly lines), and (3) long-run, continuous-process production (such as, oil, chemical). She found that the more successful firms using each of these three technological processes had different organization structures. As complexity increased from small batch to continuous process, the number of levels and the span of control increased. Likewise, line organization was more suitable to the simpler processes, and line–staff–functional patterns were best in the more complex. In general, organization of firms with small-batch and continuous-process production tended to be consistent with the human participative theories. The large-batch and assembly operations were organized along classical and bureaucratic lines.

If contingency theory, with emphasis on the impact of technology, is used in a large company with different production processes, the design of structure in one part of the company will tend to differ from that of another part using a different technology. Therefore, it becomes possible to fine-tune the organization structure to fit the technological situation.

matrix approach

In this fine tuning, many have found the *matrix approach* to design to be useful. This approach matches the type of task to the type of personnel needed to perform it. Four situations are identified in the approach, calling for different structures:

1. The routine task situation that requires repetitive solutions by personnel with technical backgrounds. (Taylor and scientific management proposed functional specialists in the design for this situation.)
2. The engineering situation that requires nonrepetitive solutions by personnel who are professionally educated. (A professional staff usually appears in the structure to analyze and advise the line manager.)
3. The craft situation that deals with uniquely different but repetitively processed outputs. (This situation requires a flexible and person-oriented structure.)
4. The heuristic situation that deals with unique and nonrepetitive tasks, with the output ill defined. (A flexible and group design is called for in this situation.)

[10] Joan Woodward, *Industrial Organization: Theory and Practice* (London: Oxford University Press, 1965).

The matrix approach encourages the adapting of organizational structure to the situation existing in different parts of an enterprise and can result in different organizational designs being used, depending upon differences in environment, tasks, and personnel involved. For example, the manager of a machine shop would face the routine situation in a department having automatic equipment and semiskilled personnel; he would have the engineering situation in the task unit that plans and designs products; he would operate in the craft situation for his die makers; and he would experience the heuristic situation in the research and development unit.

Project organization

Matrix thinking leads to new organizational structures uniquely adapted to the task. *Project organization* is one that can be tailored to a particular mission or project, to coordinate actions toward the completion of the project while retaining the advantages of functional specialists. Whereas the classical approach is built around authority centers and the behavioral approach is built around people, project organization is designed to meet the demands of a particular job. A functional specialist can be loaned out for a particular project and will answer to the project manager as in a line organization, but when the project is finished, he returns to his functional department and gains the advantage of relationships with others in his specialty. This approach leads to the development of temporary structures that are tailored to the successful completion of a project, as illustrated in Figure 6.9.

The project type of organization was very effective in the space program, because it was capable of adjusting to the changing needs of the specific environment. When production involved high uncertainty of results and the application of new scientific knowledge, a project manager coordinated production by using line authority. Functional specialists (including specialized scientists) were borrowed by the project manager from functional departments for the length of time required by the project and returned to their functional departments at the termination of the project.

Project organization has been found to fit a number of widely differing situations, from building contractors and advertising agencies to accounting and consulting firms. The increasing complexity of projects that require the highly specialized experts and rapid changes from one project to another that are needed in modern society often demands the flexibility provided by project organization. A project structure accommodates the formal ideas of classical thinking, together with the team and participative ideas of behavioral contributions.

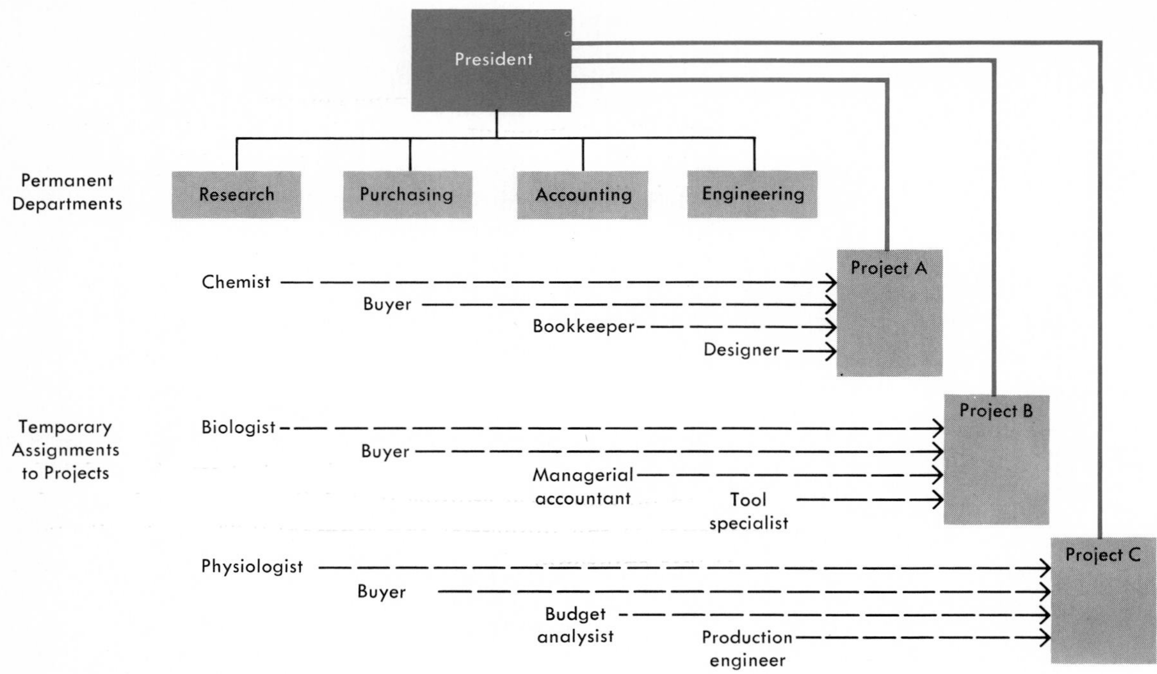

FIGURE 6.9 Project organization

Environment's Impact on Organization Design

Environment

Contingency theories of design of organizational structure increasingly consider the varying characteristics of different environments in which organizations function. *Environment* is generally defined as all factors outside the boundaries of the entity under consideration. The environment of a single worker includes all other workers, his working conditions, and all other factors outside himself. Likewise, the environment of an organization includes all factors outside the organization. The study of an organization's environment can be viewed as concerning successively larger circles of factors as one proceeds from those immediately outside to the broader and more inclusive. We can classify this continuum in three degrees of scope: (1) the immediate organization environment that is most directly, closely associated with the organization, such as the local labor market, the size of the firm, the professional support services of bankers and lawyers, and the organization climate; (2) the task or industrial environment, which includes the industry in which the organization competes and which provides services, supplies, and revenue to sustain the organization (and, in a regulated industry, including the regulatory bodies and legal structure constraining certain actions); and (3) the societal and cultural environment, which includes the sociological, cultural, political, and economic framework underlying the broadest and most indirect factors.

As one might expect, organization designers have given their initial attention to the immediate environment. Early scientific managers concentrated on such subjects as lighting, color, and working conditions. Behavioral researchers have focused on communication systems, intergroup relationships, and what they refer to as organization climate.

In the last decade, contingency theorists have expanded their attention to the characteristics of the industrial setting, our second classification. Paul Lawrence and Jay Lorsch have formulated a theory based on empirical studies that differentiate with regard to characteristics of the industrial environment.[11] They identify three classes of this environment: market, technical-economic, and scientific (which in general correspond with sales, production, and research and development functions). Each of these environments may vary as to (1) the rate of change experienced in the industry, (2) the degree of uncertainty of information about the situation, and (3) the length of the feedback time in which results become known.

Lawrence and Lorsch studied three industries: plastics, food, and containers. They first studied the plastics industry, because it represented a diverse and dynamic environment. The food and container industries were added at a second stage to provide a comparative approach with more stable industrial environments. In all three, they used three key concepts: differentiation, integration, and environment.

Differentiation

Differentiation involves "difference in cognitive and emotional orientation among managers in different functional departments."

Integration

Integration involves the unity of effort among the subsystems. The organizational pattern for a given firm and its different departments was found to require a satisfactory accommodation of the demands for differentiation and integration in the light of the environment.

Lawrence and Lorsch found not only that the environment resulted in different structures in the three industries, but that within the plastics industry, varying structural theories were employed. The production departments were more highly formalized

[11] Paul R. Lawrence and Jay W. Lorsch, *Organization and Environment* (Homewood, Ill., Richard D. Irwin, Inc., 1969).

for routine procedures; the sales departments were less formally organized because of the greater competitiveness and uncertainty experienced in the situation; the research and development departments used propositions from the human and participative theories. Thus, environment not only affected the general organization pattern but caused variations of organization structure within a given firm.

Most recently, the third and broadest view of environment has received attention. Comparative research across national boundaries has studied the similarities and differences among organization structures as they are affected by moral values, political systems, stages of economic development, educational systems, and culture. The emergence of multinational corporations that must adjust to a variety of national environments has required the development of structures to suit the worldwide scope of operation. The ecological awareness of the balance in nature to which organizations must adjust introduces structural concepts to fit the issues of conservation of energy, pollution of the environment by industrial processes, urban sprawl, and general recognition that economic growth will in the future be constrained by the available resources in limited supply on this earth. Organizational design models for this broadest scope of the environment are in their infancy; however, at least the scope is now recognized.

CHANGE AND UNCERTAINTY AND ORGANIZATION DESIGN

No organization design should remain unchanged. People change, technology changes, the environment changes, and the organization itself grows and matures. These changes continually introduce uncertainty that managers must learn to cope with.

The various stages of the life cycle of an organization, introduced in Chapter 1, determine design changes. During the start-up stage, the manager tends to concentrate on functions other than design, because initially the design can be simple and informal. As the firm grows, more managers are needed, and each must be aware of the activities expected. During this growth stage, the top manager still tends to feel that he can centralize authority, and he "keeps on top of his job" by delegating only well-defined duties.

With continued growth, central direction becomes impossible, and middle managers have had time to grow into their jobs; generally, at this stage decentralization evolves, or the formal design is changed after a complete study of the situation. With increased decentralization, problems of control and coordination develop. At this stage, added staff specialists are needed, and central coordination may be achieved by the establishment of committees and conferences. It is at this time that the bureaucratic model tends to develop weakness as viewed by the members of the organization. Collaborative and participative techniques are then introduced to keep the organization alive. If these changing needs of the organization are not met, the organization may be threatened with the declining stage of the cycle. In many cases, decline may be averted by merger with an organization that has been more successful in meeting the needs. In the future, many organizations may have to adjust to a change from a growth situation to one in which the organization must adjust to the improvement in the quality and efficiency of operations rather than to an ever-increasing quantity of sales or services.

Throughout the various stages in the life cycle, the manager has available various options in organization design. These options enable him to reassert his power to continually revitalize his organization. The choice of a design is not simple, but that is what makes management interesting.

SUMMARY AND PROPOSITIONS

Organizational behavior is much broader than the conscious planning of formal organization structures, yet a manager is typically most interested in how he can organize his department. He thus wants guidelines of the type supplied in this chapter. These guidelines, however, must be understood in the light of the discussion of spontaneous informal groups in the preceding chapter. We have seen in this chapter that it is desirable to distinguish among three types of authority: line, staff, and functional. We have summarized certain principles of organization and described some of the models available to aid in designing satisfactory organizational structures.

This subject of organization structure is well suited to the following concise restatement of basic propositions:

1. If you have had no previous experience or education in planning an organization, certain prescriptive "principles" serve as a point of departure in a number of industrial settings: unity of command, exception principle, span of control, scalar principle, departmentation, and decentralization.

2. The degree of autonomy allowed to subordinates in an organization depends upon the amount of information available to subordinates, the ability and experience of the subordinates, and the need for stability and consistency apparent in the situation.

3. The design of the most effective organization is dependent on the characteristics of the cooperating personnel, the state of the technology, the degree of uncertainty and tendency for change inherent in the situation, the characteristics of the environment in which the organization exists, and the size and complexity of the organization.

4. The consistency of the organizational goals with the individual personal goals of the members of the organization determines the suitability of the organizational design to the actual organizational behavior of the individual parts.

STUDY ASSIGNMENTS

1. *Can an organization exist without any structure? Give the reasons for the existence of formal organization.*

2. *Why have organizations developed staff and functional authority to help support line authority?*

3. *In the introductory vignette, "Who's Boss?" how is it possible for Larry to feel that staff really could be the boss? Can you think of illustrations where "advisors" have great authority?*

4. *Discuss how informal groups, as discussed in Chapter 5, are related to the idea of informal organization as discussed in this chapter.*

5. *Draw an organization chart for a club, church, business firm, or government agency in which you have been active. How does this chart help you understand the structure better? What things cannot be shown on the chart?*

6. *Explain how the chief accountant in Figure 6.3 can have line, staff, and functional authority at the same time.*

7. *How can the exception principle enable a manager to increase his ability to get things done within the limited time available to him?*

8. *What are some of the guides for deciding what activities to group together in departments?*

9. *Why has decentralization become a most important concept as organizations become larger?*

10. *What types of organizations could best use Weber's bureaucratic model?*

11. *Is Likert's idea of linking pins inconsistent with Weber's model? Explain.*

12. *Of the factors considered in contingency theories, which one do you consider to be most important? Explain why you selected it.*

13. *Your interest in a political campaign makes you decide to form an organization to promote your favorite candidate. Using the propositions, analytical methods, and principles in this chapter, outline how you would create a useful organization to accomplish your objective.*

14. *Why don't organizations find the one best structure, so that we would find all organization structures to be alike?*

15. *How does the structure of organizations depend on the knowledge explained in Chapters 3 to 5?*

situational episodes

1. Recently you have become disturbed over the fact that perfectly good furniture, appliances, and supplies are being thrown out as trash. You and your friends reason that you can perform a useful service to the community by organizing a nonprofit firm to collect the good equipment, make simple repairs and paint these items as needed, and sell or donate these products to people who cannot afford the price for new items. Your group reasons that this activity will save the community in hauling expenses and will reduce the need for ever-increasing landfill (dumps). With the cooperation of government agencies and civic groups, you and your friends have decided to form an organization to achieve your objectives. The available personnel at the beginning will be three full-time paid managers and fifty people who have volunteered 15 hours per week. You have already identified organizations that will underwrite the costs of the first three months' operations. Several trucks will be made available whenever they are idle in business firms. The city has agreed to provide trucks for the initial collection of items.

   The idea has caught the imagination of a large number of people in the community. The chief problem now is to design an organization structure that will be suitable to this unique activity. Up to this time, little attention has been given to the organizational problems. You happen to have just read the organization chapter in this book, and now you are sitting down to outline the organization. You have promised to present your plan to a committee by the end of the week.

   a. What classical principles seem to be of greatest help?
   b. What characteristics of the situation above are most important for you to consider in structuring your organization?
   c. Will the ideas of line, staff, and functional authority be used? of project organization?
   d. Prepare the skeleton of your proposal to be presented to the committee.

2. Your younger brother has just secured three newspaper delivery routes. He now finds that he will need to hire two teen-age boys to help him deliver the papers. Since this is his first experience in

directing the efforts of others, he has asked you to help him organize this activity. Although this task first appeared to be very simple, your brother has asked a number of key questions about what he should do: Should he allow each boy to run the route as though it were his own? Should he closely supervise their work? One boy has a car, the other a bicycle—should they work together to increase their efficiency? What other organizing questions should be answered in planning the activities?

You are now outlining your response and hoping that your short study in organizing can give you some clues as to how to advise your brother.

management systems

SEVEN

OBJECTIVES YOU SHOULD MEET

Define *system and its related terminology.*

State *the characteristics of open systems.*

Outline *the nine hierarchical levels of general systems theory identified by Boulding.*

Identify *five subsystems of a business firm, and* illustrate *how they fit into a management information system.*

Define *routinization, and* identify *those aspects of management that can be routinized.*

Summarize *the steps in programming repetitive activities for computer applications.*

Describe *the basic components of computer equipment.*

CAN MAN CONTROL MACHINES?

"I'd like to talk to you about how I can fit into your computer-controlled organization, Frank. I don't know anything about computers, but it seems that anything I do in my job of personnel selection runs into printouts from your monster."

"Sure, John, I'd be happy to chat about it; however, I would say that I run this computer center as a service to people like you and that we don't control anything or anybody. We merely process information to help you do your job better."

"Hold on, Frank. I've known you a long time and we can be candid with each other. You mean to tell me that all that stored-up information on your tapes—I think you call it your data bank—doesn't pose a threat to every person in the organization? You've got more inside dope on me than I can remember about myself. Any time the president wants to nail me on an issue, he can ask you to punch a button and he's got enough to fix me. If I wanted to specialize in blackmail, I'd just become a computer operator."

"Don't blame an efficient data-processing system for the sins of man! The computer, like any other good tool, can be used for good or evil. You can't argue that the wheel is a monster because it's on an automobile that kills people. The human being is the controller of the automobile—if it does something bad, don't kick it; blame the guy at the wheel!"

"Well, OK. But let me try to explain what's really eating me. It seems that I have to change my way of doing things so that you can program that computer, as though you're trying to program me to fit the computer rather than programming the computer to fit my needs. Frankly, I like a little variety in life, and that computer is certainly reduc-

ing everything to a standard way—I'm getting tired of reading all those reports printed in the standard, unpersonalized printout style. Every time I want information from the computer, you give me that peculiar-looking form that's designed to feed so much info into the computer storage. Frankly, I don't worry about all the deep and long-run problems of mankind; but I am darned concerned about how all this technological stuff is going to affect me. Am I becoming obsolete? Will the company decide that I'm an inefficient machine and replace me with one of those electronic wizards?"

"Now, John, if it's your job you're worried about, I assure you you're not the type to be replaced by a computer. You just said you like a little variety, and I've known you long enough to know that you enjoy doing things that are nonrepetitive. People who repeat a simple, standardized process are the ones who might be replaced by the computer, not you. The computer gives the promise to thinking human beings that they no longer need to handle the lower-level, mechanical processes. You can concentrate on those higher-level human activities a computer can never compete with. Even though you argue that computers have a dehumanizing tendency, the fact is that the computer is now giving people an opportunity to think and not be poor substitutes for a machine."

"Well, actually, my advice to young people that I interview for jobs is to become prepared for positions that require judgment and creativity rather than a nice little routine that can be repeated. Sometimes I tell them about the trend in one of the jobs for your shop. Ten years ago, everybody was yelling for more programmers, so we pushed new schools to teach people to program computers—that was a hot job possibility then. Now it appears that much of the programming is being handled by the different computer languages, and I read that soon the computer itself will handle its own programming. The guy who ten years ago decided to focus on systems and higher-level stuff now has it all over those people who got into a field in which they were competing with your monster."

"Look, just as you seem to be understanding the issues, you use that word 'monster' again. This is not 2001 and my computer is not named Hal!"

"OK, I'll stop calling it a monster—but is it going to program my activities in personnel, or am I going to program it? If my job as a manager is just a link between your computer inputs and outputs, where's the job satisfaction? I guess I'm saying that there's a limit to the information I need. All I want is the relevant information to answer a managerial problem, not mountains of printouts—I'm snowed under reports now."

"Well, that's exactly how computers are developing. Pretty soon the output will be shown on TV screens. Have you ever gone to a broker's office to ask the price of a stock and seen the exact information pop right on the screen? And even on printouts, the information is becoming more relevant. If you make airplane reservations, the clerk can quickly reproduce your entire confirmed schedule and hand it to you.

With this information, you can better control whether you will be able to get on the airplane at the right time."

"Yeah, I see that, but I still think I'm being forced by the machine to adapt to it. I just can't see that a master should be required to adapt to the slave. Man is surely going to have to continue to fight to keep from becoming the slave. But I guess I have some reassurance as long as I know that you're over at the computer center trying to control that computer!"

We saw in this vignette how computer technology affected one manager. But the new computer technology has much more widespread applications. As a result of the "information explosion" made possible by developments in computer technology since 1960, great emphasis has been placed on a systems approach to management. The foundation for this emphasis and approach was laid at the very birth of professional management—in the initial contributions of scientific management.

In the last two decades, the systems approach has developed so greatly that knowledge of the systems concept, the systems terminology, and the computer hardware and software is essential to any manager. The present chapter summarizes these essentials. This knowledge is closely related to the preceding chapter, on organization design, since organization structure can be viewed as a system of organizational relationships.

THE SYSTEMS CONCEPT

Scholars in a variety of disciplines, disturbed by the tendency toward fragmentation and specialization of knowledge and the increasing complexity of phenomena, have recently attempted to find a unifying framework for knowledge. A biologist, Ludwig von Bertalanffy, led in the development of a general theory of systems that could be applied to any arrangement of elements or combination of elements, such as cells, atoms, human beings, societies, planets, or galaxies.[1] Norbert Wiener, a mathematician, observed that information and communications serve as connecting links for unifying fragments.[2] His *systems concept* of information theory and cybernetics, showing the parallel between the functioning of human beings and that of electronic systems, laid the foundation for electronic computers. Kenneth Boulding, an economist, further developed the systems concept by identifying nine levels of system organization, which range from the simplest and most static to the self-directed and dynamic.[3] H. A. Simon, a political scientist, brought the systems concept into the study of organizations by viewing them as systems that make decisions and process information.[4]

systems concept

As a result of pioneering work in other disciplines, management writers have recently attempted to view the previous developments in accounting systems, production-control systems, procedural systems, and other parts of the management process as a "total system." The problem is that it is much easier to talk about "total systems" than it is to develop the necessary linkages among the various parts. Yet the idea of systems can be most practical and necessary in conceptualizing interrelationships and integration of operations, particularly as computerization has increased.

System and Its Terminology

system

A *system* may be defined as an orderly grouping of different, interdependent components or combinations with the intention of attaining a planned goal. Any system, therefore, must have three characteristics: (1) It must be an orderly grouping, (2) there must be linkages of communications and influence among its components, and (3) its design must be oriented to goal attainment. The essence is in goal attainment; thus, the whole is the primary concern, with parts important only as they relate to the whole. Furthermore, since parts are interdependent, any change in one part will probably create changes in other parts.

[1] Ludwig von Bertalanffy, *General System Theory* (New York: George Braziller, Inc., 1968).

[2] Norbert Wiener, *Cybernetics* (New York: John Wiley & Sons, 1948).

[3] Kenneth Boulding, "General Systems Theory—The Skeleton of Science," *Management Science,* April 1956.

[4] Herbert A. Simon, *The Shape of Automation for Men and Management* (New York: Harper & Row, Publishers, Inc., 1965).

The terminology used by systems experts is generally standardized, and it is desirable for a manager to learn the proper language so that he can utilize the skills of systems analysts. Five basic aspects serve as a foundation:

Components. These are the parts of the system.

Attributes of components. These are states of the components that can be measured; e.g., color, weight, height, age, width, length.

Relationships among components. We find that the attributes measured in the system vary together; that is, components are related through their attributes. For example, the manager might find that the speed of an assembly line is related to the quality of his employees.

Process or action. This is the behavior of the system.

Function. Here we ask about the goals of the system. What does it accomplish? What influence does it have on its environment?

The description of a system employs certain language that facilitates the mental process of building an orderly arrangement.

Subsystem

Subsystems are conceived as components of larger systems, depending on the analytical objectives of the manager. Each system is viewed as having inputs, throughputs, and outputs.

input

The *input* of a system may be information, materials, or energy from outside the system.

output

throughput

The *output* is the product of the system that is transmitted outside. The *throughput* is the transformation or process performed by the system; for example, a transformer in an electrical system receives electrical current at one voltage and changes it to a different voltage for transmission outside. It is not mere coincidence that systems terminology borrows from the terminology of electrical systems, for one early use of the systems concept was in electrical engineering. The idea of the "black box" in systems terminology is a case in point. The electrician, focusing on the input and the output of his system, often places a black box into the system, to perform some transformation without his knowing (or caring) just what goes on in the black box. Systems terminology, therefore,

black box

uses the term *black box* to refer to a component that can be assumed to perform in a stable and predictable manner without our knowing what goes on within it. For a manager with the limits of human attention, the idea of a "black box" permits him to proceed to operate his system without getting lost in details.

boundary

A particular system can further be defined by its *boundary*. We said that a system (or subsystem) has inputs from the outside and outputs delivered to the outside. The limits of the mental concept of a system are clearly identified and viewed as boundaries. Explicit identification of these boundaries is critical to the entire systems approach. For example, systems may be classified as machine systems, man-dominated systems, and man-machine systems. The machine system is bounded by the limits in which machines operate, without direct interrelationships with elements outside the immediate system. In a house, the plumbing (pipes) can be viewed as a system separate from the electrical (wires). Where the plumbing system must function in coordination with the electrical system, the boundaries of the two subsystems must be clear.

Closed systems

Open systems

Two types of systems are defined in terms of the nature of their boundaries: closed systems and open systems. *Closed systems* operate without any exchange from the outside. For purposes of simplifying a mental process and to gain the advantage of rigorously handling all possible conditions of a system without introducing outside factors, closed systems have a special place in theoretical development. *Open systems* interact with their environment—the factors external to the system. They influence and are influenced by their environment. Open systems have purpose—to survive and to grow; in short, to maintain their orderly arrangement and to fight the underlying tendency to disintegrate. Figure 7.1 is a simple representation of an open system, showing its interaction with its environment at its boundaries.[5]

HIERARCHICAL LEVELS IN A GENERAL SYSTEMS VIEW

Can life be viewed as systems of differing complexity?

Since management systems, as we saw earlier, are an outgrowth of new developments in many disciplines, they can be viewed as a part of a unified attention to general systems. Kenneth Boulding classified nine levels of a hierarchy of complexity of basic units of behavior.[6] His scheme offers both greater breadth and depth for understanding the place of management systems. His "system of systems" starts with the least complex and moves to a ninth level of complexity:

[5] W. Warren Haynes et al., *Management: Analysis, Concepts and Cases,* 3rd ed., p. 442. Reprinted by permission of Prentice-Hall, Inc.

[6] Boulding, "General Systems Theory."

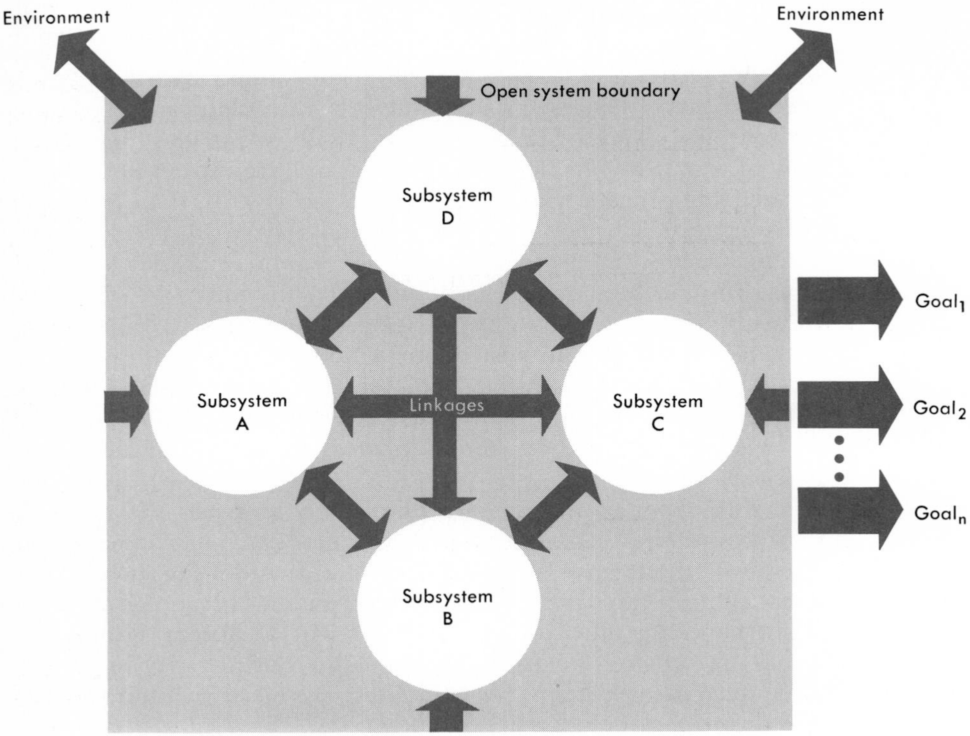

FIGURE 7.1 An open system consisting of four subsystems

1. The first level is the static structure, or *framework;* it includes the geography and anatomy of the universe, from the micro patterns of atoms to the map of the solar system and the universe.

2. Second is the level of simple dynamics, or *clockwork* of basic motions; it includes basic mechanics, from levers to the chemical tables and economic models.

3. Next is the self-regulated control system, one that moves to maintain an equilibrium, which he nicknames the *thermostat* level; this level includes all control systems (biological, mechanical, electronic, economic, and management) that have the characteristic of self-correcting performance.

4. Open system or self-maintaining structure is the level that introduces the distinction between life and nonlife, succinctly referred to as the *cell* level; it includes systems that reproduce themselves and maintain themselves.

5. Next in the hierarchy is the level of the *plant;* this level includes the botanical systems.

6. The sixth level is the *animal* level, in which the system has mobility and self-awareness; this level includes the systems of information receivers and the organization of knowledge into images.
7. The *human* level is the level of the human being, who not only knows, but knows that he knows; of course, this level includes systems of the type discussed in Chapters 3 and 4.
8. One of the most complex systems is the *social* interrelationship among individuals; it includes social groups, organizations, and the relationship between an individual personality and the role in which others perceive him, as we discussed in Chapters 5 and 6.
9. At the highest level is the transcendental, which includes the ultimates and the absolutes; this level includes all those things that may be systems, about which we can only ask questions but have no answers.

This hierarchical level of systems offers management a concept by which it can analyze the simplest systems as springboards to understanding greater complexity. It can enable us to relate our ideas of management in a broader horizon and to recognize gaps in our knowledge and attention. Furthermore, it offers a notion of how decisions and functions influence other levels. In management terms, it promotes perspective that includes a micro-macro continuum from details of equipment, to the individual, to groups, to the environment, and to ultimate purpose or goal.

MANAGEMENT AS AN OPEN SYSTEM

Can management be viewed as an open system?

In Chapter 6 we saw that the classical approach to organizational structure developed principles that were proposed as universal guides without regard to the specific situations in the environment; in short, design was viewed as a closed system. We also saw that the modern approach is a contingency view in which the structure depends on factors outside the organization; in other words, this approach views organization as an open system. Using the terminology of the systems concept, we will now identify the characteristics of management as an open system. Focus on these characteristics is particularly timely in the light of present-day social concerns relating to ecology, energy, and social responsibility of managers. Whereas the behavioral aspects of management discussed in Chapters 3–5 are focused on internal relationships within the organization, management as an open system tends to expand the scope of management thinking to relationships across the boundaries of organizational systems, to the outside adjustments necessary to adapt to the broader considerations in the environment.

Daniel Katz and Robert Kahn have identified nine common characteristics of open systems:[7]

> *Importation of energy.* Open systems are not self-sufficient or self-contained; they receive stimulation, information, and energy from the outside. For example, an industrial organization must import raw materials, finances, new personnel, and services from outside its boundaries.
>
> *Throughput.* Open systems convert, transform, and process. In short, they contribute a "product"; they perform work; they yield a "value added" to the "work in process."
>
> *Output.* Open systems export some product to the outside. This output enables the system to maintain itself and to yield a contribution to its environment. The nature of this output depends upon the goals of the system. A manufacturing system exports a physical product; a data-processing system exports information; a service organization offers a service to its environment; an educational institution generates and distributes knowledge.
>
> *Cycles.* Open systems operate in cycles, with inputs, throughputs, and outputs following a continuous flow path. For example, funds for purchasing the input are provided by sale of the output. These activities are repeated in a cyclical pattern.
>
> *Negative entropy.* A universal law of nature (entropy) is that all forms of organization have a tendency toward disorganization. Open systems develop means by which this tendency is arrested—thus, they must have negative entropy. In economic terms, a business organization must provide a marginal product that is greater than its marginal cost or sacrifice. The pressures of entropy toward randomness are illustrated in Figure 7.2 as being countered by a system's forces of negative entropy.[8]

FIGURE 7.2 Entropy and negative entropy

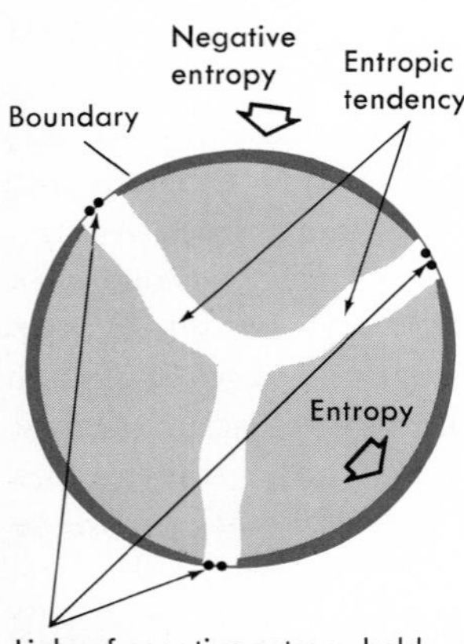

[7] Daniel Katz and Robert L. Kahn, *The Social Psychology of Organizations* (New York: John Wiley & Sons, Inc., 1966).

[8] W. Warren Haynes et al., *Management: Analysis, Concepts and Cases,* 3rd ed., p. 443. Reprinted by permission of Prentice-Hall, Inc.

Information feedback. By maintaining a flow of information concerning its activities and the events in its environment, an open system receives warnings of points where it may be deviating from the course toward its goals. This information is necessary for the maintenance of the system and its continued life.

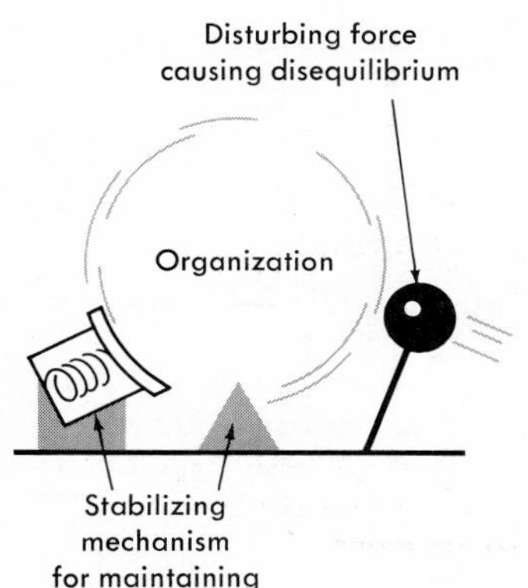

FIGURE 7.3
Dynamic homeostasis

Dynamic Homeostasis. Open systems have a basic tendency toward equilibrium. When this equilibrium is upset, forces are actuated to return the system to a steady state, as illustrated in Figure 7.3.[9] Furthermore, the system can increase the level of equilibrium by developing a higher base line around which future variations will oscillate.

Differentiation. Open systems have a tendency toward increasing specialization of functions and toward greater differentiation of their components. This characteristic explains the increasing complexity of higher forms of systems when compared with primitive forms. In a business organization, the roles of people and equipment both tend toward greater specialization, resulting in increased interaction among the components. This characteristic offers a compelling reason for the concept of systems' increasing value to management thinking.

Equifinality. Open systems can achieve their objective through differing courses of action and methods of attainment. There is no single path necessary for attaining the system's goal, but rather a network of possible paths. The search for the "one best way" or for an optimum solution is a continuing search with no end.

An understanding of these nine characteristics of open systems is fundamental to helping the manager identify his role, carry out his functions, and relate his activities to the attainment of the objectives of his organization as they contribute to society across the boundary from his internal operations. Since the manager has the power to establish operational systems, he deals with *manmade* systems, and thus operational systems are not natural like biological systems. Managerial systems are social systems held together by psychological factors, such as attitudes, values, habits, and expectations, so a manager must be cautious in using analogies of physical or biological systems in interpreting their opera-

[9] W. Warren Haynes et al., *Management: Analysis, Concepts and Cases,* 3rd ed., p. 444.

tions. As man-made systems can be changed at the discretion of the manager, he is able to adjust to rapid changes, as we shall discuss in Chapter 8. While he must attempt to provide maintenance mechanisms that ensure that the subsystems remain in balance and in adjustment with the environment, he must include adaptive mechanisms that will respond to changing internal and external requirements.

effectiveness

Let us now return to our definition of system as an orderly grouping of components for the attainment of a goal. The *effectiveness* of a system can be viewed as the optimum balance between maintenance and adaptation in order to achieve a goal. For it to be effective means that the system will, in fact, contribute toward goal attainment. However, one might be effective and not efficient; that is, one might reach a goal but only with extravagant use of physical and human resources. A manager must also consider his *efficiency*—that is, the maximization of output while minimizing input. Systems design should be oriented to both effectiveness and efficiency.

efficiency

MANAGEMENT INFORMATION SYSTEMS

How can you improve the flow of the information explosion?

The idea of the general systems approach provides a conceptual framework for unifying a wide variety of management topics. Individual and group behavior can be viewed as behavioral systems in whose functioning the manager is directly involved. The most advanced development in applying the systems approach has been in the creation, storage, and distribution of information throughout the organization. *Management information systems* (MIS) serve as connecting links for cementing operations into a coordinated effort for meeting organization goals. In the past, many independent information systems have been contrived for different functions, such as accounting systems, production-control systems, office systems, marketing systems, financial systems, and so on. With the advent of the computer, it became evident that much of the information in one system should be interrelated with the information in another. In short, each available previously independent system should become a subsystem of a larger system. Figure 7.4 sketches some of the currently available systems, illustrating how they can have subsystems and how they can themselves be viewed as subsystems to a total organization system (shown by the central, darker circle that intersects all existing systems).

The value of a systems approach is that information available in one system (say, the accounting subsystem) could be available for other systems (such as salesmen, personnel managers, and production foremen). If information is available in a central computer, it can be retrieved for use by many different departments. In this way, information on inventory would not be kept in the separate systems of accounting, production, marketing, and finance, but one central data bank would be available to all the subsystems. The advantages of such an approach are (1) cost saving, (2) greater precision of data, (3) coordination through unifying the concepts of each subsystem, and (4) more rapid access by managers to the information that they need quickly.

FIGURE 7.4 Systems and subsystems in a business firm

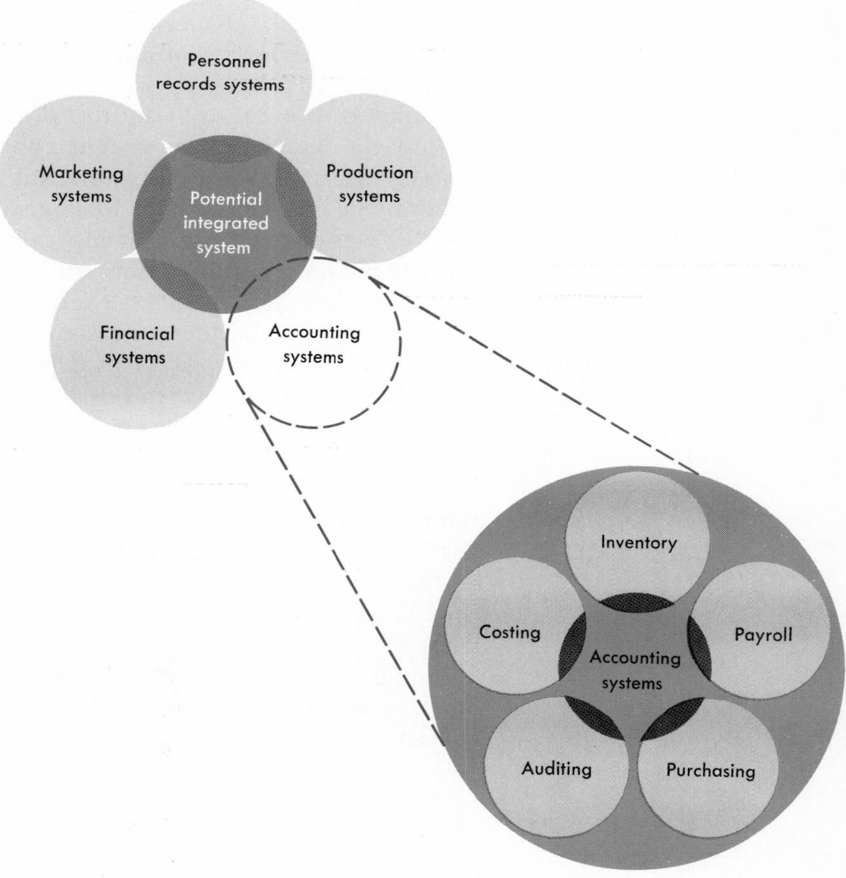

Management Information Categories

What can information be used for?

Management information may be categorized conveniently into three main areas: (1) strategic planning information, (2) management control information, and (3) operational information.

Strategic planning information

Strategic planning information relates to top-management tasks of deciding upon the objectives of the organization, the levels and kinds of resources to attain the objectives, and the policies that govern the acquisition, use, and disposition of the resources. Strategic planning depends heavily upon information external to a specific organization. When the external data are combined with internal data, management can make estimates of expected results. The specifics of this information are often unique and tailor-made to particular strategic problems.

Management control information

Management control information sheds light on goal congruence; it helps managers take the actions that are in the best interest of the organization and enables them to see that resources are being used efficiently and effectively in meeting the organizational goals. Robert Anthony has pinpointed three types of information needed for management control: costs by responsibility centers, direct program costs, and full program costs (including allocations or indirect costs).[10] Management control information ties together various subactivities in a coherent way, so that managers can gauge resource utilization and compare expected results with actual results. Management control information is often interdepartmental, in that the inputs come from various organizational groups, cutting across established functional boundaries.

Operational information

Operational information pertains to the day-to-day activities of the organization and helps ensure that specific tasks are performed effectively and efficiently. It also includes routine and necessary information production, such as financial accounting, payrolls, personnel rosters, equipment inventories, and logistics. Since this information relates to specific tasks, all inputs generally come from one established department.

These three categories are useful when developing management information systems, because they point out a continuum from the more *well-defined* type of information typical of operational information to the other extreme of *ill-defined* information characteristic of strategic planning information. This continuum is

[10] Robert N. Anthony, *Planning and Control Systems: A Framework for Analysis,* (Boston: Harvard Graduate School of Business Administration, 1965).

central to the problems of utilizing computers as the central hardware for systems design. A well-defined body of information can be reduced to a series of written instructions; that is, it can be *programmed.* A programmed information system involves specific elements that remain unalterable and thus subject to straightforward calculation. For example, the usual payroll information can be reduced to a definite rate per hour multiplied by a number of hours worked. Some programmed information may be quite complicated, but as long as each element can be precisely defined, the result can be precise and calculable. Strategic planning information tends to be nonprogrammed, because it defies routine specification; however, with the development of rigorous planning models, some strategic planning has been programmed.

programming

March and Simon have put forth a proposition of particular importance to a manager's reaction to programmed and nonprogrammed tasks: When a person is faced with both highly programmed and unprogrammed tasks, he will give greater attention to the programmed at the expense of the unprogrammed.[11] Most of us have observed or experienced situations in which nonprogrammed tasks are delayed or avoided while programmed work receives immediate attention.

INFORMATION SYSTEMS AND COMPUTERS

What is the place of computers in management systems?

Technological advances, along with the increasing complexity and size of organizations, have enabled men to improve management techniques. The principal hardware provided by technology has been the large, high-speed electronic computer. The basic principle of management for employing this hardware is to reduce to a routine and repetitive form anything that can be programmed either for human manipulation or for electronic processing. In the operation of the system, judgment is minimized by the establishment of decision rules and guides that enable the system to operate with a minimum of managerial attention. Programmed and routinized procedures thus relieve the manager of time-consuming attention to details and afford him the opportunity for handling strategic problems that often have unique solutions and therefore demand human attention.

[11] James G. March and Herbert A. Simon, *Organizations* (New York: John Wiley & Sons, Inc., 1958).

Routinization

Let us now concentrate on those parts of management that can be routinized, programmed, and systematized. The human nervous system provides an analogy. Certain body functions are performed without conscious attention to details. The development of good habits in early childhood enables a person to concentrate later in life on higher, nonroutine choices. Personal habits, clerical routines, standard operating procedures, and other "programmed" activities make it possible for a person to carry out repetitive activities with minimum effort and to be free for important decisions that require the use of the human brain.

Can computers help increase the personal, human touch in management?

Many of us are like John in the story at the beginning of this chapter—we like variety, and we don't like to feel that a machine is controlling our activities; however, we frequently fail to see that reducing some details to habit or checklists makes it possible for us to complete the necessary everyday chores more efficiently, so that we will have more time to think and be creative—in other words, to be more *human*. Managers who tend to focus on the routine operations of their jobs find that they never have time to handle its more important aspects. The exception principle, discussed in the last chapter, helps us understand that, as managers, we must delegate the well-structured operations to others and then handle ourselves only those aspects that are exceptions.

The parts of management that can be routinized will always be a challenge to you as a resourceful manager; however, a few clues can help you meet this challenge. First, routinization can be achieved for those activities that you can define explicitly—that is, those that you predict will recur in a clear pattern. Second, identification of the common components of operations reinforce the systems thinking. For example, if you find that you must write a large number of letters to similar correspondents, you can develop standard paragraphs so that someone else (say, a secretary) can write the letters for you. You would then need to compose only those paragraphs that give a personal touch and answer unique questions. In this way, not only can you turn out more letters but the letters will handle the subjects better, since you can use the best ways of expression repeatedly. Third, the development of checklists and standard operating procedures enables you to leave the detailed checking to others and to be more confident that you didn't forget important items. Inspection and control activities tend to be subject to routinization. Finally, once you find the right way to do something, you can standardize it. This standardized way can be better; it is more predictable by others; it is subject to routinization.

How can the manager make best use of a computer?

In order to program repetitive activities, it is necessary that the manager study the activities and predict the type of actions that will recur often. Then he must make his instructions explicit. Whereas it is *desirable* for a manager to be explicit in his instructions to human beings, he cannot utilize the capabilities of the computer without providing a detailed and explicit set of instructions; that is, *he must program the computer.* Finally, in routine and repetitive systems, techniques of measurement in quantitative form become essential. In other words, the computer must be given explicit numerical guides for its routine processing.

Improvements in Computer Systems Design

How have computers been improved?

Computer technology has developed at an extremely rapid pace since the first units in the early 1950s. These *first-generation* computers utilized vacuum tubes in their electronic circuitry. With the advent of the transistor, the *second-generation* computers were born. The use of transistors represented a technological breakthrough in the cost of producing computers, their reliability, and the size of hardware necessary. In 1964, the *third-generation* computers were born. These computers were microminiaturized and permitted relatively inexpensive communication between computers and other devices, such as teletype, typewriters, or other computers. People began planning for computerized information systems in which all company transactions were entered into storage units accessible to computers, then classified, tabulated, and catalogued in such a way that any arrangement of information was easily retrievable. "Total information systems" became possible.

Although a fourth generation of computers is becoming available, managers are still challenged to make proper use of the third generation. Most computer systems obtain inputs from one or a few departments and were designed to solve specific operational or reporting needs of those departments. Attempts are now being made to tie together several of the existing operational systems to gain from the computer the ability to interrelate different kinds of information that can prove useful to a number of departments. One approach is to systematize islands or blocks of operational data about each department and then tie the blocks together. Another approach begins with a comprehension of an overall design and finally fits each individual operational system into a grand plan. Such an all-encompassing system appears to require a first look from the top, in the strategic planning area, then a view of management control information, and finally a look at operational information. The conflict between these two approaches tends to retard the development of an overall systems approach.

Operational information needs are invariably met first in practice, because they can be economically evaluated and justified, and also because some of these operational systems already exist. As a result, existing fragmented systems tend to retard the comprehensive systems approach. The old systems cannot be abandoned, because they fill operational needs, and for the same reason, a new, more global system cannot be easily implemented without temporarily duplicating many functions at high cost. Opportunities for young managers in computerized information systems, therefore, are great. In order to meet these opportunities, the young manager must understand something about the anatomy of a computer, in addition to understanding the nature of the relevant information to be requested from it.

Computer Equipment

What is a computer?

Computer systems are composed of three main parts: (1) storage, (2) processor, and (3) input and output devices.

Computer storage

Computer storage records and retains information such as letters and numbers. The main storage is composed of a large number of storage locations, each with a unique address. These storage locations are analogous to post-office boxes, each with an address, each with storage capacity. Any combination of letters, numbers, or special characters can be stored in a computer storage. These kinds of information are referred to as *data*.

data

In addition to data, computer storage holds instructions, which are also combinations of numbers, letters, and special characters. These instructions command the computer to perform certain basic operations, such as add two numbers, compare two names, read or write information. The ability to retain and comprehend these instructions is what differentiates the computer from simple devices such as adding machines and calculators. A set of these instructions, written in some language, is called a *program* and is written by a computer programmer. The two most common computer languages in use are COBOL and FORTRAN.

program

Processor units

Processor units house the control unit, which interprets and executes the instructions, and an adder, which can add rapidly. The processor is analogous to a brain performing interpretive functions.

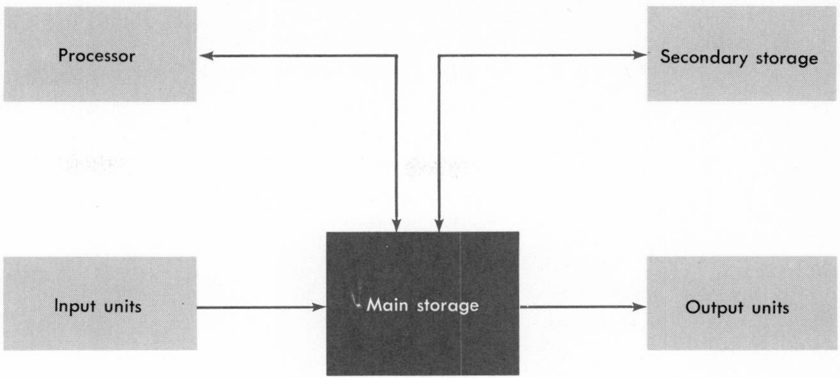

FIGURE 7.5 A computer system

Input and output units

Input and output units provide an ability to enter information into computer storage in the form of punch cards, magnetic tape, paper tape, or written documents, or to convert internal computer representation to a form suitable for either human interpretation or further processing or storage. Figure 7.5 is a schematic drawing of a computer system.

multiprogramming

In the past, computers were operated on batch machines, in which only one job was processed at a time. Third-generation computers use a technology called *multiprogramming,* whereby multiple jobs reside in storage, thus enabling the computer to schedule a number of jobs almost simultaneously. In multiprogramming, the processor handles the jobs to be accomplished by overlapping or interweaving their execution in a manner that most fully uses the processor's components. The results of multiprogramming have revolutionized systems design concepts. Great flexibility exists, since the computer can process a number of jobs while remaining available for unpredicted demands for management control and strategic planning information. While the computer is processing its regular information, the manager can submit questions to it through direct coupling without waiting for the work in process to terminate.

in-line modes

real time

In computer terminology, the manager can use *in-line modes* in which he has a direct connection to the computer; if this response is extremely fast, he is said to be dealing in *real time.* A manager at a remote terminal (a device to receive or transmit information to or from a computer located at a geographically distant location) can ask a question that immediately becomes active, and thus the information can be retrieved immediately, even though the manager is located at some distance from the major computer installation.

time-sharing

A variant of multiprogramming is *time sharing,* where several computer programs are given a "slice" of computer time in a round-robin fashion. In this manner, several users can simultaneously receive a small amount of computer service. The time-sharing characteristic provides an important potential for using a single computer for a number of systems and tying them together in an overall, comprehensive systems approach.

SOCIAL IMPLICATIONS OF USING AVAILABLE COMPUTER TECHNOLOGY

Designers of management information systems try to use common data to satisfy the information requirements of many types of managers. Some redundancy is desirable in any language or communication; however, many middle managers tend to maintain their own sets of information, thus increasing costs significantly.

data bank

The storage capacity of modern computers permits the retention of a very large volume of information inexpensively. This large amount of data is often called a *data bank*. The concept of large data banks has been viewed as an ideal. If one were available, individual managers could then go to the data bank (computerized library of data) and retrieve just that relevant and significant information they need. The progress toward large data banks depends upon making each of the separate systems compatible with all other systems and with the total system.

All contemporary managers need to develop an appreciation of the opportunities and challenges involved in taking a systems approach to management. Those at the first or second levels of management can in this way better understand how their own units fit as subsystems into the overall functioning of the larger systems; as a result, they can clearly identify how their own contributions interrelate with the other parts of the organization and with the organization as a whole. Higher-level managers using a systems approach can plan the interrelations of the various subsystems so that each subsystem contributes effectively to the objectives of the organization. In recent years, this challenge of the systems approach has been so great that a new type of management specialist—the systems analyst—has evolved. This new development opens up career opportunities for people who are looking for promising avenues for entering management. As a systems specialist, you would have attractive job opportunities and at the same time would be involved on the frontiers of management improvement in challenging and interesting activities.

Technological developments in computer hardware, and the rapid progress made in utilizing this hardware by means of entire libraries of computer programs and other "software," have raised new problems in the social and ethical dimensions. Norbert Wiener, one of the pioneers in computer technology, early expressed concern about the ability of human beings to remain in control of electronic computers: "It is my thesis that machines can and do transcend some of the limitations of their designers, and that in doing so they may be both effective and dangerous."[12] Even granted that computers are governed by the programs given them by humans, Wiener argued, computer systems may take actions at such speeds that the human control may be too late to ward off disastrous consequences. He cited the analogy of a driver of a speeding automobile who is unable to correct the path of the machine before it hits a wall.

The rapid progress in systems design and computers has made available a powerful tool for management—so powerful, in fact, that society needs to improve its processes for controlling the vastly increased available information. Information necessary for one system of decision making may pose threats to individual rights if allowed to enter other systems for which it was not planned. In the 1970s, the issue received national attention when it was discovered that tax information collected by the Internal Revenue Service had been made available to other government agencies and threatened to serve as political blackmail. Rigid restraints have been imposed by the Department of Health, Education and Welfare on the access to student grades in educational institutions by unauthorized people. Disclosure of the existence of large files of information held by the FBI and CIA raised serious questions about the potential misuse of information stored in large data banks.

Systems analysts have been so effective in tying large information banks into a total system that they must now be particularly aware of the boundaries of their systems. If they are not, the counteracting threat to securing information necessary for decisions may result in unnecessary constraints imposed by society in the name of human rights. Breakthroughs in assembling information pose new challenges to managers for ensuring that information systems are designed in such a way that they continue to provide valuable information for improvements in society without the costs of improper uses.

[12] Norbert Wiener, in *Science*, May 6, 1960.

SUMMARY AND PROPOSITIONS

This chapter has introduced the terminology and classifications important to viewing management as a system. It has concentrated on systems of information because, as a result of the rapid development of the computer, the systems approach has matured and developed most in content and techniques. It dealt with a short description of computer hardware and the potentials of computer systems. It concluded with the view that the very success of information systems and computer development creates new challenges for attention to higher levels of complexity, as identified in Boulding's eighth and ninth levels of systems.

We can state some of the kernels of thought in the following propositions:

1. Management can be viewed as a system that integrates and interrelates a number of subsystems.
2. Management thinking can best be developed in terms of open systems that import ideas and energy from across boundaries.
3. Systems thinking can most easily be demonstrated when routinization of repetitive activity can be programmed.
4. Modern electronic computers provide more than adequate means by which management can implement the ideas of systems.
5. Routinization is desirable chiefly because it relieves key human beings of work and thus increases their time available for ill-defined and often broader, more fundamental issues.
6. Computer technology tends to develop more rapidly than the skill with which managers can make efficient use of it.
7. Information is a major source of power to managers; this power has the potential for great improvements, yet it is a power that has potential dangers.

STUDY ASSIGNMENTS

1. *Can computers and machines replace managers as well as laborers? What implications does your answer have for the type of education you should seek?*
2. *Give examples from your experiences that illustrate the issues raised in the vignette.*
3. *Why have total integrated systems been difficult to achieve?*
4. *Why has routinization received new attention since the wide adoption of computers?*

5. *Give examples of each type of information—strategic planning, management control, and operational.*

6. *Do you feel that management can best be viewed by use of the systems approach? What are its strengths? Does it tend to focus on the broad view at the expense of analysis?*

7. *Considering the constraints imposed on the flow of information by emphasis on an individual's right to privacy, do you think there is a threat that managers in the future may have difficulty in obtaining relevant information even though they have the means with which to obtain it?*

8. *With your present understanding of systems, give your reasons for changing the order of topic discussion in this book. Could systems approach be the introductory chapter? Could it be the concluding chapter? Can you support the authors' view that it is essential knowledge that can best be understood after understanding the behavioral material, but that it should not be left to the end because you would have too many parts to wrap together?*

situational episodes

1. A local housing contractor has offered you a part-time job to help him systematize his operations. He builds 200 houses annually. In the past, he has depended on a group of foremen to coordinate activities. He tells you that he has grown so fast that he has never had anyone look at his operations as a whole and attempt to gain advantages from his larger scale of operations. His business has grown bigger, but he has evidence that his costs of building a single house have increased because he has failed to interrelate the activities of the foremen. He read an article in a trade-association journal describing the systems approach in house construction. It pointed out that subcontractors (plumbing, electrical, heating and air conditioning, carpentering, brick laying and masonry, etc.) should be viewed as subsystems. It went on to identify the boundaries of his house-construction system with zoning and government regulations, union organizations, individual buyers, the IRS, and other environmental constraints outside. He recently arranged with a computer installation to handle not only his costing and financial reporting but also his scheduling, purchasing decision, and job orders for his foremen. He has searched for a person experienced in systems work but found only one consultant, who admittedly did not know much about housing construction. For this reason, he decided that a bright person with some introduction into systems thinking could assist him in developing a systems view of his operations. You report to him next Monday and are now searching for ideas that will impress your new boss.

   a. Although you don't yet know all about the details of housing construction, what conceptual framework is available as a first approximation?
   b. Diagram the subsystems so that you can identify the critical interfaces and points that require close coordination.
   c. Do some of the open-systems characteristics give you clues to ideas that you should apply in the construction business?

2. You have been a bank clerk for three years. You have noticed that many of your duties are routine and could easily be adapted to computer utilization. You tend to get bored in your job and find that the bank has a computer with considerable idle time available for performing other jobs.

a. Would you be afraid of "working yourself out of a job" if you made proposals for explicitly defining your duties in preparation for having the computer perform them?

b. Would this situation offer you opportunities for demonstrating that you are manager material and thus upgrading yourself?

c. What would be some of your considerations in making this important decision?

managing change
EIGHT

OBJECTIVES YOU SHOULD MEET

Identify *the significant changes in the manager's world.*

Define *the role and limitations of the manager in the change process.*

Diagram *the relationship between the planned-change model and the managed-change model.*

Describe *the psychological factors in resistance to change.*

List *the advantages of and limitations to three approaches to managed change.*

CHANGE ONE BEGAT CHANGE TWO

"I wonder where I went wrong. Did I get bad advice, or didn't I implement the advice right? Should I call Professor Elsea again?"

Watty Evans had had many second thoughts about the organizational changes he had made. At first, when he had started to implement his plan, things seemed to go just the way the professor had predicted. Actually, the professor had answered Watty's question with a series of other questions, as professors frequently do. At the business school, Dr. Elsea had suggested the use of information and knowledge from the behavioral sciences by those in positions of leadership in organizations. And that's exactly what Watty had tried to do. He decided to write the professor a letter, since getting things down on paper frequently helps clear up the problem. The letter read as follows:

Professor William Elsea
Department of Business Administration
College of Business and Economics
University of Kentucky
Lexington, Kentucky 40506

Dear Professor Elsea:

I am faced with an organizational problem I would like to share with you. You may recall our phone conversation two years ago, dealing with the specific problem of reorganization in my department. I know you recall the problems the department had when our president-appointed task force uncovered many morale problems using the survey you conducted.

You may also remember that when I pressed you for solutions at the debriefing meeting, you replied that since I was the one who had to be part of the dynamic plan of action, I should be the one to develop the solution. At the time, frankly, I felt you had let me down. . . . I guess I was hoping for some miraculous, university-endorsed solution. You turned out to be very prophetic.

You asked me to recall some of the information from your course, Analysis of Organizational Behavior, and use some of the tools and techniques of analysis as well as some theoretical models of organizational behavior. You agreed that the Homans A-I-S thoughts and Leavitt's Structure-Technology-People model might apply. Using those ideas, I developed a scheme that my boss approved.

I asked my secretary to draw up a blueprint of the physical location of all 40 people in the department. Next, I had a management trainee in the company do a kind of work-flow analysis. After looking at both the reports and diagrams, I decided to make structural changes in the physical locations of the people so that their behavior might be changed.

Based on my analysis of the type of work to be performed, I found all the workers doing a similar function. Next, I took a blueprint of the office space and diagrammed where each of these functional groups should be located and had the Office Construction Department erect partitions in what was the large "bullpen" area. Now the large area was divided into five sub-areas. I also asked the construction people to make signs designating the functional title for each area. Knowing how people sometimes resist change, I informed all employees of the impending change, and on a holiday weekend, we paid double time to have the partitions put up.

Initially, there was a little static and resistance, but most of the people responded and adjusted quickly. Within six months, communication improved within each of the functional divisions, new cliques formed, workers identified with the goals and norms of the functional unit, and the process time for auditing functions in the whole department speeded up. With all this success, you probably wonder why I am writing you with a problem.

Coordination between the functional units is at an all-time low. Where I have been able to promote identification within the unit, I now find there is almost no identification or loyalty to the department I manage. While there seems to be good cooperation and communication within the units, there is almost no cooperation or communication on projects that take the efforts of more than one auditing unit. Whenever I have staff meetings with the highest-grade personnel from each of the units, there seems to be a reluctance by anyone to put himself out for the sake of another unit. I can even sense that the units are becoming jealous of each other, and I have to be very careful with the verbal rewards I make.

I guess I had to give something up in order to gain the within-unit cohesiveness. Now, what I want to know from you is what to do about getting identification on group projects. Surely, if the behavioral-science theory and research studies were able to contribute so much to my first success, they should be able to help me out in this new problem.

I look forward to your reply and also a possible visit from you. Is there an ethical question involved when I make use of the behavioral-science data to change, or as some say, "manipulate," the environment or structure and thus have people do what I want them to do?

Sincerely,

Watson B. Evans, Manager
Auditing Department
Smyth Industries, Inc.
Wadsworth, Ohio

Sometimes it seems that our solutions, managerial or otherwise, get us from the frying pan into the fire. Certainly Watty, the writer of this letter, displays this mood. One of the harsher realities in business is that a vital, growing organization will constantly have problems because growth means change.

Change is one of the most important organizational facts of life. By definition, any living organism is constantly undergoing change. The manager is part of this change environment in a number of ways: He is changing because of his own biological composition, his world is constantly changing, and the people he works with are under constant conditions of change (Figure 8.1).

Since there is no way to get around change, the best approach might be first to examine more closely *where* the manager's world is changing. After we see in what ways his world changes, we will need a more careful analysis of the change process. Then, finally, we will be ready for the discussion of managerial alternatives to effect change.

CHANGES IN THE MANAGER'S WORLD

What are some of the changes?

Most changes in organizations are beyond the control and influence of the manager, yet they still have an impact on what he does and on the success of any of his change strategies. We know that change is one of the most characteristic features of management and the manager's job, and we also know that leadership can be seen as an attempt to implement change.

Much of the information you have already read here testifies to the fact of change: Textbooks written in the 1970s are unlike those written in the 1960s, 1950s, or decades earlier. The changes highlighted here are in the following areas:

Changes in knowledge, information, and techniques

Changes in the scope of management

Changes in the issues and problems facing managers

Changes in the environment

Changes in the rate of change

The Changing Knowledge Base

The early chapters of this book offer concepts and language unknown to the nineteenth-century manager of the small factory. The profession of management had its roots in the engineering problems of production. Although the management field has advanced greatly in technical ways, another area emerged in this

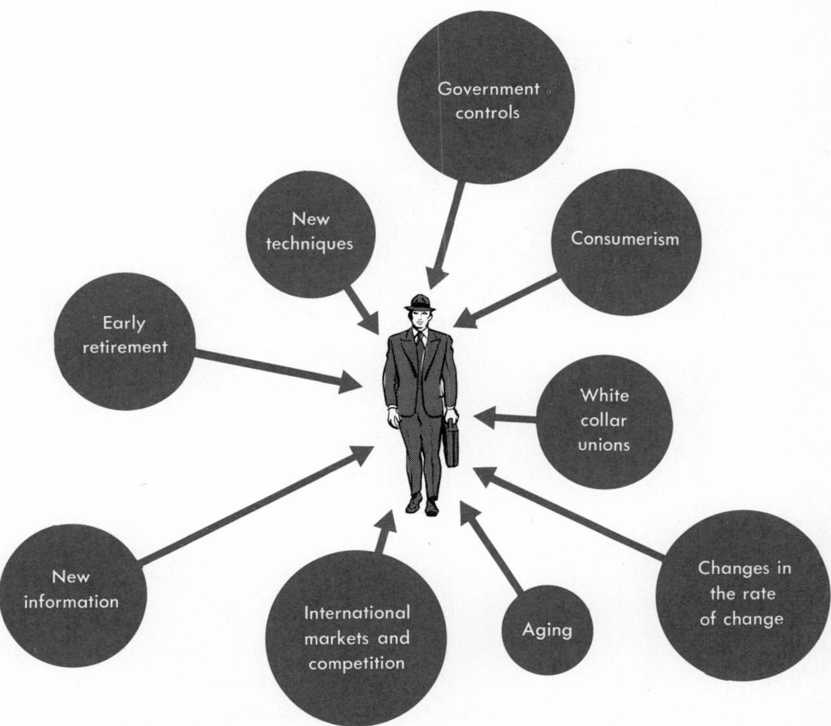

FIGURE 8.1 Some changes in a manager's world

century and received the most attention during the 1960s—the area of behavioral sciences.

Do the behavioral sciences have the answer?

Whenever a manager must relate to other people, some aspect of behavioral science comes into play. Although the application of behavioral science to the management field has had top priority in management programs in recent years, expectations of dramatic results from "behavior management" should not be too high. Machines are usually more predictable than men, and advances in the technical areas of management since the Industrial Revolution will not be easily matched in the behavioral field. Even when scientists can identify the significant factors in individuals, groups, or societies, the relative weight of each factor constantly changes. For example, group identification and belongingness may be important in one period of time, but not in another.

Man and his environment continually change, and the difficulties facing the behavioral scientists are great. Perhaps all that can be expected for the next few decades is a bare understanding of the problem rather than a specific model that improves the predictability and control of behavior.

The Changing Scope of Management

How has management changed?

There was a time when the field of management spoke primarily to the managers of industrial plants. Recently, managers in the public sector and managers of educational institutions, medical clinics, employment agencies, consulting firms, and staff units of religious organizations have found that they have many common problems. Thus, the application of management concepts and techniques to varied organizations spreads and will continue to spread as the makeup of organizations changes.

The broadening of the scope of management should bring greater demand for specialization of the application of management knowledge. There will be more research studies dealing with the management of organizations concerned with poverty, voluntary groups, political units, and other newly formed groups. The early statements about the universality of management will find expression in specific applications and interpretations of insights in differing new contexts.

The Changing Issues and Problems Facing Managers

A pronounced trend in the American management scene is the growth of educational preparation and training programs. Each year, beginning workers at all levels of the organization (machine operators, secretaries, supervisors) enter their careers with higher levels of formal education. More companies and universities offer training programs for advanced study.

This educational trend has caused an increase in the *career mobility* of the work force. Each graduating class is expected to make an increasing number of job or career changes during the lifetime of its members. A graduating senior may expect to make at least seven changes in career or company, not including changes in geographical location within the company.

Another change in the work force under the manager is a *change in composition.* Fewer jobs are available to the blue-collar worker. Automation and technological changes in the nature of work have stimulated the growth in white-collar positions. Each year the ratio of blue to white collar changes, which means that today's manager must deal with a more educated and mobile subordinate. Furthermore, managers themselves have become more educated and mobile. Companies are finding that the traditional motivational techniques no longer yield the expected results, and inroads are being made into the once "loyal" members of the organization.

The white-collar workers and public service employees will be a challenge to the skills of management. The question of *legitimacy* of organization has not been clearly defined for many of the new groups seeking or contemplating some form of collective representation. Teachers in several cities went on strike in the 1960s and 1970s and will continue to use the strike as a means of power equalization. New groups have considered taking some form of collective action against what they think are autocratic institutions and practices. Groups that contemplated action in the 1960s (for instance, ministers and priests) may express themselves more dramatically if changes do not meet their expectations.

What changes are still to come?

The future holds much uncertainty in the relations between organizations and individuals. The security derived from educational training and mobility of the labor market gives rise to a situation where subordinates no longer automatically yield to hierarchical authority. The question of *governance* (who has rights) will continue to be crucial in the interpersonal relationships.

governance

The Changing Environment

The increasing consumer markets and the segmentation of markets into strata (age, ethnic groups) are obvious changes. Patterns vary and are in constant states of change; thus, the manager must continually search for market information to help him make sound decisions. Values, expectations, and aspirations are continually being transformed.

Other environmental changes relevant to management are pollution and social changes in the city. Pollution (air, water, land, noise) and the exploitation of the resources of the country seem to be the cost of industrialization. What makes the topic critical in the second half of the twentieth century is that many *ecologists* (scientists who study the relationship of living things to their environment) foresee the possible destruction of irreplaceable resources. Managers in organizations as well as in the professional and academic communities are now starting to show interest in this subject. The crisis in the cities and urban centers increasingly affects management. The interdependence of the many factors of society make one problem the problem of many. Thus, management in the 1970s and 1980s may become more oriented to the problems of the environment.

ecologists

The Increasing Rate of Change

The changes facing the managers of organizations today are made even more significant by the increased *rate of change*. Figure 8.2 shows some of the dimensions of change during the last 100 years. You can see that these dimensions change with varying speed. This, of course, creates many problems. Assume that you have an acre of land and that only ten people live on and produce their food from that land; if the population figure increases at a rate greater than the ability to produce food, you will have a serious problem. If you drove to work or school today and faced transportation problems, you are very aware of another problem caused by different rates of growth—the use of cars is growing at a rate faster than our ability to build roads. The types of change and the differences in rate of change will create an organizational world

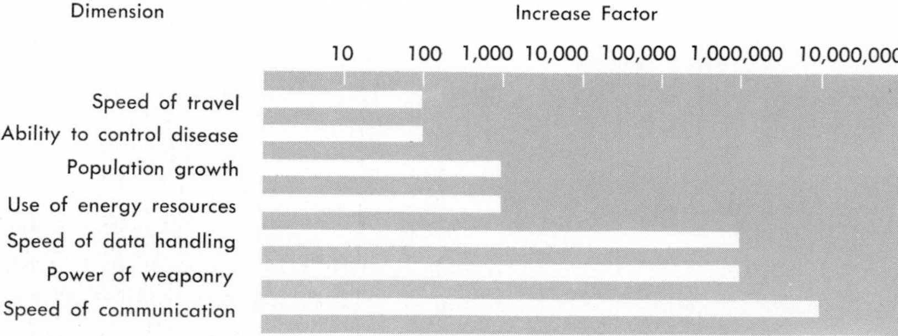

FIGURE 8.2 Dimensions of change during the past 100 years. [Based on data from Warren H. Schmidt, *Organizational Frontiers and Human Values* (Belmont, Calif.: Wadsworth, 1970), p. 28]

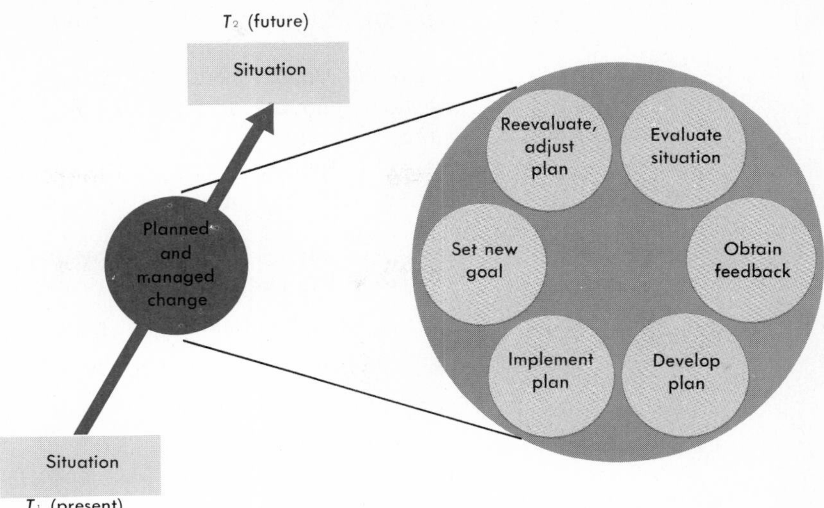

FIGURE 8.3 The scope of planned change

filled with uncertainty and problems. The manager facing the possibility of change must be prepared and willing to accept the conditions of uncertainty and conflict.

In the next section, we look more carefully at the process of planning change, to establish a basis for our final discussion of managerial approaches to planned change.

PLANNED CHANGE

The preceding section, on the changes in the manager's world, represents one facet of change. But many changes are beyond the manager's control and influence, so that all he can do is respond or be affected. In Chapters 1 and 2, we said that the manager's job was one of *action* as well as response, and it is to the action phase of change that we now move.

The Setting for Planned Change

Planned and managed change

Planned and managed change is the preset method a manager uses to move a situation toward a specific, predetermined objective. Figure 8.3 pictures the scope of planned-change activities. At T_1 (time 1), some situation develops that is not wanted: Production or sales drop, there is a possibility of a strike, personnel turnover is higher than anticipated, the government changes a regulation, a competitor comes on the market with a new product. The manager wants to be in a more favorable situation at T_2. All the things he thinks about doing to the situation can be covered by the term *planned change*, and all the things he does by the term *managed change*.

Can change be planned?

The following list outlines the steps in the planned- and managed-change process.

1. A *situation evaluation* takes place that results in dissatisfaction with the present condition, so that
2. A new *objective* or goal gets set, and then
3. A *plan* is developed to reach the goal.
4. Then the manager *implements* the plan, using the resources of the organization.
5. Next, the manager gets *feedback* on the results of the plan, and
6. *Reevaluates* and *adjusts* his objectives or plan.

The process is frequently repeated. Since the steps of this process may seem very logical to you, you may fail to find the problem areas in the change process. What's so difficult about moving from T_1 to T_2?

Human interpretation and individual differences present most of the challenges in planned and managed change. In every one of the steps in the change process, you might expect at least three responses from the people involved:

1. Acceptance and positive support
2. Compliance and minimal support
3. Resistance

These three conditions can occur at any point of the process. For example, not everyone may agree with your *evaluation* of the situation or with your *objective, plan,* or method of *implementation.* Frequently your decision is based on your personal interpretation, your values, and your priorities. The assessment in such subjective areas varies from person to person.

The Language of Planned and Managed Change

The sociologists, anthropologists, and educational psychologists have given us the language and theory for the planned-change process. For instance, you as the manager would be classified as the change agent

client-system

change agent, that person brought into or from the system to help resolve the conflict of differences, induce change, diagnose problems—to make something happen. The person or unit in need of or desiring the change is the *client-system.*

Included in the concept of planned change is the idea of a preset, definite goal or objective, and the problem is one of moving or directing all the efforts of resources to the prescribed goal. Learning fundamentals are also integral to planned changed, for people will need to direct their behavior (that is, change or learn) to this new goal. Some approaches to managing change are discussed later in this chapter, but first we should consider one reaction managers frequently face—resistance to change. It's one thing to be the management change agent when the client-system wants or needs the change and looks forward to your efforts; it's another and more difficult task when the client-system resists change.

Resistance to Change

Why do people fear or resist change?

At the base of all change is uncertainty. By definition, if something is to change, it means that the state of the event in the future will be different from the state of the event in the present. It is not always possible to know in advance the exact state of the event in the future. Thus we deal with uncertainty.

We know from earlier chapters on human motivation and individual behavior processes that people come into an experience with different self-concepts, dominant needs, and perceptual frames of reference. This means that an event that is really a changing event may be perceived favorably by one and unfavorably by another. You know of people who are very comfortable with the past and with the status quo. Yet you also know of people who are eager to change, to get themselves out of a kind of patterned behavior. The spectrum, therefore, is broad in terms of acceptance or resistance to change. If we accept for the moment the fact that change also breeds uncertainty, what is it that uncertainty breeds?

To some, uncertainty is perceived as natural and healthy, so that change is expected and accepted. And some find their present situations so unbearable that change is viewed as a necessity for continued survival. Most people, however, exist somewhere between these two points. To them, change has the potential for creating resistance to that change. Resistance to change arises from three possible sources:

1. The change may threaten psychological safety.
2. The change may require a shakeup and revision in the psychological world.
3. The change may have economic impact.

To many people, change and uncertainty present the opportunity for personal *failure*, and thus they have an emerging sense of *fear*. To the person who is not confident of himself (has a weak self-concept), new and changing situations with a great deal of uncertainty will be perceived as threatening his psychological safety (Maslow's second need area).

How does change affect your perception?

Change will also require a revision in the behavioral processes of perception. New stimuli must be filtered and interpreted, and the changing motives of people will also come into the picture. The traditional and patterned defense mechanisms must now

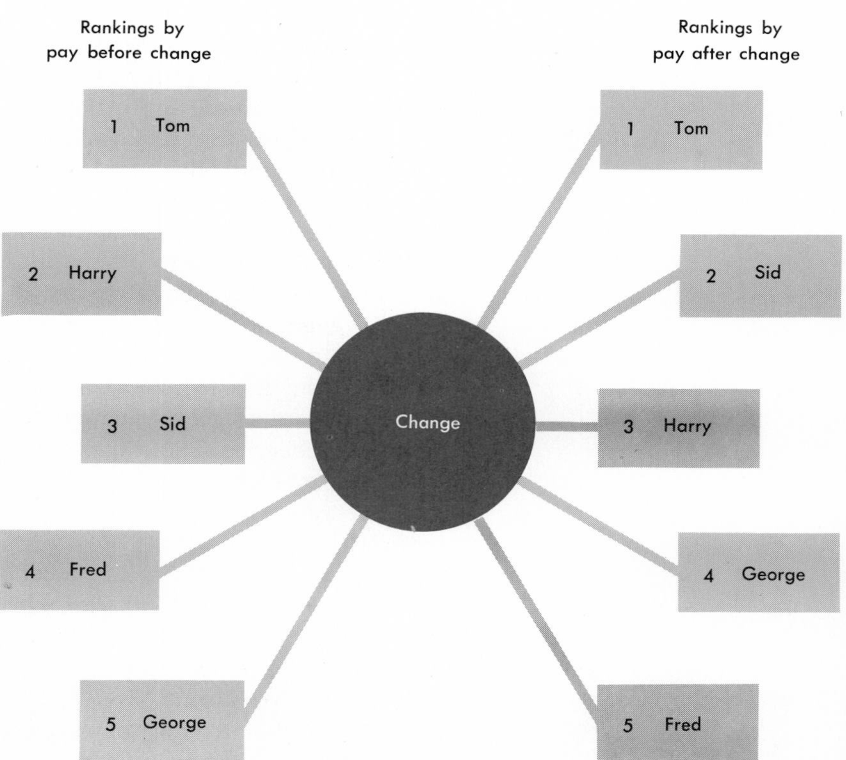

FIGURE 8.4 The social consequences of change

be revised as well. The total psychological processes that perhaps placed a man at a point of psychological equilibrium will all be affected because of the newness of the situation. Certainly, change will demand at least a reorganization of the behavioral processes.

Not all resistance is only psychological. There are changes in jobs or duties that will alter the worker's productive capacity and thus his opportunity for organization rewards. One obvious reward is money, and if the change results in a change in the person's economic condition, there may be resistance to it. The psychological aspects of economic changes must not be overlooked. There may be a change in the nature of a job, which results in an economic gain to a person. He may resist the change, however, if some of his peers receive gains greater than his own. He'll also resist if the change brings about a difference in the rankings within his present work group. Figure 8.4 shows this situation. Note that all five of the men ranked in Figure 8.4 could resist the changes in pay. If you will remember our discussion of groups in Chapter 5, you will recognize that not all the men may want to disturb the cohesiveness, norms, or status positions already established.

Usually, resistance is a warning signal to the manager, for nearly all change brings a change in the social patterns and individual behavior processes. Managers should expect and anticipate resistance when change occurs. Knowing how to overcome resistance begins with knowing why it exists, and the past few paragraphs have focused on some reasons for resistance.

We have now considered the theory behind change (the knowledge base), but we are also interested in the implementation of that knowledge. The emphasis in Part 2 has been on the knowledge base; in the remaining sections of this chapter, we anticipate Part 3 by considering the process base. Thus, we next discuss some possible approaches managers can take to the ever-present and ever-pressing existence of change.

APPROACHES TO MANAGING CHANGE

Can change be managed?

The approaches to change described in this section are based upon the assumption that a manager of an organization is interested in reducing any resistance to change where that resistance would be harmful to the organization. In one broad way of thinking, the approaches could be classified as those by which the *structure is changed,* the *technology is changed,* or the *decision-making technique is changed.* In these general approaches, the objectives are still the same: to create the desired behavior. In some cases, the approach works more on attitudes than on behavior, but the ultimate objective still rests with the behavior change. (See Figure 8.5.)

Changing the Structure

Is it simple?

This change method is probably obvious to you from reading the previous chapters. In this approach, the manager who has direct authority and influence over the structure of the organization changes behavior by changing the structure.

Assume that you are a political appointee in the state office of personnel. When you come into your new job, you find that the people (managers and nonmanagers) are considered either employees or political supporters. Because part of the work situation is federally controlled through civil service (employees cannot be fired arbitrarily after each election), you find yourself with a number of people belonging to the Republican party and a number belonging to the Democratic party. Assume further that one person in your office has an exceptional amount of power and influence in the political arena of the state capital, and she knows of this power, as do other employees. You go to others for counsel, because she is not only unproductive in your work unit but also disruptive and annoying. All your friends and associates remark to you that the situation is a fact of life and cannot be changed. You are at a loss to make any kind of shift through firing or job rotation. You instruct a consultant to do a work-flow analysis of the materials being processed in your unit. The consultant performs

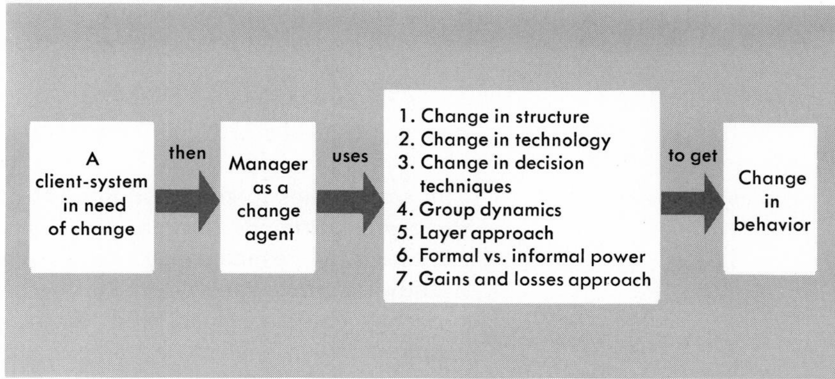

FIGURE 8.5 Managed change

this function and submits recommendations. You go ahead with the recommendations and are delighted by the results. Under the previous situation, your problem employee was allowed to behave in a very annoying manner. Under the new situation, she is placed in a position along the flow of work that gives her something to do and makes her dependent on others in the office. It is not long before she finds that she cannot take this kind of situation, and she resigns. You find later that she makes no political problems for you or the commissioner, and the whole operation of the department has been improved by her absence, the work study, and the redesigning of the organizational structure.

The vignette at the beginning of this chapter highlights the structural approach to changing behavior. Watty Evans was making use of the activity–interaction–sentiment model of George Homans; that is, as manager, he determined the activities that the individual or group would be required to perform. The manager may attempt to influence the interaction around those activities as well as the activities themselves.

Changing the Technology

How does the type of work affect change?

The management of the organization's technology is another approach to changing attitude and behavior. This approach was shown clearly in the research studies of Leonard Sayles, referred to in Chapter 5. Sayles identified four work groups of people who displayed similar behavior: apathetic, erratic, strategic, and conservative. He suggested that the behavior of each group was influenced by the type of job performed. It follows, therefore, that the manager of an organization can influence the behavior of work groups through the decisions he and others make about the types of work to be done in the organization.

Why are some waitresses unhappy?

A research study done by William Foot Whyte on the restaurant industry reveals the impact that work flow (technology) has upon the behavior and satisfaction of work groups.[1] Whyte found that there was a difference in the satisfaction or the tension of waitresses, even though the women might have had similar position descriptions and even similar authority over others (similar structure). Where the flow of work required a person of low status to start the interaction with one of higher status, neither found satisfaction in her workplace.

[1] William F. Whyte, *Human Relations in the Restaurant Industry* (New York: McGraw-Hill, 1948).

Cooks in most restaurants have more status than waitresses. Thus, if the work flow requires the waitress to give orders to the cook, tension should follow. This would be an example of a lower-status person initiating the interaction with one of higher status. When managers change technology they must be aware of the behavioral changes too.

More illustrations are possible, but perhaps the point has already been made: The manager of an organization has at least two approaches in the attempt to influence and change behavior—he can affect the structure or he can affect the technology. The third approach to be discussed deals with the decision-making techniques of the manager.

Changing the Decision-Making Techniques

In most organizational decisions, the manager has at least three options. He can make the decision by himself, he can let subordinates make the decision, or he can participate in a mutual decision-making experience.

If you recall the steps in the planned-change process, you can see the possibility of the three decision-making options to the problems of evaluation, objective setting, plan development, and implementation. Is there a management decision-making approach or technique that will improve the success of planned change and the reduction of resistance to change? Setting objectives or goals is one area where we have some insight in knowing how to manage change and reduce resistance.

Does it help to let people in on the action?

There is an increasing body of research that suggests that goal setting is directly related to goal achievement; that is, the conscious setting of goals results in behavior toward that goal. David A. Kolb and Richard E. Boyatzis identified characteristics of the goal-setting process and found that five factors were important for goal setting to result in goal achievement: awareness, expectation of success, psychological safety, measurability of the change goal, and self-controlled evaluation.[2] To have successful participation in goal setting that will lead to the planned behavior change, you will want to be sure these characteristics are present.

What does awareness mean?

If *awareness* exists, it means that the subordinate in an objective-setting session is able to focus clearly on the role required for

[2] David A. Kolb and Richard E. Boyatzis, "Goal Setting and Self-Directed Behavior Change," in *Organizational Psychology*, eds. David A. Kolb et al. (Englewood Cliffs, N.J.: Prentice-Hall, 1971), pp. 317–37.

the goal achievement. Such a person will be more aware of the forces that are related to the change goal and will have a reality orientation rather than being naive.

Does success breed success?

A person who expects to succeed will be confident that the goal is possible, feasible, and within his grasp. Thus, the *expectation of success* may help one to achieve and be successful.

With *psychological safety*, the person feels psychologically free and safe and is therefore open to realistic feedback and results. He is less likely to use defense mechanisms to cover up his weaknesses and has a healthy attitude toward the results of his efforts.

The *measurability of the change goal* is also a critical characteristic, for if a goal does not have the potential of being measured, feedback and progress toward that goal will be superficial and unreal. If a person has identified a goal with a specific target date and specific methods of achieving it, he should be able to get feedback on his progress and move more successfully toward that goal. It may even be necessary for him to make modifications in his productivity rate or in his methods, or even in the goal itself, as he gets the feedback from his efforts.

The final characteristic is the *self-controlled evaluation*. The person will only be going through the motions if the goal that is set comes from the organization or the boss and progress is viewed as some kind of a forced requirement. If he has some control over the process and regards the goal-setting method as important as does his superior, the whole process will be improved.

The management technique of subordinate objective setting will lead to behavior change if the goal-setting process has the *self-directed feature* to it and contains the five characteristics just mentioned. Another management approach is needed to ensure behavior change; it is called the coaching relationship.

Management coaching

How does coaching work?

Management coaching is just what it says. The management superior attempts to establish a helping relationship with a subordinate to "bring him along." It is an on-the-job technique that includes performance and evaluation as part of the process. Frequently, the coach is not the immediate superior of the individual, so that openness and direct communication are more possible. Kolb and Boyatzis offer suggestions for the type of model to best give behavior change in what they call the helping intervention (coaching) experiences. Figure 8.6 shows this model clearly.

How does helping intervention work?

You can see that some of the features of the goal-directed and self-directed process are contained here, so that psychological safety, goal awareness, self-control, expectations of success, attempts to achieve the goal, feedback from the environment, and behavior change are all part of the full cycle. Important to the manager who wants to fulfill the role of helper or coach are the descriptive statements on the spokes of this wheel. Notice the terms that the two authors use: The manager should develop a climate of *supportiveness,* there should be *collaborative goal setting,* there should be emphasis on *self-direction,* the manager should feel free to *manipulate expectations,* there should be *behavior monitoring and control,* there should be *selective reinforcement,* and the manager should feel free to *manipulate the results.*

Other Approaches to Managing Change

There are some other methods that may affect both behavior and attitude simultaneously. The logic behind these methods is very simple: Rather than getting involved in debate over which comes first, attitude or behavior, the proponents of these methods are concerned with the immediate output of change more than whether intervening variables are changed before other variables.

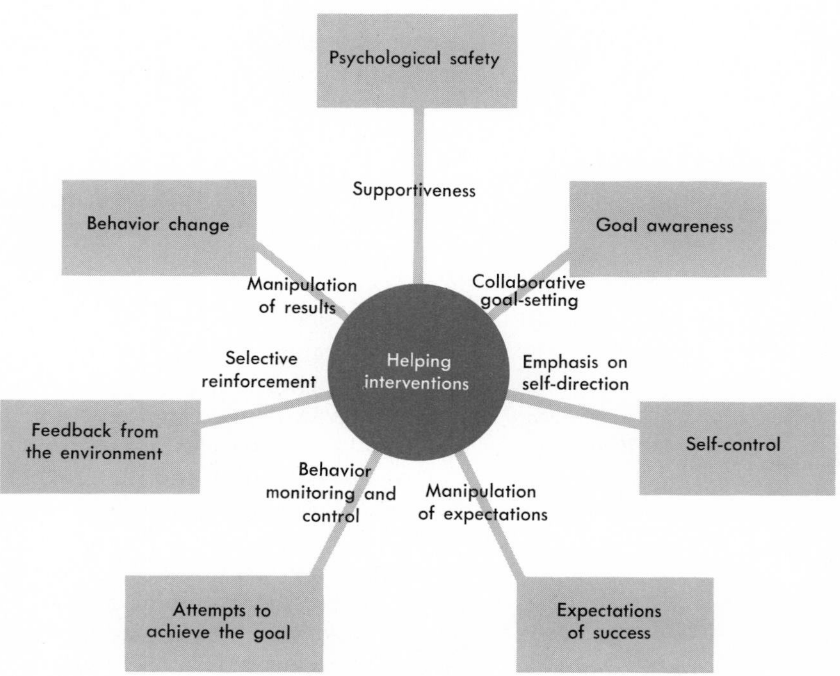

FIGURE 8.6 A model for helping interventions [Adapted from David A. Kolb and Richard E. Boyatzis, "Goal Setting and Self-Directed Behavior Change," in *Organizational Psychology,* Kolb et al., eds. (Englewood Cliffs, N.J.: Prentice-Hall, 1971), p. 333]

There are four approaches that we want to share with you: the group-dynamics approach, the formal versus informal power and influence approach, the "layer" approach, and the gain-and-loss approach.

GROUP DYNAMICS In the group-dynamics approach, man is assumed to be primarily a social animal. He functions almost constantly with other people and thus uses or needs other people for three reasons: (1) to give him insight into himself, (2) to determine a bench mark or standard of acceptable behavior, and (3) to serve as a trial-and-error base for experimental behavior. Sensitivity training, encounter groups, and T-groups (training groups) are some of the vehicles for the changing of behavior.

What does a trainer do?

The trainer of a group establishes some minimal ground rules, and the group proceeds with its learning. Discussions and reactions are usually limited to *here-and-now* situations. In other words, the group creates experiences that are shared by all the members in that group at that time—thus, all the members have a common bond, and the experiences are real and highly personal.

Is this the "tell it like it is" idea?

The second ingredient that the trainer usually introduces into the group is the idea of feedback. Each participant is encouraged to respond to (to feed back) the experiences he is having in the here-and-now situations. He is asked to state exactly how he views the experiences and to express the impact they have on him. Reality is defined in the perception that each individual has of the behavior, not in any "should" or "ought" or "I didn't mean it that way" type of context. People are encouraged to give "gut level" feedback, and it is assumed that the sender of the initial message will be able to handle the feedback and also be able to come up with the *behavioral adaptations and changes.* In many situations, the group training experiences are quite traumatic.

FORMAL VERSUS INFORMAL POWER This approach to attitude-behavior change can best be illustrated by a concrete example. A church group was sponsoring a People's Organization in a predominantly black, low-income area. The neighborhood people wanted to plant gardens in their area and asked for assistance from the university and other groups in town. They received the seeds and planted them. A drainage problem developed, however, during one of the first major rainstorms; directly across the street, the drainage pipes from warehouses were turned in the direction of the vegetable garden. The problem was brought to the church board of directors, and two approaches were suggested. One approach required using formal channels of communication and power, even to the point of a picket or march on the homes of the owners of the warehouses. The other approach, which eventually won, was to use more informal and subtle techniques. The manager and owner of the warehouses was identified and found to be a member of the affiliated churches. A phone call was placed to the minister of his church, and the minister in turn relayed the request and problem to the manager of the warehouse. Soon the drainpipes were realigned so that the flooding stopped.

In this example, the informal, nondirect approach seemed preferable to the direct use of power through formal channels. In another situation, formal power may be necessary and more effective. In our case, however, the parties (the client-systems) were never given an opportunity to generate resistance to change. They were not put into embarrassing situations where they might lose face. They were not presented an issue that gave rise to emotional overtones. The issue was fed through the informal channels where the action was immediate and successful.

THE LAYER APPROACH The layer approach recognizes the differences in people and their natural tendency to resist change. For example, suppose a black man is the director of an OEO project in a city and wants to effect change in either attitude or behavior of white people who have very low income levels. No mat-

TABLE 8.1 The Gains and Losses Approach to Proposed Change of Secretaries from Personal to Pool Assignment

Gains	Losses
To Secretaries	
More money.	No sense of loyalty.
Specialization of talent.	Loss of pride and identity with specific job.
Greater socialization with other secretaries.	Boring.
	Less chance to broaden growth through varied experience.
To Bosses	
Greater efficiency.	Possible loss of power.
Reduced manpower costs.	Loss of status symbol.
Impersonal—few personnel problems.	Loss of personal services.

ter what the black man does, he cannot become white, nor can he shed the characteristics of his education and affluence. If he goes directly to these people, they are apt to greet him with distrust and suspicion, wondering what it is he wants from them. Using a layer approach to change, the director would relay and communicate his change plan to his subordinates, and so on down the line, until two people with similar orientations are able to communicate with each other with no distrust. For example, perhaps the assistant director is white and is able to talk with someone who has had a difficult financial time and is thus in the deprived group (the target for change). This same layer approach works upward as well as downward in organizational hierarchy; it recognizes the facts of organizational life and the psychology of individuals.

GAINS-AND-LOSSES APPROACH In this approach, the manager performs a process of analysis prior to any kind of action. He makes up a simple T-account form and asks one question: If the proposed change were to take place, what would be the gains and losses to the people affected by the change? In Table 8.1, for example, the proposed change from personal secretaries to a pool of secretaries in an office may have an economic advantage but psychological disadvantage. What the manager would do in this case is to list the gains and losses from the viewpoint of the managers, secretaries, and others, and also attempt to identify within each the importance of the factors. For example, a change might give financial improvement to a group of workers, but the informal leader of the group might not rank economic gains very high. This would be especially true if, in order to get economic gains, the informal leader were to be relocated into some corner and thus cut off from the communication processes of the other workers.

This approach takes into account some important features of change. Looking at change from the perspective of the people involved reminds us of the importance of individual processess, especially the process of individual perception. The changes contemplated by any manager have a meaning above and beyond the meaning that the manager simply states. Much friction, frustration, confrontation, and organization disarray can be prevented by the use of so simple a process as this behavioral analysis of change.

SUMMARY AND PROPOSITIONS

Among various approaches to the management of change we found changing the structure, technology, decision-making technique, and others. You will remember that we arrived at the discussion after first discerning the ways the manager's world changes and then analyzing the change process itself.

The manager of an organization will have to learn to live with change. Frequently, change is like the wind, in that it is neutral in its effect. There are times when the wind can be refreshing and there are times when it can be destructive and harmful. We hope the ideas presented in this chapter give the manager a perspective on the topic of change so that he approaches the organizational world with confidence rather than fear.

1. Change is an organizational fact of life.
   a. Changes outside a manager's control have some bearing on how he does his job.
   b. The manager continually faces change and resistance in his personal relationship with bosses, peers, and subordinates.

2. Individual behavior is susceptible to influence.
   a. Influencing behavior through structure and technological forces is easiest, most subtle, and least likely to create resistance.
   b. Face-to-face contact is a difficult way to effect behavior change.

3. Resistance to change is to be expected and can be used advantageously.
   a. Since organizations and humans are imperfect mechanisms, there will always be incomplete communication and perception of the events of change.
   b. Resistance can be a warning signal, alerting the manager to the necessity of taking additional action.

4. Participation of those involved in changes is fundamental in making change decisions.
   a. If people help make the change, they will work harder to make the change successful.
   b. In participation, anticipated fears and problems can be identified and studied for solutions.

5. The layer approach to change works best when there are major differences between the individuals or groups.

6. Change is necessary for organizational and personal growth.

a. Poor management practice creates many of the problems relating to changes.

b. Managing change is primarily a function of managers and cannot be done easily by subordinates or peers. It takes hierarchy.

STUDY ASSIGNMENTS

1. Did Watty Evans get bad advice from Professor Elsea, or did he implement the advice incorrectly? Explain.

2, Is there an ethical question when you make use of behavioral-science data to change environment or structure? Explain.

3. Describe specific ways in which changes in the following would affect the manager's job:

a. More government controls

b. White-collar unions

c. Early retirement

4. How can a manager discuss planned and managed change at the same time he discusses his dynamic, unpredictable world?

5. Is resistance to change to be expected? Why do people resist change? How do you overcome the resistance?

6. Try to identify change and resistance in your own personal life.

a. What are some of the changes in your recent past?

b. In what situations have you resisted change? supported change?

7. Changing the structure of the organization is a management technique. Do you think the consultant and manager (in the example of the state office of personnel) were ethical when they changed the structure?

8. Give three examples from your personal observation where the type of job and its technology influenced the behavior of those in the job.

9. Develop arguments for and against your participating in setting the objectives and goals in this class.

10. Evaluate the layer approach. Have you ever experienced this approach?

11. Why might Proposition 2(a) *be true?*

12. *Why is face-to-face contact the most difficult way to effect behavior change?*

13. *What aspects of Chapters 3, 4, and 5 have relevance to change?*

14. *Is participation in decision making always good? Explain.*

situational episodes

1. You have worked for two weeks in the cafeteria. The money helps you defray expenses while in school. The new assistant manager is a recent graduate of a business school, and you feel comfortable around her. You observe that the flow of people through the line causes delays and even some nasty remarks. Some customers want only a light lunch—soup, salad, beverage; others want a complete meal. The ones wishing the light lunch complain about standing in the long line. When they cut out to get just soup, for example, others resist letting them back in line. There is one cashier. The staff members have become specialized and like being known as "the dessert lady" or "the main-dish lady." When you suggest changing the flow, the assistant manager asks if you have considered the consequences of the change on the staff. What consequences would you mention? How would you prepare the staff for a change in the flow of work?
2. Alan has just joined your department. He seems very eager to do well and has many ideas; in fact, he comes in at least once a day to suggest changes for the department—and you agree that the department could use some change. You have a mixed department in terms of age, time on the job and with the company, etc. How do you determine what should change, how much to change, who should be involved in change, and who may get the credit for the change?

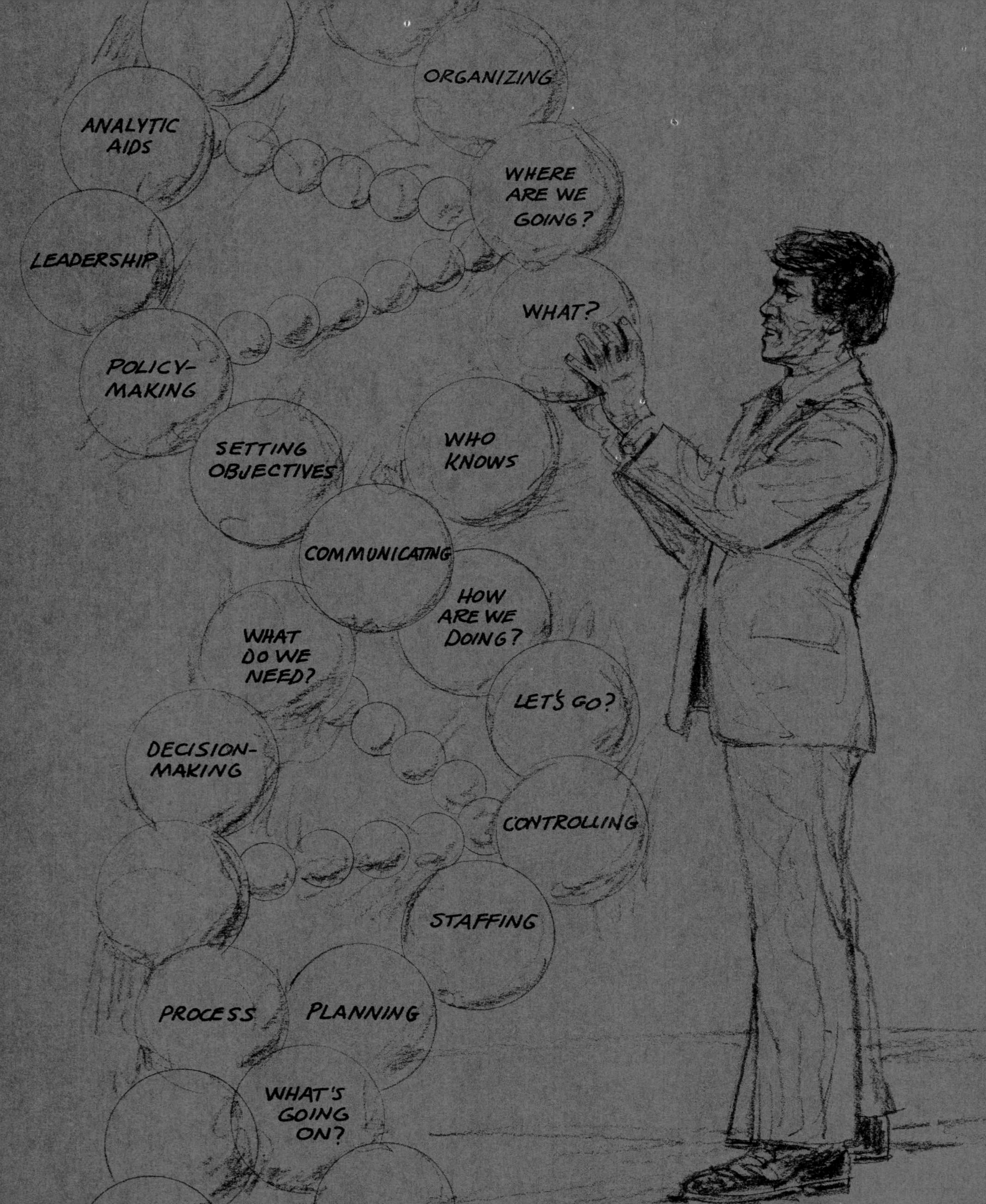
ORGANIZING
ANALYTIC AIDS
WHERE ARE WE GOING?
LEADERSHIP
WHAT?
POLICY-MAKING
SETTING OBJECTIVES
WHO KNOWS
COMMUNICATING
HOW ARE WE DOING?
WHAT DO WE NEED?
LET'S GO?
DECISION-MAKING
CONTROLLING
STAFFING
PROCESS
PLANNING
WHAT'S GOING ON?

management fundamentals: the processes for managing

3

Using the knowledge base about people, groups, organization, and systems from Part 2, we are now ready to analyze the things that managers do. In Part 3, we discuss in detail each of the seven functions of management outlined in Chapter 2.

Chapters 9 and 10 describe the decision-making process and offer valuable aids from accounting, economics, and management science. In Chapter 11, we focus on setting objectives. People usually assume that the manager acts to achieve objectives set by owners; however, management by objectives now places the manager in the active role of setting his own objectives.

In Chapter 12, planning and policy making are seen as functions that help maintain the organization. In Chapter 13, we build on Chapters 6 and 8 by discussing how staffing of the structure with human beings can best be accomplished. Chapter 14 develops methods for improving communications. Chapter 15 offers guides for effective leadership for the directing and supervising functions. Finally, the control function is seen as universal, providing means by which actual performance is checked against expected performance.

These management processes are generally performed simultaneously. A manager does his job without consciously thinking that at one time he is planning and at another time he is controlling; however, the study of these functions is simplified by analyzing each separately. We can then improve the total process by improving each element.

the decision-making process

NINE

OBJECTIVES YOU SHOULD MEET

Define *a decision; include its three essential characteristics.*

State *five elements of the decision-making process.*

Outline *the advantages and disadvantages of committees for making decisions.*

Summarize *the principles of group participation.*

HOW DO I GET A DECISION MADE?

I was in the western part of the state today and got back early, so I punched out earlier. But I got paid the full day, since I had to travel so far, so I stopped in at the tavern for a beer. Soon I spotted a friend. "Hey, Eddie, come over and join me."

"Harry, old buddy, how are you? Gee, I haven't seen you in months . . . since I quit the company. Harry, this is a friend of mine—Joe, Joe Norman. Joe and I work the rig together with Central Power. Mary Ellen, a round of drafts!"

"So you work for Central Power now. That's funny . . . you working for the same kind of outfit. . . . How do you like working for them?"

"Better than working for Northwestern Power. In Central, the guys let you alone and don't bother you as long as you're doing the job. And they don't ask how we do our job so long as we do it. Not like that cotton-pickin' dynamite job we had in Northwestern that finally got me to quit. Joe, you wouldn't believe the stupidity of that company. Harry will, 'cause he was there when it happened and can vouch for everything I say.

"Remember when the government passed that new law about the use of dynamite?—had something to do with trying to put down the violence of crowds and things like that, OK? Well, the law says that before I can get dynamite I have to file for a permit, and to get the permit I have to give them the Social Security number of the company. . . . Well, I don't think that's any big thing, so I ask my boss to get me the number, OK? So he says he'll get it soon.

"Well, I get this order from the dispatcher to take a bunch of guys to Brookneal, you know that town and area, just east of Smith Mountain Lake. It seems that some lines are in need of repair, and we may even

have to put up some new poles. Well, I know that area pretty well; I know how hard that rock is and that we'd be digging for months unless we can blast. I check our listing and see that we have the OK to blast in that area, and then I go to my boss to get the Social Security number so I can draw out dynamite.

"Do you know, that pencil-pushing jerk tells me that he doesn't have the Social Security number! I ask him how come, and he tells me the request is being processed! And what am I doing in the meantime? How can I break rock without dynamite? He finally agrees to call his boss and explain the problem. His boss, Mr. Arthur, says that he doesn't know the company number and also doesn't have the authority to give it out if he did have it. But he would look into the matter.

"Get hold of that answer. Here I am with a crew of men, trying to meet the lousy standards, and I'm told by a pretty high-up boss that he'll look into the matter. By this time, it's time for me to have my break, and boy, I'm in a mood to have one. What I really needed was some suds, but I knew the mangement would blow their lid if I took off. I go for my coffee, and who do I bump into but Harry here. Harry can see that I'm hot to go and asks me the problem. After I tell him, he tells me that he had the same problem two months ago and was still waiting for an answer! The problem is in the hands of the security people. It seems that the VP of operations is afraid that when we give out the company Social Security number, all hell's going to break loose. Boy, they must know something I don't know!

"So I ask Harry what he's going to do about it, and he says he's waiting for the brass to make a decision. In the meantime, he's got his men doing other kinds of work that don't require blasting. I wasn't about to take that 'sit and wait' approach. I sent too many requests up the line that took weeks and weeks to get solved. So I miss my standards, and when I tell my boss the reasons, he said I was giving excuses, not reasons. They weren't going to play games with me any more."

"What'd you do, Eddie?"

"I took the crew out to the job. I got off the truck in town and borrowed a guy's car who works for the telephone company. I drove out to the Deep River Project area and slipped some of the guys a few bucks for some dynamite. I took the blasting stuff to the job, and we got the work done. It took two days instead of one, but if I waited it would have put me back a week.

"I'll tell you what, though. When I saw how slow the higher management was and how they didn't care about my problems, yet were going to hold me responsible, I decided, right then and there, to get with a company that knew which end was up. Higher management sits at their fancy desks in nice offices at headquarters and doesn't give two hoots for us in the field. They couldn't make a decision, which forced me to, and to stick my neck out!

"Harry, was anything I said a lie?"

"No, but you just don't realize that higher management has other things on its mind. Besides, let's stop complaining. Drink your beer, I gotta go soon . . . tonight's barbershop practice."

Since early childhood, we have all made thousands of decisions. Some we have felt were good, and some bad. Many of us like to make decisions, many of us try to avoid them. For many, the right to make one's own decisions is a matter of "principle." Yet even though we sometimes like to feel that we have the power to make decisions, we may be happier when someone else "sticks his neck out" and makes the troublesome ones. A hermit on a desert island may make difficult decisions, but he doesn't have the problems associated with relating them to the decisions of others. Often we find ourselves in situations like Eddie's, which caused him to quit; he could not get a decision from his boss and had to go ahead on his own.

In this chapter, we discuss the decision-making process, which is fundamental not only for each individual but also for any manager. In fact, all a manager's functions involve decisions; thus, we discuss the decision-making process as the first function of the management process. A manager is oriented toward making decisions rather than toward performing the actions himself; the actions are carried out by others. A manager may therefore be viewed as a specialist in the art of decision making.

What is a decision?

The decision-making process of management is affected by the environment of the decision maker, the role that he assumes, and the mental process developed in his past experiences. The product of the process is called a *decision*—a course of action consciously chosen from available alternatives for the purpose of achieving a desired result. Thus a decision is (1) a choice, (2) the

decision

result of conscious mental activity, and (3) directed toward a purpose. For example, if we have no choice among alternatives, we cannot make a decision; if we act without conscious effort, we merely act without a decision; if we have no purpose, we have no target for a desired result.

When do you make a decision?

The manager must be conscious that his decisions occur in sequence. One decision may be required before another, and therefore, the time for making a decision is itself an important decision. For example, if you are reading this sentence, it is the result of a prior decision to start this chapter. You always have the choice of stopping immediately or continuing to read.

A manager must develop the art of deciding upon the proper time for making a decision. This art involves several subdecisions: Is the question now pertinent? Do you understand enough about the matter, or should you seek more information? Do you have the time for further deliberation? If you make the decision, can you make it effective? Should the decision be made by someone else? Should other people be involved in making it? How will this decision affect your future decisions? It is clear that even a simple decision raises important questions.

When one realizes that he, as an individual, has limited knowledge, limited time, limited mental ability, and limited possibilities for making a decision effective, it is clear that any discussion of the decision-making process must involve a simplified picture of the real situation. In this chapter, we describe a simplified logical process by which an individual manager can proceed. Second, we see how many manager's decisions are in fact influenced by others, individually or in groups. In the next chapter, we offer some of the most important aids to decision making that have evolved from several other approaches: techniques developed by economists to optimize, techniques developed by management scientists that help in situations of risks and uncertainty, and concepts developed by behavioral scientists.

A SIMPLIFIED RATIONAL PROCESS

Although decision making cannot be reduced to any formula, it is useful to develop a simplified approach for reaching decisions. Outstanding practicing managers are at a loss when asked to describe just what they do. In evaluating a past decision, the results of that decision (satisfactory or unsatisfactory) must not be the only consideration, since chance may have been a significant factor in the result. It is helpful to use certain elements of decision making as guides both to improve one's decision-making process and to evaluate decisions after they have been made. These elements may occur in the order in which they are discussed here; however, the sequence is not rigidly fixed in actual practice.

So you want to be logical —what's the pitch?

A logical process for developing a rational decision includes (see also Figure 9.1):

1. Consciousness of the problem-provoking situation
2. Diagnosis, recognition of the critical problem, and problem definition
3. Search for and analysis of available alternatives and their probable consequences
4. Evaluation of alternatives and selection of a course of action
5. Acceptance of the solution by the organization

Consciousness of the Problem-Provoking Situation

A good decision depends upon the maker's being consciously aware of the factors that set the stage for the decision. Past actions and decisions provide clues. The situation surrounding the maker sets the stage for determining whether matters are within his power and whether any decision by him is feasible. Predetermined objectives provide the focus for the decision at hand.

Many decisions seem to be simple at first glance merely because the maker fails to comprehend the number of factors that affect his situation. An open mind, breadth of knowledge, and past experience may tend to complicate the task of decision making by increasing his awareness of the number of factors involved.

What is relevant?

Confusion is not uncommon or unhealthy at this stage; however, the decision maker must recognize that he cannot consider

FIGURE 9.1 The five basic elements in a rational decision-making process

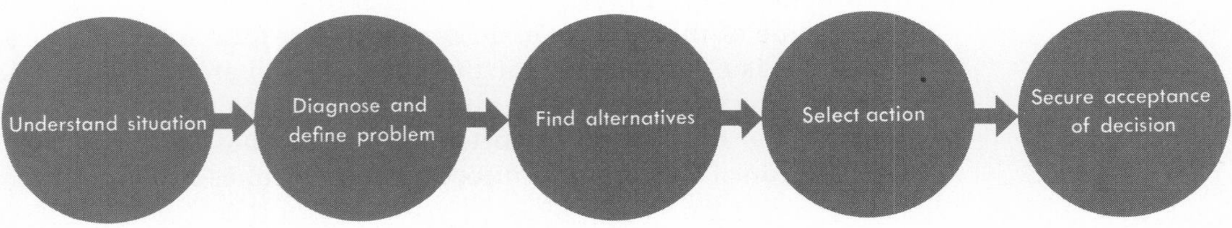

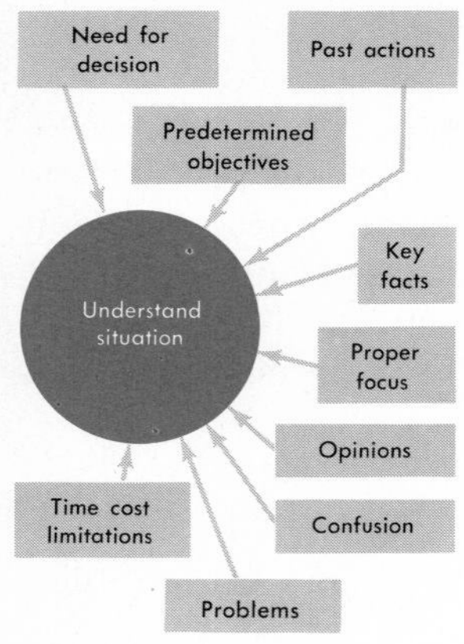

FIGURE 9.2 Inputs to diagnosing and defining the problem

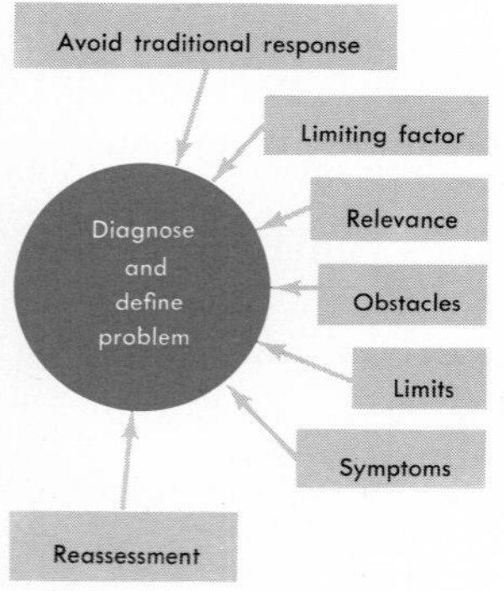

FIGURE 9.3 Inputs to understanding the situation

all the facts and that he must develop a selective approach for keeping the most important and relevant facts in mind. He may saturate his mind with facts about the situation, yet by concentrating on the key aspects, he may avoid factual indigestion.

At this stage, your creative ability is put to the test. If time is available, you, the decision maker, may find that allowing the facts to simmer in your mind will provide opportunities for sudden insights. Some people find that discussing the situation with others tends to lubricate their own thought processes. You may "brainstorm" with a group of your associates. The key at this stage is to refrain from jumping to a single conclusion no matter how fine it sounds, or from laughing at a contribution no matter how silly it appears. This first step too often is neglected; however, there is no substitute for attempting to lay a good foundation by *understanding the situation* (Figure 9.2).

The consciousness of the situation will emerge gradually, raising doubts and confusion in your mind. At this stage, you might appreciate the wisdom of those who say. "If you can keep your head in all this confusion, you don't understand the situation." If you realize that confusion is inherent in the decision-making process, you may avoid some frustration.

At this first stage, you as a manager must face two questions: To which of your many problems should you direct your attention? and, How much time, effort, and expense should you invest in resolving uncertainty about that problem? The answer to the first question determines whether you concentrate on obvious day-to-day problems, or search out a deeper and more fundamental problem whose answer will solve the more immediate ones. The answer to the second question determines whether you settle for satisfactory answers or continue to search for the best.

It is at this stage that you must continue to be practical in your attitude. Do not create in your mind problems that do not exist—you have enough real problems. It is at this stage that you will need to stay on top of your job and not have the job crush you.

An alert, creative, and intelligent manager will usually find in any situation more problems than he has time to give his attention to. For some of these, he may delegate the last four steps to a subordinate. It is at this stage that the manager will show whether he has a tendency to run away from important major problems by spending his time on unimportant problems that he can answer easily. He must beware of a directive once emphasized by a large organization: "Make a decision, right or wrong, but make a decision." It is true that one weakness of some managers, like those in Northwestern Power in the vignette, is the reluctance to ever make a clear decision. On the other hand, before going to the second stage in the process, the manager must be alert to the possibility that many problems exist.

Diagnosis: Recognition of the Problem and Its Definition

Once the manager is aware that something needs attention, he proceeds to diagnose the situation. Since it is impossible for him to weigh all the facts, the manager must develop a means of sifting out the relevant ones (Figure 9.3). In the classification of these facts, he can then define the problem. The more completely the problem can be stated, the easier the other steps will be. By this time, you, the manager, should have cleared your mind of any habitual or traditional responses to the situation. If the habitual had been sufficient, there would have been no problem. Even when current operations appear to be proceeding nicely, the good manager will not relax and assume that there are no problems.

limiting factor

The proper definition of the right problem depends on the use of the concept called the *limiting factor.* In identifying the limiting factor, the manager seeks a clear definition that will strike at the heart of the issue and provide residual answers to lesser problems. A key problem has the characteristic of being closely related to a series of other problems. The most damaging proof of a poor definition of the problem is to find that the problem remains after you have identified the limiting factor and tried to solve it.

diagnosis

A good *diagnosis* includes both the reasons leading up to the need for decision and the obstacles standing in the way of achieving your objectives. A diagnosis consists of a search for symptoms. Many of the techniques described in Chapter 10 will help in this search. The search must be based on a clear recognition of the desired results, the obstacles faced, and the limits within which a solution must fall.

definition of the problem

A clear *definition of the problem* is needed. Consider a doctor who is informed by a patient that his stomach aches; the doctor would be no better than a layman if he merely recorded "stomach aches." He must use tests to determine the reason for the ache, exactly what is causing it, and the limitations of the solution. An aspirin may resolve the ache, but it may not treat the cause of it. Or

Just what is a "clear definition"?

perhaps you have seen someone trying to get a car started. The driver makes the statement, "The car won't start"; this may indicate a problem, but it does not include a good diagnosis or a definition of the problem. An experienced mechanic will quickly seek to determine whether the battery is turning the engine over. He would not start to look into problems of compression, the generator, or the distributor until he defined more clearly the exact problem—it might be merely a dead battery!

The diagnosis and definition of the problem is a recurring process. Reassessment and reconsideration of the issues help keep the decision-making process realistic and in touch with a changing set of conditions.

Search for and Analysis of Available Alternatives

Recent studies have emphasized the third phase of the decision-making process—the search for potential courses of action and the quantitative analysis of the probable consequences of each perceived alternative (Figure 9.4). This phase then involves a search process and an analytical process. The first is a creative art, but the second has developed into a scientific field of study based on probability concepts.

How can you come up with a bright idea?

THE ROLE OF CREATIVITY Creativity in a manager is always assumed to be a most important and desirable characteristic; however, it is generally difficult to capture in a nutshell just how a person can develop his creative talents. The painter, the musician, the architect, and the inspired marketer seem to develop this skill to a greater degree. Many successful firms have been chiefly the result of a simple creative idea on the part of a promoter-enterpriser who may have had little skill in other management aspects. Each of us has some potential for developing a new idea, but we must not smother these possibilities through stereotyped thinking. This phase is dependent upon developing an *attitude* toward viewing life's experiences and an independent way of thinking that asks, "Why not be unconventional?" We shall look further into this attitude in our discussion of innovation in Chapter 21.

FIGURE 9.4 Inputs to finding alternatives

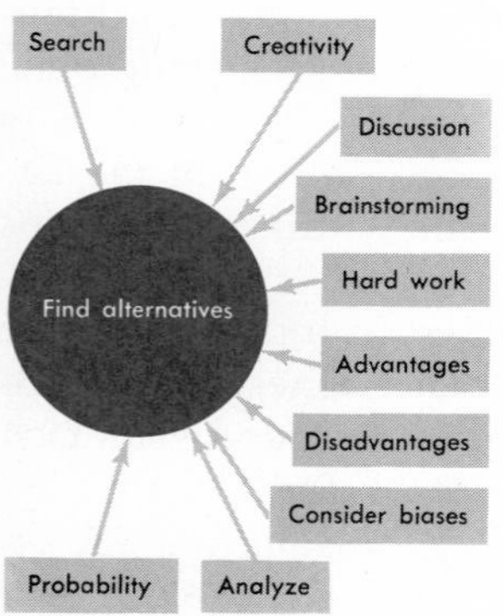

From time to time, writers have proposed systems for encouraging creativity, apparently failing to see that any such system must create constraints, since these are inherent in all systems. However, you may profit from checking some books on how to be creative.[1] Some simple examples might give you a hint as to how to improve your own creative ability:

1. "Picking the brains" of others, by personal discussions with people who appear to reach out for new ideas
2. *Brainstorming,* in which a group of people meet and toss out ideas to each other, recording them for further study without evaluating whether they are brilliant or silly

NARROWING DOWN THE ALTERNATIVES The search for possible alternatives can often be organized by identifying the desirable characteristics of a good solution. As Edison explained, his search for the proper element for his electric light bulb was a matter of *perspiration* rather than *inspiration.* All of us, however, tend to have sporadic new ideas that flit through our minds and then are quickly forgotten. Try writing down these ideas for future consideration. As you develop a series of alternatives, it is a simple process to list the advantages and disadvantages of each. However, do not fall into the trap of selecting an alternative with ten advantages over one with five advantages; weigh *each* advantage and disadvantage carefully.

How many possibilities can you juggle in your head?

The number of alternatives to be considered is itself a difficult decision. In order to make a choice, there must be at least two alternatives. However, the human mind seems to have difficulty in handling more than six or seven alternatives. Thus, the development of a few alternatives by a process of elimination is generally a first step. Often three are studied in some detail. A decision tree, a useful graphical device for clearly showing different alternatives and the consequences of each, will be described in the next chapter.

If . . . then . . .?

LOGICAL PREMISES Each decision involves a large number of mental "if–thens"—"if we do this, then that result will occur." A general error in making quick decisions is to consider the result without clearly recognizing the "if." It is necessary to train oneself to search for assumptions, many of which might be unconscious,

[1] See Calvin W. Taylor, ed., *Creativity* (New York: McGraw-Hill, 1964); Derek Castle, *Creativity: A Tool of Development in Business* (Sydney, Australia: West Publishing Corporation, 1963); R. W. Gerard, "How the Brain Creates Ideas," in *A Source Book for Creative Thinking,* eds. S. J. Barnes and H. F. Harding (New York: Scribner's, 1962); and Carl E. Gregory, *The Management of Intelligence* (New York: McGraw-Hill, 1967).

factual premise
value premise

or at least concealed. Decision-making premises may be factual or a matter of judgment based upon one's values. The distinction is important when testing the validity of premises. A *factual premise* can be proved by observable and measurable means. A *value premise* can be only subjectively asserted to be valid. In considering value premises, it is desirable to recognize our biases. If we feel that we can eliminate our biases, we may be failing to consider value premises to which we have long been attached. Whenever we can base a decision on factual premises, we eliminate biases; yet often we must rely on value premises, and we must understand that they are subjective and subject to errors in judgment.

THE ROLE OF PROBABILITY The consequences of each alternative are usually a matter of probability—what is the chance that the result will turn out in different ways?—because most decisions involve uncertainty. Great advances have been made in techniques for handling decisions under conditions of risk, and we shall outline these techniques in Chapter 10.

SEARCH FOR FACTS The analysis of each alternative depends upon determining the *relevant* facts of each, relating facts in such a way that derived facts emerge, and rechecking validity by continued search. Intensive search for more facts is costly, and the value of added information reaches a point of diminishing usefulness. The decision maker needs to remain conscious of the relation of the value of added facts to their costs. The greater the number of alternatives considered, the greater the need for facts. A critical element of judgment involves the time in which sufficient facts and alternatives have been considered so that one can proceed to the next step of evaluation.

Evaluation of Alternatives and Selection of a Course of Action

OK, now, what's the answer?

The crucial step in the decision-making process, of course, is the selection of the solution (Figure 9.5). At this stage, the ranking of preferences is important. The manager who must make decisions quickly may have to settle for only a satisfactory solution; often, what is theoretically best may be only slightly better than a number of satisfactory decisions. The consequences of an alternative occur in sets, some favorable and some unfavorable. A selection involves a comparison of these sets and picking the alternative that appears wisest under the specific circumstances. This

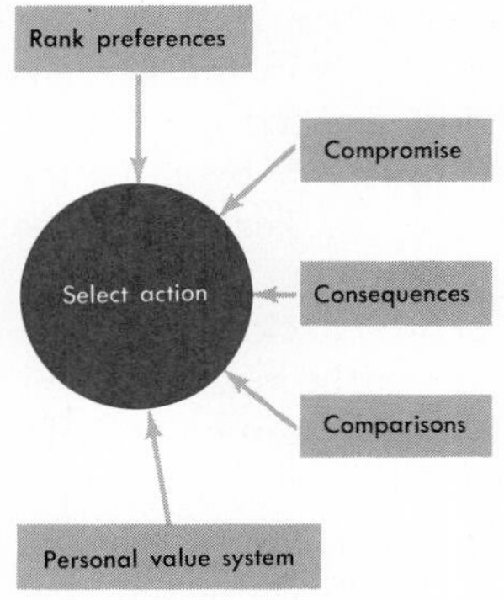

FIGURE 9.5 Inputs to selecting action

comparison may be reduced to a weighing of the values and costs of each alternative. The best technique will depend upon the problem at hand, the situation, and the person making the decision. If the selection appears to be simple, it may indicate superficial consideration of the factors (which is bad) or great skill of the decision maker in reducing the essential elements to a clear-cut set (which is good).

An important factor in this stage of the decision-making process is the preference of the decision maker. He may tend to select the alternative that is the least risky; he may want to select the alternative that gives him more security in his mind. Many times his selection depends on whether he wishes to decide in a manner that will meet others' expectations or one that will indicate his own power. At this stage, the decision maker must consciously outline for himself just what his preferences are.

No matter how much factual information and scientific analysis are used in the decision-making process, the actual selection of the alternative is based on the decision maker's own value system. Thus, he will do well to understand his value system, so that he will have certain guides for making the final selection.

Securing Acceptance of the Decision

Will the decision make any difference in actual practice?

The decision process is directed toward securing action (Figure 9.6). If others are affected, the decision must be communicated to them; they must be motivated to implement the decision; furthermore, control provides information for future decisions. Whereas this element might be considered to be outside the decision-making process, it frequently affects the other elements of the process and should be considered as its final phase. At times, the manager may treat his decision as tentative until he tries it out on his colleagues. Often at this stage, he may desire to restate his decision differently from the way he had conceived it. At times, a decision may be made and held in mind—the manager may not communicate it to others or attempt to implement it immediately.

FIGURE 9.6 Inputs to securing acceptance of the decision

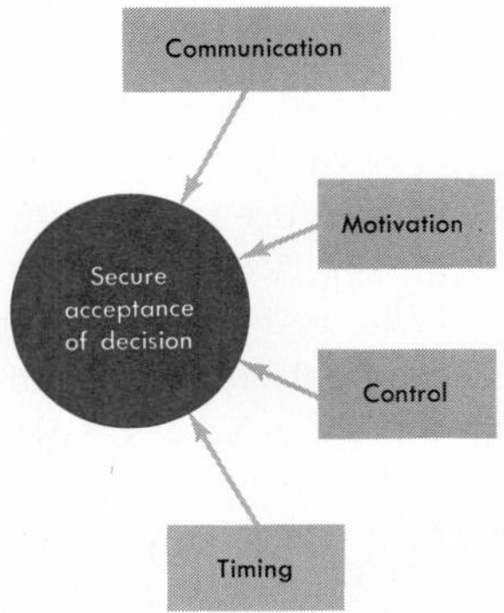

A managerial decision's success depends not only on its quality but also on the effectiveness of its implementation. A decision may appear as a good one to the maker but to others as poor. Implementation of a decision is the product of the avoidance of conflict of interest, the recognition of the risk factor, and the degree of understanding by those who must carry out the decision. Thus, the organization must not only be given the decision but be made aware of the key factors that were considered in reaching it.

The five steps outlined above form a framework for the decision-making process; however, the techniques used in the process may vary depending upon the type of decision making employed. Two types of decision can be distinguished: decision by *initiation* and by *approval.* In the first type, the decision maker originates the process; in the second, the decision maker receives recommendations that he approves, disapproves, or sends back for further study. The qualities needed by managers in initiating decisions are different from those needed in approving recommendations. When decision by approval is used, group interactions become more important.

This five-step simplified process is sometimes criticized, because in practice even good decisions involve emotional overtones and complications that are not explained by any rational process. Moreover, many decisions are made by several people, often acting as a group. Since group decision processes may be more complex, the following section focuses on the factors involved when groups effect decisions.

DECISION MAKING BY GROUPS

Should others help make a decision?

In a cooperative endeavor, one person may appear to have made the decision when, in fact, that person has performed only one step in the process. Managers usually make decisions in a social environment. *A* may provide a fact; *B* may provide a premise; *C* may provide a value judgment; *D* may supply one complete alternative; *E* may supply a second alternative. Even if not all are present at the time of the final choice, each has had a definite part in the process. In fact, organization may be viewed as an interrelationship of decision centers. Cooperative decision making is a process by which a group attempts to develop a composite or organization mind.

In large firms facing complex problems, decisions emerge from a series of meetings in which managers jointly approach problems. These group meetings may be called conferences, committees, boards, task forces, or merely staff meetings.

Decision making is just one of many possible assignments for committees. Furthermore, formal committees constitute only one of the many possible forms of group decision making. As a result, the manager must develop an understanding of these possibilities so that he can answer, to his own satisfaction, several important questions:

Are committees worth the time spent in meetings?

1. Should group decision making be used extensively in the organization?
2. What types of problems are best tackled by groups?
3. If groups are used, how should the meetings be conducted?

Should you use committees as a chief decision technique?

Operating managers usually have strong opinions on the answers to these questions; however, opinions range all the way from outlawing any idea of group decision making to continual use of groups. Whether to use a committee or some other group method of decision making is a question that can be approached by comparing the advantages and disadvantages listed in Table 9.1.

Some problems lend themselves to committee action better than others do. Any decision requiring deliberation by a group of specialists tends to encourage the committee approach. Often, the conclusions of a committee are said to be advisory, the actual decision being made by a single line officer. In practice, if the members have maintained close contact with the appointing authority, the "advisory" committee report becomes the basis for action on the decision.

A decision involving implementation by several departments

TABLE 9.1 Advantages and Disadvantages of Decision-Making by Committees

Advantages	Disadvantages
A decision can be approached from *different viewpoints* by individual specialists on a committee.	Considering the value of the time of each individual member (as measured by his salary), committees are costly.
Coordination of activities of separate departments can be attained through joint interactions in meetings.	The length of time a committee requires to reach a decision makes its use inadvisable if a decision must be made promptly.
Motivation of individual members to carry out a decision may be increased by the *feeling of participation* in the decision-making process.	Group action may lead to compromise and indecision.
Committees provide a means by which executives can be *trained* in decision-making.	If the superior line executive is present at a meeting, the decision may be made individually by him with subordinates attempting to appear competent by proposing ideas they believe he likes.
Committees permit *representation* of different interest groups.	Committee decisions may result in a method by which no one is held responsible for a decision; thus "buck passing" may result.
Group discussion is one method of *creative* thinking; a fragmentary idea by one member may create a chain reaction in the minds of others present.	

calls for some means by which the departments become involved in the decision making. Committees are means by which each department can obtain the benefit of comments from other departments. The joint decision made in a committee tends to be a balanced decision that takes into account interactions of different viewpoints. Planning decisions lend themselves to committee work, whereas implementation of orders tends to be clearer when made by a single line executive. Committees are extremely weak when forceful, immediate action is needed.

How should you handle a decision-making meeting?

Many criticisms of committee activities result from the lack of thought about how to handle a group in the process of making a decision. Typically, if advance thought is given to a meeting, the chairman often assumes that *Robert's Rules of Order* will provide the "best way" to handle the meeting. Because group interactions are time-consuming, business managers make use of formal devices, such as agenda for the meeting, minutes of the secretary, and motions and votes on motions, to expedite the business of the group. Often, a formal meeting merely rubber-stamps a decision previously arrived at by a line executive or a staff group.

Research on small groups has indicated several principles of group participation that provide guides for group interaction:[2]

1. The physical layout, size of the group, and general atmosphere are important factors determining the effectiveness of problem solving. For example, a meeting located in the boss's office will be entirely different from one held in a "neutral" conference room. If the committee has only three members, it may not have enough "interaction"; if it has thirty members, it is difficult for each member to participate freely.
2. Threat reduction is an important objective in the planning for group action so that the group will shift from interpersonal problems to group goals. Any tendency to put a member "on the spot" or to force him to "take sides" will increase the debating-society feeling and will result in an increase of tension.
3. The best group leadership is performed by the entire group; it is not the job of the "chairman," "secretary," or other formal leader. A group that functions well tends to function informally, with no single person providing all the leadership. Leadership may shift, and different types of leaders may evolve. One member may serve as the social leader, another

[2] E.g., see J. R. Gibb, G. N. Platts, and L. F. Miller, *Dynamics of Participative Groups* (St. Louis, Mo.: Swift and Co., 1959).

may serve as "questioner," another as "clarifier" or "summarizer," and so forth.

4. Goals should be explicitly formulated by the group. The group should refrain from being "fenced in" by predetermined rules. The objective is to increase the involvement of each member in the decision-making process.
5. An agenda should be formulated by the group, but it should be changed as new goals develop from new needs. Preplanning for meetings should retain flexibility so that the group maintains its ability to meet new issues.
6. The decision-making process should continue until the group formulates a solution upon which it can form a consensus. If the group action results in a minority opinion, the group has failed to maximize its effectiveness. In a group that emphasizes this principle, there is no formal voting. Discussion continues until no one in the group can add any improvements to the solution.
7. Any group should be made aware of the interaction process by which it arrives at solutions. In this manner, the skill of being a member of a group becomes a distinguishable skill that the executive can develop. This principle leads to the idea that group actions are important subjects for study; continual evaluations should be made of group processes.

The need for improvement of group decision processes is great in all types of organization. The foregoing principles offer a definite viewpoint that may be helpful in crystallizing thought about group decision making.

Decisions vary in complexity and importance, whether they are made primarily by individuals or by groups. The more complex and important a decision, the greater the need for useful decision rules. The complexity of a decision increases as the number of variables to be considered increases, as the degree of uncertainty increases, and as more value judgments are required. The importance of a decision increases when more decisions are dependent on it, when more subordinates are involved, and when the financial consequences are more critical.

SUMMARY AND PROPOSITIONS

Decision making is so important to management that some authorities feel that, in the final analysis, it is the single function of management. As you continue to study this book, the decision-making process will become clearer and progressively more usable. All other managerial functions have a decision-oriented component. Thus the subject of decision making is interrelated very closely with other subjects of this book. In the next chapter, we summarize some of the aids available for use in the process.

You will need to make continual reference to this chapter's ideas in your further study of this book; therefore, the following propositions can help you:

1. A human being intends to be rational in making his choices.
   a. One process for increasing rationality includes five elements: consciousness of the problem-provoking situation; diagnosis, or the recognition of the problem and its definition; search for and analysis of available alternatives; evaluation of alternatives and selection of a course of action; and securing acceptance of the decision.
   b. What may be rational to one person may not appear to be rational to another; therefore, each person should check his own intended rationality by examination through a different perspective.
2. The decision of whether or not to make a decision is critical to good management.
   a. At times, a manager may not want to stick his neck out; he may leave the decision to someone else, so that he allows himself more room to maneuver later if the decision is poor.
   b. Successful decision making depends on postponing questions that are not now pertinent or on which not enough information is available; not making decisions that cannot be made effective; and not making decisions that someone else should make.
   c. Each decision requires time, effort, and expense; thus, the cost of making a decision should be considered.
3. Having a large number of people involved in the decision-making process tends to appear democratic (and thus good) and to improve the acceptance of the decision.
4. Group decision making diffuses the responsibility for a decision and thus protects the individuals from embarrassment from mistakes.
5. The quality of a decision should be evaluated on the basis of the situation confronted by the decision maker at the time of the decision, not on the developments (some chance and some out of the control of the decision maker at that time) that later appear.
   a. Even a perfect decision (at the time of the decision) may, in fact, later turn out to be unfortunate.

b. Even the worst decision made with no thought at all may turn out to be favorable.

STUDY ASSIGNMENTS

1. If Eddie (in the vignette) was frustrated by management's indecision on giving out the number he needed to obtain dynamite, what other alternatives did he have to resolve the problem?

2. What considerations important to management, but about which Eddie was not aware, could have been reasons for the "red tape"? Should management have made these clear to Eddie? How could they have improved their handling of the matter?

3. What are the reasons that many argue that decision making is the most important managerial function?

4. What guidelines are available for saying whether a decision is a good one or a bad one?

5. Why is a good diagnosis necessary before looking for answers in the decision-making process?

6. Show how the identification of "limiting factors" can help in a diagnosis.

7. How many alternatives do you feel are best to consider before making a decision? Can there be too many? Can there be too few?

8. Many writers do not include "securing acceptance of decisions" as part of the rational decision process. Give the reasons that support the inclusion of this final step in the process.

9. How can group decision making result in better decisions? What reasons can you think of for not *bringing others into the decision process?*

10. Discuss your reaction to each of the principles of group participation. What reasoning supports each? What criticisms may be relevant for each?

11. Consider an important decision that you have made recently. Review in your mind how the five steps discussed in this chapter could have helped you in reaching that decision.

12. Suppose you are asked to help a friend make an important decision. Show how this analysis permits you to contribute to his process of thinking and prevent his jumping to a conclusion.

situational episodes

1. You have a four-year-old car that has cost you 100% of its "Blue Book" value to maintain during the last year. Like a typical American, you like the convenience of having a car to commute 15 miles to school (a city bus could take you from home to school with a total walk of four blocks), to see the girls on weekends (you have a number of friends who have cars), to take off to Florida during spring vacation, and to use in emergencies—for example, if you get sick, or simply must have a beer at the tavern. You don't trust used-car salesmen, but you don't know enough about mechanics to really identify a lemon or handle any major repair on your old car. You like to think of yourself as a person who doesn't throw money away, but you might be rationalizing when you think you should buy another car. You are thinking to yourself, "How should I make this decision? Should I first determine how to pay for it? Budget? Borrow? What other factors should I consider? What else do I need? This isn't one decision—if I think much more, I'll be making a number of decisions. Maybe I'd better ask my buddy to decide for me. But *that's* a decision! I don't like decisions—I might make a wrong one—But dammit, *that's* a decision! Maybe that professor in class today was right when he said, 'The decision-making process is not only critical for managers; this part of the course could help you in just living.' Well, anyway, I'll check that chapter and see whether it will help me decide on what to do about putting wheels under me!"

   How does this chapter help you decide on purchasing a new car?

2. You have been married for six months and want to continue your college education. You have been supported about 50% by your parents; your wife is attending the same college as you are; you have a part-time job that keeps the wolf from your door.

   You received a long-distance call last night that your father had died suddenly. You are getting ready to go with your wife to be with your mother and to attend the funeral. You are confident that your mother will have enough from your father's estate to live on, but she will not have enough now to provide the 50% support for your schooling. You are pretty upset and confused now, since you were close to your father. Yet you know that you will have a big decision to make: whether to drop out of school and get a full time job, or somehow continue your schooling.

   You haven't had time to think much about it, and you will

need to obtain more facts. Your present feeling is that it will help you psychologically if you at least make a decision as to how to make the college-vs.-job decision. Since you had just been studying about the decision process, you are glad that you have some general guidelines. But on the other hand, what real help can all that textbook stuff be in a real-life decision crisis?

a. What further thought should you give to the five-step decision process to help you decide whether to decide? or when to decide? or whether to leave it to your wife to decide? or to decide to make the final decision in a couple of weeks?
b. What additional facts should you secure before you make the school-vs.-job decision?
c. Will it help to write down all alternatives that come to your mind?
d. What criteria do you feel will be most important in choosing among your alternatives?
e. Is this decision irreversible? Can you later make a different one if you find that you first made a bad decision?

Concepts and Techniques of Decision Making

TEN

OBJECTIVES YOU SHOULD MEET

State *the concepts of optimization, suboptimization, opportunity costs, and incremental costs.*

Construct *a simple breakeven chart.*

Illustrate and interpret *three financial ratios that have most value in decision making.*

Explain *what a funds statement can tell a manager.*

State *the concept of satisficing used by administrative man.*

Define and illustrate *the meaning of probability and three methods of estimating it.*

Construct *a payoff table and a decision tree.*

WHAT TECHNIQUES CAN I USE IN DECISION MAKING?

The board of directors of HCC had just reviewed the operating reports for the past month, presented by the controller and each of the division managers. Mr. Parker, the chief executive, asked for questions concerning the reports and then commented that the reports had been improved in the last two years, since the company had installed a computer—the information for the past month was now available to operating personnel within ten days after the end of the month, and information about each manager's own operations was now available to all operating people, and not just sitting in the accounting department.

"It is now possible for each manager, including every first-line supervisor, to have timely information for making daily decisions," Mr. Parker said, "but we now must face up to a new problem: How do we develop each of our managers so that they can make best use of the mass of information flowing from the computer in the accounting department? I have asked Bob Seeger in our management training department to develop a program focusing on interpretation of our operating data by managers at all levels. Even those of us on the board of directors have difficulty in pinpointing the most relevant information, and so I am sure that our young managers will have difficulty in making use of the reports flowing from accounting. We hired our operating people for their technical know-how, and we have been doing a pretty good job in our training sessions to help them adjust to the human factors of their job. Bob will now concentrate on some training sessions for managers on techniques for understanding numbers.

"Bob has some ideas of offering some short courses in accounting, economics, and statistics, but he prefers to organize these sessions around daily problems that will be more meaningful to our own people, and not merely offer some dry academic lectures. He has asked me to

find out from you what type of problems you feel would help most in answering decision issues in our own operations. Got any suggestions?"

The first to speak up was John. "Mr. Parker, this idea is really getting down to what we need—not a lot of theory, but refining some basic things that help in our decisions. Yes, I have one issue that recurs continually when I talk with division managers. We have each division set up as a profit center, with contracts and revenue handled within the division, but the division people can't understand why they are charged for administrative overhead. They understand that gross profit is merely gross revenue minus cost of goods. They also see that selling expenses and the overhead of their own division must be covered by their operations. They can visualize the breakeven concept for their own division, but they get upset when we point out that the corporation's administrative costs—your salary, accounting costs, company training, and so on—must be covered before the company can realize a net profit! They're always telling me that they are making money in their division but that the reason the company profits are so low is that company administrative costs are usually 10 to 15% of gross revenue. Could Bob direct some of his attention to explaining the idea of contribution toward fixed costs and profits, and demonstrate some of the basic things about breakeven analysis?"

"John, that is the type of suggestion I'm looking for. As one of those whose salary is in the central office and therefore a part of administrative overhead, I would think our divisions should be aware of the fact that even decentralized divisions must be oriented to the good of the entire company. Do any others have any other specific suggestions for our training program?"

"Yes, Mr. Parker," said Pete, a division manager, "I must continually review our bids for new jobs, and my people do a good job in building up our estimates with current costs for each part—materials, labor and so forth. But I have problems getting them to build into their thinking that even though these costs may be true at the time of the bid, in times of inflation a job that takes two years to complete will face probable overruns because of price increases. I haven't thought through the details of what I would like Bob to cover, but I would say that the big problem is to cover some of the ways that the degree of risks we face in carrying out a job after we are successful in bidding can be spelled out. You see, I must choose which bids are possibly most profitable, but I need more definite information for determining the margin of profit to add to our costs in bidding. We used to add 10 percent for the profit margin, but now we know that we end up losing money on some of our bids because risks are higher in some jobs—I mean, we take chances on the weather, changes in prices, and the chance that our subcontractors won't meet their schedules. Concisely, we are trying to develop means by which we add a risk factor to our thinking so that we can make our bidding better. Several of us can agree that the risks are greater in Job A than in Job B, but we need to determine by how much. Then we can arrive at a better planned profit

margin for each job. This type of training for all our manager personnel would pay out directly in better profit projections."

"Pete, that area is very important. Bob, are you taking notes? . . . Let's keep going—this board meeting is turning out to be really useful, and not just rubber-stamping of management's actions. Any more ideas?"

Ed spoke. "Well, boss, I'm not sure whether my suggestion is as fundamental as John's and Pete's, but I'll add my two cents for the training program. Mine relates to our critical problem of cash flow and to our current ratio in the range of 1.3. I know we are growing and making money, but I'm worried whether we might go bankrupt amid all this profit. The problem appears to be that our divisions make increased sales by dealing with some people who don't pay their bills on time. The division managers don't worry about this very much, since the accounts receivable are handled on a companywide basis and the tardy payments don't appear in their profit centers as a cost; they end up as general administrative costs—higher interest charges. Bob could review the impact of these tardy payments and show how we should all focus on improving our cash flow, or else we may all be out of a job, with no flow!"

"These three suggestions have been very helpful," said Mr. Parker. "We don't have any more time now, but I want each operating manager to submit requests to Bob for other specific aids to our decision making. If we don't keep up with the current techniques, our competitors will; then, we will lose out even if we are technically sound and keep satisfied employees. This discussion has impressed on me that we all need to attend Bob's sessions and do a little more homework on our own decision making."

The discussion of the decision-making process by individuals and groups in the preceding chapter was both prescriptive (identifying what steps should be taken) and simplified for practical use (focusing on real problems and their solutions). The discussion was kept simple so that you could view the process as a whole and see why it is central to a manager's duties. The subject, however, has received a large amount of attention by specialists in many disciplines that have produced a number of key concepts and techniques fundamental to the development of improved managerial decisions.

What fields of study offer aids to making better decisions?

This chapter summarizes selected concepts from several disciplines and explains some of the principal techniques generally in use by managers, techniques that have been refined rigorously for the purpose of making the decision process more scientific, or at least more systematic. We start first with the classical economics approach and explain how some of the most-used techniques employed by economists and accountants can help in analyzing the factors introduced in the decision-making steps of diagnosis, search for alternatives, and selection of a course of action. Then we proceed to a behavioral description of decision making, with its emphasis on psychological and sociological aspects of human behavior. Finally, we outline the recent contributions of management science and its quantitative contribution to decision theory.

This interdisciplinary perspective of decision making will help you make use of knowledge available in courses in other disciplines and should encourage you to integrate the most important concepts and techniques in your own managerial decision making.

ECONOMIC CONCEPTS USEFUL IN A MANAGER'S DECISION MAKING

Optimization—The Manager as an Economic Man

economic man

optimization

Do people really act like economic men?

The subject of economics, in its focus on scarce resources (supply) in the satisfying of human wants (demand), assumes that man is motivated by economic matters and that a manager will make decisions as an economic man. As an *economic man,* he will act rationally—that is, he will decide on the allocation of scarce resources in such a way as to maximize profits. The objective of the manager as an economic man is assumed to be *optimization*—that is, the obtaining of the best results from maximizing revenue and minimizing costs. The assumptions for this rational approach are (1) that a manager will have complete knowledge of all alternatives available to him, and that he knows the consequences of each alternative; (2) that he has the ability to order his preferences, and to obtain, process, and use all this information in making optimal decisions; (3) that all the information regarding goals, outcomes, and alternatives is readily available and free of cost to the decision maker; (4) and that there are no noneconomic conflicts among organization members.

Although you may quickly notice that the assumed world of the economist is most difficult, or even impossible, to reproduce in the real world of the manager, the rigor of economics made possible by these limiting assumptions provides the manager with certain concepts important in his decision-making process.

suboptimize

Certainly, it is helpful to seek an optimum solution and to utilize techniques that will help analyze revenue and costs in a manner that will approach the ideal or optimum. Furthermore, the field of managerial economics has provided useful guidelines for attempting to optimize. One problem in applying economic concepts and techniques is that a manager must consider other objectives in addition to the purely economic ones. Also, in an organization, a marketing manager may view volume of sales and revenue as the central objective for him, whereas a production manager may view reduction of costs as the central objective. Each of these managers may thus *suboptimize*—that is, seek an optimum solution for a lower-level objective, such as maximum sales or minimum costs. Using our previous discussion of subsystems, it is helpful to visualize a best possible solution for one subsystem, as long as we keep in mind that the best solution for one subsystem may not be compatible with the best solution of another, and thus the optimal solution for the entire system may not be the simple summation of suboptimal solutions. Nevertheless, the manager's thinking can be improved if he seeks to discover certain best solutions for a clearly defined part of his problems under explicit assumptions. In short, the economists' concepts are extremely valuable and important as a means of allocation of an organization's resources to continue to meet the economic needs of its customers.

Cost Concepts as Viewed in Economic Reasoning

economic cost

To an economist, the basic idea of *cost* is that it is a sacrifice. Measurement of cost involves an attempt to determine the amount of sacrifice that will be made in a particular decision. Because a decision is made in the present with consequences that will occur in the future, the manager's judgment may be important in estimating the total costs or sacrifices involved in the decision. Several cost principles are basic to this analysis.

Why does an economist differ with an accountant as to the meaning of costs?

Future Costs Are the Important Costs Only those costs not yet incurred are relevant to a manager's decision. The manager makes decisions for future action. His viewpoint, like that of the managerial economist, requires that he be concerned with future as well as with past costs. The basic criteria for current decisions are the expected benefits to be realized as a result of the decision as compared with the expected sacrifices that will need to be made. The regular books of an accountant show past costs only, and thus the manager cannot depend solely on the accountant's cost information; he must look to the future, using the economist's viewpoint.

opportunity cost

Opportunity Costs Since the manager is interested in selecting the best alternative available, he must concentrate on the various opportunities open to him. A basic principle of economics is the principle of *opportunity (alternative) cost:* The cost of any kind of action or decision consists of the opportunities that are sacrificed in taking that action. In deciding to use an hour of your time to file correspondence, you are sacrificing the chance of doing anything else with that hour. What is the cost of your filing correspondence for one hour? It depends. If you would otherwise have been waiting for someone and thus would have been idle, the cost is zero. If the services that you could perform in this hour were very valuable—say, worth $100—the cost of filing the correspondence would be $100. Of course, it is often difficult to comprehend all the alternatives available, and thus it is difficult to know all opportunity costs; yet the basic idea of opportunity cost is invaluable in helping to allocate resources properly. (Thus, your cost of reading this chapter is your sacrifice in not doing something else with your time.)

incremental cost

INCREMENTAL COSTS A most valuable concept in decision making is *incremental cost,* defined as the additional (change in) cost that results from a particular decision. Incremental analysis involves a comparison of changes in revenue and changes in cost associated with a decision. The idea is simple—you will want to do something if, and only if, you can expect to be better off than you were before. In a business firm, the manager would want to make sure that the *additional* total revenue would be greater than the *additional* total cost.

The logic of incremental reasoning is clearly sound. The greatest problem in the use of this reasoning is in the search for all variables that should be considered and the actual measurement of all costs.

TECHNIQUES USING ACCOUNTING DATA FOR IMPLEMENTING ECONOMIC REASONING

accounting functions

Economic concepts offer the theoretical basis for many decisions; however, the manager also needs techniques for analyzing the information usually available to him. Accounting has been a basic tool of management since the introduction of double-entry bookkeeping in the fifteenth century, because its major functions concentrate on organizing revenue and cost information. The *functions of financial accounting* provide the manager with information by (1) recording and classifying resources and obligations for the purpose of providing a historical review of transactions, (2) reporting by consistent statements the status of the firm at certain times, (3) measuring revenue and expense over periods of time, and (4) auditing records and reports so that outside interests (stockholders and creditors) can receive information about the operations of the firm.

For many years, the economic concepts developed independently of the accounting functions. The economist argued that the relevant information for decisions should be *future* revenue and costs, and the accountant developed sophisticated methods for recording and interpreting *past* revenue and costs. Neither alone appeared very useful in helping a manager make decisions. We are fortunate that some economists and some accountants in the past several decades have developed techniques for interrelating these two fundamental fields. Managerial economists and managerial accountants now offer a number of techniques directed at aiding a manager in his decisions. Two such techniques, breakeven analysis and tailored cost analysis, are simple and important ways that economic reasoning can be implemented with the usually available information. In addition, two accounting techniques, ratio analysis and funds analysis, offer information in a form that improves decision making.

Breakeven Analysis

breakeven point

Breakeven analysis implies that at some point in the operations, total revenue equals total cost—this is the *breakeven point.* The simplest method of handling this analysis is by means of a breakeven chart; however, before we can construct a breakeven chart, it is necessary to classify total costs into at least two types, fixed and variable.

Why do fixed costs cause so much worry for businesses?

The short run

variable cost

fixed cost

Distinction between Fixed and Variable Cost The basic distinction between fixed and variable costs involves the consideration of a period of time in which costs can be changed; the economist refers to this period as the short run. The *short run* is a period of time in which it is possible to vary the rate of production, but it is too short to vary the capacity or scale of operations. In this period, some costs will be *variable* with the change in the rate of operations, but other costs will be *fixed*—that is, they will remain constant regardless of the quantity of output. The manager must frequently classify total costs as either variable or fixed costs in order to determine the correct cost for a given decision.

The process of classifying costs as fixed or variable is a necessary first step in breakeven analysis. Sometimes it is easy to identify a cost as variable. For example, when a worker's pay is based on the number of pieces that he produces, if that worker produces no output, then the cost of his wages is zero; if he produces a number of pieces, the cost can be computed by multiplying the number of pieces by the rate per piece. If we plot this cost on a chart, it will originate as zero and be a straight line sloping up-

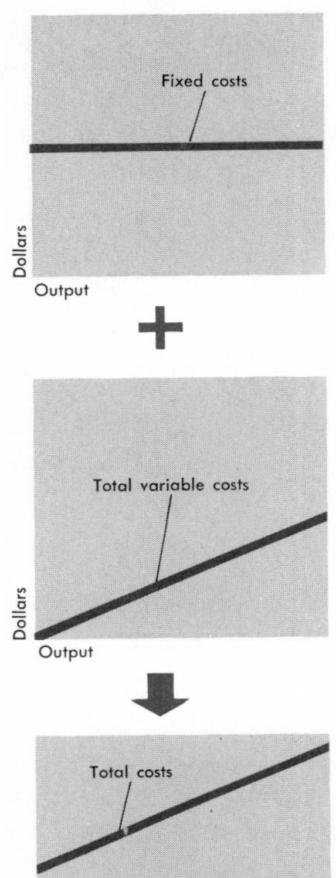

FIGURE 10.1 Derivation of the total costs curve

ward (typically, the economist places quantities on the horizontal or x axis and dollars on the vertical or y axis). In most industries, variable cost per unit can reasonably be assumed to be constant, and thus total variable cost will appear as a straight line (linear) when plotted against various quantities of output (see Figure 10.1). On the other hand, certain costs are clearly fixed—that is they will continue regardless of the rate of production. For example, the cost of the fire insurance premium on an office building will continue unchanged regardless of the output by people within the building.

Many costs are partly variable and partly fixed; in this case, the manager must analyze in more detail just what part of the cost varies with the rate of production and what part remains constant. For example, an electric bill may be composed of electricity for lighting, which will be constant regardless of the number of people in the building, and electricity for operating machines, which will vary with the rate at which the machines are used.

CONSTRUCTION OF A BREAKEVEN CHART The breakeven chart is a graphic representation of the relationship between cost and revenue at a given time and shows the point (volume) where they are equal (breakeven). Figure 10.2 is a typical breakeven chart. Many times, fixed costs are shown as a base with variable costs shown above this base. For purposes of understanding the idea of incremental cost, it is preferable to use the form in Figure 10.2.

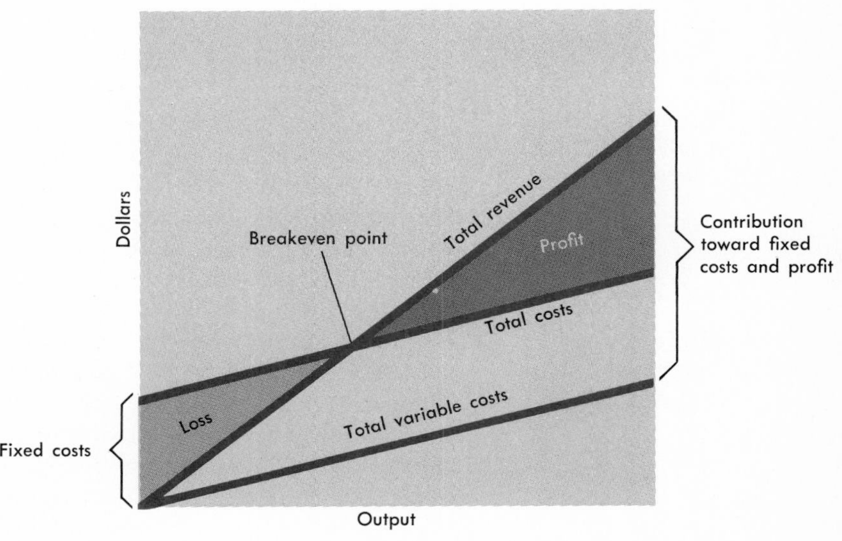

FIGURE 10.2 A simple breakeven chart

How can you construct a breakeven chart?

The simplest breakeven chart makes use of straight lines that represent revenue, variable cost, and total cost. The construction of this chart requires only that the cost and revenue be known at two points (volumes of output), because only two points are required to draw a straight line. The point at the y intercept (left-hand side of the chart) is given by definition: The revenue line will start at 0 (0 volume); variable costs will also start at 0 (0 volume); fixed costs will be a given level on the y axis, because by definition they will exist even if there is no production. Cost and revenue data at an actual volume level provide the basis for the necessary second point. All other points on the lines are the result of the assumption of linear relationships for both revenue and cost.

The simple analytical device is very useful if interpreted properly but can cause trouble if the following assumptions upon which it is based are forgotten:

1. The linear revenue line indicates an assumption that the price at which any quantity of the output can be sold is fixed and does not change with output. In other words, at any point on the line, the value is determined by multiplying the price by the number of items sold.
2. Variable costs are assumed to be proportional to output; in other words, the variable cost per unit does not increase or decrease with the rate of production.
3. The product mix (the percentage of each of the several types of products produced) remains constant.
4. Fixed costs and variable costs are clearly distinguishable.

Why should you consider whether variable costs are covered first?

INTERPRETATION OF THE BREAKEVEN CHART The value of the breakeven chart lies in the simple and straightforward manner in which it illustrates some important economic concepts. One obvious observation is that profits do not appear if any costs are fixed until a given volume of output is reached. Once this breakeven point is reached, profits appear and increase at a faster rate than do total costs.

contribution toward fixed cost and profit

The idea of *contribution toward fixed cost and profit* is clearly indicated in Figure 10.2. This idea is one of the most basic for a manager to understand; yet many errors creep into managers' decisions on this point. We can simply state that a decision to produce extra volume depends upon whether the extra revenue will at least cover variable costs; in other words, will new revenue provide extra funds to contribute toward fixed costs and profits?

Many forms of breakeven charts have been developed. Figure 10.2 shows costs and revenue plotted against output or volume in number of units. At times, you may want to use gross sales or percentage of capacity of operations instead of output in units. You can easily adapt this simple technique to your own particular situation, be it a newspaper route, benefit dance, or automobile or airline company, and thus better understand whether the activity is sound in terms of revenue and expenses.

Computation of profit is directly affected by the determination of what costs should be subtracted from total revenue. Because the conditions under which one decision is made may differ from the conditions under which another is made, costs should be tailored to one decision only. (See Table 10.1 for different cost concepts.)

TABLE 10.1 Comparative Cost Concepts Important in Business Decisions

Concept	Related Concept	Distinction	Example of Use
Variable costs	Fixed costs	The costs that vary with changes in the rate of production versus those that remain constant.	Breakeven charts; shutdown plant?
Implicit costs	Explicit costs	The sacrificed alternatives resulting from the use of facilities for a particular purpose versus the actual expenses recorded.	Total costs including those found and not found in accounting records.
Escapable costs	Nonescapable costs	Those costs that could be avoided versus those that would continue after the decision was implemented.	Decision to eliminate a product, type of customer, plant, etc.
Out-of-pocket costs	Book costs	Costs that involve actual payments of cash versus those that are recorded but do not involve cash outgo (e.g., depreciation).	Estimate of cash flows.
Traceable costs	Common costs	Those costs that can be identified easily with a unit versus those that cannot be separated. (Accountant refers to direct versus indirect.)	Precision of knowing exact costs per unit.
Incremental costs	Sunk costs	Those costs that are affected by the decision versus those that have been incurred in the past and will continue regardless of the decision.	All decision-making
Short-run costs	Long-run costs	Those costs associated with changes in the rate of use of fixed facilities versus those involved in changing the size or scale of operations.	Building a new plant or more intensive use of current facilities.
Controllable costs	Noncontrollable costs	Those costs that can be affected by the decisions of a given executive versus those that are out of the power of the given executive.	Organizational control of costs.

SOURCE: Joseph L. Massie, *Essentials of Management,* 2nd ed. (Englewood Cliffs, N.J.: Prentice-Hall, 1971), p. 114.

In our discussion of breakeven analysis using Figure 10.2, we find that by increasing volume, the extra revenue is greater than the extra cost. We said that the difference was a contribution to fixed cost and profit—in other words, the increment gained by deciding to increase volume. If the revenue realized from each unit of production is less than the variable raw-material cost, obviously you would lose money on the first item of production. In this case, increasing production would in fact increase your losses, since you would lose on each additional unit produced.

Breakeven analysis is a very simple analytical tool, yet it has power in improving decisions, since it applies basic economic theory using data usually available from accounts. After costs are segregated into fixed and variable, the number of units that must be sold to break even is simply the amount of fixed costs divided by the contribution of each unit (which, as we have seen, is the price of each unit less the variable cost per unit). Charting of different values for price, fixed cost, and variable cost per unit enables a manager to visualize the effects of alternatives available and within his control.

Tailored Cost Analysis

Using routine accounting methods, the manager can easily comprehend his total revenue and total cost, and by identifying his units of output, he can develop his average revenue per unit and average cost per unit. These are valuable items of information for some purposes; however, many of our decisions on a day-to-day basis require tailored cost analysis to support our incremental thinking.

How much does it cost to drive an auto on a planned trip?

A classic illustration of tailored cost analysis involves the determination of how much it costs to run a personal automobile. The user could total the cost of fuel, oil, lubrications, maintenance, licenses, garage rent, insurance, depreciation, and taxes and check the beginning and ending mileage on the car. If he divided the total number of miles into this total cost, he could come up with an average cost per mile. This information could help him decide whether to operate an automobile during the next year. But would it give us enough information to decide whether to fly or drive the car on a 600-mile trip tomorrow? We could multiply the average cost per mile computed on last year's experience by 600 and obtain a cost that could be compared with the air fare. But does this computation really analyze those costs that are relevant? If we drive, are the cost of licenses, garage rent, insurance, and obsolescence going to be any greater than if we left the car in the garage? Was the opportunity cost of our added time for driving (instead of flying) important? We have learned that we should consider only those costs that will be affected by the decision, and we have learned to consider the alternative use of our time. For a truly rational decision, it is necessary for us to tailor our analysis to individual decisions.

pro forma statements

We could organize the foregoing information by making two *pro forma statements* (estimates)—one for the airline travel and the other for the automobile travel. Estimated revenue and expense, using the future orientation and opportunity-cost principle, help the manager visualize his expectations before he takes an action. Estimated statements, therefore, are hypothetical (or simulated) exercises that can identify potential troubles and thus give the manager a chance to avoid the results of bad decisions that he could have made.

Ratio Analysis

ratio

How can relative figures give new meaning to two absolute figures?

An interpretation of the information provided by an accounting system can be improved by relating absolute amounts to one another and expressing these relationships as ratios. A *ratio* may be expressed as a common fraction with a numerator and denominator, or as a percentage. The simplest financial ratios compare costs and revenue for one period. For example, if we use total sales as the denominator, we can develop much greater insight about priorities by relating individual elements of revenue and expenses to the total. One important ratio relates the cost of goods sold to gross revenue. Other financial ratios compare two or more periods; a ratio might relate sales for this year with sales for last year.

Ratio analysis involves very simple computations and thus is a general-purpose analytical device open to a manager with limited background. Although there are many standard ratios (see Table 10.2), the manager has the opportunity to develop special ratios to improve his understanding of quantitative data.

Can percentages mislead the user?

The chief problem of ratio analysis is not computational but interpretive. Two interpretive problems of ratios are oversimplification and confusion resulting from changing denominators. The first limitation is inherent, since the very purpose of a ratio is to simplify; thus it must be carefully guarded against. To really understand the basic data in the numerator and denominator, it sometimes helps to retain the absolute values without reducing the ratio to the least common denominator. One of the trickiest

TABLE 10.2 Checklist for Financial Ratio Analysis

Name of Ratio	Formula	Industry Norm (assumed merely as illustration)
1. *Liquidity Ratios* (measuring the ability of the firm to meet its maturing obligations)		
Current ratio	$\frac{\text{Current assets}}{\text{Current liabilities}}$	2.6
Acid-test ratio	$\frac{\text{Cash and equivalent}}{\text{Current liability}}$	1.0
Cash velocity	$\frac{\text{Sales}}{\text{Cash and equivalent}}$	12 times
Inventory to net working capital	$\frac{\text{Inventory}}{\text{Current assets} - \text{Current liabilities}}$	85%
2. *Leverage Ratios* (measuring the contributions of financing by owners compared with financing provided by creditors)		
Debt to equity	$\frac{\text{Total debt}}{\text{Equity}}$	56%
Coverage of fixed charges	$\frac{\text{Net profit before fixed charges}}{\text{Fixed charges}}$	6 times
Current liability to equity	$\frac{\text{Current liability}}{\text{Equity}}$	32%
Fixed assets to equity	$\frac{\text{Fixed assets}}{\text{Equity}}$	60%
3. *Activities Ratios* (measuring the effectiveness of the employment of resources)		
Inventory turnover	$\frac{\text{Sales}}{\text{Inventory}}$	7 times
Net working capital turnover	$\frac{\text{Sales}}{\text{Net working capital}}$	5 times
Fixed-assets turnover	$\frac{\text{Sales}}{\text{Fixed assets}}$	6 times
Average collection period	$\frac{\text{Receivables}}{\text{Average sales per day}}$	20 days
Equity capital turn-over	$\frac{\text{Sales}}{\text{Equity}}$	3 times
Total capital turn-over	$\frac{\text{Sales}}{\text{Total assets}}$	2 times

SOURCE: Joseph L. Massie, *Essentials of Management*, 2nd ed. (Englewood Cliffs, N.J.: Prentice-Hall, 1971), p. 211.

TABLE 10.2 (continued)

Name of Ratio	Formula	Industry Norm (assumed merely as illustration)
4. *Profitability Ratios* (indicating degree of success in achieving desired profit levels)		
Gross operating margin	$\frac{\text{Gross operating profit}}{\text{Sales}}$	30%
Net operating margin	$\frac{\text{Net operating profit}}{\text{Sales}}$	6.5%
Sales margin	$\frac{\text{Net profit after taxes}}{\text{Sales}}$	3.2%
Productivity of assets	$\frac{\text{Gross income less taxes}}{\text{Total assets}}$	10%
Return on capital	$\frac{\text{Net profit after taxes}}{\text{Net worth}}$	7.5%
Net profit on working capital	$\frac{\text{Net operating profit}}{\text{Net working capital}}$	14.5%

problems, and one that causes many mistakes in interpretation of ratios, is the problem caused by changing the base of comparison, the denominator. One method of playing games with ratios is to fail to point out the absolute figures used. (Many governments as well as businessmen do this when it is to their advantage.)

If you are trying to fool someone else, the ratio offers real opportunities; however, many managers tend to fool themselves (and that is not good). Suppose that we want to determine our current financial solvency—that is, our available cash compared to our immediate obligations to creditors. Many businessmen think that a current ratio of 2 to 1 has some mystical support as being good. If our current checking account has a balance of $500, and total short-run debts are $400, our ratio is 1.25 to 1. If we use $300 of our checking account to pay off some of those bills, we could then improve our ratio to 2 to 1 ($500 minus $300 equals $200, and $400 minus $300 equals $100). Now, have we really improved our financial condition? It depends—and what it depends upon is the important factor in interpreting these ratios.

It is often helpful to use standard ratios so that you can compare yourself to others. Therefore, it will be useful for you to understand the ratios given in Table 10.2, which are some of the most used expense, operating, and financial ratios. This set of ratios can be viewed as supporting one of the most fundamental—the rate of return on investment. In fact, we shall see in Chapter 11 that the ratio of net profit to investment can be assumed to be the primary objective of a business firm; it is the one economists assume to be optimized.

Funds Analysis

If a manager is to maintain a viable organization, he must continually decide where to invest additional funds and where to obtain the funds. A business firm must not only make profits but also maintain its ability to meet its obligations for payments when they come due. A very profitable firm may go bankrupt if it places all its funds into assets that cannot be used to pay its debts. Thus, a systematic method of watching the flow of funds is a most critical aid for a manager. Even in public agencies and nonprofit organizations, managers must reckon with problems of funds to pay their personnel and to satisfy cash demands on their operations.

Historically, most people who have learned a little accounting develop their accounting skills around the balance sheet and the income statement (illustrated in Table 10.3). Although they are

TABLE 10.3 Simplified Balance Sheet and Income Statement for Joe's Hot Dog Stand

Balance Sheet as of Dec. 31, 1990

ASSETS		*CLAIMS AGAINST ASSETS*	
Cash	$ 1,000	Debts to suppliers and banks	$ 1,500
Inventory	3,000	Long-term liabilities (mortgage)	8,500
Store and equipment	11,000	Joe's net interests in his business (equity)	5,000
Total assets	$15,000	Total claims	$15,000

Income Statement for the year 1990

INCOME		*EXPENSES*	
Sales of hot dogs	$20,000	Selling expenses	$3,000
Cost of buns and meat	−8,000	General expenses	6,000
Gross income	$12,000	Total expenses	$9,000

Net income before taxes: $12,000 − $9,000 = $3,000

fundamental for many people interested in a firm, neither of these statements keeps track of the flow of funds through the operations.

funds statement

To a manager, a *funds statement,* often called a statement of sources and application of funds, is particularly important for day-by-day decisions. In simple terms, the manager needs to know where he got his funds and where they went. He also needs a framework for estimating his working capital (funds) for some future period of time, so that he can feel confident that he will have sufficient funds to satisfy the demands of his proposed level of operations.

The flow of funds originates from the sources available for these funds and is directed to various applications where they will be used. Both the statement of source and application of funds and the projected estimations of future conditions of funds summarize the sources and uses of funds of the organization. Generally, the elements of the source of funds are (1) sale of assets no longer needed; (2) sale of stock ownership, or borrowing of funds through bonds, or loans from a bank; (3) reduction of inventories, accounts receivable, or other current assets; (4) net earnings retained in business from normal operations; and (5) provision of depreciation on fixed assets (which is treated as an expense in determining net earnings but which requires no cash expenditure). The elements of the uses of funds include payment of dividends, purchase of fixed assets or investments, payment of long-term debts, and increases in inventories, accounts receivable, or other current assets.

Most illustrations of funds statements become involved with the accounting techniques for relating them to the balance sheet and the income statement; however, the essential nature of the statement can be made very simple without getting into the refinements of accounting. Table 10.4 illustrates a funds statement for a family drugstore.

Although there are many more complicated analytical techniques available to the manager from economics and accounting, the four simple ones discussed above—breakeven analysis, tailored cost analysis, ratio analysis, and funds flow—offer a good introduction to how management thinking has been improved by ideas from these two disciplines.

ADMINISTRATIVE MAN—A BEHAVIORAL CONCEPT

The classical view of economic man—attempting to optimize in the future using historical data provided by the accountant—has often been frustrating to managers, since they have found too large a

TABLE 10.4 Smith's Pharmacy: Source and Application of Funds Statement

Sources of funds (where got)	
Net income from operations	$ 3,000
Sale of stock to brother	5,000
Sale of delivery truck	1,000
Depreciation on store fixtures (noncash expense charged in determining above net income)	1,000
Reduction in merchandise inventory	500
Total	$10,500
Application of funds (where gone)	
Payment of mortgage on store building	$ 5,000
Payment of dividends to stockholders	1,000
Increase in credit to customers	4,000
Purchase of typewriter	500
Total	$10,500

gap between prescriptions of what they should do and their observations of actual possibilities. H. A. Simon, in his research, focused on describing decision making in organizational behavior and emphasized several concepts that further help us understand organizational decision making. He used the term *administrative man,* instead of economic man, as his prototype.[1]

administrative man

The administrative man is more human—that is, he seeks to be rational within the limits of human capabilities. He usually seeks a satisfactory solution, which is often not the optimal solution. Simon referred to a concept of bounded rationality as being more useful in describing managerial decision making. Concisely, *bounded rationality* recognizes human limits to a person's knowledge of all alternatives and their consequences, and focuses on the fact that only a few things can be done at a time, making use of only a small part of the information presented by the environment. Consequently, a manager makes decisions in sequence; he searches for new alternatives only if he is dissatisfied with present outcomes. The determination of whether he is dissatisfied will depend on his *level of aspiration* and the expected value of the outcome. Figure 10.3 illustrates the process used by the administrative man.

bounded rationality

Take the case of an employee who is dissatisfied with his pay. He searches for alternatives to improve it. He may seek an-

[1] Herbert A. Simon, *Administrative Behavior,* 3rd ed. (New York: Macmillan, 1976).

other job with a higher salary. The higher salary leads to higher levels of satisfaction, but the higher pay may increase his level of aspiration. Whether the net effect is greater satisfaction depends on which is rising faster, the expected value of the outcome or the level of aspiration.

The central issue in this behavioral description of the decision-making process is the matter of reaching a satisfactory outcome, not necessarily the optimum or best. Simon observed that, typically, a person attempts to make a decision by searching for satisfactory alternatives, and he called this attempting to *satisfice* rather than, as with the economic man, attempting to optimize.

satisfice

This description of the administrative man has several implications. First is the decision maker's use of the most convenient, least costly information—he recognizes that he cannot obtain perfect knowledge of all information. Second, the process is repeated, depending on the relationship between actual outcomes and aspirations. Third, an integral part of the process is an ordering of preferences, which are influenced by perceptions, training, experience, goals, beliefs, and values.

The result of this description of the administrative man is that *rationality* is defined in terms of whether one's decisions are consistent with achieving one's goals. Thus, what may appear to be rational for one person with one set of goals—say, high income and status—may not appear to be rational for another person with a different set of goals or preferences—perhaps, security and sufficient leisure.

rationality

When we shift our view of decision making from individual terms to an organizational context using this behavioral description, we see that the problem is to achieve a satisfactory integration of decisions among a number of people with varying orders of preferences. This integration results from cooperation and

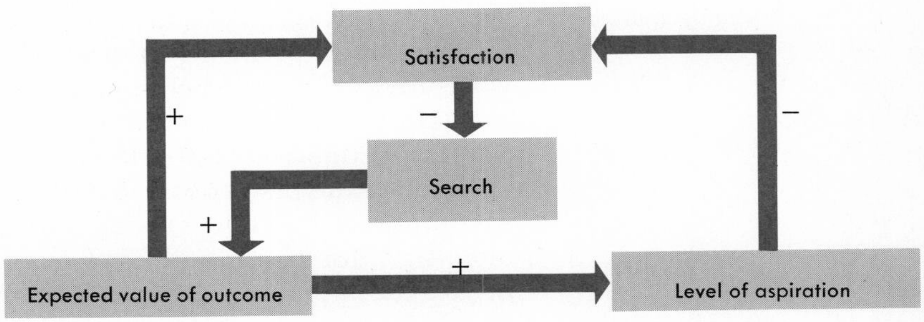

FIGURE 10.3 General model of adaptive motivated behavior

acceptance by individuals of a common set of organizational objectives. In organizational satisficing, the individual recognizes that he has limits to his discretion. These limits are social controls that limit one's freedom in making decisions. Organizational objectives and policies (to be discussed in the next chapter), constraints set by the external environment (culture, government, customers, and so on), and a person's value system provide the framework for individual decisions in an organizational context. For example, if a manager is faced with a decision of increasing the salary of a subordinate or losing him to another firm, he attempts to reach a satisfactory solution after considering such factors as the availability of funds, the productivity of the subordinate, company pay policies, legal regulations, and many other considerations that limit his discretion. In view of all these considerations, the manager necessarily strives to reach a good solution (one that is acceptable to all) that tends to approach, but not reach, the single best solution.

The behavioral concept of the administrative man offers a model that makes refinements in the conceptual framework for decisions. The third approach, management science, offers both conceptual help and rigorous analytical techniques. We now turn to a summary of this approach to decision making.

MANAGEMENT SCIENCE

Some of the most promising advances in making the decision process more scientific have been made in the field of management science. This field concentrates on quantitative concepts and techniques built upon the foundations of mathematics and statistics. The field is closely related to an approach generally called *operations research* (OR). Although many of the concepts and techniques are beyond the scope of this book, it is becoming increasingly clear that managers must be able to understand the basic terminology and approaches of management science, so that (1) they can at least *state* their problems in forms that permit utilizing specialists who provide valuable help in carrying out the rigorous techniques, and (2) they can *interpret* the answers obtained by the number of available refined methods of analysis. In this section, we shall clarify some of the key terms used in management science, explain the conditions of decision making in which quantitative approaches offer significant aid, and offer examples of several simple techniques for improving decision making.

Why can't you avoid quantitative approaches in management?

Terminology

Because even simple decisions involve complex elements (numerous causal variables, many possible alternatives, and different values of each possible outcome from each alternative), even the administrative man who attempts to satisfice must seek ways to handle complexity. The usual approach is to break the problems down in a more clearly defined manner, so that he can determine definite answers. For this reason, management science makes use of *models,* simply defined as abstractions of real-world situations. We are all familiar with toys that are *physical* scale models of the real things. *Iconic models* graphically or pictorially represent certain important characteristics of the real world, such as in photographs or artists' drawings. An *analogue model* represents some set of properties of a real situation; for example, having water in a series of pipes and containers represent money flowing through an economy or a business firm. The most generally used type of model in decision making is a *symbolic* or *mathematical model* that uses symbols to specify important properties to be considered. Symbolic models can be constructed to show the relationships among variables; these symbols can be expressed as equations.

models

How can models help simplify a complex decision situation?

Mathematical models are powerful tools of analysis in decision making, because each symbol representing a variable can be explicitly defined and the relationships of the most relevant variables can be stated. Typically, a decision model consists of the most important assumptions, variables, and relationships relevant to a decision. In short, a symbolic model focuses on the quantitative aspects of a problem and restricts one's consideration to a stated group of factors by clearly stating assumptions. Thus, by treating the situation as a closed system, limited by explicit assumptions, the decision maker can determine more rigorously the relevant factors, available alternatives, and possible outcomes. Models, therefore, are excellent ways of handling certain well-defined problems, but since they represent only a limited set of characteristics of the real world, the decision maker must still interpret the results of his computations by bringing in other factors not included in the particular model that he has selected.

objective function

Any decision model consists of (1) an *objective function*—a symbolic statement of an objective of the decision making, such as maximizing profits, minimizing costs, and so on; (2) a set of *constraints* or relevant factors that are important for consideration; (3) and *hypotheses* of the relationships among the factors. Management scientists refer to those factors that are not within one's control as

states of nature

strategy

decision rules

states of nature, the uncontrollable possible events that affect outcomes of alternatives. On the other hand, the decision maker has control over his choice of a *strategy*, a statement of preference for a certain pattern of his response, and he can identify certain guidelines for his decisions, which are called *decision rules*. For example, a businessman may select a marketing strategy of providing a full line of products, with a clear-cut decision rule of dropping any product that does not cover variable costs.

deterministic model

probabilistic model

Conditions under which managers make decisions vary along a continuum from those of perfect certainty to those of complete uncertainty. He can assume certainty and use a *deterministic model*, one in which all the factors are assumed exact, with chance playing no role. If he wishes to treat chance quantitatively in his model, he may construct a *probabilistic model*, one in which a quantitative representation of probability is included.

Degrees of Uncertainty

How do you make a decision that takes a calculated risk?

Since the idea of chance implies that there is a large number of unknown forces about which we have little information, a decision involving chance will never turn out to be correct 100 percent of the time. The best we can do is to "play the averages" and make decisions that will be satisfactory more times than they will be unsatisfactory. The manager's attitude is that when faced with chance, he must still make a decision, for indecision is viewed as a cardinal weakness. Thus, a manager must take chances, but he must develop an approach by which he can better understand the possible outcomes and be able to estimate the *probable* outcomes. A first step in facing uncertainty is to be aware of the existence of chance in the decision situation.

conditions of certainty

If the manager has sufficient information about all the elements affecting the outcomes of the decision, so that he can predict the outcomes 100 percent of the time, we can say that he is operating under *conditions of certainty*. For example, if the decision involves action in the immediate future and if he has made this decision a number of times with the same results, he may assume that he knows and can determine the expected outcome. Under such rare conditions, he does not need to analyze the chance elements. We may view this degree of certainty as one extreme along the continuum illustrated in Figure 10.4.

If a decision involves conditions about which the manager has no information, either about the outcome or the relative chances for any single outcome, he is said to be operating under

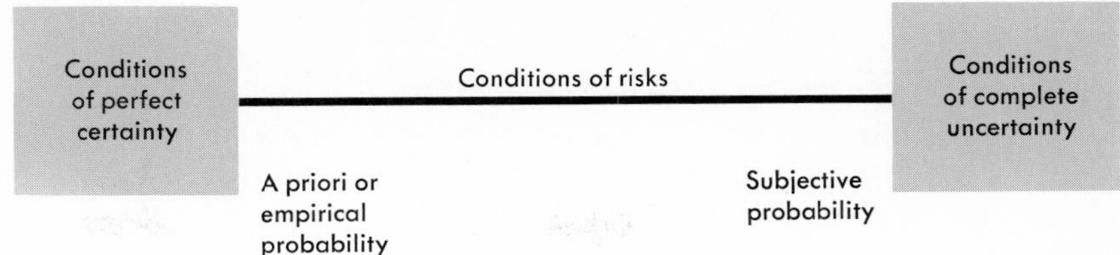

FIGURE 10.4 Degrees of knowledge available in decision situations

conditions of uncertainty

What strategies are available to a decision maker under conditions of complete uncertainty?

conditions of uncertainty, as illustrated in Figure 10.4 at the opposite extreme from certainty. Under these conditions, he has no information on which he can develop any analysis, and thus, the best he can do is be aware of the fact that he has no chance of predicting the events.

Yet, even in cases of total ignorance, under conditions in which the decision maker has no historical data or any idea of the effects of states of nature or what action others will take, several approaches have been suggested for making decisions.

First, if he thinks optimistically, he may select a strategy under which he has the possibility of receiving the greatest return, referred to as the *maximax criterion.* Using this criterion, he ignores possible losses or failures. Probably, prospectors for gold, buyers of lottery tickets, or the most venturesome entrepreneurs who "go for broke" face uncertainty with the maximax criterion.

Second, if the manager decides upon believing that only the worst possible outcome will occur, he will tend to use a strategy that maximizes the *least* favorable result, generally called the *maximin criterion.* Viewing uncertainty in this pessimistic manner, the manager seeks to make the best of adverse effects of states of nature, so that he can be assured of the best outcome under the worst conditions.

Finally, if a manager has no information about the probability of states of nature, he may select an approach that assumes that each state of nature has the same chance of occurring. In this way, he treats the situation in the same way as he would in those cases in which he has some knowledge of his risks (near the right side of Figure 10.4), except that in the absence of any knowledge, he merely assumes the chances for each state of nature occurring as being equal.

Thus, even in the case of complete uncertainty, the decision maker has options for making decisions. The criteria above provide some framework for choice even under the most uncertain type of situations.

We are fortunate that in modern society we have developed a great many facts and much technical scientific data that provide information to the manager, so that he does not normally operate under conditions of pure uncertainty even though he does not have complete certainty. A third condition, *conditions of risk,* illustrated in Figure 10.4, makes some analytical devices possible. Under conditions of risk, the manager has sufficient information for estimating the probability of outcomes. *Probability* (usually represented by the symbol P) can be defined as the percentage of times in which a specific outcome would occur if an action were repeated a very large number of times.

conditions of risk

Probability

All the analytical aids for dealing with probability depend upon the various methods by which the manager can estimate P. Probability is usually stated as a fraction or a percentage; for example, $P = .5$ means that the chance of the occurrence is one out of two, or that it would occur 50 percent of the time.

There are three methods of estimating the probability under conditions of risk:

How can you quantify risks?

A priori probability

1. *A priori probability* is obtained through deductions from assumed conditions. For example, you know that the probability of a head on the flip of a fair coin is .5. Through the knowledge of the conditions of the coin, you can deduce the probability of the results, although you cannot predict with certainty the outcome of any single toss.

Empirical probability

2. *Empirical probability* is based on recording actual experience over a period of time and computing the percentage of times that each event has occurred. Management generally has considerable historical data and can compute the percentage of occurrences of past experiences. Life insurance companies predict probabilities of death by using tables based on past experience. In recent years, meteorologists have stated predictions in terms of probabilities—for example, stating that there is a 50% probability that it will rain. Since there are numerous variables affecting the weather, the weatherman bases these estimates of probability of rain on past experiences involving a number of variables.

subjective probability

3. When a manager does not have sufficient knowledge of conditions to use a priori probability and does not have sufficient data to develop empirical probability, he may still estimate P by using judgment. This less exact type of probability, called *subjective probability,* is available in most situations. For example, you might state the subjective probability of your passing this course as .90; since you have no "track record" in this course and no logical basis for predicting the actions

of your present instructor, your statement is purely a matter of opinion. This approach has been criticized because it encourages the manager to pull a probability estimate out of the air; however, subjective probabilities make it possible for the manager to state his assumptions to someone else explicitly and quantitatively and help in his own logical processes when dealing with conditions of risk. (Your estimated grade in this course can be compared with your estimate for passing other courses you are now taking and help you in your study plans. Your estimate of .90 is also a more precise way of telling your parents that you really think you will pass.)

Decision Techniques under Conditions of Risk

Management science offers an expanding number of rigorous techniques for helping the decision maker face conditions of risk. Since most real situations faced by a manager are situations in which he has some information about the possible states of nature and the probability of the outcomes from his alternatives, these techniques are important to the practicing manager. He may feel that some decisions involve so much exact knowledge that he need not consider probability and can use any of the available deterministic models. Many formulas for setting prices, fixing levels of inventory, balancing production lines, and determining standards of work fall in this category. We shall not discuss these deterministic models because they are beyond the scope of this book and because the operating manager usually faces conditions in which probabilistic reasoning is most useful.

Under conditions of risk, the decision maker has several alternative courses of action (strategies), but he does not know the expected consequences of each; however, he has some knowledge of the probability of the different outcomes. In such cases, he can receive great help if he can organize his information in such a manner as to explicitly identify the available alternatives, the outcome of each, and the probability of each outcome's occurring.

Three steps are basic to organizing the factors to be considered in a decision involving probabilities: (1) The decision maker should first lay out, in tabular form, all the possible alternatives or *strategies* that he thinks are reasonable for him to consider, and all the possible states of nature that affect the *outcomes* of these strategies. (2) He must then state in quantitative form a probability distribution in which he forces himself to state his feelings about the chances of each outcome that might result from each alternative strategy. In this step he may use a priori or empirical methods, or he may only be able to subjectively assign probabilities that he feels are reasonable. The key to this step is to state explicitly the various probabilities that might be attached to each act–outcome situation. (3) Then the decision maker must determine the value, usually in dollars, of each outcome.

To illustrate the use of these steps in a simple decision, let us assume that a store manager must choose between stocking Brand A and Brand B in his store, since he cannot stock both. If he stocks A and it is a success, he feels that he can make $200, but if it is a failure, he stands to lose $500. If he stocks Brand B and the outcome is successful, he can make $400, but if the outcome is unsuccessful, he would lose $300. Which brand should he stock? Without some idea of the probabilities of success and failure, he cannot quantify his thinking. He therefore estimates the probability of each outcome: If he stocks Brand A: chances of success, .80; chances of failure, .20. If he stocks Brand B: probability of success, .50; probability of failure, .50.

PAYOFF TABLE The store manager can present this information in tabular form, showing the conditional values for each strategy (choice of brand) under each state of nature or competitive action (the combination of uncontrollable factors, such as demand, that determine success or failure). This simplest payoff table is illustrated in Table 10.5 as the first step in stating strategies and possible outcomes.

With the information in Table 10.5, the store manager can use his subjective estimates of risks by multiplying the conditional values by their probability of occurrence. This calculation will result in their *expected values.* Table 10.6 illustrates this expected-value payoff table.

expected values

From the expected-value payoff table, the store manager can determine the *total expected value* for each strategy by obtaining the sum of the expected values for each state of nature. If Brand A

total expected value

TABLE 10.5 Payoff Table

Strategies	State of Nature (Demand)	
	Success	**Failure**
Stock Brand A	$200	–$500
Stock Brand B	$400	–$300

is stocked, the total expected value is $60; if Brand B is stocked, the total expected value is $50; therefore, under the assumptions in this case, the store manager would decide to stock Brand A, because its total expected value is $10 more than if Brand B were stocked. Obviously, if the total expected value for stocking each brand had been negative, he would decide not to stock either, because the probability would be that he would lose using either strategy.

decision tree

DECISION TREE A graphical method for identifying alternative strategies, estimating probabilities, and indicating the resulting expected payoff is a *decision tree.* This graphical form visually helps the decision maker view his alternatives and outcomes. A decision tree for the store manager and his choice between Brand A and B is illustrated in Figure 10.5.

Note that in the decision tree, the decision maker states in some form his estimate of the expected outcome for each of the expressed alternatives. One approach would be for the decision maker to state these expectations in verbal form, such as "almost certain, very likely, likely, unlikely, very unlikely, and almost never." However, it is very useful to make these statements of expectations in quantitative values of P using one of the three methods previously discussed for estimating probabilities. The key to this step is to state explicitly the various probabilities that might be attached to each act–outcome situation (as is shown in Figure 10.5), the alternatives, each of the outcomes for each alternative, and the probabilities for each outcome. All we need is to develop some measure that will distinguish among each of the outcomes, for there will probably be greater value for certain outcomes than for others. A useful yardstick used in the illustration above is a monetary unit—for example, dollars. In this last step, we merely assign the value of each outcome as a certain number of dollars (as was done in parentheses on the middle limb of the tree in Figure 10.5).

TABLE 10.6 Expected Value Payoff Table

	State of Nature	
Strategy	**Success (P)**	**Failure (P)**
Brand A	$200 × .80 = $160	–$500 × .20 = –$100
Brand B	$400 × .50 = $200	–$300 × .50 = –$150

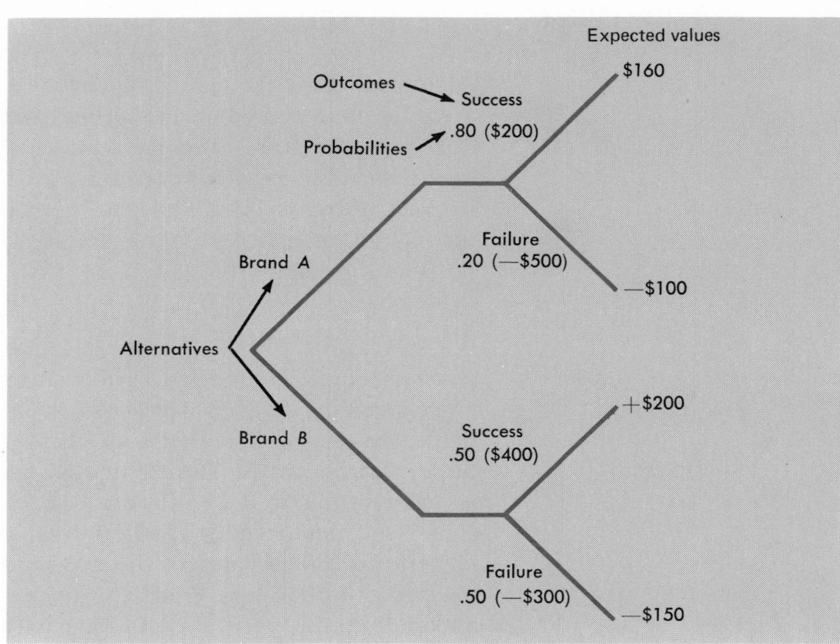

FIGURE 10.5 Decision tree

SIMULATION TECHNIQUES Many managerial decisions under conditions of risk are so complex that models become too involved and estimating probabilities is very difficult. Simulation techniques are often helpful in such situations. In this way the manager, with the aid of a computer, can rapidly try out proposed strategies without committing himself to large expenditures by trying them out in real situations. Simulation is a way that a manager can learn from simulated experiences in place of actual trial (and possible error). One type of simulation is used in queuing problems, problems in which the need for personnel or equipment varies over a time period but the determination of the peak demands cannot be estimated because the occurrence is random or due to chance. With this approach, he can then try out his available strategies as they might result in different outcomes depending upon probabilities from a table of random numbers.

For example, the store manager may wish to determine the work schedules for three salesmen to serve customers and whether he should add a fourth salesman. His problem is that he does not know when customers may appear in the store. He may have some experience indicating the probabilities that at some hours of the day all three salesmen would be serving customers, but that at other times, the salesmen will be idle. In simulating the traffic for a day, he may wish to use subjective probabilities for those times in which he has no data from experience; but even if he has no experience data, he can still simulate activity by using random numbers. In this type of problem, the store manager may generate simulated activity in place of the pure trial-and-error method by varying actual salesman schedules or number of salesmen.

SUMMARY AND PROPOSITIONS

The viewpoints of the economist, the accountant, and the statistician can help the manager make better decisions. The ideas of opportunity costs and incremental thinking are extremely valuable to anyone who is allocating his precious resources to alternative commitments. Ratio analysis, funds analysis, and tailored cost studies are managerial techniques that can give added meaning to the records and reports of the accounting department. Such techniques as expected monetary value and tree diagrams can help the manager face the risks and uncertainties inherent in his operations. Thus, even though these techniques are borrowed from other disciplines, so that for further details you must study other books and in other courses, our discussion should challenge you to broaden your understanding to incorporate any tools that can be helpful to you as a manager.

Since this chapter covers a number of aids to decision-making, it will help to summarize the essence of these aids.

1. Only those costs not yet incurred are relevant to a manager's decision.

2. Costs represent the sacrifice that must be made in the future if a certain decision is made.

3. A breakeven chart is a simple graphical device by which total revenue and total costs can be compared at various rates of production, so that the manager can better plan for profit (and avoid loss).

4. Interpretation of accounting data can be improved by relating two quantities (e.g., sales and costs) in the form of a ratio.

5. Funds-flow analysis involves the identification of each source of funds and the determination of the applications and uses of these funds.

6. The model of an administrative man who attempts to obtain a satisfactory answer (satisficing) is more realistic than the one in which an economic man attempts to optimize.

7. The law of large numbers, assumed in employing probabilities, states that mass phenomena tend toward regularity and thus it is

possible to predict that a certain percentage of events will happen even though we cannot predict what will happen in a specific event.

8. An expected value is merely the value of an outcome weighted by an estimated probability of the outcome.

9. In making decisions under conditions of risk, we can never prove that we will be right; however, we can state the results in a form that will indicate the chances that we will be right (or wrong).

STUDY ASSIGNMENTS

1. *Explain how the distinction between fixed and variable costs depends on the length of the time period involved in the analysis.*

2. *In using a breakeven chart, which costs (variable or fixed) must be covered at all times by total revenue? Explain the reasoning for your answer. How does this explanation help show the importance of incremental thinking?*

3. *Airlines use the percentage of capacity at which their planes are loaded with passengers as a measure of operating efficiency. Draw a rough illustration showing a sample breakeven chart for a 747 and list some of the probable fixed and variable costs in operating the plane.*

4. *How does the idea of bounded rationality relate to the tendency for the administrative man to satisfice?*

5. *Why is it difficult for an accountant to record opportunity costs?*

6. *Is the classification of controllable costs, explained in Table 10.1, more important to managers than the classification of out-of-pocket costs? Explain when each classification is important.*

7. *Explain the reasoning behind a payoff table and show the relationship of this reasoning to the contruction of a decision tree.*

8. *If you show an increase in sales of 10 percent in one year and a decrease of 10 percent in the next year, would total sales be the same as when you started? Show your calculations and then explain why it is important to identify the base (denominator) of a ratio.*

9. *Is the stub on your checkbook more similar to an income statement, balance sheet, or funds statement? Explain your answer.*

10. *At which accounting statement (balance sheet, income statement, or funds statement) would you look for the following information:*

a. The total amount of your current debt

b. The size of your past expenses in an economizing program

c. Evidence of the degree of risk of going bankrupt

11. *Under conditions of risk, how can a manager improve his chances of success through analytical precision? What special type of information is needed to help him avoid conditions of pure uncertainty?*

12. *Illustrate three methods of approximating* P *(probability) for estimating the chances of operating a delivery truck for 20,000 miles without an accident.*

situational episodes

1. A company has the following cost situation for one of its products:

Fixed costs:	$300,000
Variable costs:	$4.00 per unit
Sales price:	$6.00 per unit

   a. What is the contribution to fixed cost and profit for each unit?

   b. Construct a breakeven chart for this operation.

   c. The management is considering an increase of the price to $8.00 in the event that the fixed costs rise to $400,000. Show in a chart the effect of these two changes.

2. You are planning to sell Christmas trees in your community for the next season. You have decided to price the trees at $4.00 per unit; you have a commitment for buying any quantity of trees to be delivered to your lot for $2.00 per tree. Your problem is that you cannot order any additional trees during the season. Any unsold trees will involve a total loss.

   Your risk involves the number of trees that you should order. You have made subjective estimates of the probability distribution relative to the demand in your area:

   100% chance that you will sell 1,000 trees or more
   75% chance that you will sell 1,300 trees or more
   50% chance that you will sell 1,500 trees or more
   25% chance that you will sell 1,800 trees or more
   0% chance that you will sell 2,400 trees or more

   How many trees should you stock? Give your reasoning for your answer.

3. You are planning to drive your own car to a destination 1,000 miles from home. You hit on the idea that you have "idle capacity" in your automobile and could take three passengers. In attempting to determine what to charge three people interested in going with you, you want to identify your detailed costs tailored to this decision. Specify the costs relevant to the decision.

setting objectives

ELEVEN

OBJECTIVES YOU SHOULD MEET

Distinguish *between objectives and plans.*

Explain *how a person relates his personal goals to the goals of the organization.*

Illustrate *how goals may conflict with one another.*

Illustrate *how objectives form a hierarchy in an organization.*

State *the characteristics of sound objectives.*

Describe *how MBO affects a manager's selection of the means to achieve objectives.*

WHERE AM I GOING?

I had just returned from one of those semiannual sessions with my boss in which he keeps pressing me to tell him exactly what I expect to do in the next six months. On my way from his office, I had mixed feelings: On the one hand, I felt that the hour-long talk with him helped me to understand some pieces of my own life, since he kept asking me just what I wanted from my job; on the other hand, it's always a trying experience to try to pin down exactly what targets you're aiming at, especially since I know that after six months, I'll be asked to go over with him just which of these I hit and which I missed. I hoped that I said the right things and that I didn't overstate just what I could do. You always have a tendency in these chats to want to sound good at the time, but then you realize that what sounds good also puts you on the spot to do what you said you would do. Just as I was about to turn into my office, I ran into Bob, a friend who manages a department similar to mine.

"Hi, Bob—well, I've just had my talk with the old man. Your 'Where am I going' session with him last week and your advice to me were really helpful. But I'm afraid I was too frank with him, and I guess I agreed to some pretty high objectives."

"Yeah, Joe, I know it's hard. My reasoning, though, is that if the boss really means that I can set my own objectives, he's giving me the chance to be sure that I set them at a level I'm sure I can meet. He did manage to raise some of them, but I came out with detailed objectives I think I can meet."

"My trouble when I talked with him, Bob, is that I really do think that I can reduce the scrap in my shop, and so I agreed to an objective to reduce it by 25 percent in the next six months. Now, maybe I'll only

reach 20 percent, but I hope that when we look over my record he won't focus on the failure to reduce by the extra 5 percent—I think he should look at the performance as being darn good."

"That's the trouble with this management-by-objective stuff. The higher you set the targets, the greater the risk that your performance will be less than the target. So my pitch is to keep the objectives as low as I can get away with. When it gets down to it, my sole objective is to make as much money as possible with the least effort and worry. I get my kicks out of going hunting, and I don't see that my job can be made as much fun as some of those guys in the personnel department try to tell me."

"I don't know, Bob, I really do like my job, and I have to admit that I get a kick out of getting my boys to turn out a good product. We kid around a lot but we do the job. Frankly, the way things are at home with Sara and those three teen-agers, I come to work sometimes with the idea that I can get away from all the fussing at home and enjoy the gang in the shop. I doubt that I would be as happy as I am now if I suddenly inherited a million dollars and could quit my job and stay home. I think I would go nuts."

"Boy, Joe, the boss must have really sold you a bill of goods. He's some smooth character, with all his psychology and manipulating you. I think he really convinced you that you can get satisfaction out of working your heart out for good old ADC, Inc. I go along with this objectives stuff just because I can see that I won't get promoted unless I do. I really think it's just one big game—I bluff the boss into thinking my job is really tough and the objectives are really awfully high, when I really think I could beat them all the time if I wanted to. Maybe I'd have to admit that I get a lot of fun in this company just playing games with the boss on his objectives stuff."

"Maybe you're right, but I have a hard time in this bluffing game. I actually feel a need to be sincere and straightforward. When I talked with the old man, I got the idea that he was really trying to help me. He wasn't just trying to make himself look good for his promotion. He actually said that he would support me in my idea to pack those boxes in a different way. I got the feeling that if I goof, he'll give me credit for trying and I'll be better off than if I just continued to do it in the same old way."

"All I've got to say, Joe, is that you sure have your neck stuck out. Sure, I might try some new ideas, but I don't want to commit myself to their success before I try them. I'm not about to tell the boss that I can do something until I have already done it. In that way, the results will speak for themselves. A bunch of high-sounding objectives makes me nervous. If I'm going to be happy in the job—and that is *what they seem to be shooting for—I don't want to create more pressure for myself. If I can push my boys to increase their production, it's going to make me look good. My chief problem is that I've got a couple of boys who want to quit. Today, I'm going to talk to them and tell them that there are plenty of good men who'd like their job and that they have got to get with it or ship out. My idea is to run a tight ship, and I don't see*

any point in one of the objectives that the boss set for me—I didn't want it but I finally agreed—to reduce the high turnover of people in my department. I see nothing wrong with getting rid of people that really are no good."

"Well, I've got different problems—all my people are really good, and I'd be sunk if several of my diemakers quit. My big problem is that my people want each item that they turn out to be so good that it will win a prize. I don't have problems with my quality objectives, but I have got to figure out how we can look good on the quantity targets. The kick I have with my objectives is that it's a lot easier to measure the quantity that our department turns out—you only have to count them—but how can I show the boss that each item we turn out is really high quality? Sure, I can show that our defective rate is low, but I wish the boss had a way to demonstrate that my gang turns out good stuff—he always talks to me about turning out more."

"Say, Joe, I have to run—I've got to get back to the salt mines; when I'm away from the shop, I get the feeling that my boys start goofing off. I guess you just can't wait to get back to your happiness boys. Have fun."

Managers are people of action who participate in decisions about the planned changes of their work groups. These three ideas—action, decisions, and planned change—were the basic topics of Chapters 2, 8, and 9. In this chapter, we want to see where objective setting fits into the management processes. Stated simply, *objectives* are ideas and statements that give the direction and goal to behavior and effort. We saw in the foregoing vignette that managers have different attitudes toward objective setting. In this chapter, we consider how objective setting relates to the manager's world of action, decision making, and planned change.

objectives

OBJECTIVE SETTING AND MANAGEMENT

You may recall the steps in the planned-change process in Chapter 8. In this process, a number of decisions or choices must be made. A situation has to be evaluated, and if a new objective is needed, it must be set; a plan must then be developed and implemented into the work setting. You could almost think of the situation evaluation as related to objectives, since your evaluation must be made against some predetermined goal or plan. If your objective or goal is to be the number one firm in the industry, for example, all decisions will be evaluated with this objective in mind. So the setting of objectives is a critical first step in managing an organization.

Plans flow from previously set objectives. Whereas objectives

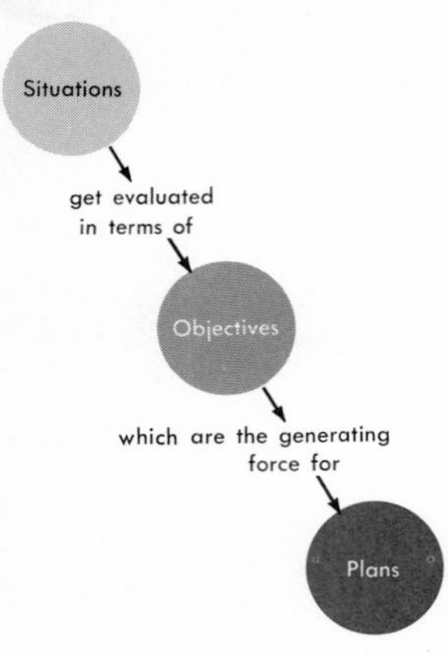

FIGURE 11.1 Relation of objectives to plans

answer the questions of *what* we are doing and *where* we're going, plans give us an idea of *how* to reach objectives. Figure 11.1 highlights this simple relationship.

You may also recall from Chapter 8 that implemented plans are the factors that trigger change or resistance to change in situations. Table 11.1 shows the relation of objectives to the notion of management action. Most of a manager's day will be spent on some phase shown in Table 11.1 The problems you face as a manager emanate from the interplay of objectives with other aspects of organizational activity. An organizational problem will exist for you as a manager under a number of possible conditions.

1. The objective set may be achievable and feasible, but the plan or implementation may be poor. A company currently ranked eighth in sales in an industry may set an objective to be ranked sixth. Their plan may call for increased production at the expense of quality and cost control.
2. The plan may be good but the objective impossible. An excellent advertising and promotion plan may not be able to move your firm from eighth to first.
3. A good objective and sound plan may be too difficult to implement. The extra effort of salesmen may not come when they receive a directive telling them they'll have to work harder.

Other combinations of these conditions are possible, but the illustration should be clear now. Management decision making

TABLE 11.1 The Place of Objectives in the Management Process

Phase	Decision To Be Made	Action State	Interpersonal Change Impact
Situation evaluation	How does the situation compare with objectives?	Preaction	Little
Setting objectives	What direction should we go? Where should we be in the future?	Preaction	Little
Plans	What is the method to better reach the objective?	Preaction	Some
Implementation	What is the way to insure changed behavior and reduce resistance?	Action	Much

and problem solving frequently hinge on the topic of organizational objectives. The previous paragraphs show you how pivotal and critical the topic of objectives is. There are also several important questions in this area that managers will have to answer. *What* are objectives? In what *areas* of activity are they set? *How* are objectives set? *Who* sets objectives? What is the *relationship* between personal and organizational goals? These questions will be answered in the remaining parts of this chapter.

PERSONAL AND ORGANIZATIONAL GOALS

In what direction should the organization head?

Human beings attempt to be purposive; that is, they try to act in a manner that will enable them to reach certain personal goals. In a free and open society, each person is allowed and encouraged to set his own life goals. He may clearly visualize at an early age that he wants money, fame, freedom, a happy family life, excitement, security, or any of a number of other broad and general goals. On the other hand, he may live from day to day and assume some of these goals without clearly directing his own effort. He may borrow his personal goals from those with whom he has close contacts, such as his parents, his close friends, people with whom he is associated in a variety of organizations in which he finds himself, or from writers, speakers, or leaders who appeal to him. In any case, he will need to assume some goals if he is to develop rational behavior, for rationality, as we have seen, may be defined in terms of whether actions are conducive to the achievement of predetermined goals.

Are your goals consistent with the goals of the organization?

When a person joins an organization or becomes closely identified with several others in a social group, he is continually faced with estimating whether his personal goals are consistent with the goals of others. Informal organizations are developed spontaneously by people who discover that their interests and goals have elements in common. In each case, the goals of one person may not be exactly the same as the goals of others in the group; in fact, there are usually conflicts of personal goals.

Organizational goals are derivatives of personal goals; throughout life, a person either consciously or unconsciously continues to check whether his own personal goals are consistent with the goals of social groups to which he belongs. He will remain in organizations that generally support his own goals even though there are day-to-day conflicts.

zone of indifference

Some people have a broad *zone of indifference;* that is, they remain loyal to an organization in spite of many slight differences between their personal goals and the goals of the organization. Others have narrow zones of indifference, which means that they do not tolerate association with people with differing goals. In such cases, they may "drop out" as a result. However, even the most individualistic person with a narrow zone of indifference generally finds that it is to his advantage to perceive his personal goals as being fairly consistent with those of some organization.

Do your personal goals conflict with one another?

Individuals and organizations tend to have many goals. Some tend to conflict; some are more important than others; some are short run and some are long run. Moreover, the priority of goals tends to change for both individuals and organizations. For example, a young person selecting a job may not consider retirement benefits important; but as he becomes older, security in his old age may take on greater weight. A person may tentatively state that his goal is to get the greatest amount of money. When offered this maximum amount of money for a particular job, however, he may find that the job requires him to risk his life, work under unfavorable conditions, or perform activities that have no interest for him. Thus he may find that his single goal of money is actually qualified by a number of other goals that are as important or more important to him. In other words, a person continually faces conflicts among his own goals. In such cases, it is very helpful for him to recognize what he really wants and establish priorities among his own conflicting goals.

coalition

Now let us consider an organization as a *coalition* of twenty people who have a variety of goals and each of whom has a variety of priorities among his own individual goals. If this group is to cooperate toward common organizational goals, it must evolve an official set that will motivate the individual members within their zones of indifference to participate toward the achievement of the organizational goals. These official organizational goals are usually stated in broad terms so that they can accommodate the conflicting order of preference of the personal goals of individuals in the organization. If an individual is to accept organizational goals, he must feel that achieving them will satisfy, or at least not conflict with, his own personal goals. Organizational goals therefore serve as common denominators for the entire group. Thus, organizational goals must be clear but general, if for no other reason than to make it possible for the individual members to be aware of the direction in which the organization is headed. In fact, quite often, if organizational goals are well stated and are meaningful to an individual, he will tend to adopt them as his own personal goals.

How can personal goals also be organizational goals?

As an open system, an organization generally imports its official goals from across the boundary of the organization—from the external environment. Legally, society permits the formation of a corporate organization by granting a charter that states generally the goals and mission of the organization. Within this highest level of goal formulation, the organization as a coalition interprets these broad goals through continually bargaining and shifting among often conflicting personal goals of its members. At the organization level, goals may be inconsistent and ambiguous in order to accommodate the variety of preferences among individual members. One accepted view of goal formulation by organization members is that the organization must provide *inducements* (by means of money, status, challenges, and other evidences of achievement), so that each member perceives his *contributions* as not too great for him to remain in the organization. A middle manager views the official goals as imposed from outside the organization (that is, from society), and he continually participates in internally interpreting the goals of the whole organization. But operationally, he has the influence to *set* objectives for himself and his immediate subsystem or department. The remainder of this chapter will focus on objective setting at this level, since it is here that specific objectives can serve as the foundation upon which all management activities can be built.

Hierarchy of Objectives

Organizational objectives give direction to the activities of the group and serve as media by which multiple interests are channeled into joint efforts. Some may be broad objectives of the organization as a whole; some may serve as intermediate or subobjectives for the entire organization; some are specific and relate to short-term aims.

There is a hierarchy of objectives in an organization: At the top, the entire organization aims in a given direction; each department in turn directs its efforts toward its own objectives; each division of each department has its own meaningful aims; and finally, each individual position can be assigned definite objectives, which can clarify the role of the person that fills that position. Table 11.2 illustrates this hierarchy for a middle-sized company.

Are some objectives more important than others?

In Chapter 6, the idea of a hierarchy was introduced in the development of an organizational structure. In this structure we saw that there was a need for a job pyramid in the statement of what was called the scalar principle. In that chapter, we focused on

TABLE 11.2 Sample of a Hierarchy of Objectives in a Middle-size Company

Top Management

1. Represent stockholders interests—net profits of 10% or more.
2. Provide service to consumers—provide reliable products.
3. Maintain growth of assets and sales—double each decade.
4. Provide continuity of employment for company personnel—no involuntary layoffs.
5. Develop favorable image with public.

Production Department	Sales Department	Finance & Accounting Dept.
1. Keep cost of goods no more than 50% of sales. 2. Increase productivity of labor by 3% per year. 3. Maintain rejects at less than 2%. 4. Maintain inventory at 6 months of sales. 5. Keep production rate stable with no more than 20% variability from yearly average.	1. Introduce new products so that over a 10-year-period, 70% will be new. 2. Maintain a market share of 15%. 3. Seek new market areas so that sales will grow at a 15% annual rate. 4. Maintain advertising costs at 4% of sales.	1. Borrowing should not exceed 50% of assets. 2. Maximize tax writeoffs. 3. Provide monthly statements to operating depts. by 15th of following month. 4. Pay dividends at rate of 50% of net earnings.

Foremen	District Sales Managers	Office Managers
1. Handle employee grievances within 24 hours. 2. Maintain production to standard or above. 3. Keep scrappage to 2% of materials usage.	1. Meet weekly sales quotas. 2. Visit each large customer once each month. 3. Provide salesmen with immediate follow-up support.	1. Maintain cycle billing within 3 days of target date. 2. Prepare special reports within a week of request.

authority, responsibility, and the departmentation of the necessary activities of the organization. In this chapter, we are focusing on the question, "Organization for what?" and we are giving a partial answer to that question by observing that each individual in the organization must have a clear understanding of what he is trying to accomplish and must see how these objectives interrelate with the broader and longer-run objectives of the larger group. In other words, we are focusing on a pyramid or hierarchy in which the top is supported by the individual building blocks (individual objectives) used by each member of the organization.

The hierarchy of objectives provides a structure by which each member in a group effort can concentrate on interrelating his own output to the total and on clarifying each contribution to the broader and longer-run goals. The process by which this idea can be put into practice is management by objectives, introduced by Peter Drucker, as noted earlier.

MANAGEMENT BY OBJECTIVES

management by objectives

How can you direct others toward better use of objectives?

The hierarchy of objectives has recently been systematized and called *management by objectives* (MBO). Its basic idea is the joint participation of subordinate and superior in the establishment of clear and definite objectives for each individual and unit (as illustrated in Figure 11.2). The usual approach is for each manager and his subordinates to get together at the beginning of a period and discuss objectives until an agreement on clear objectives is reached. In this discussion, each subordinate has the opportunity to set his own objectives. Of course, if these objectives are not satisfactory to the superior at this time, it may become evident that the subordinate's zone of indifference is not broad enough; that is, that he does not want to accept the organizational objectives set by the higher managers. In this case, however, it is much better for these differences to be brought to light, since all concerned can then adjust their expectations to reasonable, jointly understood targets. If there is agreement, management by objectives can provide

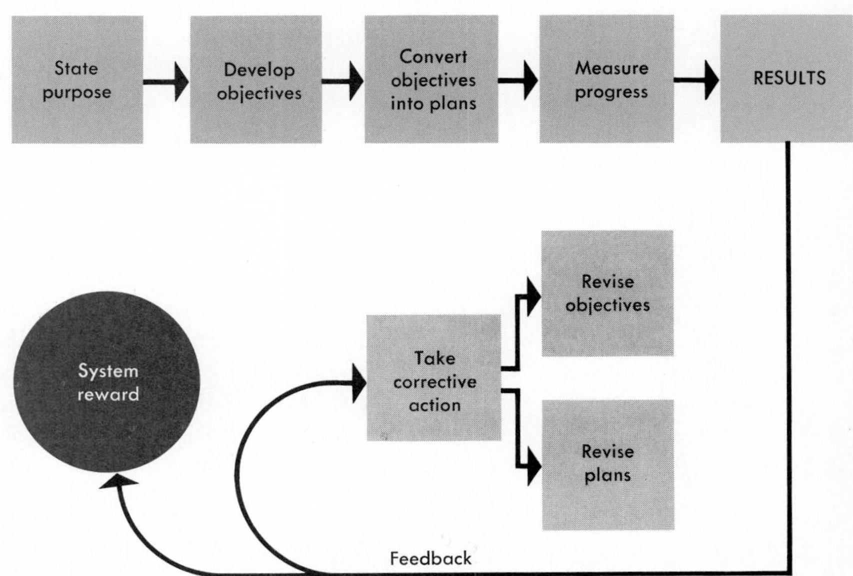

FIGURE 11.2 MBO model

a fundamental base for carrying out activities in a coordinated manner. Many problems can develop, as we have seen in the discussion between Joe and Bob in this chapter's vignette; yet different attitudes are possible for resolving the issues between superior and subordinate.

Management by objectives is also called managing by results. It involves setting yardsticks of effectiveness for each managerial position and a periodic conversion of these yardsticks into usable objectives. Many advantages are claimed by proponents of MBO:

1. A subordinate learns at the beginning of a period what is expected of him, and thus there is less chance of frustration.
2. A subordinate agrees on a clear method of measuring his performance, and therefore feels a sense of participation.
3. Since a manager has helped set his own objectives, he is motivated to hit his targets and not seek excuses.
4. Superiors feel more security in forecasting results and in planning future activities.

In many organizations, MBO has been successful in motivating managers and in measuring performance; yet research has shown that problems can develop unless implementation is carefully planned. Top management must give active support. Each individual must perceive that objectives jointly arrived at will be applied, and feedback from actual performance will serve as the basis for revising objectives in a future period. MBO is a dynamic process that has potential for changing the climate of the organization.

Characteristics of Sound Objectives

How can objectives be made meaningful to the individual using them?

We may agree that orientation to results, participation in setting objectives, and the availability of yardsticks all sound fine and good; but how can sound objectives be set for each individual and unit in an organization? Let's get down to the specific requirements. Assume that a subordinate and a superior have met and agreed that (1) the subordinate will improve performance, (2) he will work harder, and (3) he will motivate his workers. Now, all these objectives are commendable, but none satisfies the following basic requirements for sound objectives—that they must:

1. Be measurable and usually quantitative
2. Be specific

3. Identify expected results
4. Fall within the power of the individual manager or unit (not allow buck passing)
5. Be realistic and obtainable
6. Clearly state time limits for completion

Other characteristics of sound objectives have been proposed: Objectives should make people reach a bit; they should allow for creative methods and thus should not predetermine the means for achieving them; they should be known to all workers so that the workers understand the targets for their own work and how they relate to the broader objectives of the organization; they should be periodically reconsidered and redefined; and they should not be too numerous or complex.

When a subordinate and superior are involved in the process of searching for sound objectives, they have the opportunity to select the specific objectives from a number of sources. First, an objective may be built upon past experience; for example, cost will be reduced by 10 percent, or sales will be increased by 5 percent. Or the objective can be based upon some outside authority; for example, a consultant may have research information to indicate that a fair day's work for a reasonable standard would be *X* number of units, *X* number of dollars in profit, *X* amount of cost, or a given percentage of a total. The objective may also be based upon an average of similar operations by other organizations. Thus, the Jones Company may be producing twenty units per worker, whereas ours is producing fifteen. Finally, the objective may be based upon response from the customer or user of the output; for example, the number of complaints must be kept below five per 100 sales transactions.

The implementation of management by objectives is becoming more and more difficult. Increasingly, units of an organization perform a service or provide some intangible contribution. It may be easy to set objectives for a salesman in terms of the units he sells, or for the production worker based upon the amount of products he produces; however, difficult problems develop in measuring the performance of managers responsible for research activities, public relations, and supportive ideas for other units. Nevertheless, an attempt to identify the exact nature of expected performance is superior to methods in which the manager is evaluated by such other measures as number of hours worked, opinions as to whether he is a nice guy, or maintenance of a customary policy.

Frequently, the statements of objectives are too general and vague to be operational. Many are mere platitudes and assert obvious generalizations such as service to society, profit maximization, protection of the ecological environment, and employee satisfaction. In order to be effective, the statements of objectives that can be useful to a lower or middle manager must be stated in terms that motivate him to identifiable results consistent with the broad, companywide objectives. In the preceding section, we summarized the desirable characteristics of the operational objectives; in this section, we give a specific illustration and describe just how a superior can build up the objectives for each subordinate in order to meet his own specific objectives.

How can you develop useful statements of objectives?

George Odiorne, one of the outstanding recent proponents of MBO, has suggested that the superior meet with each subordinate in order to establish objectives in three major categories: routine objectives, problem-solving objectives, and innovative objectives. For each of these categories there should be an agreement on three levels of achievement: pessimistic (absolute minimum), realistic (normally expected), and optimistic (ideal). This structure helps both parties, since it gives the superior targets that he can support with his bosses, while it gives the subordinate a framework by which he can check himself on a day-by-day basis.

Operational Objectives for a Store Manager Consider the specific example of a manager of a roadside ice cream and hamburger store with ten employees; our manager reports to a regional manager who sets the operational objectives for the store. The regional manager wants to develop some reasonable basis for being kept informed about how the store manager is doing; the store manager wants to feel that he is accomplishing something. An explicit statement of the objectives of the store manager will help both.

Tentative statements of objectives can be made by each manager. A definite time period for meeting the objectives is necessary if the objectives are to be operational. After some interchange (by written statements and by oral discussion) between the two, the form shown in Table 11.3 could be effective in developing a process of managing by results.

How can you improve the statements of objectives?

The form of Table 11.3 could be improved by adding a range for the objectives and by refining the units of measurement for each objective. This approach provides an example of how two managers can jointly develop specific objectives that will be meaningful to each. Each position may list a different set of objectives, and the degree of detail may vary; however, the essential elements require a clear statement of the objective, a means of measuring the performance, and a review of accomplishment based on the agreed-upon measures. Practice in stating objectives that satisfy these elements can improve managerial performance.

How can you "study by objectives?"

OPERATIONAL OBJECTIVES FOR A STUDENT The first page of each chapter in this book is an example of objective setting in an educational context. The idea of instructional objectives (performance objectives) for courses and textbooks is to make clear to the student what is expected of him when he studies a subject. Our objectives in this book have the same characteristics as objectives

TABLE 11.3 Objectives of a Store Manager

Objective (and expected completion date)	Measurement Used	Review Dates	Evaluation (percentage of objective achieved)
1. Number of customers attracted to store will be increased 5 percent monthly.	Actual count by sales tickets		
2. Expenditure per customer will increase by 5 percent yearly.	Sales tickets		
3. Promotion of a new item will be emphasized so that 10 percent of all customers will try new item by end of first month; 15 percent by end of second month; etc.	Special coupons		
4. No customer will be kept waiting for more than three minutes.	Sampling using direct observation		
5. Employee turnover will be reduced.	Personnel records		
6. Operating costs will be kept at the same cost per hamburger as in the past year.	Accounting records		
7. Waste of food will be controlled and the number of garbage cans used limited.	Focus on ratio: percent of food costs to sales		
8. The store will be kept clean so that at no time will there be more than five paper cups, napkins, or plates lying in the customer area at any time.	Inspection		
9. Safety of employees will be maintained so a maximum ot three hours per month will be lost due to burns, cuts, etc.	Time loss records		

for MBO: They are directed toward the end performance that is desired; they are in terms that are measurable—that is, showing the level of satisfactory performance in explicit terms; and they indicate the conditions under which your performance is satisfactory.

The statement of objectives at the beginning of each chapter has given you the opportunity to study by objectives that we have set. Your instructor will probably further delineate the objectives for your course. For these objectives to be operational, you should commit yourself to achieving them and making them your own. Studying by objectives presents problems similar to those we noted in the conversation between Bob and Joe. First, you certainly must read the objectives carefully and work to attain them. Second, the entire process can become a semantics game among the author, teacher, and student, in which each plays along with the idea because it is the currently accepted practice, but without really giving the objectives a chance to help in the education process. Yet as you continue to study this book with the use of explicit objectives, you should see clearly what the process is all about.

SUMMARY AND PROPOSITIONS

This chapter has concentrated on goals, that part of management built on philosophy and value judgments. Specific objectives have been viewed as a derivative of organizational goals and as yardsticks for measuring the success of the organization. The decision process discussed in the preceding two chapters is important both in the setting of clear objectives and in implementing performance to meet the objectives. In the next chapter, planning and policy formulation is shown to be a process for meeting the future challenges and in providing guides for individual decision and day-by-day action.

Since objective setting is basic to other chapters in this book, it will help to restate the basic ideas of this chapter.

1. Organizational goals and objectives serve as common denominators by which individual members decide whether they will cooperate in the organization.
   - *a.* Personal goals may conflict with one another and with organizational goals.
   - *b.* The zone of indifference identifies the latitude with which an individual will permit organizational goals to vary from his own personal aims.
2. Organization objectives form a hierarchy from the broad aims of the organization to the specific objectives of the lowest subunit and of individual members.

3. Management by objectives can make it possible for each subunit of a group to have more freedom in selecting its *means* of achieving the output desired by top management and the overall organization.
   a. Aids in setting objectives consist of the development of indicators of good performance that can be set at the beginning of a period, used during the period, and evaluated at the end of the period by a superior.
   b. Sales quotas, production standards, and financial budgets tend to make MBO easier to implement.
   c. In service industries that are hard to measure, indicators can be made more definite by inventing ratios or percentages (e.g., batting averages), indexes (e.g., composites of personnel turnover, number of grievances, and failures to meet deadlines), and scales (e.g., opinions by consumers, marked on a scale of one to ten, indicating satisfaction with performance of the individual manager).

STUDY ASSIGNMENTS

1. *Based on the conversation between Joe and Bob in the vignette, summarize the character of each man. Compare the men's actions and responses and show how they differ. Do both have some characteristics in common?*
2. *Do you think that each of these managers will be successful? What guidelines would you use in defining success when answering this question?*
3. *Show how the discussion in Chapter 3 and the models of organization in Chapter 6 can help in clarifying the differences in Bob's and Joe's approaches to managing.*
4. *If you could choose the department in which you would work, would you choose the one managed by Bob or Joe? Why?*
5. *List some possible goals for individuals. List possible goals for organizations. Relate these two lists and show how organizational goals may be inconsistent with personal goals.*
6. *Give illustrations from Table 11.2 showing that objectives form a hierarchy.*
7. *What are the basic requirements of sound objectives in MBO?*
8. *Study critically the objectives of the store manager in Table 11.3. Point out those objectives that satisfy all the requirements you have listed in answer to question 7. Make improvements on the objectives that you feel to be poor.*

9. *We have provided you with performance objectives for each chapter. One requirement of MBO is that each person should be involved in setting his own objectives. How can this requirement be satisfied in your classroom?*

10. *How can you estimate the width of your zone of indifference relevant to the educational institution you attend? What happens when zones of many participants are very narrow?*

11. *Explain the reasoning that supports Proposition 3.*

12. *Show how you, at this stage of your course, can better relate your daily study objectives to your long-run goals. Consider such topics as grades in the course, new knowledge, new perspectives, and the relation of these to your prospective life's work.*

situational episodes

1. You have just obtained your first full-time job with a real estate agency. The owner-manager of the agency has just introduced you to most of the 20 full-time salesmen, who receive a percentage of the total commission for their efforts. Some tend to specialize in the type of property they handle—homes, apartments, farms, commercial businesses, or industrial sites. Your manager has asked you to concentrate on expanding the agency's listings of homes available for sale. He explains that this activity is an excellent way for you to learn the real estate business; furthermore, it is most important, because before the agency can earn a commission for selling a house, it first needs to secure a listing of the property and thus the right to make the sale. Your compensation will be determined by the number and type of listings you obtain. It will be highest for an exclusive right to sell by the agency; lower for a multiple listing, in which other agencies may participate in the sales campaign but the listing agency will receive a portion of the commission regardless of who sells; and lowest for an "open" listing, in which all agencies may sell but only the one that makes the final contract receives the commission.

   You are just beginning work, and your personal objective seems clear to you—to make the most money you can. In your first week on the job, however, you observed several incidents that cause you to seek clarification as to exactly what targets you should shoot at. (1) You found one homeowner who wanted to rent his house. (2) You got a tip about another who might "rent with an option to buy." (3) Your first chance to sign an exclusive contract involved a client who had previously made contact with another member of the agency. (4) You got the feeling that some other members of the agency were trying to use you as a general flunky who should help them do the routine legwork in obtaining a listing.

   a. At the end of the first week, you ask the owner-manager to chat so that you can clarify your objectives in relation to the agency's objectives. How should you raise the subject?

   b. After noticing that the older salesmen tend to form cliques for helping one another, you are trying to find out how you can "learn the ropes" and avoid conflicts in objectives. What potential conflicts are indicated from your first week's experience?

2. With the financial help of your uncle, you have obtained a franchise for a gasoline service station from a major oil company. The facilities available enable you to sell three grades of gasoline (regular, unleaded, and premium); lubricate, wash, and make minor repairs on automobiles; and sell auto supplies, soft drinks, and sandwiches. In the past, the station has maintained a high volume of gasoline sales and has been known as one of the few 24-hour stations in the area. You have decided to retain an experienced mechanic for daytime hours and need to hire at least three more attendants. You understand that the previous owner of the franchise had difficulties making a profit primarily because his fixed costs were high and because his employees failed to see how their efforts were appreciated by the owner. You have heard about large companies and their use of MBO, and you are now developing in your mind how you might turn the operations of the station around by focusing on relating your objectives to your employees.

   a. How should you state your specific objectives for the station in terms of gallonage, auto service, food sales, labor costs, hours of work, etc.?

   b. How would you handle your discussion with the experienced mechanic? Should you ask him to participate in setting his own objectives?

   c. In interviewing for the new attendants, should you seek to determine the objectives of the applicants? Should you "lay down the law" as to what you expect of them?

planning and policy-making

TWELVE

OBJECTIVES YOU SHOULD MEET

Describe *the planning process.*

Outline *a procedure for forecasting future conditions.*

Illustrate *the procedure for constructing a budget.*

Construct *a simple network showing the critical path.*

Compute *the payback of an investment.*

Define *policy.*

Outline *the characteristics of good policy statements.*

CAN PLANNERS HELP ME GET A JOB DONE?

"Mr. Jones, now that I've been with the corporation for six months after completing my degree, I'm still having difficulty in seeing how my textbook knowledge is valued by you line people with 15 and 20 years of service with the company. My job in the planning department has been interesting enough, and I've been working with some of the techniques that I learned in college, but most of my time has been spent in training seminars or conferences and the remainder in pencil pushing and routine chores. Next month our plan for a new plant will be due, but as of this date I have little perspective of what we are turning out—I can see only a couple of trees in the forest, and I really can't see how those trees are very important to the company."

"Well, Skip, I don't know anything about those powerful planning tools that you all talk about. My job is running my department, keeping my people reasonably happy, and keeping our costs in line. The reason that I got to know you soon after you arrived was that you looked like a regular fellow who might help me keep in touch with the new ideas and thinking of the Young Turks. I suppose that some of the policies and guidelines that come down to us originate in staff departments like your planning bunch. But some of that stuff is really out of touch with what we can and will do. In fact, I have to plan for the future of my department, but my experience has been that some of the plans that come from your bunch are not relevant to my problems by the time we hear about them. Things are happening so fast in our line department that we need to take action on matters that you in planning don't seem to have considered."

"Of course, you must realize that much of our work—and especially some of the details that I handle in the planning process—is sup-

posed to give you information upon which our projections are based, so that you can modify your actions to fit the changing scene. You have told me many times that you stay so busy keeping day-to-day production going that you don't have time to see the big picture. That's why the corporation has a group like ours, to concentrate on long-run developments to give you support in adjusting your bread-and-butter operations. What eats at me is that people like me are so separated from the actual operations that we can't get a feel of how our plans are being implemented. The reason I have enjoyed our chats here in the dining room is that you help me keep in touch with reality. I'm still convinced that planning specialists should turn out material that is necessary to the company's survival and growth, but from my restricted viewpoint in my own job, I must take most of this on faith. I wish I had more feedback as to whether our plans are really useful or whether they're just filed away. In our business, we can't make money selling plans—we planners are out of a job if you people don't come up with the revenue. Sometimes I feel like asking to be transferred to where the action is."

"Skip, I see that both of us are frustrated, but for different reasons. I'm getting older every day, and I'm getting tired of repeating the same experiences over and over again; I'm out of touch with new ideas that you had a chance to get in college. Sometimes you use words and express thoughts that I don't really understand. You seem to be up in a department where you should be able to know where we are going, but you can't tell how your map is being used. Now you tell me that you don't have a chance to see the entire map because you are so involved with the details of part of it. I wonder whether the big boys in headquarters realize that their attempt to separate planning from operations ends up in making both groups frustrated. I wonder what would happen if they suddenly put you in my job and me in yours. I guess we would both be uncomfortable—my experience couldn't substitute for your up-to-date knowledge, and you might find yourself facing issues in my operations with no experience of how to handle them. I still think that one of the reasons the company places most college graduates in staff positions is to give them time to learn about the company operations and keep them from messing up the assembly line by taking actions that sound good in theory but won't work in practice. I guess the reason they keep me to handle everyday problems is that they know I don't have the knowledge to come up with well-balanced plans for the future."

"Maybe you're right, but I can't see why they don't give each of us a chance to take a project and plan it and then try to carry out the plan. That way might improve our planning by fitting it to up-to-date experiences, and it would give you a chance to get your nose away from the grindstone so that you could develop some ideas for the future. It would keep us both alive."

"I can give you another reason that combining the two might help. I don't think I ever told you that some of those ivory-tower plans that come from your bunch make those of us in operations feel as if we're being manipulated at the end of a string—like puppets! We tend

to view plans as a set of straitjackets. For example, that budget I got last week really is tight in some places, but in others I'm going to have to figure out ways to spend that much money. If they just gave me a single figure and told me to use it any way that I thought best, I believe I could plan my expenditures so that something would be left over. But your costing boys seem to think they know best. Some of your budgets merely encourage people like me to play games—I think you call it 'budgetmanship.' Before the corporation set up your planning department five years ago, I thought the company was making a lot of money. I'm just not sure whether we would be making more money by eliminating the costs of people like you, sitting in planning instead of learning operations on the firing line. It seems that you might be happier also."

"Anyway, it seems that the corporation is heading in the opposite direction. I heard just the other day that they're talking about a separate staff department—this time, it's to be called Organizational Planning. Now there will be a superplanning department to handle such topics as those we are talking about. Now, if I could get into that department, I might be able to influence the organizational boys into coming up with an idea of temporary internships within the company—you could take my job and I could take yours. But then, I guess, we might end up messing up the organization by developing a structure that's out of tune with the times."

"Oh, well, maybe the company is better off leaving us to chat about these matters over lunch where it won't hurt anything. If we were able to put talk into action, things might be worse. Anyway, I've got to get back to operations—I've got a guy who thinks he can do his job in a way that I told him wouldn't work."

"See you—I've got some more data to collect so that you will have a new memo next week as to where you should be in two years."

The planning function has received increased attention as organizations have grown and the subject of management has developed. The need for planning becomes more obvious as people and organizations develop an awareness of the precise nature of their objectives, as discussed in Chapter 11. Planning focuses on estimating the future and establishes the "ballpark" in which decisions are made. Policies provide the cement that holds the many individual decisions together by serving as guides for decisions and relating individual actions to goals and objectives. In this chapter, we explore the basic ideas of planning and policy making that provide consistency and direction toward objectives.

Typically, planning and policies are discussed as they relate to top management; however, these concepts are essential for all levels of management. We saw in the vignette that Skip was assigned to a specialized planning department immediately after he was graduated from college, and how he reacted to his isolation from the day-by-day operations. Many companies have set up separate planning departments to ensure that they focus on adjustments to changes in the future; yet planning is so important that each manager at every level should be aware of the planning element.

PLANNING

Each individual in an organization must have some idea of the general plan set by his superior. With this understanding, the employee can then lay out his own concrete plans. These plans at the lower levels will be for short time periods, and they will be specific. Since planning is such a crucial managerial talent, we shall first discuss the five basic steps in the planning process.

Steps in the Planning Process

How do you set up a plan for the future?

The first step in the planning process is to *identify the goals* of the organization. In this step, the middle managers not only must give lip service to the general goals as stated by their superiors, but must restate these goals in a form that will be useful to their own subunit. In other words, the broader goals must be restated in definite terms that will encourage checking and measuring performance against the expected performance in the plan. Examples of such definite statements are scheduled completion dates, specifications of acceptable quality, standards for quantity of output, limitations of cost for a project, and sales quotas for marketing personnel.

Second, planning involves a *search for opportunities.* This step requires the collection of data that tend to guide the planner toward discovering the needs of potential customers, clients, or others to be served. In this step, the manager must attempt to break out of a fixed way of thinking, leaving his mind open to new ideas for product, methods, and services that would fit the situation. This step includes forecasting events and identifying changes in demand, competition, technology, finances, and industrial structure. Later we shall discuss some of the techniques available for forecasting.

The third step in the planning process is the *translation* of the opportunities *into selected courses of action.* In this step, the plan itself emerges; here, it is placed in writing and becomes a formal document.

The fourth step involves *setting specific targets*, quotas, and quantified statements. At this stage, the plan may be called a budget, a schedule, a routing, or some other specific statement of targets.

The last step of the planning process is *continual review and revision* of the initial plan in the light of its effectiveness in actual performance. It is this final step that checks to see whether the plan is purely a matter of "hot air" or whether it is actually having an effect upon the activities.

Let us illustrate the planning process by a simple example. Assume that you own a car (your capital equipment) and that you set goals to earn a living, to remain independent, and to do something that "turns you on." Let us further assume that you like to see interesting places and show others these places. First, you would check out these goals in relation to your resources (you and your car), and second, you would search for opportunities. Third, if you found that there was a lack of tour agencies for your locality, you could translate these alternative opportunities into a selected course of action. Fourth, if you chose to start a tour agency, you would set up your targets concerning source of customers, schedules for tours, costs of operations, expected number of hours a week for conducting tours, and so on. Fifth, you would check out the various possibilities for revising the plan by hiring a bus, conducting walking tours, expanding your geographical area. Such a use of the planning process would enable you to develop your managerial talents and to put these ideas into practice.

Planning Techniques for Operations

Many techniques and aids are available for improving the planning process. Of course, techniques depend on the type of activity and the dimensions to be planned. In predicting the future, various techniques of forecasting are pertinent, including forecasting economic conditions, sales for a particular product, supply of scarce resources, and availability of skilled workers. *Budgeting* is merely a planning technique in which specific amounts of revenue and costs are planned for a given period of time. In many activities, planning your time is critical; thus, scheduling activities constitutes a specific form of planning. The operation of an office, store, or plant usually involves working within a definite space constraint. Such activities as plant location, plant layout, and channels for transportation involve pictorial diagrams using general concepts similar to those used for mapping of geographical areas.

Since planning always involves looking into the future, one is always faced with errors in the estimating process. Therefore, many planning techniques utilize approaches for handling decisions under conditions of risk discussed in Chapter 10. We outline in greater detail here some of the specific planning techniques available.

Is there a substitute for the crystal ball?

FORECASTING In planning for future actions, a person must identify explicitly how the future conditions will affect his own activities. If he does not have good estimates, he must make clear assumptions. If he does not have the time and skill for good forecasting, he may use the forecasts of others that are published in

forecasting

periodicals, newsletters, and trade association reports. Generally, *forecasting* is of two types: predicting general economic conditions, and predicting market conditions for the products and services offered by an individual firm.

gross national product (GNP)

Forecasting general economic conditions has developed through the use of elaborate econometric models of the economy, which consist of a large number of equations needing a computer solution. The manager should keep up with these predictions of specialists published in newspapers and magazines. However, if he wishes to check his agreement with these by a simple model, he can use the *gross national product (GNP)* model, which has four major components: consumer purchases (durable consumer goods, nondurable consumer goods, services); private investment expenditures (construction, durable equipment, building up inventories); and government expenditures (federal, state, and local spending). Using the GNP model, one merely estimates specific values for each of these components. The manager, with the help of forecasts of others and this simple model, can arrive at his own expectations of general economic conditions, such as that they will improve by 5 percent in the next year, will stay about the same, or will contract by 5 percent. He can *extrapolate* (extend a time series into the future based upon past tendencies) or he can use percentages of GNP as guides.

extrapolate

Using the results from looking at the general economy, the manager is then interested in focusing on the industry and the segment that most affects his organization. The demand for the industry can be viewed as consisting of such components as sales of products to new customers, sales of additional products to old customers, replacement sales for products that have worn out, and sales affected by recent technological developments.

The manager has a number of available approaches for forecasting from which he can choose:

1. He may study the past and assume that what has occurred will continue to occur. In short, he can extend the trends of the past into the future.
2. He may identify key phenomena that have shown a cyclical or seasonal pattern and assume that this pattern will repeat in the future. For example, sales of a product in the past may have consistently been low in the summer and high in the winter, causing him to predict that the pattern will continue.
3. He may find some other phenomenon that is closely correlated with the variable he wishes to predict. Using facts

about the other phenomenon, he can base his prediction on the close association of the two. For example, if his company sells household furnishings, he may use facts about housing construction to help predict demand for furnishings.

4. He may identify some underlying cause for the variable to be predicted and focus on the results expected from this cause. For example, he may find that sales are directly the result of the number of contacts by his salesmen and predict that for every five contacts, one sale will result.
5. He may infer from the results of a small sample of responses to a questionnaire that the total he is predicting will perform in the same way as his sample results indicate.

After the industrial forecast has been made, the manager is interested in just what share of the market he can reasonably expect his company to capture. Past market share may serve as a base, but supplemental data should be obtained from sales personnel and other people who are close to the specific conditions. Thus, reports from the actual markets can make the specific predictions more reliable. In general, the forecasting of future demand provides specific predictions upon which to build a clear plan for the future.

Why do you hear more and more about budgets?

BUDGETING Business budgets are the principal financial means by which the manager can formalize and express his plan in terms of revenue and costs. Accounting data generally give the manager a foundation of historical costs and revenue upon which he can build his projections into the future. Budgets also serve as control mechanism (discussed in Chapter 16) for activities of various functions and operating segments of the firm. Figure 12.1 shows that comprehensive budgeting consists of a number of budgets, with the sales budget usually serving as the focus of the process. The production budget is based on the sales budget, and all others in turn are constructed on consistent assumptions concerning the future.

Budgets reflect joint planning of all operating segments, and so budget committees usually develop plans in order to ensure the cooperation and understanding of all principal parties who will later be affected by the budget.

The period of time for the budget is an important issue for a manager to resolve. Two factors provide a range for the length of time: First, it should be short enough to permit the making of fairly accurate predictions; second, it should be long enough to

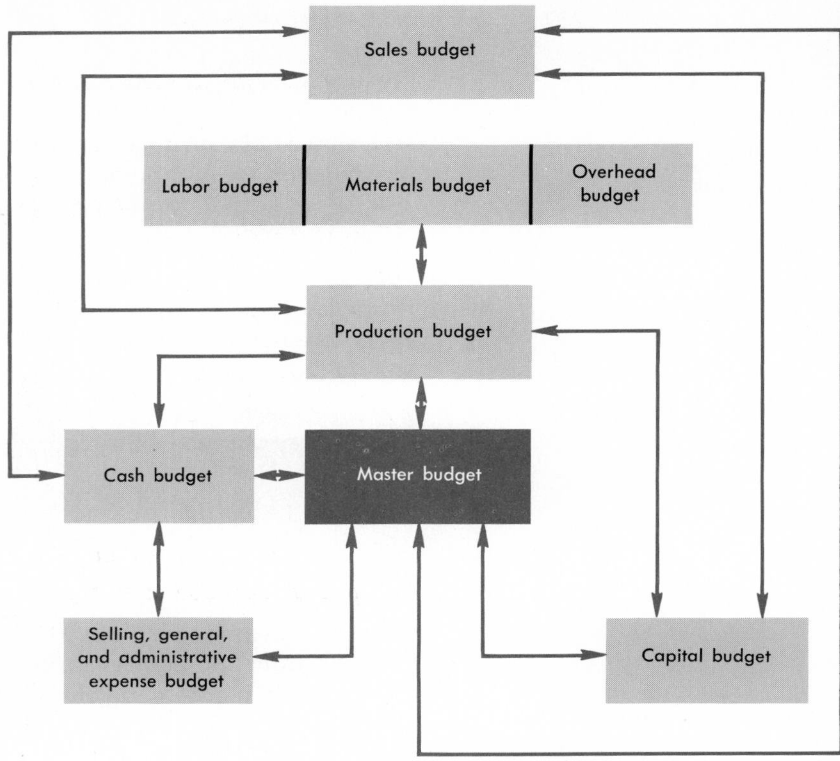

FIGURE 12.1 The coordinating nature of the various budget types

identify significant problems. A number of factors can affect the length of the budget period: the availability of factual information; the stability of the market faced by the firm; the rate of technological progress; the seasonal characteristics of the industry; the length of the production cycle; the customary credit extension time for customers; and delivery times of both raw materials and finished products. In addition, the budget period must coincide with the accounting period so that the comparisons between actual results and budget amounts can be made routinely.

fixed budget
flexible budget

A budget for a stated future period of time that does not make allowance for cost changes owing to possible changes in the amount of output is called a *fixed budget*. A *flexible budget* shows expected costs of production at various levels of production. Table 12.1 illustrates a flexible budget. The prerequisite for flexible budgeting is the separation of fixed and variable costs. Once the flexible budget is formalized and reports are flowing to management, opportunities for analysis are open. The advantages of flexible budgets are that (1) cost variations due to output changes are indicated; (2) the segregation of fixed and variable costs is useful for other management functions; and (3) standard costing is more easily implemented.

Budgets are important planning techniques available not only to the manager but to individuals and heads of households. Such estimates improve one's approach to the future and allow less hesitancy in decisions than would be true otherwise.

How can you do things at the right time?

SCHEDULING ACTIVITIES Scheduling is the term usually used for planning the time for the use of physical and human resources and for the various activities of an organization. Numerous scheduling techniques are available, ranging from simple, everyday devices, such as appointment books, reservations for use of space and equipment, and rough notes on a memo pad, to complex mathematical programming involved in the production of complex and sophisticated activities of the moon shots, missiles, and large airplanes. In this section we concentrate on the proven, simple graphical devices used in scheduling.

As the expected use of equipment, space, or human resources approaches capacity, the manager needs better scheduling devices. Moreover, when one operation cannot start until a previous operation is completed, scheduling tends to become tighter.

Gantt chart

The *Gantt chart,* a general-purpose tool for scheduling, is a bar chart with time on the horizontal axis and the factor to be scheduled on the vertical axis. Gantt charts are used as progress charts (which show the various articles to be produced), machine record charts (which show the available machines and time at which different jobs are planned), order charts (which indicate the

TABLE 12.1 Flexible Budget

	Rate of Operations (output; 000 omitted)			
Types of Costs	**700 units**	**800 units**	**900 units**	**1,000 units**
Manufacturing costs				
Direct labor	$ 350	$ 400	$ 448	$ 497
Raw materials	700	800	900	1,000
Overhead	400	415	425	435
Selling costs				
Salesmen (on commission)	700	800	900	1,000
Advertising	200	200	200	200
Administrative costs				
Fixed	200	200	200	200
Variable	50	55	58	60
Total	$2,600	$2,870	$3,131	$3,392

time to start different orders and the time of completion), and man charts (which show the work planned for each worker or group of workers, as illustrated in Figure 12.2). Special adaptations of Gantt charts involve the use of acetate, pegs in a board, and lights that indicate planned usage.

Critical path analysis

In the last decade or so, network analysis has developed into a general-purpose planning device to indicate all the interconnecting links in a system. *Critical path analysis* uses networks for scheduling production, construction projects, and research and development activities that require estimates of time and performance when it is important to identify the sequence of activities that will set the tightest limits on completion (thus the "critical path"). PERT (Program Evaluation and Review Technique), first developed for use in defense projects, is now a generally accepted network technique for planning all the links in a complex program.

network

A *network* is shown by a line graph (instead of a bar diagram as in a Gantt chart) because it is necessary to clarify the relationship of each task to each other task. Such a network is viewed as a system and subsystems in which the elements interconnect and interact at one or more points. Figure 12.3 illustrates a simple network.

activity

event

The first step in network analysis is to separate each element or link and describe it in terms of other elements in the system. In order to present a network pictorially, as in Figure 12.3, you must distinguish the activities and events involved. An *activity* is a time-consuming effort necessary to complete a particular part of the total project; with the numbers along the line denoting the time, the lines represent the activities. An *event* is a specific instant of time that denotes the beginning and end of an activity; an

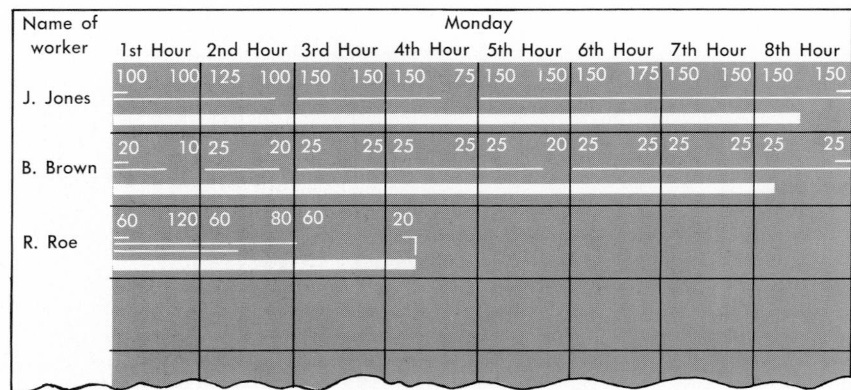

Name of worker
Monday
1st Hour 2nd Hour 3rd Hour 4th Hour 5th Hour 6th Hour 7th Hour 8th Hour
J. Jones
100 100 125 100 150 150 150 75 150 150 150 175 150 150 150 150
B. Brown
20 10 25 20 25 25 25 25 25 20 25 25 25 25 25 25
R. Roe
60 120 60 80 60 20

FIGURE 12.2 The Gantt chart for scheduling workers' activities

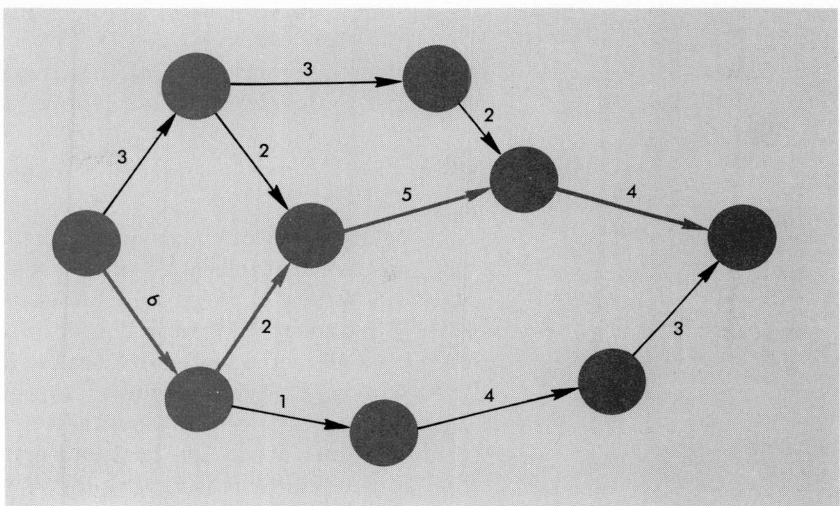

FIGURE 12.3 A simplified network. This network is merely a pictorial device to indicate the following: After event *A*, there are two activities, one taking three minutes ending in *B*, and one taking six minutes ending in *C*. Likewise, after event *B*, two activities occur, one taking three minutes leading to *E*, and one taking two minutes leading to *D*; and so on to the terminal event *I*. With this device, you can see which activities take the longest time (thus, *critical*). You can also quickly see that reducing the activity time between *A* and *B* would not speed up final completion at all (since it is not on the critical path). You would therefore look for means of shortening activity times between *A* and *C*, *C* and *D*, *D* and *G*, or *G* and *I*. Of course, if you could reduce the activity time between *A* and *C* to two instead of six minutes, this improvement would change the critical path to *A* to *B* to *D*.

event is represented by an ellipse or circle. An event cannot be accomplished until all activities preceding it have been completed. All activities begin and end with an event. The event is a milestone or signal for dependent succeeding activities to begin. Events are usually assigned numbers sequentially for identification and analysis. In thinking through the process, you should repeatedly check three questions about events and activities: (1) What must be accomplished before a given event? (2) What cannot be accomplished until an event is completed? and (3) What can be accomplished concurrently? After a network has been prepared and times for each activity have been noted, it is then possible to determine the path that consists of those events and activities that require the maximum time (by adding the times for all activities along the path). The *critical path* (the brown line in Figure 12.3) identifies the sequence of activities that will determine the earliest time at which the project can be completed.

critical path

Many variations of these graphical devices are available;

however, the simple idea of charting time makes it possible for the manager to develop his own tailored techniques.

Planning Techniques for Resources

Many types of charts and maps are available for planning the use of space, capital, and human resources. Planning of space involves a variety of maps with dimensions, conventional signs, and lines for transportation or communications. Office and plant *layouts* may be represented by scaled diagrams or models showing the space and physical equipment needed for the activities. Using these simple devices, the manager can simulate his entire operation and thus avoid the trial-and-error method of moving the actual equipment or reassigning the space.

layouts

Capital budgeting

payback period

How can we choose among investment opportunities?

Capital budgeting is a plan for the long-range financial investments required to obtain benefits from alternative uses of capital. Several approaches to the evaluation of investment opportunities provide estimates for planning to satisfy capital needs. The *payback period* is an estimate of how long it will take for the investment to pay for itself. This period is then compared with some standard period. If the asset will pay for itself in less time than the standard period, the investment should be made. The payback formula is simple:

$$P = \frac{C}{R}$$

where P represents the payback period, C the cost of investment, and R the expected net annual return from the investment. For example, if a new machine will cost $10,000 and produce $5,000 in extra revenue per year, its payback period would be two years.

present value

A more precise method for evaluating capital expenditures is to determine the *present value* of the net cash benefits, from widely available tables that discount at the cost of capital rate of interest. If the amount computed is greater than the new investment, monetary gain should result from the outlay. Assume that the cost of capital is 10 percent after taxes, and the benefit after taxes for a $10,000 investment is $4,500 per year for three years. Using present-value tables, we find that the present value of this stream of income discounted at 10 percent is $11,192, or a net realizable gain of $1,192. Since tables are available for finding present values, it is not necessary to work out each formula computation or to understand all the theory behind the formulas and tables.

Planning for human resources involves a systematic method for identifying future personnel needs for a particular project and making a manpower inventory of available personnel. Two essential aspects for manpower plans are description of the necessary jobs and specification of the qualifications of people needed to perform the jobs. In other words, any planning for manpower requirements necessitates a description of the entire operation, in which individual positions are clearly defined in terms of their function, authority and responsibility, and relationships. With this information, one can identify the skills, aptitudes, interests, and educational background necessary to perform the job, and a recruiting program can be developed to locate people with the required qualifications. We shall discuss this subject further in Chapter 13.

Estimating Risks in Planning

In using the planning process just described, it is very valuable to identify the risks involved in each opportunity and to relate these opportunities and risks to the basic goals of the organization. Again, it is desirable to use probability estimates to help in the selection of the proper course of action. One fairly clear but simple approach is to divide the various degrees of risk into three classifications: conservative, normal, and speculative. This is similar to classifying horses at the racetrack as favorites, probable winners, and long shots. It might help further to quantify the risks involved in each class of opportunities—such as those with a 75 percent chance of succeeding, those with a 50 percent chance of succeeding, and those with a 25 percent chance of succeeding. Consider an operation that depends upon assuming risks of weather conditions. Current weather reports are now expressed in terms of the percentage of chance of rain. If the operation involves outdoor activities that would be halted by rain, you need only make use of the weatherman's probability as an estimate for the weather risks of the operation.

It is helpful to be aware of the assumed risks, but a plan should also include alternatives available for handling the risks; for example, if it rains, we could pitch a tent or move inside for alternative operations. Thus, good planning includes selecting the primary course of action and developing plans for alternative courses of action if certain things occur.

POLICIES AS USEFUL GUIDES

Policies flow from planning and are the extremely useful connections between goals and action. As previously explained, we concentrate here on the idea of policy as a useful day-by-day guide. It is true that large organizations have broad policies such as diversification, social involvement, equal employment opportunities, attitudes toward unions, and prices. The middle manager must be well acquainted with these general policies and use them as guides for his action, but he is also in a position to set more specific policies that will guide his subordinates in their decision making.

A policy should be distinguished from certain other closely associated terms. Table 12.2 offers a summary of some of these terms. As a guide for making decisions, policies provide important advantages:

Are policies important to all managers?

1. They tend to serve as precedents and thus reduce the repetitive rethinking of all the factors in individual decisions; they save time.
2. Policies aid in coordination; if a number of people are guided by the same policies, they can predict more accurately the actions and decisions of others in the organization.
3. Policies provide stability in the organization and thus reduce frustrations of members.
4. Clear policies encourage definite individual decisions, inasmuch as each manager has a clear understanding of the *range* within which he can make decisions and thus feels less uncertainty about whether he can give answers to subordinates without getting into trouble.

An important characteristic of a policy is that it provides a guide and a framework for subordinates' decisions. Therefore, strong and clear policies encourage the delegation of decision making; they do not predetermine the decisions. For example, a personnel policy by a department manager may state that each person is allowed a fifteen-minute coffee break each half-day and that as long as the obligations of the job are satisfied, he may have some leeway concerning the times of reporting and leaving each day. Such a policy provides clear limits to the range in which individual decisions can be made: Coffee breaks are limited to fifteen minutes but may be taken at different times; an employee must get his work done, but his pay is not reduced if he is one minute late.

Good policies provide definite and clear direction by management and at the same time allow subordinates to make their own decisions within clearly stated limits. A good policy has the following characteristics:

1. It should be related to an objective of the firm and be explained to all those to whom it applies.
2. It should be stated in understandable words and in writing.
3. It must prescribe limits and yardsticks for future action.
4. It must be subject to change but relatively stable.
5. It must be reasonable and capable of being implemented.
6. It should allow for discretion and interpretation by those responsible for carrying it out.
7. It should be subject to periodic review.

Whenever a manager is required to make a decision on a matter that he has not considered before, he should check all existing policies. If there has been no previous policy statement, he

TABLE 12.2 Policy and Related Terms

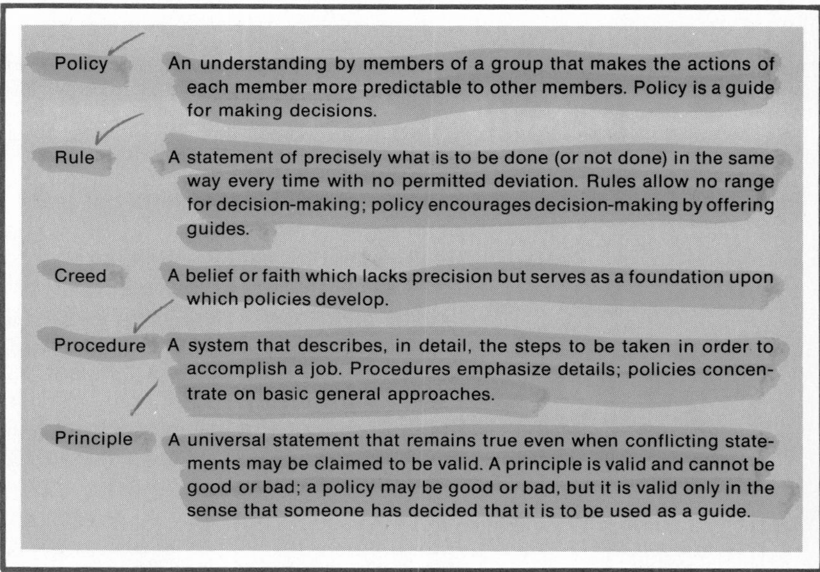

Policy	An understanding by members of a group that makes the actions of each member more predictable to other members. Policy is a guide for making decisions.
Rule	A statement of precisely what is to be done (or not done) in the same way every time with no permitted deviation. Rules allow no range for decision-making; policy encourages decision-making by offering guides.
Creed	A belief or faith which lacks precision but serves as a foundation upon which policies develop.
Procedure	A system that describes, in detail, the steps to be taken in order to accomplish a job. Procedures emphasize details; policies concentrate on basic general approaches.
Principle	A universal statement that remains true even when conflicting statements may be claimed to be valid. A principle is valid and cannot be good or bad; a policy may be good or bad, but it is valid only in the sense that someone has decided that it is to be used as a guide.

must still make a decision in the individual case. However, he should be aware of the potential future *policy implications* of his single-shot decision, since it may be referred to in a later situation as providing a precedent for other decisions. Every manager is involved in making decisions that have such policy implications. In fact, if a written policy is continually ignored by a number of managers and if the superior knows of this practice and does nothing about it, it means that a new policy is evolving—that is, the policy generally is to ignore the previously written statement of policy. In this way, it can be seen that policy guides are either written or unwritten statements actually used in helping make decisions consistent.

Since policies evolve from good plans, and since the actual performance of duties and activities depends upon some means of directing future actions, planning and policies are fundamental to the management of an organization.

SUMMARY AND PROPOSITIONS

All managers are involved in planning for future action. Top management makes long-range plans (e.g., ten to twenty years), and subordinates must be acquainted with some of the details of these plans and their assumptions. Middle managers make plans of their own for shorter periods (usually one year); these medium-length plans must be consistent with the long-range ones and make it possible for the lower-level managers to make their own plans. The lowest-level managers make their own plans (usually for days, weeks, and months).

We have seen that planning can be viewed as a five-step process: (1) identification of goals, (2) search for opportunities, (3) translation of opportunities into selected courses of action, (4) establishment of definite, quantifiable targets, and (5) continual review and revision of plans.

Although planning may appear to be vague and general, there are many techniques available to the manager to help him create clear and definite plans: Forecasting techniques offer means of predicting the future; budgeting enables managers to formalize their planning of financial needs and resources; scheduling techniques, such as Gantt charts and networks, help in determining the timing of future operations; and capital budgeting can make investment planning more rational.

With the development of clear plans, policies can be set to give useful guidelines to other managers for making decisions and implementing plans. The subject of policy is important to all managers for two major reasons: (1) Each manager must learn how to use the policies set by his superiors to help him make decisions that are consistent with those of others; and (2) each manager makes his own policies so that his subordinates can have a definite understanding of his thinking and make day-by-day decisions that are consistent with that thinking.

Finally, the ideas for planning and policy making can be summarized into the following useful propositions:

1. In the busy life of a manager, there is a basic human tendency for day-by-day activities and decisions to drive out thought about planning for the future and establishing unambiguous paths for future action directed toward goals and objectives.
   a. "Putting out fires" of daily crises, the proverbial "rat race," and dealing with the run-of-the-mill routine chores about which questions of relevance continue to haunt people indicate conflicts between "doing" and "thinking."

   Gresham's law of planning

   b. This proposition has been called *Gresham's law of planning*—bad uses of time tend to drive good uses out of circulation.
2. The importance of planning increases as changes in the environment accelerate.
   a. In traditional societies (those that maintain their ancient cultures, such as in India and Africa), cultural institutions, habits, and customs provide the guides for decision making, because change is relatively slow and the individual does not feel the power to affect his own destiny.
   b. Rapid changes in technology (e.g., computers), government policy (e.g., ecological awareness), economic growth, and social norms in modern society demand that managers devote more time to planning and adjusting plans.
3. Flexible plans can form the basis for enabling the organization to adapt more quickly to new situations.
4. A plan for the organization should be built from the bottom up, with each subunit preparing its own plans and integrating into the general plan.
5. An effective plan depends upon relating commitments among human, financial, and physical resources sufficient to make the accomplishment feasible.
   a. The development of plans has little effect unless these plans are actually used and are built upon capabilities for implementation.
   b. A simple plan that is used is better than a complicated plan that is ignored because it appears to be a "pie in the sky."
6. Policies clearly define the range within which individual decisions can be made and thus encourage clear and forceful decisions.

a. By identifying the limits for individual decisions, policies direct performance toward long-range goals.

b. By providing deliberations on basic issues, policies save the time of decision makers by reducing the need to consider factors outside the range of the individual decisions.

STUDY ASSIGNMENTS

1. How is planning different from decision making? Can a person be a good planner and a poor decision maker? a poor planner and a good decision maker?

2. Using the five steps in the planning process, prepare a plan of study for becoming qualified as a manager.

3. Show how forecasting is desirable for planning work at the first or second level of management.

4. Can budgets provide means by which management by objectives (MBO) can be made meaningful to each level of managers? Give several examples of how these two ideas are related.

5. Is budgeting less important in a rapidly changing situation than in a stable situation? How does the flexible budget (Table 12.1) help answer this question?

6. Prepare a Gantt chart for scheduling work in a shop in which a number of customers' orders are to be processed on a first come, first served basis.

7. In Figure 12.3, assume that the activity between C *and* F *will temporarily take seven minutes (due to the breakdown of a key machine) instead of one minute. How does this affect the critical path and the final completion time?*

8. How can clearly stated policies enable managers to make better decisions without continually checking with their superiors?

9. Using Table 12.2, classify the following statements as to whether they are examples of policy, rule, creed, procedure, or principle:

a. An order form shall be completed in triplicate.

b. No smoking is allowed in this area.

c. A district manager may make expenditures for supplies not exceeding $50 without obtaining higher approval.

d. The government prescribes that we cannot sell products at less than cost.

10. *Make a policy statement for employment of workers, using the guides listed in the text.*

11. *Have you found that Proposition 1*(a, b) *is valid in your own experience? Explain, using an example.*

situational episodes

1. You are planning to construct a small cottage on a lake. You hope to perform most of the carpentry work yourself and to subcontract the electrical, plumbing, and foundation work. With the help of a friend who is a general contractor, you have identified the major steps for the work, but you need to estimate the time for each activity so that you can have an idea as to the overall time it will take to complete the cottage. You have thought of preparing a network chart that includes your estimated times for each activity. With this preliminary network, you will be in a better position to check with your friend, who has agreed to check your estimates and the proper sequencing of the activities. Prepare the first draft of your network in preparation for talking with your friend, who will then revise your estimates in line with his experience on such jobs. The major activities are these: lay foundation, frame the shell of the house, do rough plumbing, perform basic electrical wiring, do roofing, install interior paneling, install windows, install plumbing fixtures, install electrical outlets and lighting fixtures, lay floor tile, paint, and do general cleanup and finishing.
2. You have formed a parcel-delivery-service company. You are considering the purchase of a new truck that will cost $5,000. You have estimated that this new truck will provide additional revenue of $2,500 per year over and above all operating expenses. To help you in your planning for this capital expenditure, you want to compute the payback on the truck. After making this computation, you should interpret the payback so that it will help you be more certain as to the advisability of deciding whether to buy the truck.
3. As a new office manager for an insurance agency, you supervise five secretaries and clerks. In your first month on the job, you find that in the past there have been problems in handling schedules for lunch hours, leaves, and certain official holidays, and in providing for possible absences owing to sickness. Your supervisor has delegated to you the authority to handle work times for your subordinates as long as the office remains open for business between 8 A.M. and 5 P.M. The agency will not pay overtime (above 40 hours per week). In order to reduce the present friction among your personnel regarding the fairness of working hours, you have decided that you need to prepare a memo stating policies relative to assignment of working hours. You want to be sure that your policy statements will be feasible and will serve as useful guides in the future for your decisions in making equitable assignments to meet the needs of the office operations.

staffing:
relating people to organization structure
THIRTEEN

OBJECTIVES YOU SHOULD MEET

Describe *three approaches for fitting people into a formal organization structure.*

Prepare *a complete personal data sheet for yourself that will be useful to potential employers.*

State *the guidelines for establishing a merit rating system.*

Outline *the chief issues of wage and salary administration.*

State *the guidelines for conducting an interview.*

Define *the different types of standardized tests.*

Identify *the several approaches to manpower planning.*

Explain *Follett's approach for the resolution of conflicts.*

Describe *three methods for people to adjust to the pressure of organizations.*

WHAT KIND OF PEOPLE DO WE NEED IN OUR ORGANIZATION?

Johnny Moss had decided four years ago, after graduating from the state university business school, to join his father in the family's rapidly expanding lumber and building-supplies company. His father had organized the company in 1946 and had purchased five lumber businesses in neighboring towns in the 1950s and 1960s. Johnny realized that his father had keen business sense in spite of his lack of formal education—he was a typical successful independent enterpriser. However, Johnny felt that his father's abilities lay in running a small, informal, personalized company and that the continued growth of the company was dependent upon adding key middle managers.

When Johnny first came with the company, he tried to fit in with his father's philosophy and avoid confrontations. He knew that his father was a strong person, so he would have to go slow in trying to introduce ideas that he had learned from his business courses. In addition, he knew that he himself had a lot to learn about the lumber industry and that any bright ideas he had would have to be tested before he tried to introduce them into the company. In the past year, his father had gradually started to depend on him to manage the main plant and sales office while the old man spent more time negotiating big contracts and searching for going firms that he could buy. Gross sales of the company had increased by 50 percent annually in the last few years, but net profits were no greater than they had been when Johnny started with the company. After thinking the matter over for several weeks, Johnny decided to have a heart-to-heart talk with his father about finding two or three people who had the training and experience to stay on top of the many problems of the growing company. The chance arose one Saturday morning when they were alone in the office.

"Dad, we have both been so busy in the last few months that we haven't had a chance to face up to a basic problem—we need to add several people to our management group who can help us handle the new customers we've been attracting and to help us control our costs. We need some new blood."

"Johnny, I agree with you. In fact, I've been talking to Fred Koster's boy about coming with us. Fred is one of our loyal people who joined us when we bought his company twenty years ago. He's worried about his son because the boy spends most of his time demonstrating on social issues and seems to be having trouble settling down. Although Tom Koster doesn't have any experience or business training, I'm sure that, being Fred Koster's boy, he would give us a loyal and intelligent employee who could develop in the same way that you have."

"Now, Dad, you have hit on the point that I'm most worried about. Everybody we've added to our organization has been one of our close friends, owners of companies that we have bought, or someone who has political connections. That may have been all right when we were smaller, but now it's clear that we must have several people who fit the needs of our larger organization. We don't just need good men, we need some guys who know accounting, computers, and how to make use of cost information. Also, we have a lot of skilled cabinetmakers, but we don't have anyone who can manage our shop and who can plan, coordinate, and control the work of the twenty people in it. I've been trying to help out from the front office, but we're getting too big to run the shop by remote control. Then, our purchasing of lumber needs to be organized—sure, you and I can jump at good buys sporadically, but we can no longer depend on past sources of supply on a piecemeal basis. We need to plan our growth in personnel to meet our real needs. You and I should take an inventory of the people we have and determine who can be promoted. Then, we should look outside for the specific skills that we don't now have in the organization."

"Johnny, I know you think I operate too informally, but from all my years of experience I feel that the best way to pick a man for our team is to find a good, clean, loyal, intelligent person and to teach him our way of doing things. You get a good man that fits in and you'll find that he can adjust to our needs. Anyway, the kind of fellows you're talking about would be expensive—a controller, a production manager, and a purchasing agent would add to our administrative overhead, and you know our costs keep rising so that we don't have any increase in net. Bigger companies can afford to have those specialists, but we need people who can get things done and not spend their time devising new systems and plans that will upset our organization. Maybe Fred Koster's boy is not the one, but I know several others who would fit in. Take Jim Walker, the house builder; he's had seven years of experience in house construction, and I understand that he's thinking about getting out of that rat race. His luck hasn't been good lately, but he knows people and how to get along with carpenters and other people in our business."

"You still don't see what I'm talking about. We are a big organization for our region in lumber now; we can't continue to operate as

though we were small. We've gotten caught in our growth between the small size of firm that can be handled on a personal basis and the large bureaucracy that's big enough to hire professionals and to coordinate operations on an impersonal basis. I agree with you that we can't afford to add a lot of professional people because we can't stand the overhead—but we must evolve into an efficient organization by recruiting some *people on the basis of what they know, not who they are, or what good fellows they are, or how they will fit in."*

"OK, Johnny, let's try to resolve our differences in our approach to staffing our organization. I'll make a list of the people I have confidence in and give it to you so you can check out their 'professional' qualifications. You make a list of the jobs that you feel are critically needed and how you would go about finding your 'experts'. Do you want to advertise in the Wall Street Journal, *or register with the placement office at the university? The chances for a company like ours in finding the type of expert that will fit in from those sources are small. I'd rather see the fellows in operation over a period of time than depend upon interviews, standardized tests, and so on."*

"Dad, I know how you feel, and I'll look for a way to find people who are qualified for our specific needs and at the same time will fit in."

The chat between Johnny and his father deals with a critical and continuing issue of management—selecting and developing people to meet the needs of the organization. Both agree that a growing organization is dependent upon the human factor, but they approach the issue from different perspectives. In this chapter we discuss the staffing function—the manning of the organization in such a way that its objectives can be achieved. This managerial function makes use of the behavioral knowledge contained in Chapters 3–5 and relates it to the organizational concepts explained in Chapter 6. Because of its importance, many firms assign some of the staffing functions to a special department with a title such as Personnel or Industrial Relations; yet staffing is always of primary importance to any manager, from the first-line supervisor to top management.

staffing

The *staffing* function can be viewed as the process of building up the most valuable asset of an organization—human resources. Although the usual accounting records and reports do not include a dollar figure for this resource, there has been a trend toward treating the investment in people more objectively. *Human-asset accounting* attempts to record the significant costs of recruiting, training, and servicing the human element and to recognize the long-term investment in human resources on the balance sheet. This attempt is consistent with what managers have long recognized—that even if the physical assets are suddenly destroyed, the human organization, if staffed properly, can rebuild and maintain a viable firm.

Human-asset accounting

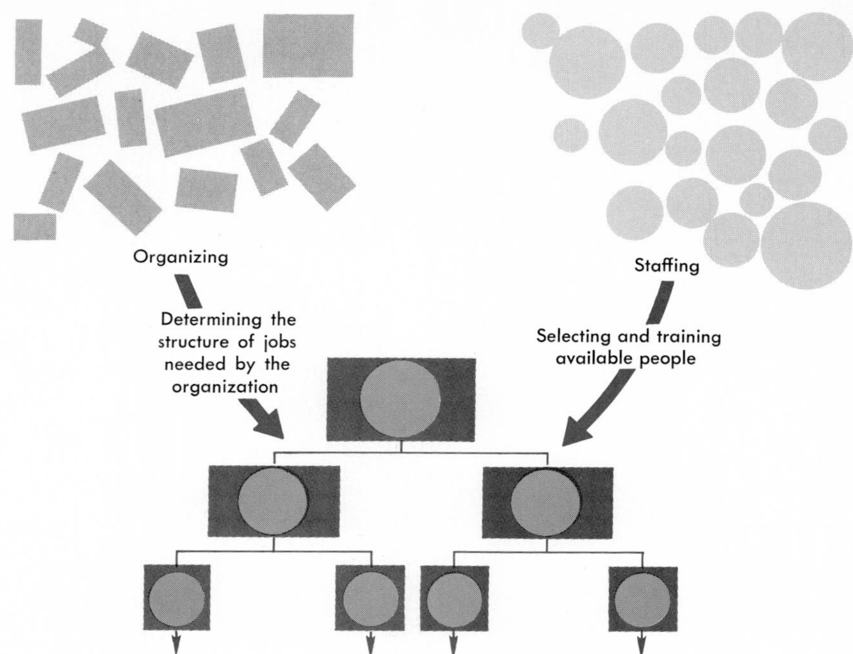

FIGURE 13.1 Matching jobs and people

In this chapter, first, we outline the process of matching jobs and people; second, we discuss the continuing process of managing human assets; and finally, we see how to adjust so as to meet changes in the organization.

MATCHING JOBS AND PEOPLE

How are organization structure and staffing related?

Any organization requires a variety of people, and the supply of people consists of differing types. The staffing function includes the process by which the right person is placed in the right job. There are three ways of handling this matter: (1) Design the jobs first and fit people into the spots; (2) hire people and build the organization around them; (3) do both simultaneously and develop a contingency approach (let the organizing and staffing depend upon the individual situations).

The first has been used by many larger firms for the last half-century; it has the advantage of being implementable in a systematic manner and appeals to engineers, who argue that the design of an organization (like the design of a machine) must come first, but it tends to depersonalize the organizational structure. The second and third ways have received considerable support from behavioral scientists because of their emphasis on the human factor. Nevertheless, in practice, most medium and large firms continue to use a number of processes that assume that people should be fitted into job slots; therefore, even if the behavioral scientists are correct, a person who is a manager in an existing organization, or plans to become an operating manager, certainly should be aware of the structured approach to personnel matters existing in many business firms. Figure 13.1 summarizes the relationship between organizing and staffing.

Determining the Job Structure

The formal structure of the organization (discussed in Chapter 6) is generally assumed to be the foundation on which individual positions are rationalized. Many companies systematize organizing in the four steps shown in Figure 13.2: job analysis, job specification, job description, and job evaluation.

Job analysis
What is the job like?

JOB ANALYSIS *Job analysis* is the orderly and systematic assembling of all the facts about a job. The purpose is to study the individual elements and duties that will make the formal organization structure meaningful and eliminate gaps and overlaps of responsibilities of the total organization.

job description

JOB DESCRIPTION The *job description* is a written statement that defines the duties, relationships, and results expected of anyone in the job. It usually includes a job title, the title of the immediate supervisor, signatures of those who prepared the description, a brief statement of the purpose of the job, and a list of duties and responsibilities. Table 13.1 is a simple job description for a bank supervisor.

The job description is invaluable to a person immediately after he accepts a position, because it offers at least a first overall picture of just what he is supposed to do. When new jobs are created or when reorganization takes place to keep in tune with the needs of the organization, the job description is basic for handling these changes. It is definite and explicit and thus can reduce frustrations. Even if no formal job descriptions are prepared (they seldom are in small firms), each person in a specific job will find it helpful to write down exactly what he perceives his job to be; then he can check with his supervisor to determine whether he is on the right track. Unless there is a common understanding, disagreements between the superior and his subordinate may cause unnecessary friction.

FIGURE 13.2 The process for determining job structure

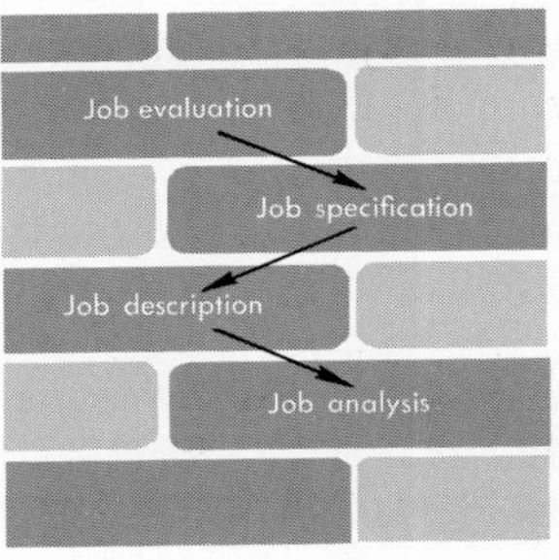

TABLE 13.1 Job Description in a Bank

DEPARTMENT: Trust
JOB TITLE: Supervisor, Trust Accounting
DATE:

The Trust Accounting Supervisor is directly responsible to the Trust Department Head for duties and responsibilities as outlined herein:

Primary Responsibility

Perform diversified assignments to supervise the accounting activities of the Trust Department.

Typical Duties

Verify commissions taken on the trust accounts and approve for posting.
Verify and approve interest calculation on mortgage payments received.
Prepare purchase tickets on new mortgages.
Maintain an inventory of supplies and requisition additional supplies as needed.
Assist the Data Processing Department in programming and processing Trust Department systems.
Assist in the operation of the accounting function as work requires and time permits.
Perform such other duties as may be assigned by the Department Head.

General Information

The Supervisor must possess a complete and thorough knowledge of procedures related to Trust and other departments. He must keep abreast of the latest developments in trust accounting systems.
He is responsible for training personnel assigned to this section and for employee evaluation in the section.

Prepared by:

job specification

What kind of person does it take to do the job?

JOB SPECIFICATION The *job specification* sets forth clearly and specifically what kind of person it takes to do the job—it gives the qualification requirements. The specification includes the degree of education required, the desirable amount of previous experience in similar work, the skill required, and the physical (health) requirements. In applying for a job, it is very handy to have a clear job specification, so that one can estimate how his own background fits the specifications desired by the employer.

Job evaluation

What factors determine the ranking and rating of jobs?

JOB EVALUATION *Job evaluation* is the process of studying job descriptions and specifications to determine levels of responsibility and difficulty for grading and pay purposes. Normally, the ingredients of jobs can be measured in terms of mental requirements, skill requirements, physical requirements, responsibility inherent in the job, and working conditions. In evaluating jobs, it is desirable to find ways in which these ingredients can be measured and handled objectively. For some ingredients, it may be useful to use a point system, in which points are given (say, from 1 to 10) for each requirement; the points can then be totaled and compared with those of other jobs, and the totals ranked in order of the overall level for the job. It is at this stage that jobs are grouped into ranks and grades. Table 13.2 illustrates the factors and the point values that may be used for evaluating some jobs. After the total points are computed for each job, the jobs then can easily be ranked as to their relative value and level.

Determining People's Qualifications

After the needs of the organization are determined through a rational job structure, staffing involves locating suitable people to fit the jobs. Several general techniques are available to help determine the qualifications of available people: (1) personal data sheets, (2) tests, and (3) interviews.

What are your qualifications?

PERSONAL DATA SHEETS You will do well to maintain a concise personal data sheet (resumé) to help you fit into the staffing needs of an employer. In this way, the matching process involves a comparison of the job specification with the personal data of the applicant for the job. This record not only helps an applicant when he is being considered for a new position, but it also serves as a personal scorecard that organizes information about his past performance and facilitates planning his direction in life.

In preparing one's own personal data sheet, one should include all factual information that will be relevant to the person who is seeking to fill a spot in his organization. The sheet is often the first demonstration by the job seeker of his ability to communicate; therefore, not only does it provide factual information, but through its organization of the information it tells the recruiter something between the lines about the type of person seeking the job. If it is poorly organized, it transmits an image of a person who is disorganized. If it is cluttered with unimportant details, it tells the reader that the job seeker has problems in focusing on important matters. If the applicant has information about the company and what it considers to be important, he may want to tailor his resumé to meet the needs of the employer. Table 13.3 illustrates a simple example of some of the information that will usually be helpful to the employer. Since the resumé is generally the first contact with the employer, it necessarily performs the function of attracting attention to one's capabilities and interesting a prospective employer to proceed with other stages in the employment process.

TABLE 13.2 A Point System for Job Evaluation

Rate each job using the following job factors, assigning points by picking the statement that most closely describes the requirements for the job.

	Points					
Job Factors	**0**	**2**	**4**	**6**	**8**	**10**
1. Details to be organized	Few details; little organizing	Well-routinized	Varied work with some need for organizing	Numerous details; organize work of others	Many details that cause problems	Cannot be routinized
2. Supervision of others	None	Two subordinates with routine duties	Small group doing individual work	Large group in routine tasks	Several groups with varied work assignments	Important work that requires individual attention
3. Education and experience needed	High school education; average intelligence; no experience	Minor special training; e.g., typing, operating simple machines	Experience in lower level job; post high school courses	Knowledge of special field	Thorough knowledge; short courses	Knowledge of several fields; wide experience
4. Time required for training	Very little	One month	Three months	Six months	One year	Two years or longer
5. Resourcefulness	Very little	Requires little interpretation	Independent thinking at intervals	Independent thinking regularly	Much initiative and thought	New issues faced constantly
6. Personality required for dealing with others	Rarely in contact with others	Contact with small group	Contacts with public on routine basis	Employees, customers, public on routine basis	Major contacts with key customers, employees	Ability to get along with others most important
7. Responsibility required	Work under direct supervision of another	Any failure noticed immediately	Handles cash and payrolls; audited frequently	No close check by superior	Responsibility for expensive equipment and large funds	High dedication and trust required

The personal data sheet supplies the introductory information to the employer so that he can screen the qualifications of applicants and determine which are compatible with the needs of the organization. The recruiting organization usually provides an application form that organizes the factual material about the applicant to guide the further investigation in the selection process.

With the personal data sheets and the application forms, the recruiter possesses initial information about the total number of people who may have the qualifications to fit the needs of the job(s) that he wishes to fill. Often, the total number of applicants is large, and he must proceed to screen those that best match his needs.

What can be learned from standardized tests?

STANDARDIZED TESTS One source of additional information at this stage is the applicant's performance on standardized tests. Well-developed standardized tests are available for a number of

TABLE 13.3 A Personal Data Sheet

John W. McCable

Home Address: 3 High Street, Centre City, NJ 07632 — Phone: 201 592-7766

Birthplace:	Centre City, NJ
Date of Birth:	February 4, 1956
Marital Status:	Single
Work Experience:	
Nov. 1975 to Present	Centre City Memorial Hospital Admissions Clerk with responsibility of scheduling rooms
1973–75	United Parcel Service, Newark, NJ Parcel Delivery Driver (part time, on night shift while attending school)
Education:	Centre City High School, graduated with honors Centre City Community College, 1973–75
References:	Dr. James Roe, Superintendent, Centre City Memorial Hospital Mr. John Franks, Manager, United Parcel Service, Newark, NJ Rev. Charles Rich, Centre City Community Church Dr. James Rosenberg, Asst. Professor, Centre City Community College
Avocations:	Photography Citizens Band Radio
Aspirations:	To complete my college education possibly in night school To obtain experience in some health delivery organization
Comments:	My father died when I was 15 and I have partially supported myself in part time jobs since his death.

purposes. These tests have been scientifically checked for *validity* (Does it measure what it is supposed to?), *reliability* (Will the test give approximately the same results if repeated a number of times?), and the establishment of *norms* (What standards of results for comparison and interpretation are available?).

Achievement tests
aptitude tests
proficiency tests
personality tests
interest tests

Tests are available for measuring different things. *Achievement tests* measure past accomplishments; *aptitude tests* are designed to predict future potentialities of a person, such as verbal, quantitative, and manual skills; *proficiency tests* measure the attained skill in a task in which the applicant has past training or experience; *personality tests* reveal characteristics of a personality that may affect a person's success in adjusting himself to his work; *interest tests* help a person identify just what type of work he likes. The availability of many different types of tests increases the possibility that a manager may misinterpret test results by failing to recognize what the test does *not* measure. Even the results of the most outstanding test need to be interpreted correctly.

When the recruiter has collected information about the most suitable applicants, he normally checks with references to determine how the selected applicants have performed in school and on other jobs. The most promising candidates are then asked for interviews.

INTERVIEWING The art of interviewing is important to a manager from two perspectives: as one who is being interviewed for a managerial position, and as a manager who is staffing his organization.

From the former perspective, an applicant scheduled for an interview with a prospective employer can assume that the interviewer has studied the information obtained from the data sheet, applicant forms, and test scores and is seeking to supplement this information by personal contact. The applicant is understandably apprehensive. How can he prepare for the interview? How should he act? What should he say? Several generalizations are helpful: (1) Since the interviewer has shown interest in the applicant by obtaining information, the applicant can prepare himself for the interview by prior study about the company he seeks to join. This preparation will enable him to identify with the company and its needs. Furthermore, it will indicate to the interviewer that the applicant is interested in the particular company and not in just landing a job. (2) The applicant's initial appearance and behavior will have a great effect on the interviewing process; therefore, he should dress neatly and try to be at ease. (3) By the applicant's being himself and not trying to act in a role different from his own personality, the purpose of the interview will be better achieved. The recruiter is trying to match a person with the organization's needs, but the applicant is also trying to find out whether he will fit into the company. An honest exchange of comments will support the objectives of both parties. (4) The tone of the interview will be set by the interviewer, and the applicant should speak freely but refrain from "taking over" the interview. Answering questions concisely and to the point will provide a favorable reaction by the interviewer. In addition, if the applicant asks pertinent questions, the interviewer can further evaluate the manner in which he will act on the job if hired.

From the perspective of the manager who is conducting the interview, the interviewing process offers many opportunities. Interviews in general may be either directed or nondirected. In the *directed interview,* which is generally suitable for employment interviews, the interviewer knows what he wants to cover in order to obtain the necessary facts. The *nondirected interview* is more free-flowing, for the purpose of not only finding facts but building confidence in the interviewee and permitting him to talk freely about matters important to him. In both types, however, the interviewer must continually try to allow the interviewee to talk; the interviewer must be a good listener.

directed interview

nondirected interview

Some guides for the interviewer are these:

1. Before the interview, he should review the specific situation so that he has the basic facts in his mind for the talk. He should receive the person being interviewed promptly at the appointed time, plan the physical layout (location of chairs) so that the person will be comfortable and at ease, and try to avoid interruptions by other visitors or the telephone.
2. He should provide an informal, friendly opening to set the tone of the entire interview.
3. In conducting the actual interview, the interviewer should use questions that clarify facts previously stated in writing (in the application form, letters from the applicant's references, etc.); however, he can obtain information from nonverbal sources such as personal appearance, voice, general personality, and emotional characteristics of the applicant. Thus, observation is often as important as listening.
4. He should jot down several words during the interview and dictate or write down the important impressions and facts immediately afterward. If the interview is short, there may be little need to take notes while the applicant is present.

5. He should face emotional overtones and evidence of resistance frankly and not avoid them. A wealth of information may be available from unexpected reactions of the applicant if the interviewer allows him to express himself.
6. He should plan the conclusion of the interview. The last few remarks by each party in an interview give a lasting impression.

An interview is one method by which a manager adds to the information obtained from other sources. Throughout the manager's work, he will conduct numerous interviews, such as employment interviews, exit interviews (when a person leaves employment), counseling sessions, and the handling of grievances. A basic requirement of all interviews is that the interviewer show real interest in the matter, be himself, and encourage the one interviewed to express himself openly.

MANAGEMENT OF HUMAN ASSETS

The staffing function includes not only the matching of the needs of the organization in recruiting new people but also the dynamic process of retaining the best people in the organization. This management of human assets uses many ideas discussed in Part 2 of this book, but it will be helpful to discuss the following chief elements of the staffing function as viewed in a formal organization.

Performance Appraisal

How am I doing?

Job evaluation rates and ranks jobs; performance appraisal rates people's performances in their jobs. Systematic procedures for rating a person's performance are referred to under several headings (all meaning about the same thing), including efficiency rating, merit rating, merit review, progress appraisal, and performance appraisal. All ratings yield several returns to the company: They supply a control function for people (to be discussed in Chapter 16); they are closely related to motivation theory (discussed in Chapter 3); they encourage an objective basis for pay increases to people who continue in the same job; they enable the company to develop an inventory of people for promotion; and, most important, they provide each person with an answer to the ever-recurring question—"How am I doing?" In short, merit ratings challenge people to perform well. Table 13.4 is one example of a merit rating form.

Merit rating systems must be built carefully; if installed too soon, they can fail miserably. Some guidelines are as follows:

1. Good systems depend on day-by-day measures of performance of both good and bad points; for example, if a system involves semiannual reviews, the supervisor should keep good records throughout the period and should not depend only on the performance at the time of the review.
2. In any merit system, each subordinate should be told how he is doing. If a person is not performing properly, he should be told as soon as possible after it becomes clear that he is not measuring up. The human tendency is to avoid such difficult interviews and to let mistakes build up to an explosion point—at which time it might be too late to effect a change in the performance.
3. Good systems encourage involvement by those being rated. Those being rated should know clearly the "rules of the game" and on what basis they are being rated.
4. Systems should rate the *performance* of the person, not the person himself.
5. The system should be consistent with the training program; for example, a new supervisor should be allowed a learning period and should not be rated on the same basis as those who have had time to develop their skills.
6. Some clear method of describing levels of performance should be developed. Some systems use numbers for identifying quality of performance; others use such terms as outstanding, satisfactory, improvement needed, unsatisfactory.
7. The standards of performance should be as objective as possible. We have seen in Chapter 11 that management by objectives (MBO) is a means of using stated objectives as standards.

Personal data sheets and merit rating systems help determine the qualifications of people working in the formal job structure of an organization. With this knowledge of the people and their jobs, we can now explain briefly how money payments to workers are administered.

Compensation

The money paid to each participant in an organization is administered with attention to the three basic subjects illustrated in

TABLE 13.4 A Merit Rating Form

Employee ______________________ Job Classification ______________________ Date __________

THIS REPORT IS MADE OUT FOR (CHECK ONE):

( ) 90 days	( ) 6 months	( ) Annual
( ) Promotion	( ) Transfer	( ) Exit

This rating sheet provides a practical method through which the ability of the individual can be judged with a reasonable degree of accuracy and uniformity. Indicate your opinion of this employee by placing an "X" in the block by the phrase which seems to fit the person best. Please follow these instructions carefully:

1. Use your own independent judgment.
2. Disregard your general impression of the person and concentrate on one factor at a time.
3. When rating an employee, call to mind instances that are typical of his work and way of acting. Do not be influenced by UNUSUAL SITUATIONS that are not typical.
4. Make your rating with the utmost care and thought. Be sure that it represents a fair opinion. DON'T ALLOW PERSONAL FEELINGS TO GOVERN YOUR RATING.

I. ATTENDANCE
1. Punctuality
   a. ( ) Always on time
   b. ( ) Occasionally late
   c. ( ) Requires occasional reminding
   d. ( ) Often tardy—job apparently of secondary importance
   e. ( ) Always tardy
2. Dependability
   a. ( ) Perfect record since last rating
   b. ( ) Rarely absent
   c. ( ) Frequently absent—but for cause
   d. ( ) Poor record—requires counseling
   e. ( ) Unsatisfactory—work suffers

II. PERSONAL QUALIFICATIONS
1. Appearance
   a. ( ) Neat and in good taste
   b. ( ) Neat but occasionally not in good taste
   c. ( ) Sometimes careless about appearance
   d. ( ) Untidy
   e. ( ) Unsuitable for job
2. Personality
   a. ( ) Exceptionally pleasing—a decided asset
   b. ( ) Makes good impression—wears well
   c. ( ) Makes good *first* impression only—doesn't wear well
   d. ( ) Makes fair impression only
   e. ( ) Creates unfavorable impression
3. Tact and courtesy
   a. Shows exceptional tact and courtesy
   b. ( ) Tactful and considerate of others
   c. ( ) Occasionally untactful and inconsiderate
   d. ( ) Attains goal but arouses antagonism
   e. ( ) Often breeds trouble

III. CAPACITY
1. Ability to learn
   a. ( ) Learns with exceptional rapidity
   b. ( ) Grasps instructions readily
   c. ( ) Average ability to learn new things
   d. ( ) Somewhat slow in learning
   e. ( ) Limited in learning new duties
2. Initiative
   a. ( ) Always finds extra work to do
   b. ( ) Pushes work through on own initiative
   c. ( ) Normal supervision required—not a self-starter
   d. ( ) Needs considerable supervision
   e. ( ) Must always be told what to do
3. Judgment
   a. ( ) Outstanding ability to reach sound and logical conclusions
   b. ( ) Action generally based on good reasoning
   c. ( ) Average judgment
   d. ( ) Usually makes decisions without considering all alternatives
   e. ( ) Conclusions often faulty

IV. ATTITUDE TOWARD JOB
1. Interest
   a. ( ) Shows intense enthusiasm and interest in all work
   b. ( ) Shows interest; enthusiasm is not sustained
   c. ( ) Passive acceptance; rarely shows enthusiasm
   d. ( ) Shows little or no interest
   e. ( ) Dislikes work
2. Cooperation
   a. ( ) Goes all out to cooperate with associates and management

TABLE 13.4 (continued)

b. ( ) Promotes cooperation and good will
c. ( ) Moderately successful in cooperating with others
d. ( ) Cooperates reluctantly and sometimes causes dissension
e. ( ) Uncooperative; often breeds trouble

3. Responsibility
   a. ( ) Seeks additional responsibilities
   b. ( ) Willingly accepts additional responsibilities
   c. ( ) Reluctant to accept additional responsibilities
   d. ( ) Avoids responsibility
   e. ( ) Cannot be depended upon

V. JOB PERFORMANCE

1. Accuracy
   a. ( ) Rarely makes mistakes
   b. ( ) Above average
   c. ( ) Average
   d. ( ) Below average
   e. ( ) Highly inaccurate
2. Neatness
   a. ( ) Takes pride in appearance of work. Has "sense" of neatness
   b. ( ) Usually turns out neat work
   c. ( ) Apparently lacks "sense" of neatness. Requires reminding
   d. ( ) Too often sacrifices neatness for quantity
   e. ( ) Majority of work must be done over
3. Quantity
   a. ( ) Unusually high output—meets emergency demands well
   b. ( ) Consistently turns out more than average
   c. ( ) Finishes allotted amount
   d. ( ) Does just enough to get by
   e. ( ) Amount of work done is inadequate

1. How long has this person been under your supervision? ________
2. What do you consider his (or her) STRONGEST POINTS? ________
3. What do you consider his (or her) WEAKEST POINTS? ________
4. What steps are being taken to correct this (or these) weaknesses? ________
5. Give a brief appraisal of employee's potential for promotion: ________
6. Has this report been discussed with employee?
   ( ) Yes ( ) No If not, why? ________

________ Signature—Employee

________ Signature—Dept. Head or Supervisor

________ Title

Figure 13.3: the general (community) level of wages and salaries, the internal equity of pay scales, and incentive pay systems.

How much is the job worth?

The general wage level is determined by economic forces. Productivity, collective bargaining, and rates paid by competitors for similar services are important factors treated by labor economists in explaining wage determination. Each company must obtain factual information about wages currently paid in its labor market. From time to time, the company will make a "labor survey" to determine the supply of labor in its market and the going rates of pay.

The internal equity of a company's pay scales depends on relating the value of each person's contribution to that of each other person and to the needs of the company as a whole. An employee's satisfaction with his own rate of pay is determined greatly by how he feels his pay relates to that of others with whom he has constant contact. Even a person receiving a very generous wage will consider it unsatisfactory if he finds that others who he thinks do not deserve it are actually receiving more. Thus, the manner in which job evaluation and merit rating are translated into money terms is very important in the development of a wage and salary structure that contributes to the long-range goals of the organization.

Systems for providing money incentives have the objective of relating money payments directly to productivity. Piece-rate plans are the simplest and oldest. In these plans, the worker's pay is calculated by multiplying the quantity of products produced by a money rate per piece. Hourly pay systems are often modified by the addition of an incentive element. Merit ratings can be translated into money terms for pay purposes. Many variations of incentive systems are available; however, each company tends to adapt the money-incentive concept to fit its own particular situation.

Training and Management Development

How do companies fit into the educational system?

People never stop learning. Organizations never stop educating and training. Thus, the training function takes the present personnel as raw material and improves and develops them to their highest potential. The direct line supervisors continually serve as on-the-job instructors; however, the personnel department provides a number of training programs to support the improvement of personnel: *orientation sessions*, in which employees are made familiar with the services available, procedures, policies, and objectives of the organization; *worker training*, in which the employees are taught the necessary skills for their individual jobs; *supervisor training*, in which foremen and first-line managers are developed; and *executive development programs*, in which currently available potential managers can be developed to their highest potentials. Numerous methods are available to further the training objectives.

orientation sessions

worker training

supervisor training

executive development programs

Apprentice training

Apprentice training is a method in which the learner is made an understudy of an experienced person. The apprenticeship usually lasts for a fixed length of time, after which the learner "solos," or goes it on his own.

Formal *short courses* are offered by the personnel department to cover a certain subject in the classroom, seminar, or conference. This method is similar to the experience that you are getting in this course on management in a college.

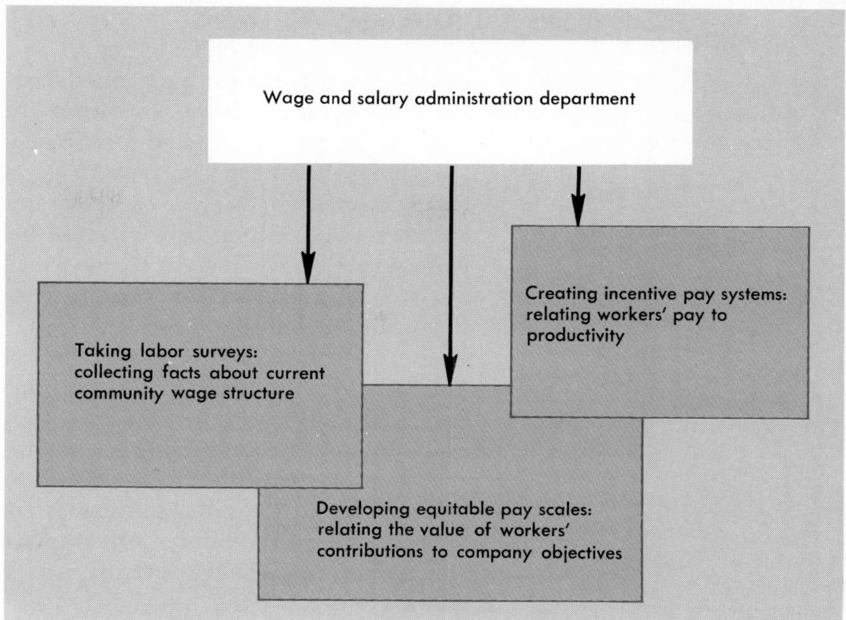

FIGURE 13.3 Duties of a wage and salary administration department

Programmed instruction

Programmed instruction is a newly developed technique in which the student can take a programmed book, a learning machine, or a set group of exercises and teach himself at his own rate of learning. The keys to this type of instruction are a well-motivated learner and frequent self-feedback to the learner as to how he is doing.

Coach-and-pupil method

Coach-and-pupil method is a technique that economizes on experienced teachers, in that two students teach each other through continually alternating between the coach role and the pupil role.

Since the training function employs many of the educational concepts of high schools and colleges, we believe that you can develop your own thoughts on this subject without further discussion in this chapter.

Handling Grievances

How can you handle what's "bugging" employees?

An organization that claims to have no complaints or grievances may be in worse shape than one with a record of complaints and their satisfactory resolution. Subordinates generally have numerous questions and criticisms; if they are not being expressed, they are being submerged and may cause bigger problems later. Therefore, any organization should maintain an appeals process, complaint procedure, and means by which this information can flow to the person who can correct the situation.

grievance procedure

In companies with unions, the *grievance procedure* is included as part of the union contract. In general, the procedure is to have the person with the grievance attempt to resolve the matter with his immediate supervisor with the help of the union shop steward. If it cannot be resolved at a lower level, it is referred to higher levels in both union and management organizations. Figure 13.4 outlines this procedure.

Any complaint procedure should make it easy for the complainant to initiate action. It should be clear, simple, prompt in handling the cases, and fair. An "open-door" policy by managers helps answer minor problems before they become deeply rooted. The frequent trouble is that even though the manager may feel that he has an open door, subordinates sometimes think they will be penalized if they enter. On the other hand, the perpetually critical person who seeks attention may clog up the channels with trivial issues if the procedure is not implemented in a firm manner.

Counseling

empathy

Good counseling on both a formal and an informal basis is a prerequisite to a smooth-running organization. *Counseling* involves informal techniques and attitudes that are sincerely directed toward helping others achieve their aspirations. It involves the ideas about communications discussed in Chapter 14. In addition, it depends on *empathy* (viewing problems from the other's viewpoint), listening attentively, patience, goodwill, and rapport.

ADJUSTMENT TO CHANGES IN STAFFING

Organizations are dynamic; that is, the situations continually change and thus cause demands for reorganizing. Furthermore, staffing is always involved with requests for additional personnel, replacement of those who retire, and development of an inventory of promotable people who can fit the positions left vacant from transfers. In this section, we offer some guidelines for managers who face increasingly rapid changes.

Why can't we set up a good organization and keep it? Why do we always have to change?

The structured approach described earlier, which is used by many business firms, has the disadvantage of tending to become rigid. Even if a firm has developed ideal organizing and staffing procedures to meet today's problems, the system must be elastic enough to permit needed changes tomorrow. A joke in one well-known firm is that IBM stands for "I've been moved." This may be a joke, but it has profound implications; and it is no joke at all

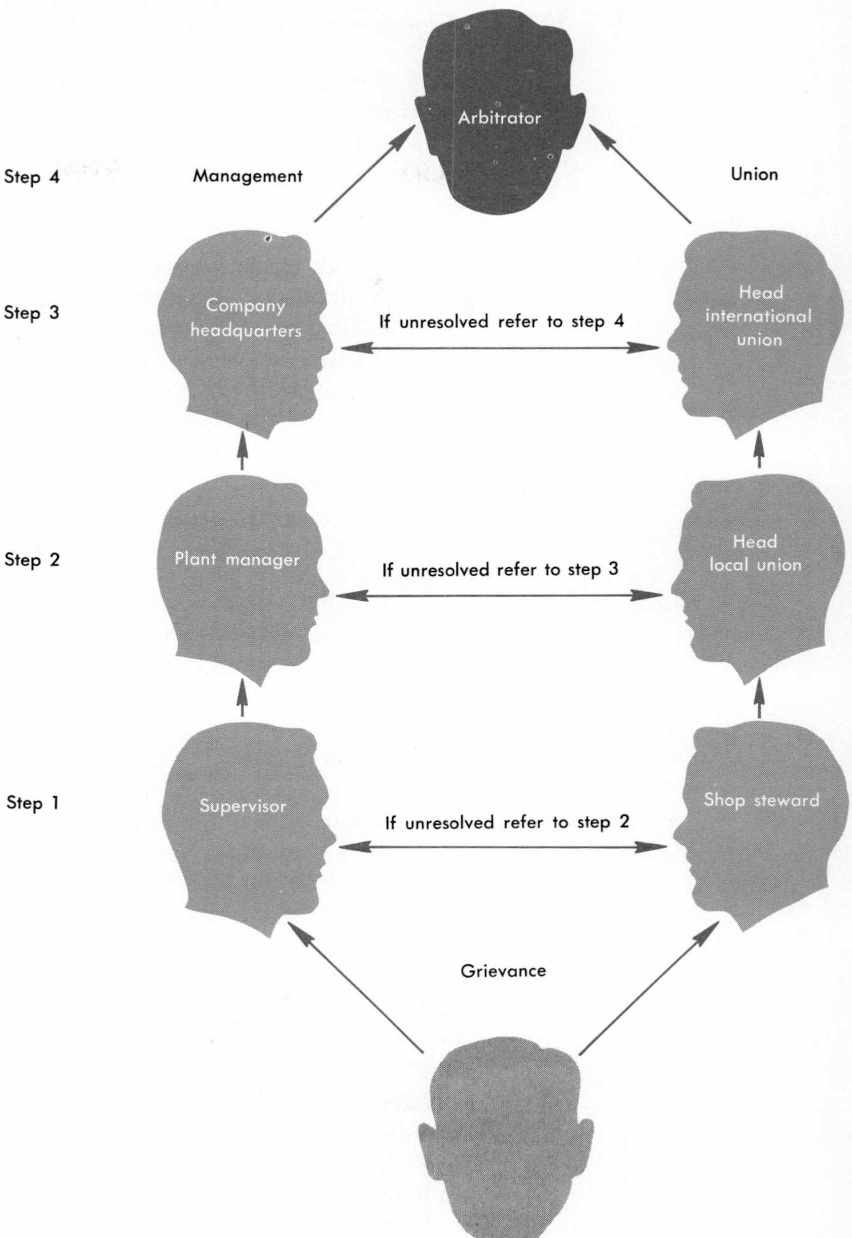

FIGURE 13.4 Grievance procedure in a unionized company

to those managers who must continually adjust to new situations. However, in a growing and successful firm, we must expect this condition. Smaller, rapidly growing firms have tended quite often to avoid rigid procedures by hiring good people and fitting jobs to them. However, even where people are fitted to jobs, we find considerable effort devoted to reorganization. It has been said that General Electric reorganizes every two years. The human reaction to frequent reorganizations is that the original organization must not have been the best and that the executives are merely searching for an answer. The more reasonable cause for such frequency, however, is that the situation beyond the company's control changes, and it is necessary to adjust to the new set of conditions.

Staffing involves continual changes even in a stable organization structure, because people are continually moving from one company to another, being promoted, retiring, or dying. Thus, a critical need in staffing is to plan a reservoir of replacements. Let us then look at the ideas of manpower planning and inventories of human resources.

Manpower Planning

Who can expect to move up in the organization?

In recent years, many large firms have purposely recruited a pool of personnel beyond their current needs. Some members of this pool are engaged in training programs, some are serving as assistants to key executives, and some constitute a "floating" group of personnel in the process of "being moved." Ford Motor Company lays special stress on human-inventory planning by having three people planned for each critical position: one who is currently in the position; one who could take over immediately in the event that, for some reason, the current executive is not available; and a third person who is "heir apparent" and who has experience enough so that he can fill the position within one year.

manpower audit

A *manpower audit* provides the basic information about managerial personnel so that the available resources can always be tapped quickly. This information about each person is stored in the computer: (1) age; (2) years of service; (3) current performance (from merit rating); (4) promotability, and how soon; and (5) possible replacements, with similar information about them. This audit must be kept highly confidential; if those involved knew of the estimates, they might consider that they "had it made" and become complacent, or they might lose heart and leave the organization because they were not one of the "crown princes."

Another approach to filling vacancies is to "advertise" them and allow anyone who feels qualified to bid for the choicer spots. At times this approach may run into unforeseen difficulties, since many workers and managers feel that seniority or length of service is the chief criterion. The problem with length of service as the only basis for advancement is that some people develop more quickly than others. For example, a principal of a school was criticized by a teacher with twenty years service when a young teacher with four years of service was selected for the better position. The answer of the principal to the older teacher was, "Mrs. Jones, you do not have twenty years of experience, you have merely repeated the same experience twenty times."

Promote-from-within policies have the advantage of providing greater incentive to lower levels; however, the policy can result in "inbreeding" and a failure to learn new ideas from people who have worked successfully in other companies. The recruitment of college graduates for choicer jobs also causes continual concern by those who lack educational opportunities. However, although no amount of experience will substitute for education in professional and technical jobs, no amount of education is a substitute for developing a person who has come up through the "college of hard knocks." Thus, the need for understanding the complex issues involved in manpower planning is essential for maintaining a manpower supply that is balanced and "alive."

Labor–Management Relations

How can unions help in staffing?

The staffing procedures of unionized firms differ from those of nonunionized firms because of the existence of the union's organization structure and the legal aspects of the union contract and collective bargaining. The subject of union–management relations is beyond the scope of this book, but perhaps we can give you some idea of the complexity of this area.

The question of union or nonunion labor is not one of all good or all bad. The existence of a union organization can support company personnel practices and can provide the company with procedures and opportunities that could help management. The chief question is whether the labor–management relations are handled in a favorable climate—one of mutual respect and understanding. The existence of a union can also help the company meet the continual changes that both union and management must face. Since the union is the official representative of all member employees, management need convince only the union officers of needed changes and leave to the union the problems of bringing the membership into line with the changes.

Resolution of Conflicts

In any problem of organizing and staffing, conflicts naturally develop. An organization without conflicts may be dead. The problem is to develop a means of resolving conflict. One useful

How can you get people who differ to make a real cooperative effort?

framework was proposed by Mary Parker Follett over forty years ago. She argued for integration of social relationships. Since conflict is usually present, she observed, the manager must handle it by domination, compromise, or integration. She strongly advised integration wherever possible. If domination is used, the conflict is merely submerged and will probably reappear later in a more virulent form. If compromise is used, Follett argued, neither party will be completely satisfied. But if the bases for *integration* are discovered, the differences are brought into the open, "reevaluation" occurs, and each party anticipates the responses of the other. The final result of integration, illustrated in Figure 13.5, is that a third position (which is the position of neither party at the start) will appear. Often, both sides can agree on this third position, and thus both can come out with true satisfaction.

integration

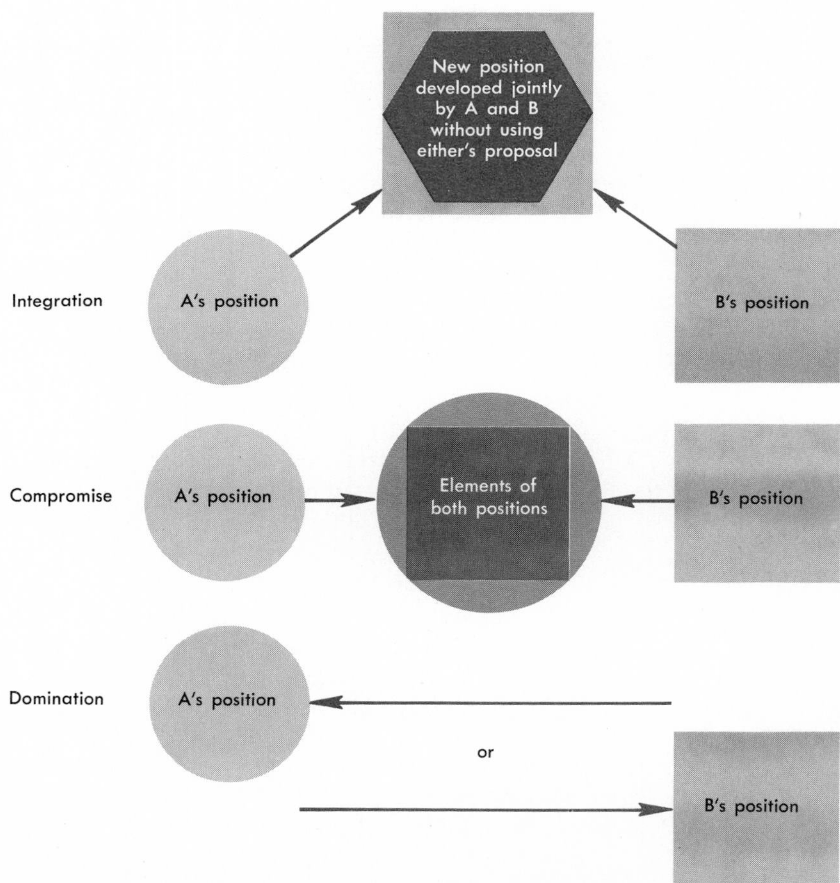

FIGURE 13.5 Methods of resolving conflict

Procedures for handling conflict continue to be developed. Behavioral scientists are coming up with scientifically supported results that will greatly affect staffing and organizing. The reasoning in Part 2 provides the introduction to a number of ideas from behavioral scientists that tend to conflict with some of the current personnel practices.

ADJUSTMENTS OF PEOPLE TO PRESSURES IN ORGANIZATIONS

In the last several decades, new techniques have been tried to meet the growing pressures in organizations caused by rapid changes. We shall conclude this chapter with three approaches that have been advocated: job enrichment, sensitivity training, and transcendental meditation. There are many more, but this sample of three very different approaches will indicate how modern society has searched for methods to meet the increasing pressures in relating people to their jobs.

Job Enrichment

Studies have shown that workers are alienated in their jobs because, although they expect to find meaning in their work, the structure of organizations tends to give them simplified assignments. One earlier approach, which emphasized grouping of a number of activities for each person to perform, was *job enlargement.* This idea focused on remedying the boredom resulting from routine and repetitive duties. It proved successful in many cases, but many workers demanded more; they wanted increased recognition, advancement, growth, and responsibility. Texas Instruments, AT&T, Volvo, Saab, and many other companies have changed their entire production processes to provide this enrichment. *Job enrichment* attempts to structure the job so that each worker can plan his own work and control its pace and quality, and in this way relate to it better. The basic idea of job enrichment is to provide challenges in the organization so that people will view the pressures as interesting and satisfying.

job enlargement

Job enrichment

Sensitivity Training

Another technique used to help managers adjust to the pressures in organizations is an approach focusing on helping people understand themselves and others in groups; it is known as *sensi-*

sensitivity training

tivity training. The technique is built around extended small-group interaction under stress in unstructured encounters, which demand that people become sensitive to each other's feelings. The proponents argue that after participating in *T groups*, as they are called, people are more open, more receptive to what others say, and more aware of their own feelings and the feelings of others. Results from this technique are mixed. Some claim that the experience is extremely helpful to the participants when they return to the everyday organization activities; others say that there are no changes; still others argue that the experience can be devastating to some people and can have lasting detrimental effects. One thing is clear—sensitivity training must be conducted by a highly trained discussion leader and should not be handled by untrained and inexperienced group leaders. The popularity of this technique illustrates how people will try new approaches to help adjust to the pressures in modern organizations.

Transcendental Meditation (TM)

transcendental meditation

Whereas job enrichment is initiated by the organization to help people search for meaning, and sensitivity training is built around voluntary group encounters, *transcendental meditation* is a unique mental technique by which each person in the organization gains profoundly deep rest and insures normalization of the nervous system through the natural release of stress. The method for taking the awareness within to the source of thought, the pure field of creative intelligence, is very simple and easily learned by anyone but the proponents[1] claim that a teacher personally trained by Maharishi Mahesh Yogi, founder of the Science of Creative Intelligence, is required if the full benefits are to be realized. Personal instruction takes place in private with the trained teacher. The student is given a mantra, or sound, which he uses during two 20-minute sessions each day, one in the morning and one in the evening, before meals. The purpose of the two periods of meditation is to provide the mind and body with deep rest so that stresses may be released and so that the person can return to his activities after meditation with renewed energy and a clearer, more orderly mind.

Once begun, the meditation is effortless and automatic, using the mantra as the vehicle for minimizing mental and physiological

[1] Harold H. Bloomfield, M. P. Cain, and Dennis T. Jaffe, *TM Discovering Inner Energy and Overcoming Stress* (New York: Delacorte Press, 1975). Important contributions to this section were made by Wayne L. Schmadeka, Maharishi International University, Fairfield, Iowa, and Carol N. Massie, teacher of the Science of Creative Intelligence and Transcendental Meditation.

activity. The key is to allow the nervous system to normalize itself since control or effort of any kind only interferes with the mind's natural tendency to gravitate in the direction of "pure awareness" or "pure consciousness" which, in the terminology of physics, is parallel to the vacuum state of quantum field theory, a state of orderliness and no activity.

An analogy that serves as one basic explanation of what happens in meditation involves two laws of thermodynamics—the second law of thermodynamics, which defines the nature of entropy stating that entropy tends to increase (that is, that there is a natural tendency toward disorganization and randomness) if contact with a continuing source of order is not maintained—and the third law of thermodynamics, which connects entropy with activity stating that greater orderliness in nature occurs when temperature and activity are lowered and that order is perfect when temperature and activity are zero. During transcendental meditation, activity of the mind is reduced to such a degree that orderliness increases naturally.

Scientific validation of the effects of TM involve research in physics, physiology, psychology, and other sciences. The method has been advocated by many managers as a means of enabling organizations to develop people whose minds are less tense and more ready to adjust to new challenges. More than one and one half million people from all walks of life, nationalities, and religions around the world have become meditators. Many testify that meditation for 40 minutes per day prepares them for greater and better-directed activity for the remaining part of the day, with a capacity to handle stress and pressures. Because the effects are cumulative, practitioners claim that continued practice and involvement in the TM program for systematic development of the full potential of the individual helps to develop their creative intelligence, increase alertness, expand awareness, and to reduce anxiety, boredom, frustration, and discontentment at work thus improving both job performance and interpersonal relationships. Many firms have encouraged the use of this technique in their organizations. The Foundation for the Science of Creative Intelligence at World Plan Centers throughout the world offers programs to business and government and teaches basic and advanced courses for executives.

Modern management is challenged by increasing rates of change and the increasing pressures on individuals in organizations. The staffing function, relating people to the organization structure, will continue to search for better means for adjusting people to their jobs. The examples outlined above take different levels of approach; job enrichment approaches the problem from the initiative of the entire organization; sensitivity training approaches the problem by small-group encounters seeking to understand individual feelings; TM focuses on the individual and allowing the mind to automatically refresh itself so that it will be better able to cope with increased organizational stress. All are seeking to improve the staffing function of management in a rapidly changing world.

SUMMARY AND PROPOSITIONS

The person who plans to be a manager in today's world needs to understand the current procedures and practices for staffing and to keep up with new developments and research in the behavioral sciences. We have seen in this chapter that firms continue to use a structured approach to job evaluation, merit rating, wage and salary administration, and grievance procedures for handling conflict.

We can summarize some of the basic ideas for relating personnel to their work in the following propositions:

1. Most companies benefit from a functional department (usually Personnel) that specializes in helping to satisfy the staffing needs of a firm using techniques such as job analysis, job descriptions, job specifications, job evaluation, merit rating, and wage and salary administration.

2. Staffing faces continual changes to meet new situations.
   a. Behavioral scientists are continually supplying new insights into means by which the personnel activities of both personnel and line executives increase productivity and satisfy the needs of employees.

   b. Resolution of conflicts is a permanent function of managers that requires the searching out and facing of grievances and complaints by members of the organization.

   c. New techniques, such as job enrichment, sensitivity training, and transcendental meditation, are being developed to meet increasing pressure on people in their relations to formal organizations.

STUDY ASSIGNMENTS

1. *How does a good organization structure depend on clear job descriptions?*

2. *"The most difficult problem is to find good people. You can always build a sound structure if you have good people." Discuss the problems of organizing and staffing implicit in these statements.*

3. *Describe the procedures used in determining the job structure of an organization.*

4. *How does a job description differ from a job specification?*

5. *Prepare your own personal data sheet.*

6. *Using Table 13.2, evaluate a job with which you are familiar.*

7. *In the absence of a good merit rating system, how can a manager determine the quality of performance of his subordinates? Is length of service of employees a desirable basis for advancements?*

8. *Give your evaluation of the merit rating form illustrated in Table 13.4.*

9. *What are some helpful guides for a person who conducts an interview? for the one being interviewed?*

10. *What types of standardized tests are most relevant in helping to select a new machine operator? a new first-line supervisor? a new receptionist?*

11. *"An organization that claims to have no complaints or grievances may be in worse shape than one with a record of complaints. . . ." Explain why this statement in the text is valid.*

12. *Explain how Follett's idea of integration differs from compromise.*

13. *Do organization structures need to be changed continually? Explain the reasons for your answer.*

14. *Explain three approaches to meeting the increasing pressures of formal organizations.*

situational episodes

1. You have worked for an independent fast-foods restaurant for the last three years. For the first year, you were an order taker at the counter. During the second year, you filled in for cooks in the kitchen. For the last ten months, you have served as assistant manager in charge of the 5 P.M. to 11 P.M. shift. The manager works during the daytime and leaves the hiring and training of the nighttime workers to you. Since the turnover of personnel is high, you must spend considerable time in recruiting to maintain the necessary work force of six.

   The restaurant has developed no guidelines for measuring the performance of employees. After talking with the manager, you are proposing to experiment with a simple merit rating system on the night shift. You are in the process of identifying the three or four basic criteria for rating the performance of your subordinates.

   a. What criteria should you select?
   b. Do you think that a merit rating system might reduce employee turnover?
   c. How would you weight the performance factors?
   d. Should you confer with your subordinates during the development stage?

2. You have a full-time job with a large retail store. Your progress has been rapid since your employment five years ago, and now you are manager of sporting goods. The store is planning to open several branches in malls and shopping centers and will need to add a number of managers. The general manager has asked you to help his personnel department by visiting your former educational institution and making screening interviews of potential manager personnel. The personnel department has provided you with the store's hiring procedures, application forms, and policy statements. In addition, they have given you an interviewers' report form that you are to use for each interview. Since this is the first time you have conducted such interviews, you are preparing your notes to guide you in them.

   a. What actions should you take prior to your trip to the campus?

b. Should you use the report form as an outline for structuring the interview?

c. During the interview, should you allow the candidate to chat about his interests and abilities without questions from you? Or should you concentrate on merely obtaining the information that you will need for your report?

interpersonal and organizational communications

FOURTEEN

OBJECTIVES YOU SHOULD MEET

Identify *the terms generally used in a communications model.*

Describe *the managerial roles in communication.*

Distinguish *between the two types of communication networks.*

Discuss *the importance and function of the "grapevine."*

Describe *two examples of nonverbal communication.*

Outline *the barriers to good communications.*

Describe *the approaches to improve interpersonal and organizational communication.*

DO YOU GET WHAT I MEAN?

"Mr. Perry, I'm afraid we have a bad situation developing between some people in your marketing division and the personnel department. We in personnel try to do the best job we can for the company. We also consider ourselves professionals and will do only what we feel falls within our duty to our profession and the company."

"Wait a minute, Mr. Lumous. I don't know what you're talking about. Obviously, you're upset about something. Just what is it?"

"Do you have a Mr. Harold Martin working for you?"

"Yes, I do."

"Mr. Dan Taylor of your division called our people last Friday and asked us to do an investigation of Mr. Martin, and I want to tell you right now that my department does not perform private detective services for anyone in this company. If you have some reason to investigate Mr. Martin, you should—"

"Whoa, Mr. Lumous! Just hold on a minute. There's obviously a misunderstanding between my request and your response. Did Mr. Taylor tell you what our problem was, and why we needed additional information on Mr. Martin?"

"No, Mr. Taylor did not give us any information other than a bare request that we perform an investigation on Mr. Martin."

"We are considering Mr. Martin for a promotion and transfer to a new area where he would work with U.S. government contracts and the contracts of other national governments. To comply with government regulations, we must file documents with certain information and data about Mr. Martin. I cleared all this with Mr. Martin first, and then told Taylor to contact you. I didn't use the term 'investigation.' I told Taylor to ask you to help gather additional data to help us comply with regu-

lations and help Martin get the promotion and transfer. Now, I don't see how this violates company policy—do you?"

"Mr. Perry, I owe you an apology. Your request, as you've just stated it to me, is a legitimate one and one that we will get to right away. Thank you."

"Ginnie, have Dan Taylor come in to see me. . . ."

Every first Monday of the month, the executive staff had a luncheon meeting. Today we were to discuss whether to go with the new product line. The whole question started out rather quietly, as the executive VP outlined our present financial position and problems. I then talked about our market analysis and projections for the success of the new product. Ed, our production VP, spoke about the production problems of the project, and as he spoke, I could see that Milt, from Product Development, was beginning to appear tense and anxious—he was breathing harder, his face was turning red, and he was chain-smoking. I tried to be as objective as possible and not say anything that could be interpreted personally by Milt, but Ed was going way beyond me. Now he was commenting that this was the third new product idea in the last three months from Milt's people, that all three had cost everybody time and money, and that in every case the decision had been the same, no go. I could see the daggers in Milt's looks at Ed, and I waited for Milt to explode.

"I'm getting a bit tired of having to defend our proposals every time," said Milt. "Six months ago, the president asked all of us to give that extra effort to overcome the crisis our company faced. We in Product Development have done all that we have been asked to do." Milt's voice had started out in a low tone, but it now reached a higher pitch. His pattern of speech had become more rapid-fire, and everything was coming in short bursts.

"It's not my job," continued Milt, as he looked directly at Ed, "to point an accusing finger at anyone. As members of the executive staff, you have the power to do as you will. I no longer care if the project goes or dies. It certainly doesn't matter to me. If you'll all excuse me, I have another important meeting to attend."

I looked at Ed—he now knew that it mattered a great deal.

It had been a rather full day, but I thought I'd stop back at the office before leaving. It was now 4:30—I was just in time to pick up the mail. There in the pile of mail was this memorandum that made me pause:

MEMORANDUM

DATE: February 14

TO: Division Vice-Presidents

FROM: Art Moss, Controller

According to the instructions from the Corporate Headquarters Financial Staff, the printouts you recently received from them should be returned with corrections and comments. Each division should check that the printout data correspond with the previously published budget data.

AEM:gg

P.S. THE DEADLINE FOR THESE PRINTOUTS TO BE TURNED BACK TO US IS FEBRUARY 14.

Art Moss wanted the information back the same day he requested it! It was 4:30 now, so I couldn't possibly meet this request. I wondered if Art really meant us to respond by February 14. Art had done this before, and his "emergency memos" usually meant that we add three days to his deadline. Since today was Tuesday, I had until Friday, and even though I had to fly to Chicago tomorrow, the checking could get done. I dictated a memo to Miss Johnson to have all the reports on my desk by Thursday. That way, I was sure they'd be on my desk by Friday.

Just think of the confusion Art's memo caused. Why can't people say what they really mean?

Communication is essential to management. A manager can make a sound analysis of a situation, generate outstanding solutions or alternatives, anticipate the impact and consequences of planned changes, organize the elements needed, and set controls; yet his best plans might frequently fail because of communication shortcomings. Managers often find they cannot transmit ideas clearly or concisely to others; costly misunderstandings frequently arise in oral, written, and even nonverbal communication.

Chet Perry asks the question at the end of the vignette that many managers ask daily: "Why can't people say what they really mean?" Just think how many years each of us has engaged in communicating messages to others. Why is interpersonal communication so difficult? What can a manager do to improve the communications within an organization? If we are successful here in communicating meaning in the written word, you will soon have the answers to both questions.

You already know from personal experience that interpersonal communication is difficult; but is this fact of any significance to a manager? Prof. Henry Mintzberg reported on a study of both British and American managers on the topic of communication. In the British studies, managers spent from 66–80 percent of their time in verbal (oral) communication. In the American study, the figure was 78 percent.[1] Thus, an understanding of inter-

[1] Henry Mintzberg, "The Manager's Job: Folklore and Fact," *Harvard Business Review*, Vol. 53, No. 4 (July–August 1975), 52.

personal and organizational communications has high value to prospective or practicing managers.

THE ANATOMY OF INTERPERSONAL COMMUNICATIONS

Communication

A simple interpersonal-communication model contains three elements: a sender (S), a message (M), and a receiver (R). *Communication* can be defined using these three elements: the process of transmitting the ideas and images of one person to another person. But you can see that in using such a definition, we also include all the possibilities of errors, poor communications, and misunderstandings that we want to avoid. From a managerial perspective, therefore, a better approach is to work for *effective communication*. When effective communication occurs, the receiver understands the message sent by the sender, and the sender realizes that the receiver understands it—a far more complex but also more realistic process. A meaningful exchange between two parties has taken place. Effective communication is thus the objective of managers.

effective communication

What else need we know about the S-M-R communications model so that effectiveness can occur? In Figure 14.1, we present an overview of the refinement of the simplistic model.[2] As can be seen in the figure, the first refinement we need is the knowledge about the *situation* surrounding the communication event. Communication effectiveness between S and R will differ if S is sending messages to R when both are in a boat about to capsize, as opposed to a situation with S and R exchanging messages in some secluded lovers' spot. To sense the effectiveness of communication, then, you must be aware of the situation surrounding the event and realize the impact the situation will have upon the total process of interpersonal communication.

A second ingredient added to our situational S-M-R model is the *personalization* of both S and R. We know the significance perception makes from our reading of Chapter 4, and we can sense the differences in the effectiveness of communication by knowing

[2] The ideas behind this refinement model were developed from a reading by Arlyn J. Melcher and Ronald Beller, "Toward a Theory of Organization Communication: Consideration in Channel Selection," originally published in the *Journal of the Academy of Management*, March 1967, but more recently published in *A Contingency Approach to Management: Readings*, eds. John W. Newstrom et al. (New York: McGraw-Hill, 1975), pp. 383–95.

who S and R are. For example, if S is your boss, perceptional filters operate in terms of how and what M is sent as well as how and what M is received. In most instances, subordinates more willingly accept an order from a boss, since the order fits into the expectation of both parties. Suppose, however, that S and R are peers, working at the same organizational level; then the meaning of the communication in terms of the different perception fields would vary. You can easily think of other examples in which the people involved—independent of the situation—make for important differences in communication (boss–boss; mother–daughter; friend–friend; rival–colleague).

Identification of the situation and the people involved in the communication process represents only a portion of the completed dynamic model. We must add the *content of the message* to get a fuller understanding. Factual statements ("Your budget for the next year is $50,000") may be understood differently from evaluative or

Simple Model
Sender — Message — Receiver

Refined Model

Model	Refinement
Situation S-M-R Situation	The situation surrounding the communication event
Sp-M-Rp	The sender and receivers personalized
S-M_{co}-R	The content of the message
S-$M_{w/o}$-R	The method of the message: written or oval
S-M-R CRE	The climate for the response exchange
Intended S-M-R Unintended	The body language—intended and unintended meaning

FIGURE 14.1 Interpersonal-communication model for effective managerial communication

judgmental statements like, "Your performance last year was not up to par." Orders ("Please finish the report by the 15th") differ in terms of potential communication misunderstanding from opinions ("I feel the organization is growing beyond us").

So far, our illustrations have been primarily oral. But often the communication between S and R will be written, not oral. The effectiveness of the communication *method* will again vary: In an oral message, you frequently have the opportunity of immediate feedback from the other person; then the message can be changed and revised until understanding is reached and effectiveness occurs.

The aspect of feedback just mentioned suggests another dimension to the model. Since effectiveness appears to improve with the amount and type of exchange between S and R, the *climate for response exchange* between S and R is an important dimension in understanding our ever-expanding model. A receiver will sense whether the sender wants feedback—that is, additional messages to confirm or clarify the initial message received. The S who shouts, "Are there any questions?" or who destroys the attempted feedback by using defensive behavior (either with aggression or rationalization) will quickly produce either an artificial response or none at all, hardly effective communication.

nonverbal behavior

The final aspect of the model deals with the differences between *intended and unintended messages.* Our model, although complex, would lack reality if we didn't include the whole range of *nonverbal behavior.* Nonverbal behavior or communication is "communication in addition to the words themselves."[3] The tone of the response, the inflection of the voice, the frown on the face, and other forms of body language frequently convey more meaning than the actual spoken word. Or, as is frequently the case, receivers perceive body language in a way that is different from that intended by the sender. More on this topic is developed later in this chapter, but for now we can see that both the sender and the receiver need to be made aware of these different interpretations as possible sources for miscommunication.

To move from a description of a communication model to the context of organizational life requires that we isolate and examine the interpersonal aspects of the manager's communication world. Once this world is disclosed and explained, we will move to the dimensions of organizational communication.

[3] Bobby R. Patton and Kim Giffin, *Interpersonal Communication* (New York: Harper & Row, 1974), p. 316.

Organizational life requires managers to behave and communicate in a number of varied roles. (See Figure 14.2.) Four important ones follow.

A manager engages in communication with his boss and/or individual subordinates in a *one-to-one relationship*. He also communicates with *subordinates as a group*. Managers find themselves frequently *members of groups* or committees. And managers spend many hours in *lateral or diagonal relations* with peers or people outside their immediate departments—dealing with external work flows (developed more fully in Chapters 18 and 19).

The differences in roles add variations to the communication processes for managers. For example, in the first two situations,

FIGURE 14.2 Organizational roles in managerial communication

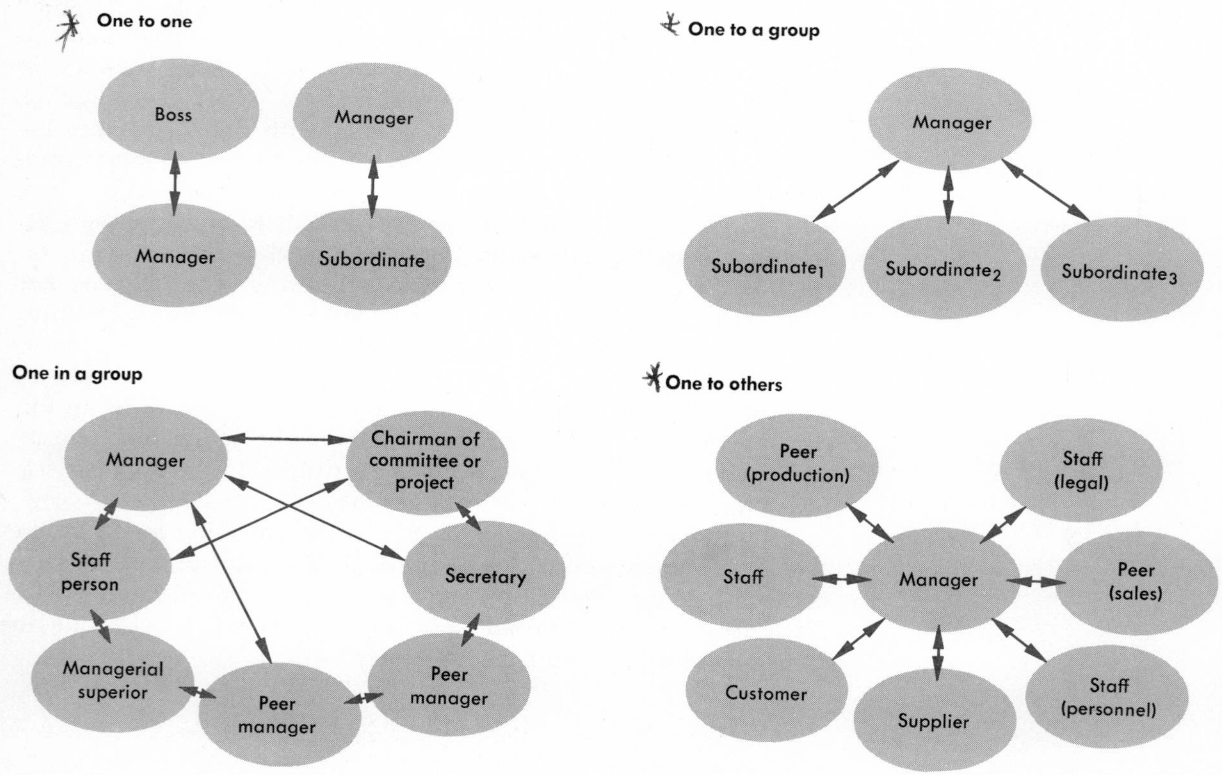

the senders and receivers share a work environment and experience that probably create some common elements in their perception fields. Greater role certainty exists and expectations are clear. In the other two roles, communication is more difficult because of the differences in the use of words (staff personnel frequently use more technical and sophisticated language), perception fields, goals and objectives, and climate for response feedback. The meaning given a message will differ also according to whether the receiver is alone (as in the first role above) or is subject to the interpersonal pressures of the group (as in the second and third roles). The manager probably initiates more of the messages in all situations except as a committee member, and thus has more control over the successfulness of the communication.

You can see, therefore, the basic interpersonal-communication process: A sender transmits a message to a receiver. Optimally, the meaning given to the message by the receiver corresponds with the meaning intended by the sender. As a sender you attempt to send messages as clearly as possible by keeping them short, simple, and void of ambiguous words. You can also encourage the receiver to give you feedback either in terms of behavior or in terms of oral or written messages. Armed with this information, you can conclude either that the communication was effective (that is, the behavior complied with the instruction), or that there is need for revision in the communication message. This process may also be repeated when you are the receiver.

You can see also that the interpersonal roles a manager faces in organizations call for different communication skills and approaches. The specific approach should be related to the communication channels and networks existing in the organization.

ORGANIZATIONAL COMMUNICATION CHANNELS AND NETWORKS

Communications permeate every organization. Some messages are sent and received clearly and effectively; others cause confusion and errors. In addition, some messages that are sent throughout the organization contain misinformation or secret information that may impede organizational processes. In this section, we describe the networks that carry messages so that you can see how to use the channels to enhance the smoothness of the managerial process.

Formal communication networks

The channels can be broadly classified into formal and emergent. *Formal communication networks* are those designed by the organization and known by all. In most instances, legitimate organizational means are used to transmit messages along formal lines—direct mail, closed-circuit television, called meetings, telephone, and so on. *Emergent communication networks* arise to fill needs not met by the formal channels; they are networks not necessarily known to corporate officials or used by all managers or employees. They are those channels developed to transmit sensitive or personal information. The messages are usually oral, rarely written.

Emergent communication networks

These two forms require elaboration to show their importance for organizational communication.

Formal Communication Networks

One way to view the communication in an organization is by the nature and direction of the flow: vertical flow and/or horizontal flow (see Figure 14.3). Generally, the first of these is used formally when the manager issues orders to others further down in the hierarchy and expects feedback from subordinates concerning the effectiveness of the communication. In vertical flow, considerable attention is given to downward and upward flows of communication through the formal structure. Organizational charts (described in Chapter 6) show the flow of authority, and these channels are used also as vertical communication channels. In vertical communication channels, many of the messages are written and deal primarily with information and instructions. The organization tries to simplify this type of communication by going to planned forms; verbiage is reduced and respondents frequently just check boxes to give higher management necessary feedback data. Monthly personnel reports, expense statements, and budget comparisons are examples of the kind of feedback reports sent up the communication channel.

Horizontal channels provide means for managers on the same level of an organization to coordinate their activities without referring every matter to their superiors. In this way, many matters can be handled on the same level of an organization, thereby speeding action while at the same time relieving superiors of unnecessary problems. For example, multiple copies of memoranda flowing to all positions needing information increases coordination and effectiveness.

With this background of the formal channels and networks, coupled with insights from the refined interpersonal-communication model, you might see how a manager could improve communication effectiveness by asking questions like the following:

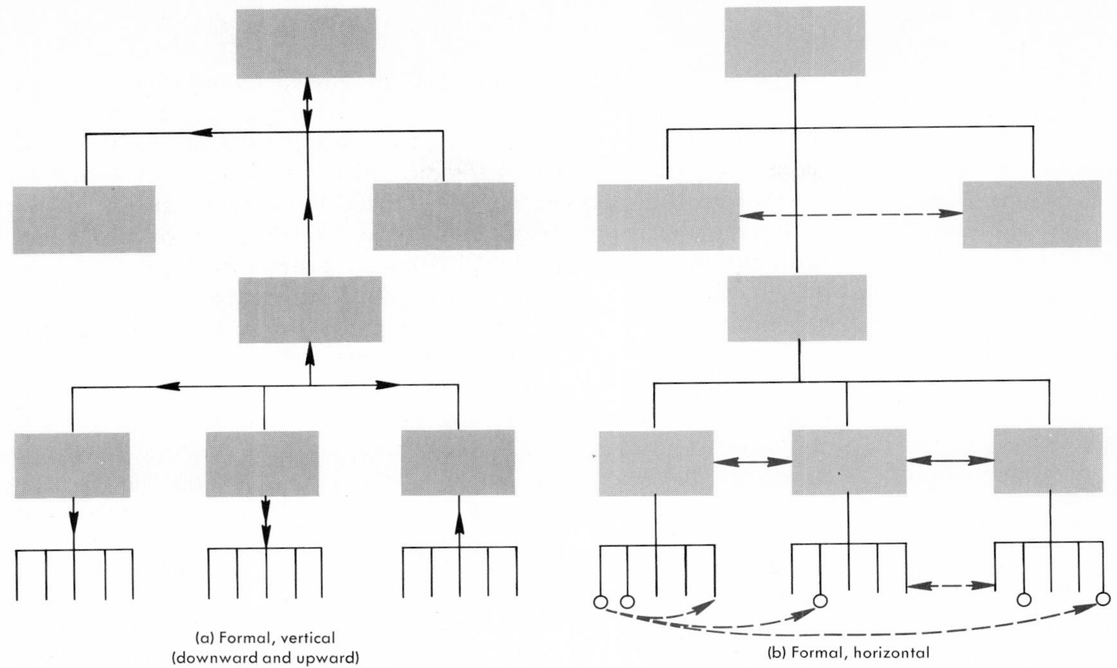

FIGURE 14.3 Formal communication networks

Are the receivers of the communication socialized or trained well enough so that language and terms will not be misinterpreted?

Is the message constructed in such a way that clarity is ensured?

Has the sender determined who should be on the communication channel? (Sending information to people who don't need it or don't know what to do with it is communication overkill and sets up dangerous expectations for future informational messages.)

Do the receivers know why they are receiving the message?

Do the receivers understand why the information is being requested, what objectives have priority, and what role organizational members are to assume if they have the data or come into contact with the data later?

These sample questions give you some idea of what managers must ask in their efforts at planning for organizational communication.

It is no great revelation to anyone in or out of organizations to say that the formal channels account for only a small percentage of the total communications transmitted between members. In the same way that organizational members form informal and emergent groups (mentioned in Chapter 5) to meet needs not fulfilled by the formal structure, they also develop emergent channels for communications.

There are at least three major emergent communication networks in organizations: (1) lateral, (2) informal, and (3) grapevine. In the first, the participants are primarily managers, staff personnel, or even customers of the organization. This channel is termed *lateral* or *diagonal.* (In Figure 14.2, the "One to others" is also lateral or diagonal). One manager will be on many of these networks, since the networks are generated from a particular person's trying to get specific information about a project or problem. Face-to-face contacts and telephone conversation are the primary means of communication.

lateral channel

Another characteristic of a lateral network is that it rarely goes beyond one or two people. Suppose you discover a problem in a project you are responsible for. Your boss has been putting the pressure on you for early completion and you run into a snag. You do not feel free to go to your boss for help, so you call a fellow manager in another plant or company whom you know from earlier days. He gives you the clues to solve your problem and meet the deadline. The communication channel between the two of you was not formal; rather, it emerged so that you could resolve a work conflict. Most likely your friend will feel free to reciprocate and call you when faced with a problem or in need of a favor.

Many researchers of management behavior believe that much of a manager's time is spent in relationships outside the immediate work scene—relationships not with superiors or subordinates. In these external relationships, you face an entirely new situation from the one under the formal structure. You have little or no direct organizational authority over the other person. People cannot be forced or coerced into giving information. Terms like *trading, mutual,* and *reciprocal* replace terms like *procedures, rules,* and *policies.* Communication guidelines effective under the conditions of a formal channel may no longer prove useful. Managers must be aware, therefore, of the differences in these channels and adapt their style to fit the situation.

In a second emergent network that exists among organizational members, the manager stands on the outside as an observer.

From the materials in Chapter 5, we know that informal groups will emerge to meet needs and perform functions that the formal structure doesn't provide for. This informal or emergent group will have a leader, a set of norms, a process for giving sanctions (either rewards or punishments), and a communication network. This network is that of *informal or emergent communications* within both formal and informal groups, as well as between them.

informal communications

What can a manager do about the informal communication network in his work unit? Years ago, managers might have been told to try and destroy the informal group and its communication network. Today, contemporary managers are told that the informal organization is not necessarily destructive to the overall effectiveness of the organization. Its presence acknowledges the fact that differences exist between those in authority and those responsible to the formal authority figures. Managers are encouraged to accept the informal group and recognize the positive as well as potentially negative features. The negative communication aspect is that the group will search out and at times invent information to meet its need for certainty. To relate well to the informal communications, the manager has to ask what information the group is searching for. If the need is task-related (for example, Will there be overtime work next month?), the answers should be found and supplied to the work force. If the need is to find out how management ranked Susan's performance with Rick's performance, management may not want to supply this information.

The emergent or informal communication network extends beyond the manager's immediate work group. There may be informal work groups in other departments or units of the organization. Communication will most likely travel between departments as well as within departments, and the information on this network may be work-related or it may be of a social nature. Managers must realize these many different channels and learn to cope with them.

grapevine

The last example of an informal, emerging communication network is the one some managers find most frustrating to deal with, the grapevine. The *grapevine* is a communication network that spontaneously emerges to disseminate information from the point of origination to other points throughout the organization. Items on the grapevine are random—whatever seems to sound like something someone else would want to know.[4] In some instances,

[4] Keith Davis suggests that the grapevine is "an expression of a natural motivation to communicate." See Davis, *Human Behavior at Work* (New York: McGraw-Hill, 1972), pp. 261ff.

the information is factual; in some, it is partially factual and partially fabricated; and in some instances, the information is totally "created"—simply what people want to hear. Examples of grapevine communications range from overheard comments from the president on the elevator or in the washroom to the names of workmen on the promotion list. "Created" information examples would include the "early" announcement of the signing of a peace treaty during wartime, the "word" that a new plant is coming into town and planning to pay higher wages, and a rumor that the president of the university is being sued in a class-action case.

The organization form or route that the grapevine takes varies. For example, some information will flow through routes that are fairly consistent. People on this grapevine are there not because of an election by their peers or friends, but because of their positions in the organization. Their positions are usually close to the information source (executive secretaries, mailboys, sweepers, and relief personnel on assembly lines). Other information may start in a car pool and then travel by telephone to friends or by word of mouth to people contacted during the day. Much of the conversation during coffee breaks and lunch hours contains the material for grapevine dissemination.

Some other characteristics offered by Professor Davis are important for an understanding of this communication channel in an organization:[5]

> News that is recent is most susceptible to the grapevine.
>
> In normal work situations, well over 75% of the grapevine information is accurate.
>
> Grapevine information is usually incomplete. One story may contain bits and pieces of three or four events.
>
> The information may be either helpful or harmful to the organization. There is no built-in screening of the information.
>
> Information travels quickly.
>
> The most damaging information on the grapevine is rumor—that is, information communicated without secure standards of evidence.

Managers interested in creating effective communication will be those who are aware of all the channels of communication.

[5] These statements have been generalized from two sources: Davis, *Human Behavior at Work;* and Keith Davis, "Communications within Management," *Personnel,* Vol. 31 (November 1954), 212.

They will try to get information from the informal, emerging networks so that corrections of misinformation can be sent. They will not overreact to grapevine communication and will realize that much of the information has been filtered. They will not view the informal channels with hostility but rather as necessary, and thus use them themselves to improve the communication throughout the organization.

In the description of interpersonal and organizational communication in this section, you have read of the refined and more dynamic S-M-R model, of the manager's involvement with interpersonal communication, and finally of the communicative networks of organizations. With an eye toward developing effective communication, we have suggested some of the problems that can develop in both the formal and emergent networks. There are other barriers to effective communication that are important to identify. In the next section, we shall discuss these, then in the last section, we shall deal with suggestions for overcoming them.

COMMUNICATION BARRIERS

Problems of communication directly retard the success of managers in the performance of their function. If messages are poorly transmitted, or if action is not effected, management cannot plan or control activities properly. The barriers and some of their remedies are summarized in Table 14.1.

Distortion

Distortion may be noise in transmission or it may result from inadequacy of the words in carrying the precise ideas of the sender. If an accountant submits a report on costs to an economist,

TABLE 14.1 Some Barriers and Remedies to Communication Problems

Barriers	Remedies
1. DISTORTION—from differing reference points	1. EMPATHY—place oneself in another's shoes
2. FILTERING—intentional sifting of information; complication of perceptions	2. RAPPORT—listen to subordinates; reduce fear of failure
3. OVERLOADING—of channels with irrelevancies	3. PRIORITY—monitor systems for important messages
4. TIMING—releasing messages at the wrong time	4. SEQUENCING and SELECTIVITY—tell a few or everyone at once or in some order
5. ROUTING—sending to wrong people	5. PLANNING—proper planning of a communication system

distortion may result because of differences in the meanings of the word *cost.* If the industrial engineer receives the report, he may get ideas entirely different from those of the accountant or the economist. The financial manager will view costs as outgo of funds; the production manager may think of unit costs of the manufactured product; the marketing manager will think of cost as a part of the total selling price; the industrial relations manager may view cost as a social factor of employment. Each of these specialists will tend to have a different frame of reference within which he interprets the communication. An important means of overcoming the distortion barrier is to expand the horizons of each member of the management team so that each can understand the meaning in the minds of other members. Another means is to use what the psychologists call *empathy*—to attempt to project oneself into the viewpoint of the other person. In short, distortion involves confusion between words and ideas.

empathy

Filtering

Filtering is a barrier to communication when the sender intentionally sifts the information so that the receiver will look favorably on the message. No one likes to show his mistakes to someone else, especially to his boss. The boss, on the other hand, wants to secure information about what is actually going on, especially those actions that need his attention. If a manager is not careful, he may encourage a free flow of just those messages that contain little information. The remedies for filtering are a well-designed control system, the development of rapport with subordinates, listening to subordinates with an understanding attitude, reducing the fear of failure, and increasing the awareness of management to problems of subordinates.

Overloading

Overloading of communication channels (sending too much) can cause the network to be jammed with irrelevant messages. Too often managers assume that improvement of information will be achieved by increasing communication flow. But increasing communications may merely overload the channel with dribble (the slang for nonsense), gobbledygook (the bureaucratic specialized language of big words that mean nothing), or routine memoranda that nobody reads. Managers can literally be buried in memoranda and reports with no hope of digging themselves out. The answer to this problem lies in monitoring the channels to clear messages in order of priority and importance. More messages do not necessarily mean more information. The communications system should provide for editing by devices or people to regulate the quality and quantity of communications with regard to the sufficiency of information for decision centers.

Timing

Timing of communications (when to send) can result in problems for management. Some messages need to be released so that everyone will receive them simultaneously. Other messages being transmitted should be timed sequentially so that receivers will not be confused by issues that are not important to them at the moment.

Routing

Routing of communications (to whom to send) should provide sufficient information for the decision to be made by the proper person. The route may be determined by the content of the message and the language in which it is stated. If official information is received first by the grapevine, the employee may be placed in an insecure position. If the information that affects an employee is publicized first in the newspaper or on TV, he is frustrated by the feeling that he is left in the dark. The answers to this problem are in the proper planning of a communications system and the recognition of its human elements.

MANAGING INTERPERSONAL COMMUNICATION

In a previous section of this chapter, two dimensions of managerial communication were mentioned: the organizational dimension and the interpersonal dimension. You have just read of the communication barriers in organizations and, generally, what might possibly be done to overcome some of them. A more specific and perhaps more helpful way to view the problems of interpersonal communication is in the context of change, a topic you have been exposed to earlier.

Is most of the communicating in organizations interpersonal?

In Chapter 8, our discussion of change put the manager in a context of action and change. If we now integrate the ideas from that chapter with some ideas on communication, we may see the relationship between communications and managed change. Assume for the moment that, as a manager, you want answers to the following questions:

What is to be communicated?

How is it to be communicated?

What results can be expected from the communication?

Table 14.2 shows a few possible answers to these questions. Now assume that the situation requires you to manage a change in the behavior of another individual or group. The questions about communication asked earlier may now be reordered to give us a different

TABLE 14.2 A Managerial Communication Model

Communication Question	Possible Answers
What to communicate?	Factual information. Information about opinions and attitudes.
How to communicate?	Verbally (oral and written). Nonverbally.
What to expect?	Compliance behavior. Changed behavior.

TABLE 14.3 Communication for Managed Change

Communication Question	Possible Answers
What to expect?	Managed change.
What to communicate?	Attitude information.
How to communicate?	Verbally—oral.

sequence of analysis (Table 14.3). This assumed model of communication for managed change may not be too far from reality.

Much of the first- and second-level managers' world involves attempting to change the behavior of others. So the possible answer, "managed change," rings true. We have information that changes in knowledge or factual recall (the first outcome of Table 14.2) show little correlation with changes in attitudes or behavior; there seems to be little relation between what a person learns, knows, or recalls (with just knowledge or factual information) and what he does or how he feels. Thus, stressing opinion, value, or attitude information has greater promise for behavior change. And verbal communication makes up most of the communication world of the manager. Hence the model described in Table 14.3 has a reality base to it. An example of how to use the communication process for the purpose of behavior change is given by two authors interested in communication.

Does the model seem real to you?

Attitude Change and Communication

Can attitudes be managed?

Philip Zimbardo and Ebbe B. Ebbesen have written an informative and delightful book entitled *Influencing Attitudes and Chang-*

ing Behavior.[6] They look at attitude change as the *target* or *objective* that someone is trying to achieve. This objective is usually approached through the communication process, so the process itself is broken down into the elements of *source, communication* and *audience.* In other words, who says what to whom and with what effect will influence the effectiveness of the attitude change.

Can attitudes be changed through communication?

Another way of looking at the communication attitude-change model is to think of it in terms of a psychological-process model. In this model, Zimbardo and Ebbesen identify four elements: (1) the person's *initial position* with regard to the attitude; (2) his *attention* to the communicator and the message; (3) his *comprehension* of the arguments, examples, illustrations, and the conclusion; and (4) his general and specific *motivation* for accepting the particular new position. If you combine the communication and psychological model, there are five specific persuasion techniques that may be used for attitude change.

Are you influenced by a sender's credibility?

THE SOURCE Suppose you are a manager and must deal with another person (your boss, your peer, or your subordinate). What you would like to do is to change the person's attitude on a particular topic. According to the Zimbardo-Ebbesen suggestions, you as the source and persuader might do any one or more of the following: First, you might try to have *high credibility* with the other person, for the higher the credibility, the greater will be the chance of the desired opinion change. If the topic is, say, the U.S. government's position on war, you might mention your own military experience as an attempt to show your expertise on the subject. You might also attempt to show your trustworthiness on the subject by suggesting that you had nothing particular to gain by taking such a position and that you are only making your comments based upon your experience and your desire for truth. Second, you might *feel out the other person's position* on the topic, for your effectiveness is improved if you initially express some views also held by the other person. The old technique used by preachers in getting people to say "amen, amen, amen" (signs of agreement) is a technique for getting people to move toward some kind of attitude change. Finally, you might attempt to ask for an *extreme opinion change* from the other person or persons, expecting that by asking for the extreme you increase the chances of getting some actual change in attitudes.

THE MESSAGE If you are trying to change an audience's attitude on a topic and are the only speaker, present only *one side of*

[6] Reading, Mass.: Addison-Wesley, 1969.

the argument. You will have a greater chance to get immediate, albeit temporary, opinion change. If the audience starts by disagreeing with your position, or if you can anticipate that they will disagree, or if it's likely that there will be another person presenting the other side of an issue, start by *presenting both sides* of the argument. Finally, if two opposite views are to be presented, one after the other, be sure to *present your view last.*

Are you willing to try some of these ideas?

THE AUDIENCE Try to get some kind of a reading on the *intelligence level* of the audience, for this will determine the effectiveness of your appeal. It will help if you can find some *common personality traits* in the audience; for example, people of low self-esteem are easily influenced. If a person plays a role previously unacceptable to him, the chances for a change in behavior improve.

THE INFLUENCE OF GROUPS Try to *encourage group discussion* and decision making, for this helps to overcome individual resistance. Realize that an opinion that a person makes *before a group* will be harder to change, because he will lose face if he changes before the group. Most people value groups; they will probably resist an attitudinal change that the group would not accept and will not change if the change is in conflict with the group. Thus, if you want to change the attitudes of a group, *try to get at least two people to agree,* for this weakens the powerful effect of the majority opinion.

THE PERSISTENCE OF OPINION CHANGE If you want opinion change to continue, remember to *reinforce* the changed behavior or to repeat the communication asking for the change. Generally, the effects of a persuasive communication tend to wear off, but this erosion can be delayed by letting the *receiver actively participate* in the communication.

We have seen how the communication process can be used by a manager to get behavior change through changing attitudes. There is a less obvious aspect of communication that permeates every managerial interaction. This is the nonverbal side of communication.

Nonverbal Communication

Much of the communication that a manager must deal with involves the behavioral dimensions. We have seen the role of perception as the sender and receiver filter messages. You may also recall that in the vignette, Milt, the manager from Product Development, transmitted nonverbal as well as verbal messages (both of which are behavioral).

nonverbal communication

In very basic language, *nonverbal communication* is the message transmission between sender and receiver that does not use speech or formal language. The meaning of a message is transmitted through the eyes, an eyebrow, facial expressions, hand positions, and even body movement.

Is there any nonverbal communication going on around you now?

We do not have the space here to develop the area of nonverbal communication. Much of the interest in this field grows from developments in training laboratories, sensitivity sessions, encounter groups, body awareness, and other research. To the disciples of these training methods, the nonverbal communication is the human and emotional expression somewhat unique to man.

Do you believe there is any value to understanding the nonverbal field?

Even more subtle nonverbal behavior is being examined as potential transmitters of messages and meaning. Professor Albert Mehrabian, in reviewing experimental findings dealing with the posture and position of the sender and the relative attitude and status of the receiver, found some interesting ramifications of the nonverbal field. For example, people of equal status sit closer than do people of unequal status; the distance between communicators gives clues to the degree of negative attitude; eye contact is minimal for disliked communicators; and when a communicator is in a standing position, hand relaxation is greater when communicating to a low-status than to a high-status person.[7]

Managers must be aware of nonverbal communication for at least two reasons: (1) to be able to pick up the signals and meanings from the communication process of others; and (2) to be aware of the effect of their own nonverbal communication on others. Frequently, greater significance is placed on how you appear than on what you say.

GUIDELINES FOR COMMUNICATION IMPROVEMENT

With the knowledge we now have of the setting, types of problems, networks, interpersonal features, and barriers to communicating, we can summarize some ways to improve this important managerial function. An awareness of these points is of basic importance to good communication: the symbolic nature of languages and messages (words and symbols represent ideas); the filtering

[7] Albert Mehrabian, "Significance of Posture and Position in the Communication of Attitude and Status Relationships," *Psychological Bulletin*, Vol. 71, No. 5 (1969), 359–72.

process, and the distortions that can be expected; the effects of the receiver's attitude and his background of experience. You should have a tolerance for misunderstanding when it does occur.

The message sender should also remind himself of these attributes of good communication:

Fairness, openness, and straight talk will reduce distortion.

The sender should not only encourage feedback and response from the receiver but do everything possible to expedite this feedback.

Effective listening is equal to or more important than effective sending. Listening involves attempting to understand the meanings that the sender is attempting to transmit. It is more than merely being able to repeat the words in the message. Have you every experienced a situation in which you were talking and felt that the receiver was not actually listening but, when challenged, he repeated words that you had said—and at the end you were still convinced that he did not try to understand your meaning? Try to fit your thoughts into the framework of the sender; don't try to force the sender into your preconceived framework.

Using a number of different channels (appealing to all five senses) will help neutralize the noise in any one channel.

Words should be selected, carefully avoiding emotionally loaded terms that will cause the receiver to jump to an incorrect conclusion.

Repetition is a good form of learning and is helpful in communication. Redundancy is a key to neutralizing distortion, filtering, and noise.

Using the method of written and/or oral communication that is appropriate to the situation will improve effectiveness. Generally, oral (for face-to-face contact and the opportunity for feedback) followed by written (for a record of the specific message) is the best method.

Many problems of communication are problems of managing or leading. If managers are effective in their styles and relationships, communications tend to be effective.

SUMMARY AND PROPOSITIONS

Because communication is an integral part of almost all segments of management, it deserves very close attention. We have attempted to give it this by describing the setting of the process first. After this description, we looked at communication problems and then considered how content gets processed through networks. These sections were then followed by a discussion of some important interpersonal aspects of communication. Finally, some communication barriers plus guidelines for improvement rounded out the scope of coverage. Let us proceed now to the propositions:

1. What the formal organization does not communicate, the informal organization will.
   a. People and work groups have a need for information and will actively seek it out.
   b. Informal communication tends to be less accurate and more impressionistic than formal communication.

2. Managers are not well prepared to handle nonverbal communication.
   a. Managers rarely receive any training in the nonverbal area.
   b. Managers in the United States have a culture that puts emphasis on "frank" verbal communication and plays down the subtle nonverbal aspects.

3. One major barrier to communication is poor listening habits of both senders and receivers.
   a. Managers tend to dominate in originating communication, thus they are poor listeners.
   b. Since evaluation is so common in organizational life, managers spend much of their "listening time" preparing answers to personal criticism.
   c. Listening usually means silence, a habit that is contrary to American culture patterns.

4. Communication techniques differ in effectiveness.
   a. One-way is faster than two-way communication in transmitting messages.
   b. Two-way is more accurate than one-way communication.
   c. Psychological stress varies with the type of communication method: In one-way, the receiver feels more stress than the sender; in two-way, the sender feels more stress than the receiver.
   d. Oral and written methods combined are more effective than oral only or written only.
   e. The fastest and most effective method is two-way communication (both written and oral) followed by one-way communication.

5. Effective communication does not just happen. It requires the application of management functions to the structure, technology, and human factors of the organization.

STUDY ASSIGNMENTS

1. *In the vignette, Chet Perry faced three communication problems. What are some reasons for these problems? (Include both organizational and personal reasons.)*
2. *Explain this statement: "Information is a measure of your freedom of choice when you select a message."*
3. *How does a person's perception affect his communication processes?*
4. *Language is central to communication yet contributes to a semantics problem. To get a better feel for the semantics problem, answer the following:*
   a. *List words that belong to only one culture or country.*
   b. *List words that have different meanings depending on which groups use them.*
   c. *List words that are unique to one group.*
   d. *What is the significance of the fact that the Eskimo people have many words for snow and no word for war?*
5. *Consider the communication situations you have been in during the past few days. Analyze these situations using the "possible outcomes" from Table 14.2.*
6. *As a sender in the communication process, you can communicate verbally through oral or written means. Which do you prefer using? Why? As a receiver, which do you prefer? Why?*
7. *Consider a speech you have heard or read whose purpose was to influence attitudes and change behavior. Use the five persuasion techniques from the text to analyze your experience.*
8. *Go back to the vignette and identify Milt's nonverbal messages. Why doesn't Milt use verbal means?*
9. *List some nonverbal communication you have observed in this class. What kinds of messages are sent nonverbally? Can you control your nonverbal communication? Should managers try to develop more or less nonverbal communication?*
10. *Do you accept proposition 2*(b)*? If so, why do you believe it is true? If not, explain.*
11. *Explain the reasons why you would accept or reject Propositions 3*(a), (b), (c); *4*(c).

situational episodes

1. You are a manager of a marketing group and overhear the following conversation:

   Market Researcher: Our data show, with a 98% confidence level, that your market share was 20% last year.

   Sales Manager: What do you mean, only 20%? I know we got close to 40% of the market. What is this 98% confidence level?

   Market Researcher: Our computer testing of the data base indicates that we would expect to get the same answer 98 times out of 100. So we have a 98% confidence level.

   Sales Manager: I don't care how many times you get an answer—the thing is, is it the right answer? You interviewed only a few of the banks in our area. How can you say what our market share is when you haven't talked to all the banks?

   Market Researcher: The sample size was more than adequate. We calculated the required number of interviews ahead of time, taking into account the confidence level we wanted and the number of degrees of freedom in our matrices.

   a. Is there effective communication between the two? Why, or why not?

   b. What action would you take to improve communication?

2. As project manager of an engineering group, you overhear the following conversation:

   Engineer: You've done it again! You salesmen are all alike. Our equipment won't do what you've promised this customer unless we modify it.

   Salesman: Well, it won't take much to modify it. All you have to do is add a few relays and a couple more wires.

Engineer: That's easy to say, but the cabinet won't hold any more. We'll have to not only redesign the circuits but go to a special cabinet and modify the printed circuit boards. I also think it will take a larger power supply to drive the extra circuits.

Salesman: Yes, but once that's all done, we'll have a design we can use for other customers. In fact, I could have gotten a couple of sales earlier this year with this modification to our units.

Engineer: You'll have to sell more than a couple to pay for the redesign and tooling, but since you've already sold this guy one, I guess we'll build it.

a. Is there effective communication here? Why, or why not?

b. What action would you take to improve communication?

leadership

FIFTEEN

OBJECTIVES YOU SHOULD MEET

Distinguish *between management and leadership by giving two examples of each.*

Describe *the relationship among the three determining factors of leadership.*

Identify *four generalizations on the nature of effective leadership.*

State *two ways of affecting the climate of an organization to achieve some leadership goal.*

Diagram *the relationship between the two-factor and four-factor leadership models.*

State *a clear, encompassing definition of leadership.*

Define *the term contingency attitude.*

HOW DO I DIRECT OTHERS?

"Did you get the assignment?" Phil asked Jack.

"Yeah, I think so. Boy, in these nonstructured classes where the prof has no assignment sheets, you really have to stay awake to catch the things he dropped."

"I know what you mean, Jack," Birl, who had just caught up with the others, added. "My mind was off somewhere and I just managed to grab onto his last words about leadership."

"You guys got time for some coffee? Let's not go to the student union—that stuff tastes like liquid volcanic ash."

The conversation continued later at the Paddock, when Phil asked, "What example can you think of on leadership?"

"Oh, we're back to the prof's assignment, eh?"

"Well, I'll probably give him examples of Churchill, or Roosevelt, or Malcolm X, or maybe Indira Ghandi. To me, they're great leaders; they're what I'd call 'natural-born' leaders. I've read that natural leaders may not be the ones with the highest intelligence, but they do have drive, energy, forcefulness, and the ability to inspire the people under them. Could you imagine any of these 'naturals' not being a leader of the group he's in with? I think people either have it or they don't have it as far as leadership goes, so I'll give my natural-born leadership examples. What about you, Jack?"

"Oh, I don't know. . . . I was thinking about that newspaper article I read last night—the one where five men survived a plane crash in the mountains. Man, what an experience they had."

"What's that got to do with leadership, Jack?"

"Well, the article went on to tell you more about the five men. Most of them were in some kind of management positions in com-

panies, and yet the guy who became their leader for survival was a high school biology teacher who knew something about living off the land. The VPs of the bank and corporations would have died within the first five days. And to think they all made it through fourteen rough days. It's funny how a situation will bring out the leadership ability of a person."

"I'm going to just go back to last year, when I finished my two years in the infantry. Boy, did we have examples of leaders! The leaders in the military all seemed hung up on their rank. All infantry sergeants were the same. They were all a bunch of rotten apples. No matter where I got stationed, they were all hard-nosed and tough. And what made it worse was that you had to take all that stuff from them. Even the physically weak sergeants were strong because of the threat of court martial. If you were to disobey any order they gave you, you had had it. The same thing seemed to be true with second lieutenants. Frequently a second lieutenant would tell you that when you had to salute him, you were saluting that bar, and it seemed that both the bar and the stripes had a whole series of punishments behind them that made all of us jump."

"Gee, these examples sure are different. I wonder what the prof's going to do with them. I wonder if we're giving him what he wants."

"I'm not giving him anything like you guys are," Harold said. "I've been listening to you and I wonder if I understood the assignment."

"What are you going to turn in?" asked Birl.

"Well, my father works for the government. He's a budget officer with the Internal Revenue Service, and he's just been picked to attend an executive seminar at Oak Ridge, Tennessee. It's sponsored by the U.S. Civil Service Commission."

"What's all that got to do with leadership?"

"My example of leadership will be my old man and the kind of training he's going to have at Oak Ridge. After all, a bunch of management professors teach there, so the topics must have something to do with leadership."

"Like what topics will they have?" asked Birl.

"I've got the program in my notebook here."

"Man, look at those things—they sound just like our class." Jack took the program and scanned the first few pages. "Listen to these!" Jack said. "Myths of Management; Management Theory; Group Communications; Conflict; Productivity; Decision-Making Functions of Management under Pressure; The Manager and the Bureaucracy; Management by Objectives; Management and Motivation Principles. . . . Hey, Harold, do you think this stuff is what the prof wants?"

Three of the examples in the vignette show the complex and differing views of leadership. In no way can we say that leadership is an easy topic to discuss. Even though there have been leaders since the beginning of man, a formal discussion of leadership is still very difficult.

In this chapter, however, we attempt such a discussion because managers are often in a leadership role. After we describe and identify leadership more specifically, we consider the factors that shape the leadership function. Finally, an explanation of effective leadership approaches ends the chapter.

LEADERSHIP IDENTIFIED

Leadership

Leadership occurs when one person induces others to work toward some predetermined objective. Although this definition is very close to that of managing, it emphasizes the personal relationship through the use of the word "induce." Perhaps the leader is one who "inspires" others to work toward goals. At any rate, leadership has to do with the *dynamic* quality of a relationship—the action-reaction phase of managing others.

Are all managers leaders?

When the three illustrations in the vignette are compared with the previous fourteen chapters, you can see that managing is different from leadership. In Figure 15.1, you see that much of what a manager does is nonbehavioral. A manager must plan, frequently makes physical checks of inventory, may do a lot of in-

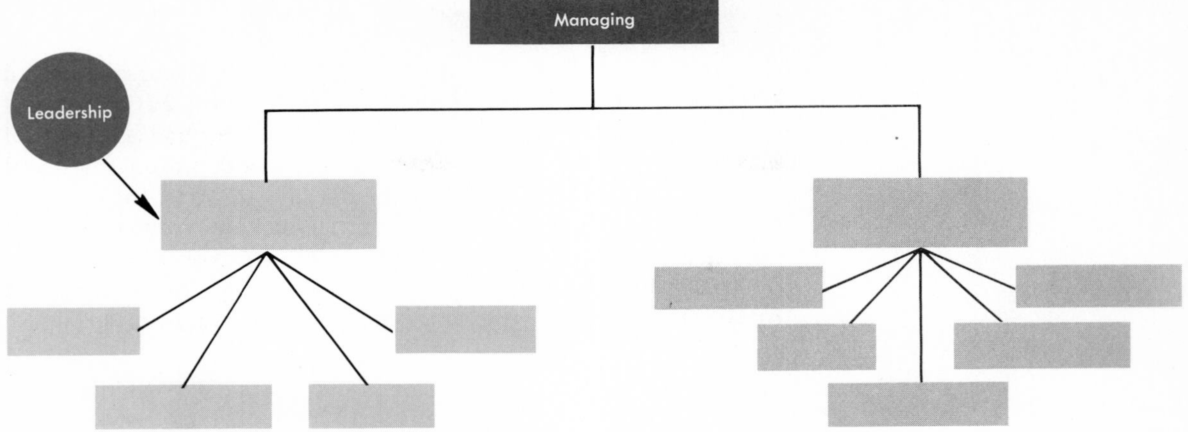

FIGURE 15.1 Relationship of leadership to managing

dividual analysis of data, and does a great deal of thinking in his job.

When we talk about leadership, we are thus talking about a situation in which a person is inducing another person or a group of people to produce some output or specific performance. In this chapter and throughout this book, we consider the behavioral part of leadership to be its critical feature.

The manager of an organization has a title and position with prescribed responsibility and authority. He knows basically what it is that he is to get done. But how to get things done through and with other people is what makes leadership a challenge. One first step in meeting this challenge is by understanding the factors that contribute to effective or ineffective leadership. In this next section, we scrutinize such determining factors.

THE DETERMINANTS OF LEADERSHIP

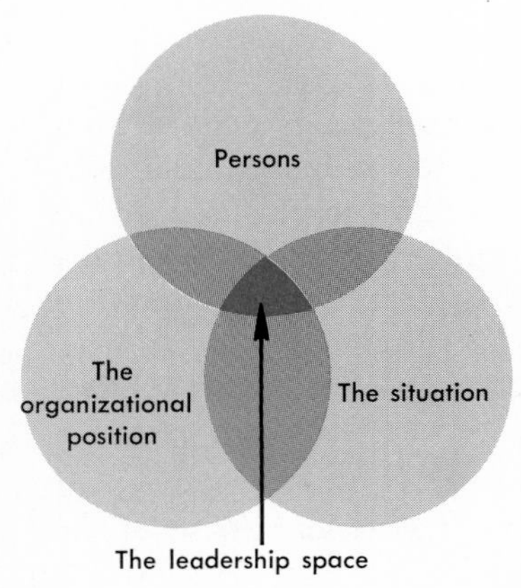

FIGURE 15.2 The determinants of leadership

The discussion so far gives us an insight into the character of the leadership process. If we examine Figure 15.2, we find that:

- Leadership is interpersonal.
- Leadership operates from some organizational position.
- The act of leadership occurs within a specific situation.

The leadership act takes place when these three factors all interact with each other. For example, when danger threatens a crowd and the crowd becomes a mob, the behavior of the mob is very unpredictable and uncertain. The situation is there, the people are there, but there is no leadership, for the organizational position does not exist. Similarly, a manager with authority and responsibility may be unable to direct and supervise a group of workers who feel their protection is in the form of union rules and regulations. No matter what the manager says or does, they feel he has no influence or power over them, and thus, repeated leadership attempts fail to become leadership acts. For leadership to operate, there must be a dynamic interaction and the existence of all three of these factors—person, position, and situation.

The Person Factor

Obviously, people are involved in leadership. Such a simple statement, however, is not enough to help the manager develop leadership qualities. What in the person factor helps a manager become a more effective leader?

How does personality relate to effective leadership?

The leadership concept often focuses on the leader's personality or personal characteristics. Centuries ago, men believed that kings and nobles had a divine right to rule, and thus leadership was assumed to be a hereditary feature. Even though monarchy remains in only a few countries in the twentieth century, the notion survives in a "great man" theory of charismatic leadership that exists with us today. If you reflect on the recent history of the world, the names of Winston Churchill, Dwight Eisenhower, Adolph Hitler, Charles deGaulle, and others would suggest that the idea has support but the "great man" theory, although interesting, is not too useful for those of us who have more common talents and characteristics. Yet our personal experiences suggest to us that there are individual characteristics of people that work for or against them as leaders. Most organizations have been looking for the secret formula to identify the traits that make successful leaders. Are there traits that can be learned so that managers may improve their leadership?

What is known about leaders and nonleaders?

Research studies done on leaders and nonleaders suggest that leaders tend to be brighter, to be better adjusted psychologically, to display better judgment, to interact more than nonleaders do, to give more information, to ask for more information, and to take the lead in interpreting a situation.[1] A. Paul Hare says, "There are indications that certain traits such as intelligence, enthusiasm, dominance, self-confidence, social participation and equal-

[1] E. P. Hollander, "Emergent Leadership and Social Influence," in *Current Perspectives in Social Psychology: Readings with Commentary,* eds. E. P. Hollander and Raymond G. Hunt (New York: Oxford University Press, 1963), pp. 468–75.

What are some traits of successful leaders?

itarianism are frequently found to characterize leaders."[2] The industrial psychologist William Henry, doing research in the late 1940s, found a definite personality pattern in a study of more than 100 successful business executives; he found traits such as powerful work motivations and desire for achievement, warm feelings for superiors (with whom they identified) and detached attitudes toward subordinates, stable and well-defined self-conception, ability to see relationships and make decisions, high degree of activity and aggressiveness, interest in practical realities here and now, smooth relationships with superiors, and a certain insecurity about their abilities to achieve.[3]

In a more recent work, Edwin E. Ghiselli continued the examination of managerial leadership traits.[4] Among two groups of 105 people each, Ghiselli found that the traits of supervisory ability, intelligence, and initiative related to success in managerial positions.

Supervisory ability

Supervisory ability is the ability to direct the work of others, to organize and integrate activities so that the goal of the work group can be obtained. Of these three abilities, Ghiselli says that supervisory ability and intelligence are the major aspects of managerial success.

Can you learn traits?

There are certain personal characteristics that cannot be altered—physical build, facial characteristics, perhaps voice, and other aspects of the biological makeup. Intelligence seems to be subject to change, for we know that scores on intelligence tests can be improved through training. Many of the traits that Ghiselli describes seem to be a product of a certain environment and thus susceptible to learning. Indeed, the purpose of the third part of this book is to develop your knowledge and insights about supervisory skills and ability. Business schools and management training programs exist for this purpose. Self-assurance and decisiveness, although difficult to train and develop, are usually the goals of Dale Carnegie–type training programs. And McClelland has run experimental training programs to develop the need for achievement and power.[5]

[2] A. Paul Hare, *Handbook of Small Group Research* (New York: Free Press, 1962), p. 292.

[3] William E. Henry, "The Business Executive: The Psychodynamics of a Social Role," *American Journal of Sociology*, Vol. 54 (1949), 286–91.

[4] Edwin E. Ghiselli, *Explorations in Managerial Talent* (Pacific Palisades, Calif.: Goodyear, 1971).

[5] David C. McClelland, "That Urge to Achieve," in *Organizational Psychology*, eds. David A. Kolb, Irwin M. Rubin, and James M. McIntyre (Englewood Cliffs, N.J.: Prentice-Hall, 1971), pp. 123–30.

Thus, personality characteristics of people involved in the leadership act contribute a great deal to the effectiveness or ineffectiveness of the act itself, and some of these characteristics seem amenable to education and training.

The Position Factor

We have seen how the person factor contributes to the effectiveness of a manager as a leader. But the personal characteristics of the organizational leader do not operate in a vacuum; the position factor puts structure or conditions on the person factor. The position factor provides the *meaning* the organization (people) intends the person to give to a function, duty, or job. Labels are the best way to start understanding this factor. Think of the labels you use to define the jobs of different organizational participants: student, teacher, professor, president, chairman, co-director, group leader, mayor, minister, assistant store manager.

How do you know what to do in a job?

role concept

role expectation

role

Probably every person has some kind of an image of the way he should act in a given position, and this image is often called the *role concept.* Those who must come into contact with the position (either the bosses, peers, or subordinates) also have an image about how the person should act in the position, and this is called the *role expectation.* Both these images are important to the understanding of the human behavior that flows from the position factor of leadership. Whenever we use the word *role,* we are referring to what a person is *supposed* to do. We have touched very briefly on ideas that influence the role concept—the person's image of what he is supposed to do in a role. There are at least three sources of role expectations (see Figure 15.3). Knowing about these is important to the manager, for trouble results if a manager is unable to meet these expectations.

Are the role expectations of others important?

PERSONAL EXPECTATIONS Personal expectations are the ways in which people expect the leader to behave. In every group, there is a pattern of expectations—the group expects the leader to do certain things and to refrain from doing certain things. For example:

1. The group expects certain patterns of behavior from its formal leader.
2. The role the leader plays depends upon the role expectation of the followers. If the followers want to participate in a decision and the leader makes all the moves, tension and frustration will result.

3. The leader tends to be selected by the nature of the role; that is, certain roles attract certain people. Foremen in foundries are usually rough, tough, and physically strong men.
4. All members of a group have roles, and these roles are related to one another. One member, for example, may assume the role of the "joker" so that group tensions and frustrations are released.
5. Roles are related to the people in them. Certain professional quarterbacks influence the style of play of the whole team.
6. Roles are related to the situations in which they are played. The behavior of a union steward may depend on whether the company is near a strike.

What do organizations expect of leaders?

ORGANIZATIONAL EXPECTATIONS Many companies have definite and specific expectations about the behavior of their managers and leaders. These expectations are frequently written into formal position guides or job descriptions. As mentioned earlier, most jobs have some heritage within an organization, so that the previous person in the job helped develop the expectations that people have for the job now. In addition, there are both *technical and nontechnical organizational expectations.* The job behavior of a manager of a live TV production would be quite different organizationally from the job behavior of a manager of a taped program, which has a different time dimension. Nontechnical organizational expectations also differ in terms of what is allowed in personal habits, status, group relationships, coffee breaks, and the place you may or may not park your car.

Why do accountants wear green eyeshades?

CULTURAL EXPECTATIONS In addition to the specific personal and organizational patterns of role expectation that contribute to the shaping of the leadership role, there are also cultural expectations of many types. One of these is the industry culture. The banker and the CPA may be expected to be serious, conservative, and cautious. The advertising-agency man may be expected to be creative. The politician is expected to shake hands, kiss babies, secure appropriations for his territory, and make extravagant promises that are reassuring but not taken too seriously. The tax collector is expected to be rather suspicious and perhaps hostile. The military leader is expected to be gallant, fearless, and conscious of his status.

FIGURE 15.3 Sources of role expectations

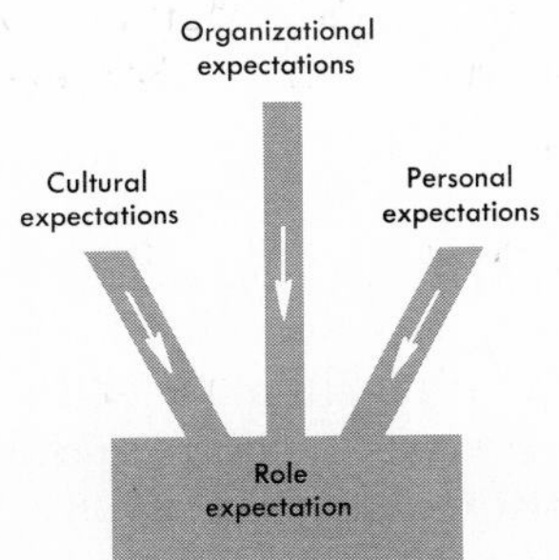

Cultural expectations became pronounced during the late 1960s and early 1970s with respect to clothing and hair. Many members of older generations have a certain kind of role-behavior expectation toward any younger man with long hair, sideburns, or a mustache. Clothes also became a symbol and signaled a series of behavioral expectations that may or may not have been warranted.

The Place or Situational Factor

How does the situation trigger the other P's?

This factor is a very obvious one. Some writers have suggested that, for example, Winston Churchill would not have made the imprint that he did upon civilization if World War II had not demanded from him the talents he had. (This illustration shows the relationship between the person, position, and place factors.) Churchill was a member of the English government for years prior to his election as prime minister, but his greatest success came in what others would refer to as his retirement years—when he was well over 65.

President Truman was also a leader whose talents seemed to flourish in a particular situational context. But President Richard Nixon found his credibility in domestic affairs different from his credibility in foreign affairs. Watergate was unlike detente with China or Russia. You can probably think of many illustrations where the relationship between the leader and the group changes because of a different situation.

Why is it important to know what situation you are in?

Different situations may call for different leadership roles and different personality characteristics; thus, in the course of their growth, companies usually appoint different kinds of leaders. It is common for new companies to be led by the charismatic leader—one who leads through sheer force of personality. Later, leadership may be more bureaucratic and impersonal, or it may reflect the company's need for specialized skills in engineering, marketing, design, labor relations, or finance. (This point will be clearly illustrated in Chapter 17, when we look at the lessons that can be learned from companies in terms of dynamic leaders.)

We can see, then, that the leadership act that occurs within a group depends upon the person performing it, the parameters of the position, and the expectations and skills demanded by the situation. These three factors are not of equal weight, for a strong, dominant person may force or influence the group's expectations of behavior and thus define the situational needs to fit his own abilities. But the model seems clear: For leadership to be effective the person performing the leadership act must meet his own needs, the needs of the group, and the needs of the situation. With this conceptual foundation behind us, we now turn to more pragmatic suggestions for improving leadership effectiveness.

EFFECTIVE LEADERSHIP BEHAVIOR

Is it just an individual thing?

There is no magic formula for becoming an effective leader. Management is no easy job, and the leadership function of a manager frequently requires many difficult decisions. Not all people, obviously, have the physiological, psychological, and sociological makeup to be leaders. Yet there is a need and challenge for leaders. Companies would greatly benefit if someone could devise a formula for the early identification of effective leadership and managerial success, but as of this writing, no such formula exists. The eight statements that follow are no formula, but simplified statements or generalizations. We have said repeatedly that truth comes from many sources, and this will be very clear when we talk about leadership behavior.

Some Generalizations

BE YOURSELF This statement reflects the ideas of the trait school. The adherents of this approach would recommend that every aspiring manager try to find out as much as he can about himself through assessment tests, personality tests, sensitivity training, encounter-group experiences, and the like. What is important, these people say, is not only what you do, but who you are. Others will quickly find out if you are playacting in a role, so manufactured behavior is only short-lived. If you can find yourself and know yourself, the behavior will take care of itself. Obviously, this advice is excellent.

Why are others important?

BELIEVE THE BEST ABOUT OTHERS Douglas McGregor was able to highlight this point very clearly in his *Human Side of Enterprise*.[6] You should remember from Chapters 3 and 6 that McGregor contended that the leader's behavior and the response to his behavior depend upon beliefs about the nature of man. In what has become known as the Theory X philosophy, McGregor said that if you believe man is lazy, hates work, does not want responsibility, works as little as possible, is motivated by money and fear, and is basically uncreative, you will tend to expect this behavior from him. McGregor believed that the manager who believes this and behaves accordingly will create just such behavior in others.

McGregor offers to the manager a substitute theory, Theory Y. Supported by behavioral research, this theory, McGregor says, is that

[6] Douglas McGregor, *The Human Side of Enterprise* (New York: McGraw-Hill, 1960).

the nature of man would suggest that he is intelligent, creative, wants to work, to achieve, and to solve problems, and will initiate programs if placed in a suitable organizational environment. To McGregor, who followed a Maslow need-hierarchy theory of motivation, workers will respond and move to the higher need levels of self-esteem and self-actualization in a work climate that can be created by the manager. What is needed initially, however, is a revision in the assumptions that the manager makes about the nature of man.

Why not push for production?

CHOOSE YOUR OWN STYLE Much of the industrial work on leadership done in the early 1900s seemed to stress productivity and output of work units. The effective manager during this period would have been the one who put high stress on performance, and who saw to it that the work was well planned and well organized and that the workers were trained in the most efficient work methods to get the job done. If we add to this highly efficient model the carrot of money or the whip of firing or discharge, the leader should get effective performance from subordinates.

In later research studies of leadership, this one-factor leadership model was expanded to include two factors. Research data from some industrial studies in the 1930s suggested that man in his workplace was more than a simple economic factor of production. He was a human being who related to the work environment as a human being, and therefore the model of a manager or leader was described in two ways: production-centered or employee-centered. Figure 15.4 gives a number of synonyms for these two factors. Supervisors are placed into one of the two leadership categories according to some measurement scale, and then the productivity of the work group is identified. For years, the behavioral scientist hoped and expected that the more human-oriented leadership style would result in the highest productivity. According to an article in *Personnel Psychology,* however, a potential leader cannot assume that if he stresses one dimension at the expense of another, he will automatically be able to get high productivity.[7]

Which type wins?

ADOPT A CONTINGENCY ATTITUDE The search for the one best way of leading others will probably never end. But more and more researchers and practicing managers are coming to a similar conclusion: Questions on leadership effectiveness cannot be an-

[7] Abraham K. Korman, "'Consideration,' 'Initiating,' and Organizational Criteria—A Review," reproduced from *Personnel Psychology,* in *Readings in Organizational Behavior and Human Performance,* eds. L. L. Cummings and W. E. Scott, Jr. (Homewood, Ill.: Irwin-Dorsey, 1969), pp. 627–35.

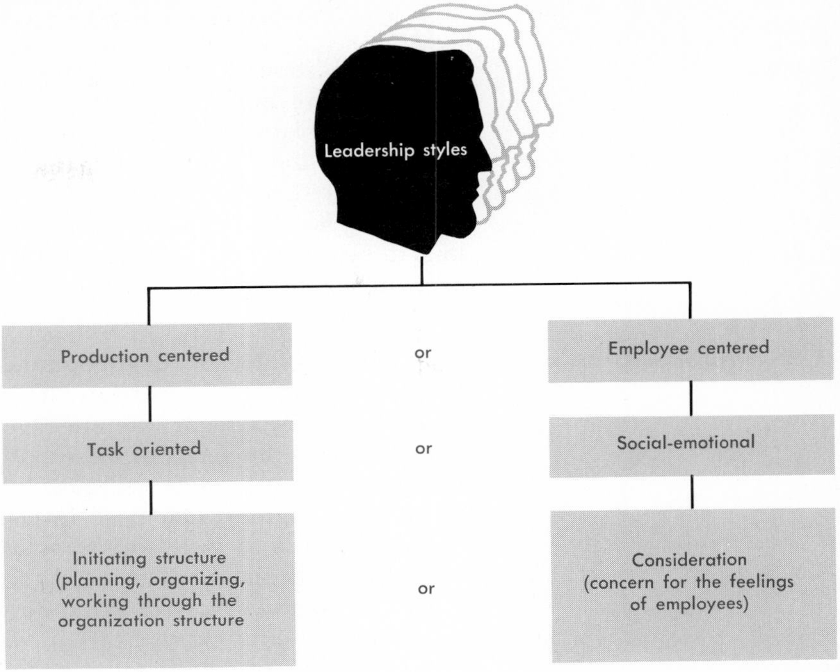

Leadership styles

Production centered	or	Employee centered
Task oriented	or	Social-emotional
Initiating structure (planning, organizing, working through the organization structure	or	Consideration (concern for the feelings of employees)

FIGURE 15.4 Contemporary terms in a two-factor leadership model. The usual objective of a leader and his group is output, which may be expressed in terms of productivity and satisfaction. Leadership styles for achieving output are, however, frequently one-sided: They stress either productivity, or the satisfaction and welfare of employees.

swered with simplistic solutions. There are too many verified studies showing that a leadership style successful in plant A was unsuccessful in plant B. What seems to be the best answer is, "It all depends."

contingency attitude

An "it all depends" attitude is a *contingency attitude,* one that is conditional upon certain factors. For a manager to be freed from rigid and static leadership approaches, he must be able to ask what seems to be the most appropriate approach given the forces in:

The manager

The subordinates

The organization

The situation

You can see that it's highly unlikely that these four forces would ever be identical, and therefore, effective solutions at one time might not carry over to another time.

For example, in a study of four organizational units, it was found that the managers in one plant worked in a very formal setting and thus allowed minimal participation in decision making.

Such a condition should have affected their motivation negatively; yet they were highly motivated. Conversely, managers in a low-performing plant were in a freer setting, participating in decision making; yet they were not as highly motivated as the first group. McGregor's Theory X and Y assumptions did not seem to hold up.[8] According to these researchers, there must be a fit between the task to be performed, the organization, and the people. The manager must condition his style to the task being performed by the group he manages.

What do subordinates want?

MEET THE NEEDS OF SUBORDINATES This, of course, is a simple statement of the Maslow-McGregor thinking. Given the assumptions of McGregor, the effective manager is the person who is able to have the needs of his subordinates met in the workplace; as the lower-level needs are quickly met, we find workers operating in the higher-order need levels. The obvious difficulty with this approach is as clear to you as to any practicing leader. What do you do with those whose needs do not seem to find satisfaction in their present workplace? What do you do when there is a poor, bad, dirty, unfulfilling type of job, which has to be done, that has a low potential for a need satisfaction? How do you get the people who report to you to agree with the organizational goal? McGregor specifically addressed himself to this question by recommending a kind of behavior that included subordinate participation and dialogue on such things as goals and objectives.

Are there other ways of being effective?

GET WHAT YOU WANT THROUGH CONDITIONING Robert A. Stringer, Jr., writes about achievement motivation and management control. Stringer says, "By creating the right kind of climate, managers can have a definite impact on the achievement motivation of their subordinates. They can present these individuals with new sources of satisfaction and new opportunities to achieve, thereby arousing achievement motivation."[9] Stringer gives a very clear picture of a model in which the objective is to improve the level of performance of others, an obvious objective for any effective leader. Stringer believes the organizational climate can be affected and controlled so as to influence the output of individuals.

Other researchers speak in the same tone: Control the envi-

[8] From an article by John J. Morse and Jay W. Lorsch, "Beyond Theory Y," in *A Contingency Approach to Management: Readings*, eds. John W. Newstrom et al. (New York: McGraw-Hill, 1975), pp. 273–84.

[9] Robert A. Stringer, Jr., "Achievement Motivation and Management Control," in *Motivation and Control in Organizations*, eds. G. Dalton and P. Lawrence (Homewood, Ill.: Irwin-Dorsey, 1971), p. 331.

ronment in such a way that the individual's behavior is affected in a predetermined direction. Nord, in defending the value of B. F. Skinner and his conditioning ideas for management, looks at the positions of Douglas McGregor, Abraham Maslow, and Frederick Herzberg and finds that these three men, although not directly using the Skinner language or approach, are in effect suggesting a conditioning type of management behavior.[10] Each is suggesting that the leader can change, influence, or create the environment that will be supportive and reinforce the behavior desired. Managers use *behavior modification* by controlling the immediate consequence of the individual's behavior.

behavior modification

Nord takes the Skinner idea of reinforcement and talks about a theory of management through positive reinforcement. Rather than trying to go back into the inner depths of man, or searching for man's essence, Nord suggests training and personnel development, compensation, supervision and leadership, job design, organizational design, and organizational change as the areas for the systematic use of positive reinforcement. The Skinner approach is a behavioral approach, which is not concerned with motivation or philosophical questions about the nature of man.

Is expediency the answer?

USE WHAT IS AVAILABLE In this approach, the leader is not spending a great deal of time in analysis of motivation or in the debate on animal psychology and conditioning. The leader uses personal experiences to form a simple, concrete, day-to-day working model. He looks at the areas within his control that others view as important and uses these as reward areas. Monetary rewards are usually under his control, and the effective leader acts with this knowledge. The effective leader is aware that there are nonmonetary rewards that are also important to people. He may use status, or competition, or information and communication as valuable techniques for achieving change in behavior and performance of goals. The leader also recognizes the value of punishment or the threat of punishment; he realizes the importance of power and influence and that his own effectiveness is improved if others feel he has influence and power to get things done.

What do people respond to?

The effective leader, using a very pragmatic approach, will realize that there are times when subordinate groups in competition with each other will do many negative and destructive things in order to win. He may then have to use the notion of *superordinate*

[10] Walter R. Nord, "Beyond the Teaching Machine: The Neglected Area of Operant Conditioning in the Theory and Practice of Management," in *Motivation and Control*, eds. Dalton and Lawrence, pp. 352–77.

superordinate goals

goals, goals that require the cooperation of two units for completion. For example, during World War II, Russia and the United States became allies because of the attack by Hitler on Russia. The superordinate goal (to defeat the Nazis) demanded the cooperation of the allies and thus directed a great deal of behavior.

The manager cannot escape his leadership responsibility, for even if he sits in his office and does nothing, others will perceive him as withholding the rewards and punishments due them.

EMPLOY AN INTEGRATION APPROACH Perhaps the best ending for this discussion of leadership behavior is with an integrating theory of leadership from David Bowers and Stanley Seashore, who suggest that four factors emerge from various research studies.[11] These four dimensions are behavioral, in that they are something that a manager *does* in order to become effective. Notice how these four factors cut across and integrate much of what we have already presented to you in Parts 2 and 3.

To Bowers and Seashore, leadership behavior should do four things:

1. *Create support.* This behavior will let others feel that they are of worth and importance.
2. *Facilitate interaction.* This behavior will encourage members of the group to develop close, positive, warm, satisfying relationships.
3. *Emphasize goals.* This behavior will stimulate an enthusiasm among people to meet the performance goals of the group.
4. *Facilitate work.* This behavior is related to goal attainment and includes scheduling, coordinating, planning, and providing technical knowledge, tools, and materials.

You can see from this four-factor theory of leadership that the earlier thoughts of the 1900s (points 3 and 4) are included with the later developments of man as a human resource (points 1 and 2).

A Concluding Thought

The topic of leadership is more complex than the four-factor theory of leadership seems to imply. It would be no great revelation to you that work has to be done, and it has to be done by

[11] David G. Bowers and Stanley E. Seashore, "Predicting Organizational Effectiveness with a Four-Factor Theory of Leadership," in *Readings in Organizational Behavior,* eds. Scott and Cummings, pp. 441–54.

people who want to be treated like human beings. For some reason that has defied research and experimentation, managers and leaders have tended not to treat others as they themselves want to be treated. Many managers describe their subordinates in derogatory terms and feel that their insights constitute a law of human nature. They are amazed, surprised, and embarrassed when they find that their bosses describe them in the same way. The challenge to those managers who want to fulfill the leadership function and become effective managers and leaders is to recognize the dual and complementary objectives of both getting a job done and getting it done through human beings.

SUMMARY AND PROPOSITIONS

So end our thoughts about the leadership function residing in the managerial role. We have made some progress in identifying this elusive quality. We have also thought about the determinants of the leadership role and provided some generalizations about approaches to effective leadership behavior. The following propositions should help to integrate these ideas:

1. Management is more than leadership, although leadership is important.
    a. Many preaction functions and mental activities do not involve leadership.
    b. Since organizations involve people, leadership is one of the most critical functions of management.
2. A wise leader will not try to be "all things to all people."
    a. Most situations and groups have a definite leadership need, and the effective manager will act to meet the need.
    b. Most people have a specific self-concept and become artificial leaders if they try to satisfy everyone.
3. Personality factors are more important to an *emergent* than to an *appointed* leader.
    a. Emergent leaders usually have no official position authority and must satisfy the needs of their peers to become the leader.
    b. Appointed leaders have organizational authority and can get performance even if they have some personality limitations.
4. A rewards approach in leadership will have a longer-run benefit than a punishment approach.
    a. Rewards are pleasing and thus have benefits beyond the immediate performance—they affect expectations positively and carry over to other areas of performance.

   b. People will perform quickly to avoid pain (punishment, either physical or emotional), but threats of punishment induce only minimal compliance.

5. An effective manager will see that the leadership needs of the formal and informal organization are met.

6. Contingency thinking is a must for managers in the 1980s.

STUDY ASSIGNMENTS

1. What specific determinants of leadership are developed in the vignette?

2. Can anyone become a manager? a leader?

3. In what ways can you distinguish between management and leadership?

4. Give personal examples to show that the leadership act takes place when the three determinants of leadership interact with each other.

5. Is one of the three P's more important than another in determining leadership? Explain.

6. In the person factor of leadership, a number of traits and abilities are mentioned.

   a. Make a list of the traits and abilities that seem related to becoming a successful leader.

   b. Make a list of your own traits and abilities at this point of your career.

   c. Compare the two lists.

   d. What training or learning experiences do you need to develop as a leader?

7. "The most popular person is not always the best leader." Explain.

8. What qualities in a person would make you want to follow him?

9. Write out the role expectation you believe exists for the following:

   a. Your teacher's expectation of your role as a student

   b. The community's expectation of the student role

   c. Your expectation of the student role

   d. Your role expectation for the brightest student in class

10. Give examples in which the situations seemed to determine the effectiveness of leaders.

11. *Eight statements are given for effective leadership behavior. Answer the following questions about these statements:*
    a. *If effective leadership is as simple as following eight simple rules, why aren't more managers effective leaders?*
    b. *Why are the statements about being yourself and choosing your own style critical statements?*
    c. *Is the Theory X–Theory Y statement at odds with the situational factor in leadership? (In other words, people are not "X" or "Y," but rather respond to a specific situation.) Explain.*
12. *Give reasons why you would accept or reject Propositions 2; 3, 3(b); 4; 5.*

situational episodes

1. Suppose a friend of yours comes to you for advice. He wants to know what he should do to become a leader. You reflect on what you know of your friend: He is outspoken, frank, and frequently critical; he rarely wins any popular elections in clubs or schools; he has average or above-average intelligence; and he seems to be very competitive. What do you tell him?
2. Roger and Harry were in college together. Both participated in football and basketball, although Roger played first string and Harry was a substitute. Harry ran on the track team and also loved music. Roger was elected president of the fraternity, president of the junior and senior classes, and president of the student council, and he was selected as the outstanding male in the graduating class. Harry was business manager of the touring choir, was appointed as chairman of the senior-prom committee, and was selected by the student council to be its financial manager. Can you predict what management success and position each holds twenty years later? Explain your answer.

controlling

SIXTEEN

OBJECTIVES YOU SHOULD MEET

Define *control when used as a managerial process.*

State *the four essentials of a control system.*

Define *and* ***illustrate*** *closed-loop feedback.*

List *the six functions of a production control system.*

Outline *the questions answered by an inventory control system.*

Show *how a quality control system indicates points at which attention is needed.*

Paraphrase *the key points to consider in a performance evaluation system.*

WHO'S CHECKING THAT OUT?

"Hey, Jim, I sure do need some help. We district managers seem to be caught in the middle. What do you do about all this red tape? Headquarters is bothered about the way people are padding their travel expenses and, of all things, long-distance calls. More red tape is their answer."

"Well, Frank, I don't know, but I'm feeling the heat too. They tell us to keep contact with our customers and be sure to meet our quotas. So we push the salesmen to phone our best outlets and to see them frequently. I have a dickens of a time getting my men reimbursed for their travel expenses. Now headquarters is kicking because we spend a few measly bucks on long-distance calls that save traveling."

"I don't know what to do, Jim. I'll admit that some of my boys tend to charge the company for expenses that are for their personal entertainment. How can I tell whether they're buttering up a customer or just living it up on the company? Headquarters does have to require some receipts and records to support salesmen's expenses. But I think that getting a receipt from a taxi driver is carrying this control stuff too far. You know, the other day, I parked my car at the airport and forgot to keep the charge receipt from the parking lot—I'll bet I have a hard time getting that money from the company even if I sign a notarized affidavit."

"Well, the way I handle those things is to charge the company for more tips than I actually give—and you know, they don't require receipts for tips yet. I just don't know how to decide whether those expense vouchers that I sign for my boys are legit. If I call the guy in and ask him some questions about items on his expense voucher, he acts as though I'm charging him with grand larceny. So far, I've decided to

sign whatever vouchers they turn in and leave it to the treasurer's office to clamp down if they want to. The trouble is that I have no guidelines as to what is 'reasonable.' Don't you think the company should make clearer what charges are permissible?"

"Yeah, but I don't want to ask questions about that, because it would just result in more doggone straitjackets," Frank said. "It isn't up to me to be a policeman for the company. The accounting department sits back looking at all those figures—they should watch expenses. I ran into one of them the other day on what he called an internal audit trip, and he told me that they *aren't in a position to say whether a twenty-dollar dinner at a restaurant is necessary to make the sale. He said that the charge was made by one of my men and that I should check it out! Gosh, am I a salesman or am I an accountant? I've got enough to do meeting my district quota with my fifteen salesmen—I can't go snooping around to find out whether my men are taking advantage of the company. The men may get the idea that I don't trust them, and I've always heard that business depends on trust."*

"Well, I must say the brass is getting hot about a small problem. A little fudging on an expense account isn't going to break the company, but if we don't get in there before International Dynamics captures the entire market, then we'll be broke. I learned the other day that I.D. doesn't require any *receipts—they just give a per diem for travel and let the salemen spend it however they want to, just as long as they don't go over the allowed amount for the days that they're on sales trips."*

"Now that sounds like a good idea," Frank replied. "It sure would make my life easier. I don't want to get a guilt complex about signing travel vouchers that may look a little out of line. Why should I call a salesman on the carpet for some small expense he swears was really the reason he got the sale? Selling is our job, so why can't the company leave us alone? They should let us decide what it takes to make a sale. Then, if we don't produce enough sales, we'd catch the dickens about something that's important—not about these trifling details."

"Frank, I've got to run now, but honestly, if I were you, I wouldn't worry so much about these Mickey Mouse controls. I'm going to just do my job and fill in the cotton-pickin' forms in a way to stay out of trouble on the details. It's not worth getting upset about."

"Thanks for the advice, old man. But all I can say is that headquarters had better do something about this mess or I'll lose some salemen. And maybe I'll quit myself."

Controlling

Managing an organization requires many skills and techniques. Having already presented six of the seven management functions, we turn now to the function many consider the most basic and critical—controlling. *Controlling* is seeing that actual performance is guided toward expected performance.

The control function of management relates to all other management functions, and most of the others cannot be completed effectively without recognition of the control function. Here, as an integrating and ending chapter of Part 3, we first present a brief look at some relationships of controlling to other management functions to show the vital role that control plays. Then we continue our discussion of control by answering the following questions: What are the essential features of controlling? What are some of its technical aspects? What are some of its practical applications? And finally, what are some of the human features of controlling?

THE RELATIONSHIP OF CONTROLLING TO OTHER MANAGEMENT FUNCTIONS

Recall for a moment the other management functions: Managers make decisions, set objectives, plan, organize and staff, communicate with others, and lead through the process of directing and supervising. These functions usually involve the managers and oth-

How can I find out what's going on?

ers—bosses, peers, or subordinates. What controlling does is to provide the means for consciously knowing what's going on. When control exists in an organization, people know what targets they are striving for, they know how they are doing in relationship to those targets, and they know what changes, if any, are needed to keep their performance at a satisfactory, expected level.

Managers cannot make sound decisions unless they have performance data, are able to relate these data to some standard or expected level, and are able to determine the significance of any deviation from the standard. Objective setting is meaningful when the statements are translated into specific targets with the potential of being measured. Plans, derived from objectives, must also be viewed in terms of the control process so that the decision maker anticipates changes in plans based upon the anticipated reporting back of performance results.

In the functions of communicating and leadership, control plays a different part. You could think of organizational communications as necessary ingredients of control. And managers as leaders can also be seen as people who ensure that the control function operates within the organization. Thus, overall, controlling is an extremely fundamental and essential management activity.

THE ESSENTIALS OF CONTROLLING

One way of achieving a clearer understanding of the control function is to explain what we do *not* mean by control. The word *control* has a number of meanings; some of them are part of our common language and some are part of a technical language.

How can you avoid fuzzy thinking about control?

Some people think of control as coercion, force, or power: "Control the flood waters. . . . Man must control the environment. . . . Our pitcher has lost control of his curve ball." These are examples of control in the "power over things" sense. The controlling function of management used in this chapter does not have this interpretation.

Another interpretation is the notion of control as any form of social influence. In this sense, authority over others is control. Informal groups thus exercise control of work performance when they use their informal means of rewards and punishments to hold back the productivity output of rate-busters. This interpretation also differs from the one in this chapter.

Controlling is the activity that measures performance and guides actions toward some predetermined target. At this point in our understanding, we want to look at the simple questions of what controlling is and how it gets done. Who should control, the more difficult question, comes later in the chapter.

The term *control* as we use it has many synonyms. Words like *regulating, checking,* and *monitoring* convey the meaning of control we are trying to develop. Imagine an organization without control. You would find chaos and confusion. People would not know where they were or what they were doing, or how their work fit into plans. As a consumer, you can probably cite case after case where there seems to be an absence of control.

Another way to develop insight into this concept is through an example you may have experienced. Suppose you have an objective or goal for a course in school. This objective could range from just passing to gaining understanding and growth. Your plan for this goal will include study habits, preparing for class and assignments, and performing on exams, discussions, and other projects. Assume you take the first exam (performance) and receive a grade of 63. Control comes into this picture when you receive additional information about your grade. For example, where does the 63 rank in regard to the rest of the class? Does the instructor grade on a curve, or does he use absolute standards (90–100 = A)? Will the instructor value improvement of performance during the course, or will every test grade be weighted the same? In other words, until you receive some control information, you do not know how to guide any future behavior or action; you do not know how to guide yourself toward your target.

In the classroom illustration and the examples of the control synonyms, certain essentials of the controlling process are evident. In any control system, there is some *predetermined target,* a means for *measuring* actual accomplishments, a means for *comparing* actual performance with the target, and a means of *correcting* performance to meet the target. Because these four essentials exist in any control system, and because they are used extensively in later portions of this chapter, each will receive further attention at this point.

Setting a Target

Why should you set targets?

This first element is the foundation upon which the entire process is built: You must determine what the results should be, or what can be expected. In short, planning must precede control.

The first element of the control process demands a look into the future and a prediction of a definite feasible *target.* This element may be in the form of a scientifically established standard, such as the weight-bearing limits of a bridge; it may be borrowed from information about what others have been able to accomplish—for example, par for a golf hole; it often assumes that future performance is directly related to experiences in the past, as with profits for the last twelve months; it may be merely a target agreed on by the manager and his workers to be reasonable.

In the preceding vignette, Jim, as manager of salesmen, should reasonably expect the company to make clear what expenses are allowed for reimbursement. If the company expectations remain vague, Jim will continue to ignore one important managerial function—control of expenses.

Measuring Performance

The second element in any control system is the *measurement* of actual performance. This element usually requires the greatest amount of work, since it involves keeping records of the results of one's effort.

How can you measure performance?

Although the discussion of a control process appears rather late in this book, it is obvious that this element must be considered at the beginning of operations if one is to collect information about what a person is really getting done. Let us consider some examples of such measurable units: In production, it may be in physical units, such as number of units of output, or units per man-hour, or pounds of scrappage per unit of output. In financial questions, it is generally stated in terms of dollar revenue or dollar cost or ratios of cost to revenue. In marketing, the target may be stated in terms of number of units sold, percentage of the total market to be captured by the manager's unit, or the number of visits to be made by salesmen. (Jim's department's travel and phone expenses could be related to the amount of sales generated by each salesman.)

The following are key considerations in selecting the unit for measuring performance:

1. Targets and results must be stated in the same units. For example, if the target has been set in dollars, performance should be stated in dollars.
2. The unit should encourage prompt reporting of actual performance. For example, if physical volume of output is available on a daily basis, daily volume is preferable to some other unit that is available only weekly.

3. Since all measurement is accurate only to some limited degree, the relative accuracy in the unit is very important. Unnecessary accuracy may be costly and of little use; on the other hand, "fudged" figures will not help in interpreting the data either.

Making Comparisons

Why compare?

The third element of any control process is the comparison of actual performance with the expected target. This step adds meaning to the data. Some variation in performance can be expected in all activity; therefore, the manager must determine what amount of variation is significant and worth attention. For this reason, the technique for comparison should indicate clearly and quickly the size of the variation. The simplest technique is to record the target and actual performance near each other and, by visual inspection, to determine which is larger. Here are two other simple techniques that make comparisons easier:

1. Record current activity and the targets in a line chart (Figure 16.1).
2. Develop ratios of actual performance to the targets, such as: current expenses running over 10 percent of the target.

Taking Corrective Action

The fourth element of a control process is the action phase of making corrections. If the comparison indicates that performance is satisfactory, no action is needed. If, however, the comparison indicates a large variation, the manager uses this information to signal corrective action.

Two basic types of error face the manager when taking corrective action. If the control devices are in error, he may take action when none is required. For a similar reason, he may also delay action too long. For example, the dashboard of an automobile consists of lights and dials for controlling temperature, oil pressure, and other characteristics of engine operations. If the oil-pressure warning light goes on, the driver should stop the engine immediately to prevent engine damage; however, if the oil level indicated on the dipstick appears normal, the trouble may be in the functioning of the control light or in the operation of the oil pump. Corrective action may be needed either in the functioning of the engine or in the functioning of the control light. In any case,

FIGURE 16.1 Performance compared with targets

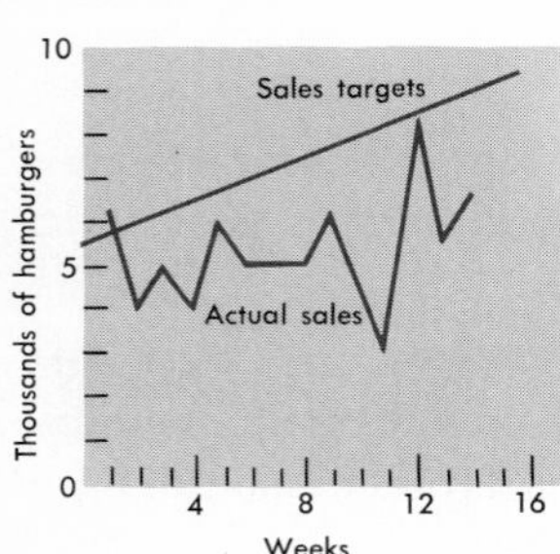

the control light only provides warning of the existence of a problem, it does not automatically provide the necessary corrective action.

SOME ASPECTS OF CONTROLLING

When you design and implement a control system, you should consider some basic aspects for making it efficient and effective. Two of these, feedback and strategic-point control, will be explained here.

Feedback

Feedback

How do you get feedback?

Feedback is the process of adjusting the future action based on information about past performance. Although applications of the idea date back to controls on windmills, the flyball governor of Watts's steam engine, and the steering of steamships, recent developments of electronic hardware for automatic controls have reinforced the importance of this principle.

closed-loop system of feedback

open-loop system of feedback

The engineer refers to a *closed-loop system of feedback* when the information on actual performance is fed back to the source of energy by electrical or mechanical means in an endless chain without human intervention. An *open-loop system of feedback* involves a situation in which electronic or mechanical devices are supported at some point by human intervention. Figures 16.2 and 16.3 illustrate these two systems, using the heating of a house as an example.

Note that the concept of feedback is a precise way of illustrating our four essentials of any control system. Many automatic appliances use the closed-loop feedback concept; however, a number

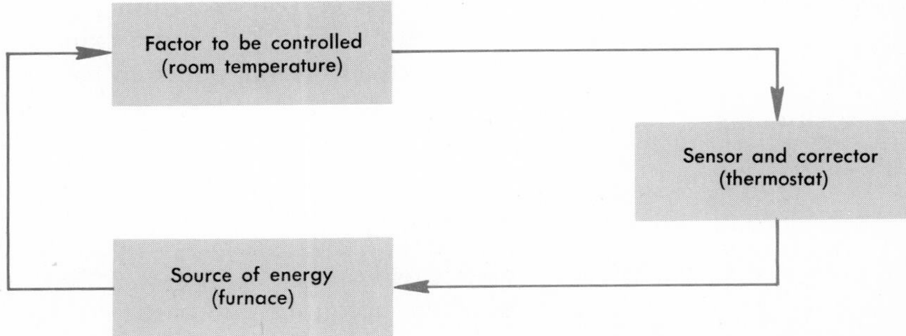

FIGURE 16.2 Closed-loop feedback

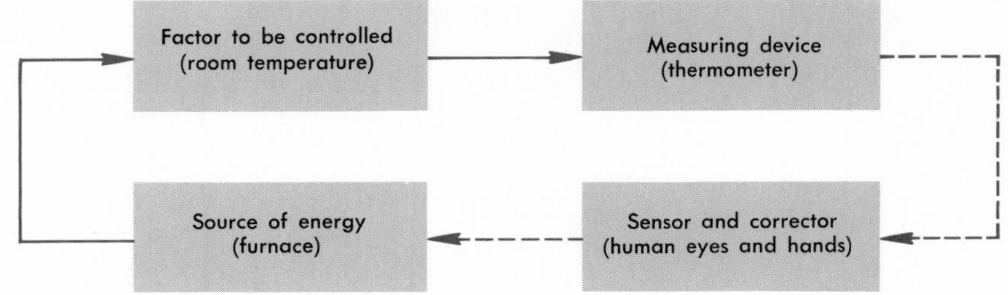

FIGURE 16.3 Open-loop feedback

of so-called automatic systems do not. For example, an "automatic" electric toaster uses the closed-loop feedback principle only if it is designed to turn off the current when the bread is toasted to a specified degree. If the toaster is designed to proceed through a cycle regardless of the condition of the bread, it is often called automatic, but it does not involve closed-loop feedback. In the latter example, one could end up with a burnt piece of toast!

Strategic-Point Control

How can you minimize costs of controlling?

Optimum control can be achieved only if critical, key, or limiting points can be identified and close attention directed to adjustments at those points. Thus, increased control does not necessarily mean better control. The *strategic points for control* can be identified by a careful study of operations and by relating the control system to the organizational structure. In this study of the situation to be controlled, you search for those points at which knowledge about comparisons of actual performance with targets will help explain whether performance at other points is satisfactory (see Figure 16.4). For example, a traffic engineer who designs a system of electric traffic signals will make studies of traffic density at numerous points. He will locate those intersections that, if controlled with a traffic signal, will regulate traffic smoothly through other intersections without using signals at each intersection. Careful attention to these key strategic points will usually result in better overall control of traffic in the area than if the engineer had planned for a more expensive system of additional traffic lights and additional police to monitor the performance of drivers.

An airport is a strategic point for controlling the flight of aircraft. Very expensive and sophisticated equipment is used to control air traffic around airports, whereas less control is maintained in the air space where plane density is at a minimum.

The degree of control at strategic points directly affects the degree of control needed at other points. In a business organization, the accounting department collects data on receipts and expenditures as materials or products move from one department to another. In this way, the performance of each department and its manager can be checked against company targets. In addition, each manager is given information about those matters over which he has authority to take remedial action.

If the organization focuses on strategic points of control, it can maintain effective controls without trying to control all details. Furthermore, this method permits subunits to maintain self-control and thus reduces the feeling that members have little freedom for meeting situations as they see them.

You will see in the following section that a clear understanding of the essentials of control and these additional ideas of controlling can be applied in many different types of situations.

SOME APPLICATIONS OF CONTROL

At this point, you may think that you understand the essentials and ideas of control, but you also probably feel the need for more specific applications of these ideas to organizations. We therefore turn here to examples of applied control systems. In these examples, we show how each of the elements appears in actual control systems. In addition, we outline some of the special techniques for applying these essentials to the operational areas.

Controlling Products

Some organizations specialize in purchasing products, manufacturing products, or marketing products. Some do all three. Regardless of the nature of this specialization, managers need to con-

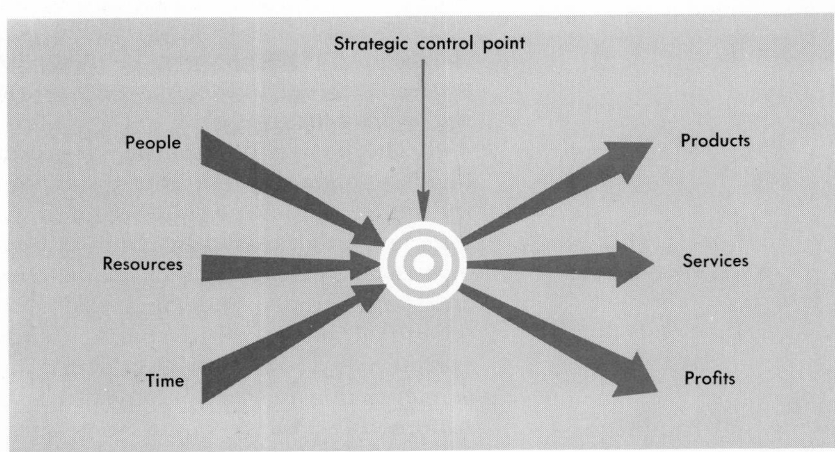

FIGURE 16.4 Strategic-point control

trol the path and timing of the flow of products, the quantity of products available, and the quality of the products. Therefore, we shall describe an application of controlling products to meet each of these needs. Controlling the timing and path of the flow usually is called *production control.* Controlling the quantity available is called *inventory control.* Controlling quality is called *quality control.*

PRODUCTION CONTROL Production control consists of five functions:

Routing

1. *Routing* determines the operations to be performed, their sequence, and the path of flow of materials through a series of operations.

Loading

2. *Loading* is the function of assigning work to a machine or department in advance.

Scheduling

3. *Scheduling* of production determines the time at which each operation is to take place.

Dispatching

4. *Dispatching* is the process of actually ordering work to be done.

Expediting

5. *Expediting* is a follow-up activity that checks on whether plans are actually being executed.

Production planning and control are often handled by one department, which directs the operation of a number of subsystems of control. Figure 16.5 illustrates the relationships of production control to typical departments in a manufacturing organization.

The first three of the functions of production control aim at setting specific targets, our first essential of control. Dispatching directs actual performance, the second essential, and expediting is involved with initiating corrective action, our fourth essential. The physical work is performed by operating departments, with the production-control function serving as the nervous system, providing signals for control.

job lot

What affects the design of a production control system?

product basis

The design of a particular planning and control system depends to a great extent on the state of the technology of the industry. Some industries produce products for a particular order and thus use *job-lot* methods of controlling production. The production of this textbook, from final manuscript through typesetting, galley and page proofs, indexing, and final binding, was routed and scheduled on a job-lot basis. Other industries concentrate on assembly-line methods, by which machines are placed along a conveyor in a planned manner so as to mass-produce the product. Automobiles, TV sets, and home appliances use this *product basis*

continuous processing

for planning and control. Still other industries, such as chemical and oil refining, are adapted to *continuous processing*, and depend upon a careful production and control system's being built into the manufacturing processes. Other industries need still other types of control systems; for example, in the construction industry, machines and materials are transported to a particular spot for erection of the structure. Thus, variations in technology have been found to influence not only methods of control, but also the management style of the company.

FIGURE 16.5 Relationship of production planning and control to other departments of a manufacturing company

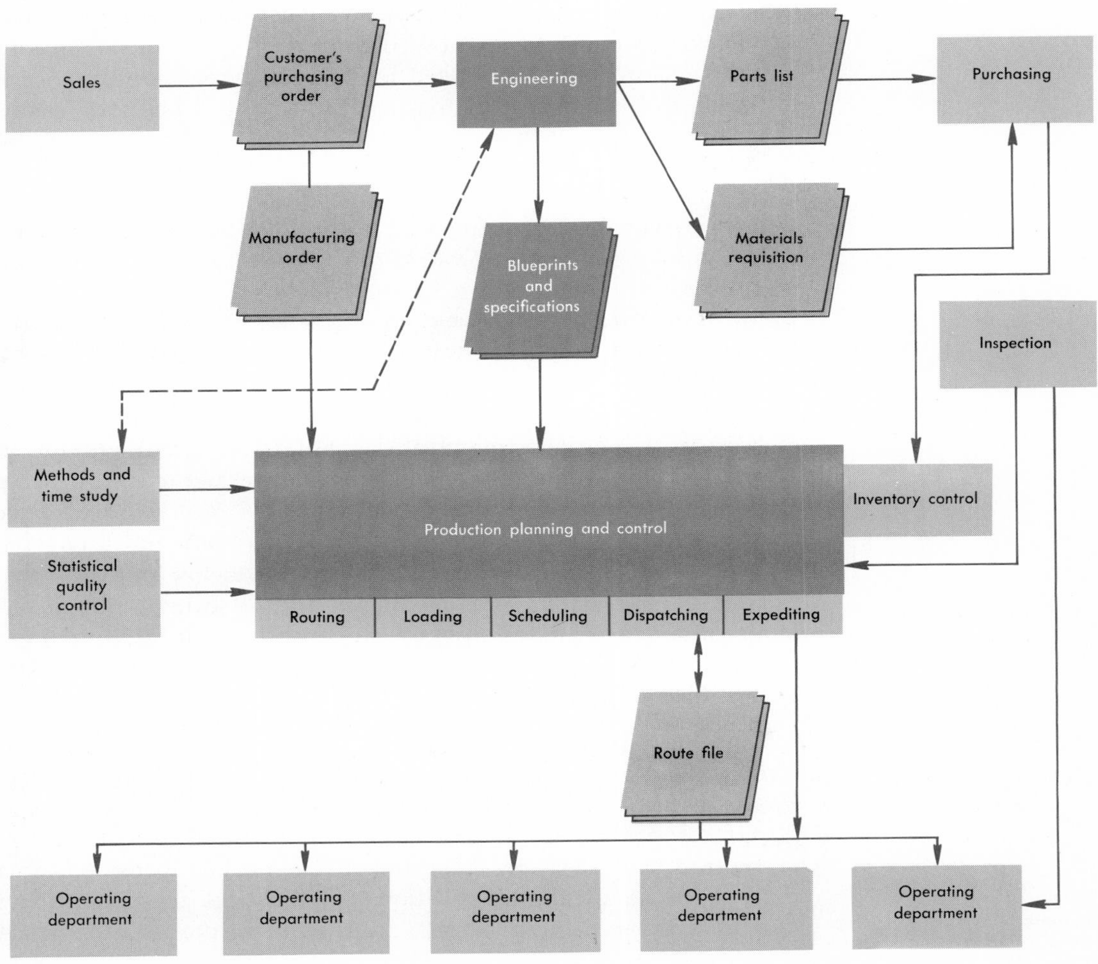

How much inventory do you need?

INVENTORY CONTROL Inventory control is a product-control system that relates to purchasing, production, and sales. The types of inventory to be controlled are (1) raw materials and parts, (2) work in process, and (3) finished goods. Inventory control handles the following questions:

1. What is the optimum amount of inventory to carry?
2. What is the economic lot size for an order?
3. What is the record system for showing the status of inventory on hand?

Targets should be set for four aspects of inventory: maximum inventory, minimum inventory, the reorder point, and the order size. Figure 16.6 illustrates how these four targets relate to each other. When such a chart is used for control, actual performance is plotted on the same sheet so that comparisons can be made easily. For example, usage of the product will cause the quantity on hand to decline. Before the minimum inventory is reached, an order must be issued for the amount of the economic ordering quantity. When it arrives, the quantity on hand would reach the maximum level. If the replenishment process is dependable, with few delays, then minimum inventory can be set very low, since the chief reason for having minimum inventory above zero is to serve as insurance for delays and to reduce the chance that continual corrective action will be needed.

Since the subject of inventory control is of great importance—the manufacturing department must maintain sufficient supplies to be worked on, and the marketing department must make available goods that can be sold—various systems of inventory control have received special attention in recent years. In some industries, it has been possible to introduce closed-loop systems for such commodities as oil, water, and chemicals. In the future, new techniques promise improved systems for other industries, but these improvements will be merely extensions of the simple framework we have introduced here.

FIGURE 16.6 Inventory control

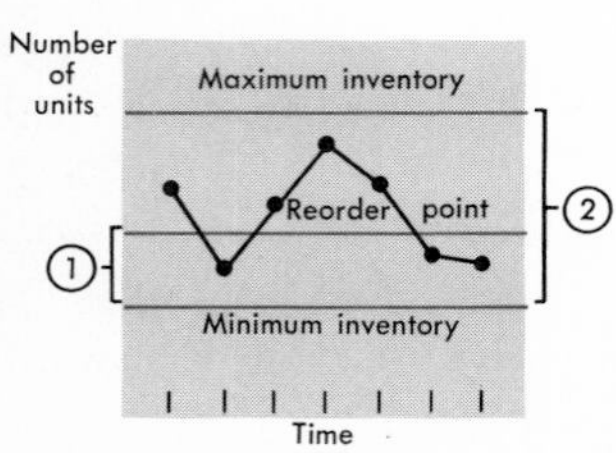

QUALITY CONTROL Controlling quality of products (also called quality assurance) has greatly improved in the last fifty years as a result of refinements in systems that have become available for comparing the quality of products with standards set by engineers and designers. This improvement has been possible chiefly because of the application of statistical methods using probability theory. Using samples from work in process, the prod-

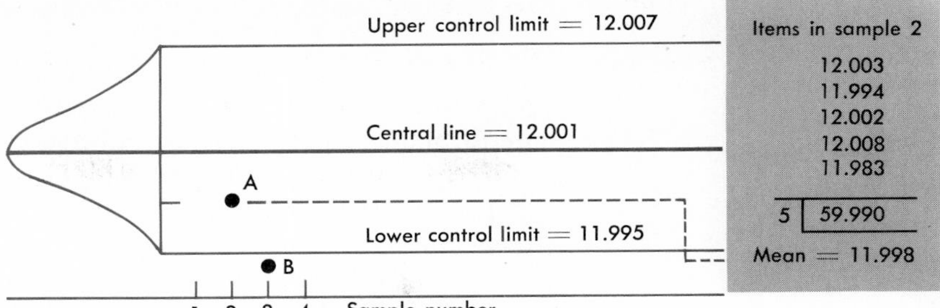

FIGURE 16.7 A quality-control chart for producing a 12-inch ruler

How do you measure quality?

uct can be checked against standards so that the output will contain a minimum number of rejects. The quality targets are set by engineers. Samples of products in production are tested at intervals to provide data on the current quality. These samples yield data that may vary from standard for two reasons: because of the chance selection of the items in the sample, or owing to some "real" cause, such as the wearing of a cutting tool. The problem in controlling quality using samples is in differentiating between these two factors, so that corrective action is taken only when it is probably needed.

Statisticians have provided tables for determining the size of samples, degrees of risk for inference from samples, and other data using probability reasoning. The important skills needed by the non-statistics-oriented manager are (1) a familiarity with the powerful tools provided by statisticians, and (2) an ability to interpret the output of their work. Quality-control charts offer a graphical means by which the manager can interpret this information supplied by the statistician.

Figure 16.7 illustrates one type of quality-control chart. Let us study that figure. From past production figures, we have calculated the mean length of all rulers and plotted this as a central line—12.001. The upper control limit, 12.007, and the lower control limit, 11.995, are found from statistical tables that give the spread of sample means that would be expected owing to chance. If variations are due to chance, they will have a stable character; that is, the results will tend to cluster around a central figure, and a plot of their distribution will appear as a "normal" curve (shown to the left of the figure). Since this variation is predictable using this normal distribution, we can say that a mean of a sample of five items picked at random from the production line is probably due to chance or not due to chance, depending on whether the sample mean falls inside or outside the control limits.

The mean of sample 2 in the figure, 11.998, falls within the control limits (point *A*) as illustrated, and its variation from 12.001

would be considered to be due to chance. The results of this sample indicate that the process is probably under control; that is, performance does not vary enough from the target for us to take corrective action. If another sample is taken and its mean is found to be 11.994, as illustrated by point *B* on the figure, then the variation would be too great to attribute to chance and the process would probably be out of control, and corrective action would be needed. You will notice that in interpreting the results from both samples, we say that the conclusions are *probably* correct.

Controlling Finances

In any organization, there is a need to establish systems for controlling revenues and costs. If costs exceed revenues over a long period of time, the organization is not performing the function expected of it. We shall discuss two systems for controlling finances: standard costs and budgetary control.

How can you tell when costs are too high?

STANDARD COSTS In accounting, standard cost systems are based on predetermined costs developed from either past experience or expected future manufacturing costs. In standard costing, the unit cost of a particular product is the sum of (1) the standard labor costs, (2) the standard material costs, and (3) the standard overhead costs. As products are completed, the inventory of finished goods is charged with standard costs of completed units. Actual costs are collected, and then the manufacturing cost variances result from a comparison of the standard costs and the actual costs.

We can illustrate how standard costing uses the four essentials of any control system by studying the comparison in Table 16.1. The targets or standards have been placed in the first column and the actual costs in the second. The resulting variance has been recorded in the third column and gives a comparison that enables a manager to see that corrective action is needed. The fact that the cost of raw materials has exceeded the standard by $0.08 per unit

TABLE 16.1 Comparison of Actual and Standard Costs per Unit (in dollars)

	Standard	Actual	Variance
Raw material	0.42	0.50	0.08 over
Labor	1.04	1.06	0.02 over
Overhead	0.52	0.53	0.01 over
	1.98	2.09	0.11 over

gives the manager a signal to check whether there is waste in the quantity of raw materials being used; it is also possible that the prices paid for the raw material have increased from the prices used in setting the standard. The labor cost is also excessive, indicating that the time taken to produce the product may have been longer than expected or that the wage rate has increased. The slight variance in overhead indicates that the indirect costs of administration are higher than standard. A number of reasons for this problem are possible: The rate of production may have been lower than expected, or the number of administrative personnel may have increased.

The use of standard cost systems thus makes possible an analysis of different classifications of cost variances and pinpoints the areas in which corrective action is needed.

BUDGETARY CONTROL In Chapter 12, we saw that budgets are principal techniques for planning receipts and expenditures. We developed some of the guidelines for constructing budgets. The discussion here focuses on budgets as a set of targets of income and expense. Budgetary control is a system of using the targets established in a budget for guiding actual performance.

Budgetary control is a simple and direct application of our four essentials of control. After budget figures are set, records of actual receipts and expenditures are kept. For each item, the budget is compared with the actual performance, and variances can then be noted—over or under budget. The manager then has the necessary information upon which he can take corrective action—(1) to increase receipts, (2) to reduce expenditures, or (3) to revise the budget. This process enables the manager to check continually and to locate problems in finances early, before they develop into large figures to threaten the very existence of the organization.

Controlling Manpower

Applications of the essentials of control are varied with regard to manpower. In Chapter 13, we discussed how the personnel specialist defined jobs and positions and staffed them with personnel having the required qualifications. In the language of control, the jobs and positions are the targets, and the manner in which the people do the jobs is the performance that must be measured.

Are you doing your job?

A manager must always determine whether people under him are "doing a good job." He may leave such evaluations to his own judgment; however, such a tendency may cause personal biases (whether he likes the subordinate or not) to affect his judgment, and it will be more difficult for him to point out to the subordinate the basis of his judgment. Therefore, some system of performance evaluation is usually desirable to help the manager control performance. We introduced this idea in Chapter 13 under merit rating; however, the control aspects need further emphasis.

Of course, the first step in deciding whether a worker is doing a good job is a clear understanding by the subordinate and the manager of exactly what the job is. Considerable effort has been devoted to establishing a "fair day's work"—that is, the reasonable effort, skill, and output that should be expected. After the target is clearly set, a system of performance rating must keep records on the actual performance. When the product of the job is measurable in quantitative units, such as number of pieces produced, profit in dollars, or a score in an athletic contest, actual performance can be objectively measured.

However, many jobs, such as college teaching, have as the product a service that is difficult to state in numbers. In these cases, it is desirable to develop an index of performance that is affected by a number of factors. This index could include such objectively measurable factors as total student credit hours taught by the instructor (number of students in classes times the number of credit hours); it can also include subjective rating systems, in which the superior rates quality on the basis of some scale—for instance, 1 through 10 for each factor important to the job. This rating system can incorporate opinions of the customer, student, or user of the product. For example, the quality of an instructor's performance could be evaluated by the students in his class, by the employers of the students when they take a first job, or by instructors who teach courses that make use of the knowledge contributed by the one being rated.

These examples of control systems apply the four basic essentials of control and are representative of the large number of control systems possible. You should constantly be aware of cases in your own practice where you might develop your own tailored control system, using these same four essentials as guides.

HUMAN FACTORS IN CONTROL

How can controls backfire?

The human element is central to the effectiveness of any control system, for humans design, create, and implement the systems, they respond to the systems, and frequently they resist the systems.

So far, most of our descriptions of controlling have answered the questions of what is to be controlled and how a manager uses control. We have talked of a control process and its essentials without locating the control function in the organization and without reference to the specific person exercising the control. The literature in the behavioral-science field is full of examples of employee and subordinate reaction to control. Much of the criticism directed at managers is due to the *misuse* of control. Where in the control process must managers look for the dangers of misuse? What are the points of potential conflict as you implement the ideas of controlling? Answers to these questions dealing with the human elements in control form the subject matter of this last section.

Misuse of Control

When the control process is used to create power or for the purpose of coercion, the misuse is obvious and the reactions fairly predictable. This concept of control has no place in our definition or presentation. Our premise is that the application of control to the work of an organization improves the relationships, reduces the uncertainty, and results in benefits to both the organization and its members. Our concept of managerial control is a positive one and is as natural in its behavioral implications as the other management functions. One example of misuse will illustrate the potential dangers for managers.

A nonmanufacturing organization was experiencing difficulty with mailing costs. Each month, costs were increasing. A quick check of the source of the increase suggested that one department contributed to most of the increase. The investigating manager, having authority over the secretaries of the departments, instructed all secretaries to log in the mail of the managers of the department. He felt that some managers used the company mails for personal correspondence.

The reaction was predictable. The secretaries were agitated because of the increased burden placed upon them, and embarrassed at having to log in the managers' mail. The department managers became furious, since most knew that the culprits were few in number and possibly were not aware of policy restrictions on the use of the mail.

The secretaries did as directed, but their productivity suffered. In order for the managers to compensate, they reduced the use of the mails even on company business. The improper implementation of controls resulted in lost productivity and human resentment.

Why do controls create conflicts?

The major source for conflict centers on answering the question of who controls. The control process deals with work flow from the target date to completion date. But this process also involves people—managers, staff personnel, and subordinates. Real and legitimate differences of opinion may exist on such questions as the following: Who sets the targets? Who determines what unit is to be measured? Who decides on what is to be compared, and how and when it is compared, and who does the comparison? Who participates in determining when and what kind of corrective action should take place? To every question there may be at least three sources of involvement: the line manager, the staff manager, and the worker.

Illustrations abound of potential conflicts arising from the involvement question. For example, some managers, fearing failure, might set their targets too low, thus ensuring that they always reach the goal. Other managers enjoy overreaching and setting goals very high. The second group may outperform the first but might not be rewarded if some boss worships "reach the goal."

Conflict may arise between line and staff over the authority in the control process. If staff personnel set the targets, do the measuring and comparing, and expect the line managers to take corrective action, conflict is almost inevitable.

Another source for conflict emerges from the sanctions placed in effect after the corrective action has been decided. If managers or employees are punished for not meeting targets, the targets may get met at the expense of something more important. For example, one small manufacturing firm was having quality-control as well as production-control problems. The first- and second-level managers were given training in human relations, since the company assumed that the cause of the problem was in the relationship between management and the workers. A training consultant worked with these men and had all of them take a series of simple tests. To his amazement, a few of the managers did not know the difference between the simple geometric outline symbols for a triangle and a rectangle. In further discussions with these men, some of whom had come up through the ranks and were now in production control, the observation was made that the third level of management, mostly college-trained and from the home office, resented the local men. There was no way for these local men to inform higher management of their problems without fear of sanctions being applied against them by the third-level managers. For years, these men had been able to get by without detection. Thus, the way managers treat or are expected to treat information they receive greatly affects the kind of feedback they actually receive.

Corrective action is a crucial last step in controlling. Whether it is taken by the manager as boss or by the worker as subordinate, certain options are open and some may create conflicts. When data are compared, the decision maker has two options—to make some change or make no change. Assume that some change is required. Now the options expand: The target or standard may need revision, the measuring process may need reviewing and change, the work pace or method may have to be completely changed, or the worker's effort may need correction. At every point just mentioned, there is the potential for change and thus resistance to change.

The manager who sees that the controlling function is being performed is a manager who is living in a dynamic, changing environment. As a manager, you must expect the problems just mentioned. Some of the leadership approaches in Chapter 15 may appeal to you, especially the McGregor and contingency models. McGregor emphasizes the importance of mutual target setting and self-control as the best approach. There are times, however, when subordinate participation may not be feasible, and thus you may approach the problem from a situational or contingency context. You must identify the conditions in the situation that will aid you in deciding the questions of what, how, and who is controlling.

SUMMARY AND PROPOSITIONS

This chapter has focused on the last function of management—control. We have attempted to show how control is an integral part of all functions of management that ultimately lead to performance. For controlling to be effective, all other functions of management must be working properly.

The integral nature of control—its relationship with other management functions—was stressed in the initial section of the chapter. Then the four essential stages of controlling were considered. After discussing two aspects of control, we illustrated the dynamics of control through a few applications dealing with controlling products, finances, and manpower. The central position of the human element in the effectiveness of any control system was the subject of our concluding section.

The elusive function that is control permeates the complete spectrum of management. The following propositions help us focus on its chief points:

1. An optimum control system maintains control on only those activities that have significant impact on the achievement of objectives and offer an opportunity for conscious attention to remedial action.

   a. Control necessitates the establishment of predetermined goals.

   b. Control processes are useless unless comparisons can be made between actual performance and projected performance.

   c. Corrective action is the remedial phase.

   d. Control does not produce a product other than information, and since it generally increases costs, control costs should themselves be controlled.

2. Feedback is a basic principle of control. Closed-loop feedback involves the direct feedback—without the interference of human beings—of information on actual performance for comparison with a preset target.

3. Controls should be tailored to fit the organization, so that the person who has the power to effect remedial action can be clearly identified as responsible. Factors beyond the control of a manager at a given level should not be intermingled with those factors over which he exerts control.

4. Any control system should be responsive to changing conditions, including the possible failure of the control system itself.

5. Maximum use should be made of systems of self-control existing within the unit or individual being monitored.

6. Control systems should be designed to be generally acceptable to the people being controlled.

7. Direct control between the controller and the controlled should be maintained as far as possible, and so the immediate supervisor remains the most important element in any control system, regardless of the number of control systems available to him.

8. Optimum control can be achieved only if critical, key, or limiting points can be identified and close attention directed to adjustments at these strategic points.

STUDY ASSIGNMENTS

1. Contrast the idea of control in the managerial process with other meanings of control.

2. Does a good control system depend on other functions of management? Planning? Decision making? Organizing? Communicating? Give examples of the interrelationships.

3. *"The predetermined target and the record of actual performance should be stated in the same measurable units." Explain the importance of this statement.*

4. *What are the advantages of using open-loop feedback? What are the advantages of using closed-loop feedback?*

5. *Does an electric signal at an intersection use closed-loop feedback? Explain your reasoning for your answer.*

6. *"If you try to control everything, the results will be that you will control nothing." Discuss.*

7. *How can you locate the strategic points for control?*

8. *Who would perform the functions of production control if no special department existed?*

9. *Explain how inventory control affects each of these: the sales department; the production department; the purchasing department; the finance department.*

10. *Some cost control systems do not make use of standard costs. What essential control systems may be missing in these systems? Make a personal budget for the next six months. Explain how this budget can be used in controlling your finances over the period.*

11. *Control of cheating on tests is an important subject in education, both to the teacher and to the student. How would you develop an effective control system using the ideas in this chapter?*

12. *Control systems affect your daily life. Express your reactions to these systems. Do they infringe on your personal freedom of action? Do you try to "beat" the system? What does your cooperation with a system depend on? Would your reactions be similar to those of Jim or of Frank in the introductory vignette?*

13. *Explain the importance of Proposition 3.*

situational episodes

1. In operating a service station, you become concerned about the fact that the total of gallons of gasoline purchased is greater than the total gallons sold (measured by the gasoline pumps). Should you expect some differences without suspecting a thief? For what reasons? How can you establish guidelines that will help you decide what type of corrective action to take?
2. Jane and John have been married for two years. Both are continuing their education, and both have part-time jobs. As a result of their limited total income and the erosion of their purchasing power because of inflation, they continually face a shortage of cash to pay their bills. They use a joint bank account, with each being able to write checks on the account. Recently, the account has been overdrawn, because each has written checks without knowing that the other had withdrawn funds. In the past, the couple has tried to make a budget covering the upcoming semester of course work. John has recently been studying budgeting in one of his courses and has proposed that he and his wife develop a system by which they use their budget not only for planning purposes but for control of income and expense. They are sitting down together over the weekend prior to the beginning of a new semester to outline how they can improve their control of expenditures.

   a. Outline the elements for their six-month budget. Assume that each has an income of $200 per month from their part-time jobs. Assume that their chief expenditures are for food, rent, transportation, and academic costs.
   b. Devise a simple system in which their budget can be used as a basis for a control system for their expenditures.
   c. Explain the advantages of the development of some control system to meet their needs.

3. You have just been hired as operations manager for an independent auto repair and service garage that employs eight mechanics and five body-shop specialists. The company also has a sizable car-wash installation and a road-service section with AAA listing.

You have little mechanical knowledge, but the company is looking to you for guidance in improving its planning and control of operations.

a. Devise a control system that will handle the usual production-control functions of the garage.

b. In your planning, identify the strategic points for control.

c. At what points would you make use of feedback in your system?

MANAGER'S GAME
POLITICS
PROMOTION
RISKS
PROFIT
MERGE
ITT
IBM
BLUFF
MUDDLING
STRATEGY
POWER
GM

4 management fundamentals: the reality of managing

Managers live in the real world. This means that they must deal with situations as they find them, not as they would like them. Managers are susceptible to the temptations and pitfalls present in all vocations.

Throughout this book, we have tried to emphasize the importance of reality. There is little value in reading a book on management that assumes an unreal world—a book that prescribes what *ought* to be rather than what *is*. Some managers, although well acquainted with the material presented to this point, are ineffective managers. And some who would fail a simple test on this material are the most successful. The missing ingredients may be found in the chapters that follow.

So far, you have studied ideas and techniques that are logical and sensible within the academic world; yet the complete picture cannot come from these sources alone. In Part 4, we expand our search for insights, disregarding traditional and sometimes narrow-sighted limitations of scholarly work to examine the "fundamentals" of practicing managers.

Lessons from the leaders of American organizations and foreign practices in Chapter 17 start the view of the practicing manager. In Chapter 18, the topics of authority, power, and politics are highlighted and integrated with the interacting behavioral world that the manager must face. Then in the final chapter of Part 4, we return to a more personal context, to round out the broad scope of the manager's world with a discussion of integration and innovation, necessary in a changing world.

lessons from managers in practice

SEVENTEEN

OBJECTIVES YOU SHOULD MEET

Distinguish *between the initiator and the organizer in the evolution of a company.*

Explain *Sloan's idea of decentralization.*

Explain *the importance of Watson's five lessons for IBM.*

Summarize *the chief reasons why Sears has remained successful throughout the last 75 years.*

Illustrate *the idea of locating niches for the operations of small and growing companies.*

Discuss *what you can learn from the mistakes of well-known companies.*

Summarize *two managerial ideas developed by management in foreign countries.*

CAN I FIND A COMPANY WITH A PHILOSOPHY THAT FITS MINE?

"Say, guys, how about that blowout that business threw for us at the civic center! I'm not sure what I learned, but the free lunch at the hotel impressed me. Also, I'm trying to figure out why all those companies spent their money in that Careers on Parade program. Of course, they said that the reason was to explain promising job opportunities. I'm just a little skeptical of all those grey flannel executives of the Establishment and their smooth talk about the companies they work for. Sure, their talk, brochures, exhibits, and movies sounded good—in fact, they sounded too good, like they were tossing us a lot of propaganda."

"Gosh, Frankie, I liked it. Why do you always look for ulterior motives when successful businessmen are involved? My worry is that they talked about the fine jobs we might get when we finish college, but I doubt whether they would actually offer me a job, with my average grades and test scores. My reaction is that if I could get in on some of that bread, I'd give my big toe! The discussions concerning their philosophy, policies, and approach to management turned me on more than all that theory and research junk that the profs hand out in the management course we're taking. I felt those people knew what they were talking about, since they were actually practicing what they were saying. They talked my language when they explained what they were doing to get a jump on their competition. They didn't just talk about principles, theory, research findings, and all that academic stuff. I could understand why they did their thing in the way they explained."

"Yeah, I did think it was worth my time not only to get free food but to learn something about the real world, but my reaction is that I'm more confused now than with the ideas in Management 101. Frankly,

Paul, I can get hold of some of the ideas in the course because the text and prof appear to draw a more rational picture of how management should approach their decisions and actions. The course, at least, gives me some organized idea of what to look for when I talk to practicing managers. For example, I can tell you more about the knowledge I have gotten in the course than what I learned in the Careers on Parade thing. For one thing, I talked with several of the discussion leaders after the panel presentations. That guy from PDG, Inc., explained how his company has a training program covering six months for new college graduates. He went on to tell me that the company policy was to teach the new employee PDG's way of doing things. I got the idea that the company wants each PDG manager to learn to think 'the company way.'

"Then I talked to that VP from Technotronics, and he said his company encouraged each new manager to express himself and do things the way that seemed most natural to him. Technotronics seems to let its managers take off and do their own thing, without any bureaucratic straitjackets. Then I talked with the old guy who was owner of that independent discounter downtown, and he didn't think we were learning the right things in college. He said that business was quite simple—he found that he just had to roll up his sleeves and work hard, and always keep two things in mind: to find out what the public wanted and to be sure that he gave it to them before one of his upstart competitors did. He came out and said that he could beat the pants off those big boys who spent most of their time planning, reorganizing, and issuing directives instead of getting out and selling their wares. I guess he's "from the old school," but judging from his success, he has been able to make a lot of money without taking a single course in management. But when it comes down to which company I might like to work for, I would feel more at home in PDG, because they seem to have a clear idea of where they're going, and they give the new guy a chance to learn the company's way of doing things. They even knew what I was talking about when I asked them whether they use Theory X or Theory Y."

"Jim, I was in the same panel discussion with those people from PDG, Technotronics, and the discounter. I agree with you that I'm more confused now on what the correct management approach is, but I learned something else that I never thought about before. I now see that there are a lot of different types of companies and a lot of different practices, so it's darn important to try to get a job in a company that fits your own preferences and attitudes. When I get into the job market, I'm going to investigate how the company operates. I find that I do better when I don't have too much pressure on me, and I felt that PDG has a lot of pressure. I get uptight when I take a test in school, and I don't want to continually feel that I'm being tested every day in a job. Technotronics seems to look for good people who want to get something done in their own way, yet they don't throw company policy, 'the company way,' or anything else at you to restrict your development. I like that. Jim, you can have PDG and I'll take Technotronics. I'm sure glad

that not all companies are like PDG, so maybe it's good that all companies aren't alike."

"Well, this is interesting—Frankie, Jim, and Paul sure did have different reactions to the Parade. I was in a different set of panels, and I spent a good deal of time wandering around the exhibits of a number of companies and glancing over their brochures. I found several companies that wouldn't fit any of the molds that you all have been talking about, yet most of the representatives seemed to use a lot of the same buzz words—systems, participative approaches, service, being a good corporate citizen, company loyalty, and so on. What amazed me was the way they seemed to talk the same language and still meant different things when they used the same words! I got the idea that the common denominator of most executives at the Parade was the jargon. Except for the self-made owners, they all seemed to lean on the same pat set of terms. In several cases, I felt they had all been indoctrinated with a course like Management 101 and then in practice interpreted the words in their own way. Maybe that tells us something—one reason for taking a course like 101 is to give all of us a common body of words and techniques, and then when we get into an actual job, we can use those words and ideas as a security blanket or as a badge for showing that we have joined the club. One thing for certain is that I saw a lot of different interpretations, some of which, as the old prof would say, are mutually exclusive. I was glad to get a chance to find that some of the stuff I've been memorizing for the test may possibly be useful to me in a job; but the disturbing thing is that there are so many differences in management practices based upon the same group of academic generalizations. Now, I'm not sure just what is the right way."

"Well, all you future executives can stand around and talk about the differences in company practices, but there's the bell. Let's go to class and hear about the 'rational' approach to management as pitched out by a doctor who's never tried to manage a hot-dog stand. For me, I don't care about all the talk about different management philosophies, but I was glad to go to the Parade for one reason—I think I made several good contacts so that I can get a job. I spent most of my time snowing those boys, and I think the chief factor for success is acting like just the fellow they're looking for so that you can join the club. Those representatives didn't seem so smart to me—they just seemed to fit the characteristics that recruiters look for. Anyway, it's not what *you know, it's* who *you know."*

"See you later, fellows. My question is, With all those different practices, isn't there some right way to manage? I'm going to pop up in class and ask Dr. Jones that one. I wonder what he'll say."

How can you develop as a manager outside of studying a textbook?

A manager may develop his skills and techniques through a number of approaches:

1. He can develop the knowledge base discussed in Part 2 in formal educational programs.
2. He can observe managerial practices as a researcher, visitor, or apprentice.
3. He can concentrate on reading business histories and numerous case situations in an effort to sift out the key elements from practical situations.
4. He can learn on the job through trial and error from his own experiences.

Examples of how people have developed into successful managers through any one of these routes are numerous; however, a more efficient and practical approach for modern managers is to use each route as it fits their own individual opportunities and needs.

In the nineteenth century, many managers developed successfully on the job and later picked up ideas from other sources. In most countries outside the United States, many managers still develop primarily on the job; however, the pressure from the increased complexity of modern conditions has demanded that future managers accelerate their development by focusing on formal education initially.

What is the practical value of theories?

No one can become a successful manager in practice without practicing; thus, there is a limit to what studying any book can accomplish for you. Nevertheless, this book can help you plan to use each of the four routes for developing your own skills. Part 4 is devoted to viewing management in practice, and this chapter focuses on lessons learned from business leaders in the real world. With the knowledge developed in Part 2 and an understanding of managerial functions from Part 3, here we seek to learn from the experiences of others—key people and companies that in the past have evolved important insights from actual practice.

Fortunately, many books and periodicals have recorded events and key ideas about management in action.[1] A number of business leaders have recorded their own observations. Thus we have the opportunity to learn from the experiences of others who have "actually met a payroll." Our discussions of the life cycle of a company in Chapter 1, of formal organization charts in Chapter 6, and of the managerial functions in Part 3 are all helpful here, for they can give us a framework for relating these practices to one another.

In scanning American corporations, we find that large size, rapid growth, and sustained profitability are typical. In this section we survey several well-known corporations in search of basic ideas that help explain their ability to achieve these objectives. Each of the corporations has been fortunate in having a series of capable chief executives, but in each case we can identify one clearly outstanding person who developed managerial ideas that have proved to have lasting importance to the continued success of his company. These ideas will further expand your understanding of how to become a better manager, no matter what level you attain.

Two quite different people have been important in the development of a large number of well-known companies:[2]

initiator

1. The *initiator*—an entrepreneur, promoter, and inventive person

organizer

2. The *organizer*—a manager who builds the structure and lays the foundation for permanent life of a corporation (not dependent on the life of any single individual)

[1] Back issues of *The Wall Street Journal, Fortune* and *Business Week* are filled with sketches of management in practice.

[2] Alfred Chandler concluded from a study of a number of firms that "the empire builder rarely became an organizational builder." Alfred Chandler, *Strategy and Structure* (New York: Doubleday, 1966), p. 391.

We shall see that the major source of new basic managerial concepts is the person who has served in the second role, the organizer. The role of the initiator is dependent on personality traits—such as charm, imagination, brilliant flashes of insight, intuition, hunches, venturesomeness—which are not learned easily through intellectual endeavor and thus are less transferable to others through study. Therefore, let us look at some of the basic organizing ideas and identify the great organizers who have contributed them.

IDEAS OF EXECUTIVES OF WELL-KNOWN FIRMS

We have chosen three very large and well-known companies to represent the strategic sector of the American economy: General Motors Corporation, the world's largest manufacturing firm; International Business Machines Corporation, the leader in the computer industry; and Sears, Roebuck & Company, a leader in mail-order and retail sales. Each of these firms has become so large that it may give an initial appearance of an impersonal entity; however, each is a product of one or two great organizers. Although the histories of these corporations and biographies of these great men are interesting, we are primarily interested in the *ideas* that have contributed to the successes of these firms.

Decentralization in Administration, and Coordination through Policy

General Motors Corporation developed through the two stages of leadership discussed above. William C. Durant created General Motors in 1908, using the Buick Motor Company as his base. With great vision and energy, he included Olds, Oakland, and Cadillac in early consolidations. Durant's financial skill and sales promotion ability were essential elements in the rapid growth of the company.

Why did General Motors survive when many auto companies dropped out?

Durant was prone to keep information in his head, to take risks without analyzing detailed facts, and to run the company as a one-man operation. In the early days of the company, this approach fostered growth through flexibility and informality. However, during World War I and immediately thereafter, Durant, failing to use accounting information and inventory control, ignored advice from his experts and faced a business-cycle crisis with few resources to combat the problems. The result was that in 1920, General Motors faced collapse; it was averted only by prompt action of key stockholders.

Alfred P. Sloan, who was already a part of GM, presented a comprehensive organization plan to the board of directors in 1920, and in 1923 was made president of the corporation. (He remained president until 1937, after which he served as chairman of the board until 1956.) Sloan's 28-page program for GM, prepared in 1920, provided new ideas for administrative thought that have served as guidelines for GM management to the present day. Sloan's program was based on two basic concepts:[3]

> "The responsibility attached to the chief executive of each operation shall in no way be limited." [*Decentralization of operation*]
>
> "Certain central organization functions are absolutely essential to the logical development and proper coordination of the Corporation's activities." [*Centralized staff services*]

Sloan early saw the necessity for group management in a large organization and the advantages of giving full authority to operating-division managers, who could make decisions coordinated by the general policies set by the central office. An elaborate control system was defined so that the central office would have detailed information concerning the activities of the divisions and their profitability.

The basic ideas instituted by Sloan in General Motors were being developed by other companies, but Sloan's 1920 idea has continued to serve as a basic principle for GM. The succeeding chief executives of General Motors perpetuated the decentralization plan with central policies as a medium of coordination. Sloan's ideas have also been valuable to managers in other large corporations over the past five decades.

Respect for the Individual, Service, and Superiority

The spectacular growth of IBM can be explained by a number of factors, such as the rapid growth of the new computer industry and fortunate events outside the company's control, but we are most interested in learning the management ideas and beliefs that have made it possible. Again, the original concept of the firm was

[3] Alfred P. Sloan, Jr., *My Years with General Motors* (New York: Doubleday, 1964), p. 53.

developed by one man, Thomas J. Watson, Sr., who came to the corporation in 1914 and was active in management until his death in 1956. His son, Thomas J. Watson, Jr., continued to emphasize certain tenets of management established early in the history of the company. He summarized these tenets in a series of lectures in 1962:

Do high ideals work in business?

1. Respect for the individual and development of the human resource
2. Emphasis on service to customers by helping customers solve their problems
3. Superior effort as a way of life

Using these three tenets, Watson outlined some of the lessons that the company learned from its experiences. Since these lessons have wide applicability for all of us who are interested in improvement of management, we quote them here:

1. There is simply no substitute for good human relations and for the high morale they bring. It takes good people to do the jobs necessary to reach your profit goals. But good people alone are not enough. No matter how good your people may be, if they don't really like the business, if they don't feel totally involved in it, or if they don't think they're being treated fairly—it's awfully hard to get a business off the ground. . . .
2. There are two things an organization must increase far out of proportion to its growth rate if that organization is to overcome the problems of change. The first of these is communication, upward and downward. The second is education and retraining.
3. Complacency is the most natural and insidious disease of large corporations. It can be overcome if management will set the right tone and pace and if its lines of communication are in working order.
4. Everyone—particularly a company such as IBM—must place company interest above that of a division or department. . . .
5. Beliefs must always come before policies, practices, and goals. The latter must always be altered if they are seen to violate fundamental beliefs.[4]

[4] Thomas J. Watson, Jr., *A Business and Its Beliefs: The Ideas That Helped Build IBM* (New York: McGraw-Hill, 1963), pp. 71–73.

IBM has become well known throughout the world not only as a rapidly growing, profitable business organization but as an innovator of managerial practices within the foregoing beliefs. It has minimized the number of levels in the organization through *job enlargement,* the provision of more interest, responsibility, and discretion to all jobs by broadening the responsibility of each worker. IBM has expanded its internal educational activities through company schools for employees, customers, and other educators, and it has sent many of its managers to executive development programs sponsored by universities. And it has continued to lead its industry in making its sales organization a service-oriented activity.

job enlargement

IBM has not only succeeded in attaining large size, maintaining rapid growth, and sustaining high profitability, but it has also participated with educational and government institutions in the development of management thought. Research receives special attention and large expenditures by the company. IBM's practice of management, as a result, has been in close contact with the development of management theory as discussed in this book.

Low-Cost Merchandising and Market Analysis

Sears, Roebuck & Company is another organization illustrating the two stages discussed earlier.[5] It was created before the turn of the century by one man, Richard Sears, who was an expert promoter and salesman and a spectacular advertiser. Sears responded to the needs of the isolated farmers of the late nineteenth century through the innovation of direct-mail advertising and direct mailing of products. Under Sears, the company's operations were more a series of astute purchasing deals and mass distributions than a coordinated, long-term business venture.

Was the success of Sears merely a matter of luck?

Managing the large number of transactions began to create serious problems, and again an organizer appeared who could build a firm foundation for the large organization. Between 1895 and 1905, Julius Rosenwald originated several basic ideas that have continued to serve the company through the years: (1) systematic development of low-cost merchandising sources, (2) a factual, comprehensive mail-order catalogue, (3) implementation of the policy of "satisfaction guaranteed or your money back," (4) scheduling and routing of the large, central mail-order plant, and (5) recruit-

[5] Boris Emmet and John E. Jeuck, *Catalogues and Counters: A History of Sears, Roebuck & Company* (Chicago: University of Chicago Press, 1950).

ment of professional managers. Supporting the fifth idea was Rosenwald's recruitment and backing of another innovator, Otto Doering, who designed and built the first large mail-order plant in Chicago in 1905. Doering concentrated on operating efficiencies by breaking down work into simple, repetitive operations at the time that Frederick W. Taylor was becoming known as a scientific manager in manufacturing firms. Doering used the mass-production techniques of the conveyorized assembly line, standardized and interchangeable parts, and detailed planning and control in the Chicago plant almost a decade before Henry Ford became known as a mass producer in the automobile industry.

Julius Rosenwald was the leading organizer of Sears during the peak centralized mail-order phase of distribution; however, Sears's continued success in the marketing field was fostered by a second major organizer, General Robert E. Wood, who appeared when marketing channels changed as a result of widespread use of the automobile. Wood contributed new ideas to meet the different situation that developed in the 1920s—the growth of chains of retail outlets. Management concepts thus were adapted to the changing situation by providing the following:

1. A strong decentralized organization with managers who could make most decisions at the store level
2. An incentive system through profit sharing and stock ownership
3. Strong emphasis on the human element

Sears offers an excellent example of how the management processes can be changed to meet changing social and economic conditions. The company needed two great organizers, Rosenwald to refine mail-order distribution for the rural markets of the early twentieth century, and then Wood to change the direction of distribution through retail stores for the growing urban markets of the mid-twentieth century.

Many other interesting historical and contemporary examples of successful management of large firms could be studied in detail, and you will want to continually search for those ideas that have proved useful in practice. These three companies are especially important, for all three have found answers to the demanding problems of directing and controlling large, complex organizations. All three have also led their industries in research and innovation. All three have achieved a dominant position in the American economy, and thus each must respond to demands of social responsibility.

When Charles E. Wilson, a former secretary of defense and chief executive of GM, said, "What is good for GM is good for the country," he provoked considerable discussion. No one can deny, however, that the quality of management of such a large firm as General Motors is of vital concern to many citizens, whether they be employees, stockholders, customers, or suppliers.

IBM has led its industry in rate of growth in the United States, and, in recent years as a multinational company, it has led the world in the computer business. Whereas both GM and IBM are manufacturing firms, Sears has grown solely in the sales and distribution field. Today, over 60 percent of those employed in the United States work in service industries; assuming this trend in services continues, then significant improvements in managing in the 1970s and 1980s will probably be made through extending the practices of leading firms in manufacturing and marketing into the service industries.

IDEAS OF EXECUTIVES OF RAPIDLY GROWING FIRMS

Why is it important to search for niches in business?

niches

Opportunities continually appear for new firms to satisfy consumer needs when the managers of these firms focus on the gaps or niches not being serviced by the larger, well-established companies. These *niches* may be in the form of new products, new services, new managerial practices, or new ideas. The history of business enterprises is rich with examples of how unconventional or new ideas have continued to revitalize the economic system. In this section, we discuss two cases showing the advantages of maverick activities.

Flexibility and Informality

Should a manager use "textbook learning" without modifications?

The first thirty years of the Ashland Oil & Refining Company were characterized by rapid growth based on the unique ideas of its chief executive officer, Paul G. Blazer. In the oil industry, twenty very large and powerful firms had controlled refining, transportation, and distribution of oil products. In this environment, Blazer organized a very small refining company in 1924 with $250,000 in capital and directed its activities until, by 1957, the date of Blazer's retirement, it had become one of the large firms in the industry, with $113 million in capital. In spite of the depression of the 1930s, the company never showed a loss for a single year.

Flexibility

The ideas that contributed to this success were a strong emphasis on flexibility of operations and informality in organizational behavior. *Flexibility* refers to the quality of adaptability to external changes, resiliency of policies, and responsiveness of the entire organization to meeting new problems. Blazer prided himself on being "unconventional" and felt that it was an advantage to do things differently from his competitors: He concentrated on profits from refining when the industry focused on profits from crude-oil production; he depended on barge transportation of crude oil, which enabled him to move in and out of markets, whereas his large competitors relied on fixed pipelines; he was a "price marketer" and sold through numerous private brands, whereas the industry was structured on price leaders and well-defined brands and territories; he developed markets for fractions or cuts from refining that did not sell in volume but had high profit margins, whereas his large competitors tended to overlook these opportunities because they were not worth the trouble. In short, Blazer's emphasis on flexibility enabled him to shift quickly into typically unnoticed profitable niches.

How can flexibility be valuable?

The type of organization needed for this degree of flexibility differed from the highly structured plans of the larger companies. Blazer abhorred organizational charts; he intentionally refrained from developing clear job descriptions ("If you had really sharp departmental lines, you would find people telling others 'it is none of your business' or 'leave that to me' . . . you get more cooperation from people if your organization is so set up where they have to cooperate to get along");[6] he did not use his office (it was handled by his secretary) and did not give specialized titles to his top managers (no names or titles appeared on doors); formal channels of communication through different levels of the hierarchy were continually violated (if something needed to be done, he would often give orders directly to a worker). In fact, many of the propositions of previous chapters were disregarded.

The usefulness of the ideas of extreme flexibility and informality is dependent on certain conditions: (1) an exceptional executive who works long hours and is highly respected; (2) personnel who grow up with the company and who "learn the ropes" of the

[6] Joseph L. Massie, *Blazer and Ashland Oil* (Lexington: University of Kentucky Press, 1960), p. 207.

particular organization; (3) strong loyalty of all personnel to the chief executive and the organization (wives of Ashland executives were known as "Ashland widows"); (4) a relatively small number of people in the company, who can keep in mind the unwritten procedures and policies and who have a high tolerance for frustration; (5) a clear understanding of usual management concepts and their rationale so that when exceptions are made, techniques are available to handle the inevitable disadvantages.

The chief lesson that we can learn from this unusual example is that all of us have the power to develop new and unique approaches if only we understand the reasons for established guidelines and adapt our ideas to each new situation. For those who tend to fight the use of a standard, routine way and seek new, different, and possibly better ways, the established way must first be studied very carefully to find out why it has been adopted. With this historical perspective, you then have a better chance of avoiding problems that previous managers have already solved. The story of civilization is one of building on the accomplishments of predecessors, not one of tearing down past accomplishments and starting over.

Promotion of a New Idea and Franchising

American ingenuity is legendary. The ability to "find a better mousetrap" is at the heart of many business successes. One of the most recent and spectacular ideas came to "Colonel" Harland Sanders, who had already passed the usual retirement age. As a restaurant owner, he had discovered a way of cooking fried chicken using "eleven herbs and spices" and a pressure-frying cooker. In 1964, Colonel Sanders sold his idea and his already rapidly growing business to a newly formed company, Kentucky Fried Chicken Corporation (KFC). The central concepts of the company were (1) aggressive promotion of fried chicken through the image of the white-suited, white-haired colonel, (2) the standardization of preparing fried chicken in many outlets using the secret eleven herbs and spices, and (3) the franchising of retail outlets to owner-operators.

Can aggressive promotion of a new idea be the basis for success?

KFC was fortunate that consumer patterns were ready for the expansion of the fast-foods industry; the consumer was interested in buying ready-cooked food at outlets just around the corner. Within five years, the company was able to sell 6,000 franchises and thus become an American institution, well known not only in the United States but around the world. However, with this rapid growth came increased competition from numerous other firms, which recognized the opportunities of the fast foods industry.

With the company's rapid success and growth, including expansion outside the fried chicken specialty into fish and chips, beef products, and plans for chains of motels and related activities, KFC management needed to develop a large organization quickly. Many franchisers became millionaires, and KFC viewed franchiser's profits as potential profits to the company if the stores had been company-owned; thus, KFC developed a program of purchasing back a number of these franchises for operation by a company-owned division. This program greatly increased the problems of developing a large, well-managed organization.

KFC again illustrates the validity of the stages discussed at the beginning of this chapter. Colonel Sanders, the creator of the idea, and John Young Brown, Jr., the president of KFC, were experts in promoting and franchising fried chicken. The need for an organizer became evident at the beginning of the 1970s, when the problems of growth overtook not only KFC but all its competitors in the fast-foods industry. KFC attempted to answer this need in 1971 by merging with a large, well-established firm.

Kentucky Fried Chicken was built on the foregoing three concepts of the firm, which proved to have great advantages. However, as is often the case, rapid growth and quick success tended to entice promoters and entrepreneurs to forget where their strengths had been. At this stage, the concepts of management planning, organizing, and controlling became paramount. Unless management takes stock of its resources through well-thought-out objectives and policies, successful firms may grow to such size that administrative problems outweigh the original advantages. Large size has many advantages, but they can be gained only if answers to administrative complexity can be obtained through thorough understanding of the ideas in this book.

LESSONS LEARNED FROM MISTAKES OF BIG BUSINESS

Why not learn from the mistakes of others?

Much of this book describes ideas and techniques of successful management. Such "positive" thinking is informative, but we all know that a very good way to learn is from mistakes. All managers will make their share of mistakes; the good managers, however, will learn from these experiences and not repeat them.

In this short section, we cannot cover all mistakes, but we can focus on several that have received wide attention because they were big mistakes made by managers of big companies. There are many of these: Henry Ford's authoritative methods of the 1940s; Sewell Avery's failure to expand activities of Montgomery Ward because he was expecting a great depression after World War II; Olin Mathieson's superdiversification program, which should have given warning of the problems to be experienced by conglomerates during the 1960s; Crane Company's crisis, caused by a single company-plane crash that killed most of its top management; the Edsel disaster in the Ford Motor Company of the 1950s; the Penn Central bankruptcy; Lockheed's problems, which became national issues in the 1970s; and RCA's retreat from computers in 1971, costing it over a quarter of a billion dollars.

We offer two examples that have fundamental implications for management: the moral crisis of the General Electric antitrust case of the early 1960s, and the General Dynamics management crisis.[7]

Decentralization without Control, Leading to Irresponsibility

General Electric Company has long been a leader in the electrical industry. Since it is a very large firm, it has continually faced problems relating to the antitrust laws of the United States; and, also because of its size, along with other large electrical firms, GE has led in the promotion of the idea of decentralization of authority—it has established about 100 profit centers that operate with considerable autonomy. These two situations laid the groundwork for one of the most serious management crises in the last several decades.

Do actions speak louder than words?

In 1961, the Department of Justice was successful in a court case in Pennsylvania in convicting 29 companies and 30 executives of conspiracy to fix prices on heavy equipment. Seven top executives went to jail. Ralph Cordiner, the chief executive officer of General Electric, was able to show the court that he had no knowledge of the conspiracy and, in fact, could point to a strongly worded antitrust directive from his office and speeches that strongly opposed any attempt to create cartels.

[7] The facts in these examples are drawn from Richard A. Smith, *Corporations in Crisis* (New York: Doubleday, 1963), pp. 113–66 and 207–49.

Does decentralization have weaknesses?

The irony of this example is that although the headquarters of General Electric was well aware of the problem the company faced in complying with the long-standing antitrust laws and had issued directives to make sure it complied with the laws, the actual results were that, because of the strong emphasis on decentralization, the chief executive of the large company did not know what was going on in his divisions. The result was a failure in management, at both the moral level and the technical level. Headquarters had placed extreme pressure on its divisions to earn a respectable profit but had not followed up to find out just how the profits were made or whether the division executives were complying with directives from headquarters.

Decentralization in administration with coordination through policy, as applied by Cordiner and General Electric, required further elaboration—control and follow-up to determine whether clear policy statements from headquarters were being implemented. Delegation of authority and responsibility to divisions can never relieve the chief executive of his own responsibility of directing the entire company. The reasoning behind decentralization of large firms was, and still is, sound; however, it took the government's antitrust action of the early 1960s to teach proponents of this useful concept that the importance of the flow of information upward in the organization through reports and personal inspections cannot be minimized. If managers are to manage, they must develop techniques whereby they know what is going on in the company. Furthermore, the case raised serious moral questions about management's objectives and methods of achieving those objectives.

The General Electric antitrust case underscores the importance of our previous discussions: in Chapter 6, on proper organization structure, in Chapter 11, on the setting for each unit of clear objectives that are consistent with the long-run goals of the company and society; and in Chapter 16, on the essentials of all control systems. The managers of General Electric apparently thought they had established the predetermined target (no collusion with competitors), yet their measurement of actual performance was only in terms of profits and not in terms of how these profits might be generated. Thus, there was a failure to compare what the lower managers were doing with the clearly stated policy and, as a result, no corrective action was forthcoming. If General Electric had applied the concepts that we discussed in previous chapters, the company and a number of its executives would have been able to stay out of trouble.

Unrealistic Estimates of Cost and Market Potential

General Dynamics Corporation is a defense company that was formed after World War II and that concentrated on attracting a group of engineers and scientists with high degrees of technological skills. It became very large immediately by acquiring companies producing atomic submarines, large airframes, and space vehicles. It was conceived, developed, and managed by one exceptional leader, Jay Hopkins. During the ten years in which Hopkins was chief executive, company headquarters were successful in keeping control of the independent and forceful division managers. The success was dependent not upon any comprehensive information and control system but upon the forceful, energetic, and brilliant activities of one man, Jay Hopkins.

What can cause a large firm to get out of control?

In 1961, General Dynamics achieved a most unwanted distinction: It was forced to absorb what was then the greatest loss in a single year that any company had ever suffered—nearly half a billion dollars. Ten years later, Lockheed ran into similar difficulties but received greater attention because it sought government financial help to avoid bankruptcy. It appears that certain lessons should be learned from such situations.

Hopkins was an outstanding innovator and personal leader. However, the organization was built too exclusively around his personal leadership ability. Hopkins died of cancer in 1957, at a time in which the production of jet airliners was being planned. The difficulties of the next four years can be traced to this "act of God"; however, the failure to fill the need for an outstanding organizer can be identified as causing the tremendous loss of 1961.

The problems developed in the large Convair division, in the development and sale of the Convair 880 and 990 jet airliners. At the death of Hopkins, Frank Pace, a skillful public administrator and government-relations expert, suddenly assumed the position of chief executive officer of the sprawling, decentralized company. The Convair division was in the process of estimating costs and breakeven points for the 880 and, later, the 990. To remain competitive with Boeing and Douglas, it proceeded to assume the risks of developing a medium-range airliner for one main purchaser, Howard Hughes of TWA. It based its cost estimation on assumed total sales to TWA, Delta, United, and American airlines; however, as the situation unfolded, it became clearer that the cost estimates were too low, the estimated number of units that would be sold was too high, and the untested jet engines and airframe design required expensive modifications.

At different stages, management decided on a "double or nothing" policy—that is, since it had sunk large sums in the 880, it would be necessary to put additional large sums into the project or lose all that it had previously invested. And so the company got deeper and deeper in the hole.

These problems arose in a period in which the headquarters of General Dynamics had not developed an information system between the divisions and headquarters that would facilitate top management's control of the company. The result was that the chief executive officer of the company failed to obtain information as to how bad the situation was until after it was too late. For example, a decision was made by the division managers to develop the 990 "as a modification of the 880" without this most critical question's being brought before the board of directors.

Cost estimates were continually increased without complete explanations being made to the chief executive officer. Top management found itself on many occasions forced to approve actions that had already been taken. Headquarters had lost control of the company and in fact could not exert any effective remedial measures because it did not even know what the problems were until it was too late.

The General Dynamics experience in this period emphasizes that large size brings more than economies of scale of production; it brings problems in administrative control systems. "The bigger they come, the harder they fall." Management must take risks in many of its activities; however, through rigorous study of the facts of the situations, the risks can be calculated and decisions made based on reliable information. In the four years preceding 1961, General Dynamics continued to increase its risks without even knowing its problems, let alone the possible alternatives available to meet them.

The mistakes of General Electric and General Dynamics are, of course, only samples of mistakes made by managers of well-known business firms. Many others have been publicized including illegal political contributions by the large oil companies, large "gifts" made by aircraft manufacturers to influence the sale of their products, and insolvency of Franklin National Bank and W. T. Grant. Many other examples could be offered involving smaller, less dramatic cases. The student of management, by recognizing current examples of mistakes made in actual practice, has the opportunity to learn from the mistakes of others and thus to improve his own ideas and practices.

LESSONS LEARNED FROM FOREIGN PRACTICES

Can American managers learn from foreign practices?

The management ideas and techniques discussed in this book have developed primarily in the United States and Western Europe. These ideas have been transferred to other countries and, on the whole, have improved the management process, especially in developing countries. The reason for this American orientation is that business management has been emphasized in the educational system of the United States; until recently, management education in other countries has been minimal or at a lower level of prestige. However, in the last two decades, other countries have begun to study management and to develop concepts from within—not imported from Western countries. With this development, a source of knowledge is available other than from research and practices of U.S. organizations.

In this section, we select two foreign sources of management practices and identify several additional basic concepts. Of course, these practices are dependent upon the environment in which they developed and may not be transferred directly without modification. As we have pointed out throughout this book, theories and practices are contingent upon the environment in which the organization exists. Nevertheless, management seriously needs help from whatever sources are available.

Loyalty, Cooperation, and Lifetime Employment in Japan

Today, Japanese businesses have grown to be some of the main competitors of American products, not only in the foreign markets but also in the American domestic markets. The Japanese society is different from Western society, and these differences can also be seen from their management practices. Let us observe some of the basic practices in most Japanese firms.

LIFETIME EMPLOYMENT Traditionally, when a young man has secured a permanent job with a firm in Japan, the commitment by both the firm and the individual covers the lifetime of the young man. The firm assumes responsibility for the individual's employ-

Does a company have obligations to its employees?

ment for his entire life and for not only his development but also non-job-related aspects, such as housing, sports, medical care, and social life; any change of employers implies a violation of the *firm's responsibility* or the *individual's loyalty*. Thus, until recently, Japan has had minimal job mobility. The impact of this practice, rooted in the culture that has evolved over centuries, has far-reaching effects on management. This management philosophy calls for cohesion within the company and tends toward a type of paternalism. The basic objective of the Japanese firms is to make employees devote their full concentration to the firm's activities in a peaceful state of mind.

ASCRIBED STATUS Respect for age, seniority, and educational foundations are keys to the role of Japanese management. A young manager, in his ambition to excel, refrains from activities that might be interpreted as undercutting the respect and authority of his older superiors and those who have a longer length of service. The result is that courtesy and ritual are an important part of the leadership style in Japan. Status in the organization is ascribed to the position the manager has and is less dependent on achieved status. For example, if the performance of an older, respected manager shows that he is making mistakes and is not really competent in a present job, his subordinates refrain from "showing him up" but attempt to courteously support his actions. If top management feels the necessity to replace him, it will transfer him to a position with at least equal status but one in which his actions will not damage the efficiency of the organization. In short, management attempts to maintain a strong, aggressive, efficient management group, but not at the expense of shirking its responsibility to the lifelong welfare of individuals.

Do cooperation and competition conflict?

COOPERATION Government and business view their relationships as supportive of one another. People within the Japanese firm focus on cooperative efforts rather than competitive rivalry, and business firms as a group tend to view the government as an ally, cooperating toward the goal of improvement of Japanese society as a whole. The result is that Japanese business and government present a formidable team when they compete with outside groups—foreign multinationals, export promotion in markets outside Japan, and other non-Japanese elements.

RINGI SYSTEM OF DECISIONS Formally, decisions appear to be centralized in a small group at the top, since superiors must approve many decisions with the appearance of little delegation.

However, Japanese management uses an unusual method of decision making, causing one observer to state that in effect, authority has been delegated to the middle-management level.[8] This paradox can be better understood with a short explanation of the *ringi* system of communication and decisions.

ringi system of decisions

Assume that management is faced with an important decision. The first step in the *ringi* process is the drafting of a plan by middle management. (If the draft actually originates at lower levels, it will carry the name of a superior in middle management.) The papers *(ringisho)* stating the alternatives and proposal are then circulated horizontally among positions with the same rank, and each manager attaches his seal to provide a record of their journey. They are then presented vertically up the organization to several superiors with higher rank who attach their seals, so that by the time the decision is firm, the *ringisho* will consist of a dozen or more seals. The system results in obscuring the locus of authority for carrying out the decision and responsibility for its effects; in short, no one person clearly assumes the responsibility for the decision, and if it later turns out to be poor, no one will "lose face" or feel that he alone is responsible.

The *ringi* system represents a device for knitting together as many people as possible in decision making. Many are given the opportunity to contribute, with the objective of seeking a unity of thought and unanimous consent. The real decision-making process involves subconscious and informal activities that do not appear when we study the formal organization only.

Assimilation of Diverse Practices A popular view is that the Japanese are skilled at copying technologies, products, and practices from others. However, this conduct is more related to their receptiveness to new or different ideas and skill at assimilating them into the traditional and customary Japanese set of practices. At times, this skill appears as another paradox, since some apparently conflicting practices are adopted. The entire culture of the Japanese can be viewed as a historical stream of customs and traditions that do not reject flows from tributaries from abroad. For this reason, an observer may be fooled by noticing radical changes in the last few decades in management practices, if he does not search deeper to find that these changes have been assimilated

[8] Noda Kazuo, *Big Business Executives in Japan* (Tokyo: Diamond Press, 1960), p. 117. The discussion in this section is based on William Brown, "Japanese Management—The Cultural Background," Selection 32 in *Culture and Management,* Ross A. Webber (Homewood, Ill: Richard D. Irwin, 1969), pp. 428–42.

with tradition. In short, Japanese management has the capacity to import and transfer ideas from other management approaches without radically and suddenly changing its own basic traditional approach.

Can Japanese practices work in the United States?

The characteristics of Japanese management have become quite relevant to American management approaches recently, inasmuch as some Japanese firms operating in American society are introducing elements of their approaches in the United States. For example, Sony has experimented in California with a Japanese approach to American employees. Of course, for some years, American multinational firms have operated in Japan with American approaches. In the future, it seems, lessons from foreign practice will increase in importance.

Self-Management in Yugoslavia

Yugoslavia's managerial and economic system is a unique experiment. The country entered the post–World War II period with a highly centralized economic planning and control system similar to the one then in use in the Soviet Union. But Yugoslavia chose to pursue its independent goals. A rupture of political and economic relations between Belgrade and the Kremlin in 1948 forced Yugoslavia to depend upon her own resources, as the former trade with her Communist neighbors was curtailed. Military and economic aid from the West, including substantial amounts from the United States, helped to fill the gap and enabled Yugoslavia to solidify her position of individuality in the community of nations. In the past two decades, a unique managerial system, referred to as *self-management*, has been evolving. The following elements of this system can be viewed as lessons from management in a foreign country.

self-management

DECENTRALIZATION Since Yugoslavia consists of a diverse group of people and cultures, using two different alphabets and several languages, the Yugoslavian government chose to focus on decentralization of authority and decision making. This approach contrasted with its initial attempt, immediately after World War II, to follow the Soviet Union in its central planning and the typical organization used by Communist countries in Eastern Europe. The result of decentralization has been to allow the local communities through their communes to plan their own development. In management as well as in the political and economic areas, Yugoslavia is charting a third communist approach, depending on neither Russian nor Chinese leadership.

workers' council

Election of Managers The local enterprises are operated under a *workers' council* that consists of workers in the enterprise who are elected to the council for one year. Rotation of membership results from limiting the number of terms that one can serve. In this way, it is possible for a large number of workers to serve in a managerial capacity. In short, workers actually participate in managerial decisions, since the council makes the important policies and decisions for the enterprise. It is said that all workers are managers.

The effect of this concept of election of managers is to deemphasize the professionalization of management, since the managers are not required to be technical experts or to have obtained a minimum level of education. Of course, it is recognized that management involves specialized skills; however, the view is that the workers will choose those best qualified, in their own self-interest, since bonuses and the welfare of the workers are dependent upon the success of the enterprise.

The Director The director of the enterprise is elected to perform its technical-organizational functions. He serves for several years. His authority is no longer based on his position in the hierarchy; he is elected and controlled by those whom he leads. It is said that his position is thus based on achieved rather than ascribed status. The manager is in a position of having to "sell" his ideas about investments, new technology, and other matters to the council and to the workers, so the degree of confidence the workers have in him has a direct bearing upon the influence he can exert. The director is the guardian of the legality of the enterprise, and as such he must give his attention to the protection of the interests of the social collective. The role of the director is an ambivalent one, since he is responsible both to the government and to his workers' council. In practice, this role creates tensions that result in making the position of director none too attractive to the people who are best qualified to aspire to it. Frequently, the director is a specialist, such as an engineer, lawyer, or economist, but in the course of performing his duties, he may lose contact with his own profession.

Managerial concepts and practices in Yugoslavia integrate elements from both communist and capitalistic countries. The members of the Communist party provide a countervailing power in the operation of enterprises, yet the concepts of profit and locally controlled acquisition of capital are central to their system. One commune may find that it is competing with another commune for its products and services.

The experiment has encountered a number of difficulties, which are being met pragmatically. (1) Since the constitution has granted local workers' councils basic powers to set their own work rules, wages, and objectives, coordination toward national objectives has become more difficult. (2) The role of the managing director of a factory is made especially difficult by his lack of power to fire employees, to institute efficiency measures, and to allocate resources to more productive projects. (3) New developments in property rights raise many questions; property is defined as social and not state. If one local commune decides to "invest" in a productive activity in another commune and the project is successful, can the new activity declare itself independent and thus eliminate any return on investment to the aggressive commune?

The experiment in Yugoslavia is trying out many new approaches, and it will be interesting to see how the practices work out in the long run.

SUMMARY AND PROPOSITIONS

Improvement in the practice of management can be achieved through empirical research and conceptual model building, discussed in other parts of this book, and also through understanding the business histories and experiences of practicing leaders. In this chapter we have reviewed the experiences of five successful firms—General Motors, IBM, Sears, Ashland Oil, and Kentucky Fried Chicken—two firms that made big mistakes—General Electric and General Dynamics—and practices employed in Japan and Yugoslavia and other countries. Our chief purpose in this chapter has been to focus on the *ideas* of the practicing managers, not on their interesting lives or exotic settings.

We are trying to find those ideas that are *transferable* to you, so that you can be successful in your own managerial experiences. Therefore, we shall summarize some of these ideas as propositions, without identifying the company that contributed the idea; we shall leave it to you to recheck the chapter to match the ideas with the well-known firm.

1. Decentralization of authority, responsibility, and operations enables a large firm to maintain vitality and initiative while a centralized staff and policies provide control and information for the corporation headquarters.
   a. Each division can be operated as an independent company, resulting in a reduction of bureaucratic constraints.
   b. Each division can compete aggressively with other divisions of the same company.
2. The successful implementation of plans is dependent upon the development of people and a cooperative climate through motivation and education.

3. Standardized, interchangeable parts that are purchased, processed, and distributed through a well-designed and scheduled system reduce the cost of a product to the consumer.
   a. Mass production and distribution enable a firm to reduce prices and thus make quality goods available to more people.
   b. The development of systems for handling instructions, customers orders, and payments becomes mandatory as operations increase in scale.

4. A smaller firm has significant advantages in its responsiveness to new opportunities through flexibility and informality.
   a. By identifying niches for operations and understanding clearly the guiding concepts of the firm, small firms may find tremendous opportunities that are ignored through the inertia of their larger competitors.
   b. As a firm grows, the need for attention to explicit organization problems increases.

5. Regardless of policies of delegation and decentralization, the top executives retain ultimate responsibilities for a company's action, and thus information and control systems become especially important.

6. The *ringi* system of communication used in Japan and self management in Yugoslavia are samples of ideas that may be learned from foreign practices.

STUDY ASSIGNMENTS

1. *Explain how each of the methods of developing managing skills can contribute to your own personal development.*

2. *Describe the characteristics of the initiator and the organizer and show how they are different.*

3. *Compare the results of decentralization in General Motors and in General Electric. What are the arguments for and against decentralizing authority?*

4. *Explain how Sloan's basic concepts supplement the discussion of organization structure in Chapter 6.*

5. *How do T. J. Watson's tenets for IBM relate to McGregor's Theory Y?*

6. *How does the story of Sears illustrate the need for an organization to adapt to changing situations?*

7. *Were the contributions of Julius Rosenwald to practices in Sears of the same type as the contributions of F. W. Taylor to scientific management? Explain the similarities and differences.*

8. *"You get more cooperation from people if your organization is set up so that they have to cooperate to get along." Point out the dangers of this position with reference to the discussion in Chapter 6.*

9. *Is flexibility necessary for any organization? Identify the conditions under which the extreme flexibility used by Ashland Oil can be effective.*

10. *What are the problems created by large size, as demonstrated in the cases of General Dynamics and General Electric?*

11. *State the basic concepts underlying the management of IBM, Ashland Oil, and Kentucky Fried Chicken. Are these concepts applicable in other firms?*

12. *Explain how the facts in the discussion of General Dynamics demonstrate the importance of the essentials of control discussed in Chapter 16.*

13. *Match the propositions with those companies discussed in the chapter that best illustrate their validity.*

14. *"Each company should clearly identify the niche into which it fits in industry." Discuss this statement as a means of identifying a company's objectives.*

15. *Do any of the practices described in this chapter conflict with propositions stated in preceding chapters? Discuss.*

16. *Are some of the ideas developed in Japan and Yugoslavia of potential use in the United States? Does culture have an effect on their practicality?*

situational episodes

1. You are preparing to be interviewed by a representative of a company in an effort to obtain a full-time position. You wish to impress the interviewer of your sincere interest in the company he represents, and therefore, you have decided to do some research on the company. If the company is a large national one, you know that you can find information in *Business Week, The Wall Street Journal, Fortune, Forbes,* and other business periodicals. Also, you may find that the chief executive has written a book or the company has produced a volume covering its history. A focus in the research is to uncover certain practices and policies of the company that could make a fundamental contribution to your development as a manager; therefore, in your research you will attempt to identify certain basic concepts used by the company, such as those discussed in this chapter. To help you in this project, the following questions can serve as a guide:

   a. What key factors have been important in explaining the company's success?

   b. Is the policy of the company to specialize in a specific service or product, or can you identify a trend in diversification?

   c. Is there one person in the company's history who was a great initiator? a great organizer?

   d. Does the company stress a particular approach to management? a type of organization? a special type of marketing strategy? an appeal to its employees?

   e. Are union–management relations of particular importance to the management?

   f. Is the company especially aware of its effect on the environment?

2. In discussing your interest in management with your friends, you find that some have fundamental criticisms about "the industrial–military complex," the quality of consumer products from Ralph Nader's standpoint, the Establishment and the power in corporate hands, illegal political contributions, and other subjects by which they are "turned off." These friends tend to argue with you that you are "selling out" if you aspire to become a manager. Prepare a constructive outline of arguments that you can use to defend your position.

the political world of managing

EIGHTEEN

OBJECTIVES YOU SHOULD MEET

Distinguish *among the definitions of authority, power, and influence.*

State *and* ***describe*** *at least five sources of power.*

Differentiate *between the negative and positive faces of power.*

Identify *the relationship among power, influence, and dependence.*

List *five personal examples of negative power.*

State *the role of power for effective managing in an organization.*

I THOUGHT AUTHORITY WAS ENOUGH

I wondered what had happened to Dan. He seemed to be walking on air. I hadn't seen him so excited since he had described in detail his catches of big fish. Finally he came into my office, with a twinkle in his eye and a bounce to his step. "OK, Dan," I said, "what is it?"

"Burke, I've got a tremendous offer for another job! It's the kind of thing I've always wanted. In fact, you'd probably like it too. Why not come along with me?"

"Whoa! Before you get me to come along with you, why don't you start from the beginning and fill me in on all the details."

"Well, you know how we've always wanted to be in positions of power and influence so that our ideas of education could be put into effect? Well, this is our chance. I'll be able to see that all new courses developed in the program will have a behavioral orientation. You know how often both of us have said that teaching behavioral-science courses by themselves doesn't give the student any feel for the area—he doesn't know how to relate the ideas in the social-psychology courses to the business world—and that what should be done is to have behavioral-science concepts taught as part of the finance, marketing, management, and quantitative courses. Now's my chance to see that that happens."

I was still confused, but I could see that Dan was too excited to be organized, so I thought I'd better ask questions about the situation rather than try to get the story straight out.

"What kind of job is it? Where's the school? What's the teaching load? And how much money is involved? What's your title?"

"I'll be the assistant to the president. It's a new university. In fact, the students won't start until a year after I arrive, so I'll have a year to develop curriculum and hire faculty members. The president, a friend of

mine, wants me to make the behavioral-science inputs. The other deans and chairmen are coming from first-class schools all over the states, and we should have a great university. I'll have to hire 50 people the first year, and then 25 each of the next three years until we get a faculty of 100. Just think of the opportunity to make a significant impact on business education."

The phone rang, and my secretary reminded me that I was already late for an ad hoc university committee meeting on a faculty appeals case.

"Dan, I'd like to talk with you and Phyllis about the new job. I have more questions I want to ask. Why don't Marilyn and I run over to your house for coffee tomorrow night, and we can talk?"

I didn't listen very well to the vice-president's introductory comments about the procedures for our appeals committee—my mind was recalling the events of the past five years. Dan had been hired from a West Coast school by the man who had preceded me as chairman of the department. His first full year as a faculty member was my first full year as a department chairman, so we grew and developed together. Dan quickly proved to be an invaluable faculty member. He was an excellent committee member, too, willing to put in the kind of time needed to get a project completed. In fact, it was Dan and Charlie who helped me put together our new graduate program in business. Dan seemed to thrive on developing ideas, analyzing events of the past and putting them into the context of the present, anticipating problems of program implementation, and planning for the execution of the whole project. He was an excellent staff man.

But Dan was also outspoken, and in recent years he had provoked a number of faculty members and others in administrative positions. And because he was reluctant to publish just anything, he had not been productive enough, in the eyes of the present administration. Consequently, his ideas were not given much support. It seemed to me, coming back after I had resigned as chairman and taken a year's leave for a sabbatical, that Dan was being tolerated rather than encouraged and supported by faculty and administration. As an ex-administrator, I could see the situation from both sides and did not feel particularly hostile to the faculty or the administration. Dan was unable to function the way he wanted, and the environment had changed for him. In all honesty, I had to say that Dan was not receiving respect from either his superiors or his peers. In both groups, the absence of "professional productivity" set the stage for a holding operation. I could see that a move by Dan at this time could be beneficial to him and would be one way of resolving the conflict. But there was something he needed to know about becoming effective in organizations. Dan had to learn how to become political.

The next night, I tried to show Dan that he needed to develop many bases for power—he needed to get faculty as well as administrative support. He replied by saying that he would have all the power he needed. "My authority as assistant to the president will be enough." I wondered if indeed it would be enough.

For the full reality of the manager's world to be understood, another dimension of managerial activity must be explored. The contemporary manager in a changing world uses strategy and tactics to deal with the dynamic character of the organizational environment. The examples from the cases of Chapter 17 offer many lessons and many questions in this area. Would the Blazer approach work with IBM? Could Colonel Sanders have innovated at Sears? Might General Electric have avoided problems if Watson had been its head?

With so many different examples, it is apparent that no one approach will guarantee success or survival. The somewhat static knowledge base for management you received in Part 2, coupled with a knowledge of the processes for managing, may not be enough. You must also relate to an ever-changing dynamic environment and to less traditional aspects of managing.

The first three parts of this book have described and discussed professional aspects of management in organizations. The discussion highlighted the official features of organizations and management processes. We now turn to the unofficial world that oils the working parts of any organization. To fully understand the manager's position in the world of power and politics, we must understand that this is a world different from the one that was described earlier. For a moment, think of the topics and discussions that have come before this chapter, and compare them with the following advertisement from *The Wall Street Journal*, about *The Enjoyment of Management*, by Frederick C. Dyer and John M. Dyer, published by Dow Jones–Irwin, Inc., a book that is supposed to aid in improving management:

> Authors Frederick C. Dyer and John M. Dyer are wholly concerned with how a good manager can bring out the best in his people by recognizing their contributions to the company; by turning their negative qualities into positive forces; by motivating this work force instead of browbeating it; etc. The authors used interesting examples and colorful terms to illustrate their principles and to make their point. One chapter, "Algren's Doctrine Applied to Management," takes novelist Nelson Algren's three rules—never eat at a place called Mom's, never play cards with a man named Doc, and never sleep with someone who has more trouble than you have—and shows how these rules apply to management. Another chapter, "The Rumpel Theorem of Management," demonstrates that, just as in the old fairytale in which Rumpelstiltskin did all the work, but got none of the credit, there are people ("Rumpels") in every company who do more than their share of the work, but never seem to get any of the credit for it. Packed with so much excellent material on the human relations aspects of management, the book will be useful to management at all levels.

There is a flavor in this ad that you will not often find in textbooks on management. Management authors (especially those writing for college courses) rarely present such "down-to-earth" materials to prospective and potential managers. Yet, such nontechnical topics are important.

Look how important the nontechnical area is to Dan in the vignette. You sense the different concepts of organizational life held by Dan and Burke. Dan sees the life in very simplistic terms. "If I have authority, people will do as I say and I'll be successful as an administrator." Burke, on the other hand, displays an organizational wisdom developed from some personal wars. He is trying to explain the other world of organizational life. This other world, the unofficial world, does not exist on charts or diagrams. In fact, to some people it is invisible. It's the world of power, politics, tactics, and conflict resolution. It's the world of managerial reality.

Figure 18.1 shows the three sectors of the manager's reality world. Sector 1 contains the information and skills applied to the nonbehavioral aspects of the organization. Most of the materials in Part 3 dealt with developing management skills in decision making, planning, organization, and control. Sector 2 deals with the behavior dimensions—the relationships between the leader-manager and others (bosses, peers, subordinates, groups, and so on). Many of the skills used in sector 1 apply to sector 2, but because of the interaction characteristics of the behavioral factors, managers must view many of their approaches in terms of a contingency posture (see Chapter 15).

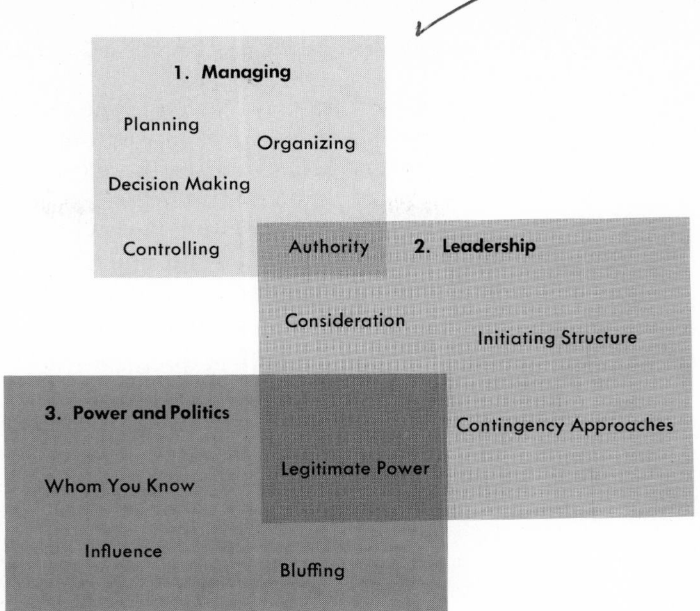

FIGURE 18.1 The three dimensions of a manager's world

In this and the remaining chapters, sector 3 is presented. The leader-manager may be successful in the very-short-run time period but not effective if he doesn't see the factors of power, politics, and tactics operating in his world. In Chapter 18, therefore, we present this subtle, unofficial, but critical world. To some, this picture will appear bleak and unattractive; to others, it will support perceptions you have had throughout the earlier sections that the whole truth was not being told. To both groups, we offer suggestions in Chapter 19 for coping successfully and effectively.

In this chapter, we begin our exploration of this new world by first presenting a description of its characteristics. You should then want to know more about it, and we give you this by looking at the terms in this world: *influence*, *power*, and *authority*.

CHARACTERISTICS OF THE POLITICAL WORLD OF ORGANIZATIONS

In a lead article in the National Observer, the characteristics of organizational politics were described.[1] Author Chew quotes liberally from many management experts, and in sum, the following features seem to stand out:

[1] Peter Chew, "Backstabbing, Inc.," *National Observer*, Vol. 13, No. 4 (week ending January 26, 1974), 1 and 18.

It exists in every firm. Politics is unavoidable. "Since power exists in every group or organization, politics must exist in every firm. You can therefore get away from politics only by becoming a hermit." [Professor Alan Schoonmaker, Carnegie-Mellon University] "In every company there's an 'informal organization' on the upper levels with power centers that are often at variance with what the company organization chart suggests." [Auren Uris, author of many management books]

It's subjective. The political world judges behavior on a different set of criteria. In a study of 3,000 U.S. businessmen, Dale Tarnowieski, director of the American Management Association survey, reported that "52% of all respondents believe that advancement and promotion . . . are most often based on a largely subjective and arbitrary decision . . .; 88% say a dynamic personality and the ability to sell yourself and your ideas is more of an attribute to the manager on the move today than is a reputation for honesty or firm adherence to principles; 82% believe that pleasing the boss is the critical factor in determining promotability in today's organizational environment."

It's on the rise. "In uncertain times such as these, politicking invariably increases markedly, says Uris. Not to be liked by a key man has immediate and very serious implications for a guy's future in the company and his peace of mind. . . . In recessions, it's the middle managers who are always bounced out of an organization." Two statements by the Research Institute of America show the significance of organizational politics to aspiring or practicing managers: "(1) Today, when business can least afford a dissipation of effort, office politics

TABLE 18.1 Relationship between Influence, Power and Authority

Term	Feature
Influence	Broad . . . An objective of interpersonal relations. Something someone does. Active effort.
Power	Less broad . . . A means to achieve influence. Describes the capacity you have to influence. Deals with potential acts.
Authority	Most restricted term . . . A form of power. Power associated with a given organizational position. The right to command.

is on the rise within many companies. As a menace to individuals and organizations alike, it deserves more concentrated study than anyone has given it. The price of office politics is tremendous, both to management and the individual; and (2) To ignore the existence of company politics, when others in an organization are dedicating much of their time to it, can be as impractical as assuming that the right-of-way is always an assurance of safety in traffic."

With this background, we are now ready to explore more fully the specific features of the political world—influence and power.

THE RELATIONSHIP AMONG INFLUENCE, POWER, AND AUTHORITY

influence

In one way of thinking, the objective of most interpersonal acts by managers is influence. Put simply, *influence* is any behavior by one person that produces an effect on the behavior of another person.[2] It is also a psychological force. As a manager, you might like your subordinates to produce more, to produce at an even rate, to reduce the number of processed defective parts, to accept a new person into their work group, or to become more cooperative. This attempt to influence behavior is not limited to subordinates, for you also want to affect the behavior of your boss, peers, staff or line personnel, and/or customers. Thus, for our purposes, influence will be considered as a very general term.

The relationship between influence and other concepts appears in Table 18.1. In this table you see that influence is the most general, inclusive term, that power is one way to get influence, and that authority is one way to get power. An illustration will develop the idea of authority a bit more.

What does authority mean to a manager of a bowling center?

In Chapter 6, "Design of Organization Structure," we talked about the idea of authority. You read that when a person joins an organization, he is usually put into some kind of an organizational position or job, a job with a list of duties and expectations. If you become a manager of a bowling center, the owner will neither tell you, nor hand you a sheet of paper that describes, what it is you are to do. You may be expected to open the bowling center, to

[2] This definition is approximately that found in *The Social Psychology of Organizations*, by Daniel Katz and Robert L. Kahn (New York: John Wiley, 1966), pp. 218–20.

check the roster of people assigned for the day's work, and to see that the various people get started on their jobs. You may have a maintenance group cleaning the lanes; you may have others cleaning out the ashtrays and picking up the litter from the previous night; you may have people working in other areas selling soft drinks and other refreshments. There may even be a supply store with bowling accessories.

There are many things that would have to be done before the bowling center opens for business. You may even have to make a physical count of cash and a physical check of inventory, and place some orders for materials that you anticipate needing in the future. The owner may expect you to hire part-time help, to see to it that ads are placed in the paper, and that innovations and special promotions are communicated to the public. There are numerous things that have to be done to run a bowling center, and you, as the manager, are probably the one responsible for getting everything done. We could go on with the various duties of the manager of a bowling center, but perhaps the point becomes obvious—the complete description of the job might take more paper than this textbook.

It is likely that if a job description is written, the statements are very broad and lack detail. How a manager gets the job done is usually a matter of individual and personal discretion. What the owner will do, however, is identify for the manager the rights and authority that he has in the job. A manager will know how much money he can spend, whom he can and cannot hire and fire, what disciplinary action he can take, and what rewards he is able to pass out to those working for him. The job has *authority,* which is the right to command action from others. Thus, authority is a source of power.

authority

POWER

Suppose you are the owner of a number of car-wash operations in a city, and you have a local manager for each of these operations. As you look over the performance of these operations, you find that one is more successful than another. You might ask why, for each is located in a similar traffic pattern, each manager is approximately the same age, has approximately the same training, and supervises the same number of men.

Why is one manager more effective and successful than another?

If you were able to visit the car-wash operations and make yourself invisible, you might find that the difference among the managers could be best described in terms of the power that each has. You might find that all the managers started with the same authority, yet one seems to be more successful in dealing with his subordinates than another is. The power of this man is greater than that of others.

What is the nature of this power? What are its sources?

The Nature of Power

Power is a topic of new interest in organizations. Swept under the carpet for years, the subject was the theme of a best-selling book during the mid-seventies. In this book, *Power! How to Get It, How to Use It,* author Michael Korda views power as an instinct in men and women and says that the will to power is an essential expression of our humanity.[3] Korda also states that although there are primarily four reasons for working—habit, pleasure, money, and power—it is primarily the desire for power that keeps most people working. He cautions, however, that power must be your servant, nor your master.

Robert N. McMurry, management consultant, speaks dramatically of this topic when he states that "the most important and unyielding necessity of organizational life is not better communications, human relations, or employee participation, but power."[4] To these two contemporary writers, power is natural and expected to exist among people in organizations. You have heard power called an instinct and a necessity. Conceptually, power has another meaning.

power

From reviewing Table 18.1, you see that *power* can be defined as that force others perceive you to have that gives you the capacity to influence them. Power refers to a *potential set of acts,* not a specific act occurring at the present time. As mentioned earlier, the objective of power is influence over others.

When we talk of influence, we speak of it in terms of *psychological force.* For example, when one person wants something that another person has, he attempts to influence the second person in order to get it. If a manager wants subordinates to work harder, he attempts to influence them to do so. If a secretary wants her boss

[3] Michael Korda, *Power! How to Get It, How to Use It* (New York: Random House, 1975), p. 10.

[4] Robert N. McMurry, "Power and the Ambitious Executive," in *Management in the World Today: A Book of Readings,* eds. Don Hellriegel and John Slocum, Jr. (Reading Mass.: Addison-Wesley, 1975), p. 294.

to think she is very valuable to the office, she will try to influence him to think she is indispensable.

Power also operates in social interaction. A man marooned on an island has little power or influence if he is the only person on that island. Power and influence are forces that exist between people—that operate in social interaction. These features of power are shown in Figure 18.2.

The nature of power, then, becomes clearer to us. A person can be said to have power over others when those others believe that they should act the way he wants them to. Power, then, depends upon the perceptions that people have of one another and the situation that they are sharing. It is a psychological force and one that deals with the potential acts of others.

An effective manager needs authority as well as power. A realistic manager is one whose authority defines the rights he has to operate with those people reporting directly to him (his subordinates), and who has been able to establish sufficient power in the eyes of his subordinates, his peers, and his boss.

In a traditional sense, we know how a person gets authority—by being appointed into the hierarchy of an organization. When a person becomes a manager, he also becomes a person with authority. But how does the manager with authority establish his power? How does he develop this potential capacity to exert influence over others? We have seen in earlier sections of this book that when we talk about leadership we talk about the leadership act, an act that may be exercised by people not in formal positions of authority. This same thinking applies to power. Power can be held by people who are not in the formal, official chain of command. Earlier reference to informal leaders and the power they have from their fellow workmen suggests that a manager not aware of such power could possibly make grave errors in judgment. To avoid errors in judgment, we turn to finding the sources of power.

FIGURE 18.2 What power is

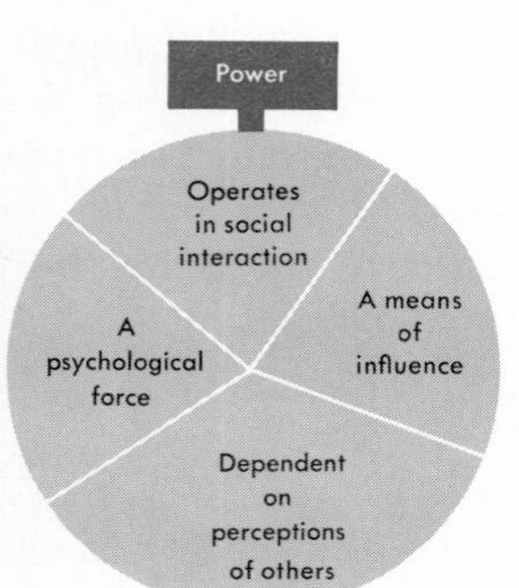

Sources of Power

When we speak of the sources of power, we do so with the understanding that people may use power derived from upward, sideways, or downward sources. Whereas authority is primarily a downward-flowing concept, power flows in all directions.

Why would A do what B wants him to do? Why would A be dependent upon B? Why does B have power over A? How is C able to resist the efforts by B? These fundamental questions give a focus to the topic of power and the sources of power. Let us explore some possible answers to these questions. An overview can be seen in Figure 18.3.

Can legitimate power come from subordinates?

legitimate power

You may do what someone else tells you to do because he is your boss. Since he is your boss, it follows that he has a position in the organization, and that position gives him the right to do many things. The power that he has is *legitimate power,* and it comes primarily from the organization. So the first reason why one person is influenced by another is legitimate power. This legitimate power obviously comes to you when you become a member of the organization and others in the organization accept and expect you to have power. Authority is legitimate power.

Why do certain people emerge from a group as leaders?

Suppose a group of you are interested in playing volleyball, and only one of your members is very familiar with the rules. After a number of heated arguments between the two teams because of a lack of rules, one person may emerge from either side as a leader, someone with power. Each of you in the group gives him the right to influence your behavior because you view his knowl-

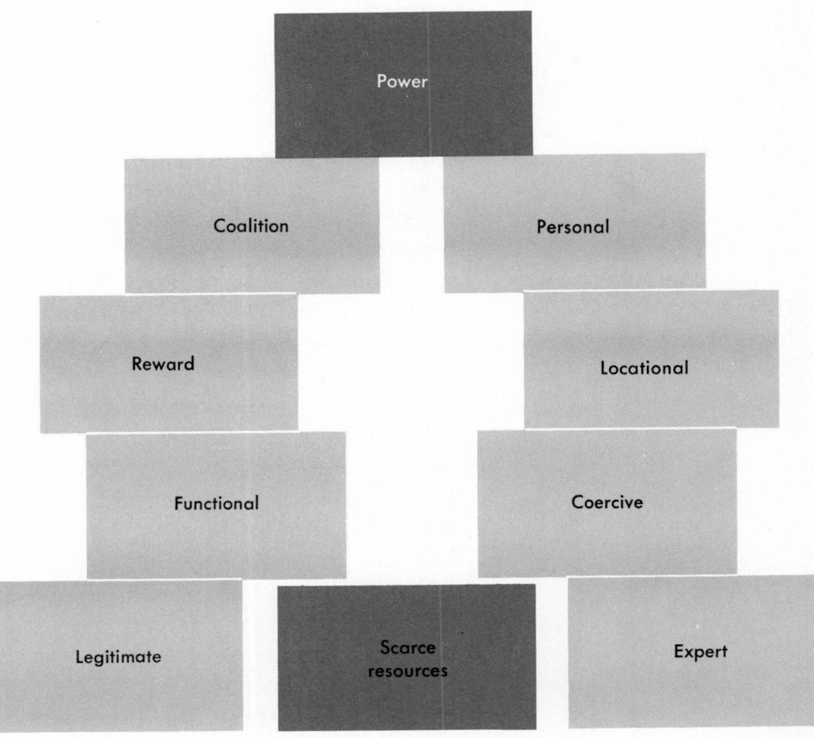

FIGURE 18.3 Sources of power

edge of the game as important for the play of the game. If this person with the *expert power* tells you to play at the back of the court and hit the ball to a center-set person, or to take up a position in the front line and spike the ball, you will do so because you can see the advantage of his knowledge and experience in trying to win the game. Thus you have the elements of an organization. All those on a team have decided that they would like to compete and even win; but they recognize that they are unable to win without someone to direct their efforts. When they sense the need for a leader with knowledge of the rules and strategy of the game, they give power to such a person and allow him to influence their behavior.

expert power

In the business world, expert power is frequently in the hands of engineers, accountants, technical experts, or people who have been in the company for years and who know things that others do not know. Whatever the shape and form, what is true about expert power is that the organization senses the need for this knowledge and willingly yields to its influence.

functional power

Power frequently rests with those people who perform certain functions; this could be called *functional power*. For example, if an organization is very conscious of its spiraling costs, the members who keep records and report back to higher management about cost information undoubtedly have power because of the function they are performing. Often older, experienced, "tough" managers will respond very meekly to the young clerk who is checking on cost information. The manager allows the clerk to influence his behavior because he senses the power that the clerk has owing to the function he performs.

coercive power

Do muscles ever help?

Another kind of power is *coercive power*. This is power that is based on fear. The fear can take many forms, and the punishment that is potentially forthcoming from the person can also take many forms. You may have been a member of a group in which you were readily influenced by a more powerful person because, if you did not do as he said, you would get a sharp punch, which might be very, very painful. Or if you want very much to be a member of a group, for example, and it is obvious who its leader is, you will allow him to influence you so that he does not punish you by keeping you out of the group. Coercive power with physical punishment is not very common among managers of organizations, but the notion of coercive power and some of the nonphysical punishments is one that should not be overlooked or forgotten.

Reward power

Reward power is very different from coercive power. In this case, you recognize that there is someone who gives the rewards,

Will people give you power in exchange for rewards?

and you willingly allow that person to influence your behavior. You do what he wants because you would like the reward. In some instances, the rewards will be monetary, and thus this person is likely to have not only reward power but legitimate power, in that he is probably your formal boss. In other cases, however, this person may reward you with a compliment or with a statement that gives you a feeling of being accepted. A group or informal leader can be the source of reward power in organizations.

Is locational power the same as authority?

locational power

Your actual physical location or position in an office may give you power. For example, if you are located near the water cooler and thus have opportunity for a great deal of contact, interaction, and communication with others, you undoubtedly have power. Another simple example of *locational power* is in a workplace where the work of one person is fed into the work of a second and a third, and so on. If the first person does not perform his operation correctly, none of the others is able to complete his task. Thus, the position in the flow of work gives rise to different positions of power and potential influence.

Michael Korda devotes one chapter of his book to locational power; he calls it the power spot. Offices are filled with power spots—corner offices, offices with a view, offices with proximity to important people. Corners are power spots at office parties but not necessarily at conference meetings. The power spot is at 12 on a clock face, the second most powerful person is usually at 1 o'clock and the least powerful at 11.[5]

coalition power

Anyone with military experience should recognize the next source of power—*coalition power*. Where a large number of draftees (men who have a U.S. prefix to their serial numbers) are in strategic positions throughout an army base, powerful coalitions develop. For example, a high-ranking military officer may desire some medical supplies for his wife but finds that the normal channels are blocked to him. The drafted clerk assistant in his office may be able to make a few phone calls to other drafted low-ranking noncoms and produce the medical supplies. In all large organizations, there is a powerful unofficial, informal organization that is a coalition of people with some common bond.

Won't this lead to organizational revolution?

personal power

People may have power given to them because of their personality or physical attributes. This *personal power* may be as simple a thing as physical attractiveness. Occasionally, the secretary with quite a bit of power is the one who is the prettiest, not necessarily the one best skilled. In a similar way, Samuel, in the

[5] Korda, *Power!* pp. 63–105.

Old Testament, was admired because he stood at least one head above the rest of his contemporaries. The Churchills and Napoleons of the world may not have had the physical stature of a Samuel, but they had other personality features that made others willingly yield influence to them.

power over scarce resources

A final source of power we will list here is called the *power over scarce resources.* The example suggested by Dr. T. O. Jacobs was information.[6] Think how often people are given power when they have information that others want. It's possible that the grapevine is fed information by people with an instinct or desire for power. Any resource short in supply and wanted by others thus becomes a source for obtaining power.

The list of sources of power could continue for pages. Perhaps it is time to summarize this brief section and make a few important observations. Your ability to be powerful in an organization depends on a number of factors, especially the other person or persons and the situation. You might even have said to yourself in looking over the previous paragraphs, "I have some of these attributes of power but do not seem to be powerful." Obviously, what is happening is that the attributes you have are not perceived by others as being of value to the group in its particular situation. An expert's knowledge of lighting fires when it is raining is of value only if you need to light fires when it is raining.

Is dependence healthy?

If we were to subtitle this chapter, we would probably add, "How to Make Others Dependent on You." The objective of power is to influence others, and you can influence others only if they become dependent on you. They must see something in the situation that you have and that they need. Thus they become dependent on you and allow you to influence them so that the situation meets their needs. It is possible to summarize all sources of power as attempts to influence three features of any group or organization: (1) information, (2) facilities and machines, and (3) people. By having power over information, facilities, and people, a manager makes others dependent and is able to become extremely influential and successful in achieving the objectives of the work unit.

Suppose, however, that a manager wants to use the knowledge from this section on power sources to increase or decrease the power of his subordinates, not just himself. If we view the sources in Figure 18.3 from the perspective of manager influence or control, we find the relations in Table 18.2. A number of these insights will be developed in the next chapter.

[6] T. O. Jacobs, *Leadership and Exchange in Formal Organizations* (Alexandria, Va.: Human Resources Research Organization, 1971), p. 225.

TABLE 18.2 Manager Control of Power Sources

Power Source	Amount of Manager Control or Influence
Legitimate power	Great deal
Expert power	Some
Functional power	Great deal
Coercive power	Little
Reward power	Great deal
Locational power	Great deal
Coalition power	Little
Personal power	Little to none
Scarce resource power	Some

Isn't this manipulation?

Many of you may at this point be rather concerned about the frankness of our statement on power. You may resent and feel uncomfortable with the statement that others must be dependent on you, with the subjects of how you become a powerful and influential manager and how to be successful through the manipulation of behavior. Many people are suspicious of power figures. This is particularly true in America, where people came to escape dictatorships and oppression. American laws attempt to divide power sources and create a pluralistic type of society, where all voices are heard and a form of representative government protects minorities from majority manipulation. It would therefore be natural for many of you to feel uneasy with some of the previous statements about power. Yet power, influence, and authority are factors of organizational life. They are terms used in objective descriptions of behavior and as such are neutral in feeling. Actually, power may be viewed as having both positive and negative features.

Negative and Positive Power

David C. McClelland believes there are two faces of power, a negative and a positive face.[7] McClelland believes that too many of us think of power only in the negative way. In the negative sense, power is domination over others, submission of one person to another, and the use of all necessary maneuverings to gain an end. Such power is antisocial and obviously destructive and dangerous

[7] D. C. McClelland, "The Two Faces of Power," in *Organizational Psychology*, eds. David A. Kolb, Irwin M. Rubin, and James M. McIntyre (Englewood Cliffs, N.J.: Prentice-Hall, 1971), pp. 141–54.

to any organization, for it evolves and generates from only one person.

What will positive power do?

The second face of power is more attuned to society. This is the type of power that you can develop and make use of. A person with this type of power motive does not make the other person feel drained and sapped of energy. Rather, the other person finds himself inspired, confident, willing, and interested in moving with the power figure, and thus is more powerful himself. Positive power is not based on coercion but rather on identification with goals. In the illustration given earlier about volleyball, the emerging leader is not dominating the group; the group recognizes the necessity for his leadership and use of power and willingly submits to that type of influence. This more positive face of power is similar to the type of philosophy that McGregor and Maslow talk about. It is a kind of management and leadership that may be difficult to achieve, may not be universally applicable in all situations and at all levels, but definitely is a worthy goal.

Do all people have power?

You cannot escape the fact of power. The very fact that you finish this course will mean that you will have more power than someone else who has not taken the course if, in a group discussion, people are speaking about management and you are the only one with the information. Anyone who affiliates with an organization is a person who will be given power or who will give power. In any social relationship, we are talking about an exchange between two or more people. One person gives up something to get something else, and this process of exchange (an exchange of influence and power) is continuous.

Probably no social interaction could take place and thus little work could ever be accomplished in an organization if all persons had equal power. If no one needed anything from another person, there might be no society. It is the dependence upon each other that generates the need man has for organizations. We do not want to carry the point of dependence to an illogical extreme, but we do want to emphasize that dependence, power, and influence of themselves are not necessarily negative and destructive terms.

SUMMARY AND PROPOSITIONS

The preceding descriptions of power give a glimpse into the manager's political world. We started by examining the nature of that world, then we explained several types of power. As has been said before, the words *power* and *politics* are neutral. They become moral questions when the ends are for selfish purposes. Like parents, managers structure the environment for good purposes. Although the definition of "good" is always debatable, the power of managers is a fact of organizational life. Managers must be made aware of this power, its generation, its sources, and its political usefulness. Now that you have been introduced to these ideas, consideration of the following propositions may develop your thinking:

1. To be effective, a manager must have both authority and power.
   a. Authority usually comes from the organization and gets expressed through the duties and rights of a position.
   b. Power usually comes from others and is granted tacitly to the person in a position.

2. Power is an organizational concept and identifies the importance that others give to a person.

3. Most of the organizational power sources available to managers are social in nature.
   a. Managers spend most of their time in nonauthority interactions with other managers on their level. They must relate and attempt to influence behavior through the nonauthority methods.
   b. It is not the accepted behavior for managers to resort to punishment or the use of legitimate authority when dealing with other managers. The interactions are thus in the realm of power and politics.

4. Effective and successful managers are aware of the organizational "facts of life."
   a. Power is a necessary force for merging the human elements with the organizational elements.
   b. Effective managers realize the limits of formal authority, especially when dealing with other managers. Power and politics become the human organizational instruments in the interpersonal behavior of managers.

5. Power and politics are used more frequently at higher levels of management.
   a. There is more uncertainty in information and behavioral expectations at the higher levels of management, and thus power and politics come into play to reduce uncertainty.
   b. Performance at higher levels of management is more difficult to measure and also requires help, integration, and cooperation from the managers and personnel of other units. Power and politics become an important technique by which the manager can reach his performance goals.

STUDY ASSIGNMENTS

1. *Compare the broad meaning of Parts 1, 2, and 3 with the ad from* The Wall Street Journal. *Are we talking about the same world? What is the ad's contribution to your understanding of management in practice?*

2. *What is the difference between authority and power? Would the difference be important to you if you were a manager? Explain.*

3. *Make a list of organizations you are in. Include formal, informal, and friendship groups. Do you have authority and/or power in each group? Give the evidence for your power and/or authority.*

4. *We list nine sources of power. Can you think of any more? Which of these is the easiest to get? Which is the hardest? Which do you have in your groups?*

5. *Do you believe power is a negative or a positive concept? Explain. Why do you feel most other people believe as they do about power?*

6. *Does politics have a place or role in managing? Why, or why not?*

7. *"If people wouldn't play politics, we could get a lot of work done." What is your reaction to this statement?*

8. *Do you accept or reject Propositions 3, 3*(a), *and 3*(b)*? Explain your answers.*

9. *What insights and information from Parts 2 and 3, as well as Chapter 18, give support to Proposition 5?*

situational episodes

1. You were delighted when you read in the school paper that Sherril Bailey was returning to campus. The two of you had been roommates as undergraduates a number of years ago. Now you were here as a graduate student in educational leadership, and Sherril was here as lead minister of the campus ministry group. You wondered if things were going well—Sherril seemed disturbed yesterday when she asked you for some free time to discuss a problem.

   Put simply, her problem was this. She is responsible for making up the budget for the year, and when she presented it to the board (made up of businesspeople, townspeople, and faculty), some of them gave her upsetting advice. They suggested that Sherril add 10 percent to her budget request. When she asked why, they said that the state board always cut budget requests by some percentage. "You never get what you ask for. It's the nature of budget requests," said one businessman. "The head people in Kansas City need to feel they're important, so they cut budgets."

   Sherril then asked you for advice. She felt her budget was honest and truthful, and she did not want to lie, fabricate, or pad the figures. What made her request to you so interesting was that just last week you had finished reading a book on organizational power. What should you tell her?

2. March 17 is circled on your calendar. On that date, you received a promotion that at first seemed to be great. You had worked at the Pierce Company's Greensburg plant for the past twelve years, first on the loading dock, then on the assembly line, and eventually in most of the departments. At the end of the sixth year, you were asked to become a supervisor, and you accepted with mixed feelings. You were no longer "one of the boys," and that hurt, but you have been more than rewarded by a sense of doing a good job. You felt at home in first-level management and thought you'd stay there the rest of your life, but on March 17 you became a member of middle management.

   You had been in the job only two months when you received two visits that have you troubled. Frank Igno, manager of the accounting department, asked for your support at the next staff meeting, to block a proposed expansion of the warehouse. When you left his office, you felt confused, since Bruce Duvain, marketing manager, had also asked for your support, but to help put the proposal through. This kind of stuff was new to you, but you thought you had detected a hint from each that if you helped him on this one, he'd help you on the next one. What should you do?

managerial politics and tactics

NINETEEN

OBJECTIVES YOU SHOULD MEET

Define *a manager's job in terms of Sayles' managerial-behavior model.*

State *the four manager modifications of basic intellectual qualities.*

Compare *the attitude-modification strategy to the "muddle-through" strategy.*

Distinguish *two features of the branch approach to decision making.*

Identify *the place of politics and tactics in managerial decision making.*

List *at least two reasons why "bluffing" should be viewed as a legitimate part of managing.*

IT'S EXPERIENCE THAT COUNTS: HOW TO PACKAGE RESEARCH

I thought I had been well trained. Psychology had been an exciting undergraduate major, and the master's degree in research and statistics had rounded out my formal education. But I needed experience, so I jumped at the chance to join a management consulting firm, Sliter Associates, in Los Angeles. The firm specialized in providing consultant services to institutions and service-type agencies: universities, colleges, technical schools, libraries, housing projects, and municipal units such as the waste-control, police, and fire departments. The broad scope of clients stimulated my imagination, and I was pleased to be assigned to the Library Project Team, with Ted Sieb as project director.

Ray Founts, vice-president of Sliter Associates, said this project assignment would give me an insight into the way an experienced director relates with a client. He said I would also see how research data get translated into managerial action. Sliter Associates had worked for LARVAL before, and this time its administrative board had specifically requested Ted Sieb.

"What does LARVAL stand for?" I asked.

"Oh, that's something you'll get used to—a kind of verbal shorthand. LARVAL stands for the Los Angeles Regional Valley of Associated Libraries. It's an organization of libraries in six counties that pool their local budgets and requests into a central staff group. The central staff group performs many activities that some of the small libraries could not do. They also provide for the training and development of the local librarians and staff, and do centralized purchasing, ordering, and so on."

"Who pays for the central staff?" I asked.

"Good question. Because the state wants to encourage the more

efficient use of resources, they support the staff with a budget that comes from Sacramento, the state capital.

"You might wonder about the authority structure with LARVAL," Mr. Founts added. (I really hadn't wondered about it at all, but thought a nod of my head would show I was with him.) "Each local library has a local board, and one member from each board makes up the board of directors of LARVAL. The central staff requests everything through that board. Robin, I'm actually telling you more than you need to know. Besides, Mr. Sieb will fill you in on the details. Let's go see him now."

"Ted, this is Robin Glasser. She's assigned to you on the LARVAL project." Ray Founts introduced me, then left.

Six months later, I was a different person. I found that my formal education had prepared me for technical matters—designing a research project, developing and pretesting a questionnaire and interview schedule, running the statistical tests on the data—but I wasn't prepared for the things going on behind the scenes. For example, I discovered that Mr. Sieb and Mr. Gartling (new director of LARVAL) didn't get along too well. Mr. Sieb was very friendly with some of the librarians in the larger libraries in LARVAL. Because of their size, these libraries usually had larger staffs and budgets and had more power. Their representatives from the boards to the central staff board were more articulate and had political influence at the statehouse. Directors of LARVAL lasted, on the average, three years; some of the librarians had worked for 20 or more years.

I also discovered that the original project estimate was increased against the wishes of Mr. Gartling. He had turned down Mr. Sieb's request for an increase, and Mr. Sieb had resubmitted it to all the member libraries and received approval.

Research data for mangement purposes meant, in this case, that our figures on population needs and use were supposed to help justify a budget request for additional funding. The state board had demanded a survey by an independent research firm to determine the needs of the market area. When I asked Mr. Sieb what would happen if our data showed no need or satisfaction with the status quo, he replied that such questions are his to handle.

I had decided that I would not knowingly falsify the data. I felt sorry for Mr. Gartling. It appeared that no one had thought to develop different strategies for different outcomes from the data. What was Mr. Sieb going to do with the data? Should I talk with Mr. Gartling unofficially? Should I talk with Mr. Founts? Or should I just sit back to see what happened? Maybe these events were what my prof had meant when he said, "When you get out in the field, it's not what you know but how you package what you know."

Robin received a baptism of fire in the vignette. The politics of Ted Sieb surprised her, and she presently faced a question of determining her own tactics for organizational survival. If power and politics are so natural and necessary (as depicted in the preceding chapter), organizational participants need better equipment to face the challenges.

In this chapter, we offer you some ideas and approaches that should better equip a potential manager or member of an organization. The chapter has two basic sections. In the first, you will read a description of the type of managing world that exists and the necessary posture for successful coping. The second section offers specific approaches for you to get, hold, and use power.

THE CONTEMPORARY SCENE OF MANAGING

The contemporary scene of managing calls for the manager to learn how to manage *without formal authority*. To prepare for this situation, managers need to develop particular postures. The first deals with *attitudes* toward their environment; the second deals with approaches to take in *decision making*.

Managing without Authority

Leonard Sayles is interested in what managers *do*.[1] He has reviewed the empirical studies of managerial behavior and found

[1] Leonard R. Sayles, *Managerial Behavior* (New York: McGraw-Hill, 1964).

that there is a discrepancy between what many people say managers should do and what some researchers find managers doing. Sayles' summary of the findings of these studies gives us the following picture:

1. Management means *working with and through people.* Approximately 80 percent of a manager's time is spent in contact with other people.
2. The manager has a *wide variety of contacts.* Some of these contacts last a short time, whereas others extend for large portions of an hour or longer.
3. The manager has *breadth in the range of his contacts.* In most studies reported, the supervisor is not dealing primarily with his subordinates—his contacts include people other than those working directly under him.

external work flows

What does a manager's job look like?

After his review of the empirical literature, Sayles described what a manager really does. First, a manager is *a participant in external work flows.* This means that he spends a great deal of his time in nonauthority relationships with other managers at his own or a higher level. The second role of the manager is *the manager as a leader:* He gives direction to subordinates, he responds to the actions of his subordinates, and he functions as a representative for his subordinates in contacts with others. The third aspect of the manager's job is *the manager as a monitor*—that is, the one who watches to see that the system is running smoothly. Let us expand on these three parts of the manager's job.

Sayles believes that a large portion of the manager's workday behavior should be called lateral, horizontal, or work-flow behavior. It takes a different form from the behavior between a manager and his subordinate, because there is *no authority* between the two or more parties. Much of the behavior described in Chapter 18 on power is of this type; indeed, Sayles is describing a relationship based on exchange and power. He talks about trading, work-flow, service, advisory, auditing, stabilizing, and innovation types of relationships; in nearly all of these, he is describing the relationship that a manager has with other managers in the horizontal or external world (see Table 19.1).

Why is the description important?

The significance of this description of managerial behavior is that it points out an important area where the manager has little formal authority and control; therefore, his tactics must not assume these factors. If Sayles had described the work relationships as some authors often do, you might imagine a column on the left side describing traditional management or leadership or supervisory styles,

TABLE 19.1 The Manager's World

	First Industrial Revolution (1850s)	Second Industrial Revolution (1950s)
Management level involved:	First level: foremen, plant superintendents.	Middle and upper level managers.
Nature of manager's job:	Supervises subordinates using authority and organization control.	Views job as part of work flow system. Monitors the system to get feedback.
Scope of job	Primarily works on small jobs and with subordinates.	Deals in external work flow; minimal interactions with direct subordinates; performs monitoring function of system.
Type of decision approach:	Identifies problem, applies analysis, and makes decision.	Makes marginal adjustments to maintain continuity and movement of the system.
Attitude toward change:	Desire for stability, predictability, minimum change.	Expects, welcomes, and integrates change into a dynamic system.

SOURCE: John Douglas, "Management and Change," in Joseph L. Massie, *Essentials of Management*, 2nd ed. (Englewood Cliffs, N.J.: Prentice-Hall, 1971), p. 244.

while the right-hand column would say "*but* that is not the way the real world is." To Sayles, the second aspect of the manager's job (the manager as a leader) may represent only 20 to 25 percent of the total workday activities. Thus, the world of power and politics is definitely a world that consumes most of the manager's attention. Many of the tactical suggestions we shall discuss later in this chapter are of use here—building alliances, compromising, and so on.

monitoring

The third part of the manager's job is *monitoring*. To Sayles, this means that a manager must know *when and where change is required* in the organization. The manager does this through a series of monitoring techniques that in themselves assume little authority. To Sayles, the manager is a person whose job is to relate to the work system, a situation of constant action and reaction, movement and activity. Getting information is useless unless that information is valuable in keeping everything going. The monitoring technique may be as simple as plain observation or as complex as analysis of computer printouts. The intention, however, is to maintain the flow and dynamic equilibrium of the organization. The manager is constantly making marginal decisions to maintain movement and flow.

Table 19.1 may help summarize the ideas of Sayles as well as the contributions of earlier writers. In this table, notice that we are spanning 100 years (1850 to 1950). Sayles identifies two industrial revolutions. The first was brought about primarily by machines. In the second industrial revolution, the major change was the new awareness that the organization is really a network of work operations. Work and systems are synonymous. The efforts of individuals must be programmed so that there is flow, coordination, and interdependency. To do this programming effectively requires an attitude more in line with the changes in the manager's world.

Attitude Modification

Why is attitude important?

A manager who reads this book is exposed to a great deal of knowledge in the first three parts. Much of this knowledge is presented in an orderly, logical fashion—chapters with major headings and subsections, summaries, and so on. In addition to this kind of highly structured learning experience, the manager must also cope with the various bits of knowledge that continuously flow to him from many sources in a state of disarray.

Another model we describe sets up the type of mind or attitude that managers need in facing the ever-growing knowledge base in their field. Professor Charles Summer believes that managers of organizations must learn to use and modify the knowledge of others.[2] Since the knowledge has to be applied in the manager's world rather than in the scientific or academic world, the orientation of the manager is toward action. His payoff comes in results and problem solving. The manager must be able to relate to the ever-changing knowledge bank if he is to develop a strategy for his work world.

What is left after modification?

This simplified but useful "modification model" views knowledge and the scientific world in a way that does not require polarization; you are not forced to have your head in the clouds or your hands in the dirt. Table 19.2 shows a management modification process for relating five basic intellectual qualities of one world to fit the other. (Naturally, a manager must confront many

[2] Charles E. Summer, Jr., "The Managerial Mind," *Harvard Business Review* (January–February 1959), pp. 69–78.

more qualities than these five, but the importance of this table is to show the modification process—not the complete listing of basic qualities.) These five qualities are the factual attitude, quantitative attitude, theoretical attitude, predisposition for truth, and consistency. Summer gives many more qualities and expands on them at length, but we summarize only some of them in order to demonstrate how managers make modifications.

TABLE 19.2 Basic Intellectual Qualities and Modification for Management

Basic Qualities		Management Modification
The Factual Attitude		
The manager demands and seeks facts before making decisions	*but*	must use his own reasoning and judgment if lack of facts or time prevent a complete researching of a problem.
The Quantitative Attitude		
The manager attempts objectivity and collects "measurable" facts	*but*	does not worship mathematical systems and thus does not postpone or shun judgments when action is called for.
The Theoretical Attitude		
The manager develops an interest in searching for concepts that help catalog events into the same meaning; he also develops an interest in reasoning out laws to explain the interrelationships of concepts	*but*	realizes that reasoning and quiet thought, as well as the use of theory, can be valuable in professional practice, provided one maintains a healthy distrust and a willingness to abandon theoretical concepts if they do not fit the specific problem.
Predisposition for Truth		
The manager would like every word tested and traced to the abstract characteristics that connect the word to the object it represents in the real world	*but*	realizes that he cannot shrink from problems because some statements are impossible to define precisely.
Consistency		
The manager tries to be sure that the reasoning in his arguments is valid—that premises are consistent rather than contradictory and that statements of conclusions and decisions are also consistent with the statements of premises	*but*	he cannot expect to discover scientific laws in every decision through strictly valid arguments, and sometimes finds it necessary to substitute "reasonableness" for precision in thinking.

SOURCE: John Douglas, "Management and Change," in Joseph L. Massie *Essentials of Management*, 2nd ed. (Englewood Cliffs, N.J.: Prentice-Hall, 1971), pp. 237–38.

The language of these basic qualities (the left column of Table 19.2) may seem familiar to you; this is frequently the language of basic management courses. But this language may not always help the prospective manager of organizations; in some cases, the over-simplified presentation actually creates a damaging misconception of the real world. Note that the left column of that table describes the world in unreal and static terms. There are many unsuccessful older managers and naive young managers who have the factual attitude of seeking facts before making decisions; yet they do not realize that they need to use their own reasoning and judgment if time prevents the complete researching of a problem. There are also those managers who methodically worship the quantitative attitude and attempt objectivity and the measurement of performance. These rigid and static managers usually create all kinds of frictions, frustrations, and difficulties.

The manager who senses the importance of facts, but modifies the process, will not worship mathematical systems and thus will not sit around when action is needed. In all the modifications of Table 19.2, the process is the same. Surely, the basic qualities described in the table are valuable ones to search for and possibly achieve, but their modification is also a crucial aspect for the development of any complete management strategy. Too often, managers stay in a sputtering state of inactivity because they are unable to acknowledge realistic demands placed on them by the dynamic, ever-changing world.

This model for developing a management posture suggests a management modification of any static inputs from the knowledge world. Do not misinterpret this model—we are not suggesting that knowledge has no value and that the manager is to bounce through his management world disregarding what is known and what is available. The emphasis in this model is *modification* of knowledge.

"Muddling" Decision Making

What is being muddled?

Like the attitude-modification model, the "muddling" decision-making model is also essentially nonbehavioral. In it we are talking about a decision approach that is independent of the people affected by the decision.

The basis for the nonbehavioral model comes from a valuable article for managers, "The Science of 'Muddling Through.'"[3] As you know, managers use different approaches to decision making;

[3] Charles E. Lindblom, "The Science of 'Muddling Through,'" *American Society for Public Administration*, Vol. 19, No. 2 (Spring 1959).

Charles E. Lindblom compares two of them: the rational, comprehensive method, and the successive, limited comparisons method. You should immediately recognize the similarity between the approaches of Summer and Lindblom. To both men, the manager errs in taking a traditional, static approach to the world of management. Lindblom believes that the first method (the rational-comprehensive method) is the most common one today,[4] and that it must give way to or at least be modified by the second method when the manager is faced with complex problems. Lindblom distinguishes between the two methods by using the terms *root* and *branch* (see Table 19.3).

The root model, or rational-comprehensive method, is outlined in the left column of Table 19.3; it would receive the applause of the many managers attached to the traditional, static, single-cause-and-effect approach. Notice the logic of the method as a manager moves through the steps of decision making:

1. The administrator first identifies his values, objectives, or ends and then seeks the means to reach the ends.
2. It follows from this that a "good" policy is one that most appropriately meets the desired ends; thus, we have a connection between objectives and policy.
3. The manager then considers all the important factors, and analyzes and evaluates them.
4. This process then leads to the last step, where theory is often used, but we find that the goals and values of the manager or administrator are maximized by selecting the best solution that fits these conditions.

Many management texts use different and perhaps more sophisticated symbols to describe the statements just presented; nevertheless, their intention is the same. The assumption made is that decision making is a rational, comprehensive, step-by-step process that is amenable to learning, quantification, computerization, and perhaps simulation. The disciples of this approach believe that most organizational problems can be analyzed and that what stops man from conquering his problems in his inability to use the rational approach.

Is there another approach?

Lindblom's branch approach pictures a different kind of world—a world filled with curved and crooked lines rather than

[4] You may find some examples of this rational-comprehensive method in Chapter 17.

TABLE 19.3 Decision-Making Model for Change

Root (rational-comprehensive)		Branch (successive, limited comparisons)
1. The administrator identifies his values, objectives, or ends, and then seeks the means (policies) to reach the ends	*but*	this is almost impossible to do since determination of values and objectives is usually intertwined with the empirical analysis of the alternatives. Often a means-end analysis does not apply or is limited.
2. Thus a "good" policy is one most appropriate for meeting the desired ends.	*but*	the real test of a "good" policy should be whether there is agreement among analysts that the policy is good in itself (workable), not that it is the optimum means to an agreed objective.
3. Next, all important factors are considered, analyzed, and evaluated. The process is a comprehensive one	*but*	in dealing with real, complex problems, all important factors cannot be known, analysis must be limited, some alternative policies will be neglected, and important values overlooked.
4. Finally, theory is often used; goals and values are maximized by selecting the best solution	*but*	in reality and dealing with so many limitations, theory would be restrictive and inappropriate in most cases. The administrator gives up the search for the "best" solution. Rather he makes marginal and incremental comparisons between policies and/or solutions and finds the better one.

SOURCE: John Douglas, "Management and Change," in Joseph L. Massie, *Essentials of Management*, 2nd ed. (Englewood Cliffs, N.J.: Prentice-Hall, 1971), p. 242.

straight lines. Notice the language that Lindblom uses when he says that clear objectives may not be possible; that a means-end analysis does not always apply; that agreement among analysts defines the real test of a "good policy." The language in the branch column for item 4 (Table 19.3) could almost have been given as a reaction to the scientific-management people of the early 1900s. You may recall that the early engineer-type contributors to management were searching for "one best way." They believed that the problems of management could be solved much as the problems of machines could—but Lindblom tells us in the branch method that the manager's world, unlike a machine-type world, is an interacting world. The manager must make marginal and incremental comparisons between policies and find the *better one*—a satisfactory one, not necessarily the best one.

How do Summer and Lindblom relate?

Two of the three models offered here are obviously similar. Both Summer and Lindblom deal with nonbehavioral situations. Both present the traditional and logical approach to knowledge and decision making and then modify the thinking process. Summer would have us respect the basic qualities of knowledge and truth but modify them to fit the management context. Lindblom would have us respect the complexities, difficulties, and rigor of scientific and quantitative analysis, but he views the management approach as one of multiple marginal adjustments rather than a forced, limited approach. The picture coming from the comparison of these two ideas is clear. The decision world and the knowledge world of the manager call for adjustments, adaptation, and comparisons of alternatives emerging from the specific environments rather than decisions structured from static goals and objectives. The reality emerging from our analysis of Tables 19.1, 19.2, and 19.3 is *change,* and the management posture and strategy required is *response* and *adjustment.*

What does the "real" world call for?

We turn now to the second section of the chapter and discuss more specifically what responses and adjustments managers might choose.

POLITICS AND TACTICS

politics

tactics

Managers want the answers to the following questions when dealing with power: (1) How do you get and keep power? In this chapter, we define *politics* as those things a person does to get and keep his power. (2) Once you have power, how do you use it? Using the power you have is defined here as *tactics;* that is, the specific ways you exercise the power. (3) Finally, what can a manager do to increase or decrease the power of subordinates, peers, rivals, and bosses? Politics and tactics are both used in this area to achieve effective influence over others.

In the next few pages, specific suggestions are offered that help answer all three questions.

The Scope of Politics and Tactics

Politics deals with the tactics that people use to get and activate their power potential. Changing behavior through influence is still the objective, but now the manager wants to make use of the power he has been given by others to a constructive, positive end. Ironically, most people probably think of power as a top-down, dominating force; in the discussions in Chapter 15 on leadership, the true character of these concepts comes forth—the manager can only exercise power that others give to him.

As is true in leadership and authority, the ultimate source of power is in the group, and it is the group that decides how effective a manager will be. Thus, the real question that a manager must ask himself is this: What is it that a manager can do to influence the group, to have them give him power, to have them accept his leadership and authority, so that the goals of the organization and its members are both met? Figure 19.1 presents an overview of politics.

With the scope of politics and tactics in mind, we present two examples of politics and tactics: one dealing with interpersonal dimensions, and one dealing with the tactics of organizational bluffing.

Some Tactics of Politics

What are some ways of being political?

In a penetrating article in The *Harvard Business Review,* Norman Martin and John Howard Sims offer a number of tactics for the purpose of improving power.[5] To discover these tactics, they searched the biographies of leaders throughout history, explored the lives of successful industrialists, and interviewed a number of contemporary executives. The listing that follows corresponds very closely to their article, although the illustrations and examples differ. The question that these men asked themselves was this: What are the tactics that have proved successful for controlling and directing the actions of others?

TAKING COUNSEL An effective manager is very cautious in deciding when to seek advice. An able executive can get advice from others as soon as he initiates or asks for it. He must be continuously careful that in asking for advice, he does not show to others any weakness in himself or his position.

FIGURE 19.1 What politics is

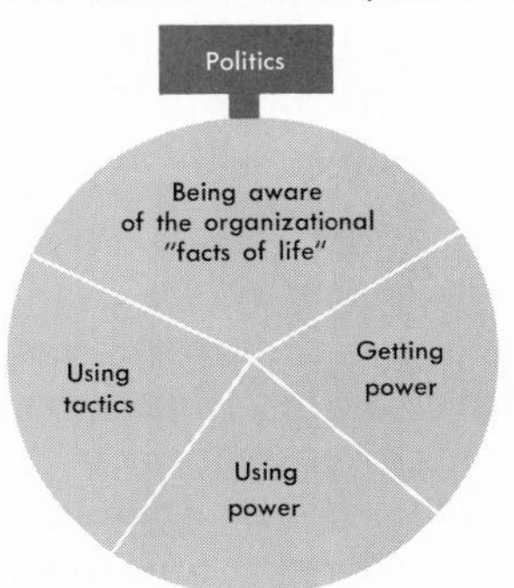

ALLIANCES Many young people in organizations have learned quickly to form alliances with others above, at the same level, and below in the organization who seem to have those characteristics and abilities that the organization wants. These are the people who are most likely to be promoted in the organization and with whom the manager has easy access, communication, and con-

[5] Norman H. Martin and John Howard Sims, "Power Tactics," *Harvard Business Review* (November–December 1956), pp. 25–29.

fidence. These alliances also help the manager gain a degree of respectability from his subordinates, for they know he has access outside a specific work unit.

Does the maneuverability tactic work against the goals of the organization?

MANEUVERABILITY The idea of maneuverability was developed early in the first chapter of this book when we suggested that a manager be careful about staying too long on a sinking ship. This tactic suggests that a manager is continuously aware of what the organization is looking for and tries to grow with these needs. The manager also maintains contacts outside the company or industry to give himself a great deal of flexibility and maneuverability within the organization. The old adage that "you are worth more to us if you are worth more to someone else" applies here.

COMMUNICATION The communication tactic would suggest that the manager is able to identify those people who have important, critical, and frequently confidential information. The insightful manager also wants to have information that other people need, so that he is a supplier of information and thus becomes more powerful. This frequently means that the manager will seek out informal channels rather than holding rigidly to formal channels, which are often slow with important information. People in certain positions in an organization are good sources of communication. For example, elevator operators will have information at certain times, as will mailroom boys or others who happen to be crossing over routine and rigid lines of organizations. You must also know when to limit information.

COMPROMISING This tactic will be obvious to those of you who have already been masters of conflict resolution. You frequently see people who are able to win one battle but in the process create enemies and thus lose the war. There is definitely an art in the ability to compromise and give up on insignificant points while being willing to fight for those points that are critical and important. A successful manager is able to recognize the stakes that people have in various matters and the potential alienation and power they have so as to be sure to move with the flow that is important.

Is negative timing like organizational sabotage?

NEGATIVE TIMING Frequently, a lower-level manager cannot get into direct confrontation with his boss about certain projects. He will be able to sense when his boss wants no more discussion, but action. It may be possible to delay the implementation of action by negative timing, a technique in which the manager starts the project in motion but may call for additional planning, additional studying, additional feedback; in doing so, he retards the movement of the project. Obviously, the manager must be fully aware of the costs and consequences of taking such negative timing and be prepared to shift into a faster gear if his boss insists upon the project or if, in hindsight, the manager feels the project is a legitimate one that should be expedited quickly.

ENTHUSIASM This technique deals with nonverbal communication. People "read" both what you say and how you say it, and therefore, the manager must be aware that both these aspects are important for him. A successful manager should have the skill (expert power) of selling projects. He is able to convey an excitement and tone that commits others to projects, and thus, if people want things done, they may frequently channel them through him.

CONFIDENCE Confidence is a must for managers. Confidence is obviously something that others see in you; yet there are techniques, skills, and tactics that a manager may develop that will improve the probability of others' viewing him as confident. Someone who is optimistic is usually viewed as confident, whereas someone who is always pessimistic may be viewed as having no confidence. A manager who reports to his peers, bosses, and subordinates in optimistic tones may well exude an air of confidence that will enhance his power position. Frequently, a manager must act as if he knew what he was doing when in fact there may be some doubt and uncertainty. In some cases, he is able to share with his subordinates his doubt and uncertainty, realizing that they are mature enough to understand that no one in the situation has certainty. But in other instances, transmitting the feeling of uncertainty to a group that needs certainty would destroy any possibility of success. Thus, being confident is a delicate but invaluable power tactic.

ALWAYS BEING THE BOSS Subordinates do not want bosses to become subordinates. A boss cannot be a boss and a subordinate simultaneously. As long as organizations have hierarchy and positions of authority and responsibility, there will be bosses and there will be subordinates. This does not mean that the boss must constantly isolate himself from his subordinates. But it does mean that boss and subordinate have a mutual respect for the roles and psychological demands that are called for. The boss must stay away from some group meetings where he knows workers will be critical of him. The criticism, the "getting it off the chest," may be very healthy for the group, and his presence would just destroy the solution. Subordinates also want you to show evidence of your status and power. Their own power is enhanced if they work for a powerful boss.

MANAGING STATUS SYMBOLS[6] You can affect the power of yourself and others by managing the symbols of status and power. Recall from the preceding chapter that author Michael Korda mentioned the existence of a power spot in an office.[7] You might have the authority, for example, to move people in and/or out of the power spot, or to improve their status by giving them more "status-looking" desks. Gold-plated thermos jugs, type of car, and number of telephones are also symbols subject to your management.

MANAGING THE SOURCES OF POWER In Chapter 18, Table 18.2, we showed the amount of management control over sources of power. For example, as a manager, you have authority in terms of legitimate, functional, locational, and reward power sources. Manipulating these will change the chances that others will perceive you as having power.

The Tactics of Bluffing

Why must you bluff?

The idea of organizational bluffing comes to us from an article by Albert Z. Carr in the *Harvard Business Review* that generated a great deal of discussion and reaction because of its openness and frankness.[8] As we present some of Mr. Carr's ideas and positions, we would have you remember that the term "business" in this context could very easily be replaced by "organization." We have said repeatedly that managers in the future will be managers of many different kinds of organizations and that the behavior found in the business organization is likely to be found in other types of organizations.

How is business like a game of cards?

Carr believes that the ethics of a business are not necessarily those of society but are rather those of the poker game, and he uses the analogy of a poker game to illustrate his point. He says that in poker, as in business, the element of chance exists, yet the person who plays with skill is most likely to come out the winner

[6] The last two illustrations of tactics are from your present authors, not Martin and Sims.

[7] Michael Korda, *Power! How to Get It, How to Use It* (New York: Random House, 1975).

[8] Albert Z. Carr, "Is Business Bluffing Ethical?" *Harvard Business Review*, Vol. 46, No. 1 (January–February 1968), 143–53.

in the long run. Now, what are the rules or elements in a poker game that might also relate to a business world? In both games, according to Carr, "the ultimate victory requires intimate knowledge of the rules, insight into the psychology of the other player, a bold front, a considerable amount of self-discipline, and the ability to respond swiftly and effectively to opportunities provided by chance."[9] Thus far, the rules sound very similar to some of the insights we have been identifying throughout the previous chapters.

Carr maintains that there is a certain code of ethics, a certain expectation in a poker game that is different from the expectation of behavior in a church. It's expected in a poker game for one man to try to bluff another man even if that other man is his friend. The good poker player is one who is able to keep a straight face and be careful about the communication signals he displays. He does not want to give the other people in the game any knowledge of the cards he holds or the excitement he feels if he is dealt a winner. Certain poker players use a strategy of voluntarily losing early games to encourage opponents to stay in the game in anticipation of winning a big pot at the end of the evening. Carr identifies the special ethics in poker and says these ethics are not dishonest. A man who cheats at the game will receive punishments from the other players, and Carr is not suggesting that businessmen become cheaters.

How should you play the game?

Carr gives more meaning to the brand of ethics used in poker: "The game calls for distrust of the other fellow. It ignores the claim of friendship. Cunning deception and concealment of one's strength and intentions, not kindness and openheartedness, are vital to poker."[10] If a special brand of ethics is applicable to the poker game, should not a special brand of ethics be applicable in certain business transactions?

Just think for a few moments of the many situations where the brand of ethics that Carr speaks of applies. Would you expect the first offer of a union official at a collective bargaining session to be his final offer? Is it not true that both the public and the parties involved in negotiation expect a bargaining relationship to exist? Do you expect the first figure quoted by a car salesman to be his final offer, or one that can be negotiated? Do you make a monetary bid for a car that is the one and only bid, or do you anticipate a kind of "auction ethics" in which there will be negotiations and a great deal of give-and-take between buyer and seller?

Can you bluff on everything?

There are some areas in the relationships among people that

[9] *Ibid.*, p. 145.

[10] *Ibid.*

are not bargainable. We are not saying here that people expect negotiation and compromise in all areas. If you are given a ticket for speeding and must appear before a judge, it is unlikely that you and the judge will enter into negotiations as to the amount of fine. If you and your boss are having a performance appraisal, and your performance is measurable and the evidence is clear-cut, you probably do not enter a bluffing and bargaining contest with your boss. You may resort to other tactics—passing the buck or finding a scapegoat—but it is unlikely that you would bluff your boss in this kind of exchange.

A few statements concerning bluffing as an ethical consideration may summarize this discussion:

1. The strategy and tactics a manager uses must relate to the mores, culture, and standards of the organization that he deals with.
2. Using ethics or standards that are foreign to the organization may result in a breakdown of relationships in the organization.
3. Conforming to the expectations of other people is not an unethical or illegal practice.
4. Business bluffing (or organizational bluffing) seems to be a natural feature of organizational life and probably applies in many instances.

SUMMARY AND PROPOSITIONS

This chapter ends the short trip into the world of organizational power and politics. Our purpose was to show you the changes that a manager must make in his perception of the organizational world, his attitudes, and his decision-making approaches.

The section on managerial tactics outlined just a few of the ways that politics and tactics can be used for managing during the active implementation of strategy. Our discussion focused first on the important concept of managing *without* authority—an informal reality of the manager's world—and then concluded with a consideration of the tactics and ethics of bluffing.

Note that the theme of modification of traditional approaches permeates the ideas in this chapter. Armed with these new views of strategy and tactics, you should now be a bit more aware of the subtle qualities required of the manager. With this perspective, think through the following propositions carefully:

1. The successful manager is the one who knows how to get and use power.

2. The "smart" manager has learned the "facts of life" on the job, not in school.
   a. Most schools have an academic orientation and omit such topics from their programs.
   b. Power almost has to be felt to be realized; on-the-job situations can be felt.
3. Managers who spend most of their time with subordinates are ineffective managers. They also tend to be nonpromotables.
   a. Influence and power come from above or outside a manager's unit.
   b. Organizations and subordinates want managers with power and influence.
4. Bluffing, not lying, is a normal practice in organizations.
5. The successful and effective manager in the long run is one who:
   a. Knows how and when to modify his decisions.
   b. Knows how and when to "muddle through."
   c. Knows how and when to make marginal decisions and operate in the external arena.
   d. Knows how and when to bluff.

STUDY ASSIGNMENTS

1. *What is the relationship, if any, between tactics and politics?*
2. *Explain the attitude-modification model. What is its value to you?*
3. *We say that the five basic qualities of the managerial mind noted in Table 19.2 frequently appear as the language of basic management courses. Compare these qualities with the language presented in this book. What do you find? Explain possible reasons for your answers.*
4. *Compare the "muddling" decision-making model with the decision-making materials in Chapters 9 and 10. Are we describing the same world from two different perspectives, or two different worlds? Explain.*
5. *Make a 2 × 2 table and label the rows "similarities" and "dissimilarities" and the columns "modification" and "muddling." Make notes in each of the four cells and comment on your findings.*
6. *How can you manage without authority? Is this where power comes in?*

7. *What is meant by the expression, "A manager is a participant in external work flows"?*

8. *Do you feel bluffing is ethical? Give some situations where you would and would not engage in bluffing.*

9. *Why can't you learn the "facts of life" in school (Proposition 2)?*

10. *Assume Proposition 3 is true. What are the implications, then, for the training and development of managers?*

11. *Compare the part-opening illustrations for Part 4 with the part-opening illustrations for Parts 1, 2, and 3. What general differences and similarities in the subject matter of these parts can you deduce from what you see?*

situational episodes

1. You are really concerned about Chris. He has been in your department six months, and you had hoped he would have worked out. He hasn't. The man before Chris, John Baumgarten, had worked so well. You even had Chris spend one month with John before John moved back into the field. You thought some of John's skills would rub off on Chris.

   Being in Personnel, Chris has to deal with people in many different departments and at many different levels. Most of the complaints center on his attitude. Chris is called "pushy" by some. Others say he has a chip on his shoulder. Some even say he lords over them because of his advanced degrees from college.

   John had a college education as well, but somehow he was able to work with all kinds of people and get their cooperation.

   You're Chris' boss, and you feel something has to be done. Just what should you do?

2. Phil's behavior has changed recently, and you wonder what you should do. Phil transferred into your unit three months ago from the prestigious research labs at Stanford University. The parent organization sends its top scientists to a ten month "educational program." The past two years were exciting for Phil. He was in England before California and now he's in the old building in New Jersey.

   When Phil first came, you showed him his office and apologized at the same time. Your facilities are old and poor: small space, poor lighting, and dirty. But Phil laughed and said that stuff meant little to him and you laughed too.

   At first, all the other personnel were interested in hearing Phil's stories and experiences in his last two positions. Lately, his pep seems low, and others have complained that he isn't pulling his weight. You wonder why the situation has deteriorated and what you should do.

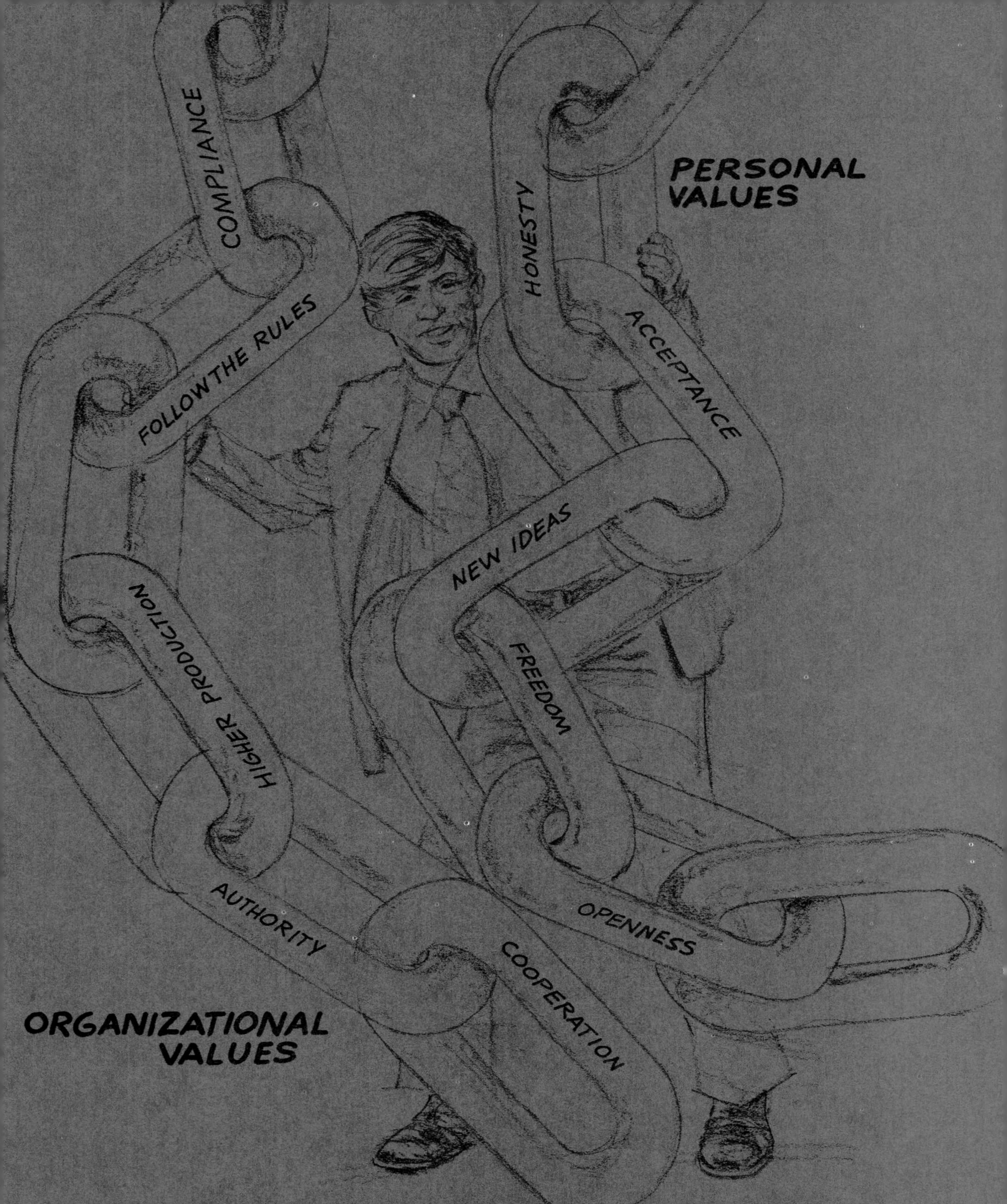
COMPLIANCE
FOLLOW THE RULES
HIGHER PRODUCTION
AUTHORITY
COOPERATION
HONESTY
ACCEPTANCE
NEW IDEAS
FREEDOM
OPENNESS
PERSONAL VALUES
ORGANIZATIONAL VALUES

the manager in a changing world

Fundamental, critical questions are being asked today by many people in organizations. What should I ultimately value? What responsibility do I have to myself and to my organization? Does an organization have a responsibility to society? Is a manager's responsibility to society different from his responsibility to his organization? These questions involve values and goals – personal, organizational, and social. In a changing world, these values also change, and this fact may be a source of major conflict.

Change affects people as well as organizations. The manager is personally involved in changes that neither occur at the same rate nor have the same source. The manager therefore frequently faces a conflict of interests and goals as he relates to the ever-occurring changes.

This last part of the book explores the subject of change and its consequences in considerable detail. Working out responses to changes and the resulting conflicts comprises a primary challenge that must be answered by the contemporary manager. Chapter 20 takes up the question of values and value changes through illustrations of value conflicts in the business world. After we explore some actual scenes of conflict, we discuss their possible causes and suggest ways of resolving both personal and organizational conflict. The managing forces of integration and innovation are the subjects of Chapter 21.

the conflict between organization and personal values

TWENTY

OBJECTIVES YOU SHOULD MEET

Identify *the types of conflict that managers face in organizations.*

Give *three examples of personal conflicts with organizations.*

Distinguish *among the three sources of personal values.*

List *four reasons why the bureaucratic form of organization conflicts with personal values.*

Identify *two reasons for and two reasons against the inevitability of conflict between man and his organizations.*

Compare *the four suggested managerial approaches with the approaches from earlier chapters on change, setting objectives, and leadership.*

TO TELL OR NOT TO TELL

"I'm in a real bind . . . don't know what to do . . . thought you might have a suggestion. . . . Do you have time for a long lunch on Thursday at the Ale House?"

Craig's call caught me off guard. I had been discussing new design changes with my people earlier and was taking a few minutes to reflect when the call came. I had known Craig for five years—we had both come to Lebanon, Pennsylvania, about the same time, lived close to each other, joined Kiwanis together, and were good golfing buddies. Even though Craig worked for a different company, we were both middle managers and shared many problems over a few beers.

"Craig, Thursday is fine. Let's beat the crowd and get there at 11:30. OK?"

Craig was obviously bothered. We had no sooner sat down at our table than he started. "Burt, you remember that I came here from our Decatur, Alabama, plant where I worked for five years. While there, I managed a group of managers." I wanted to interrupt Craig and ask what his immediate bind was—I always liked to relate to the big problem and work back from it—but I could see that Craig wanted to tell it all.

"Well, the other day, Tuesday, I was asked by my boss to give him a reading on Rick Benson, one of my managers in Alabama. Rick has requested a transfer to our plant here."

"So what's the big deal?" I said.

"Rick was a friend of mine, and the company is asking me to level with them." He paused. "Rick's an alcoholic, and I don't know what to tell my boss."

"Won't the company personnel file contain the info that Rick's got a drinking problem?"

"No. We're decentralized in personnel, and our plant manager was sensitive about keeping our problems to ourselves. He saw to it that stuff that might prove embarrassing to him never got in the files."

"Five years is a long time. Maybe Rick is over his problem." I was groping for some way to help.

"No. I bumped into a buddy on a trip to North Carolina and we talked about Rick. He's still the same. What bothers me is that I sometimes feel he drinks because of his situation at the plant. Rick's very outspoken and doesn't have good social manners, sober or high. I said to my wife Laura that if he could get out of that environment, his drinking could be stopped. So, here I am. On the one hand, I want to do right with Rick, help him if I can. I don't want to lie to my boss; but if I tell him Rick's drinking interferes with his relationships on the job, Rick won't get the job. My boss really values company loyalty, and if I withhold information from him, he'll think I'm disloyal. I've also known of cases where comments given in confidence got back to the original party."

"Craig, you really are in a bind."

The exchange between Burt and Craig is typical of the conflicts facing organization members. The issues and the decisions are subtle ones. No one is being asked to perform illegal acts. But in hundreds of ways, pressures exist to make a manager's day more than routine.

The vignette portrays another feature of conflicts—a person seems torn between two forces. On the one hand, you want to function as a responsible member of your organization; you want to be loyal. On the other hand, you want to be responsible to yourself or your friends. There are even times when the conflict arises between oneself and a group.

In most of the discussion that follows, the conflict presented is between the organization and a person. We'll look at conflict that you might experience as a member of an organization. We'll also place you in the role of a manager and face the problems of resolving the conflict. There are even illustrations in this chapter in which the manager himself is the primary cause of the conflict.

The objective of this chapter is similar to that of Part 4: to view a dimension of a manager's world in truth and openness. Differences between people and organizations are normal and expected. Frequently, these differences occur in minor and insignificant areas; but they also occur in values—areas that have deep meaning and impact. Table 20.1 shows examples of the differences between what an organization might want and what an individual might want. You can see, especially in the "Personal Wants" column, the values or beliefs behind the statements.

Value conflicts are the type we want to examine in Chapter 20, and we begin offering some brief examples of value conflicts in organizations.

TYPES OF ORGANIZATIONAL CONFLICT

Many value-conflict situations could be presented. You can think of many yourself. The Watergate affair of the mid-1970s serves as a type of value conflict generated in an organization when certain values (interdependence yet independence of the executive, judicial, and legislative branches) become confused with political goals (the reelection of the president). The price fixing and collusion of business firms make headlines in news media along with the crime and corruption found in labor unions and law-enforcement

TABLE 20.1 Potential Conflict Areas

Organizational Wants	Personal Wants
Dependability in behavior	Individual differences
Uniformity of action by management	Personalized situations
Authority in the hierarchy	Power, influence, recognition
Efficient use of scarce resources	Not to be treated like a machine
	Innovation and creativity, expression of identity

agencies. The examples that follow are intentionally selected so as to be less sensational.

Ideally, of course, you could spend a lifetime in management and not be embroiled with the volatile examples just mentioned. You might, however, find yourself in some of these situations to be presented—where your authority is challenged, your private rights are questioned, or your organizational security is threatened.

The Conflict: Authority Challenged

The first example is that of a manager in a marketing firm who has the responsibility for placing salesmen in different districts throughout the country. This manager started in the industry with the most competitive, dog-eat-dog firm. He moved to his present firm eight years ago and rose rapidly through the management levels to a vice-presidential position.

The job and its opportunities are so challenging and rewarding to him that he has turned down opportunities to move into other industries and other jobs. His family situation is organized and planned around his development in the firm, so that all things were looking bright.

One day he was called in by his boss and asked to reorganize one of his territories. He asked his boss why the reorganization was necessary and was told that the change was needed to accommodate one of the major stockholder's interests. This stockholder wanted one of his relatives to have responsibility in a particular new territory. When the manager balked at this recommendation, his boss told him that the stockholder owned more shares in the company than either of them and that they had better go along with his requests or look for employment elsewhere. The vice-president decided that the issue was not important enough to fight and that he would make the accommodation and change as requested.

Do managers get much outside pressure?

This incident is probably a common one among managers. They find that the formal job description of their position gives way to "special requests" from higher levels of power. The relationship between the vice-president of marketing and the major stockholder is fuzzy, but both the vice-president and his boss can sense the power of the major stockholder. At times like these, the vice-president may question how much freedom he has over his work unit; he may even recall that he has probably acted in the same manner with his own subordinates or peers, suggesting the power he has in order to influence their behavior. People caught in the middle of an authority and power squeeze frequently have to assess their personal values and priorities. If the issue is perceived as being "not too significant," accommodation and change probably take place.

The Conflict: Private Rights Questioned

The next illustration concerns a company, an individual, and the notion of "private citizenship" in community life.

On March 16, 1964, the Bethlehem Steel Company fired Philip B. Woodroofe, supervisor of municipal services at the Bethlehem, Pennsylvania, home office. The charge was that Woodroofe and his wife refused to comply with a company demand to resign from the Community Civic League, an organization to improve interracial relations. Woodroofe was the founder of the organization.[1]

The major events of this situation were as follows. The company, Bethlehem Steel, is the second largest steel company in the United States and dominates the economic and social life of the city of Bethlehem, Pennsylvania. There have been no civil rights demonstrations in this town, even though there has been a problem of inadequate housing for the poor and a high dropout rate for blacks in school.

Bethlehem Steel has demonstrated its consciousness of the civic community in a number of ways: It participates in air-pollution controls; it encourages its employees to participate in civic activities; on the surface, it seems supportive of active roles.

In May 1963, the Right Reverend Arthur Lichtenberger, presiding bishop of the Episcopalian Church in the United States, appealed to all church members to take an active and positive role in solving the country's racial problems. Philip Woodroofe took the appeal personally and started informal meetings between local black and white leaders to develop a new organization. On March 15, 1964, that organization was created, the Community Civic League.

Two days before the organizational meeting of the league, Woodroofe was informed by his superiors that they were not pleased with his involvement in these activities. He was advised to get out of the league, and they gave him a few days to make his decision. Woodroofe decided to remain with the league and was released from the company the next Monday at 10:15.

[1] Discussion of the Bethlehem Steel Company and the Woodroofe incident is found in F. Prakash Sethi, *Up Against the Corporate Wall* (Englewood Cliffs, N.J.: Prentice-Hall, 1970), pp. 215–22.

Bethlehem Steel told the press that Woodroofe had resigned, a statement that Woodroofe denied and one that the community would not accept. The company later made an official statement that it would be willing to send an official representative to the Community Civic League.

The league's board of directors rejected the offer by Bethlehem Steel, saying that it wanted members to serve willingly as individuals and not as representatives of any church, industry, business, or profession, but it took no official position on the Woodroofe incident. On June 30, 1964, Philip Woodroofe resigned from the board of directors, since he planned to move to New York where he had reportedly accepted a real estate job.

This incident has an ending different from the first illustration. Again we see a conflict between what a manager believes he has the freedom to do and what the company believes is in its best interests. To Philip Woodroofe, his life as a responsible private citizen was beyond the scope of company influence and control. It is difficult to tell from the data in this incident whether Bethlehem Steel was opposed to the idea of a Community Civic League or to the role Woodroofe played. Whatever the motive, we know that Bethlehem Steel fired Woodroofe. They apparently felt his role was not beyond their scope of influence and authority.

Do organizations have any "rights" over you as a private citizen?

This conflict becomes increasingly important as the movement for responsible managerial participation in community affairs increases. You can anticipate the problems that would arise if you, as a member of a firm publishing high school texts, get elected to a school board that has the authority to decide on textbook selection. Other "difficult sets" include a member of a community board on pollution control who is a management member of a chemical plant, a major area polluter; a volunteer member of a nonprofit housing board who works for a local general contractor; a faculty member of the state university who is a member of a committee studying the ethical behavior of state legislators. The conflict area, therefore, will account for many crises of values.

The Conflict: Organizational Rights

In this conflict situation, the question of due process of law is raised, and our illustration is not an incident but rather a descriptive paragraph from a professor concerned with this problem. Prof. William M. Evan speaks of the organization man and due process of law.[2]

[2] Charles E. Summer and Jeremiah J. O'Connell, *The Managerial Mind* (Homewood, Ill.: Richard D. Irwin, 1968), pp. 85–89.

Evan compares the organizational man (that is, the manager) to the unionized manual worker and finds that the manager comes off a poor second. The manager lacks the right of appeal, he is at the mercy of the decisions of his boss, he does not have the protection of any outside occupational organization, he does not have a code of professional ethics to govern his relationships, he does not have the protection of peer control, and he learns to meet the expectations of his superiors because his own performance is usually subjectively evaluated. In one way, the organization of man's life is the process of adapting himself to the expectations and behavior patterns of his superior.

Evan's analysis may be applied to the case of Philip Woodroofe. You may have felt that an injustice had fallen on Woodroofe. Why should a private citizen be fired for trying to be a responsible member of the community? It is unlikely that Woodroofe would have been fired for the same activity if he had been a union member, fully protected by contract and federal law. Thus, managers are second-class citizens in terms of their own labor relations.

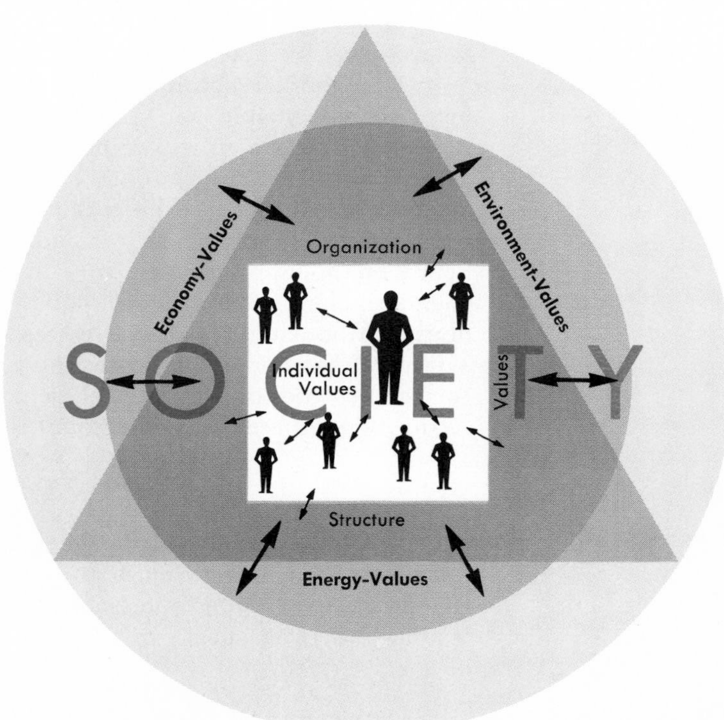

FIGURE 20.1 Causes of value conflicts

TABLE 20.2 Basic Value Perceptions

Category	Source	Instrument	Major Value	Term
1. Religious	Deity	Faith	Charity Love of God Neighbor	Moral theology
2. Philosophic	Man	Reason	Justice Exchange Equity	Ethics Descriptive Normative Critical
3. Cultural	Society Nation Ethnic group Corporations	Experience	Progress Pluralism Competition Individualism	Mores

SOURCE: Clarence C. Walton, *Ethos and the Executive* (Englewood Cliffs, N.J.: Prentice-Hall, 1969), p. 24.

When conflicts in values arise between managers and organizations, must there be such an imbalance of power between the two parties?

In many examples of the types of conflict that exist, the confrontation seems to be one of differing values. The individual comes into the organization with one set of values that dictate a particular form of behavior and finds himself in an organization that may have a totally different set of values. Much can be learned if we take time to search out the possible causes of these value conflicts. (See Figure 20.1.) Four such causes are (1) the differing sources of values, (2) the differing values of organizations and individuals, (3) the bureaucratic structure itself, and (4) the disagreement within society's goals and values.

POSSIBLE CAUSES OF VALUE CONFLICTS

Multiple Value Sources

Could the problems come from your own values?

People are in conflict over values because values differ. One reason these values differ is that they come from different sources. Table 20.2 suggests why you may find conflict within yourself. For instance, your value of individualism may conflict with your value of equity when the issue is the employment of minorities.

You can see from Table 20.2 that the source of religious values is a deity, that the instrument of this source is faith, that the major value is charity, or love of God and neighbor, and that the major term for expressing the value is *moral theology*. So too with the philosophic category of values, whose source comes from man. The basic instrument is reason, its major value is justice, and the term that identifies the value is *ethics*. In the cultural category, the society is the major source, with nations, ethnic groups, and corporations contributing to the cultural values. The instrument for the value is experience, and the value expressed is progress, in terms of either pluralism, competition, or individualism. When we speak of values in the cultural category, we are usually talking about the mores of a people, nation, or group.

This table enables you to see the potential conflict between personal values and organizational values. For example, you may have a value of charity for your neighbor and find that this comes into direct conflict when your neighbor happens to be a competitor of your firm. You may value progress but find that the value of competition runs into direct conflict with the value of individualism. The importance of this discussion is that managers must continually keep in mind the individual value differences of others as well as themselves. Of course, this is only one cause of value conflict. The dissimilarity between individual and organizational values constitutes another major cause of conflict.

Idealized Personal Values vs. Realistic Organizational Values

In Table 20.1, we pictured the tugs and pulls on an employee as the organization demands behavior at odds with personal wants. Basic to those behavior descriptions are differences in what an organization values and what an individual values. Differences will always exist but these differences frequently stem from idealized personal values. Many of the personal values held by Americans seem more appropriate for the 18th rather than the 20th century. Values born in a country with openness, much inhabitable land, and mobility will conflict with values in a country plagued by overcrowded cities, large populations, and limits on growth.

Such conflicts between individuals and organizations are the subject of a book edited by Kuhn and Berg.[3] The following state-

[3] James W. Kuhn and Ivar Berg, eds., *Values in a Business Society: Issues and Analyses* (New York: Harcourt Brace Jovanovich, 1968).

ments, paraphrased from selections throughout this work, are given with the intention of showing the areas of potential conflict in personal values. Notice how many depict the idealized-realistic conflict.

> Americans have traditionally been hostile toward organizations and bureaucracy: big government, big business, and now big schools, unions, churches, and so on.
>
> We value self-employment. We have a Small Business Administration, and the Defense Department favors small business in its contracts.
>
> Employees respond to "normlessness" and rootlessness of urban life by becoming members of work groups.
>
> Employees become dependent on corporations to give their lives direction and meaning. Such dependence allows them to escape the burdens of personal responsibility.
>
> Industrial engineers design jobs to serve machines, not men.
>
> Although individualism is highly praised in America, bureaucracy, which often requires that the individual be treated impersonally, has become our way of life.
>
> Efficiency, valued as highly as individualism, regularly demands that certain organizational needs have higher priority than the rights of individuals.

Notice from reading these statements how often the organizational goals and values find expression in a certain structure (bureaucracy). We know from earlier study (Chapters 3, 6, and 8) that structure, either in design or in procedures, rules, and regulations, greatly determines behavior. In fact, the purpose of Part 3, "The Processes for Managing," is to influence the behavior of others in the attainment of some work goal. Thus, structure is an important source of value conflict, as you will see more vividly in the following paragraphs discussing the work of Marshall Dimock on bureaucracy, Chris Argyris on the personality and the organization, and Raymond Baumhart on the relationship of work to business ethics. The topic we discuss now is bureaucracy, the form of organizaton structure that is most applicable to large organizations. What are some features of bureaucracy?

The Bureaucratic Structure Itself

ITS MEMBERS When organizations grow large, it is necessary to make a distinction among types of workers. The top level of management is comprised of *executives*. These are the people who either own the corporation or establish the major goals, objectives, and policies. At the other end of the personnel picture we find the *workers*, a group that performs directly on the product of the organization. The group in the middle, the middle managers (also called *bureaucrats*), is charged with executing the policies and practices of higher management. Each group has its own culture and values. They frequently see things differently and thus form a source of conflict.

bureaucrats

Bureaucracy

ITS FORM In a *bureaucracy*, certain characteristics are present. Some of these are:

An emphasis on form. Bureaucracy is a form of organization.

An emphasis on hierarchy. All the units of an organization are under the control and supervision of some higher unit of the organization.

An emphasis on specialization of work. The work in the organization is clearly defined and specialized as much as possible. People are hired to perform specialized tasks.

A spirit of competence. The task specializations are well known, and members are aware of the specialists in all parts of the organization. People tend to do only what they are assigned to do.

Established norms of conduct. People throughout the organization have confidence that a great deal of behavior is predictable. Policies, procedures, and rules are very explicit, and individual behavior is defined very narrowly within the organizational constraints.

Many records and reporting. To ensure the predictability of performance within a bureaucracy, the behavior of individuals is reported to higher levels of management so that control can be maintained.[4]

Are bureaucracies good?

There are many management writers who delight in attacking the essential features of bureaucracy, and there are many who delight in supporting those essential features. There is obvious value in efficient administration under a system of law and rules, and in a hierarchy that gives some predictability to behavior, outlines precise job jurisdictions, calls for specialization of effort, promotes the professionalization of a management group, favors impersonality of attitude and procedure, and stands for continuity of

[4] Adapted from John M. Pfiffner and Frank P. Sherwood, *Administrative Organization* (Englewood Cliffs, N.J.: Prentice-Hall, 1960), pp. 56–57.

office and function. You can see why the ideal bureaucratic model first described by Max Weber was attractive to American businessmen, for Weber wrote during the early stages of organizational growth in this country, when managers faced many problems of structure.[5] You can also see why the form of bureaucracy is a source of potential conflict. A bureaucrat values the six characteristics just mentioned. In a contemporary world that emphasizes involvement, individuality, freedom, and personal growth and worth, the bureaucratic description of organizations often runs counter to the demands and needs of many of its members.

Much of the material in Part 3 of this book is an outgrowth of the knowledge of the bureaucratic form of organization. The idea that managers are professionals or that management is a separate field for study and training is also a product of the bureaucratic form of organization. Thus, managers live with this structure and behave within its definitions and limits.

The bureaucratic model of formal organization is just that—a description of how an organization should function. We are familiar with the weaknesses of bureaucracy as we try to live with the problems of large organizations. A few of the most frequent inefficiencies of bureaucracies emphasize the point that any descriptive model works only when its human inputs are added and cooperating.

Why can't you ever get a direct answer from a large organization?

Its Problems Marshall Dimock writes about bureaucracy and lists 26 distinct pathologies or weaknesses.[6] A few of these pathologies will give us an idea of what he means, for most of us have experienced some. They include excessive red tape, runaround, buck passing, indifference, impersonality, duplication, inflexibility, complacency, waste, featherbedding, and conformity.

Dimock believes that problem behavior in bureaucracies is due to an imbalance between the role of the individual and that of the group. He states that people in a bureaucracy tend to react to such imbalance in three ways:

> People working in large organizations tend to become *self-centered.*
>
> People working in large organizations tend to *avoid responsibility* if they can.

[5] Max Weber, *The Protestant Ethic and the Spirit of Capitalism,* trans. Talcott Parsons (London: George Allen and Unwin, 1930 and 1948).

[6] Marshall E. Dimock, *Administrative Vitality* (New York: Harper & Row, 1959), pp. 102–4.

> People working in large organizations tend to compensate for their declining status by attempts to *exert their power.*

Are there no positive responses to value conflict in bureaucracy?

It is difficult for us to avoid judgment and evaluation of these three responses. From an organizational point of view, they do not seem to be the kind of behavior that is wanted or rewarded. This type of behavior might even be called dysfunctional, or harmful to the overall interests of the organization. From the viewpoint of the individual member of an organization, organizational members who are self-centered, avoid responsibility, and take advantage of their power do not have the behavioral characteristics you would consider valuable in a subordinate, peer, or boss.

What are some "truths" about big organizations?

Another tendency in bureaucracies is to increase staff and budgets with little regard to objectives or necessity. The "ballooning" effects of bureaucracy are perhaps best identified by C. Northcote Parkinson.[7] In his short work, Professor Parkinson describes some of his "laws." He states that work expands to fill the time available for its completion. Bureaucratic officials make work for each other and expand their staff by hiring inferior personnel, since an official wants to multiply subordinates, not rivals. More time is spent considering trivial than important projects, committees expand and become less effective as they grow, and organizations devote more and more attention to form and less to substance. Another "law" applicable to our interests says that as budgets grow, the work expands to fit the budgets. Although some managers and professional people feel that Parkinson was writing with tongue in cheek, there are many practicing managers who will verify the existence of these laws in large organizations.

What is the Peter Principle?

A similar reaction developed after the publication of *The Peter Principle.* The "Peter Principle" is simple: in a hierarchy, every employee tends to rise to his *level of incompetence.* The Peter Corollary to the Peter Principle reads, "In time, every post tends to be occupied by an employee who is incompetent to carry out its duties."[8]

Whether it be Parkinson or Peter, the message of the critics is clear: The traditional Weber model of bureaucracy falls short of its efficiency goal because of the performance of its participants. The formal organization structure undoubtedly gives rise to a kind of

[7] C. Northcote Parkinson, *Parkinson's Law* (Cambridge, Mass.: The Riverside Press, 1957), pp. 2–12.

[8] Laurence J. Peter and Raymond Hull, *The Peter Principle* (New York: William Morrow, 1969), p. 8.

behavior based upon certain organizational values, and this required behavior may come in conflict (as it obviously does) with individually desired behavior.

Why should organizations accommodate personal values?

An additional elaboration of the conflict between required organizational behavior and the individual is presented by Chris Argyris in his classic work, *Personality and Organization.*[9] In this book, Argyris argues for a self-actualization type of man, saying that the human personality wants to grow, develop, and express its psychological energy.

He believes that in most organizations, especially formal organizations based upon the rules and regulations of bureaucracy, there is a basic conflict between the needs of a mature personality and the requirements of a formal organization. For example, if the principles of formal organization are used, employees will be in a work environment where:

They have minimal control over their work.

They are expected to be passive, dependent, and subordinate.

They are expected to have a short time perspective.

Only their shallow abilities are required.

They are expected to produce under conditions leading to psychological failure.

The values identified in these behavioral expectations seem at odds with the language and insights given to us from the behavioral sciences, especially the ideas on motivation and Theory Y–type leadership styles.

Aren't all organizations somewhat bureaucratic, and thus won't values always be in conflict?

We now see better what the confrontation looks like. It would appear that the traditional goals and structure of organizations may be in conflict with the needs and goals of a developing personality.

Does it help to know how businessmen behave?

Dimock and Argyris pointed their fingers at the organization for creating conflict with the individual. In a study by Raymond Baumhart, other forces appear as contributory. In his book, *Ethics in Business,* Father Baumhart revealed the results of a survey of 1,800 businessmen.[10] Six summary statements adapted from the book are helpful in our search to see what causes value conflicts:

[9] Chris Argyris, *Personality and Organization* (New York: Harper & Row, 1957).

[10] Raymond Baumhart, S. J., *Ethics in Business* (New York: Holt, Rinehart & Winston, 1968).

Personnel problems cause the ethical dilemmas of deepest concern to businessmen.

The golden rule is not an adequate norm for solving most ethical problems.

There is a relationship between type of job and ethics. It is easier, for example, to be ethical in accounting and engineering jobs than in jobs such as selling or purchasing.

Competition is the greatest factor in influencing ethical behavior. Ethical problems arise from situations where either too little or too much competition exists.

A person with extensive formal education is usually more aware of ethical issues, but his education appears to have little effect on his business decisions. His conscience, or sense of values, developed before adolescence through parental influence, is a more powerful influence.

Church affiliation is not related to ethical attitudes.

Two of these statements stand out from the rest whenever managers consider the forces contributory to value conflicts. Competition, the hallmark of our economic system, is the greatest factor in influencing ethical behavior. Often, it is the behavior that is legal but morally questionable that causes ethical friction. In addition, the type of job affects our likelihood of encountering such conflict, since values are more likely to be challenged in a sales job, for instance, than in a research-unit position. Thus, the goals of the organization and those of the individual are frequently out of accord. Many organizations create structures and jobs that encourage behavior at odds with the values of many of its members.

Our view so far has been limited to areas of direct work-related areas. This view changes as we look to a broader spectrum. As private citizens in a changing world, we have our values challenged and sometimes changed by the myriad changes going on in our volatile society. A person today must stand ready to defend or reorder his value system as a result of challenges from people whose systems differ, from organizations that hold self-sustaining priorities, and from a society in a state of self-examination.

Disagreement about Society's Goals and Values

The values of society seem to change more rapidly each year. Beliefs we thought secure are altered as some crisis brings a reassessment. Many contemporary writers call the present period a "postindustrial state." It is known, for example, that most of the new jobs created in our economy during the years 1960 to 1970 were in the public rather than private sector. We know also that we are rapidly approaching a time when an increasingly smaller percentage of our population can contribute and produce the needs of most of society. Our nation, whose ideas and values have been based on an industrial growth model, will have to find a new model if we are entering a time when the notions of productivity, economic contributions, and economic growth no longer make sense.

The dynamic shifts in values make a complete analysis of the topic impossible, for values cherished when this book is written may be revised by the time it is read. What we offer, therefore, is a look into the types of values that are under pressure to change. Such pressure creates an instability about these values and opens the door to many personal and organizational value conflicts. The three types of values selected are (1) the profit motive, (2) technology, and (3) growth. Table 20.3 shows the converging pressures to change the three values.

For example, the profit motive is under attack by political liberals, extreme radicals, and consumer advocacy groups. But even if you belong to none of these groups, your belief in the profit motive may be shaken when you read what men do in the name of profit. Robert L. Heilbroner and other authors, most of whom were reporters, have written the true stories of executives of B. F. Goodrich, Richardson-Merrell, General Motors, Dow Chemical, and other companies. These executives, solid citizens of their communities, engaged in questionable behavior. One ordered his subordinate to fake a lab report; others bribed a city official to get a zoning advantage; and some kept selling and promoting a drug they knew had terrible side effects.[11]

Many voices are also being heard raised in protest against our worship of technology as a means to solve society's problems. You can easily understand how Americans might value technology and engineering know-how, since U.S. ingenuity was credited with the victories in both world wars. Health and food problems throughout the world are frequently solved through the use of technology. But people like Rene Dubos are troubled about our losing our humanness to our mechanized surroundings.[12] Perhaps we place too much value on technology as savior.

[11] Robert L. Heilbroner et al., *In the Name of Profit* (Garden City, N.Y.: Doubleday, 1972).

[12] Rene Dubos, *So Human an Animal* (New York: Scribner's, 1968).

TABLE 20.3 Pressures Which Cause Disagreement About Values

Forces Attacking:		Forces Supporting:
	Value: The Profit Motive	
Profits lead to exploitation	P R O	Need Profits to keep organization going
Profits become the ends rather than the means	F I T	Profits mean competition: the American Way of Life
Profits reduce man into an economic, non human factor of production	M O T I	Profits reward the strong, eliminate the wasteful, inefficient
A profit motive creates a win-lose situation—brings out the worst in mankind.	V E	Profits create jobs, new products, health in an economy
	Value: Technology	
It dehumanizes society	T E C H	Society's problems are so complex, only technology can solve them
It has caused more human problems	N O L O	The material advances are a direct result in our technological advances
Scientific thinking led to the atom bomb, nerve gas, napalm, and other instruments for the efficient destruction of man	G Y	Mankind cannot stop technology from growing. It is a product of education
The worship of technology leads man into a blind alley—believing the basic problems of man are amenable to scientific solutions.		Technology can identify the basic questions and thus allow mankind the opportunity for political or philosophical thinking
	Value: Growth	
The planet has limits	G R O	Society has no choice but to grow. No growth is death.
Growth rates of the consuming forces are exponential. Resources will be consumed faster than they will be resupplied.	W T H	Growth expands the distribution of wealth.

TABLE 20.3 (continued)

Each new level of growth brings unknown and unexperienced pressures for immediate solutions.	The U.S. must maintain growth equal or greater than the growth of its ideological adversaries.
The world is in a constant state of disequilibrium and war may seem the only solution.	Growth has been good to us and will continue to be good.
	There are untapped resources that science will discover. To deliberately stop growth would destroy a successful civilization.

Such critics often raise questions about our general approval of growth as well. For years, the philosophers who warned us about the unthinking exploitation of the world's resources were viewed as critics of the American way. The unbelievable growth of populations plus the realization of the scarcity of resources have led to some new thinking about the value of unlimited growth. Books like *The Limits to Growth,*[13] *The End of Affluence,*[14] and *The Peter Plan*[15] sound the alarm. Managers, both as citizens and as corporate decision makers regarding the use of scarce resources, now face more difficult decisions—ones based upon values. What is the price of progress? Can we grow with no regard for the impact growth has upon limited resources?

These questions will not be answered in this chapter nor in this book. They may not be answered during this century. What is important is that they are being asked. And because the values that many have taken as sacred for so many years are now being questioned, managers can expect an increase in the number of conflicts. They will face more personal conflicts when they are asked to engage in some corporate activity that they feel damages the earth. They will find more instances where other members of their organization may speak out or refuse to comply with directives that conflict with their values. Knowing that value conflict and confrontation might well be on the increase in organizations

[13] Dennis Meadows et al., *The Limits to Growth* (New York: New American Library, a Signet book, 1972).

[14] Paul and Anne Ehrlick, *The End of Affluence* (New York: Ballantine, 1974).

[15] Laurence J. Peter, *The Peter Plan: A Proposal for Survival* (New York: William Morrow and Company, 1976).

increases the need to search for some approaches to conflict resolution. The next section provides some guides for managers of organizations.

PERSONAL COPING MECHANISMS FOR VALUE DIFFERENCES

Why do you take value conflicts so seriously?

Conflicts in values can produce a deep impact on and have serious consequences for the people involved. Values are different from opinions or attitudes in that the whole person is involved in values. For example, you may have an opinion about a movie you have seen or a book you have read; you may have an attitude toward some of the human crises existing between a government and its people; you probably have a value statement about life, death, honesty, morality, or your fellow man. When you put your values on the line, you put yourself on the line. Thus, a conflict in values can be a very traumatic experience.

You respond to conflicts and attacks on your values in different ways. For example, some people respond to conflict physically: They suffer from ulcers, alcoholism, heart disease, and even mental breakdowns. The body responds to the threat or attack by reducing the tension or returning the situation to some state of balance. There are other, less drastic approaches. Some of these approaches have been mentioned throughout this book. Defense mechanisms, as discussed earlier, are an obvious form of response to conflict. Other examples are offered here as representative of some responses people make to personal value differences.

Accommodate and Suffer

Can you add some of your own responses?

This approach seems best illustrated in the incident related earlier in which the vice-president of marketing realized that his power and authority were limited and his ideas about his personal freedom got challenged from a pressure source above him. The vice-president yielded and changed for the sake of his position and future with the company. He probably had to go through the painful experience of reviewing his own personal values and concluding that some would have to be sacrificed for the sake of others.

Accommodate and Gain

This approach is the other side, a more positive side of that incident. The reexamination of personal values may result in a more realistic placement of values. It is possible that the vice-president had a set of values that had been unrealistic for years, and the revision at this point in his career might be a most favorable and healthy act. He and his family might gain from the challenge.

Fight and Lose

Another incident given earlier serves as the basis for explaining this approach. A conflict existed between Bethlehem Steel and Philip Woodroofe concerning his involvement in a community league. Woodroofe fought for his rights as a private citizen, and in the short run it may seem that he lost the fight—he was dismissed from the company. We do not know what impact his actions had on other situations in the town or in the company. He was forced out of his job and left the community for a new job and perhaps a new career. In the short run, it appears that the company was able to have its values dominate the situation.

Fight and Win

Frequently, people stand up for their personal values in opposition to the organization, and the organization is the one that gives ground. It may be the power of the issue, or the status of the individual, or a set of circumstances that develop behind the scenes that ultimately decides a specific case. It is possible, however, to fight and win on a value conflict.

Create Your Own Group

This approach develops when one unit is attacked by another unit. A scientist who finds his professional values under attack by the production department may find support from the other professionals throughout the organization. He may even pursue a deliberate course to obtain support via formal and informal meetings and luncheons with those colleagues who share similar values and positions. Our individual is thus able to protect his own position and develop security in the numbers who rally around him.

Overreact

You may overreact to a value-conflict situation and emphasize the very values and behavior you abhor. The manager who values personal freedom and privacy but sees all his peers promoted because of their country-club affiliation may suddenly go overboard in his conformity and extroverted behavior in the same club.

Go Outside for Rewards

When the individual finds himself blocked or finds that his values are at variance with those of the organization, he may turn his attention and efforts to rewarding activities outside the organization. He participates in activities that enable him to express his values.

The following illustration may help you understand the need for adaptability when values conflict. Companies usually designate after a performance evaluation whether the manager is promotable or nonpromotable to a higher position. The indication that you are nonpromotable usually means that the organization no longer cares to use its resources and reward mechanisms on you. Frequently, the nonpromotable manager has established enough "protection" within the company so that firing does not follow. An interviewer questioning one such person found the conversation to be extremely boring. As the interviewer prepared to leave the office, some word was mentioned about the outside activity of the manager, and in a few minutes the manager was excitedly telling of his involvement in scheduling the buses for the county school board. Obviously, he had a great amount of unused talent that was no longer perceived as needed in the organization. He adapted by finding his need satisfied outside the organization. From a psychological viewpoint, each day on the company job was deadly, and the manager looked forward to the end of his workday so that he could turn his attention to more exciting activities.

The options just mentioned are bleak because most of them call for the manager to be an underachiever when faced with conflict. Is there no management solution in organizations that will give hope to those facing personal value conflict? Where else can a manager learn the behavior response to some value conflicts?

ORGANIZATIONAL MECHANISMS FOR RESOLVING CONFLICT

What can you do as a manager in an organization?

In the final section of this chapter, we offer additional solutions to what seems to be a difficult crisis resulting from value conflicts. So far, we have looked at some possible responses the individual can make on his own. Now we want to see if the organization itself might offer some possibilities for working out problems in this

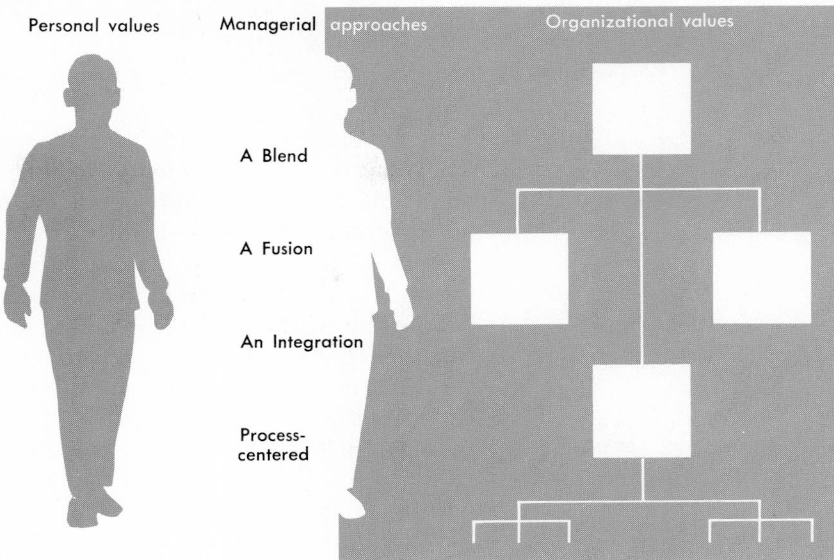

FIGURE 20.2 Conflict resolution through managerial approaches

area. What can a manager do in situations where he faces conflict but has some authority and power?

We review here the suggestions of four writers in the management field who have given much thought to new managerial styles and techniques. These four techniques—blend, fusion, integration, and process orientation—are not really different (Figure 20.2). You will sense the presence of a mood of accommodation and cooperation in each of these techniques, rather than approaches requiring highly structured and specified tools for the resolution of conflict.

A Blend

Marshall Dimock calls for a blend in administrative strategy and tactics.[16] He identifies the advantages of bureaucracy as its efficient use of technology and its orderliness. He also identifies the strong points of "enterprise"—its ability to innovate and adapt to change. Dimock calls for a blending of the two advantages into what he calls the "administrative vitality style." According to this approach, managers should attempt *administration by objectives.* Institutional objectives are democratically defined and redefined to give each unit a clear picture of its role in the total operation. Dimock's recommendations are similar to those mentioned in Chapter 11 when we talked about management by objectives.

administration by objectives

Does MBO help resolve conflict?

[16] Dimock, *Administrative Vitality.*

A Fusion

E. Wight Bakke and Chris Argyris call for a fusion process.[17] They say that people attempt to pursue their own goals so as to seek fulfillment and self-actualization. This is called the *personalizing process.* The organization, on the other hand, attempts to get people to devote their energies to the pursuit of organization goals. This is called the *socializing process.* The *fusion process* is the process by which the personalizing and socializing processes work together. Compromise and adjustment are necessary. Unifying and coordinating are called for. In the final stage of this process, the individual and organizational goals are viewed as identical or in harmony with one another.

personalizing process

socializing process

fusion process

How is fusion similar to blend?

Integration

Chris Argyris is the proponent of this idea, which is similar to the fusion process. Argyris calls for a "mix" model to achieve integration, and he identifies dimensions that are essential for any organization. According to Argyris, the healthy individual should be in a world in which he has *greater power and control* over his work world. The objectives he is achieving should be *central* ones. His *time perspective* should be expanded. To accomplish all this, the style of management would allow the individual to have a greater opportunity to *define his goals,* to *define the path* to these goals, and to develop a realistic level of aspiration, which should result in a greater probability of achievement.[18]

Centering on Processes

Warren H. Schmidt talks in terms of the need for a new kind of organization, one that is *process-centered.*[19] He talks about specific functions; for example, planning is not so much a program as a process, a social process. The planning on projects should include bargaining and accommodation among interest groups. Schmidt believes this approach will lead to innovative joint problem solving and the organization thus will be a healthy, changing, adaptive, ongoing system.

Would you like to work for a process-centered boss?

[17] E. Wight Bakke and Chris Argyris, *Organization Structure and Dynamics* (New Haven, Conn.: Yale University, Labor and Management Center, 1954).

[18] Chris Argyris, *Personality and Organization* (New York: Harper & Row, 1957), pp. 159–60.

[19] Warren H. Schmidt, *Organizational Frontiers and Human Values* (Belmont, Calif.: Wadsworth, 1970).

This problem-solving approach was the focal point of a study investigating effective methods of managing conflict.[20] Fifty-seven managers described examples of effective and ineffective resolution of conflict. Each of these statements was coded into one of the following five methods of conflict resolution:

1. Withdrawal—refraining from the conflict
2. Smoothing—playing down differences between parties
3. Compromise—splitting the difference; no one loses, no one wins
4. Forcing—a win-lose situation
5. Confrontation, or problem solving—open exchange of information; a working through of differences

Confrontation, or problem solving, was the most effective method, and forcing the most ineffective. The author goes on to describe the characteristics of problem solving and concludes with a suggestion that managers can improve their managing of conflict resolution if they can develop a more positive attitude toward disagreement. Win-lose situations, where there is a victor, must give way to a more collaborative relationship, where all win and no one loses. A "helping relationship" climate needs developing, and interpersonal skills contribute to this climate.

A FINAL WORD ON CONFLICT RESOLUTION

We showed earlier in this chapter that a conflict often exists because of the differences in values between individuals and organizations. It would be unfair and wrong to say that conflict is something that should be eliminated from organizational life. Conflict is not an evil concept, since it does highlight and pinpoint those parts in an organization that are giving honest, if negative, feedback. Thus, conflict can be viewed as constructive; yet such value conflict is very difficult to resolve.

There are those who say that organizations will fulfill their obligations to society if they keep their primary, profit-maximization goals clearly in sight, and that individuals must subordinate

[20] Ronald J. Burke, "Methods of Resolving Interpersonal Conflict," in *A Contingency Approach to Management: Readings,* by John W. Newstrom et al. (New York: McGraw-Hill, 1975), pp. 482–91.

their wills for the greater good of the organization. These people maintain that if an organization puts primary focus on the human elements, the organization may not survive. Opponents of this view say that an organization functions only as a collection of individuals and that the goals are achieved by and for people. Both these position statements contain some truth. How such different views become reconciled is a matter of conflict response.

Obviously, a dilemma exists. If left to itself, the organization will stress its goals and values; if left to himself, the individual will stress his personal goals and values. It is to the manager of the organization that the great challenge is presented. He makes the inputs that can potentially blend, fuse, and integrate. He has the power and authority to reconcile differences. He is the one who can become process-oriented so that the organization behaves like a dynamic human system.

SUMMARY AND PROPOSITIONS

There can be little doubt that confrontations between diverse values cause conflicts in the business world. We have attempted to place such clashes in a real setting in the first section of this chapter. Three different conflict situations served to illustrate the varied ways in which value conflicts occur. Generally speaking, these conflicts arise between personal and organizational goals and values.

We attempted a deeper analysis of this problem in the second section, where possible causes of value conflict were explored. The multiplicity of value sources explains why values are so dissimilar. Bureaucratic structure and changing societal values were also singled out for scrutiny. Our search found a fertile field of value conflicts, and no doubt there are many more.

The main purpose of the last sections of the chapter was to examine the ways managers can respond to interpersonal and organizational conflicts. We found that most of the personal coping mechanisms had negative effects for both individuals and organizations. Our final section on manager responses using organizational means provided the most constructive material. Here, blending, fusion, integration, and a process orientation were offered as approaches suggested by other authorities. Actually, all four are similar and represent a flexibility and openness toward the settling of conflict.

Additional insights may be developed by viewing the following propositions:

1. Much of the behavior conflict in organizations stems from value conflicts.
   a. Few people are fully aware of their values, and they relate to values only through behavioral clashes.

   b. Values are what make the human resources of an organization human.

   c. Values "run deep" in people and are the base by which many people "interpret" behavior.

2. Change is a threat to values.

   a. People have trouble adjusting to rapid change, for it shakes them up.

   b. If managers can manage change, they may be able to reduce value conflict.

3. Conflict between organizational and personal values is a fact of life.

   a. The organization must develop values for a world that includes many external forces (government, competitors, customers).

   b. Individual values tend to be personal and confined to a smaller world.

4. Although the bureaucratic form of organization has been under constant criticism, its efficiency and the increasing size of modern organizations will cause the form to remain a source of value conflicts.

5. Without managerial intervention, individual responses to conflict resolution have only short-run use.

   a. Individual responses tend to be directed toward tension reduction and not at the cause of the conflict. The conflict may reappear.

   b. Dialogue with your managerial superiors is critical for there to be any long-run growth from the conflict situation.

6. Religious forces have little influence on the ethical practices of businessmen.

   a. The businessman has been able to create two worlds for himself. In his business world, religion plays a small part.

   b. Most religious guidelines are too idealistic for managers who must live in a "situational" world.

7. Greater organizational growth and production can coexist with greater individual growth, productivity, and satisfaction if the values and goals of both are in harmony.

   a. Reliance on authority measures can get only minimal results. When forced to comply, members will not voluntarily pick up organizational slack.

b. Most people in organizations would rather function in harmony than in disharmony.

8. Member participation in organizational functions is the most critical factor in conflict resolution.

STUDY ASSIGNMENTS

1. *In the example of value conflict, the authority of the vice-president is being challenged by his superior. Give other examples where authority is challenged by subordinates.*

2. *Give some illustrations from your own community of conflicts over the question of "private citizenship." Are there any generalizations you can draw from these illustrations? What is your personal opinion about the rights of private citizenship?*

3. *We presented seven paraphrased statements from Kuhn and Berg's* Values in a Business Society: Issues and Analyses. *Show how belief in these statements would cause conflict in an organization.*

4. *Review the five summary statements from Chris Argyris. Do you accept them as some of the requirements of a formal organization? Give some personal examples, if you can, where you have experienced the behavior that illustrates such statements.*

5. *What are some examples of bureaucracies you deal with frequently? Compare some of your experiences with the pathologies offered in this chapter.*

6. *"If you're a businessman, you must always be concerned about profits. People are considered as costs, and thus business managers will always try to exploit you." Discuss.*

7. *Is it inevitable that the goals of individuals and organizations will be in conflict? Explain.*

8. *Is it inevitable that the goals of organizations and society will be in conflict? Explain.*

9. *What do you believe is the most fundamental reason for the conflict of personal and organizational values?*

10. *What is your usual response to conflict? Give examples of value conflicts you have had with individuals or organizations. Are there any generalizations you can make?*

11. *Four approaches are mentioned in the last section of this chapter: blending, fusion, integration, and a centering on process. What are their similarities and differences? Under which of the four would you prefer to work?*

12. *Compare the four approaches with the materials offered in Parts 2, 3, and 4. What differences do you see?*

13. *How does Chapter 15's discussion of leadership relate to these approaches?*

14. *Do you agree with Proposition 6, 6*a*, and 6*b*? Why? Why not?*

15. *Why would member participation help in conflict resolution?*

situational episodes

1. Even though everything you have read said undergraduate grades were not too important, company interviewers and graduate and professional schools now seem very interested in your grade point average. In fact, one company has posted a notice that people with less than a B average need not apply.

   The professor had said all along that the final exam would not be comprehensive—it would only cover the chapters from the last test. But then, last Tuesday, he dropped the bomb that he had changed his mind—there will be five essay questions in addition to the multiple-choice and true-false. You were very upset to be told this one week before the exam, especially when you were on the borderline between a B and a C. If you blow the final, it might affect your job and work career.

   You have just received an invitation from the other guys in your class to study for the final. One of the guys dates a girl who is a work-study student, and she was typing in the prof's outer office when she heard him discuss the essay questions with other faculty members. So now the guys basically have the five questions and want you to help develop essay answers. What should you do?
2. You really are enjoying your new job. It's been five years since you left school, and you are now with your third company. The move to the second company was your own decision to improve your opportunities, but then you were laid off, the reason given being the slowdown in the economy.

   The phone rings. You are at first pleased to hear the voice of Harvey Bell, the public relations assistant from Quarton Associates, one of your company's large accounts. You have worked on the account; in fact, your boss, Jack Session, has given you authority over most of Quarton's business. Harv hits you with a strange request. His boss has received a call from the top brass asking for a favor from your advertising firm. It seems that the company needs to rent a fashionable apartment for "entertainment purposes" when important customers came to town. Harv was told to call you and ask that you add an additional $5,000 to their bill. The company will pay the bill and you'll send back the $5,000 to Harv, who will lease the apartment for the year. Harv tells you your company has done this favor for them in the past and that no problems have ever developed. You tell Harv you'll have to check it out and will call him back.

You don't like the idea and wonder what you should do. Suppose you go to Jack Session and he says to go ahead? If you go to Jack, will he view your question as a sign of weakness? What should you do?

managing forces in change

TWENTY-ONE

OBJECTIVES YOU SHOULD MEET

State *three current indications of changes in your personal work experience.*

List *three environmental changes affecting managers.*

Discuss *the role of integration as a force to meet change.*

Identify *six stages in the creative process.*

Describe *the role of innovation in creating change.*

O.K. NOW, LET'S PUT IT ALL TOGETHER—WHAT HAVE I LEARNED?

"Well, Johnny, now that you have taken some courses in college, I sure would like to know whether my money has been well spent in making it possible for you to get an education. You are just completing that course in management. What have you learned? You know that I never had the chance to go to college, and I would like for you to tell me about some of the key things that you feel you have learned."

"Gosh, Dad, I don't know. I've studied for each assignment and listened pretty well in class. The teacher was pretty good, and we've learned a lot of different new words, techniques, and ideas, but they're a collection of different topics about dealing with people, the functions that managers perform, and some samples from practice. I'm getting ready to study the last chapter now and prepare for the exam. Frankly, I think I've psyched out how to get a good grade in the course, but I'm not sure what I've learned that could help you down at the plant."

"Sure, son, I know that it's taken me a number of years to learn my job at the plant and finally to become a supervisor, so I wouldn't expect for you to learn in one course all that I have in twenty years. But the best reason for taking courses is to find out early what some of the ideas are, so that you can test them out when you get into a position to start using some of the knowledge. I can tell you one thing, though—things have changed a lot, and it surely would help to have an idea of how to keep from getting frustrated by all these changes."

"That's funny, the text and prof have emphasized change all the way through the course. What worries me is whether some of the things that I've learned in the course will be changed by the time I need them. I've learned several pieces of things and several alternatives for applying them, but I'm still uncertain as to what's the best way. For example,

in organization they stress what they call the contingency approach—that is, the structure depends on the environment and tasks in the company. At one time, the book talks about participation of employees in leadership and decisions, and at another time about systems and control, where you need to have enough information to make a good decision. Another place it talks about fitting the organization to the people available, and then about fitting the people to meet the needs of the organization. I've learned some good arguments for doing things in different ways, and I have some details and pieces."

"That doesn't sound bad, Johnny. I've found from experience that one time a thing will work and the next time it'll cause problems. I'm glad you aren't just planning to use the book learning like a cookbook. Sounds like you've developed some sound reasons for doing different things. That ought to help, as long as you don't get the idea that you have all the answers just because you've been to college."

"Well, that's for sure—I probably have more knowledge about topics that a manager must deal with, but I'm at a loss to answer your first question, What have I learned that would help you in the plant? Let's see, I just read the last chapter, and the authors are talking about integration and innovation. I get the idea that it's not enough to learn about all the pieces of a manager's job—I've got to fit them together. They call that integration. Then, with everything changing, it seems obvious that we all have to keep up with things and get new ideas; but that's not all, we've got to make use of those new ideas—I guess that's what they mean by innovation. But I'm sure you must have known that."

"That's right, but when I look back on my actions in the plant, I've had to relate how one experience helps me meet a new situation better. That's not easy, because I've been so busy meeting schedules that I've had little chance for sifting out some generalizations."

"Say, that gives me an idea. The book finishes each chapter with what they call propositions. Some of those are fairly straightforward, and maybe they would help me show you what I've learned. We might look at some of those. It might help me answer your question and also help me review for the exam."

"OK, let's try that."

"All right, now, the first thing is for me to find out what type of problem you want me to tackle. Early in the course, I did get the idea that in making a decision, you've got to start with understanding the problem. What type of problem do you want me to tell you something about? Then, I'll know how to get started."

"That's fair. Let's start with a problem I've had with Tom Jennings. He seems to be a good worker when he wants to be, but I have trouble keeping him interested in his job. He always wants to talk about things instead of getting the job done."

"Say, I have *learned something about that. It's back over here in Chapter 3 in what they talk about under motivation; these propositions are nice generalizations, but I guess I must get into some of the theories. Let's see, Tom must have a number of types of needs, and the area*

of social needs sounds as though they're important to him. Then, you have certain objectives such as meeting your schedule, and that's covered in Chapter 11. Say, let's work with this—all that stuff in Chapter 3 does relate to Chapter 11. I've got it—they talk about something they call MBO, which involves your talking with Tom about what objectives he has and what objectives you have. Then, you two come to some agreement as to what he should do to satisfy both yours and his. The idea is that if he participates with you in setting objectives, he might get with it and start doing something. The prof might say that you would be satisfying his social needs by talking with him, and if you can give him some recognition for the work that he gets done, he will be trying to satisfy a different set of needs that they call need for achievement. But then I have to mention that there's something else in Chapter 12 about planning and in Chapter 16 about control. You see, if we can get Tom to plan ahead and understand your viewpoint and schedules, he might pitch in. Also, if you keep track of his actual work and compare it with what you two agree on as being your targets for a period, you can keep better control on your operations."

"Wait a minute, son, you're jumping around in different topics and chapters. I thought we would go through and check out individual propositions on a single subject. You're confusing me now. I do see that I've got to motivate Tom, but what's this about bringing in objectives, planning, and control."

"Well, Dad, maybe I'm learning more in trying to tell you about the subject than I'm getting across to you. It just dawned on me what the book was driving at when it talked about integration. Sure, I've learned something about individual topics, but now I see that they are *interrelated. I'm unconsciously trying to put some things together in my mind when I'm trying to help you use some of my learning in dealing with Tom. Let me try again and bring in some more ideas. I don't know whether they'll help you, but talking with you has turned me on. Maybe I have learned something! Now, let's see if I can convince you that it might be helpful in your situation. If I can keep going, I might find that I can send you a bill for consulting services."*

"Yeah, that's fine, but I'll just charge it against that prepaid tuition account for your education. Let's keep going before your mother interrupts us. I want to see some more samples from that book of yours."

Change has been an integral element in all parts of this book. The manager's world is changing, the manager is changing, and the processes of managing are undergoing continual change. For the purpose of clarity, we have had to treat some of the forces of change as though they were constant in our presentation.

The descriptions of the related knowledge and critical managing processes start you in the right direction as a manager. If you apply the knowledge through the management processes to your contemporary world, you should have confidence in the outcome. You should perform satisfactorily. Why, then, is there a need for another chapter?

How does change affect your career decisions?

Change and its impact permeate the manager's world so completely that another perspective of managing must be presented. In this final chapter, managing forces in change is the central topic. To develop an understanding of some forces in change, we look at areas of personal concern to you. We refocus our attention on a few significant developments in change that will affect your career choice, your managing methods, and your relationships to the management profession. With these developments presented, we then turn to the important question: How do you live and manage under conditions of constant change? Since this chapter concludes the book, an overview of all materials precedes the final summary and propositions.

A REFOCUS ON CHANGE FORCES

To be accurate, this section should be written in fading ink and on loose-leaf pages, for what are "truths" today may not be "truths" tomorrow. Many products you use daily may not exist in a few years, and much of your future living style is already on the drawing boards of firms throughout the world. What follow, therefore, are a few examples of change trends in areas that may have a direct effect on you personally.

Personal Change Forces

Many of the personal change forces are operating now. You will want to make career decisions because of your awareness of the following changes.

Where are opportunities the greatest?

SERVICE-ORIENTED ECONOMY The 1970s saw the United States move into a service-oriented economy. A formerly agrarian society has thus moved through both the industrial and manufacturing stages in less than 200 years. We tried to reflect this development by giving you illustrations in fields like marketing, recreation, auto repair, and housing. Regardless of the new fields and careers opening up, the demand for managers will increase and opportunities for managing should abound.

PUBLIC-SECTOR GROWTH In the recent past, the number of new jobs has been increasing fastest in the public sector of our economy. Jobs will always exist in the private segment, but new opportunities in federal, state, and local government will offer you challenges full of uncertainty and excitement. Environmental management demands new ideas and approaches. Developments in publicly supported recreational, educational, transportation, and housing areas are a few examples of areas where traditional methods of managing will be replaced by newer approaches.

INTERDEPENDENCE OF PARTS The world is growing smaller and more complex as each part needs the other part for existence and growth. Consumer groups gain in power daily. Residents of communities want a voice in industrial developments. Educators and public and private officials are being held accountable for their actions. Throughout the structure of all institutions, people in subordinate roles are no longer content with traditional submissive and passive roles. As a manager in either a public or private organization, you will have to work with and relate to all parts that interact. There will be a greater need than before for managers with the abilities to see interdependence and to respond accordingly.

SMALL-BUSINESS OPPORTUNITIES This development is not new. What may be new, though, is your involvement in small business. Many in small business enter the field as a second career choice. They may try employment with a large firm and become dissatisfied; they may go into small business because of family connections; they may enter the field because of its lower educational requirements.

Many of the concepts in this book apply to managing in a small business. The opportunities for variety and challenge in small business make this field worthy of your consideration.

Can managing be relevant work?

WORK IS CHANGING The concept of work, its place in a total career plan, and its contribution to the growth of the economy all change constantly. Compare your own generation's ideas and experiences with those of your grandparents, and you will find radical change in such things as (1) number of hours worked per week, (2) paid vacations and holidays, (3) retirement plans, and (4) working conditions. Fewer and fewer people are needed each year to produce the goods and services needed by the whole population. Employment and work have traditionally been the vehicles through which income has been produced. Employment and work, however, may be quickly disappearing for many as the *primary* source of income. Yet income, as purchasing power, is essential for an economy to continue.

Questions about the nature of work will grow more relevant in the coming years. You will be confronted with these changes as you participate in society as a consumer and as a member of an organization. Other changes are also on the horizon. Although less directly personal, they nevertheless contribute to the forces you must live with.

Environmental Change Forces

Changes in the wider environment are so varied and pervasive that we shall list only a few of the major ones. Each of these will have a significant impact on you and your managing processes even though some of them now seem to be quite indirect.

Is increase in population good or bad?

POPULATION EXPLOSION AND URBANIZATION Population will continue to increase rapidly in the next few decades, even though the proponents of planned parenthood and zero population growth may have a significant impact. Even if the birthrate does decline, the absolute number of babies born will still cause the total population to continue its increase. This increase will expand markets for consumer goods, services, and education, but at the same time it will cause extreme pressures on land utilization.

Not only will urbanization of the countryside continue, but it is predicted that entire stretches of land 300 to 400 miles long will become belts of megalopolises. These areas will require that managers concentrate on the interrelationships of a large number of people in groups and subgroups—central cities, suburbs, and community centers. The impact of this concentration of people will be evident in the need for improved planning, organization, and control of new clusters of people. The demand for managing skills will clearly be tremendous.

TECHNOLOGICAL CHANGES The rapidity of technological changes is evident to every person in modern society. Technological means for improving society have been discovered at a much faster rate than have the social means by which society can accommodate the contributions. Managers will continually be faced with having to adapt to rapid obsolescence of their present plants and equipment. Let us list some of the areas in which technological improvements will continue to add pressures on the manager's world:

1. New transportation methods will result in greater speed of air, land, and sea vehicles. Jet airplanes, rapid transit systems on land, huge cargo ships, and the inevitable expansion of national highway systems will bring people closer together. On the other hand, the manager will face delays through congestion, claims of damage to the environment, and increased attention to the need for planning unified networks of all transportation systems.
2. Communications will bring faraway plants and offices within instant contact. One author has predicted that the information industry will expand at a greater rate than any other because of the increased demand to secure rapid access to all types of information about an increasingly interdependent society.
3. New sources of energy must provide answers to current worries about power shortages. Solar energy, nuclear energy, fuel cells, and greater efficiency in using fossil fuels will require

continued study by public and private managers to ensure that they move with the times. In the last decade, the need for changes in the attitudes toward conservation of energy has received increased attention.

4. Technological support for life processes will improve health and extend life. Control of disease in animals, plants, and humans, new foods and new packing of foods, better fertilizers, new pharmaceuticals, and many other health aids will all improve the quality of life. These improvements will offer new opportunities to perceptive managers. Environmental protection can be viewed not only as a problem and constraint on managers but as an opportunity for managers who recognize change.

Should managers think globally?

√GLOBAL INTERDEPENDENCE Because of improved transportation and communication, the entire globe has become closely interdependent. What happens 10,000 miles away can immediately become of importance to a local community. International markets and sources of supply are available for even the small firm that in the past thought in terms of a radius of 100 miles. Effects of unstable international money markets, shipping strikes, changes in international transportation rates, and changes in the weather in some faraway place may now have an immediate effect on managing in the local plant or shopping center. Here are several specific ways that this global interdependence increasingly has a direct impact on domestic managers:

1. Multinational firms have expanded in the manufacture of automobiles, electrical products, petroleum products, pharmaceuticals, and many other products in daily use. These firms have seen the economic advantages of viewing the entire world as a market and have expanded accordingly. Competition in an increasing number of industries is now on an international basis.
2. Intercultural exchanges of ideas, products, and customs have enriched the variety and diversity of formerly isolated separate cultures. Modes of dress and style, philosophy and religion, languages and methods of expression in music and the fine arts, and new ideas of social organization are rapidly influencing significant changes in even the most provincial sectors of society. These changes at times cause disruptions in the old ways of living and force people to come to some accommodation with an increasingly diverse and pluralistic

society where differences must be not only tolerated but encouraged.

3. Small, previously domestic-oriented businessmen will find that tremendous opportunities await them if they tap the resources available in world markets. For example, a small retail store can specialize in exotic products from foreign countries, a lumber processor can import unique woods for furniture and houses, a local travel agent can promote charter flights to faraway places, or a photography specialist can offer products made in four or five foreign countries. The horizons for new opportunities for managers in a variety of endeavors is unlimited if only the effects of global interdependence are recognized.

RELATING TO CHANGE

A review now of the manager's world discussed in Part 1 should reveal to you the sense of movement and change pictured there. Such a condition of constant change might suggest a world with much uncertainty, one dominated by fear and worry. You can view change in a positive way, however, for there is certainty in knowing there will be uncertainty. The terms are relative, for, as a manager, you will have to live in a number of different worlds, each with a different time frame. You will have some knowledge about the past and near past; you will have some feeling about what will occur in the future or near future; you will make decisions and implement plans in the present. In addition to the foundation of knowledge that we have already given you for managing change forces, two approaches will be mentioned here.

When faced with the problems of adapting to known change, you may want to use the *force of integration.* When faced with the problem of initiating change, you may want to use the *force of innovation.* The contemporary manager who makes use of both integration and innovation should be able to relate successfully to change.

Force of Integration

In preceding chapters, we analyzed the many elements of knowledge, processes, and practices important to managing so that you could more easily and clearly understand each part of the subject. As we proceeded through these elements, we continually pointed out their relationships. For example, we emphasized how the structure of organizations depends on an understanding of human individuals and groups. We saw how each managerial function was dependent on other functions—control on planning, staffing on organizing, and so on. We observed how practicing managers apply their knowledge base to their actual processes. In short, you have been encouraged throughout the book to interrelate these parts. We are now ready to answer two questions: What do we mean by integration? Where is integration needed?

integrate

MEANING OF INTEGRATION The word *integrate,* according to the dictionary, means "to form into a whole; to unite or become united so as to form a complete whole; unify." The term is closely related to *synthesis,* which means the combination of parts into a whole, or a process of building up simpler elements into more complex combinations. Lately, managers have emphasized the idea of *synergism,* which points out that the total effect of independent parts is greater than the sum of the individual effects. All these terms have one thing in common: They assume that no matter how much we know about simple parts of a whole, something of a very complex nature can be added. Thus, although we have attempted in this book to reduce ideas to simple fundamental language, the very nature of integration means that we cannot employ the same approach when talking about it.

synthesis

synergism

Can you see the whole picture?

With respect to the essentials of management, we have provided the building blocks in this book; however, a manager must constantly develop the *vision* and *wisdom* for putting these blocks into a meaningful whole. As the modern world becomes more complex, as specialization increases, and as the rate of change accelerates, the need for integration by a manager becomes more critical.

The subject of management as a separate field of study has existed for only seven or eight decades. During the first three decades (1900 to 1930), most of the writing, thinking, and action of management centered around the *integration of things;* the areas of concern in this period were mechanization, efficiency, productivity, and economic exploitation of natural resources. During the second three decades (1930 to 1960), the focus of management was on the *integration of people;* the important concepts during this period were increasing satisfaction, participation, motivation, providing employment, and human relations. By 1960, the subject of management became more of an *integration of ideas;* the central ideas of this period are systems, organizational behavior, information retrieval, social responsibility, and the meaning of life. In other words, in these three periods the idea of integration has persisted, but the scope of integration has changed: In the first, it was an integration of things; in the second, it was an integration of people; in the third and present period, it is and will be an integration of ideas.

What parts need to be integrated?

WHAT MANAGERS MUST INTEGRATE We can improve our understanding of integration by outlining subjects that need to be integrated. The chief reason that we tend to confuse another person when we use the word *integrate* is that too often we fail to identify what is to be integrated. Therefore, we try to focus here on things that managers should integrate.

How do you make theory useful?

1. *Theory and Practice.* One is always faced with the distinction between the thinker and the doer, between the ivory tower of educational institutions and the raw world of action, and between highly sophisticated theories (ideas) and the very complex nature of the real world. The manager must meet a happy medium and attempt to integrate his ideas with his actions. He must think before he acts, but he must not think so long that he does not get anything done; yet, he certainly should not jump into action without any thought whatsoever. Thus, in a simple sense, the idea of integrating theory and practice involves the conceptual process of relating the mind to the hand.

The managerial mind translates theories into action and searches for theories that help it understand the complexities of the real world. For example, we saw in Chapter 3 that there are several theories for motivating others to act in a way that will further organizational objectives. Even the most "practical" manager assumes some motivational propositions, and in modern management he spends increasingly large amounts of time in the mental processes of planning and decision making. In fact, the manager's job has become so exclusively a mental activity that he must consciously work at physical exercise to maintain his physical fitness to support his mental processes.

2. *Operations and Activities.* The degree of difficulty a manager faces in gaining the extra force from integration is directly related to his level in his organization's hierarchy. The worker has only a minimum need for integration; he is given a specific job and tends to leave this complex activity to his superior. The first-line supervisor integrates the activities of his subordinates, but these activities are generally similar and easier to integrate. The second- and third-level managers need to integrate production, sales, and financial activities, and sometimes also community concerns. Top-level managers are increasingly being pressed to in-

tegrate the activities of the entire company with those of other companies and social interests.

How can you develop your integrating ability?

Typically, the second- and third-level manager is promoted from a first-level management position in production, sales, finance, personnel, or engineering. If he has been a sales-oriented person in the past, in his new job he must concentrate on integrating entirely new activities of production, finance, and so on. If the manager has previously been an engineer or a technically oriented person, he must broaden his interests and attention to sales and finance. In fact, a manager's promotability to higher levels of management is dependent on the development of the force for integrating varied activities.

MBA programs have become popular for helping specialized managers become more generalized in orientation. Job rotation has been used for the same purpose. In the final analysis, development of this force is dependent on each individual manager's recognition of its need.

Do you need to be expert in everything?

3. *Types of Knowledge.* In Part 2, we discussed in some detail the types of knowledge needed by a manager. We saw that he needed knowledge about human beings, groups, organizational structure, technology and systems, and change. Each type of knowledge has been developed into a different art, science, or professional discipline, such as psychology, sociology, anthropology, semantics, engineering, computer science, accounting, economics, mathematics, or statistics.

There is such a broad base of knowledge on which management is built that it is impossible for the manager to be an expert in all these subjects. A manager may develop confidence and security in his decisions if he has developed a fairly deep understanding of one or two of these areas. Generally, his development involves a sequential process of adding knowledge from other subject areas onto some initial confidence in one. If he tries to learn a little bit about everything, he may not be able to do anything on his first management job. He needs to be a generalist, but as we have said, he needs to know something in depth at the first level in order to get started.

There have been several studies concerning the question of what knowledge base is most fruitful for developing good managers. These studies have not been conclusive, because there are a number of possible starting points in the development of a fully integrated, thinking manager. The answer for you is to learn some field well so that you will have confidence in yourself and to understand how that field fits into the broader managerial viewpoints.

How are managerial functions interrelated?

4. *Functions and Processes.* In Part 3, we identified a number of the processes performed by managers, including planning, organizing, staffing, and controlling. We have seen that these functions are interrelated and cannot stand alone: Controlling depends on good planning; staffing depends on good organizing; supervising depends on good communicating; and all these pairs depend on each other. The successful manager develops each of these separate functions; jointly and simultaneously, he also needs to develop their interrelationships. The integration of functions and processes into a well-balanced whole is therefore a principal characteristic of a good manager.

Do you like to do what you can do?

5. *Skills and Interests.* A manager should also be able to integrate the skills that he has acquired with his own interests and his attitudes toward a job. A manager may be highly skilled in certain functions, mental processes, and operational activities, but if he has little interest in them and his attitude about them is negative, he will be continually at war with himself. He may like to do something that he cannot do; or he may be able to do something well that he does not like to do. He must continually integrate his interests with his abilities. For example, one man's personality may help him become a good salesman, but he may not like selling or managing salesmen. Generally, this type of integration is not a serious problem, because people generally like to do things that they do well.

Ideas Related to Integration Now that we know the meaning of integration and have seen what needs to be integrated, we shall conclude our discussion of integration as a force for adapting to known changes by considering some other terms associated with this force. We have already seen that integration is closely related to synthesis. In management circles, the word *coordination* also continually appears. A person who is well coordinated physically can generally do better in a variety of sports.

Coordination

Coordination in this sense means that a person acts in a harmonious and concerted manner. A manager can develop his own mental capacity for coordination through understanding the various topics in this book and their interrelationships.

The idea of *equilibrium* is related to the idea of a manager as an integrator. A *well-balanced* and stable interaction is fundamental to equilibrium. However, in a changing world, the idea of a manager operating in a "moving equilibrium" is probably closer to describing his activities as an integrator. At any one time, he seeks to maintain some stability or equilibrium; yet change continually upsets equilibrium. For example, the business manager tends to

What is a "moving equilibrium"?

produce items that can be sold and sell items that he produces. If he is especially successful in sales, he will cause a shortage of his output related to sales and thus will have to concentrate on increasing production—he has a moving tendency toward upsetting equilibrium. Just as soon as he solves a problem with respect to one set of constraints, he finds that he must give attention to a new set.

Has dependence increased in modern society?

The successful manager recognizes his *interdependence* on other managers, processes, and technological developments. This recognition of his interdependence sets the stage for integration. He depends on some stability in his external environment; he depends on other people; he depends on his own judgment; he depends on probability concepts in facing risks; others depend on him, but he must depend on others.

interface

Throughout this book, other terms have continually implied the idea of integration. One of these is the technological term *interface,* which indicates the point where one mechanical or electrical system is connected to another separate system. This term was in common usage during the Apollo moon program, in which one stage of the propulsion system was linked to another.

You should now see how a whole can be greater than the

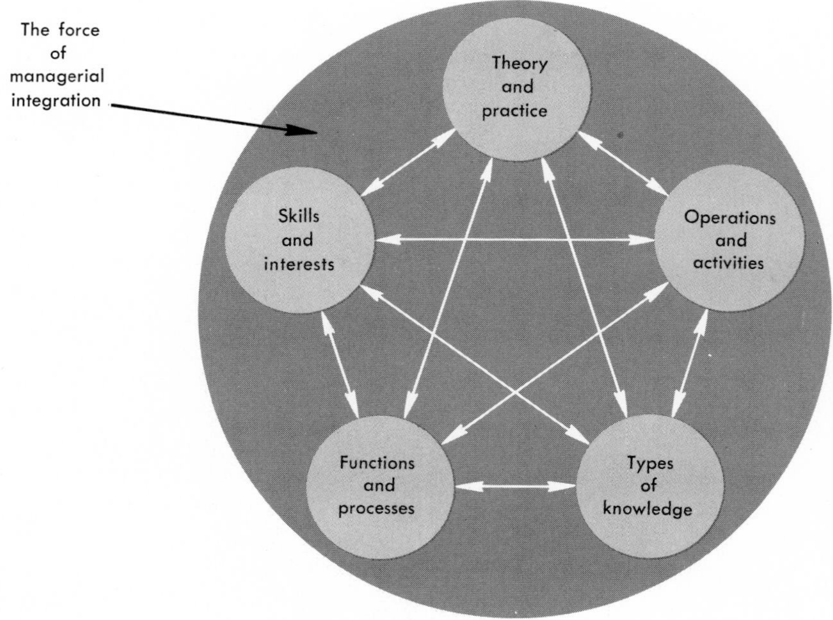

FIGURE 22.1 Managerial integration

sum of its parts—it is the complex and crucial relationships of parts that create this extra force. You should also recognize that the manager can be the key element in the creation of this dynamic synergism. The manager in the contemporary world can thus be of immeasurable value to an organization if he is in real control of the many objects of managerial integration (Figure 22.1).

Force for Initiating Change

The manager not only uses the force of integration in adapting to known change but he is also in a unique position to initiate change. He continually searches for new products, new methods, new information, and new technologies to help him improve the performance of the organization. He commands a powerful force for directing change through creativity, research, and innovation.

CREATIVITY Some people tend to be naturally more creative than others; however, there is considerable evidence to support the idea that anyone can learn to be more creative by becoming aware of the conditions that support and promote creative thinking.

How can you stay out of a rut?

Creativity is dependent on more than a rational, orderly process of the conscious mind; it also depends on supportive conditions in which emotion, dreaming, and the subconscious are allowed free rein. These conditions provide a bypass of the filter system that each of us has blocking our "preconscious" or subconscious mind. The key to this bypass is an uninhibited and free opportunity for the individual to become aware of the large number of ideas that rapidly flash into his mind.

George M. Prince, after studying creative practices, points out the need for a different attitude toward new ideas:

How can the subconscious mind help in creativity?

> Free speculation and disciplined reaction to it is of urgent importance, for there is a relentless gravity-like force working against speculation. This force is dangerous especially because it is so easily justified as realistic thinking. It is a well-kept secret that people in general . . . are determined enemies of free speculation. Each of us pays convincing lip service to his willingness—even eagerness—to consider new thoughts and ideas. But a thousand [recording] tapes, such as we have made, make liars of us all. People use remarkable ingenuity to make clear by tone, nonverbal slights, tuning out, supposedly helpful criticisms, false issues, and outright negativity, that they are not only against ideas and change but also against those who propose them. We humans habitually try to protect ourselves *even from our own new ideas.*[1]

[1] George M. Prince, *The Practice of Creativity* (New York: Harper & Row, 1970), p. 9.

We saw in Chapter 17 that the initiators of some of our best-known businesses were not the same people that served as the great organizers. In the future, however, since change has accelerated, it appears that all managers will need to be not only organizers but creators. Furthermore, various topics covered in the previous chapters and the propositions advanced are themselves subject to change—you should not assume that these ideas, no matter how good, are immutable. You should take them as points of departure and develop your own creative approaches.

Each of us can probably identify an example of some simple, new, and original idea developed by someone else as one that we could have, or have had, ourselves. A knowledge of some stages of the creative process can help you to develop your own ideas for change. We shall identify six.

Why is it important to keep up with what's new?

1. *The Familiarizing Stage.* If we hope to come up with a really new and original idea, we must first become familiar with the related ideas that others have had previously. In this familiarizing period, we seek the basic facts, characteristics, and reports of others related both to the specific issue at hand and to all other possible aids. The creator must immerse himself in all aspects that have any possible relevance to the issue at hand. In short, creativity involves *hard work.*

Does thinking help?

2. *The Mulling-over Stage.* Since, by definition, a creator can have no pattern for reaching a breakthrough to an original concept, he cannot say what material is relevant or how he should classify the information obtained in the familiarizing stage. This second stage is then one of deliberation and a general mulling over of the situation. Some approaches to consider are (1) finding a new use for a known product or process (possibly in a new field), (2) substituting a better way to accomplish an existing activity, (3) experimenting, and (4) recognizing the significance of a lucky event.

Where does imagination come in?

3. *The Speculating Stage.* In approaching a problem that requires some real breakthrough in thinking, one must shake off inhibiting forces that tend to restrict thought to past conscious patterns; in other words, the manager in such situations must be free to allow the wealth of subconscious elements to break through the barriers into his consciousness. Deliberation then is not enough; it must be followed by speculation, and this speculation should be as imaginative as possible. Some thoughts might appear to the creator or others as crazy, wild, irrelevant, or out of this world.

At this stage, the creator might be the target for ridicule. If he is working on the idea individually, he must be tolerant of his

brainstorming sessions

own half-baked ideas. If he is expressing new ideas in a group, the atmosphere must be permissive and tolerant of *any* idea. Group approaches to creativity have been called *"brainstorming" sessions.* The rules for such sessions are as follows: (1) criticism of ideas must be withheld until after the session; (2) the group must welcome freewheeling and encourage the wildest of ideas; (3) developing a greater quantity of ideas increases the likelihood of having one really useful idea; (4) each member of the group should improve and relate his own ideas to the ideas of others.

4. *The Gestation Stage.* If a person is directed toward a truly original idea, there is a period of frustration and helplessness. During this stage it may help to go to sleep, or possibly undertake TM or some other technique for refreshing the mind. Or you may go fishing and get away from it all. Generally, relaxation is a key to this period.

Can you recognize a good new idea if it hits you?

5. *The Insight Stage.* Generally, the period of insight is very short. Often the original idea occurs in a flash. The key to this stage is to be receptive to the new idea and to be able to recognize it as a breakthrough. Many people may have had the same insight, but the creative person is the one who can recognize its significance.

6. *The Testing Stage.* During the testing period, the creator checks to see how the idea can be refined and whether it can be useful in practice.

These stages in the creative process help us understand just what creativeness is all about. There are several concepts that can help the process. First, the creator must continually fight barriers to creative thoughts, such as social custom, religious institutions, and perceptual one-track approaches. For example, in viewing another culture in which people behave differently from what he is accustomed to, the creator will view these differences as interesting—not as either right or wrong according to his own cultural background. Perceptually, the uncreative person tends to have a very narrow and dogmatic reaction to what he sees. For example, if he views a growing tree, his perception may be restricted to only one or two attributes of the tree. From a broader perspective, a simple growing tree can be perceived in many ways (lumber for a house, shade from the sun, a living thing, leaves to be raked, a place for a treehouse, a thing that can be involved in an automobile accident). The creative person tends to see more of these numerous attributes.

A second concept that is most interesting to observe in practice is serendipity. Quite often, we stumble on something new and entirely different from what we are looking for. *Serendipity* is the

Serendipity

Can you stumble on something original while doing routine duties?

finding of things not looked for. Many things found from basic research are discovered without any previous goal being set for their discovery. Indeed, the by-product of an activity can be more valuable than the reaching of the original objectives.

RESEARCH ATTITUDE Research is another force by which the manager can create change. Typically, research processes are considered as activities separate from managing, yet the position of a manager offers opportunities to encourage this systematic search for new ideas. Even a first-line supervisor with a positive attitude toward the value of research can direct attention to discovering small bits of new knowledge.

You, as a manager, may not be directly involved with research projects that seek new knowledge as an end in itself, but you can certainly make use of this new knowledge if you keep up with reports on research results. In this book, many of the propositions are based on research findings. By using a "research attitude," you can do your own testing of these propositions and generate data and experiences that either support or reject the findings flowing from research projects. In the final analysis, a research attitude searches and re-searches why things are the way they are. The tools of the researcher are questions.

INNOVATION Either creativity or research, and sometimes both, are necessary for innovation; yet they alone are not enough to actually fill the needs of society. In order for an idea to have an impact on society, it must be developed and distributed to those who can gain the benefits from the idea (see Figure 21.2). *Innovation* is the application of new ideas to specific, perceived needs through the development of techniques that will make the idea feasible for economic production and then distribute the results of the new idea to those who need them.

Innovation

How can new ideas pay off?

Although not as spectacular as discovery, innovation is the force that enables the manager to offer to the public a commercial success and to secure the payoff from the idea. The biographies of many inventors end with the statement that the inventor died penniless or with small financial return for his efforts. The usual reason in these cases is that the inventor is oriented to creating new ideas but is neither interested nor skilled in exploiting possible commercial uses for them. The innovative manager has both the skills, the interests, and the opportunity for using this force to change conditions of society and to lead in progress.

Some firms and even entire countries seem to have a knack for excelling in innovation, rather than in creativity and basic re-

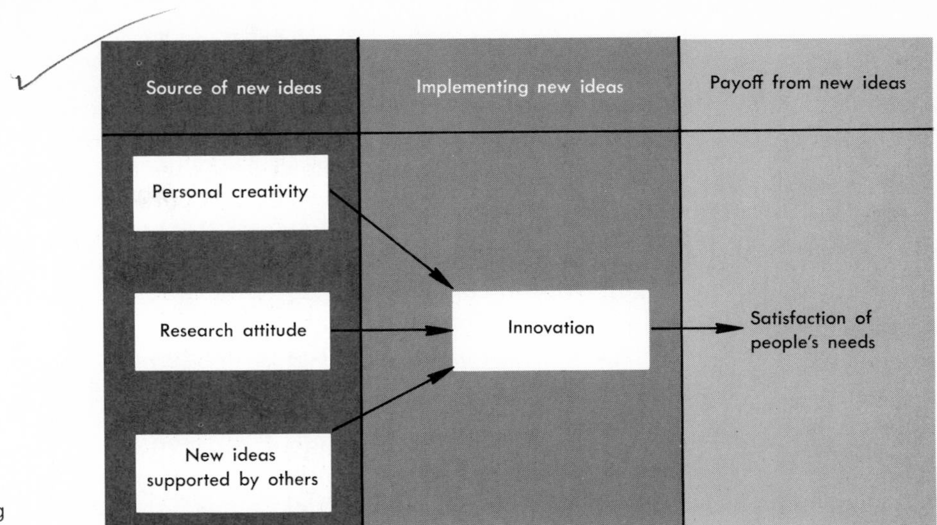

FIGURE 21.2 Initiating change

search. For example, Great Britain and Germany have, in the past, excelled in research, and the United States and Japan have been especially successful in innovation. Jet planes and oxygen converters for the steel industry are among the numerous innovations created in one nation and developed by another. Often, small companies in the United States come up with new ideas that can best be exploited by large firms. Merger of the small with the large has been one answer to this division of skills. The key, of course, is to balance the creation of the fund of new ideas with the capabilities of exploiting them into useful products that can be distributed to people who want them.

Historically, innovation has been an important force used by a single entrepreneur who with his own money and effort launched a new product or a new way of doing something. He assumed the risks of the venture and followed through with its promotion, production, and distribution. This opportunity remains for you in modern society as government and industrial firms support new ventures. You, however, have increasing opportunities for innovative efforts in modern, complex, large firms using ideas developed earlier in this book. Suggestion systems that provide payoffs for new ideas, decentralized organizations that encourage decisions at lower levels, and management by objectives (MBO) are only a few of the approaches that encourage the innovative manager.

Innovation as a force in change has been credited as being the basis for economic development and as an explanation for periodic surges in rates of growth of entire national economies. New industries in the past, such as railroads, telephone companies, and electric utilities, have provided the impulse for renewed growth. Each of these has a life cycle, as we discussed in Chapter 1, and so continued overall growth is dependent on innovations in new fields. Computers, photography, copying machines for the office, plastics, car washing, pharmaceutical products, and many more are continued evidence that innovations offer managers a powerful force for invoking change.

Up to this point, our illustrations of innovation have been of sensational, great new ideas; however, the important point for each manager to understand is that many innovations are possible for all levels of managers. Most of us are not inventive geniuses who will become well known, but we do all have the capability to create changes that yield small improvements. Even if we never have a sudden new insight or fundamental breakthrough, the opportunities to observe new ideas already available and to apply them to our own situation remain great. The manager who keeps abreast of ideas reported by others can use this innovative force in his own department to institute change.

THE MANAGER'S WORLD REVISITED

We have now come full cycle. The manager's world, simply depicted in Part 1, now shows many signs of complexity. But living with complexity is the mark of a contemporary manager. A brief review of each part seen from a different perspective may indiciate the interesting paradox of management: You simultaneously deal with complexity and simplicity, with stability and change, and with the processes of integration and innovation. In each of the following paragraphs we see this paradox.

Will you view the knowledge base presented in Part 2 as the beginning or end of your learning? While you received much information about human motivation, individual behavior processes, groups, organization structure, technology, and change, you may have sensed that these fields are relatively young and insights are being added daily.

What will you conclude about the materials on management processes discussed in Part 3? The seven functions of managing represent one cornerstone of your education in management. You now know the importance and interdependence of decision making, setting objectives, planning, organizing, staffing, directing, communicating, and controlling. You know that objectives without plans are meaningless; that decision making is enhanced through good communication; that leadership problems may be reduced through participation in objective setting.

Do you see the role of the three chapters in Part 4 in our introduction to managing? You would be naive to generalize that power, politics, and tactics are the only means to achieve the success of a KFC, IBM, or Ashland. You will have developed your insight if you can see that the men behind these companies' successes made use of managing processes within the context of their unique situations. They were no mere automatons blindly managing "by the numbers." They related their own personal capacities to a particular aspect of their environment.

Do you recognize that the notion of individuality in Part 5 is the ingredient giving managers and firms their uniqueness? The topic of values and conflict resolution highlights the differences among people and among organizations. Differences, however, can be a positive feature. Your values set you apart from others and give you an identity. An organization can spend many dollars to convince the marketplace that its products and services are different from those of the competition. Firms know the value of hiring personnel with varied backgrounds and abilities. Managing such forces of change and differences became the theme of this final chapter.

Managing in a contemporary world means living with uncertainty and differences. You also live with one eye on the internal parts of the organization and one eye on the external environment. If you only integrate (put the parts together), you may miss opportunities to grow and develop. If you only innovate, you may overstimulate the organization to a point of exhaustion. Balance is essential.

You must be ready to continuously adapt if you are to manage in the contemporary world. You must sense how much seasoning to add. You must be aware of the advantages and disadvantages of integration and innovation, of bureaucracy and entrepreneurship, of formal and informal organization, of subordinate involvement in decision making, and of many other variables.

We have discussed those features of managing in the contemporary world that we believe will prepare you for entry into the management profession. We have stressed throughout that the background of a successful manager will include a balance between "book learning" and practical experience in managing. We have provided you with your initial education, the first general admission ticket to the world of the manager; you must now have the desire to continue to learn and develop as a potentially dynamic, constructive force in today's society.

SUMMARY AND PROPOSITIONS

This chapter completes the discussion we promised. In checking the questions on the first page of Chapter 1, you will probably find that the answers to those questions are quite easy now; you know who managers are, you know what managers do, and you know what management is. You may also have noticed that the subject of Part 5 may be less clear to you than the subjects of other parts unless you stop and think while reading the material. Resolution of value conflicts is a most important dimension of a manager's work, even though it is not a simple topic.

In the last chapter, we have summarized some expected changes in your personal world and in the broader environment. We have discussed two approaches for relating to change: integration for relating to known changes, and innovation for creating changes. A manager might be able to do an acceptable job without knowing much about how to handle these forces, but for those of you who want to be particularly successful in managing, these forces are powerful and will help separate you from the merely satisfactory manager.

Managing not only deals with changes but is changing rapidly itself. For this reason, the last chapter should be not a conclusion but a springboard to other thoughts and experiences in managing. Our propositions and study assignments for this chapter encourage you to review and interrelate topics discussed earlier and to prepare your own restatements to help you as you move into your next encounter with managing.

1. The world of the manager is changing in both subtle and dramatic ways.
   a. Recognition of changes in work opportunities will help a manager adapt to this new world.
   b. Significant long-run changes in the environment set the stage for new challenges that management will face in the future.
2. The fundamental purpose of integration is to bring related parts together.
   a. A manager with varied experiences and broad educational background is generally better able to integrate the elements important to managing.
   b. The greater the trend toward specialization, the greater the need for an integrating ability on the part of managers.
   c. The need for integrating ability increases as one moves to higher levels of an organization.

3. Innovation is the payoff stage of carrying a new idea from inception to the user of the idea; thus, the manager is in the fortunate position of being able to promote change.
   a. Some people are more creative than others, but all can develop greater creativity.
   b. A research attitude is helpful to a manager, especially during periods of rapid change.
4. A manager may have two roles relative to change: He may continually adjust to change initiated by someone else, or he may initiate change through his own efforts.

STUDY ASSIGNMENTS

1. *Give your own examples of how environmental changes will require you to adapt to them.*
2. *"The total effect of independent parts is often greater than the simple summation of the parts." Explain why this is true.*
3. *Show how the design of an assembly line requires the ability to integrate things.*
4. *Show how the design of an organizational structure requires the integration of people.*
5. *Show how the resolution of value conflicts requires the integration of ideas.*
6. *Show how sound theories can be useful in the day-to-day operations of an industrial plant.*
7. *Name some methods by which you can develop the force of integration.*
8. *Do you agree with the quotation from George Prince in the chapter? Explain how your answer relates to improving your management of change.*
9. *Focusing on what stage of the creative process offers the greatest opportunities for improving your creative powers?*
10. *Give examples of serendipity from your own experience.*
11. *What is the meaning of a research attitude? Does this attitude differ from a creative mind?*
12. *What innovation by a person with whom you have had direct contact has had a significant effect on your own activities?*
13. *Discuss supporting reasons for Propositions 1*a *and* b.

situational episodes

1. You have developed some contacts in three companies as a basis for a possible job offer when you complete school. One company is in mass transit for a large city, one is in electronics, and one is in sales of aluminum windows for homes and industry. You are interested in joining a firm that has "growth potential," and you are wondering which firm might be in the right industry for you.

   a. Starting with some of the general environmental changes discussed in the chapter, make a list of some specific environmental factors for each of the three industries that will help you appraise the opportunities you might have in that company.
   b. For these three companies, what types of innovations appear to be likely in the next decade?

2. Following the vignette at the beginning of the chapter, put yourself in the place of Johnny in trying to answer the question of what you have learned in the course. Assume that your uncle asks your advice for making a decision as to whether to install a merit rating system (see Chapter 13) that will tie in some form of incentive pay (see Chapter 3). What will you tell him? In your review of the book to prepare for a talk with your uncle, identify some of the topics that require some integration of your knowledge.
3. You have taken "liberal" courses in college—among them, courses in creative writing, in art, and in philosophy. (You may substitute three other courses that you may have actually taken in your own course work.) Using the suggested stages of a creative process, describe in some detail how you might attempt to interrelate those courses with your management course in a creative manner.

Index

A

B

D

E

T

U